Italy For Dummies, 4th Edition

Cheat Sheet

P9-CFQ-624 ...orence Transportation System

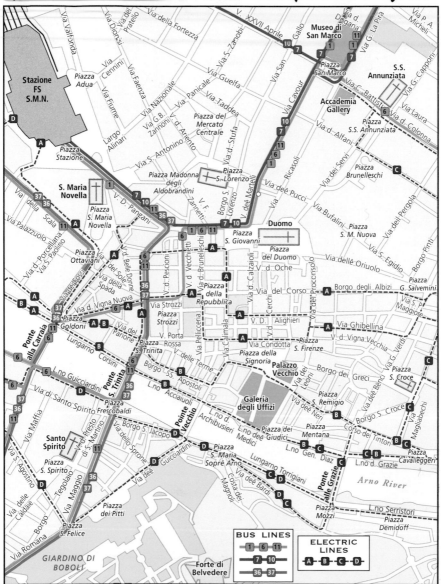

BUS LINES
1 — 6 — 11
7 — 10
36 — 37

ELECTRIC LINES
A — B — C — D

Venice Vaporetto System

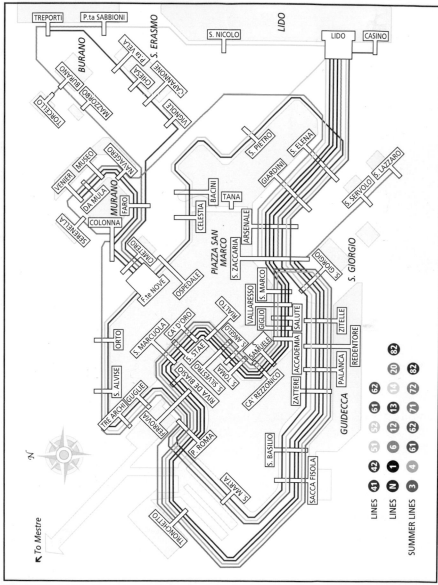

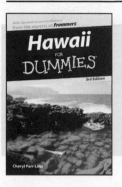
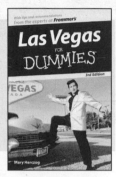
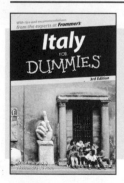

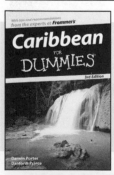
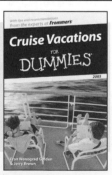

Italy
FOR
DUMMIES®
4TH EDITION

by Bruce Murphy and
Alessandra de Rosa

Wiley Publishing, Inc.

Italy For Dummies®, 4th Edition
Published by
Wiley Publishing, Inc.
111 River St.
Hoboken, NJ 07030-5774
www.wiley.com

Copyright © 2007 by Wiley Publishing, Inc., Indianapolis, Indiana

Published simultaneously in Canada

For general information on our other products and services, please contact our Customer Care Department within the U.S. at 800-762-2974, outside the U.S. at 317-572-3993, or fax 317-572-4002.

For technical support, please visit www.wiley.com/techsupport.

Wiley also publishes its books in a variety of electronic formats. Some content that appears in print may not be available in electronic books.

Library of Congress Control Number: 2006939493

ISBN: 978-0-470-06932-5

Manufactured in the United States of America

10 9 8 7 6 5 4 3 2 1

4B/QT/QR/QX/IN

WILEY

About the Authors

Bruce Murphy has lived and worked in New York City, Boston, Chicago, Dublin, Rome, and Sicily. His work has appeared in magazines ranging from *Cruising World* to *Critical Inquiry.* In addition to guidebooks, he has published fiction, poetry, and criticism, most recently the *Encyclopedia of Murder and Mystery* (St. Martin's Press).

Alessandra de Rosa was born in Rome and has lived and worked in Rome, Paris, and New York City. She did her first cross-Europe trip at age 2, from Rome to London by car. She has continued in that line ever since, exploring three out of five continents so far. Her beloved Italy remains her preferred destination and where she lives part of the year.

Dedication

We would like to dedicate this book to Sandro and Viviana de Rosa, and to Paola and Valerio Scoyni. Without their support, kindness, and wealth of good ideas, it never would have been possible. We would also like to thank our editor, Margot Weiss, who supported our work until the very day she gave birth to her son, and to Leslie Shen, who took over and did much to improve this book. A thank you also should go to Guy Ruggiero, the cartographer, who did an excellent job with the maps.

Publisher's Acknowledgments

We're proud of this book; please send us your comments through our Dummies online registration form located at www.dummies.com/register/.

Some of the people who helped bring this book to market include the following:

Editorial

Editors: Leslie Shen, Jana M. Stefanciosa

Copy Editor: Doreen Russo

Cartographer: Guy Ruggiero

Editorial Assistant: Melinda Quintero

Senior Photo Editor: Richard Fox

Cover Photos:

Front Cover Photo: © Glenn Beanland/Lonely Planet Images/ Getty Images

Back Cover Photo: © Stefano Scata

Cartoons: Rich Tennant (www.the5thwave.com)

Composition Services

Project Coordinator: Patrick Redmond

Layout and Graphics: Carl Byers, Barry Offringa, Julie Trippetti

Proofreaders: Cynthia Fields, Techbooks

Indexer: Techbooks

Publishing and Editorial for Consumer Dummies

Diane Graves Steele, Vice President and Publisher, Consumer Dummies

Joyce Pepple, Acquisitions Director, Consumer Dummies

Kristin A. Cocks, Product Development Director, Consumer Dummies

Michael Spring, Vice President and Publisher, Travel

Kelly Regan, Editorial Director, Travel

Publishing for Technology Dummies

Andy Cummings, Vice President and Publisher, Dummies Technology/ General User

Composition Services

Gerry Fahey, Vice President of Production Services

Debbie Stailey, Director of Composition Services

Contents at a Glance

Introduction *1*

Part I: Introducing Italy *7*

Chapter 1: Discovering the Best of Italy 9
Chapter 2: Digging Deeper into Italy 15
Chapter 3: Deciding Where and When to Go 32
Chapter 4: Following an Itinerary: Four Great Options 43

Part II: Planning Your Trip to Italy *49*

Chapter 5: Managing Your Money 51
Chapter 6: Getting to Italy 64
Chapter 7: Getting Around Italy 72
Chapter 8: Booking Your Accommodations 78
Chapter 9: Catering to Special Travel Needs or Interests 85
Chapter 10: Taking Care of the Remaining Details 90

Part III: The Eternal City: Rome *99*

Chapter 11: Settling into Rome 101
Chapter 12: Exploring Rome 138

**Part IV: Florence and the Best of
Tuscany and Umbria** *173*

Chapter 13: Florence 175
Chapter 14: Northern Tuscany and the Cinque Terre 223
Chapter 15: Southern Tuscany and Umbria 255

**Part V: Venice and the Best of
the Pianura Padana** *299*

Chapter 16: Venice 301
Chapter 17: Padua, Verona, and Milan 347

**Part VI: Naples, Pompeii, and
the Amalfi Coast** *379*

Chapter 18: Naples 381
Chapter 19: Going Beyond Naples: Three Day Trips 411
Chapter 20: Sorrento, Capri, and the Amalfi Coast 423

Part VII: Sicily *451*

Chapter 21: Palermo..453
Chapter 22: Taormina, Syracuse, and Agrigento 478

Part VIII: The Part of Tens *501*

Chapter 23: *Non Capisco:* The Top Ten Expressions
    You Need to Know 503
Chapter 24: Ten Great Italian Artists 506

Appendix A: Quick Concierge *510*

Appendix B: Glossary of Architectural
and Menu Terms *520*

Index *529*

Maps at a Glance

Rome Orientation 108
Rome Accommodations and Dining 116
Rome Attractions 140
The Vatican Museums 157
Florence Orientation 178
Florence Accommodations and Dining 184
Florence Attractions...198
The Uffizi Gallery 204
Tuscany and Umbria 224
Lucca 227
Pisa 236
The Cinque Terre 246
San Gimignano 257
The Chianti Region 263
Siena 266
Perugia 279
Assisi 287
Spoleto 295
Venice Orientation 305
Venice Accommodations and Dining 312
Venice Attractions 326
Piazza San Marco 333
The Pianura Padana and Milan 349
Padua 350
Verona 359
Milan..368
The Gulf of Naples and Salerno.......................................383
Naples 386
Herculaneum 417
Pompeii 421
Capri..435
The Amalfi Coast..437
Sicily..455
Palermo 457
Taormina 479
Agrigento and the Valley of the Temples....................498

Table of Contents

Introduction *1*

    About This Book..1
    Conventions Used in This Book 2
    Foolish Assumptions 3
    How This Book Is Organized..4
        Part I: Introducing Italy 4
        Part II: Planning Your Trip to Italy 4
        Part III: The Eternal City: Rome.............................4
        Part IV: Florence and the Best of Tuscany and
          Umbria...4
        Part V: Venice and the Best of
          the Pianura Padana...4
        Part VI: Naples, Pompeii, and the Amalfi Coast 4
        Part VII: Sicily 5
        Part VIII: The Part of Tens....................................5
        Appendix A and B 5
    Icons Used in This Book..5
    Where to Go from Here..6

Part 1: Introducing Italy *7*

    Chapter 1: Discovering the Best of Italy......................9
        The Best Museums...9
        The Best Churches...10
        The Best Ruins and Archaeological Areas 11
        The Best Luxury Hotels...12
        The Best Gourmet Restaurants 12
        The Best Travel Experiences 13
        The Best Traditional Italian Souvenirs.....................14

    Chapter 2: Digging Deeper into Italy............................15
        History 101: The Main Events.................................15
        Architecture: From Ruins to Rococo 20
        A Taste of Italy: Eating (and Drinking) Locally.................22
          Relishing Roman cuisine....................................25
          Tasting Tuscany 26
          Visiting Venetian and Milanese eateries 27
          Gnawing Neapolitan delicacies 27
          Savoring Sicily 28

    Background Check: Recommended Books and Movies ...29
        True stories 29
        Works of fiction 30
        The moving image...30

Chapter 3: Deciding Where and When to Go 32

    Going Everywhere You Want to Be 32
        Roaming Rome 32
        Exploring Florence and the best of
           Tuscany and Umbria...33
        Viewing Venice and the Pianura Padana.................33
        Visiting Naples, Pompeii, and the Amalfi Coast......34
        Seeing Sicily...34
    Scheduling Your Time...35
    Revealing the Secrets of the Seasons 36
        April through June..37
        July and August..37
        September and October..37
        November through March 38
    Perusing a Calendar of Events..38
        January...38
        February...39
        March/April 39
        May 39
        June..40
        July..40
        August 41
        September..41
        October 41
        November 41
        December...41

Chapter 4: Following an Itinerary:
Four Great Options 43

    Seeing Italy's Highlights in One Week................................43
        Day 1 43
        Day 2 and 3 43
        Day 4 44
        Day 5 and 6 44
        Day 7 44
    Touring the Best of Italy in Two Weeks 44
        Day 1, 2, and 3 44
        Day 4 and 5 44
        Day 6, 7, and 8 44
        Day 9 and 10 44
        Day 11 45

Day 12 45
Day 13 45
Day 14 45
Discovering Italy with Kids 45
Day 1 and 2 46
Day 3 46
Day 4 and 5 46
Day 6 and 7 46
Unearthing Italy's Ancient History 47
Day 1 and 2 47
Day 3 47
Day 4 47
Day 5 47
Day 6 48
Day 7 48

Part II: Planning Your Trip to Italy 49

Chapter 5: Managing Your Money 51

Planning Your Budget 51
Transportation 52
Lodging 53
Dining 54
Sightseeing 55
Shopping 55
Nightlife 55
Cutting Costs — But Not the Fun 56
Handling Money 58
Making sense of the euro 58
Using ATMs and carrying cash 59
Charging ahead with credit cards 61
Toting traveler's checks 61
Taking Taxes into Account 62
Dealing with a Lost or Stolen Wallet 62

Chapter 6: Getting to Italy 64

Flying to Italy 64
Finding out which airlines fly there 64
Getting the best deal on your airfare 65
Cutting costs by using consolidators 66
Booking your flight online 67
Arriving by Other Means 67
Joining an Escorted Tour 68
Choosing a Package Tour 70

Chapter 7: Getting Around Italy...............................**72**

By Plane..72
By Train 73
By Bus...74
By Ferry...74
By Car 74

Chapter 8: Booking Your Accommodations..............**78**

Getting to Know Your Options 78
Finding the Best Room at the Best Rate............................81
Finding the best rate 81
Surfing the Web for hotel deals................................82
Reserving the best room..83
Renting Apartments and Villas.....................................84

**Chapter 9: Catering to Special Travel
Needs or Interests**.......................................**85**

Traveling with the Brood: Advice for Families.................85
Making Age Work for You: Tips for Seniors 86
Accessing Italy: Advice for Travelers with Disabilities 87
Following the Rainbow: Resources for Gay
and Lesbian Travelers 88
Making the Grade: Advice for Student Travelers.............89

Chapter 10: Taking Care of the Remaining Details.....**90**

Getting a Passport..90
Applying for a U.S. passport..................................90
Applying for other passports.................................91
Playing It Safe with Travel and Medical Insurance..........92
Staying Healthy When You Travel..............................93
Staying Connected by Cellphone or E-mail....................94
Using a cellphone in Italy.....................................94
Accessing the Internet away from home 95
Keeping Up with Airline Security 97
Saving Time with Advance Reservations.....................98

Part III: The Eternal City: Rome.........................*99*

Chapter 11: Settling into Rome..............................**101**

Getting There...101
By air 101
By train...104
Orienting Yourself in Rome.....................................105
Introducing the neighborhoods 106
Finding information after you arrive 110

Getting Around Rome 111
    By subway (metropolitana)......................111
    By bus and tram..112
    On foot...113
    By taxi..113
Staying in Style 113
    The top hotels 114
    Runner-up accommodations 123
Dining Out 124
Fast Facts: Rome 135

Chapter 12: Exploring Rome 138

Discovering Rome's Top Attractions...............139
Visiting the Vatican's Top Attractions 153
Finding More Cool Things to See and Do........158
Seeing Rome by Guided Tour 161
    Bus tours..161
    Walking tours...162
    Boat tours 162
Suggested One-, Two-, and Three-Day Itineraries 162
    Rome in one day 162
    Rome in two days......................................163
    Rome in three days....................................163
Shopping the Local Stores 164
    Best shopping areas 164
    What to look for and where to find it 165
Living It Up After Dark.....................................168
    The performing arts 169
    All that jazz and more 170
    Historic cafes...170
    Wine bars and pubs...................................170
    Dance clubs 171
    Gay and lesbian bars 171

Part 1V: Florence and the Best of Tuscany and Umbria 173

Chapter 13: Florence 175

Getting There...175
    By air 175
    By train..176
    By car 177
Orienting Yourself in Florence.........................177
    Introducing the neighborhoods 177
    Finding information after you arrive 181

Getting Around Florence 182
On foot 182
By bus 182
Staying in Style 183
The top hotels 186
Runner-up accommodations 190
Dining Out 190
Exploring Florence 197
Discovering the top attractions 197
Finding more cool things to see and do.................212
Seeing Florence by guided tour 213
Suggested one-, two-, and three-day itineraries....214
Shopping the Local Stores 215
Best shopping areas 216
What to look for and where to find it.....................216
Living It Up After Dark 218
The performing arts 218
Bars, pubs, and clubs 219
Discos 219
Gay and lesbian bars 219
Fast Facts: Florence 220

Chapter 14: Northern Tuscany and the Cinque Terre 223

Lucca 223
Getting there 226
Spending the night 226
Dining locally 228
Exploring Lucca 229
Fast Facts: Lucca 233
Pisa 234
Getting there 234
Spending the night 235
Dining locally 237
Exploring Pisa 238
Fast Facts: Pisa 244
The Cinque Terre 245
Getting there 245
Spending the night 247
Dining locally 248
Exploring the Cinque Terre 250
Fast Facts: The Cinque Terre 253

Chapter 15: Southern Tuscany and Umbria..............255

San Gimignano..256
    Getting there..256
    Spending the night..256
    Dining locally...258
    Exploring San Gimignano..............................260
Fast Facts: San Gimignano..................................262
Siena...262
    Getting there..262
    Spending the night..265
    Dining locally...268
    Exploring Siena..269
    Shopping for local treasures........................275
Fast Facts: Siena...275
Perugia..276
    Getting there..276
    Spending the night..277
    Dining locally...278
    Exploring Perugia..280
Fast Facts: Perugia..284
Assisi...284
    Getting there..285
    Spending the night..285
    Dining locally...286
    Exploring Assisi..288
Fast Facts: Assisi...292
Spoleto..292
    Getting there..293
    Spending the night..293
    Dining locally...294
    Exploring Spoleto..296
Fast Facts: Spoleto...298

Part V: Venice and the Best of the Pianura Padana 299

Chapter 16: Venice..............................301

Getting There..301
    By air..302
    By train...302
    By car...303
    By ship...303
Orienting Yourself in Venice...............................303
    Introducing the neighborhoods...................304
    Finding information after you arrive.............306

Getting Around Venice..307
    On foot..307
    By vaporetto..308
    By traghetto (ferry skiff)..............................309
    By water taxi..309
Staying in Style...310
    The top hotels..310
    Runner-up accommodations............................317
Dining Out...317
Exploring Venice...324
    Discovering the top attractions........................325
    Finding more cool things to see and do............336
    Seeing Venice by guided tour..........................339
    Suggested one-, two-, and three-day itineraries....340
Shopping the Local Stores......................................341
    Best shopping areas..341
    What to look for and where to find it...............342
Living It Up After Dark..343
    The performing arts..343
    Bars, pubs, and clubs....................................344
    Cafes..344
    Venice's Casino..344
Fast Facts: Venice..345

Chapter 17: Padua, Verona, and Milan......................347

Padua: Home of Giotto's Fabulous Frescoes..................347
    Getting there..348
    Spending the night..348
    Dining locally..352
    Exploring Padua..353
Fast Facts: Padua...357
Verona: City of Juliet and Romeo.............................358
    Getting there..358
    Spending the night..358
    Dining locally..360
    Exploring Verona..361
Fast Facts: Verona...365
Milan: Italy's Business and Fashion Center..................366
    Getting there..366
    Getting around..367
    Spending the night..367
    Dining locally..370
    Exploring Milan..372
    Shopping the local stores................................375
    Living it up after dark......................................376
Fast Facts: Milan..377

Part VI: Naples, Pompeii, and the Amalfi Coast 379

Chapter 18: Naples 381

Getting There 381
  By air 381
  By train 382
  By ferry or ship 382
  By car 382
Orienting Yourself in Naples 384
  Introducing the neighborhoods 385
  Finding information after you arrive 388
Getting Around Naples 388
  On foot 388
  By subway, bus, funicular, and tram 389
  By taxi 389
Staying in Style 389
  The top hotels 390
  Runner-up accommodations 391
Dining Out 392
Exploring Naples 395
  Discovering the top attractions 396
  Finding more cool things to see and do 402
  Seeing Naples by guided tour 404
  Suggested one-, two-, and three-day itineraries 404
Shopping the Local Stores 406
  Best shopping areas 406
  What to look for and where to find it 406
Living It Up After Dark 407
  The performing arts 407
  Live music 407
  Clubs and discos 408
  Wine bars and cafes 408
Fast Facts: Naples 408

Chapter 19: Going Beyond Naples: Three Day Trips 411

Campi Flegrei 411
  Getting there 411
  Taking a tour 412
  Seeing the sights 412
  Dining locally 414
  Spending the night 415

Herculaneum...415
   Getting there..415
   Taking a tour...415
   Seeing the sights 416
Pompeii..419
   Getting there..419
   Taking a tour...419
   Seeing the sights 419
   Dining locally..422

Chapter 20: Sorrento, Capri, and the Amalfi Coast 423

Sorrento...423
   Getting there..423
   Spending the night...424
   Dining locally..425
   Exploring Sorrento...426
   Living it up after dark...................................427
Fast Facts: Sorrento 428
Capri and the Blue Grotto 429
   Getting there..429
   Spending the night...430
   Dining locally..431
   Exploring Capri 432
   Shopping for local treasures 434
   Living it up after dark...................................436
Fast Facts: Capri 436
The Amalfi Coast 436
   Getting there..438
   Spending the night...439
   Dining locally..441
   Exploring the Amalfi Coast 443
   Living it up after dark...................................449
Fast Facts: The Amalfi Coast...............................449

Part VII: Sicily 451

Chapter 21: Palermo 453

Getting There...453
   By ferry 453
   By air 454
   By train...454
Orienting Yourself in Palermo 456
   Introducing the neighborhoods 456
   Finding information after you arrive.........458

Getting Around Palermo.................................458
On foot.................................459
By bus.................................459
By taxi.................................459
Staying in Style.................................460
The top hotels.................................460
Runner-up accommodations.................................462
Dining Out.................................462
Exploring Palermo.................................465
Discovering the top attractions.................................465
Finding more cool things to see and do.................................472
Seeing Palermo by guided tour.................................473
Suggested one-, two-, and three-day itineraries....474
Living It Up After Dark.................................475
Fast Facts: Palermo.................................476

Chapter 22: Taormina, Syracuse, and Agrigento.......478

Taormina.................................478
Getting there.................................480
Spending the night.................................480
Dining locally.................................482
Exploring Taormina.................................483
Fast Facts: Taormina.................................487
Syracuse.................................488
Getting there.................................488
Spending the night.................................489
Dining locally.................................490
Exploring Syracuse.................................490
Fast Facts: Syracuse.................................494
Agrigento and the Valley of the Temples.................................495
Getting there.................................495
Spending the night.................................495
Dining locally.................................496
Exploring Agrigento.................................497
Fast Facts: Agrigento.................................500

Part VIII: The Part of Tens.................................501

**Chapter 23: *Non Capisco:* The Top Ten
Expressions You Need to Know.................................503**

Per Favore.................................503
Grazie.................................503
Permesso.................................504
Scusi.................................504
Buon Giorno and Buona Sera.................................504
Arrivederci.................................504

Dov'è 505
Quanto Costa? 505
Che Cos'è? 505
Non Capisco 505

Chapter 24: Ten Great Italian Artists 506

Giotto 506
Donatello 506
Giovanni Bellini 507
Leonardo da Vinci 507
Michelangelo 507
Raphael 508
Titian 508
Tintoretto 508
Gian Lorenzo Bernini 508
Caravaggio 509

Appendix A: Quick Concierge 510

Fast Facts 510
Toll-Free Numbers and Web Sites 515
Where to Get More Information 516
Visitor information 516
Newspapers and magazines about Italy 518
Online resources 519

Appendix B: Glossary of Architectural
and Menu Terms 520

Knowing Your Nave from Your Ambone 520
Dining in Italy, from Acqua Pazza to Zuppa Inglese 522

Index 529

Introduction

*Y*ear after year, Italy tops tourist destination lists. Year after year, we keep having the times of our lives in spite of the crowds. Really. And what's not to like? The food is perfect, the people are welcoming and friendly, the climate is pleasant, and there is art everywhere!

Modern tourism started back in the 18th century, when the literati and aristocrats bent on learning began traveling through Europe to explore the ruins of ancient Greek and Roman sites as well as to admire the rich artistic production of the Renaissance. In the 19th century, Americans made taking the Grand Tour — the classic, months-long European tour enjoyed by the rich and satirized by Mark Twain in *The Innocents Abroad* — a rite of passage for the well-heeled. Anyone who has seen a Merchant Ivory film (*A Room with a View,* for one) knows that Italy was among the most popular stops on the Grand Tour. Today, the country is still a huge destination for both cultural and religious pilgrimages. Italy retains an almost mythical status in the minds of many for its fantastic range of natural and cultural attractions. The "problem" with visiting Italy is also this country's major appeal: It's totally saturated with things to see and do (and eat and drink, too). The cultural renaissance initiated in the late 1990s has not yet given signs of abating. Old attractions are being made more tourist-friendly and new ones are opening up; brand-new hotels and restaurants are popping up throughout the country; and English-speaking staff and signs are becoming more common. Yes, things keep improving for tourists here, and we're sure you'll have the time of your life traveling through Italy with us!

About This Book

With a history stretching from the dawn of time and artwork to match, Italy definitely offers too much to see in one trip, unless you're planning a six-month-long visit. Fortunately, we've combed the country to find the best deals and things to see and do. Whether you're a first-timer or making a repeat visit to see sights you missed the first go-round, you'll find something for you in *Italy For Dummies,* 4th Edition.

Unlike some travel guides that read more like a phonebook-style directory listing everything and anything, this book cuts to the chase. It's designed so that you can quickly look up and immediately find the information you need. This means that you don't have to read the whole thing from page one, but can open it at any point and delve into the subject at hand.

Dummies Post-it® Flags

As you're reading this book, you'll find information that you'll want to reference as you plan or enjoy your trip — whether it be a new hotel, a must-see attraction, or a must-try walking tour. Mark these pages with the handy Post-it® Flags included in this book to help make your trip planning easier!

Conventions Used in This Book

The structure of this book is nonlinear: In other words, you can look up just the things you're interested in without having to read whole chapters. To help you find information quickly and easily, we use a number of visual signs (icons) positioned at the margin (see "Icons Used in This Book," later in this chapter).

We have included lists of hotels, restaurants, and attractions, and for each we provide our frank evaluation. Hotels are divided into two categories — our personal favorites and those that don't quite make our preferred list but still get a hearty seal of approval. Don't be shy about considering these "runner-up" hotels if you're unable to get a room at one of our favorites, or if your preferences differ from ours — they are still excellent choices with above-average amenities and services.

We use this series of abbreviations for credit cards in our hotel and restaurant reviews:

AE: American Express

DC: Diners Club

MC: MasterCard

V: Visa

Note that Discover is not listed. The Discover Card is unknown in Italy, so it's a good idea to carry one or more of the big three — American Express, Visa, or MasterCard.

We also include some general pricing information to help you decide where to unpack your bags or grab a bite. We use a dollar-sign system to show the price range for one night in a hotel (in a double-occupancy room) or a full meal at a restaurant (including pasta or appetizer, main dish, side dish, and dessert, but no beverages). (Note that within the restaurant listing info, we give you the price range of just the main course, referred to as *secondi*.) See Chapter 8 for a detailed chart telling you exactly what to expect in each hotel category. Here are the price categories:

Cost	Hotel	Restaurant
$	Up to 140€ ($168)	Up to 40€ ($48)
$$	141€–230€ ($169–$276)	41€–55€ ($49–$66)
$$$	231€–350€ ($277–$420)	56€–70€ ($67–$84)
$$$$	More than 350€ (over $420)	71€ and up ($85 and up)

Prices are given in euro, followed by the U.S. dollar conversion; the exchange rate used is 1€ = $1.20. Note, however, that establishments can change prices without notice and exchange rates may vary.

Another thing you will find attached to each listing is contact information. Web sites are listed whenever possible. As for telephone numbers, don't be surprised if you see ☎ **0743-220320** right near ☎ **055-290832**. The number of digits in Italian phone numbers is not standardized as it is in the United States. Area codes can have 2, 3, or 4 digits; the rest of the number can have as few as 4 or as many as 8 digits.

For those hotels, restaurants, and attractions that are plotted on a map, a page reference is provided in the listing information. If a hotel, restaurant, or attraction is outside the city limits or in an out-of-the-way area, it may not be mapped.

Foolish Assumptions

We've made some assumptions about you and what your needs may be as a traveler. Here's what we assume:

✔ You may be wondering whether to take a trip to Italy and how to plan for it. You may be a first-time visitor to Italy.

✔ You may be an experienced traveler who doesn't have a ton of time to plan your trip or to spend in Italy after you get there. You want expert advice on how to maximize your time and enjoy a hassle-free trip.

✔ You're not looking for a book that provides every bit of information available about Italy. Instead, you're looking for a book that focuses on the places that will give you the best or most unique experience in Italy.

If you fit any of these criteria, then *Italy For Dummies,* 4th Edition, provides the information you're looking for!

How This Book Is Organized

The book has eight parts, plus two appendixes. Each can be read independently if you want to zero in on a particular area or issue.

Part I: Introducing Italy

The first part is where you'll find in-depth information on Italy, from our rundown of the best it has to offer (Chapter 1) to details on its history, culture, people, architecture, and cuisine (Chapter 2). You'll also find climate information and a calendar of special events (Chapter 3), plus our suggested itineraries (Chapter 4).

Part II: Planning Your Trip to Italy

Here we give you our best tips on trip planning: from budgeting — with advice on where to save money and where not to (Chapter 5) — to figuring out the best ways to get here from abroad (Chapter 6) and to travel from one destination to another within Italy (Chapter 7). We also describe hotel standards and practices (Chapter 8) and address the special concerns of families, seniors, students, and gays and lesbians (Chapter 9). We address all other necessary details — from getting your passport to thinking about your health — in Chapter 10.

Part III: The Eternal City: Rome

This eternally lively city, Italy's capital, is as contemporary as it is ancient, a living ruin still under construction. This section includes our best tips on hotels and restaurants (Chapter 11), as well as a tour of this wonderful maze of ancient and modern treasures (Chapter 12).

Part IV: Florence and the Best of Tuscany and Umbria

Tuscany and Umbria are dotted with historic and picturesque towns. Florence's still brilliant Renaissance heritage (Chapter 13) often overshadows neighboring towns, such as Pisa and Lucca (Chapter 14), which are also repositories of art and culture. You'll find more of our Tuscan and Umbrian picks in Chapter 15.

Part V: Venice and the Best of the Pianura Padana

You will fall for Venice's mysterious and lovely villa-crowded islands that seem to float upon the water. But to avoid the city's pitfalls and stay within your budget, follow our tips in Chapter 16. We explore the best of the nearby Pianura Padana (including Verona and Milan) in Chapter 17.

Part VI: Naples, Pompeii, and the Amalfi Coast

This corner of Italy is packed with diversity and contrast — as well as an immense art endowment. Naples is a fascinating hive of activity as well as a treasure-trove of history and art (Chapter 18). It is surrounded by some of the world's greatest archaeological areas: Pompeii, Herculaneum, and the Campi Flegrei (Chapter 19). A short distance to the south is the splendid Sorrento Peninsula, with the mythical isle of Capri and the Amalfi Coast (Chapter 20).

Part VII: Sicily

A stone's throw from Africa and hundreds of miles from the Alps, the island of Sicily seems at once most intensely "Italian" and strangely different. Nowhere is the mix of cultures more dazzling than in the region's capital, Palermo (Chapter 21). And in no place is the presence of the past as ghostly as at the Greek temples of Agrigento, Selinunte, and Segesta, or fascinating as in Taormina, Piazza Armerina, Catania, and Syracuse (Chapter 22).

Part VIII: The Part of Tens

Here we've squeezed in some extra info we think you'll find useful: Italian expressions worth knowing (Chapter 23) and our favorite Italian artists (Chapter 24).

Appendix A and B

Go to Appendix A to find Quick Concierge, an A-to-Z directory that gives you the facts you need to know, such as how the telephone system works and what to expect at Customs. We also provide a list of toll-free phone numbers and Web sites for airlines, hotels, and car-rental agencies serving Italy, plus sources for additional tourist information. In Appendix B, you'll find a glossary of useful architecture and menu terms.

Icons Used in This Book

As you have already seen, we use icons throughout this book as signposts and flags for facts and information of a particular nature or interest. Following are the five types of icons:

 This icon highlights money-saving tips and/or great deals.

 This icon highlights the best the destination has to offer in all categories — hotels, restaurants, attractions, activities, shopping, and nightlife.

 This icon gives you a heads up on annoying or potentially dangerous situations such as tourist traps, unsafe neighborhoods, rip-offs, and other things to beware of.

 This icon highlights places that are particularly hospitable to children or people traveling with kids. In restaurant listings, it means highchairs and *mezza porzione* (half portions) are on offer; in hotels, it indicates cribs, extra beds, or triples and quads are available. We also mention if other amenities suitable for children — a play area, garden, pool, baby sitting — are provided.

This icon points out useful advice on things to do and ways to schedule your time.

Where to Go from Here

Now you can dig in wherever you want. The next chapter highlights the best of Italy, from museums to hotels to intangibles (experiences you may not want to miss). If you already have an itinerary in mind, you can jump ahead to the ins and outs of finding a flight and making a budget; or you can browse through city destinations you may want to visit. And if you've already traveled to Italy once or a score of times, you are still sure to find something here you haven't seen.

Part I
Introducing Italy

The 5th Wave   By Rich Tennant

"I insisted they learn some Italian. I couldn't stand the idea of standing in front of the Trevi Fountain and hearing, 'gosh', 'wow', and 'far out.'"

In this part . . .

This is where we get you excited about your trip before you go and satisfy your curiosity about this Italian world you have decided to discover. We will help you decide when and exactly where to go. We'll tell you what sort of weather to expect, where you are likely to have to deal with tourist hordes, and where, instead, you can relax in relative solitude off the beaten path. In this part, we sort through your options, showing the advantages and drawbacks of each choice and mentioning special considerations.

In Chapter 1, we highlight what we consider the best of Italy, from churches to restaurants to travel experiences. In Chapter 2, we give more information on Italy's history and culture, including the regional cuisine and local wines. In Chapter 3, we describe the best seasons in which to travel and also provide a calendar of the most important festivals and events. Finally, in case you don't want to plan your own trip or are looking for some ideas, we list four great itineraries in Chapter 4.

Chapter 1

Discovering the Best of Italy

In This Chapter

▶ From museums to ruins

▶ From churches to tchotchkes

▶ From hotels to dining

*I*taly's variety attracts all sorts of visitors. Art lovers flock to its great museums and wonderfully decorated churches and palaces, the faithful make pilgrimages to the Vatican, and gourmands devour its glorious cuisines. In *Italy For Dummies,* 4th Edition, we give you our vision of the best Italy has to offer. Here's a taste of what's ahead:

The Best Museums

Art in Italy is everywhere, but the museums, of course, enjoy the advantage of high concentrations of artwork in one place. If your itinerary takes you to any of the following cities, don't miss the selections later — even if you are not a serious museum-goer.

✔ You'll need several days if you want to see the whole art collection of the **Vatican Museums** in Rome. Not only does this include dozens of rooms dedicated to painting and sculpture, but it's also home to the **Sistine Chapel,** decorated with Michelangelo's frescoes — the most famous artwork in all of Italy, and, after the *Mona Lisa,* probably the most famous single artwork in the world. Don't forget your binoculars. See Chapter 12.

✔ Also in Rome, the **Galleria Borghese** is smaller, but houses one of the best art collections in the world. It's known especially for its Caravaggio paintings and breathtaking Bernini sculptures. See Chapter 12.

✔ The **National Roman Museum** in Rome's **Palazzo Massimo alle Terme** holds an astounding collection of ancient Roman artifacts, including unique mosaics and frescoes of rare beauty (entire rooms of Roman villas are reconstructed!). See Chapter 12.

✔ Florence's **Galleria degli Uffizi** is a required stop on any Italian itinerary for its superb pageant of Renaissance art. Only between the covers of a book could you find so many Italian masterpieces in one place. See Chapter 13.

✔ The **Gallerie dell'Accademia** in Venice houses the greatest collection of Venetian painting in the world, from the incandescent works of Bellini to monumental pieces by Tintoretto and Veronese. See Chapter 16.

✔ Often overlooked by tourists who go to Milan principally for the excellent shopping, the **Brera** is a beautiful 17th-century palace that contains the principal painting gallery in northern Italy. The collection of the **Pinacoteca** stretches from the 15th to the 20th century, including unique masterpieces. See Chapter 17.

✔ The **Museo di Capodimonte** houses its huge painting collection — the best in southern Italy — in an enormous palace high above Naples and surrounded by a beautiful park. See Chapter 18.

✔ The **Archaeological Museum,** also in Naples, is Italy's foremost museum of the art of antiquity. The splendid collection includes treasures of Pompeii that were removed from the buried city for safekeeping. See Chapter 18.

The Best Churches

Over the ages, churches in Italy have been decorated with the best works of art and built according to the designs of the greatest architects. Here are our absolute favorites from among the thousands of options.

✔ **St. Peter's Basilica** in Rome is justly the most famous church in a country filled with magnificent churches. Its majestic colonnade and soaring dome create a symbol of Rome as well as of the Catholic Church; inside are unique art treasures that include Michelangelo's *Pietà.* See Chapter 12.

✔ Among Italian churches, Florence's **Duomo,** with Brunelleschi's red-tiled dome soaring over it, is second in size only to St. Peter's Basilica. This architectural masterpiece is also known for its artworks, bell tower, and the famous doors of the nearby baptistery. See Chapter 13.

✔ Venice's **Basilica di San Marco** is as dreamlike and magical as the rest of the city. Decorated inside with 3,717 sq. m (40,000 sq. ft.) of gilded mosaics, it contains a host of marvels and has been the focus of the *piazza* that bears its name since the 11th century. See Chapter 16.

✔ The **Duomo** of Milan is a fabulous example of Italian Gothic architecture that took half a millennium to build. With its 135 towers, it may look like a whimsical construction — and to some, it resembles a sand castle. See Chapter 17.

✔ The churches of Naples are many and splendid, but if you have time for just one, make it the **Duomo.** It's actually three churches in one, from the paleo-Christian Santa Restituta (with the oldest western baptistery in the world) to the late baroque Cappella di San Gennaro. Don't miss the splendid array of artwork here. See Chapter 18.

✔ The **Duomo di Monreale,** located on a hill dominating Palermo, is a 12th-century Romanesque church whose austere exterior makes the 5,111 sq. m (55,000 sq. ft.) of Byzantine mosaics inside even more awe-inspiring. See Chapter 21.

The Best Ruins and Archaeological Areas

Say "Italy," and most people think of the ancient Romans. The country, and especially its southern half, is chock-full of archaeological remains — mostly Roman, but also Greek, including a number of the world's best. Here are our favorites.

✔ Rome's symbol and most famous ruin, the **Colosseum,** is still majestic even after centuries of decay. See for yourself where the Romans watched "sports" (read: fights to the death). Nearby are the archaeological areas of the **Roman Forum** and the **Palatine Hill,** and of the **Imperial Forums;** together they were the administrative and business center of ancient Rome. See Chapter 12.

✔ In the small town of Verona lies a great **Roman Amphitheater,** second only to the Colosseum in its state of preservation. Used as a performance hall for decades, it is still a living ruin, with a full season of concerts and opera. See Chapter 17.

✔ Who hasn't heard of **Pompeii?** The city — buried whole by Mount Vesuvius's A.D. 79 eruption — was an extremely wealthy resort during Roman times, famous for the beauty of its abodes; its frescoes are among the best in the world. See Chapter 19.

✔ Less famous than Pompeii is **Herculaneum,** a smaller town also buried by Mount Vesuvius in A.D. 79. It was a VIP resort in Roman times and remains a superb archaeological site today; many houses still have their second story preserved. See Chapter 19.

✔ The glorious Greek temples of **Paestum** lie out of the way — not far from Salerno, south of the Amalfi Coast — and are therefore often overlooked by tourists in a hurry. Try not to miss them if you're in the area. See Chapter 20.

✔ The **Valley of the Temples** at Agrigento in Sicily is the most dramatic archaeological site in Italy. A series of majestic Greek temples dominated this city, which was founded in the sixth century B.C. The ruins stand on their own in a dramatic, unspoiled landscape, and include one of the largest temples of antiquity, the **Temple of Jupiter,** which was over 30m (110 ft.) tall. See Chapter 22.

The Best Luxury Hotels

Okay, so maybe you can't afford to stay in luxury hotels every night . . . but if you want to splurge, then pick one of our favorite dream places for a special night — it will be a cherished memory for the rest of your life.

✔ In Rome, the **Hotel de Russie** holds its own against all the competition, thanks to its incomparably romantic setting and unique style. See Chapter 11.

✔ With its stylish yet welcoming interior and special children's programs, the **Hotel Savoy** tops our list in Florence. See Chapter 13.

✔ The **Brufani** in Perugia is a rare gem, boasting old-fashioned charm and courtesy coupled with modern amenities. See Chapter 15.

✔ Staying at the **Cipriani and Palazzi** on the Giudecca island in Venice will let you experience the city's grandeur in a manner that hasn't been topped since the 18th century. See Chapter 16.

✔ Housed in a former 15th-century convent, the **Four Seasons** hotel in Milan will overwhelm you with its charm and its perfect location. See Chapter 17.

✔ In Naples, the **Grand Hotel Parker's** and the **Grand Hotel Vesuvio** have very distinct personalities and so many fine qualities that both have won us over. See Chapter 18.

✔ Capri is a dream island — and the **Capri Palace** in Anacapri is the hotel to match, beginning with its ideal perch at the top of the island. See Chapter 20.

✔ The **Hotel San Pietro** in Positano and the **Palazzo Sasso** in Ravello are two jewels along the most beautiful stretch of coast in Italy, each approaching perfection in its own way. See Chapter 20.

✔ Sicily has captured our hearts, and the **San Domenico Palace** and the **Grand Hotel Timeo** in Taormina will take yours. A stay at either hotel is a feast for the senses. See Chapter 22.

The Best Gourmet Restaurants

Italians take food very seriously. Dining in one of the country's best restaurants is like a near-mystical experience: Not only is the food superlative, but nothing that surrounds you will be less than perfect, from your chair down to your napkin. Foodie or not, you won't eat in one of the following restaurants every day — few people could afford to do so — but do choose one of these places for a very special meal.

✔ For fantastic views over the Eternal City, with wonderful food to match, try **La Pergola**. This elegant restaurant will be one of your most romantic experiences in Rome. See Chapter 11.

✔ Don't miss **Cibreo** if you're visiting Florence. The restaurant's creative chef puts a unique spin on the best of Tuscan cuisine. You'll also get to taste a huge variety of the region's best wines. See Chapter 13.

✔ Hidden away from the main tourist haunts, yet within walking distance from San Polo, **Osteria da Fiore** in Venice is an address for connoisseurs. Do not miss it if you want to discover the best of Venetian cuisine. See Chapter 16.

✔ Whether you're a fan of risotto or not, visit **CraccoPeck** in Milan. Gourmands flock to this elegant restaurant just a few steps from the Duomo, as it's simply the best in the city. See Chapter 17.

✔ **Il Desco** in Verona is not only a great chef's restaurant, but also a very pleasant place where you'll feel welcome and taken care of in a wonderfully friendly way. Many foodies will tell you this is the best restaurant in Italy. See Chapter 17.

✔ The **San Pietro** in Positano — inside the hotel of the same name — is one of the best and most beautiful places to dine on this equally beautiful stretch of coast. See Chapter 20.

The Best Travel Experiences

If you love Italy, it will reward you with your own unforgettable and unpredictable experiences. Below is a small selection of our own favorites.

✔ The **Pantheon** is the most perfectly preserved building of ancient Rome. Built in 27 B.C., it was spared the looting that befell other Roman structures because it had been turned into a Christian church. It doesn't feel like a church, however. From its soaring dome (with a round opening through which you see the Roman sky) to its marble pavement, it is a stunning, airy space where you can literally walk through antiquity. See Chapter 12.

✔ Siena's **Palio delle Contrade** is more than a horse race: It's a grudge match between the city's neighborhoods that's been going on for hundreds of years. It's still carried out with all the pomp, ceremony, and costumes of Renaissance Siena. The race (quite dangerous) is held in the main square of the town — which is filled with dirt for the occasion. Imagine the Kentucky Derby being held in Times Square. See Chapter 15.

✔ Taking a **gondola ride** through Venice may be expensive and "touristy," but — especially at dusk — it is an enchanting experience. You must see for yourself the water shimmering with reflections, the imposing yet whimsical Venetian architecture, and the stillness and sheer unbelievability of it all. See Chapter 16.

✔ Crossing the **Gulf of Naples** coming from Capri or Sorrento, and entering Naples at sunset, with Mount Vesuvio in the background and the city's lights starting to come up in front of you, is truly magic: You'll now understand the old adage, "See Naples and die." See Chapter 18.

✔ Walking the streets of **Pompeii** is an awe-inspiring experience. Buried beneath volcanic ash by the eruption of Mount Vesuvius in A.D. 79, Pompeii was a flourishing Roman town caught in amber. Even corpses were turned into human statues. See Chapter 19.

✔ The **Teatro Greco-Romano (Greco-Roman Theater)** at Taormina in Sicily would be special enough as the best-preserved antique theater in Italy, where plays were staged starting in the third century B.C. But to see a play performed here today is truly amazing. See Chapter 22.

The Best Traditional Italian Souvenirs

Although you wouldn't expect to find "ethnic" gifts in Italy, there is a small selection of high-quality handcrafted goods that have been traditionally produced in Italy for centuries. They make splendid gifts.

✔ The beautiful, extensive selection of **marbled paper goods** at Giulio Giannini & Figlio in Florence are worth checking out; they make perfect gifts and come in many price levels. See Chapter 13. You can also find a large selection of marbleized paper at Piazzesi in Venice. See Chapter 16.

✔ Invest in some **Murano glass** artwork or find smaller blown-glass gift items. If it's authentic Murano, then even the most inexpensive item will appreciate in value. See Chapter 16.

✔ In Naples, select a set of **hand-modeled figurines** for the *presepio* (crèche) for someone who will appreciate them, or start your own collection. See Chapter 18.

✔ Make a gift of a beautiful **cameo jewel,** the finely carved coral or shells that have been the pride of Torre del Greco (near Naples) since antiquity. See Chapter 18.

✔ Check out the colorful **hand-painted porcelain** — dinnerware, pitchers, tiles, vases — traditionally produced according to local historical patterns in Deruta, near Perugia (see Chapter 15); in Vietri, on the Costiera Amalfitana (see Chapter 20); and in the Sicilian towns of Caltagirone, Santo Stefano, and Sciacca (see Chapter 22).

✔ And, of course, take your pick of **fashion accessories** — scarves, leather gloves, handbags, wallets, watches, sunglasses — from the many local designers in Rome, Florence, Milan, Naples, Capri, and Positano. See Chapters 12, 13, 17, 18, and 20.

Chapter 2

Digging Deeper into Italy

In This Chapter

▶ Understanding Italy, past and present

▶ Exploring 2,500 years of great architecture

▶ Savoring Italy's culture and cuisine

▶ Learning more about Italy from books and movies

*I*taly became the tourist destination of choice in the 19th century, and the first travel books on Italian culture made their appearance then. Multifarious Italian culture has puzzled visitors for centuries; here we have put together some highlights which we hope will help you enjoy a richer traveling experience.

History 101: The Main Events

If Mesopotamia is the cradle of civilization, then Italy is the cradle of Western culture. In the ancient world, Italy was the center of an empire that covered all of western Europe and much of northern Africa and the Middle East. The Romans left behind towns, roads, and aqueducts which are in large part still alive and used today. The principles of Roman (and Greek) civilization are the bedrock of modern Western values and institutions. Summarizing Italy's history in anything less than a book-length study is bound to leave huge gaps, but here goes.

Around 1000 B.C., several peoples inhabited Italy, among them the Villanova Italic tribe, which settled in the region of Rome, and the **Etruscans,** a people probably originally from Asia Minor who were famed for their seafaring, gold and metal work, and trading. The Etruscans had already developed a sophisticated culture in Tuscany and Umbria when Rome was still a collection of shepherd's huts and the first Greek colonies were just putting in an appearance in the south of the peninsula. As the Etruscans expanded southward, their culture had a huge impact on Rome — they gave the city its name, drained the swamps, built sewers, and introduced writing. Near the beginning of the

Italian history at a glance

c. 1000 B.C.	Etruscans rule central Italy; they develop large towns and commercial centers.
c. 800 B.C.	First Greek colonies established; southern Italy and Sicily become the "Magna Grecia," surpassing the mother country in wealth and success.
c. 509 B.C.	Last of the Etruscan kings overthrown in Rome: the Republic is born. It will end with Julius Caesar's tyranny (49–44 B.C.).
27 B.C.	Octavian Augustus crowned first Roman emperor. His reign will last 40 years and signal the beginning of the famous Pax Romana ("Roman peace"), a 200-year period of stability ending with the death of Marcus Aurelius in A.D.180. There is plenty of war during the "pax," but Rome brings the whole Mediterranean world under its administrative control.
A.D. 192	Assassination of Commodus and beginning of the decline of the empire.
A.D. 330	Emperor Constantine converts to Christianity and builds Constantinople.
A.D. 395	Roman Empire splits into eastern and western factions. Barbarians threaten the borders and in A.D. 410 the Goths sack Rome. Other barbarian invasions follow.
A.D. 476	Western emperor Julius Nepos executed and the German warrior Odoacer proclaimed king, effectively ending the Roman Empire. Starts the Ostrogoth reign with capital in Ravenna.
A.D. 552	Narsete — the general of Justinian, emperor in Constantinople — defeats Goths after a long war; he moves the capital back to Rome. Starts the slow rise of the temporal power of the church.
6TH–8TH centuries A.D.	Italy is divided between Longobards (ruling northern Italy, Tuscany, and part of southern Italy) and Byzantines (ruling Sicily, Rome, and some coastal towns such as Venice and Bari).
A.D. 756	"Donation of Pepin": Pepin III (predecessor of Charlemagne) recognizes the pope's right to his own state and territory, in exchange for being crowned king by the pope. The Vatican State formally begins.
A.D. 800	Charlemagne crowned emperor in St. Peter's Basilica by Pope Leo III. He establishes a kingdom of Italy as part of his new empire, but his power on the peninsula is weak. The Byzantine resist.
9th–10th centuries	Saracens (Muslim Turks) attack from their strongholds in southern Italy. Muslim Arabs colonize Sicily. Maritime republics — Amalfi, Pisa, Genoa, and Venice — start gaining power.
1030	Normans take over southern Italy from Byzantines and Arabs; will rule first Sicily and then the whole south of the peninsula up to Naples. Their reign will pass to the Swebian dynasty in 1194, the Angevins in 1266, and the Aragonese dynasty in 1442.

11th–13th centuries	*Comuni* — city-states — take over control in what had been the Longobard reign; the four maritime republics rule over the sea. Commerce flourishes.
14th century	Italian Renaissance begins: The culture of antiquity is rediscovered; great achievements in the arts and ideas will then spread to the rest of Europe. The city-states are well established. The papacy moves to Avignon, France, in 1309; it will not be back until 1377.
1542	The Inquisition begins; Naples will be the only town in the Catholic world to refuse it and resist.
1707	Austrian Hapsburgs take over the southern kingdom; they will have to give it up to the Bourbons in 1734. They will keep northern Italy, however.
1798	Napoleon invades Italy, creating two republics; they will fall with him in 1815. Papacy is restored in central Italy; Hapsburgs and Bourbons share the rest of the peninsula.
1860	Garibaldi conquers southern Italy and pushes through the Marches (belonging to the Holy See); the new Kingdom of Italy is proclaimed. The Austrians are chased from Venice, their last stronghold in Italy, in 1866. Rome is taken in 1870; it will be proclaimed capital of the kingdom in 1871.
1915–1918	Italy participates in World War I beside France and the United Kingdom; 650,000 Italians die.
1922	After the "march on Rome," Benito Mussolini obtains from the king the right to form a new government. He will rapidly transform it into a dictatorship. The fascist era begins.
1929	The Vatican signs the Lateran Pacts, agreeing to relinquish all of Rome except its churches and the territory of the Vatican.
1940	Italy enters World War II on the side of Germany.
1943	Allied troops land in Sicily, welcomed by the locals. The Italian king signs the armistice and has Mussolini arrested. The Germans occupy the country, countered by the population which, with the help of the Allies, will free southern Italy up to Naples. Rome, occupied by the Germans in spite of the resistance of Italian troops, is later heavily bombarded by the Allies. The Italian Resistance begins.
1944	Rome is liberated by the Allies on June 4. Milan will have to wait until April 1945. The Italian Republic is officially established in 1946, after a referendum decided against the monarchy. The new constitution is signed in 1948.
1957	Italy is a cofounder of the European Community.

fifth century B.C., however, the local populations began striving for independence. Weakened by their struggles with the Greeks who were colonizing southern Italy, the Etruscans lost their power over Rome — and the Roman Republic was subsequently founded in 509 B.C., when the last of Rome's kings was overthrown.

The **Roman Republic** was headed by two consuls and the senate, all controlled by the upper or patrician (aristocratic) class. The plebeians (working class) later obtained their own council and were represented by tribunes. Rome's power grew, and the city started gaining control first over the Italian peninsula and then gradually over all western Europe and the Mediterranean. Rome showed its might in decades of bloody war against the city of Carthage, whose empire spread across North Africa and into Spain. Known as the Punic Wars, these conflicts began in 264 B.C. It took the Carthaginian general Hannibal six months to make the famous march with his elephants over the Alps to attack the Romans in 218 B.C., which marked the start of the Second Punic War. His army inflicted crushing defeats on the Roman armies, but eventually the Punic Wars ended with the Romans literally erasing Carthage from the map in 146 B.C. The door was then open for Rome to spread its influence across the Mediterranean. Although the Romans have been called the "Prussians of the ancient world" for their militarism, they also strove to bring civil peace and economic development. Rome ruled its provinces through governors and allowed subject countries to retain their local governments and customs — though betrayal of Rome was brutally avenged. The republic became fantastically rich, and Hellenic and Eastern art, wealth, and cultural influences flowed into Rome and Italy.

The end of the Roman Republic and the beginning of the **Roman Empire** arrived largely through the antagonism of two great generals, **Pompey** and **Julius Caesar,** who became a tyrant after his defeat of Pompey. Following Caesar's murder on the Ides of March in 44 B.C., civil war ensued and was won by Caesar's grandnephew and adopted son, Octavian, who became Rome's first emperor, **Caesar Augustus.** His regime began a period of peace and development and turned Rome into a glowing marble city the likes of which the world had never seen. Rome became the cultural beacon for an empire that extended from the Caspian Sea to Scotland. Augustus was followed by a string of mostly debauched and even insane rulers: **Tiberius, Caligula, Claudius** (a partial exception, even though his third wife, Nero's mother, was also his niece), and **Nero.** However, in the second century, a string of "good" emperors brought order, stable succession, and civility to the state. They were **Nerva, Trajan, Hadrian, Antoninus Pius,** and the philosopher-emperor **Marcus Aurelius.** With the assassination of Commodus, Marcus Aurelius's son, in the year 192, the empire plunged once more into chaos. A period beleaguered by war, plague, barbarian invasions, and inflation spelled the beginning of the bitter end.

When **Emperor Constantine** converted to Christianity and founded Constantinople (today's Istanbul) in A.D. 330, Rome's wealth shifted east. The western empire crumbled under barbarian pressure: The **Goths** sacked Rome in A.D. 410; the Huns came next under **Attila,** and were followed by the **Vandals** of North Africa. In A.D. 476, the German chief Odoacer deposed the western Roman emperor, in effect signaling the end of the once invincible Roman Empire.

Italy was fought over by the Goths, Byzantines, and Longobards. In 552, the Byzantines chased the Goths from Rome and northern Italy, but their power was weak and they could not resist the pressure of the Longobards, who took over much of the peninsula except for Rome, Sicily, and some coastal towns.

As Rome became the seat of the Catholic church, Rome and Italy became a pilgrimage site for believers from the whole Western world. The French king **Charlemagne** tried to revive the western empire and, in A.D. 800, was crowned by the pope as the head of the **Holy Roman Empire.** His power over the kingdom of Italy lasted only during his lifetime (city-states started developing right after his death), but the system he established profoundly affected Italy's history during the Middle Ages and Renaissance. The German emperor was elected by the German princes, but only the pope could crown him Holy Roman Emperor. For the next 1,000 years, Italian politics were defined by the struggle among the Holy Roman Emperor (who was German), the pope, Spain, and France (aspiring to the imperial crown).

In the 13th century, Italy was the crossroads of the Mediterranean. A banking and commercial culture was based on the great seafaring empires of **Venice** and **Genoa,** as well as **Amalfi, Pisa,** and land-based but powerful **Florence; Milan** and other smaller city-states dominated the rest of Italy. This economic well-being and the circulation of ideas generated by trade led to the beginning of the **Renaissance** in the 14th century. This movement, which was to later inform all of Europe, was above all the rediscovery of classical learning and culture, which in turn led to an explosion of creativity, art, and exploration. The new philosophy of **humanism** promoted the dignity and goodness of the human individual and developing secularism, in contrast with the Middle Ages' emphasis on human sinfulness and doctrinal orthodoxy.

Only in the south and in Sicily, where the **Normans** (Viking descendants) founded a kingdom in the 11th century, did medieval **feudalism** take root. Later, the Spanish rulers used feudalism for their own political aims and induced it to hang on — one of the causes of north–south cultural and economic disparities that still persist.

Especially starting in the 15th century, artists and scholars from all over the Western world were drawn to Italy's burgeoning centers of art and learning, which disseminated a new way of thinking — humanism — to the rest of Europe. Unfortunately, first the Inquisition, and then the power struggle between Spain, France, and Germany, put an end to the Renaissance. City-states like Florence and Siena sought the help of those powerful larger states in their local wars, thus inviting foreign intervention in Italy. The treaty of 1559 that acknowledged Spanish claims in Italy was the start of a 250-year decline. The mercantile empires and the city-states waned, and between them the Spanish and the popes imposed a reactionary and stultifying rule that was only relieved with the arrival of **Napoleon** and revolutionary ideas.

The end of the Napoleonic era brought back reactionary regimes, with Austria dominating in northern Italy, and Spain in southern Italy, but the *Risorgimento* ("resurgence") began to gain momentum. Led by powerful political figures such as Mazzini and Garibaldi, the movement worked for the unification of Italy. Secret societies like the *Carbonari* were born. The radical **Giuseppe Mazzini** favored an Italian republic, but unification eventually came about by the creation of a liberal state formed around the house of Savoy, rulers of Piedmont and Sardinia. The revolutionary **Giuseppe Garibaldi** threw his weight and military genius behind the liberal plan. After Garibaldi conquered the Kingdom of the Two Sicilies, Umbria and Marche were annexed to Sardinia, and the Kingdom of Italy was proclaimed in 1861. Veneto was obtained in 1866 and Rome finally wrested from Papal-French control in 1870, thus completing the unification.

Between 1870 and World War I, Italy saw massive emigration to the United States and Argentina. The country was tempted by territorial promises to join the Allies in 1915 (mainly in order to get Venice back from the Austrians), and 650,000 Italians lost their lives. After **World War I,** discontent and economic depression helped **Mussolini** rise to power. Mussolini's imperialist adventures abroad were matched by repression at home, and his alliance with the Nazis was disastrous. Italians turned against him in 1943 and then continued in **World War II** on the Allied side while suffering under German occupation.

Italy rebuilt itself after the war and became a modern democratic state. It joined in the creation of the **European Community** in 1957 and has been a promoter of European unification ever since. Today, unemployment is a persistent problem, and many Italians — even those engaged in such professions as law, academics, and architecture — work for free for years just to get a foot on the employment ladder. Corruption has also been a nagging problem, but in the 1990s, a series of scandals and dramatic trials of key Mafia leaders led to a major housecleaning and the proclamation of the "new Italy." The country has received massive influxes of immigrants and refugees in recent years, and the long-term effects of these demographic changes are a great unknown.

Architecture: From Ruins to Rococo

Italy offers a compendium of architectural styles — Roman and Greek, Romanesque, medieval, Gothic, Renaissance, baroque, rococo, futurist, and contemporary. With its foot as far south as Africa and its head in the Alps, the peninsula has been a corridor for influences passing back and forth. This is perhaps most obvious in Sicily, with its mixture of Arab and

Norman architecture, but almost any church or palace (especially those like Milan's **Duomo,** which took 500 years to build) will show traces of more than one style.

Sicily's temples at **Segesta** and **Agrigento** (the famous "valley of temples") are examples of the architecture brought to Italy from Greece by colonists. These temples date from the fifth and sixth centuries B.C. and display the **Doric** style (most easily spotted in the simple rectilinear capitals at the tops of columns). Roman architecture absorbed this early style as well as later Greek developments, such as the **Ionic** capital (like a scroll) and the **Corinthian** (the most ornate capital, decorated with a profusion of leaves). The **Colosseum** in Rome demonstrates all three styles or "orders."

Byzantine style dominates the few examples of paleo-Christian architecture left — mostly churches. Of the country's Christian-era churches, the earliest to be found are in the **Romanesque** style, which, as its name suggests, drew inspiration from Roman architecture — particularly the use of the arch. Some people find the Romanesque stolid and gloomy, while to us it has an appealing simplicity (especially in comparison with some later gaudy developments in church architecture) that makes it our favorite architectural style. **Spoleto** has several Romanesque churches, including its beautiful **Duomo.**

Influence from northern Europe brought to Italy the **Gothic** style, known for its soaring towers and the flying buttresses that support the building. Not surprisingly, Italy's foremost example of Gothic architecture is in Milan — its famous **Duomo** — while the style is little represented farther south, and when used it is intermingled with other artistic influences, such as in Rome's only Gothic church, **Santa Maria Sopra Minerva.**

The architecture of **Tuscany** and **Umbria** is famous for its alternating striations of colored marble — black, white, pink, or green. This characteristic element can be found in churches considered Gothic, as in the **Duomo** of **Siena,** but also in **Renaissance** masterpieces like the **Duomo** of **Florence.** The Renaissance style stressed proportion and balance, and avoided some of the higgledy-piggledy accretions that occurred in Gothic churches built over hundreds of years. The classical orders were also employed, with the Doric in the first story of the building, the Ionic in the middle, and the Corinthian at the top. Michelangelo's **Palazzo Farnese** in Rome is a classic example of the Renaissance style, as is his dome of **St. Peter's Basilica.**

The Renaissance style evolved into **baroque,** a fuller and more ornate style. The sweeping colonnade in front of St. Peter's, designed by Bernini, is a perfect example of this style. If baroque was an elaboration of the Renaissance style, then **rococo** was overkill — the addition of all sorts of baubles and flourishes to the underlying structure. Perhaps the best word to describe rococo is "busy." With its twisting columns and encrusting of gold, Bernini's **baldacchino** (a baldaquin or canopy) inside St. Peter's shows the baroque beginning to get out of hand.

Dress code

Italians tend to dress in attire that may look rather formal to American eyes (no shorts and rarely jeans, even in the summer). This is true during the day, and even more so in the evening. As a man, you may unpleasantly stick out if you're wearing shorts and a tank top, and you may not be able to have lunch except in the most informal eateries. Shorts and tank tops (except for really stylish and elegant ones) are not a good choice for women, either, although they may pass more easily.

In Vatican territory — and that includes *all* of the churches and religious buildings in Italy — both men and women will be refused access at the entrance unless they cover up those shoulders and thighs. If you're visiting in the summer, bring a silk scarf or sweater for your shoulders, and wear a longer skirt or pants.

As a bridge between east and west, Italy's architecture shows at times a deep Eastern influence, particularly on its eastern coast. **Venice** has a style all its own, labeled **Venetian Gothic,** of which **St. Mark's Basilica (Basilica di San Marco)** is a gem. The onion domes and the ornate decoration reflect a Byzantine influence; the exotic materials, including porphyry, gold, and jewels, came from across the Venetian empire. **Sicily,** too, has its own style, which reflects Norman influence as well as Eastern art and crafts imported during the period when the island was ruled by Arabs (from their conquest in 831 until their defeat by the Normans Robert Guiscard and Robert I in 1072). The **Cappella Palatina (Palatine Chapel)** within the **Palazzo Normanni** is an astounding synthesis of Byzantine mosaics, Islamic art, and an intricate ceiling that is a masterpiece of Arab woodcarving. Later, the island developed its own version of baroque, the **Sicilian Barocco,** a captivating and ornate style that is found in many cities in Sicily and contrasts with the stark beauty of Norman architecture in Palermo.

A Taste of Italy: Eating (and Drinking) Locally

You are most certainly familiar with Italian cuisine, but you may not be an expert in the structure of an Italian meal. Although ever-expanding working hours have made it more difficult for Italians to enjoy their traditional *pranzo* (midday meal) every day, they indulge in it whenever possible: during the week for business lunches, and on the weekend with family and friends. A complete meal includes several courses and is always accompanied by wine and water (usually bottles of mineral sparkling and still).

The meal starts with ***antipasti*** (appetizers), including a variety of cured meats, vegetable tidbits, and seafood preparations, depending on the region (see later in this section). Sometimes they are served buffet-style and you can get up and choose what you want; otherwise, you can order your own individual dish — not much fun — or go the Italian way and ask your waiter to bring a selection for the number of people in your party, definitely the most festive choice.

The meal continues with the ***primo*** (first course), which can be a soup (mostly served in fall and winter) or a rice or pasta dish. The pasta dish is but another appetizer, and the real meal has yet to come. The ***secondo*** (main course) is a meat or fish dish, which you may accompany with a ***contorno*** (side dish) — but you'll have to order that separately in traditional restaurants. Only in gourmet restaurants will the chef limit your freedom and impose a specific association of flavors of his choice, serving a meat or fish preparation with a particular side dish. In most other places, you'll be able to choose from among a variety of potatoes (usually oven-roasted or french fries) and vegetables (usually cooked leafy greens, green beans, or salad).

It is nowadays quite acceptable to stop at your first course and skip the *secondo*, or to skip the *primo* and go straight for the main course. A lot of Italians will do the same, particularly during an ordinary lunch at a local *trattoria*. However, if you are in a formal restaurant and not everybody in your party chooses to do the same, you'll have to specify to the waiter that you want all the dishes brought to the table together, otherwise he will wait for everybody who has ordered a first course to finish before bringing in the *secondi*.

To finish, you can have cheese and/or dessert. This includes ***dolce*** — cake, pastry, or pudding — or fresh fruit (when in season, strawberries with whipped cream are very popular with locals). You can then top it all with *caffè* (coffee) and *amaro* (bitter *digestif* liqueur).

The ***cena*** (evening meal) was traditionally a less elaborate meal, centered on soup, cured meats, cheese, and vegetable dishes. For many working people, this has become the only meal at which the whole family is together, and therefore it has taken up many of the elements of the *pranzo*. However, most people will have a full meal only when they go out for a special dinner; otherwise, they'll choose to have a simpler meal at an informal restaurant.

What Italians call a ***ristorante*** is a formal kind of restaurant, with proper tablecloths and elegant settings, and always serving a full menu of regional and Italian specialties. You'll also find a full menu in a more casual ***trattoria*** or ***osteria,*** but these are usually smaller, family-run establishments that serve hearty and less elaborate local dishes. Whether you're at a *ristorante, trattoria,* or *osteria,* you'll still be able to have the traditional *pranzo,* at either lunch or dinner.

You can have a faster and cheaper meal in a *pizzeria,* a sit-down eatery specializing in pizza; these usually serve individual round pizzas and a limited choice of *antipasti.* Sometimes you'll find a restaurant that doubles as a *pizzeria,* in which case it will have both a regular menu and a pizza menu. Pizza is still usually considered evening fare, but thanks to an increasing demand, more and more restaurants are offering pizza for lunch as well. The typical *pizzeria antipasti* differ somewhat from the choices offered in other types of restaurants: You'll find a variety of deep-fried items, such as *filetto di baccalà* (a piece of deep-fried cod), *bruschetta* (a slice of hearty bread topped with chopped tomatoes and olive oil), potato *croquettes,* and *suppli* or *arancini* (balls of seasoned rice filled with cheese or meat and deep-fried). The pizzas themselves come with a variety of pre-established toppings; most of these combinations are rooted in long-standing tradition, such as the *margherita* (tomato, mozzarella, and basil); *napoletana* or *romana* (tomato, mozzarella, and anchovies); *capricciosa* (tomato, mozzarella, mushrooms, artichoke hearts, olives, ham, and half a boiled egg); *funghi* (mushrooms, tomato, and mozzarella); *rugola, bresaola, e parmigiano* (fresh arugula and thin slices of cured beef and Parmesan cheese, with a simple tomato sauce); *quattro formaggi* (four kinds of cheese); *broccoletti e salsicce* (broccoli rabe and Italian sausages); and so on.

Not even considered a proper restaurant by locals, a **rosticceria** or **tavola calda** is a sort of cafeteria with pre-prepared hot dishes behind a glass counter and, often, roasting chickens in the window. These are excellent places for a quick meal on the go. If you're even more pressed for time, we recommend snacking at one of the ubiquitous pizza counters that offer pizzas by the weight; these also sell soda, water, and sometimes beer, but usually don't have a seating area.

An Italian **bar** shares some of the features of a cafe: At lunchtime, bars prepare a large variety of sandwiches (filled with egg, tomatoes, cheese, and cured meats) and *tramezzino* (slices of crustless American-style bread filled with a variety of mayo-based salads). Some bars have a full kitchen and will prepare basic dishes. You can enjoy your lunch standing at the counter, Italian-style. If you prefer to eat at a table, you'll have to first sit and then order, as the menu is often different and more extensive (and a surcharge applies for table dining). Bars offer a full range of refreshments, from *cappuccino* to wine, soda to ice cream. You can easily recognize a good bar by taking a look at its glass counter: The best places prepare their own food with top-quality ingredients, and buy their bread and pastries from a reputable *forno* (bakery) in the vicinity.

Dining hours in Italy are later than in the United States. Italians sit down to dinner between 8:30 and 10:30 p.m.; lunch is between 1 and 3 p.m. Most restaurants open around noon for lunch and 7:30 p.m. for dinner. In our restaurant reviews throughout this book, we provide opening and closing times that refer to the kitchen's hours — basically, the times you're allowed to place your order. Few restaurants will keep the kitchen open past 11:30 p.m. in the city and 10 p.m. in the countryside, and only a minority will open any earlier than 7:30 p.m.

The etiquette of drinking

Don't expect to order a martini before dinner. In many restaurants, and more particularly in *trattorie, osterie,* and *pizzerie,* you probably won't find a full bar, as Italians simply don't drink liquor right before dinner. The widespread *aperitivo* is always taken at a bar before going to a restaurant, and is always accompanied by small tidbits of tasty food. If you make a bar your first stop, you can soak up the festive *aperitivo* ambience and also try the bittersweet *aperitivo* cocktail or non-alcoholic beverage Italians favor. They tend to drink wine during dinner and reserve liquor for the end of the meal, when they're likely to have a *grappa* (a clear brandy) or an *amaro* (a 60- to 80-proof bitter drink, made with herbs).

While a 10 to 15 percent charge for *servizio* (service) is usually included in the price of each dish (this will be specified on the menu; if it's not, that means the service will be added to your bill), an extra 5 to 10 percent is expected for good service. Also, some restaurants still charge a *pane e coperto* (bread and table) fee, calculated per person. This charge tends to vary depending on the elegance of the restaurant and its location (moderate and rarely assessed in Rome, it is steep and ubiquitous in Venice); it ranges between 1€ and 6€ ($1.20–$7.20) throughout the country.

Italian cuisine is really quite different from region to region, as you'll see later in our quick overview. Be adventurous, try the local specialties when you can, and no matter where you are, don't miss the local wines unless you're a teetotaler.

Relishing Roman cuisine

Traditional **Roman** cuisine is based on simple food, "poor people" fare. It may be unsophisticated, but we just love it. Among the *primi,* our favorite Roman specialty is *pasta all'amatriciana* (a tomato-and-bacon sauce with pecorino cheese) and its tomatoless relative, *gricia.* We also like *pasta all'arrabbiata* (tomato sauce with lots of hot red pepper); *gnocchi* (potato dumplings in a tomato-based sauce), traditionally served on Thursdays only; and *cannelloni* (pasta tubes filled with meat or fish and baked). Ricotta and spinach ravioli are often excellent as well. Our favorite *secondi* are *abbacchio* (young lamb) roasted with herbs or *scottadito* (small grilled cutlets), as well as *saltimbocca alla romana* (veal or beef stuffed with ham and sage and sautéed in a Marsala sauce). For the more adventurous, there is *trippa alla romana* (tripe Roman style). Desserts are few, mostly gelato (rich, creamy ice cream), creamy *zabaglione* (made with sugar, egg yolks, and Marsala wine), or *tiramisù* (layers of mascarpone cheese and espresso-soaked ladyfingers).

The best-known wines of Rome come from the nearby Castelli Romani, the hill towns to the east of the city. Our favorites are the white Frascati — very dry and treacherously refreshing — and the red Velletri.

Tasting Tuscany

Much as they hate to admit it, many Italians from other regions have to agree that the best Italian cuisine is to be found in **Tuscany.** (We don't have to tell you what Tuscans themselves say.) Many of the traditional dishes are farm-country recipes based on plenty of fresh vegetables and game, though others were refined creations for the Florentine sovereigns. We love to start our meal with *crostini* (toasted bread with savory toppings, including a sort of delicious pâté). Among the cold cuts are *finocchiona,* a fennel-flavored salami famous all over Italy. In winter, we never miss the thick traditional soup *ribollita,* made of black cabbage, bread, and vegetables. When in Siena, we always have some *pici* (hand-rolled spaghetti usually prepared with bread crumbs and tomato sauce). Another of our favorites is *pappardelle al sugo di lepre* (large fettuccine with hare sauce) or *al cinghiale* (wild-boar sauce). The best *secondo* of all — but it has to be the real thing from the Chianina cow (a breed raised only in the Tuscan countryside and blessed with especially delectable meat) — is the *Fiorentina,* a thick steak that will shame any American Westerner. One *contorno* not to miss is *fagioli all'uccelletto* (white Tuscan beans in a light tomato sauce). To end the meal, we like the simple *cantucci col vin santo* (hazelnut biscotti served with a glass of local sweet wine) and the delicious *Panforte* — a typical Christmas dessert that can be bought year-round in Siena, where it was invented.

Nearby **Umbria** has a cuisine similar to that of Tuscany, with one major difference: **truffles.** These come in white and black varieties; the former, which has a milder flavor, is the most coveted.

Farther afield, the cuisine of the **Cinque Terre** is highlighted by lots of fresh fish. Pesto sauce, now famous around the world, originated in the Cinque Terre. Another local specialty is *zuppa di pesce,* a savory, brothy fish stew.

Smoking

Italy recently instituted one of Europe's toughest laws against smoking in public places. All restaurants and bars are affected by this ruling, except those with ventilated smoking rooms. Only about 10 percent of Italian restaurants currently have these separate smoking areas. It is just as difficult to find a bar where you can smoke; only the larger places will have separate smoking areas. If smoking is important to you, call the restaurant or bar ahead of time to make sure it has a smoking area. In good weather, you will always be able to smoke on the outdoor terraces of restaurants and bars, where the law does not apply.

Chianti is perhaps the best-known Tuscan red, and is often served as table wine — even on tap, from huge casks — in Tuscan restaurants. The red Vino Nobile di Montepulciano and Brunello di Montalcino are among Italy's greatest wines. For a white, try Vernaccia di San Gimignano; for a dessert wine, opt for the famous *vin santo.*

Visiting Venetian and Milanese eateries

In **Venice,** fish and shellfish served on rice, pasta, or *polenta* (cooked cornmeal) are the staples of the local cuisine. Our favorite antipasti are *sarde in saor* (sardines in a sauce of vinegar, onions, and pine nuts) and *baccalà mantegato* (creamed codfish served cold). Among the *primi, risi e bisi* (rice and peas) and *bigoli in salsa* (whole-wheat spaghetti with anchovy-and-onion sauce) get our approval, while for *secondo,* we enjoy the famous *fegato alla veneziana* (liver sautéed with onions and wine). Pastry shops have a variety of local cakes as well as the famous *Bussolai* and *S e' Buranei* — O- and S-shaped cookies, respectively, originally from the small island of Burano.

In **Milan,** you'll find all kinds of restaurants, but we enjoy a couple of well-rounded traditional dishes: *Risotto* (creamy Italian rice cooked with fish or vegetables) was invented here, and the *risotto alla Milanese* (with saffron and beef marrow) is delectable when well prepared. For *secondo,* try the *cotoletta alla Milanese,* a tender deep-fried cutlet reminiscent of Wiener schnitzel and probably a remnant of the Hapsburg domination in the area.

Some of the best wines in Italy come from the Venetian countryside; we love Amarone and Valpolicella — earthy reds that can take the chill out of the damp weather in winter. If you prefer whites, there's Cartizze . . . but we love prosecco, a fizzy wine that we even prefer to champagne.

Gnawing Neapolitan delicacies

Naples is justly famous for **pizza** — Neapolitans claim it as their invention and indeed are masters at preparing it. But the local cuisine has a lot more to offer than just pizza, and although we really appreciate a good Tuscan meal, we are *quite* partial to Neapolitan cuisine. The fact that we love seafood probably has a lot to do with it, so if you don't, you may not share our excitement. Our favorite appetizer is *impepata di cozze* (mussels steamed in light broth with lots of pepper) or a caprese salad made with the famous *mozzarella di bufala* (buffalo mozzarella). Our absolute favorite *primo* is *scialatielli ai frutti di mare* (local home-made pasta with mussels and other seafood). For *secondo,* go for fresh fish *all'acquapazza* (poached in a light herbed broth) or the famous *polpi al coccio* (stewed octopus in a tomato sauce). Naples is also a great place for those with a sweet tooth; the *babá* is the typical pastry, a soft brioche soaked in rum and sugary syrup, served with a dollop of pastry cream. For breakfast, you absolutely have to try the local specialty: *sfogliatella,* a fragrant, crisp, crusty triangular pocket filled with sweet

Word to the wise

Italian is the general language spoken in Italy; however, if you know a bit of it, or if your ear is particularly good, you'll notice that people speak differently in different parts of Italy. Local dialects, now mostly used in the countryside, add local color but can also make things difficult for a beginner. If necessary, resort to the universal backup language: sign language. In Italy, hands talk — both to emphasize words and to convey further meaning. If you don't speak any Italian at all, most Italians will still go out of their way to try to understand you and help you out, and signs can be of great help. Also check out our glossary of Italian words (see Appendix B) and our list of what we deem the ten most useful expressions (see Chapter 23). If you're more adventurous, devote some time to *Italian For Dummies* and you'll soon become a pro.

ricotta. It's the perfect accompaniment to a Neapolitan coffee — another area of acknowledged superiority.

Naples is famous for the Lachrymae Christi (Tears of Christ), a wine made from grapes grown on the slopes of Mount Vesuvius, hence produced only in small quantities.

Savoring Sicily

When it comes to cooking (as in so many other things), **Sicily** is in a class by itself. The Sicilians perfected multiculturalism centuries ago. Here you'll find the most unique combinations — such as Italian-looking pasta served with pistachio nuts and North African spices. And because Sicily is an island, its cuisine is highlighted by tastes from the sea. Typical dishes are *pasta con le sarde* (pasta with shredded fresh sardines), *caponata* (cubed eggplant with other vegetables, spiced and sautéed), *tonno con aglio e menta* (fresh tuna with garlic and mint), and fish dishes with *finocchietto* (small fresh fennel). If you want only a sandwich, go for the typical Palermo *focacce*. It can be filled with anything, from the excellent *caciocavallo* (typical cheese) to fried spleen — yes, spleen, plus a little lung to round things out. Less adventurous "fast food" includes *arancini* (deep-fried flavored rice balls) and *panelle* (chickpea fritters). Keep in mind that Sicilians really excel at desserts and pastries. *Cassata* is a fabulous creation: ricotta mixed with sugar and candied fruit, then covered with a layer of cake and finally almond paste. Local gelato is heavenly — we quickly adopted the local custom of having it for breakfast, as the filling of a soft brioche, and accompanied by a small cup of excellent espresso. Some people even say that gelato was invented in Palermo; we nod and keep eating it. Another local specialty is *granita* (frozen coffee or lemon ice — or, best of all, almond ice).

Sicilian wines tend to be red and strong. There is a large variety; you may be familiar with the Corvo di Salaparuta, which is quite good. Our favorite is Nero d'Avola.

Background Check: Recommended Books and Movies

The number of books and films about Italy is staggering. Whether you want to bone up on history or be entertained by sights of the Eternal City, here are a few surefire favorites.

True stories

✔ **Johann Wolfgang von Goethe** was the first great modern literary visitor to Italy, and his wonderful *Italian Journey* (1816; reprinted by Penguin Books, 1992) recounts his travels there.

✔ American novelist **Henry James** lived most of his life in Europe. Some of his essays on art and culture are collected in *Italian Hours* (1907; reprinted by Penguin Books, 1995) — the pieces on Venice are particularly good.

✔ **D. H. Lawrence** wrote several books about Italy, including *The Sea and Sardinia* (1921) and *Etruscan Places* (1927); a selected edition, *D. H. Lawrence and Italy*, has been published by Penguin (1997).

✔ If you read 25 pages a day, it'll take you only about four months to get through **Edward Gibbon's** *History of the Decline and Fall of the Roman Empire* (begun in 1776), a monument of English prose. (You can find a less monumental Penguin abridged version [1983] in paperback.)

✔ **Robert Graves** wrote two novels — *I, Claudius* (1934; reprinted by Vintage Books, 1989) and its sequel, *Claudius the God* (1934; reprinted by Penguin Books, 1989) — about the best of Augustus's Claudian successors.

✔ Italian **Giorgio Vasari** was a painter, architect, and (literally) Renaissance man. His *Lives of the Most Eminent Painters and Sculptors* (1550; expanded 1568) has been criticized for inaccuracy, but is still full of interesting information about the great painters of the Renaissance. The Oxford edition (1998) is one of the many abridgements in translation of this huge work.

✔ **Benvenuto Cellini's** famous *Autobiography* (published 1728; translation reprinted by Penguin, 1999) presents a vivid picture of Cellini's time in Renaissance Florence.

Works of fiction

✓ **Ignazio Silone** was an important socialist writer who had to go into exile during Mussolini's reign. *Bread and Wine* (*Pane e vino*, 1937; translated by New American Library, 1988) is a vivid novel set during the fascist period — a modern classic.

✓ **Giuseppe Lampedusa** (actually Giuseppe Tomasi, prince of Lampedusa) wrote a single masterpiece, *The Leopard* (*Il Gattopardo*, 1958; translasted by Pantheon, 1991), about the effect on a noble Sicilian family of Garibaldi's invasion and the war of unification.

✓ **Alberto Moravia,** one of the great Italian writers of the 20th century, wrote many novels and short stories, but none as famous as *The Conformist* (*Il Conformista*, 1951; translated by Steerforth Press, 1999), a study of the fascist personality.

✓ Sicilian novelist **Leonardo Sciascia** wrote books that subtly peel apart the Mafia culture, layer by layer. Among the best of his works is *The Day of the Owl* (*Il Giorno della Civetta*, 1961; translated by New York Review of Books, 2003).

✓ **Alessandro Manzoni** wrote *I Promessi Sposi* (*The Betrothed*, 1825–27; translated by Penguin, 1984), considered one of the greatest works of fiction in any language. It's a sweeping romantic novel set in 17th-century Italy.

The moving image

The neorealist film director **Luchino Visconti** made an epic movie of Lampedusa's *The Leopard*. Also by Visconti is *The Earth Trembles* (*Terra Trema*, 1948), a version of Verga's *I Malavoglia*. **Bernardo Bertolucci** made a haunting and chilling classic out of Moravia's *The Conformist* in 1970.

Over the last dozen years or so, Italy has been the subject or the setting of several hit films. It all began with *A Room with a View* (1985), based on E. M. Forster's novel and containing beautiful scenes of Florence. *Enchanted April* (1992) is a sometimes schmaltzy but irresistible movie about a group of Londoners leaving the drizzle and fog of home for a sunny Italian villa. *The Postman* (*Il Postino*, 1994), an instant cult classic, concerns the encounter of the ordinary man of the title with the extraordinary personality of the poet Pablo Neruda, living in exile in Italy. The Oscar-winning *Life Is Beautiful* (1997), by Italy's current leading comic actor, Roberto Benigni, is set during World War II and moves from Tuscany to a German concentration camp. The comedy *Mediterraneo* (1991), also set during World War II, deals with what happens when a group of Italian soldiers are sent to garrison a lovely Greek island. Somewhat stereotypically, their Italian love of life wins out over their mission. At the opposite end of the spectrum is Nanni Moretti's *The Son's Room* (2001), about the death of a child — a film so powerful that it is perhaps the only movie ever to be given an R rating for being so *sad*.

We have to mention one of the great oldies, **Roman Holiday** (1953), the Gregory Peck/Audrey Hepburn romance that is said to have caused a surge in tourism to Rome. Another hugely popular film of the same era is **Spartacus** (1960), the Oscar-winning Kirk Douglas movie about a slave revolt in ancient Rome (we can't vouch for its historical accuracy). It was a precursor to Russell Crowe's **Gladiator** (2000), which also gives a visceral feel for the brutality of the empire at its worst.

Chapter 3

Deciding Where and When to Go

In This Chapter

▶ Exploring Italy's regions
▶ Knowing the right time to visit
▶ Scanning a calendar of the best festivals and events

*B*eneath the modernization and globalization Italy has undergone since the 1990s, the same proud traditions live on. In a country where you can't even count the number of political parties on both hands and feet, diversity is not in danger. Centuries-old traditions of independent thinking are what give Italy its unique flavors, voices, and places. Selecting your destinations from among these riches is an inspiring challenge. In this chapter, you'll find our best tips and suggestions to help guide you through Italy's maze of attractions and distractions, cuisines and subcultures.

Going Everywhere You Want to Be

Every region of Italy offers eye-popping sights as well as places to spend quiet moments. The following overview of Italy's best attractions by region will help you narrow down the destinations on your itinerary, whether this is your first trip or your fifth.

Roaming Rome

Rome is still the capital of Italy, as it was in ancient times. As the site of the Holy See, it was central to European culture for many centuries after the end of the Roman Empire — hence its unparalleled saturation of world-famous sights: the **Colosseum,** the **Roman Forum, St. Peter's Basilica** and the **Vatican Museums,** and the **Galleria Borghese,** to name a few. There are even sights underground, like the **Catacombs,** while new archaeological sites are continually being opened, such as the **Domus Aurea,** the "golden house" of Nero. As a major modern city, Rome also offers a varied and exciting nightlife, a huge selection of restaurants, plentiful and comfortable hotels, and world-famous shops. It has so much to see and do, visitors could spend months here and still find new things to savor and explore every day.

 Because of its size and energy, Rome can be quite overwhelming. You will not be able to enjoy it very much unless you're able to devote a few days here. See Part III for coverage of Rome.

Exploring Florence and the best of Tuscany and Umbria

Tuscany has been the number-one tourist destination in Italy for decades now, thanks to its lush countryside (where most people would love to own a villa) and numerous art attractions. **Florence,** with its beautiful **Duomo** (Cathedral) and museums overflowing with art treasures — the **Galleria degli Uffizi** foremost among them — is one of the finest cultural cities in the world. Florence's fame tends to overshadow its many neighboring towns, which are art gems in themselves and well worth a trip. We love **Pistoia** and **Prato,** for example — much lesser known, yet each only half an hour from Florence by public transportation; **Lucca** is another medieval and Renaissance jewel nearby. All these towns make excellent day trips from Florence.

Many are the other towns we love in both Tuscany and nearby Umbria, starting with **Pisa,** with its world-famous **Leaning Tower** (the whole complex, with the **Duomo** and the **Camposanto,** is so strikingly beautiful on a sunny day that you will not regret your visit). Two other personal favorites are medieval **Siena,** with its rusty-brick color and the exciting **Palio delle Contrade** (the horse race that occurs twice a year in the summer), as well as **Perugia,** the medieval capital of Umbria. Once you are in Umbria, you should not miss **Assisi** — with its famous frescoes by Giotto celebrating the life of St. Francis (dazzling in spite of the earthquake damage) — and **Spoleto,** with its charming medieval architecture and imposing fortress, not to mention its lively music-and-arts festival of international renown. If you have time, you certainly should visit the perfectly preserved medieval **San Gimignano,** with its soaring towers; and the **Chianti,** with its unique landscape of sweet hills dotted with vineyards, where you can taste delicious food and wine.

A little farther afield (actually located in the neighboring region of Liguria) is the park of the **Cinque Terre,** a preserved nature paradise where time seems to have stopped. It is named after the five tiny fishing/farming villages nestled along a stretch of coast that rivals the more famous Amalfi Coast in steepness and natural beauty. See Part IV for more on Tuscany and Umbria.

Viewing Venice and the Pianura Padana

Many artists and writers have been utterly smitten by **La Serenissima** (the Serene Republic), as this city called itself when it was an independent state — and we haven't been immune to its charms, either. If you have only one day in Italy, we recommend you spend it in **Venice,** which promotes dreaming like no other place. In a country lush with one-of-a-kind sights, Venice is truly in a class by itself. In addition to its glorious cultural attractions — the **Doge's Palace, St. Mark's Basilica, Piazza San Marco,** the **Gallerie dell'Accademia** — the whole town is magical, with its narrow streets and romantic canals.

The surrounding region, the **Pianura Padana,** is dotted with smaller towns, which, although they cannot compete with Venice, make very good rivals to other tourist destinations in Italy. **Verona** tops our list for both its romantic culture — Romeo and Juliet lived out their tragic affair here (supposedly) — and its architecture. **Padua** is a close second, thanks to its charming Renaissance architecture and Giotto's most celebrated frescoes in the **Scrovegni Chapel. Milan** may not be our favorite city in the world, but its attractions are first-rate: We absolutely love the **Duomo** and the **Brera.** See Part V for coverage of Venice and the Pianura Padana.

Visiting Naples, Pompeii, and the Amalfi Coast

Naples, and its surrounding region, has been one of our favorite destinations in Italy for a long time, so we're very happy that it is now receiving growing international attention. The city's huge collection of art treasures (the **Archaeological Museum,** the **Museo di Capodimonte,** the **Duomo,** the **Palazzo Reale,** the **Castel Nuovo, Santa Chiara,** and **Sant'Anna dei Lombardi,** to mention a few) and the breathtaking natural beauty of its nearby coast are enough to delight anybody for days on end. Back in the 18th century, foreign visitors spent far more time in Naples and its surroundings than in Florence and Tuscany, but decades of neglect, corruption, and crime had obscured its attractions. Luckily, a steady program of renovations and updates began in the 1990s, and Naples is now coming back.

A short distance from Naples are two of the world's most famous archaeological sites, the Roman cities of **Herculaneum** and **Pompeii,** wiped out by the eruption of Mount Vesuvius in A.D. 79. Basically in the suburbs of Naples is the **Campi Flegrei,** a protected area rich in ancient Roman and Greek sites. Farther south are the mythical **Sorrento** peninsula and the **Amalfi Coast,** much more beautiful that any postcard could ever reveal. The Amalfi Coast's famous resorts include **Positano** and **Amalfi,** both nestled along plunging cliffs. And **Capri,** the VIPs' and Hollywood stars' island getaway, is a green hill that rises steeply from the sea. See Part VI for more on Naples and environs.

Seeing Sicily

The farther south you go, the more intense Italy becomes. The rugged beauty, bountiful waters, and rich soils of **Sicily** have been fought over for millennia — and we understood why soon after visiting for the first time. You won't find such an exciting and pleasing mix of sights, cultures, flavors, and landscapes anywhere else in Italy. We love **Palermo,** a pleasant harbor town with spectacular artistic and architectural treasures — some a bit crumbling — ranging from the Byzantine **Duomo di Monreale** to the Arabic **La Zisa,** the Gothic **Cattedrale** to the Norman **Palazzo dei Normanni,** the baroque **Casa Professa** to the Liberty-style **Teatro Massimo.** We cannot get enough of the magnificent Greek temples in the appropriately named **Valley of the Temples** in **Agrigento,** as well as in **Segesta** — both easy day trips from Palermo. A bit farther, but chockfull of spectacular Roman mosaics, is the **Villa del Casale** of **Piazza Armerina.** Although we agree that the fashionable city of **Taormina** is nestled in one of Italy's most picturesque spots — overlooking the blue sea from a high cliff and dominated by the snow-capped **Mount Etna** volcano — it didn't inspire us as much as the splendid volcanic **Eolian Islands,** or **Catania** with its baroque and 19th-century palaces built of gray-lava stone, or the fascinating **Syracuse,** with its Greek and Roman **Archaeological Zone** and its baroque island of **Ortigia.** See Part VII for coverage of Sicily.

Scheduling Your Time

A quick glance at the map will reveal that the enticing attractions discussed in the previous section are spread out over a peninsula that's more than 700 miles long. A closer look will show you that Italy is crossed lengthwise by a mountain chain — the Appenines — that will make any east–west travel more complicated: logistically because there are fewer roads and railroad lines, and practically because bad weather, especially in winter, may considerably slow you down. Both these geographical characteristics can be easily sidestepped, however, by flying between your destinations. Taking the plane has become quite affordable now that many routes within Italy have opened up to small private carriers (see Chapter 7). The drawback is that flying requires advance scheduling. If you prefer a more spontaneous itinerary, one that allows you to change your destination at the last minute, then you should stick with the freedom afforded by railroad transportation (or rental car, but for countryside exploration only).

On the other hand, these geographical characteristics make itinerary planning relatively straightforward: Your travels will be along a general north–south line. Your route can be as long as your time will allow — just remember to schedule fewer destinations if you're traveling by land rather than by air.

 It used to be that all international flights arrived only in Milan or Rome. These days, you can usually schedule your flight to arrive in one Italian town and leave from another at no extra expense, which allows for much more creative itinerary planning (see Chapter 6 for more on how to get to Italy).

If your itinerary includes only the major cities, don't bother renting a car — instead, fly or take the train: You'll see far more beautiful landscapes and enjoy your vacation much more. Trains in Italy are getting better and faster by the day, yet remain very affordable (see Chapter 7).

Revealing the Secrets of the Seasons

Italy has a mild climate with well-defined seasons, drier and warmer in the south and colder in the north. The weather doesn't really influence tourism in general, as Italy is a year-round destination, but it may affect your own itinerary planning.

Table 3-1	Average Temperatures and Precipitation in Selected Cities											
	Jan	Feb	Mar	Apr	May	June	July	Aug	Sep	Oct	Nov	Dec
Rome												
High (°C/°F)	12/53	13/55	15/59	18/65	23/73	27/81	30/87	30/87	27/80	22/71	16/61	13/55
Low (°C/°F)	3/37	4/38	5/41	8/46	11/52	14/58	17/63	18/64	15/59	11/51	7/44	4/39
Rainfall (cm/in.)	10.3/4	9.8/4	6.8/3	6.5/3	4.8/3	3.4/1	2.3/1	3.3/1	6.8/3	9.4/4	13/5	11.1/4
Venice												
High (°C/°F)	6/42	8/47	12/54	16/61	21/70	25/77	28/82	27/81	24/74	18/65	12/53	7/44
Low (°C/°F)	-1/30	1/33	4/39	8/46	12/54	16/61	18/64	17/63	14/58	9/49	4/40	0/32
Rainfall (cm/in.)	5.8/2	5.4/2	5.7/2	6.4/3	6.9/3	7.6/3	6.3/2	8.3/3	6.6/3	6.9/3	8.7/3	5.4/2
Palermo												
High (°C/°F)	15/59	15/59	16/61	18/65	22/71	25/77	28/83	29/84	27/80	23/73	19/67	16/61
Low (°C/°F)	10/50	10/50	11/52	13/55	16/61	20/67	23/73	24/74	22/71	18/64	14/58	12/53
Rainfall (cm/in.)	7.2/3	6.5/3	6.0/2	4.4/2	2.6/1	1.2/0	0.5/0	1.3/1	4.2/2	9.8/4	9.4/4	8.0/3

In all major cities and towns, the off season is very short, running from mid-January to mid-March and from mid-October to mid-December. The actual dates depend on individual hotels, as well as occupancy: As a rule of thumb, high season starts earlier for smaller and cheaper hotels, which tend to fill faster, and lasts longer. The reverse is true for more expensive hotels. On the seashore and in the mountains, resorts will often be closed from November through March. Following are what we consider to be the pros and cons for traveling in each season.

April through June

This is when Italy is at its most beautiful, for the following reasons:

- ✔ The weather is mild, so you won't have to worry about either excess heat and sunstroke or the chills.

- ✔ Limited rainfall allows you to get out and really enjoy the outdoor activities.

But keep in mind a couple of drawbacks:

- ✔ Everybody knows this is a great season — including hotels and airlines, which jack up their prices. The highly desirable hotels fill up fast.

- ✔ Around Easter, vast numbers of Catholic pilgrims and large groups of *very* noisy schoolchildren from around the world descend on Italy (particularly its major destinations), making it all but impossible to enjoy many attractions.

July and August

Summertime is when many Italians take their vacations, and there are many upsides:

- ✔ The weather is beautiful throughout most of Italy.

- ✔ You can get discount rates in most towns and cities, as well as in Sicily.

- ✔ There are great art and music festivals, concerts, and outdoor events everywhere — cultural life is at its peak.

On the other hand:

- ✔ Airfares are high.

- ✔ The heat can make things quite uncomfortable — remember, Italy is still mostly a non–air-conditioned country, and Sicily is sunstroke territory.

- ✔ Mountain and seaside resorts, which can provide a respite from the heat, are taken over by Italian tourists.

- ✔ Many city shops and restaurants close during the month of August.

September and October

Next to spring, fall is our favorite time to travel to Italy. Here's why:

- ✔ The weather is usually fairly mild and pleasant.

- ✔ Many potential tourists are busy with back-to-school preparations, making crowds relatively sparse.

On the other hand:

- ✔ Airfares and hotel prices are still high.

- ✔ You have to watch for the rain, which typically starts falling in October.

November through March

More and more vacationers are reaping the benefits of traveling to Italy in the winter. Its reputation as the "off season" is fast disappearing. Here's why:

- ✔ Crowds are at their lowest at the prime attractions.

- ✔ You'll often receive better and more attentive service in hotels during this season.

- ✔ Except for the Christmas–New Year's period, airfares and hotel rates are at their lowest.

But keep in mind:

- ✔ You may have fewer lodging choices in some areas because of seasonal closures — most hotels and restaurants in Italy take a winter break of at least two to three weeks.

- ✔ Although average temperatures are mild, you'll have to put up with rain and occasionally lots of snow. It can get cold and quite foggy in the northern regions. Depending on how sensitive you are to colder temperatures, you may not be able to enjoy some of the outdoor attractions.

Perusing a Calendar of Events

Italy has many festivals and events worth planning a holiday around. Alternatively, you can use the following calendar to *avoid* big events and their attendant crowds. You'll find more information on each event in the destination chapters later in this book.

January

Celebrations of the new year are held throughout Italy. In **Rome,** a great show for children is staged in Piazza del Popolo (☎ **06-36004399**), while Florence celebrates with its annual boat race, the **Regata sull'Arno** (☎ **055-23320**). January 1.

Throughout the country, the religious holiday **Epifania** is very important for children, as they receive special gifts on this day (more than on Dec 25). On the days preceding Epiphany, open-air fairs selling children's toys and gifts are held in most towns; the best is in Rome's Piazza Navona. January 6.

February

Everywhere in Italy, **Carnevale** swallows up the week before Ash Wednesday, culminating on Fat Tuesday or *Martedi Grasso.* One of the most spectacular celebrations is in Venice, where people dress up in splendid costumes and the city organizes concerts and fireworks (☎ 041-5298711); the famous parade of floats in Viareggio in Tuscany culminates celebrations that last a whole month (☎ 0584-47503). One week prior to Ash Wednesday.

March/April

On **Good Friday,** the Catholic rite of the procession of the Stations of the Cross *(Via Crucis)* is presented in most Italian churches, often as a reen-actment with costumes. In Rome, the procession takes place at night, led by the pope, between the Colosseum and Palatine Hill. Other spectacular processions are the ones in Assisi and in several towns in Sicily. Friday before Easter Sunday.

For Easter, in Rome, the pope gives his traditional **Easter Benediction** in Piazza San Pietro, while in Florence, mass ends with the **Scoppio del Carro** (☎ 055-290832), the explosion of a cart laden with fireworks and flowers outside the Duomo. Easter Sunday, between the end of March and mid-April.

During the **Exhibition of Azaleas** in Rome, more than 3,000 azalea plants decorate the Spanish Steps. Concerts are held in Trinità dei Monti at the head of the steps. Call ☎ 06-4889991 for more information. One week in mid-April, weather dependent.

In Venice, a great procession to St. Mark's Basilica marks the city's patron-saint day, honoring **St. Mark.** Venetian men present women with a red rose on this day. April 25.

May

The first of the month is **Labor Day,** when most workers have a day off. Everything shuts down — including most museums and attractions — and public transportation operates either minimally or not at all. May 1.

Assisi's celebration of spring, called **Calendimaggio** (☎ 075-812534; www.umbria2000.it), includes singing, dancing, medieval costumes, parades, and competitions. First weekend after May 1.

Italy's oldest and most prestigious music and dance festival — **Maggio Musicale Fiorentino** (☎ 0935-564767; www.maggiofiorentino.com) — is held in Florence; you'll need advance reservations. May into June.

Each year in turn, Venice, Amalfi, Genoa, and Pisa host the **Regatta of the Great Maritime Republics,** a spectacular rowing competition between teams from each town (☎ 050-560464 in Pisa; ☎ 041-5298711 in Venice; ☎ 089-871107 in Amalfi). Second or third weekend in May.

Rowers train year-round for **Vogalonga** (☎ 041-5298711), a "long row" and major competition in Venice. Second half of May.

Rome's glamorous **Concorso Ippico Internazionale** (☎ 06-6383818; www.piazzadisiena.com) attracts the best riders and mounts from all over to beautiful Piazza di Siena in Villa Borghese. You can buy tickets at the gate. End of May.

The end of May brings the **Settimana della Cultura,** a statewide event during which admission to all the major museums is free — hence, no reservations are taken and everything becomes a zoo, with thousands of school groups roaming around. When planning your trip to major towns in Italy, take this into account. If possible, schedule your visit at a different time — we promise, it's worth it to pay admission. Last week of May.

June

Now in its fourth decade, the **Spoleto Festival** (☎ 0743-220320; www.spoletofestival.it) includes concerts, opera, dance, and theater. You'll need advance reservations for most events. Throughout June.

June marks the start of the **opera season** in Verona's Roman amphitheater (☎ 045-8005151; www.arena.it). June through September.

Florence's patron-saint day is celebrated with a tournament of rough-and-tumble Renaissance soccer, the **Gioco di Calcio Storico Fiorentino** (☎ 055-290-832). It culminates with fireworks on the Arno River. June 16, 24, and 30.

The **Roman Summer Festival** (☎ 06-4889991; www.estateromana.it) is an increasingly rich program of concerts, theater, and art events throughout Rome. Mid-June through early September.

One of the premier art expositions in the world, the **Venice Biennial** (☎ 041-5218846; www.labiennale.org), takes place in odd-numbered years in Venice's Giardini. June through October.

July

In Siena's famous **Palio delle Contrade** (☎ 0577-280551; www.terresiena.it), horses and riders wearing the colors of their medieval neighborhoods ride around Piazza del Campo in a wild, dangerous race surrounded by pageantry that lasts for days. June 29 through July 3.

Palermo's patron-saint day celebrates **Santa Rosalia** with a spectacular procession through the city and a candlelight procession up the mountain overlooking the harbor. July 11 through July 15.

Umbria Jazz (☎ 075-5728685; www.umbriajazz.com) is one of Europe's top jazz events; it is held in Perugia. Mid- to late July.

The **Festa del Redentore,** in Venice, celebrates the lifting of the plague in 1571 with boating and fireworks. Third Saturday and Sunday of July.

August

The pagan holiday of **Ferragosto** is observed nationwide. Italians vacation on the seashore and in the mountains. Most businesses are closed, so check your destination in advance to know what will be open. August 15.

Siena's second **Palio delle Contrade** (☎ 0577-280551; www. terresiena.it) is held for the finalists of the previous *palio* in July, with a similar program. August 13 through August 17.

Less spectacular and famous than the one in Siena, Assisi's **Palio di San Rufino** (☎ 075-812534; www.balestrieriassisi.it) is celebrated over four days. Renaissance costumes and pageantry precede the cross-bow competition between the town's districts. Last weekend in August.

September

Held at the Palazzo del Cinema on the Lido, the **Venice International Film Festival** (☎ 041-5218861; www.labiennale.org) is one of the top film festivals in the world. Despite the proliferation of bigwigs and wannabes, regular folks can actually get tickets to screenings. First two weeks of September.

In Venice, the **Regata Storica** (☎ 041-5298711) is a spectacular rowing event held in the Grand Canal. You'll need tickets for this one. First Sunday of September.

The **Settembre Lucchese** (☎ 0583-473129; www.in-lucca.it) opera festival celebrates the memory of Puccini in his hometown of Lucca with live performances. September.

October

Italy's patron-saint day, honoring **St. Francis of Assisi,** is observed in various towns and cities — notably Rome and Assisi — with processions, special masses, and other religious events. October 4.

November

In Venice, the **Presentation of Mary in the Temple** is a religious holiday that's celebrated with a procession that crosses the city. A bridge made of boats is strung across the Grand Canal at La Salute. November 21.

December

Hundreds of **Presepi (Crèche)** are on view in churches throughout Italy; some are truly spectacular, particularly in Rome and Naples. December 8 through January 6.

The pope gives a special **Christmas Blessing** to Rome and the world from St. Peter's Square at noon. December 25.

Partying reaches its climax at midnight on **New Year's Eve,** when Italy explodes — literally — with fireworks. In spite of the government's call for caution, everybody gets in on the act, shooting fireworks from every window and roof in the country. By tradition, fireworks are accompanied by the symbolic throwing away of something old to mark the end of the old year. Some people get carried away, so watch out for falling UFOs if you take a stroll in major cities shortly after midnight! December 31.

Chapter 4

Following an Itinerary: Four Great Options

In This Chapter

▶ Touring Italy in one or two weeks
▶ Visiting Italy with your kids
▶ Rediscovering the ancients

*I*taly offers an endless array of things to see, do, and taste — but, alas, few of us have the time to do it all. And even if you want to cram as much into your trip as possible, you still have some tough choices to make. This chapter gives some sample itineraries that won't break your budget or your back, including one for families and one for antiquity buffs. We recommend you book your transatlantic flight with arrival into one Italian city and departure from another — an option that's often affordable when you book directly with the carrier (see Chapter 6).

Seeing Italy's Highlights in One Week

You won't have much time to linger anywhere, but if all you have is one week — grab it! Think of this as a crash course in Italian life and culture.

Day 1

Fly into **Milan** and check into your hotel. Start with a visit to the **Duomo.** Afterward, proceed for a stroll in Milan's best shopping district, **Via Montenapoleone,** where you can purchase, or at least see, the latest in Italian fashion. Spend the afternoon at the **Brera,** taking in your first great collection of Italian art. Celebrate your arrival in one of Italy's best restaurants, **CraccoPeck,** where you can enjoy a view of the nearby Duomo by night (see Chapter 17).

Day 2 and 3

Take an early train to **Venice** (the trip takes under two and a half hours) and check into your hotel. Squeeze in our "Venice in two days" itinerary (see Chapter 16).

Day 4

Take as early a train as you can to **Florence,** which you'll reach in slightly under three hours. Check into your hotel, and immediately start with our "Florence in one day" itinerary in Chapter 13.

Day 5 and 6

Yes, you guessed right: Take an early train, this time to **Rome,** where you will arrive in under two hours. Get settled in your hotel, which will need to be fairly central (see Chapter 11) given the amount of ground you'll want to cover. Follow our "Rome in two days" itinerary (see Chapter 12).

Day 7

Again, take an early high-speed train to **Naples** — you'll be there in under 90 minutes. What more appropriate destination for your last day in Italy! Get settled in your hotel and follow our "Naples in one day" itinerary (see Chapter 18). Fly back home the next morning from the Naples airport.

Touring the Best of Italy in Two Weeks

Two weeks is a good amount of time — you will be able to see enough to enjoy yourself without feeling rushed all the time.

Day 1, 2, and 3

Fly into **Milan** and follow our Day 1, 2, and 3 suggestions in the itinerary earlier.

Day 4 and 5

Take as early a train as you can to **Florence,** which you'll reach in slightly under three hours. Check into your hotel; then start with our "Florence in two days" itinerary (see Chapter 13).

Day 6, 7, and 8

Take an early train to **Rome,** a trip of less than two hours. Get settled in your hotel and then start following our "Rome in three days" itinerary (see Chapter 12).

Day 9 and 10

Take the 90-minute high-speed train to **Naples** in the morning and check into your hotel. Follow our "Naples in two days" itinerary (see Chapter 18).

Day 11

Choose one of the day trips suggested in Chapter 19, visiting either **Herculaneum** or **Pompeii,** or perhaps taking the archeobus to the **Campi Flegrei.** Or you can book a car service to take you on a daylong private tour of **Sorrento** and the **Amalfi Drive** (see Chapter 20). If you opt for the latter, take your luggage along so that you can have your limo deliver you to the Molo Angioino in time to catch the Tirrenia overnight ferry for Palermo (see Chapter 21). Check into your cabin and enjoy the cruise (if you wake up at the right time in the night, you may catch a glimpse of Stromboli, an active volcano of the Eolian Islands, spewing fireworks into the evening sky). Alternatively, fly into Palermo the next morning.

Day 12

Once in **Palermo,** spend the day following our "Palermo in one day" itinerary (see Chapter 21).

Day 13

If you don't mind a lot of driving, rent a car for the next two days and drive yourself to **Agrigento** and the **Valle dei Templi** for a visit to its splendid Greek temples. Then drive on to **Syracuse** and spend the night there (see Chapter 22). For a less tiring day, take an organized bus tour to the Valley of the Temples from Palermo (see Chapter 21), and then come back to spend the night in your hotel.

Day 14

Visit **Ortigia** early in the morning and then proceed to **Taormina** — you'll enjoy spending your last day in Italy in this idyllic town. Fly home from Catania airport the next morning (see Chapter 22). Alternatively, take an organized bus tour from Palermo to Taormina (see Chapter 21) and fly home from Palermo.

Discovering Italy with Kids

When traveling with kids, the big question is how much cultural sightseeing (particularly museums) they can handle. Luckily, Italy offers plenty of attractions and sights that children will enjoy. The following itinerary is what we would do if we had only a week with our children in Italy.

 If your child is under 18 months, you can probably follow one of the other itineraries geared toward adults. Most museums have benches where you can rest or nurse, and Italians are pretty tolerant — if you get any funny looks, it'll probably be from other tourists. But if you have a rambunctious toddler or older child, you'll definitely want to switch to this kid-size itinerary.

Day 1 and 2

Fly into **Venice**, get settled in your hotel, and follow our "Venice in one day" itinerary for your first day (see Chapter 16). If there are two adults in your party, take turns visiting the **Gallerie dell'Accademia** while the other grown-up leads the kids on unending **boat rides** on the *vaporetto* transportation system (we recommend you get a day pass) or exploring the labyrinth of narrow streets and pretty bridges in the area. On your second day, visit the **Lagoon,** particularly the islands of **Lido** — where you can rent bikes and explore the beaches — and **Murano,** where your kids will be fascinated by a visit to the glass-making factories. If you have teenagers, follow the recommendations of the **Rolling Venice** program, designed particularly for them (see Chapter 16).

Day 3

Take an early train to **Florence,** where you will arrive in just under three hours. Check into your hotel and start with a stroll through town, taking in the **Duomo, Giotto's Bell Tower,** and the **Baptistery,** and going on to **Piazza della Signoria** and **Palazzo Vecchio** and the famous **Ponte Vecchio.** You can take turns visiting the **Uffizi** (make the appropriate reservations) while the other parent entertains the children in the **Boboli Gardens** or the **outdoor markets** of San Lorenzo and della Paglia (see Chapter 13).

Day 4 and 5

Take an early train to **Rome** — you'll be there in less than two hours. Get settled in your hotel and follow our "Rome in two days" itinerary (see Chapter 12), but replace the Galleria Borghese with a **boat ride along the Tiber** (or take turns at the Galleria while your children row boats and visit the kids' attractions in **Villa Borghese**). On your second day in Rome, replace the Vatican Museums with a bike tour of the **Appian Way** and a visit to the **Catacombs** there, which children usually love (alternatively, take turns at the Vatican while your children visit the wonderful Egyptian section of the **Musei Vaticani** or go on that boat ride on the Tiber).

Day 6 and 7

Take the 90-minute high-speed train to **Naples.** If you have teenagers, proceed with our "Naples in one day" itinerary (see Chapter 18), replacing the Capodimonte Museum with the **Catacombs of St. Gennaro** on your first day. Spend your second day here exploring **Pompeii, Herculaneum,** or the **Campi Flegrei.** Alternatively, take a taxi to the harbor and hop on the ferry (or hydrofoil) for a day trip to **Capri** (see Chapters 19 and 20) — you'll appreciate the chance to relax, especially if you're with younger children. If two days of hiking the island, visiting ruins, and basking in the sun seem like too much, you can always catch a ferry on your second day to **Positano, Amalfi,** or **Sorrento** (see Chapter 20). Catch your flight back home from the Naples airport the next morning.

Unearthing Italy's Ancient History

If archaeology and ancient history and culture are your thing, the focus of your visit should be central and southern Italy — Rome, Naples, and Sicily — where the main intersection of Etruscan, Greek, Carthaginian, Roman, Norman, and Arab influences took place.

Day 1 and 2

Fly into **Rome,** get settled in your hotel, and buy a combo ticket for the **110 Open Stop & Go** bus tour plus the **Archeobus.** Refer to Day 1 of our "Rome in two days" itinerary (see Chapter 12), but replace the Galleria Borghese with **Palazzo Massimo alle Terme.** On Day 2, catch an early **Archeobus** from Termini and head for the **Park of the Appian Way** and its many attractions. Upon your return in the late afternoon, squeeze in a visit to the **Pantheon** and a stroll through **Piazza Navona** and **Castel Sant'Angelo.**

Day 3

Take an early high-speed train to **Naples,** which you'll reach in under 90 minutes. Get settled in your hotel and then start with a visit to the **Museo Archeologico.** Afterward, take a local train to **Pompeii** (see Chapter 19).

Day 4

If you start early in the day, you should have time for the **Campi Flegrei** in the morning and **Herculaneum** in the afternoon; otherwise, limit yourself to one of them. Alternatively, take a day trip to visit the Roman ruins of **Capri** — they aren't as spectacular as the ones on the mainland, but they do have a strong historical and mystical appeal (see Chapter 20). Take the night ferry to Palermo or fly there the next morning.

Day 5

If you don't mind a lot of driving, rent a car for the next three days and drive yourself to **Agrigento** and the **Valle dei Templi,** where you'll spend the night. Stop on the way to see the Doric temple in **Segesta,** as well as the ruins of **Selinunte** (see Chapter 22). Alternatively, for a less tiring vacation, settle yourself in Palermo and take day trips using the excellent bus tours (see Chapter 21).

Day 6

Early in the morning, drive to **Piazza Armerina** to see the **Villa del Casale.** In the afternoon, proceed to **Syracuse** and check into a hotel. Visit the archaeological area before sunset (see Chapter 22).

Day 7

Visit the **Ortigia** early in the morning and then head to **Taormina,** where you can admire the splendid Greek theater (see Chapter 22). Fly home from Catania (or Palermo, if you chose to take day trips) the next morning.

Part II
Planning Your Trip to Italy

The 5th Wave   By Rich Tennant

"And how shall I book your flight to Italy — First Class, Coach, or Medieval?"

In this part . . .

1 n this part, we get down to the nuts and bolts of organizing your trip, including smart choices that will help you reduce costs and enjoy your vacation even more. Plus, we give tips for travelers with special interests and needs.

Chapter 5 discusses money; we deal with budget-related questions, list some tips for pinching a euro here and there without sacrificing, and suggest the best ways to handle your money. Chapter 6 concerns the various ways of getting to Italy, while Chapter 7 gives you information about getting around Italy after you arrive. Chapter 8 covers hotel options and booking your room. In Chapter 9, we offer advice for a variety of special situations, including traveling with children. Chapter 10 takes care of details that many travelers leave to the last minute, such as getting a passport, thinking about medical and travel insurance, and making reservations for special events.

Chapter 5

Managing Your Money

● ●

In This Chapter

▶ Devising a realistic budget for your trip
▶ Finding ways to save some money
▶ Carrying cash and making sense of the euro

● ●

*W*hen it comes to planning a vacation budget, you usually deal with two different numbers: what you'd *like* to spend and what you *can* spend. But if you trim here and there on the incidentals and splurge just on the things that really matter to you, you can still design a terrific vacation without breaking the bank. In this chapter, we give you some pointers on being realistic and keeping track of all the costs that you'll have to bear in mind, as well as all the necessary info on handling and carrying foreign currency.

Planning Your Budget

Italy is more tourist-friendly than ever as the level of services has increased to match the highest international standards. Globalization, though, has not come without a price: The cost of living has almost doubled since the introduction in 2002 of the euro, the unit of currency that replaced the old *lire*. You get more in hotels and restaurants now, but you pay more as well. On the other hand, many public institutions, including state museums and attractions, have maintained — or even reduced — their prices while offering a lot more than before.

We figure there are six major elements that eat up your vacation budget: transportation, lodging, dining, sightseeing, shopping, and nightlife. Knowledge is key, and we want to share with you our hard-earned experience in each of these areas.

The tables below give a sample of costs that you may encounter on your trip, both in cities and in the countryside. And if you're wondering about taxes, we cover that in "Taking Taxes into Account," later in this chapter.

Transportation

Airfare to Italy will be one of the biggest items in your budget. Keeping it low gives you a sort of cushion for the rest of your expenses. The actual cost depends on the time of year that you travel, but booking in advance helps, too: In high season, you're lucky to find a round-trip ticket for less than about $900; at other times, though, you may find tickets for half that much or even less. But if you procrastinate and wait until mid-June to reserve a flight for July, you'll be lucky to pay $1,200 — if you can find a seat at all. Be sure to check out our money-saving tips before you buy an airline ticket (see Chapter 6).

Table 5-1	What Things Cost in Rome
A metro or city bus ride	1€ ($1.20)
Can of soda	1€–1.50€ ($1.20–$1.80)
Pay-phone call	0.20€ (24¢)
Movie ticket	8€–10€ ($9.60–$12)
Caffè lungo (American-style espresso) at the counter	0.70€ (84¢)
Cappuccino (or something similar)	1€ ($1.20)
Ticket to the Galleria Borghese	8.50€ ($10) res. incl.
Gasoline	1.35€ ($1.62) per liter = 6.13€ ($7.36) per gallon
Average hotel room	200€ ($240)
Liter of house wine in a restaurant	8€ ($9.60)
Individual pizza in a *pizzeria*	8€–12€ ($9.60–$14)
First-class letter to U.S. (or any overseas country)	0.85€ ($1)

Table 5-2	What Things Cost in Greve in Chianti
A subway or city bus ride	0.65€ (78¢)
Can of soda	1€ ($1.20)
Pay-phone call	0.20€ (24¢)
Caffè lungo (American-style espresso)	0.65€ (78¢)
Cappuccino (or something similar)	0.80€ (96¢)

Gallon of gasoline	1.35€ ($1.62) per liter = 6.13€ ($7.36) per gallon
Average hotel room	120€ ($144)
Liter of house wine in a restaurant	5€ ($6)
Individual pizza in a *pizzeria*	5€–10€ ($6–$12)
First-class letter to U.S. (or any overseas country)	0.85€ ($1)

What you'll spend on transportation once you're in Italy depends a lot on your itinerary. Most towns and villages — even small ones — can be reached by public transportation, which is very affordable and has ever-improving service. Many train routes offer high-speed options as well. Traveling by train from Rome to Naples, for example, will cost you about 20€ ($24) for a full fare — or 33€ ($40) on the high-speed — while the trip from Florence to nearby Siena costs 6€ ($7.20). Buses are usually cheaper: Count on about 5€ ($6) for a ride between Florence and Siena, or 17€ ($20) between Siena and Rome.

Flying domestically has become a lot more common as the private carriers have multiplied — with the consequence that prices have dropped and you can now find a lot of great deals: Venice–Rome may cost you as little as 75€ ($90); Rome–Catania, 73€ ($88).

In contrast, traveling by car continues to be a nightmare of potential accidents and high costs — fuel hovers around 1.35€ per liter ($7.36 per gallon), renting a car is likely to be more expensive than what you're used to back home, tolls on highways are high, and parking ain't cheap, either. Long-distance trips between major destinations are best done by public transportation, which is both cheaper and a lot safer. Unless you want to meander in the countryside at leisure, skip the car rental altogether!

See Chapter 7 for more on traveling within Italy and on driving in a foreign country.

Lodging

Lodging is another big-ticket item, but one you cannot forego: After all, you do need to sleep somewhere! This expense fluctuates depending on the time of year; in high season, prices in certain destinations can double, and you'll have to book well in advance to secure the best hotels. The costs also depend on your itinerary: Cities and major towns are the most expensive, while you'll spend a bit less in the countryside; also, southern Italy tends to be less expensive than the north. For example, you can consider yourself lucky to find a nice room in high season in Rome or Venice for 200€ ($240), and it will more likely cost you 250€ ($300). You'll do better in smaller towns and in southern Italy: You should find that same nice room in Assisi for 160€ ($192), and in Naples for 180€ ($216); in the countryside, you should be able to pay about 160€ ($192) in the north and 130€ ($156) in the south.

In the hotel reviews in this book, we supply the **rack rates,** which in Italy are the highest prices the hotel can charge you (at the peak of high season and when the hotel is completely full). You should be able to do better in most cases. See the Introduction for a table indicating what the $ symbols ($–$$$$) mean.

Dining

Your expenses in this category will vary with your style: What you spend will depend on what and how you eat. Possibilities in Italy are endless and, on the whole, very satisfactory — you'll find cheap eateries and gourmet haunts and everything in between, all serving excellent food. You also have the option of buying your own food (for snacks and picnics, for example) from a wide range of choices, including small vendors, open-air markets, and supermarkets. Prices depend on the elegance of the place you choose and on the food you order, although you can count on spending more in cities and major towns and less in smaller destinations and the countryside. The north — again — is more expensive than the south. Drinks excluded, expect to spend about 35€ ($42) per person for dinner in Rome in a nice restaurant and 20€ ($24) in a less formal one, such as a *pizzeria* or *osteria;* for the same meals in Venice, you'll spend 40€ ($48) and 25€ ($30) respectively; and in Naples, 30€ ($36) and 15€ ($18). In the countryside, you should spend a bit less. For a truly special meal in one of the top restaurants, expect to spend an average of 60€ ($72) per person for a meat dinner and as much as 80€ ($96) for fish, in both cases a full meal including several courses. For a meal on the go, you can grab a bite for as little as 5€ to 8€ ($6–$9.60) in a *rosticceria* or *pizza a taglio* place (see Chapter 2 for the different types of restaurant options in Italy). Prices are not significantly different at lunch or dinner, but some restaurants serve more elaborate dishes — priced accordingly — only at dinner.

Just as with the hotel reviews, we use a dollar-sign system to indicate the average prices of restaurants; these refer to a complete meal. See the Introduction for a table indicating what the $ symbols ($–$$$$) mean. Within the listing information in each review, we give the price range of *secondi;* these are meat or fish dishes (the most expensive dishes on the menu). Keep in mind that in order to have the equivalent of a main course, you'll have to order a side dish separately — or you may be content with just a *primo* (a less expensive pasta dish). See Chapter 2 for more on the structure of a meal in Italy.

Tipping isn't a big extra in Italy because service is usually included in the prices; it's okay to leave just a small token of appreciation. Check for the words *servizio incluso* (service included) on the menu; if they aren't there, expect to pay a full gratuity of 15 percent.

A pocketful of change

In many of Italy's churches, fragile paintings are kept in semi-obscurity, but you will often find a light box nearby. When you insert a coin or two, a light pops on to illuminate a painting, fresco, or sculpture for a limited amount of time. Therefore, carrying a pocketful of coins is always a good idea.

Sightseeing

This is what you've come to Italy for: visiting attractions, attending events, and enjoying the local culture. Luckily, this expense is the most manageable: The most you'll pay for museum admission is 12€ ($14) for the whole string of museums on Piazza San Marco in Venice, and 10€ ($12) for the archaeological area of Pompeii or Herculaneum. Admission to the important museums hovers around 6€ ($7.20), and many attractions charge only between 2€ and 5€ ($2.40–$6). What's more, many attractions are free: most churches, for instance, since they are places of worship and not museums (remember to avoid visiting during mass unless you're attending the service).

If you make advance reservations for attractions, you'll be able to estimate this part of your budget before you even arrive in Italy. Most museums and attractions allow you to do so — and they sometimes grant you a discount to boot (see Chapter 10 for more on advance reservations).

Shopping

Shopping is the one expenditure that can be considered an extra: You can spend hundreds on a full-length leather coat for yourself or for a friend, or you can skip the shopping completely. Yet Italy is a shopper's paradise: The country is famous for its artwork, design, and crafts — art glass, pottery, leather, gold, and lace, among many other fine wares. Italian fashion isn't half-bad either — Versace, Dolce & Gabbana, and Armani are a few of the world-famous Italian firms. Depending on exchange rates, you may actually save by buying Italian goods in Italy. More important, though, shopping here gives you a chance to buy things that simply aren't available, or not in such variety, back home. Throughout this book, we give our recommendations for the best shops and items that each city has to offer. If your budget allows it, use your trip as a chance to pick up that special something you have an irresistible craving for — maybe a Murano chandelier, a pair of leather boots, or a Gucci handbag (you may even find a nice used Ferrari).

Nightlife

Visiting the opera, going out for a drink, listening to music in a jazz club, and dancing the night away are all extra pleasures that will make your

Follow the bouncing euro

Only a few years ago, the euro was worth about 90¢; it then bounced back strongly to over $1.30, and now it costs $1.20 to buy a euro. Such swings can make a huge difference: The 100€-per-night hotel that seemed like a bargain at $90 a couple years ago now would cost $120 (if you can still find it). Another example: Admission to Palazzo Altemps has gone down from 5.16€ to 5€, but in dollars the price has increased from $4.60 to $6. By the time you read this, the two currencies may be closer to parity, but then again, maybe not. Obviously it will help to keep an eye on the euro while you're planning your trip.

time in Italy that much more memorable. Expect to pay between 30€ and 120€ ($36–$144) for a seat at the opera, and between 15€ and 30€ ($18–$36) for a concert, depending on the performer. Cover charges for nightclubs hover around 10€ ($12), while a drink in a trendy bar will cost between 6€ and 10€ ($7.20–$12). Once again, expect higher prices in cities and large towns, lower ones in small towns and the countryside. You'll also find many serendipitous little things to enjoy that are free or nearly so, such as people-watching on a beautiful floodlit *piazza*, eating an ice-cream cone while strolling on the main street of a historic center, and ordering a coffee or drink in a classic *caffè* and soaking in the atmosphere.

Cutting Costs — But Not the Fun

Don't feel like taking out a second mortgage on your house so you can afford a vacation to Italy? Well, start thinking like an Italian. Italians have relatively less disposable income than Americans and have found many ways to enjoy themselves without going broke. Mirror the way they live and travel, and the cheaper your trip will be — and the more closely you'll get to know the Italians themselves. One thing we recommend, however: Don't skip attractions in order to save the admission price, as sightseeing isn't an area where you can save a lot of money, and you'll probably be sorry if you try. If you could enjoy the same experience from the outside, then the attraction probably wouldn't charge you for entering . . . and we would certainly say so in our write-up!

 Throughout this book, you'll see Bargain Alert icons that highlight money-saving tips and/or great deals. Here are some additional cost-cutting strategies:

  ✔ **Surf the Web.** Airlines often have special Internet-only rates that are appreciably cheaper than rates quoted over the phone. You can also find good hotel packages online.

✔ **Make your reservations ahead of time.** Flights have only so many seats at low rates, and the best moderately priced hotels fill up fast.

✔ **Try a package tour.** For popular destinations like Italy, you can book airfare, hotel, ground transportation, and even some sightseeing by making just one call to a travel agent or packager, and you may pay a lot less than if you tried to put the trip together yourself. But always work out the prices that you'd pay if you arranged the pieces of your trip yourself, just to double-check. See the section on package tours in Chapter 6 for specific suggestions.

✔ **Go off season.** If you can travel at nonpeak times (usually winter, with the exception of the Christmas and New Year's holidays), you can find airfares and hotel prices as much as 20 percent lower than during peak months.

✔ **Travel during off-peak days of the week.** Airfares vary depending not only on the time of the year, but also on the day of the week. In Italy, weekend rates are often cheaper than weekday rates. When you inquire about airfares, ask if you can obtain a cheaper rate by flying on a different day.

✔ **Pack light.** Packing light enables you to carry your own bags and not worry about finding a porter (don't forget to tip yourself). Likewise, you can more easily take a bus or a train rather than a cab from the airport, saving you a few more euro.

✔ **Book a hotel in the center of town.** If you're near all the attractions, you'll save money on cab fares and public transportation, as well as time — your most valuable asset during a vacation.

✔ **Make do with a smaller hotel room and bathroom.** It will be different from back home, but oh so atmospheric! (See Chapter 8 for more on what to expect from your hotels in Italy.)

✔ **Ask if your kids can stay in the room with you.** Many hotels won't charge you the additional-person rate if your extra person is pint-size and related to you. You can save much more if you don't take two rooms, even if you have to pay some extra euro for a rollaway bed.

✔ **Skip the breakfast at your hotel** (unless it's included in your room rate). It won't be an American breakfast, anyway (except in the most expensive hotels), and grabbing a hot drink and pastry at a bar will give you further insight into the local culture. You can also reserve a room with a refrigerator and keep a few breakfast supplies on hand.

✔ **Have lunch on the go.** Try pizza or a bowl of pasta (see Chapter 2 for more on this). Or, armed with a corkscrew and a plastic fork, you can cheaply assemble a fine picnic lunch from the supermarket, using ingredients you pay dearly for at your local gourmet shop — fresh bread, locally cured prosciutto, regional cheeses, raw or cooked vegetables, and local wine or mineral water. A picnic lunch is also a great way to visit some of the outdoor sights.

✔ **Skip the bread and sodas at restaurants.** Most restaurants impose a basic table-and-bread charge (called *pane e coperto*) of 1.50€ to 5€ ($1.80–$6), which you can avoid in some restaurants — most restaurants in Rome, for instance — by saying no to the bread basket. Also, soft drinks are relatively expensive in Italy, whereas you can order a large bottle of mineral water or a pitcher of house wine *(vino della casa)* quite cheaply.

✔ **Take advantage of combination tickets and discount cards.** We've flagged these special offers for you in the specific destination chapters that follow. (In Venice, for instance, people under 30 can receive a discount for shopping, accommodations, and sightseeing with the Rolling Venice pass.)

✔ **Don't sit to sip.** If what you're after is a coffee or a drink and not an experience, save yourself the hefty table-service surcharge at cafes and bars and have your drink at the counter. A simple coffee at an outside table in Piazza San Marco in Venice, for example, may cost the same as lunch anywhere else.

✔ **Skip the souvenirs.** Your photographs and memories could be the best mementos of your trip. If you're concerned about money, you can do without the T-shirts, key chains, salt and pepper shakers, and other trinkets.

Handling Money

If you ignore the fact that you'll probably incur more expenses while you're on vacation than you would while at home (unless you happen to eat out at every meal) and that you'll be dealing with a foreign currency, you should find things pretty familiar: The only form of payment that won't be quite as available to you away from home is your personal checkbook.

Making sense of the euro

Italy's currency, the *euro* (the plural is also *euro,* and it's abbreviated as € in this guide), was introduced in January 2002 in Italy and in 11 other European countries. You can use the same currency in Austria, Belgium, Finland, France, Germany, Greece, Ireland, Italy, Luxembourg, the Netherlands, Portugal, and Spain. The transformation to the euro has made prices much more user-friendly: 1€ is a lot easier to understand than 1,932 liras!

The exchange rate used in this book is 1€ = $1.20; we round off all dollar values above $10. Exchange rates fluctuate all the time, though, so check www.ex-rates.com for up-to-date (and historical) comparisons between the euro and your currency, whether it's the U.S. or Canadian dollar, the British pound, or something else. Another excellent Web site is www.xe.com/ucc. At press time, the British pound was at 1£ = 1.51€. These were the rates of exchange used to calculate the values in Table 5-3.

Euro €	U.S. $	U.K. £	Euro €	U.S. $	U.K. £
Table 5-3		**Foreign Currencies vs. the U.S. Dollar**			
1.00	1.20	0.66	75.00	90.00	49.50
2.00	2.40	1.32	100.00	120.00	66.00
3.00	3.60	1.98	125.00	150.00	82.50
4.00	4.80	2.64	150.00	180.00	99.00
5.00	6.00	3.30	175.00	210.00	115.50
6.00	7.20	3.96	200.00	240.00	132.00
7.00	8.40	4.62	225.00	270.00	148.50
8.00	9.60	5.28	250.00	300.00	165.00
9.00	10.80	5.94	275.00	330.00	181.50
10.00	12.00	6.60	300.00	360.00	198.00
15.00	18.00	9.90	350.00	420.00	231.00
20.00	24.00	13.20	400.00	480.00	264.00
25.00	30.00	16.50	500.00	600.00	330.00
50.00	60.00	33.00	1000.00	1200.00	660.00

Note that when saying the word *euro,* Italians pronounce all three vowels, so it's *ay*-ur-oh, not *yurr*-oh.

You can exchange money at all points of entry in Italy: You'll find automated teller machines (ATMs) as well as exchange bureaus at airports and train stations and, of course, in town. Exchange bureaus usually display multilingual signs (CHANGE/CAMBIO/WECHSEL). Rates may vary to some degree. For example, some bureaus advertise "no fee" exchanges, but then give you a lower rate so you come out the same anyway. Arriving in Italy with a small supply of euro, at least enough to pay for a cab to your hotel, is a good idea in case the ATM at the airport doesn't work or the lines are unbearably long.

Using ATMs and carrying cash

The easiest and best way to get cash away from home is from an ATM. Look at the back of your bank card to see which network you're on; then call or check online for ATM locations at your destination. **Cirrus** (☎ 800-424-7787; www.mastercard.com) is the most common international network in Italy. **PLUS** (☎ 800-843-7587; www.visa.com) exists,

The euro look

Paper bills come in 5€, 10€, 20€, 50€, 100€, 200€, and 500€ denominations. All bills are brightly colored and have a different shade for each denomination. In addition, the higher the value, the larger the physical size of the bill. Coins come in 1€ and 2€ (both thin and brass-colored); 10-cent, 20-cent, and 50-cent (all brass colored); and 1-cent, 2-cent, and 5-cent (all copper-colored) denominations. For more information and pictures of the currency, check the official Web site of the **European Union** (http://europa.eu.int/euro) or the **European Central Bank** (www.euro.ecb.int).

Don't be surprised to see different country names on euro bills and coins: One face is the European side, common to all of the participating countries, and the reverse face is the national side, where each country has printed its own design. All are valid and accepted in each of the countries.

but is less common. The Banca Nazionale del Lavoro (BNL) is one bank that does offer PLUS in its ATMs; another sure bet are the ATMs of the Italian post offices.

Before leaving for Italy, make sure that you check the daily withdrawal limit for your ATM card, and ask whether you need a new personal identification number (PIN). (You need a four-digit PIN in Europe, so if you currently have a six-digit PIN, you must get a new one before you go.) Also, if your PIN is a word, make sure you know how it translates into numbers — some ATM keypads in Italy display only numbers.

Many banks impose a fee every time your card is used at a different bank's ATM, and that fee can be higher for international transactions (up to $5 or more) than for domestic ones (where they're rarely more than $1.50). On top of this, the bank from which you withdraw cash may charge its own fee. For details on international withdrawal fees, ask your bank.

In cities and towns, ATMs are never far away, so you can walk around with little cash in your wallet, especially if don't mind paying for purchases with a credit card. Before going off on a driving tour of the countryside, however, make sure that you have a good stock of cash in your wallet; banks and ATMs are rarer there, and lots of small businesses don't accept credit cards.

If you have linked checking and savings accounts and you're in the habit of moving relatively small amounts of money from savings to checking as you need it, beware: Italian ATMs won't show you the transfer-between-accounts option, and they won't allow you to withdraw money directly from your savings account. If your checking account runs dry, you must call or write your bank to move money from savings to checking. (We did so, and our bank charged us $30. Ouch!)

Charging ahead with credit cards

Credit cards are a safe way to carry money. They also provide a convenient record of all your expenses, and they generally offer relatively good exchange rates. You can also withdraw cash advances on your credit cards at banks or ATMs as long as you know your PIN, but the interest rate is high. Keep in mind that when you use your credit card abroad, most banks assess a 2 percent fee above the 1 percent fee charged by Visa or MasterCard or American Express for currency conversion on credit charges. But credit cards still may be the smart way to go when you factor in things like exorbitant ATM fees and higher traveler's-check exchange rates (and service fees).

 Some credit-card companies recommend that you notify them of any upcoming trip abroad so that they don't become suspicious when the card is used in a foreign destination and end up blocking your charges. Even if you don't call your credit-card company in advance, you can always call the card's toll-free emergency number if a charge is refused — a good reason to carry the phone number with you. But perhaps the most important lesson here is to carry more than one card with you on your trip; a card may not work for any number of reasons, so having a backup is the smart way to go.

Toting traveler's checks

These days, traveler's checks are less necessary because 24-hour ATMs allow you to withdraw small amounts of cash as needed. Traveler's checks are still widely accepted in Italy, especially at large stores and hotels, and they'll save you the ATM withdrawal fee, but they can get stolen and you'll need to show identification every time you want to cash one.

You can get traveler's checks at almost any bank. **American Express** offers denominations of $20, $50, $100, $500, and (for cardholders only) $1,000. You'll pay a service charge ranging from 1 to 4 percent. You can also get American Express traveler's checks over the phone by calling ☎ 800-221-7282; AmEx gold and platinum cardholders who use this number are exempt from the 1 percent fee. **Visa** offers traveler's checks at Citibank locations nationwide, as well as at several other banks. The service charge ranges between 1.5 and 2 percent. Call ☎ 800-732-1322 for information. AAA members can obtain Visa checks without a fee at most AAA offices or by calling ☎ 800-339-3378. Traveler's checks are also available through **MasterCard;** call ☎ 800-223-9920 for a location near you.

 If you choose to carry traveler's checks, be sure to keep a record of their serial numbers separate from your checks in case they're stolen or lost. You'll get a refund faster if you know the numbers.

Taking Taxes into Account

You may not notice taxes in Italy because they're included in the prices that you're quoted, but do know that the **value-added tax** (known as the IVA) is a steep 19 percent. The good news is that you can get a refund for purchases costing more than 155€ ($178). Stores displaying a TAX FREE sign will give you an invoice that you can cash at the airport's Customs office as you leave Italy. You can also have the invoice from the store stamped at the airport by Customs, and then mail it back to the store, which will then send you a check or credit your charge account.

Dealing with a Lost or Stolen Wallet

Being on vacation is a blissful time of distraction and discovery. Unfortunately, this makes visitors a ripe target for pickpockets. If you discover that your wallet has been lost or stolen, contact all of your credit-card companies right away. You'll also want to file a report at the nearest police precinct (your credit-card company or insurer may require a police-report number or record of the loss). Most credit-card companies have an emergency toll-free number to call if your card is lost or stolen; they may be able to wire you a cash advance immediately or deliver an emergency credit card in a day or two. In Italy, contact these offices:

- **American Express** (☎ **06-7220348** or 06-72282 or 06-72461; www.americanexpress.it)

- **Diners Club** (☎ **800-864064866** toll-free within Italy; www.diners club.com)

- **MasterCard** (☎ **800-870866** toll-free within Italy; www.mastercard.com)

- **Visa** (☎ **800-819014** toll-free within Italy; www.visaeu.com)

If you need emergency cash over the weekend, when all banks and American Express offices are closed, you can have money wired to you via **Western Union** (☎ **800-325-6000**; www.westernunion.com).

Identity theft and fraud are potential complications of losing your wallet, especially if you've lost your driver's license or passport along with your cash and credit cards. Notify the major credit-reporting bureaus immediately; placing a fraud alert on your record may protect you against liability for criminal activity. The three major U.S. credit-reporting agencies are **Equifax** (☎ **800-766-0008**; www.equifax.com), **Experian** (☎ **888-397-3742**; www.experian.com), and **TransUnion** (☎ **800-680-7289**; www.transunion.com). Finally, if you've lost all forms of photo ID, call your airline and explain the situation; it may allow you to board the plane if you have a copy of your passport or birth certificate and a copy of the police report you've filed.

 Watch your purse, wallet, briefcase, or backpack in any public place. When walking on the street, keep your purse on the side away from traffic, so a thief on a motor scooter can't speed by and grab it from you. Better yet, carry your money, credit cards, and passport in an interior pocket, where pickpockets won't be able to snatch them.

Chapter 6

Getting to Italy

● ●

In This Chapter

▶ Checking out the major airlines

▶ Finding alternate ways to Italy

▶ Sorting out package tours and escorted tours

● ●

*I*f you live near a major city, getting to Italy may be even easier than reaching another destination in your own country, but it won't be cheaper. Italy is farther from the U.S. than England or France, for example, and airfares are significantly higher. The recent increase in fuel prices has only made matters worse: A round-trip ticket during peak times can run between $800 and $2,000, depending on how far in advance you book your trip. Of course, with the cutthroat competition among airlines, you may be able to lock in a much better deal, especially if you book well in advance and have a flexible itinerary. This chapter outlines all the ways and means you have to make getting to Italy a snap.

Flying to Italy

Because Italy is long and skinny in shape, flying into one airport at one end and leaving from another at the other end makes sense, especially if your time is limited and you want to see sights in both northern and southern Italy. If, for example, you land in Milan, you can then fly out of Rome, or fly into Venice and leave from Catania. For the right price, this plan may save you hundreds of miles of driving or sitting on the train just to retrace your steps to the airport where you entered the country.

Finding out which airlines fly there

Rome and Milan are Italy's gateways, to which you can fly nonstop from North America and other continents. For other airports in Italy — Florence, Pisa, Venice, Naples, Palermo, Catania — you will have to take a connecting flight.

Alitalia (☎ **800-223-5730** in the U.S.; 800-361-8336 in Canada; 020-8814-7700 in the U.K.; 8-8306-8411 in Australia; or 06-2222 in Italy; www. alitalia.it), the Italian national airline, offers direct flights to Rome and Milan from most major destinations in the world. It also offers connecting flights to every destination in Italy by way of Rome or Milan. Daily direct flights are scheduled from a number of North American cities, including New York, Boston, Toronto, and Montreal.

From the United States, you can also try **American Airlines** (☎ 800-433-7300; www.aa.com), **Continental** (☎ 800-525-0280; www.continental.com), **Delta** (☎ 800-241-4141; www.delta.com), **Northwest/KLM Airlines** (☎ 800-447-4747; www.nwa.com), **United** (☎ 800-538-2929; www.united.com), and **US Airways** (☎ 800-428-4322; www.usairways.com), which all offer direct nonstop flights to Rome or Milan, at least during peak season.

From Canada, **Air Canada** (☎ 888-247-2262; www.aircanada.com) offers direct flights between Toronto and Rome.

From Australia, **Qantas** (☎ 13-13-13; www.qantas.com) offers direct flights from Melbourne to Rome on a daily basis, plus flights from Sydney several days a week.

From Britain, you'll find direct flights to a number of Italian cities via **Alitalia** (☎ 020-8814-7700; www.alitalia.it) and **British Airways** (☎ 0845-773-3377 in the U.K.; www.britishairways.com). The new discount, no-frills options include **Ryanair** (☎ 0871-246-0000; www.ryanair.com) and **EasyJet** (www.easyjet.com).

Getting the best deal on your airfare

Business travelers who need the flexibility of buying their tickets at the last minute and changing their itineraries at a moment's notice — and who want to get home before the weekend — pay (or at least their companies pay) the premium rate, known as the full fare. But you can often qualify for the least expensive price, which will be several hundreds — or even thousands — of dollars lower than the full fare.

 Keep in mind that the lowest-priced fares are often nonrefundable, require advance purchase and a certain length of stay, have date-of-travel restrictions, and carry penalties for changing dates of travel.

For Italy, the high season is long and getting longer, and snagging low fares is increasingly difficult; at certain times, you may be lucky just to get on any plane heading for Italy. But fear not: You don't have to pay top dollar for your airline seat. Here are some tips on scoring the best airfare:

> ✔ **Book in advance and be flexible.** Fares can vary thousands of dollars, just depending on the season and on how far in advance you book. Changing the day of the week you travel can save a couple of hundred dollars. Passengers who can book their ticket far in advance (21 days at least), who can stay over Saturday night, and who are willing to travel on a Tuesday, Wednesday, or Thursday will pay a

fraction of the full fare. If your schedule is flexible, say so — ask if you can secure a cheaper fare by staying an extra day, by flying mid-week, or by traveling during off-peak hours.

✔ **Shop around for specials.** Airlines periodically hold sales, which tend to take place in seasons of low travel volume — for Italy, that means the dead of winter. As you plan your vacation, keep your eyes open for sales advertised in newspapers and online. Remember that if you already hold a ticket when a sale breaks, exchanging your ticket, which usually incurs a $100 to $150 fee, may pay off.

✔ **Consider non-direct flights.** On any day of the week, you can get a connecting flight through a major European city with a European national carrier, such as **British Airways** (☎ 800-247-297; www.britishairways.com), **Air France** (☎ 800-237-2747; www.air france.com), **KLM** (☎ 800-374-7747; www.klm.nl), or **Lufthansa** (☎ 800-645-3880; www.lufthansa-usa.com). In order to encourage travelers to choose a non-direct alternative, round-trip rates are often handsomely discounted, and connections often involve a layover of no more than an hour or two. By connecting in major European hubs, you'll also be able to fly into Italy's secondary airports, such as Venice, Florence, Naples, or Catania.

✔ **Join frequent-flier clubs.** Accruing miles with one program is best, as it lets you rack up free flights and achieve elite status faster. But opening as many accounts as possible makes sense, too, no matter how seldom you fly a particular airline. It's free, and you get the best choice of seats, faster response to phone inquiries, and prompter service if your luggage is stolen, if your flight is canceled or delayed, or if you want to change your seat.

Cutting costs by using consolidators

You can also check consolidators, also known as bucket shops. Start by looking in the Sunday newspaper's travel section; U.S. travelers should focus on the *New York Times, Los Angeles Times,* and *Miami Herald.* Several reliable consolidators are worldwide and available on the Web. **STA Travel** (☎ 800-781-4040; www.statravel.com), the world's leader in student travel, offers good fares for travelers of all ages. **ELTExpress** (☎ 800-TRAV-800; www.flights.com) started in Europe and has excellent fares worldwide. **Flights.com** also has "local" Web sites in 12 countries. FlyCheap, an industry leader, has become **Lowestfare.com** (www.lowestfare.com) and is now owned by Priceline (see later in this chapter). **Air Tickets Direct** (☎ 800-778-3447; www.airticketsdirect.com) is based in Montreal and leverages the currently weak Canadian dollar for low fares.

Bucket-shop tickets are usually nonrefundable or rigged with stiff cancellation penalties, often as high as 50 to 75 percent of the ticket price. Some consolidators will also put you on charter airlines with questionable safety records.

Booking your flight online

The "big three" online travel agencies — **Expedia** (www.expedia.com), **Travelocity** (www.travelocity.com), and **Orbitz** (www.orbitz.com) — sell most of the air tickets bought on the Internet. (Canadian travelers should try www.expedia.ca and www.travelocity.ca; U.K. residents can go for expedia.co.uk and opodo.co.uk.) Each has different business deals with the airlines and may offer different fares on the same flights, so shopping around is wise. Expedia and Travelocity will also send you an **e-mail notification** when a cheap fare becomes available to your favorite destination. Of the smaller sites, **SideStep** (www.sidestep.com) receives good reviews from users. It's a browser add-on that purports to "search 140 sites at once," but in reality only beats competitors' fares as often as other sites do.

Great **last-minute deals** are available through free weekly e-mail services provided directly by the airlines. Most of these deals are announced on Tuesday or Wednesday and must be purchased online. Most are valid only for travel that weekend, but some can be booked weeks or months in advance. Sign up for weekly e-mail alerts at airline Web sites or check mega-sites that compile comprehensive lists of last-minute specials, such as **Smarter Living** (smarterliving.com). For last-minute trips, www.lastminute.com (www.site59.com in the U.S.) often has better deals than the major-label sites.

If you're willing to give up some control over your flight details, use an *opaque fare service* like **Priceline** (www.priceline.com) or **Hotwire** (www.hotwire.com). Both offer rock-bottom prices in exchange for travel on a "mystery airline" at a mysterious time of day, often with a mysterious change of planes en route. The mystery airlines are all major, well-known carriers — and the possibility of being sent hither and yon before you arrive in Italy is remote. But your chances of getting a 6 a.m. or 11 p.m. flight are pretty high. For example, Hotwire has a "no red-eye" option, but be aware that it thinks a 6 a.m. flight for which you have to be at the airport two hours in advance (it's hardly worth putting on your jammies, is it?) is *not* a red-eye. Hotwire tells you flight prices before you buy; Priceline usually has better deals than Hotwire, but you have to play its "name our price" game — and with each try, you have to change something besides your bid, which is to prevent people from making endless iterations starting at 20 bucks. If you have fixed travel dates, better make a realistic bid to start or you'll have to change them or look elsewhere. In order to cover all the bases, Priceline has created/purchased **Lowestfare.com** (www.lowestfare.com), in which you don't have to bid for seats.

Arriving by Other Means

You may be adding Italy to a more extensive European vacation, or perhaps you live in Britain or Ireland. Although usually it's cheaper and faster to fly, you may be looking for other ways to get to Italy. We don't recommend driving, however, even if it may appear tempting: The drive is not only expensive (with gasoline at over $7 a gallon in Europe, plus high tolls on highways), but also *long* and exhausting (we once drove from Brittany to Rome and are not keen on repeating the experience). Here are your other options:

- ✔ **Train:** Railroads in Europe offer cheap, reliable, fast, and frequent service. Paris is connected to Italy by high-speed TGV trains to Torino–Novara–Milan. From Paris, you can also take the famous Palatino, the convenient overnight train to Rome. You can also catch overnight trains from Germany (Hanover, Düsseldorf, Köln, Bonn, and Frankfurt). **Trenitalia,** the Italian national train service (☎ 892021; www.trenitalia.it), offers excellent deals on rail passes for both Europe and Italy. **Eurailpass** grants unlimited first-class rail travel within most of continental Europe and comes in several versions for both adults and younger travelers; for example, an adult pass costs $588 for 15 days, $1,654 for three months. The pass also gives you discounts on certain buses and ferries, such as the ferry from Naples to Palermo. You can buy Eurailpasses in advance from travel agents or rail agents in major cities such as New York, Montreal, and Los Angeles; they are also available through **Rail Europe** (☎ 877-272-RAIL in the U.S.; www.raileurope.com). For more on taking the train in Italy, see Chapter 7.

- ✔ **Ferry:** Several ferry companies service the Mediterranean; you can get a ferry to one of Italy's major harbors from a number of countries in Europe, North Africa, and the Middle East. Naples-based **Grimaldi Ferries** (☎ 081-496444; www.grimaldi-ferries.com) offers service between Salerno and Palermo (Sicily), Malta, and Valencia (Spain).

- ✔ **Bus:** The leading operator of scheduled coach services across Europe is **Eurolines** (☎ 0990-143-219; www.eurolines.com), which runs buses to Italy from London's Victoria Coach Station. Its comprehensive network serves Turin, Milan, Bologna, Florence, and Rome — plus summer routes to Verona, Vicenza, Padua, and Venice.

Joining an Escorted Tour

You may be one of the many people who love escorted tours: The tour company takes care of all the details — from the itinerary to the meals, hotels, and attractions tickets and reservations — and your group leader smooths down all the occasional bumps along the way. You'll know what to expect at each leg of your journey; you'll know what your vacation costs upfront; and you won't face many surprises. Fans of escorted tours know that they can take you to the maximum number of sights in the minimum amount of time with the least amount of hassle. In this section, we give some tips on how to choose the escorted tour that best fits your vacation needs.

If you decide to take an escorted tour, we strongly recommend buying travel insurance, especially if the tour operator asks to you pay upfront. It's wise to buy travel insurance through an independent agency. (See Chapter 10 for more about the ins and outs of travel insurance.)

When choosing an escorted tour, along with finding out whether you have to put down a deposit and when final payment is due, ask a few simple questions before you buy:

✔ **What is the cancellation policy?** Can the tour operator cancel the trip if they don't get enough people? How late can you cancel if you are unable to go? Do you get a refund if you cancel? If they cancel?

✔ **How jampacked is the schedule?** Does the tour organizer try to fit 25 hours into a 24-hour day, or is there ample time for relaxing and/or shopping? If getting up at 7 a.m. every day and not returning to your hotel until 6 or 7 p.m. at night sounds like a grind, certain escorted tours may not be for you.

✔ **How big is the group?** The smaller the group, the less time you'll spend waiting for people to get on and off the bus. Tour operators may be evasive about this, as they may not know the exact size of the group until everybody has made reservations, but they should be able to give you a rough estimate.

✔ **Is there a minimum group size?** Some operators have a minimum group size, and may cancel the tour if they don't book enough people. If a quota exists, find out what it is and how close they are to reaching it.

✔ **What is included?** Don't assume anything. You may have to pay to get yourself to and from the airport. A box lunch may be included in an excursion, but drinks may be extra. How much flexibility do you have? Can you opt out of certain activities, or does the bus leave once a day, with no exceptions? Are all your meals planned in advance? Can you choose your entree at dinner, or does everybody get the same chicken cutlet?

Local travel agencies can be an excellent source for regional tours. For example, **Compagnia Siciliana Turismo (CST),** Via E. Amari 124, 90139 Palermo (☎ **091-582294;** www.compagniasicilianaturismo.it), is one of the best choices for a tour of Sicily, offering anything from short two- or three-day tours to longer two-week ones. A large number of international companies specialize in escorted Italian tours. Here is a brief list of the most reliable operators:

✔ **Italiatour** (☎ **800-845-3365** or 212-675-2183; www.italiatour.com), part of the Alitalia Group, offers a variety of tours: You can choose a regional tour or one that covers the whole country. This is the only tour operator with a desk right at the airport (at Fiumicino, in Rome) and native expertise — plus the tours are very competitively priced.

✔ **Perillo Tours,** 577 Chestnut Ridge Rd., Woodcliff Lake, NJ 07675-9888 (☎ 800-431-1515 or 201-307-1234; www.perillotours.com), has been in business for more than half a century. Its itineraries range from 8 to 15 days and are very diverse. Optional excursions are offered (at an extra charge) to allow you to customize your tour somewhat. Perillo tries to cover all the bases, and even has a package to help you get married in Italy.

✔ **Globus+Cosmos Tours** (☎ 800-338-7092; www.globusandcosmos. com) offers first-class escorted coach tours of various regions, lasting from 8 to 16 days.

✔ **Insight Vacations** (☎ 800-582-8380; www.insightvacations. com), a competitor to Globus+Cosmos, books superior first-class, fully escorted motor-coach tours.

✔ **Central Holidays** (☎ 800-935-5000; www.centralholidays.com) offers fully escorted tours in addition to its packages. Several levels of tours — and levels of "escort" — are offered.

✔ For luxurious tours, you can also try **Abercrombie & Kent,** 1520 Kensington Rd., Oak Brook, IL 60523 (☎ 800-554-7016; www. abercrombiekent.com; London address: Sloan Square House, Holbein Place, London SW1W 8NS; ☎ 020-7730-9600).

You can also choose from an increasing number of tours that address special interests, ranging from archaeology to cuisine to biking or spelunking. **Tour Italy Now** (☎ 800-955-4418; www.touritalynow.com) leads biking and hiking tours; **La Dolce Vita Wine Tours** (☎ 888-746-0022; www.dolcetours.com) focuses — obviously — on wine; and **Amelia Tours International** (☎ 800-742-4591 or 516-433-0696) concentrates on archaeology with an eye on food and wine.

Good online resources for specialty tours and travel include the **Specialty Travel Index** (www.specialtytravel.com), which offers a comprehensive selection of Italian tours, from ballooning to mushroom hunting to river cruises; **Shaw Guides** (www.shawguides.com), with links to a substantial number of Italy options, from archaeological programs to falconry excursions to tours for opera fans; and **InfoHub Specialty Travel Guide** (www.infohub.com).

Choosing a Package Tour

Package tours — airfare-plus-hotel bundles to which excursions or activities may be added — can be a smart way to go. In many cases, a package including airfare, hotel, and transportation to and from the airport costs less than the hotel alone on a trip you book yourself. That's because packages are sold in bulk to tour operators, who resell them to the public. Package tours can vary widely. Some offer a better class of hotels than others; others provide the same hotels for lower prices.

Some book flights on scheduled airlines; others sell charter flights. With some packages, your choice of accommodations and travel days may be limited.

To find package tours, check out the travel section of your local Sunday newspaper or the ads in the back of travel magazines such as *Travel + Leisure, National Geographic Traveler,* and *Condé Nast Traveler.* **Liberty Travel** (☎ **888-271-1584;** www.libertytravel.com) is one of the biggest packagers in the Northeast of the U.S., and usually has a full-page ad in the Sunday papers.

Another good source of package deals is the airlines themselves. Most major airlines, including **American Airlines Vacations** (☎ 800-321-2121; www.aavacations.com), **Continental Airlines Vacations** (☎ 800-301-3800; www.coolvacations.com), **Delta Vacations** (☎ 800-221-6666; www.deltavacations.com), **United Vacations** (☎ 888-854-3899; www.unitedvacations.com), and **US Airways Vacations** (☎ **800-455-0123** or 800-422-3861; www.usairwaysvacations.com), offer air/land packages.

Several big **online travel agencies** — Expedia, Travelocity, Orbitz, Site59, and Lastminute.com — also do a brisk business in packages. If you're unsure about the pedigree of a smaller packager, check with the Better Business Bureau in the city where the company is based, or go online to www.bbb.org. If a packager won't tell you where it's based, take your business elsewhere.

Remember that the **escorted-tour operators** discussed earlier also offer packages. For example, **Italiatour** (☎ **800-845-3365;** www.italiatour.com) specializes in packages for independent travelers who ride from one destination to another by train or rental car. Another recommended packager is **Kemwell** (☎ **800-678-0678;** www.kemwell.com).

Chapter 7

Getting Around Italy

● ●

In This Chapter

▶ Flying to and fro
▶ Traveling on land

● ●

*A*fter you arrive in Italy, chances are you'll want to explore the country a bit. Here is all the information you'll need to travel throughout Italy, plus a few tips for choosing the type of transportation that best
suits your plans. We also provide a comparison of travel times between
major destinations using different modes of transportation.

In Italy, you can get virtually anywhere via public transportation — and
quite easily: Where the air and train system stops, the bus system takes
over, and gets you into even the smallest hamlets in the countryside,
with at least a few runs per day. The largest towns and cities are connected so seamlessly — with buses, planes, and trains leaving every few
minutes — that *not* using public transportation is foolish unless you
have special reasons to need a car.

By Plane

Air travel is no longer — or not necessarily — the most expensive way of
getting from one destination to another within Italy. It also has the added
advantage of being fast, especially if you want to travel from one tip of
the peninsula to the other. **Alitalia** (☎ **800-223-5730** in the U.S., 800-361-
8336 in Canada, 020-7602-7111 in London, 0990-448-259 in the rest of the
U.K., 1300-653-747 or 1300-653-757 in Australia, and toll-free 1478-65643
or 06-65643 in Italy; www.alitalia.it or www.alitaliausa.com), the
national Italian carrier, offers flights to every destination in the country.
Other great resources are **Air Sicilia** (☎ **06-650171046**), which flies to
Sicily from a number of Italian towns; **Air One** (☎ 199-207080 within
Italy, or 06-4888069; www.flyairone.it); and **Meridiana** (☎ **0789-
52682**; www.meridiana.it).

When traveling on domestic flights in Italy, you can get a 30 percent discount if you take a flight that departs at night.

Table 7-1 provides the travel times between major Italian cities using different modes of transportation.

Table 7-1	Travel Times between Major Cities			
Cities	*Distance*	*Air Travel Time*	*Train Travel Time*	*Driving Time*
Florence to Milan	298km/185 miles	55 min.	3 hrs., 6 min.	3½ hrs.
Florence to Venice	281km/174 miles	2 hrs., 5 min.	3 hrs., 9 min.	3 hrs., 15 min.
Milan to Venice	267km/166 miles	50 min.	2½ hrs.	3 hrs., 10 min.
Rome to Florence	277km/172 miles	1 hr., 10 min.	1 hr., 36 min.	3 hrs., 20 min.
Rome to Milan	572km/355 miles	1 hr., 5 min.	4½ hrs.	6½ hrs.
Rome to Naples	219km/136 miles	50 min.	1 hr., 27 min.	2½ hrs.
Rome to Venice	528km/327 miles	1 hr., 5 min.	4½ hrs.	6 hrs.
Venice to Naples	747km/463 miles	1 hr., 45 min.	7 hrs.	8½ hrs.

By Train

Train travel in Italy is affordable and fast, and trains serve practically every destination. Trains are the best choice for medium-distance trips, and have the added advantage of extreme flexibility and convenience — you depart and arrive right from the center of town, not from a distant airport. To research how well your chosen destinations are served by rail, see the "Train Routes through Italy" map on the inside front cover of this book. You can check with **Trenitalia** (☎ 892021; www.trenitalia.it), the national train service, for all destinations and prices.

If you are planning a lot of train travel, you may be interested in purchasing the **Carta Rail Plus** — sold online at www.trenitalia.it and at all train stations in Europe — which grants a 25 percent discount on train tickets to almost anywhere within Europe; the card is valid for one year and costs 45€ ($54) for adults and 20€ ($24) for youths and seniors. Obviously, the more and farther you travel, the better the deal. You'll still need to make reservations, and surcharges may apply for the express Eurostar trains. You can also buy rail passes before you leave the United States through a travel agent or **Rail Europe** (☎ **877-257-2887** in the U.S., 800-361-RAIL in Canada; www.raileurope.com). The official U.S. representative of the Italian national rail company is **CIT Tours,** 15 W. 44th St., Suite 104, New York, NY 10036 (☎ **800-845-3365;** http://cit-tours.com).

By Bus

The bus (coach) network is very extensive in Italy, and buses connect even the most remote hamlets in the country. They are a good way to reach destinations that are not on a direct train line. We list bus companies throughout this book for those destinations where taking a bus makes sense. You won't see too many tourists on buses, which is good if you want to meet local people and get a feeling for what life is really like in Italy. It's not like the U.S. or England, where you could sit there in a clown suit and everyone would be too "polite" to speak to you. Italians will ask you who you are, where you're from, and where you're going. And if you invest just a few hours in familiarizing yourself with Italian (through *Italian For Dummies,* for example), you may be able to give some interesting answers.

Be sure to check schedules in advance — they change frequently. Tickets must be bought at the bus station; drivers don't have the cash to make change. Do not plan on using the bus to hit several small towns in a day — the bus schedules usually won't allow for it. The system is meant not for tourists, but for people who need to commute between the small towns where they live and the larger towns of the area. To see five little countryside villages in a day requires a car.

By Ferry

With over 4,600 miles of Italian coastline, ferries are an excellent resource, particularly to explore many destinations in the Neapolitan area — Capri, Sorrento, and the Amalfi Coast (see Chapter 20) — and Sicily (see Chapters 21 and 22).

If you want to bring your car on a ferry, you must make a reservation well in advance — especially during high season. Taking your car on a ferry also means you'll have to pay more. In some cases, you may save money by renting your car on arrival rather than taking it on a ferry.

By Car

While we definitely do not recommend driving between major towns in Italy (you'll do much better via public transportation), and driving *in* major towns and cities is pure madness, driving through the Italian countryside may be appealing. Here are a few things to keep in mind:

> ✔ In order to drive in Italy, you'll need to get an International Driver's License before leaving home. In the United States and Canada, you can do so at any branch of **AAA** (☎ **800-222-1134** in the U.S., 613-247-0117 in Canada; www.aaa.com) by filling out a form and providing a 2-x-2-inch photograph of yourself, a photocopy of your U.S. driver's license, and $10. Don't forget to bring your U.S. license with

you in Italy, however, because the international license is valid only in combination with your regular license. An alternative to the International Driver's License is to take an Italian translation of your U.S. license (prepared by AAA or another organization) to an office of the **Automobile Club d'Italia** (☎ 06-4477 for 24-hour information and assistance) in Italy to receive a special driving permit.

✔ Renting a car will be more expensive than what you're used to back home (see later in this section for a few tips), plus you'll have to consider fuel (at over $7 a gallon), hefty highway tolls, parking, car theft, and an aggressive driving style.

✔ Driving rules are different here (see the sidebar later in this chapter). We recommend that you: 1) drive defensively, and 2) always be ready to get out of the way. It's a myth that Italians drive badly. Italians love to drive; however, there's a reason why the Ferrari, the Maserati, and the Lamborghini are Italian cars — Italians love to drive fast. You could be going a respectable 60 mph when someone zooms up from behind, going 100 mph and flashing his lights (a perfect time to apply Rule #2, above). Italians do, however, follow the rules of the road and are usually skilled drivers (they need to be or they'd get killed).

✔ Road signs are also different. For example, you may see first a green and then a blue sign for the same destination: The first indicates the *autostrada* (high-speed, limited-access toll road), the second the local road. Once on the *autostrada,* keep your eyes peeled for exits (each marked *Uscita*): They're often indicated on the highway far in advance, and then right on top of the ramp — not a few hundred yards in advance, where it's helpful. On local roads and in town, the puzzling sign with a white arrow on a blue circle points you to the lane that you should enter or the correct way around an obstacle, a traffic island, and so forth. When you want to park, look for the blue-and-red circle with a diagonal stripe: The stripe points to the side of the street where you can't park. If the sign shows two stripes (an X), you can't park on either side of the street. The oblong blue-and-white *Senso Unico* sign indicates a one-way street.

✔ Even Italians dread driving in and near big cities and towns — Naples, Rome, and Milan are particularly notorious — not only because of the intricate network of roads, but also due to the constant traffic, the aggressive driving style, and the impossibility of finding parking. If you're planning to rent a car, we recommend that you do so from the airport, before or after your visit to a major city; you won't need a car during your stay in town.

✔ Local gas stations close for lunch and shut down all day on Sunday (except along the *autostrada*), so don't let your gas gauge get too low, especially if you're cruising the rural countryside.

✔ If you do rent a car, remember that Italian cars are small (even the big ones are never larger than an American midsize, and the trunk has half the capacity) and are standard shift. (You can get an automatic, but you will pay a surcharge and must reserve in advance, as they are not very common.)

✔ Car thefts and break-ins are widespread. Never leave your car unattended, always lock up, take out all your valuable items, and never leave luggage in a car unless it's parked in a small, manned garage.

✔ Finally, make sure you have a good road map: The best are published by the Automobile Club d'Italia and the Italian Touring Club and are widely available in bookstores and at newsstands in Italy. A lot of highway construction is going on in Italy, so maps change often.

Go online to comparison-shop for car rentals. You can check rates at most of the major car-rental agencies' Web sites (see Appendix A for a list of agencies operating in Italy). All the major travel sites — **Travelocity** (www.travelocity.com), **Expedia** (www.expedia.com), **Orbitz** (www.orbitz.com), and **Smarter Living** (www.smarterliving.com), for example — have search engines that can dig up discounted car-rental rates. If you are planning to travel by a combination of train and car, check with **Trenitalia** (☎ 892021; www.trenitalia.it), the national train service, for special car-rental and train package offers.

In addition to the basic car-rental charges, the Collision Damage Waiver (CDW) requires you to pay for damage to the car in a collision. Rental-car companies also offer extra liability insurance (if you harm others in an accident), personal accident insurance (if you harm yourself or your

---

The rules of the road

The following rules are rigidly obeyed everywhere in Italy:

Rule 1: Pass only on the left.

Rule 2: Never stay in the passing lane: Pull out, pass, and get back in the slow lane right away.

Rule 3: When you're entering a highway or any major road from a minor road and you have a sign to yield, you *do* have to yield. Often this means stopping and waiting for the merging lane to become available. Do not assume people will move over — they won't (often they can't, as there's always someone coming from behind at over 100 mph in the fast lane). The same is true when you come out of a gas station or rest area.

Rule 4: At regular intersections, the person on the right *always* has the right of way, unless otherwise indicated; in traffic circles, the cars already in the circle have priority over those trying to enter.

passengers), and personal effects insurance (if your luggage is stolen from your car). Your insurance policy on your car at home probably covers most of these unlikely occurrences, and unless you are carrying the Hope diamond, you probably don't need luggage coverage. However, if your own insurance doesn't cover you for rentals or if you don't have auto insurance, definitely consider the additional coverage (ask your car-rental agent for more information). Also, check with your credit-card company, as it may cover some of the above.

 In Italy, most rental companies will require that you pay for theft protection insurance, as car theft is unfortunately common here. Although many credit cards cover you for damage to a rental car, check with your company to see if your card's benefit extends outside the United States.

Chapter 8

Booking Your Accommodations

In This Chapter

▶ Discovering your hotel options
▶ Booking a room and finding a great rate
▶ Avoiding getting stuck without a place to sleep

*T*raveling to a foreign country can be romantic and exciting, but when we're ready for a well-deserved slumber, we like the comforts we've grown accustomed to. Although the hotel industry in Italy has made enormous progress toward standardization and upgrading of lodgings, in line with the expectations of international travelers, there are still cultural differences that are hard to iron out — and why not, since the fun of traveling also means experiencing a different culture. That's not to say you shouldn't be comfortable, though. Here we give you the lowdown on what to expect in your Italian bedroom, along with plenty of tips on choosing from among a wide, and in some cases unfamiliar, variety of choices.

Getting to Know Your Options

Italy offers a huge choice of accommodations, from very basic to supremely elegant. You'll find everything from romantic 15th-century hostels to international chains, from perfectly restored medieval towers and castles to 17th-century frescoed *palazzi,* from simple 19th-century farmhouses to ultra-modern luxury hotels, and from mom-and-pop places to the haunts of jet-setters. Travelers have journeyed to Italy for the past 3,000 years (at least), so more than a few inns can claim several centuries of service and make tradition their selling point. In contrast, a lot of newer options focus instead on sleek modern touches or immaculate refurbishing of historic buildings. With such a variety, you'll certainly find what you need, but keep in mind a few differences:

✔ Because medieval and Renaissance buildings were not designed for elevators, these are rare — and altogether absent in the cheaper hotels — and often start from a landing above street level. Steps are ubiquitous, so if they're a problem for you, make sure to call and ask.

✔ Amenities that are commonplace in the United States — big ice machines, for instance — are virtually unknown in Italy (you will find, though, a small refrigerator in all hotel rooms in the superior category); others, such as air-conditioning and satellite TV — necessary to view English-language programs — are now more the rule than the exception, although you may have to pay extra for them in smaller and cheaper hotels (we spell this out in our write-ups). By the way, regular TVs are standard in all hotel rooms, but they don't offer English-language programs. Then again, you didn't go to Italy to watch TV, did you? And you can always step out of your hotel and sit at the terrace of a nearby cafe for that iced drink.

✔ Soundproof rooms are commonplace — and even in the cheaper hotels, the thickness of the old walls helps protect you from noisy neighbors and the roar of traffic outside. Street noise, by the way, is a problem that soundproof windows cannot eliminate if you like to sleep with your window open. If that is the case, ask for an inner room.

✔ Smoking has recently been banned from public places in Italy, so all hotel lobbies and breakfast rooms are smoke-free. Guest rooms, however, are considered private; hence, you are allowed to smoke there. Make sure to specify whether you want a smoke-free room when you make your reservation.

✔ In general, rooms — especially bathrooms — tend to be smaller than what you're used at home. Space is at a premium, especially in the palaces within historic districts — which is where you usually want to be — and only the most expensive hotels can offer sizable bedrooms and bathrooms. To meet the increasing demand for ensuite facilities, many cheaper hotels (two stars and below; see later for more on this) have shoehorned bathrooms into the guest rooms, and the result is far from satisfactory: It's not at all unusual for the shower to be a wall fixture with a curtain around it (not a door) and a drain directly below it in the tiny bathroom's tiled floor. The hotels we list all have decent-size bathrooms and real showers.

✔ The majority of hotels in Italy have only one kind of bed — a large twin. In a double room, you usually find two separate twin beds. If you ask for a double bed, they will put together the two twins, making the bed up tight with sheets. You may find this practice unusual at first, but you'll discover that it's not uncomfortable. On the plus side, most hotels in Italy, and certainly all the ones in our listings, are proud of the quality of their bedding and provide good mattresses with a medium degree of firmness.

✔ The breakfast generally included in your room rate is a continental breakfast. Although an increasing number of hotels offer a buffet with a variety of choices to meet the demands of foreign visitors, eggs and hot dishes are served only at the most expensive hotels. The usual continental buffet includes a choice of breads, jams, and fruit; sometimes cakes; and usually cereals, yogurt, cheese, and cold cuts. Sometimes you can order — and pay extra for — eggs and bacon if they aren't on the spread.

✔ One more thing: When you make a hotel reservation back home, you probably don't think to ask about the flooring. In Italy, you'll often find tile or marble floors, sometimes wood, and only rarely carpeting. So bring slippers in the cooler months if you don't want to get cold feet!

All hotels in Italy are government-rated according to a strict set of rules and specifications. The system is quite reliable, as hotels are regularly inspected. The rating goes from one star for the most modest hotel — a basic room with a comfortable bed, a TV, and a shared small bathroom — to five stars for the most elegant, with an *L* added for extra luxury (such as palatial accommodations with state-of-the-art bathrooms). A *pensione* is below a hotel: a small, family-run hostel offering rooms with a bed and little else. A bed-and-breakfast is a room in a private house and can range from palatial to spartan. In the countryside, you can opt for *agriturismo:* a room in a working farmhouse, where you'll be served meals prepared almost exclusively with ingredients produced on the farm. In this category, too, accommodations range from palatial (for example, on famous wine-producing estates) to simple (but usually always very nice). They often feature swimming pools and outdoor activities.

Throughout this book, we list our favorite hotels, using cleanliness, comfort, and the most amenities at the best prices as essential criteria. We use a system of dollar signs to indicate the price categories. Table 8-1, below, explains the price scale used in this book and what you can expect to get for your money in each category.

Table 8-1   Key to Hotel Dollar Signs

Dollar Sign(s)	Price Range	What to Expect
$	Less than 140€ ($168)	No frills but dignified, usually family-run small hotels housed in oldish buildings. Rooms tend to be small, televisions are not necessarily provided, there might not be an elevator, and you may have to pay extra for air-conditioning. Credit cards may not be accepted.

Dollar Sign(s)	Price Range	What to Expect
$$	141€–230€ ($169–$276)	These are middle-range hotels: All guest rooms will have air-conditioning and a good level of amenities and service. Bathrooms tend to be small at the bottom end of the scale, but rooms are always pleasantly furnished. The category also includes some of the higher-level hotels that are located in less glamorous areas or in the countryside.
$$$	231€–350€ ($277–$420)	These are superior hotels where you get a bathroom that's really a room, not a corner, and bedrooms that are spacious and come with a number of amenities; they might even be luxurious in the less expensive neighborhoods and destinations. Service is excellent; usually a nice buffet breakfast is included.
$$$$	351€ ($421) and up	These are deluxe hotels, sometimes owned by international interests, often in new or very historic buildings (such as a former aristocratic *palazzo* or villa). They offer lots of space, attentive and professional staff, and top amenities ranging from antique furnishings and fine linens to lavish bathrooms, gyms, spas, terraces, and often gardens with pools. Usually an American-style breakfast is included. You're staying not only in luxury, but also style.

Finding the Best Room at the Best Rate

One striking characteristic in Italy is that most hotels are private businesses, don't belong to a chain, and are often still family-run, including in the super-luxury category. Some may belong to a hotel association — which fixes standards, gives a common approach, or simply allows some economies of scale — while others may belong to a group of investors. This means that room hunting follows different rules. Following are some tips on reserving your room and cutting your costs.

Finding the best rate

The "rack rate" is the maximum rate a hotel charges for a room. The rack rate is the price you'd get if you walked in off the street at the peak of high season, when the hotel is nearly full, and asked for a room for the night. You see this rate printed on the fire/emergency-exit diagrams posted on the back of room doors. We quote the rack rate for each of our hotel listings throughout this book, but it doesn't mean that's the rate you'll have to pay.

Sometimes getting a better rate is surprisingly simple: Ask for a cheaper or discounted rate. You may be pleasantly surprised.

Rates are also lower — by up to 50 percent — during low and shoulder seasons, when the hotel occupancy goes down (see Chapter 3).

If your hotel belongs to a chain, you'll usually get the lowest rate through a travel agent, online reservations service (see later), or package deal with your airline (see Chapter 6). (This is because the hotel often gives the agent a discount in exchange for steering his or her business toward that hotel.) Reserving a room through the chain's toll-free number may also result in a lower rate than calling the hotel directly.

Privately owned hotels, by contrast, do only moderate business with travel agencies and reservations Web sites. You'll often get a better discount by contacting the hotel directly or through its Web site (and be treated much better upon arrival).

Surfing the Web for hotel deals

Shopping online for hotels is generally done one of two ways: by booking through the hotel's own Web site or by going through an independent booking agency (or a fare-service agency like Priceline).

In Italy, booking through the hotel's own Web site is definitely the way to go: Many private hotels have started to offer special Internet rates, which are often even cheaper than what an agency can offer (because the hotel saves the agency fee). Some also offer significant discounts for advance booking, provided that you pay in advance. If you don't want to search the hotels yourself, use one of the Internet agencies below and then go straight to the Web site of the hotel you've selected: You'll often find that you can do better. (For hotels belonging to a chain, however, this is not always the case.)

Online hotel agencies have multiplied in mind-boggling numbers of late, competing for the business of millions of consumers surfing for accommodations around the world. This competitiveness can be a boon to consumers who have the patience and time to shop and compare the Internet agencies for good deals — but shop they must, for prices can vary considerably from site to site. And keep in mind that hotels at the top of a site's listing may be there for no other reason than that they paid money to get the placement. Among the numerous Web sites, the best is **Venere Net** (www.venere.com), which is very comprehensive and user-friendly. You may also want to check out **Giroscopio.com** (www.giroscopio.com), **Hoteldiscount!com** (www.180096hotel.com),

Italyhotels (www.italyhotelink.com), **Welcome to Italy** (www.wel.it), **Europa Hotels** (www.europa-hotels.com), and **Italy Hotels** (www.hotels-in-italy.com). For last-minute reservations **LateRooms.com** (www.it.laterooms.com) works well. Other interesting sites are **InItaly** (www.initaly.com) and **Italy Guide** (www.italyguide.com).

Most international sites tend to feature only a few hotels in Italy. Still, some may offer good deals, so it's worth checking just in case. **Expedia** offers special deals and "virtual tours" or photos of available rooms — allowing you to see what you're paying for (a feature that helps counter the claims that the best rooms are often held back from bargain Web sites). **Travelocity** posts frank customer reviews and ranks its properties according to the AAA rating system. **Hotels.com** is also reliable and easy to use. **InnSite.com**, which includes listings of B&Bs in Rome, shows descriptions written by the innkeepers (it's free to get listed), pictures of the rooms, and prices and availability.

In the opaque Web site category, **Priceline** and **Hotwire** are even better for hotels than for airfares; with both, you're allowed to pick the neighborhood and quality level of your hotel — but that's all — before offering up your money. Priceline's hotel product is much better at getting five-star lodging for three-star prices than at finding anything at the bottom of the scale. On the downside, many hotels stick Priceline guests in their least desirable rooms. Before bidding on Priceline, make sure to go to **BiddingForTravel.com**, which features a fairly up-to-date list of hotels that Priceline uses in major cities, including Italian ones. For both Priceline and Hotwire, you pay upfront, and the fee is nonrefundable. *Note:* Some hotels do not provide loyalty program credits or points or other frequent-stay amenities when you book a room through opaque online services.

 If you use one of these online booking services, remember to always **get a confirmation number** and **make a printout** of any transaction. In fact, after you've reserved your room, it doesn't hurt to contact your hotel and **request a faxed confirmation** (make sure you bring this with you to Italy) to eliminate the chance of your checking into a hotel that suddenly says it has no record of your reservation.

Reserving the best room

First and foremost, make your reservations well ahead of time (months in advance for the most sought-after destinations), especially if you decide to stay in a small hotel: The best rooms are the first to go. And ask for a large and quiet room, specifying all the characteristics that are important to you.

 After you make your reservation, asking one or two more pointed questions can go a long way toward making sure you get the best room in the house. Requesting a corner room (usually larger, quieter, and brighter than standard rooms in modern, square buildings) doesn't necessarily pay off in Italy, where so many hotels are housed in historic buildings, and where corner rooms might actually be smaller and darker.

 The prevalence of old buildings raises another issue: renovations. Always ask if the hotel is renovating; if it is, request a room away from the renovation work. Inquire, too, about the location of elevators, restaurants, and bars in the hotel — all sources of annoying noise. If the hotel is on a busy street, request a room away from the street.

And finally, remember that if you aren't happy with your room when you arrive, you can talk to the front desk about moving to another one. If another room is available, they should be happy to accommodate you, within reason.

Renting Apartments and Villas

If you plan to stay in one place for a week or more, or if you are traveling with children, renting a house or apartment makes a lot of sense. The easiest way to do so is to contact an agency.

Most of the Internet agencies listed earlier in this chapter also maintain apartment and B&B listings. Other agencies to try include **Hideaways International,** 767 Islington St., Portsmouth, NH 03801 (☎ **800-843-4433;** www.hideaways.com); **At Home Abroad,** 405 E. 56th St., Suite 6H, New York, NY 10022 (☎ **212-421-9165;** Fax: 212-533-0095); and **Rentals in Italy,** 700 E. Main St., Ventura, CA 93001 (☎ **800-726-6702** or 805-641-1650; www.rentvillas.com).

 Vacation Rentals by Owner (www.vrbo.com) has hundreds of listings (in English) of homes for rent. Each listing contains pictures, prices, and descriptions of the area where the house or apartment is located. Usually you deal directly with the owner, thus you may save considerably over the rates that would be charged for the same property by a broker.

To rent something really ritzy, like a *palazzo* or castle, your best bet is **Abitare la Storia,** Località L'Amorosa, 53048 Sinalunga (☎ **0577-679-683;** www.abitarelastoria.it), an association based near Siena.

Another option — a favorite with Italians — is *agriturismo* (staying on a working farm or former farm somewhere in the countryside). Rates usually include breakfast and at least one other meal (your choice of dinner or lunch), prepared with ingredients produced on the farm or by nearby local small farms. Among the multiplying online agencies, the best is **Agriturismo.it** (www.agriturismo.it).

Chapter 9

Catering to Special Travel Needs or Interests

In This Chapter

▶ Traveling with kids

▶ Making the most of senior advantages

▶ Meeting the needs of disabled travelers

▶ Answering questions for gay and lesbian travelers and students

*E*very traveler is a special traveler, but bringing kids along on your trip to Italy, or traveling alone as a single woman, or trying to find or arrange for wheelchair accessibility, all require extra care and thought. Seniors may be interested in special programs and activities; gays and lesbians may wonder how friendly and welcoming Italy will be. All these issues are considered in this chapter.

Traveling with the Brood: Advice for Families

 We love traveling throughout Italy with children — both our own and those of friends and family. Italy has a very family-oriented culture, which makes it much easier to travel here with your kids. In fact, Italians love children, and most people will smile at you and your children or even talk to them in public spaces. You'll find that people — including staff in hotels and restaurants — are usually ready to help you out in most situations and accommodate your special needs. They do frown upon tantrums, whining, and other outbursts, however. (Italian children are used to going everywhere with their parents, and behave appropriately most of the time.)

We also find that Italy is an easy destination for children because there are so many attractions to choose from — you're sure to find something that will please even the most difficult child (we make reservations about teenagers, though, since sometimes just *nothing* pleases them). Our strategy is to alternate: one thing that interests us and one that interests our child (in our case, playgrounds, children's museums, or outdoor activities) per day. It helps if you talk to your kids beforehand about your destinations and the special things in store for them. Italian history is so rich that you'll find many ways to keep your child interested while preparing for your trip. Involve your children in the planning and go over the list of sights and activities in the areas on your itinerary, particularly noting those labeled with the Kid Friendly icon in this book. Let your kids make their own list of things they want to do. Older children can research Italy on the Internet (see Appendix A for a list of Web sites worth checking out).

The one hump you'll face is if you don't want to have your child with you at all times. Italy doesn't have a major infrastructure of day-care and child-care services (see "Quick Concierge" in Appendix A for more about baby sitting); in fact, finding a hotel with day-care service can be difficult. If this is one of your needs, be sure to make arrangements through your hotel ahead of time. Usually the concierge will be able to help you find a baby-sitting service, even if the hotel doesn't formally offer child care.

The only thing you'll really need for your children is a passport (see Chapter 10), but you may want to check out some further resources:

- ✔ **Familyhostel** (☎ 800-733-9753) takes the whole family, including kids 8 to 15, on moderately priced domestic and international learning vacations. Lectures, field trips, and sightseeing are guided by a team of academics.

- ✔ You can find good family-oriented vacation advice at **Family Travel Forum** (www.familytravelforum.com) and **Traveling Internationally with Your Kids** (www.travelwithyourkids.com), both comprehensive Web sites that offer customized trip planning; **Family Travel Network** (www.familytravelnetwork.com), an award-winning site that offers travel features, deals, and tips; and **Family Travel Files** (www.thefamilytravelfiles.com), which offers an online magazine and a directory of off-the-beaten-path tours and tour operators for families.

- ✔ *How to Take Great Trips with Your Kids* (The Harvard Common Press) is full of good general advice that can apply to travel anywhere.

- ✔ Another good resource, *Family Travel Times* (☎ 888-822-4FTT or 212-477-5524; www.familytraveltimes.com), is published six times a year and includes a weekly call-in service for subscribers. Subscriptions are $39 per year for quarterly editions.

Making Age Work for You: Tips for Seniors

In general, Italy accords older people a great deal of respect, probably because of the continued existence of the extended family as well as the nature of the Italian language (polite forms of address are to be used when speaking with someone older than yourself). Therefore, you're unlikely to encounter ageism.

Members of **AARP** (formerly known as the American Association of Retired Persons), 601 E St. NW, Washington, DC 20049 (☎ 888-687-2277 or 202-434-2277; www.aarp.org), get discounts on hotels, airfares, and car rentals. AARP offers a wide range of benefits, including *AARP: The Magazine* and a monthly newsletter. Anyone over 50 can join.

Being a senior entitles you to some terrific travel bargains. Many reliable agencies and organizations target the 50-plus market. **Elderhostel** (☎ 877-426-8056; www.elderhostel.org) arranges study programs for those 55 and over (and a spouse or companion of any age) in more than 80 countries around the world. Most courses last five to seven days in the United States (two to four weeks abroad), and many include airfare, accommodations in university dormitories or modest inns, meals, and tuition. **ElderTreks** (☎ 800-741-7956; www.eldertreks.com) offers small-group tours to off-the-beaten-path or adventure-travel locations, restricted to travelers 50 and older.

Recommended publications offering travel resources and discounts for seniors include the quarterly magazine *Travel 50 & Beyond* (www.travel 50andbeyond.com); *Travel Unlimited: Uncommon Adventures for the Mature Traveler* (Avalon); *101 Tips for Mature Travelers,* available from Grand Circle Travel (☎ 800-221-2610 or 617-350-7500; www.gct.com); *The 50+ Traveler's Guidebook* (St. Martin's Press); and *Unbelievably Good Deals and Great Adventures That You Absolutely Can't Get Unless You're Over 50* (McGraw-Hill).

 Senior discounts on admission at theaters, museums, and public transportation are subject to reciprocity between countries. Because the United States hasn't signed the bilateral agreement (you discount us and we'll discount you), Americans aren't eligible for senior discounts in Italy. (The same rule applies to the under-17 discount.) All discounts do apply if you're a citizen of a European Union country.

Accessing Italy: Advice for Travelers with Disabilities

Italy is rapidly catching up on accessibility issues, even though it is faced with unique logistical difficulties: It is sometimes impossible to retrofit medieval or older buildings with elevators and ramps. Often the problem has been solved with separate entrances, but you usually need to be met there by an attendant — thus we recommend you always call ahead to make an appointment. Public transportation reserves spaces for the disabled, but not all buses on all lines have been upgraded, and a few subway stations are simply not accessible to wheelchairs. For the blind, special grooves in the sidewalk have been provided in major towns, and a number of street lights have been equipped with sound signals.

You can avoid some of the accessibility problems by joining a tour that caters specifically to your needs. Many travel agencies offer customized tours and itineraries for travelers with disabilities. **Flying Wheels Travel** (☎ 507-451-5005; www.flyingwheelstravel.com) offers escorted tours and cruises that emphasize sports, as well as private tours in minivans with lifts. **Access-Able Travel Source** (☎ 303-232-2979; www. access-able.com) offers extensive access information and advice for traveling around the world with disabilities. **Accessible Journeys** (☎ 800-846-4537 or 610-521-0339; www.disabilitytravel.com) caters to wheelchair travelers and their families and friends.

Avis Rent a Car's "Avis Access" program offers such services as a dedicated 24-hour toll-free number (☎ 888-879-4273) for customers with special travel needs; special car features such as swivel seats, spinner knobs, and hand controls; and accessible bus service.

Organizations that offer assistance to disabled travelers include the **Moss Rehab Hospital** (www.mossresourcenet.org), which provides a library of accessible-travel resources online, and **SATH**, the **Society for Accessible Travel & Hospitality** (☎ 212-447-7284; www.sath.org; annual membership fees: $45 adults, $30 seniors and students), which offers a wealth of travel resources for all types of disabilities and informed recommendations on destinations, access guides, travel agents, tour operators, vehicle rentals, and companion services. The **American Foundation for the Blind** (☎ 800-232-5463; www.afb.org) provides information on traveling with Seeing Eye dogs.

For more information specifically targeted to travelers with disabilities, check out the magazines *Emerging Horizons* ($14.95 per year, $19.95 outside the U.S.; www.emerginghorizons.com) and *Open World Magazine* ($13 per year, $21 outside the U.S.; published by SATH, described earlier). **Twin Peaks Press** (☎ 360-694-2462) offers travel-related books for travelers with special needs.

Following the Rainbow: Resources for Gay and Lesbian Travelers

Italy is a tolerant country, and violent displays of intolerance such as gay bashing are extremely unusual. As in the United States, there is an active gay and lesbian movement that is trying to raise public consciousness about prejudice and discrimination.

All major towns and cities have an active gay culture — especially Florence, Rome, and Milan, which considers itself the gay capital of Italy and is the headquarters of **ARCI–Gay/ARCI– Lesbica** (www.arcigay.it), the country's leading gay organization with branches throughout Italy. Its Web site has an English version. The Tuscany branch can be found at www.gaytoscana.it; for Rome, visit www.arcigay.it/roma. ARCI–Gay also has offices in Siena (☎ **0577-288-977;** www.gaysiena.it) and Pisa (☎ **050-555-618**).

Capri is the gay resort of Italy, rivaled only by the gay beaches of Venice and Taormina. The first-ever World Pride event was held in Rome in July 2000, to coincide with the Jubilee celebrations.

The **International Gay & Lesbian Travel Association (IGLTA)** (☎ **800-448-8550** or 954-776-2626; www.iglta.org), the trade association for the gay and lesbian travel industry, offers an online directory of gay- and lesbian-friendly travel businesses; go to its Web site and click on "Consumer Site."

Making the Grade: Advice for Student Travelers

If you're a student planning a trip to Italy, get an **International Student Identity Card (ISIC),** which offers substantial savings on rail passes, plane tickets, and entrance fees. It also provides you with basic health and life insurance and a 24-hour help line. The card is available for $22 from **STA Travel** (☎ **800-781-4040,** or check online for a local number in your country; www.statravel.com), the biggest student travel agency in the world. If you're no longer a student but are still under 26, you can get an **International Youth Travel Card (IYTC)** for the same price from the same people, which entitles you to some discounts (but not on museum admissions). (*Note:* In 2002, STA Travel bought competitors **Council Travel** and **USIT Campus** after they went bankrupt. Some offices still operate under the Council name, but are owned by STA.)

Travel CUTS (☎ **800-667-2887** or 416-614-2887; www.travelcuts.com) offers similar services for residents of both Canada and the U.S. Irish students should turn to **USIT** (☎ **01-602-1600;** www.usitnow.ie).

Chapter 10

Taking Care of the Remaining Details

In This Chapter

▶ Getting your documents in order
▶ Purchasing insurance — or not
▶ Staying healthy while traveling
▶ Keeping connected when you travel
▶ Understanding airline security measures
▶ Making advance reservations at major attractions

*I*f you think that having a destination, an itinerary, and a ticket in hand is enough to travel, think again: There are still a lot of details to take care of. In this chapter, we help you tie up all the loose ends.

Getting a Passport

A valid passport is the only legal form of identification accepted around the world. You can't cross an international border without it. Getting a passport is easy, though: Just follow the steps below.

 Keep in mind that losing your passport may be worse than losing your money. Why? Because a passport shows (and proves to authorities) that you are you. Safeguard your passport in an inconspicuous, inaccessible place like a money belt. Always carry a photocopy of your passport with you and keep it in a separate pocket or purse. If you lose your passport, visit the nearest consulate of your native country as soon as possible for a replacement.

Applying for a U.S. passport

If you're applying for a first-time passport in the U.S., follow these steps:

1. Complete a **passport application** in person at a U.S. passport office; a federal, state, or probate court; or a major post office (you can download the form online; see below).

2. Present a **certified birth certificate** as proof of citizenship. (Bringing along your driver's license, state or military ID, or social security card is also a good idea.)

3. Submit **two identical passport-size photos,** measuring 2-x-2-inches in size. You can often find businesses that take these photos near a passport office. *Note:* You can't use a strip from a photo-vending machine.

4. Pay a **fee.** For people 16 and over, a passport is valid for ten years and costs $85. For those 15 and under, a passport is valid for five years and costs $70.

 Allow plenty of time before your trip to apply for a passport; processing normally takes three weeks, but can take longer during busy periods (especially spring).

If you already have a passport in your current name that was issued within the past 15 years (and you were over 16 when it was issued), you can renew the passport by mail for $55.

Whether you're applying in person or by mail, you can download passport applications from the U.S. State Department Web site at http://travel.state.gov, where you can also get general information and find your regional passport office; alternatively, call the **National Passport Information Center** (☎ 877-487-2778 or 202-647-0518) for automated information.

Applying for other passports

Australians can visit a local post office or passport office, call the **Australia Passport Information Service** (☎ 131-232 toll-free in Australia), or log on to www.passports.gov.au for details on how and where to apply.

Canadians can pick up applications at passport offices throughout Canada, at post offices, or from the central **Passport Office,** Department of Foreign Affairs and International Trade, Ottawa, ON K1A 0G3 (☎ 800-567-6868; www.ppt.gc.ca). Applications must be accompanied by two identical passport-sized photographs and proof of Canadian citizenship. Processing takes five to ten days if you apply in person, or about three weeks by mail.

New Zealanders can pick up a passport application at any New Zealand Passports Office or download it online. Call the **Passports Office** (☎ 0800-225-050 in New Zealand, or 04-474-8100) or log on to www.passports.govt.nz for more information.

United Kingdom residents can pick up applications for a standard ten-year passport (five-year passport for children under 16) at passport offices, major post offices, or travel agencies. For information, contact the **United Kingdom Passport Service** (☎ 0870-521-0410; www.ukpa. gov.uk).

 When you get your passport photos taken, get six to eight photos total if you're planning to also apply for an International Driver's License and an international student or teacher ID, which may entitle you to discounts at museums. Take the extra photos with you: You may need one for random reasons on the road, and if — heaven forbid — you ever lose your passport, you can use them for a replacement request.

Playing It Safe with Travel and Medical Insurance

Three kinds of travel insurance are available: trip-cancellation insurance, medical insurance, and lost-luggage insurance. The cost of travel insurance varies widely, but expect to pay between 5 and 8 percent of the vacation itself. Here is our advice on all three:

✔ **Trip-cancellation insurance** helps you get your money back if you have to back out of a trip or go home early, or if your travel supplier goes bankrupt. Allowed reasons for cancellation can range from sickness to natural disasters to the State Department declaring your destination unsafe for travel, but not vague fears caused by airplane crashes and the like. Protect yourself further by paying for the insurance with a credit card — by law, consumers can get their money back on goods and services not received if they report the loss within 60 days after the charge is listed on their credit-card statement.

✔ **Medical insurance** may be necessary for some travelers, since most health plans (including Medicare and Medicaid) do not provide coverage for travel overseas, and the ones that do often require you to pay for services upfront and reimburse you only after you return home. Even if your plan does cover overseas treatment, most out-of-country hospitals make you pay your bills upfront, and send you a refund only after you've returned home and filed the necessary paperwork with your insurance company. As a safety net, you may want to buy travel medical insurance; try **MEDEX Assistance** (☎ 410-453-6300; www.medexassist.com) or **Travel Assistance International** (☎ 800-821-2828; www.travel assistance.com; for general information on services, call the company's Worldwide Assistance Services, Inc., at ☎ 800-777-8710).

✔ **Lost-luggage insurance** is not necessary for most travelers. On international flights (including U.S. portions of international trips), baggage coverage is limited to approximately $9.07 per pound, up to approximately $635 per checked bag. If you plan to check items more valuable than the standard liability, see if your valuables are covered by your homeowner's policy, get baggage insurance as part of your comprehensive travel-insurance package, or buy Travel Guard's "BagTrak" product. Don't buy insurance at the airport, as it's usually overpriced. Be sure to take any valuables or irreplaceable items with you in your carry-on luggage, as many valuables (including books, money, and electronics) aren't covered by airline policies.

If your luggage is lost, immediately file a lost-luggage claim at the airport, detailing your bag's contents. For most airlines, you must report delayed, damaged, or lost baggage within four hours of arrival. The airlines are required to deliver luggage, once found, directly to your house or destination free of charge.

For more information on insurance, contact one of the following recommended companies: **Access America** (☎ 866-807-3982; www.access america.com), **Travel Guard International** (☎ 800-826-4919; www. travelguard.com), **Travel Insured International** (☎ 800-243-3174; www.travelinsured.com), and **Travelex Insurance Services** (☎ 888-457-4602; www.travelex-insurance.com).

Staying Healthy When You Travel

Talk to your doctor before leaving on a trip if you have a serious and/or chronic illness. For conditions such as epilepsy, diabetes, or heart problems, wear a **MedicAlert identification tag** (☎ 888-633-4298; www. medicalert.org), which immediately alerts doctors to your condition and gives them access to your records through MedicAlert's 24-hour hot line. Contact the **International Association for Medical Assistance to Travelers (IAMAT; ☎ 716-754-4883** in the U.S., 416-652-0137 in Canada; www.iamat.org) for tips on travel and health concerns in the countries you're visiting, along with lists of local, English-speaking doctors. The U.S. **Centers for Disease Control and Prevention** (☎ 800-311-3435; www.cdc.gov) provides up-to-date information on health hazards by region or country and offers tips on food safety as well.

If you do get sick in Italy, ask the concierge at your hotel to recommend a local doctor — even his or her own doctor, if necessary. If you can't locate a doctor, try contacting your embassy or consulate — they maintain lists of English-speaking doctors. In an emergency, dial ☎ 113 for the police: They can call an ambulance or help you in many ways. If your situation is life-threatening, call ☎ 118 for an ambulance, or rush to the *pronto soccorso* (emergency department) at the local hospital.

Under the Italian national healthcare system, you're eligible only for free *emergency* care. If you're admitted to a hospital as an in-patient, even from an emergency department and as a result of an accident, you're required to pay (unless you are a resident of the European Economic

Avoiding "economy-class syndrome"

Deep vein thrombosis, or "economy-class syndrome" (as it's known in the world of flying), is a blood clot that develops in a deep vein. It's a potentially deadly condition that can be caused by sitting in cramped conditions — such as an airplane cabin — for too long. During a flight (especially a long-haul one), get up, walk around, and stretch your legs every 60 to 90 minutes to keep your blood flowing. Other preventative measures include frequent flexing of the legs while sitting, drinking lots of water, and avoiding alcohol and sleeping pills.

Area and are eligible for health insurance coverage). You're also required to pay for follow-up care. For the names, addresses, and phone numbers of hospitals offering 24-hour emergency care, see the "Fast Facts" section at the end of each destination chapter.

Staying Connected by Cellphone or E-mail

Using a cellphone in Italy

If you're from England, you're lucky: Your phone already works in Italy. If you're from another continent, things are a little complicated: The three letters that define much of the world's **wireless capabilities** are GSM (Global System for Mobiles), a big, seamless network that makes for easy cross-border cellphone use throughout Europe and dozens of other countries worldwide. In the U.S., T-Mobile, AT&T Wireless, and Cingular use this quasi-universal system; in Canada, Microcell and some Rogers customers are GSM; and all Europeans and most Australians use GSM.

If your cellphone is on a GSM system, and you have a world-capable multiband phone such as many Sony Ericsson, Motorola, or Samsung models, you can make and receive calls across much of the globe. Just call your wireless operator and ask for "international roaming" to be activated on your account. Unfortunately, per-minute charges can be high — usually $1 to $1.50 in Western Europe.

That's why it's important to buy an "unlocked" world phone from the get-go. Many cellphone operators sell "locked" phones that restrict you from using any other removable computer memory phone chip card (called a **SIM card**) other than the ones they supply. Having an unlocked phone allows you to install a cheap, prepaid SIM card (found at a local retailer) in your destination country. (Show your phone to the salesperson; not all phones work on all networks.) You'll get a local phone number — and much, much lower calling rates. Getting an already locked phone unlocked can be a complicated process, but it can be done; just call your cellular operator and say you'll be going abroad for several months and want to use the phone with a local provider.

For many, **renting a phone** is a good idea. While you can rent a phone from any number of overseas sites, including kiosks at airports and at car-rental agencies, renting the phone before you leave home may be a good idea. That way you can give loved ones and business associates your new number, make sure the phone works, and take the phone wherever you go — especially helpful for overseas trips through several countries. Phone rentals aren't cheap: You'll usually pay $40 to $50 per week, plus airtime fees of at least a dollar a minute. On the other hand, local rental companies in Europe often offer free incoming calls within their home country, which can save you big bucks. Two good wireless rental companies are **InTouch USA** (☎ 800-872-7626; www.intouch global.com) and **RoadPost** (☎ 888-290-1606 or 905-272-5665; www. roadpost.com). Give them your itinerary, and they'll tell you what wireless products you'll need. InTouch will also, for free, advise you on whether your existing phone will work overseas; simply call ☎ 703-222-7161 between 9 a.m. and 4 p.m. eastern standard time, or go to http:// intouchglobal.com/travel.htm.

 In Italy, you don't have to look for a place to rent a phone; you can make the phone come to you. **Rentacell** (☎ 877-736-8355 in the U.S., or 39-02-8633-7799 in Italy; www.rentacell.com) will deliver a phone to you anywhere for free. You can also pick it up in the U.S. before you leave. Incoming calls are free. **Easyline** (☎ 800-010-600 in Italy) also delivers phones for free.

Accessing the Internet away from home

Travelers have any number of ways to check their e-mail and access the Internet on the road. Using your wireless-enabled PDA (personal digital assistant) or laptop will give you the most flexibility, but Internet access is so widespread nowadays that you really don't need to carry the extra weight of electronic equipment, unless you need it for work reasons.

Most **hotels** in Italy — in the mid-range and up — offer Internet access from at least one computer, if not a Wi-Fi hot spot or even Internet access through the TVs in each guest room. Sometimes this service is free; sometimes you have to pay a small fee. Check with your hotel to find out. Hotel **business centers** should be avoided, however, unless you're willing to pay exorbitant rates.

You'll also find **Internet cafes** in almost every village, except the most backward ones; just ask the concierge at your hotel (you can also check www.cybercaptive.com and www.cybercafe.com, but their listings are not comprehensive). One of the leading global Internet-cafe chains is **easyInternetcafé** (www.easyeverything.com), which currently has franchises in Milan, Florence, and Rome; the company is rapidly expanding, so by the time you read this there may well be more — check the Web site for other locations. Even more prevalent is the **Internet Train** (www.internettrain.it), which not only has multiple sites in the big cities like Rome, Florence, and Milan, but also serves second-tier cities like Verona, and even smaller towns like Greve in Chianti and Agrigento.

Most major airports now have **Internet kiosks** scattered throughout their gates. These kiosks, which you'll also see in shopping malls, hotel lobbies, and tourist information offices around the world, give you basic Web access for a per-minute fee that's usually higher than cybercafe prices. The kiosks' clunkiness and high prices mean they should be avoided whenever possible.

To retrieve your e-mail, ask your **Internet Service Provider (ISP)** if it has a Web-based interface tied to your existing e-mail account. If your ISP doesn't have such an interface, you can use the free service from **mail2web** (www.mail2web.com) to view and reply to your home e-mail. For more flexibility, you may want to open a free, Web-based e-mail account through a site like **Yahoo! Mail** (http://mail.yahoo.com). Your home ISP may be able to forward your e-mail to the Web-based account automatically.

If you need to access files on your office computer, look into a service called **GoToMyPC** (www.gotomypc.com). It provides a Web-based interface for you to access and manipulate a distant PC from anywhere — even an Internet cafe — provided your "target" PC is on and has an always-on connection to the Internet (such as with a cable modem). The service offers top-quality security, but if you're worried about hackers, use your own laptop rather than a cybercafe computer to access the GoToMyPC system.

If you're bringing your own computer, the buzzword to familiarize yourself with is **Wi-Fi** (wireless fidelity) — more and more hotels, cafes, and retailers are signing on as wireless "hot spots." You can get Wi-Fi connection one of several ways. Many laptops sold in the last couple years have built-in Wi-Fi capability (an 802.11b wireless Ethernet connection). Mac owners have their own networking technology, Apple AirPort. For those with older computers, an 802.11b/**Wi-Fi card** (around $50) can be plugged into your laptop. You can sign up for wireless access service much as you do cellphone service, through a plan offered by one of several commercial companies that have made wireless service available in airports, hotel lobbies, and coffee shops, primarily in the U.S. (followed by the U.K. and Japan). **T-Mobile Hotspot** (www.t-mobile.com/hotspot) serves up wireless connections at more than 1,000 Starbucks coffee shops in the U.S. **Boingo** (www.boingo.com) and **Wayport** (www.wayport.com) have set up networks in airports and high-class hotel lobbies. Best of all, you don't need to be staying at the Four Seasons to use the hotel's network; just set yourself up on a nice couch in the lobby. The companies' pricing policies can be byzantine, with a variety of monthly, per-connection, and per-minute plans, but in general you pay around $30 a month — and as more and more companies jump on the wireless bandwagon, prices are likely to get even more competitive.

There are also places that provide **free wireless networks** in cities around the world. To locate these free hot spots, go to www.personal telco.net/index.cgi/WirelessCommunities.

If Wi-Fi is not available at your destination, most business-class hotels throughout the world offer dataports for laptop modems, and a few thousand hotels in the U.S. and Europe now offer free high-speed Internet access using an Ethernet network cable. You can bring your own cables, but most hotels rent them for around $10. **Call your hotel in advance** to see what your options are.

In addition, major Internet Service Providers (ISPs) have **local access numbers** around the world, allowing you to go online by simply placing a local call. Check your ISP's Web site or call its toll-free number and ask how you can use your current account away from home — and how much it will cost. If you're traveling outside the reach of your ISP, the **iPass** network has dial-up numbers in most of the world's countries. You'll have to sign up with an iPass provider, which will then tell you how to set up your computer for your destination(s). For a list of iPass providers, go to www.ipass.com and click on "Individuals Buy Now." One solid provider is **i2roam** (www.i2roam.com; ☎ **866-811-6209** or 920-235-0475).

Wherever you go, bring a **connection kit** of the right power and phone adapters, a spare phone cord, and a spare Ethernet network cable — or find out whether your hotel supplies them to guests.

Keeping Up with Airline Security

With the federalization of airport security, security procedures at U.S. airports are more stable and consistent than ever. Generally, you'll be fine if you arrive at the airport **one hour** before a domestic flight and **two hours** before an international flight; if you show up late, tell an airline employee and she may whisk you to the front of the line.

Bring a **current, government-issued photo ID** such as a driver's license or passport. Keep your ID at the ready to show at check-in, the security checkpoint, and sometimes even the gate. (Children under 18 do not need government-issued photo IDs for domestic flights, but they do for international flights to most countries, including Italy.)

In 2003, the TSA phased out **gate check-in** at all U.S. airports. And **E-tickets** have made paper tickets nearly obsolete. Passengers with E-tickets can beat the ticket-counter lines by using airport **electronic kiosks** or even **online check-in** from a home computer. Online check-in involves logging on to your airline's Web site, accessing your reservation, and printing out your boarding pass. If you're using a kiosk at the airport, bring the credit card you used to book the ticket or your frequent-flier card. Print out your boarding pass from the kiosk and simply proceed to the security checkpoint with your pass and a photo ID. If you're checking bags or looking to snag an exit-row seat, you will be able to do so using most airline kiosks. **Curbside check-in** is also a good way to avoid lines, although a few airlines still ban this practice; call before you go.

Security checkpoint lines are getting shorter than they were during 2001 and 2002, but some doozies remain. If you have trouble standing for long periods of time, tell an airline employee; the airline will provide a wheelchair. Speed up security by not wearing **metal objects** such as big belt buckles. If you've got metallic body parts, a note from your doctor can prevent a long chat with the security screeners. Keep in mind that only **ticketed passengers** are allowed past security, except for folks escorting disabled passengers or children.

Federalization has stabilized **what you can carry on** and **what you can't.** The general rule is that sharp things are out, nail clippers are okay, and food and beverages must be passed through the X-ray machine — but that security screeners can't make you drink from your coffee cup. Bring food in your carryon rather than checking it, as explosive-detection machines used on checked luggage have been known to mistake food (especially chocolate, for some reason) for bombs. Travelers in the U.S. are allowed one carry-on bag, plus a "personal item" such as a purse, briefcase, or laptop bag. Carry-on hoarders can stuff all sorts of things into a laptop bag; as long as it has a laptop in it, it's still considered a personal item. The Transportation Security Administration (TSA) has issued a list of restricted items; check its Web site (`www.tsa.gov`) for details.

Airport screeners may decide that your checked luggage needs to be searched by hand. **Travel Sentry certified locks** (available at luggage and travel shops, at Brookstone stores, or online at `www.brookstone.com`) are approved by the TSA and can be opened by inspectors with a special code or key. If you use something other than TSA-approved locks, your lock will be cut off your suitcase if a hand-search is required.

Saving Time with Advance Reservations

Because of long lines during peak tourist periods, many museums in Italy now offer advance ticketing. You can make reservations before you leave home (thus bypassing waits of up to three hours at the local ticket booth). The list of museums for which you can make reservations includes Rome's **Galleria Borghese** (see Chapter 12); Florence's **Galleria degli Uffizi** and **Galleria dell'Accademia** (see Chapter 13); Venice's **Palazzo Ducale** and **Gallerie dell'Accademia** (see Chapter 16); and Naples's **Museo di Capodimonte** (see Chapter 18).

Part III
The Eternal City: Rome

The 5th Wave   By Rich Tennant

ATTENZIONE!

"It says, children are forbidden from running, touching objects, or appearing bored during the tour."

In this part . . .

The seven hills of Rome have been continuously inhabited for the past 3,000 years, so it's not surprising that nowhere else will you find such cultural density and layering of periods and styles. The treasures of Rome stretch from pre-Republic ruins to Bernini's baroque marvels to the stylish, convulsive city depicted by Fellini in his famous movies.

Chapter 11 provides everything you need to know to get to Rome, orient yourself in the city, find a comfortable place to stay, and order a delicious meal. Included are rundowns of the best hotels and the best restaurants. In Chapter 12, we describe the major sites and activities — not only how to see the Colosseum and the Vatican Museums, but also where to shop and where to go for fun after dark.

Chapter 11

Settling into Rome

. . . .

In This Chapter

▶ Arriving in Rome
▶ Getting around the city
▶ Finding the best room in Rome
▶ Tasting Roman cuisine
▶ Information at your fingertips

. . . .

*A*rriving in a foreign city is always a challenge, and although Rome isn't one of the biggest cities in the world, it is large enough to be confusing, with its intricate street layout, thousands of hotels and restaurants, and complex transportation system. The narrow and winding streets of the historic center are a maze even for Romans! Sit back and relax — in this chapter, we provide all you need to negotiate the Eternal City like a native.

Getting There

Getting to Rome is fairly straightforward: The city has two airports, is a major train hub, and is served by highways from all directions. As the old adage goes, "All roads lead to Rome."

By air

Rome's main airport, Leonardo da Vinci, is located in **Fiumicino** — this is where you're likely to land if you come by plane. Charter flights and some European airlines also arrive in the smaller airport of **Ciampino.**

Navigating your way through passport control and Customs

If you've already landed in a country that is part of the Schengen European Community (which includes Austria, Belgium, Denmark, Finland, France, Germany, Greece, Iceland, Luxembourg, the Netherlands, Norway, Portugal, Spain, and Sweden), then your passport has been checked and only spot checks will be performed at the Italian border. If, however, Rome is your first port of call in Europe, then you'll have to line up at passport control. Often you'll find two lines: one for European Union citizens and one for everyone else. After having your passport checked and collecting your luggage, you must pass through Customs. Items for personal use enter duty-free up to 175€ ($210) for each adult and 90€ ($108) for each child under 15. In addition, adults can import a maximum of 200 cigarettes (50 cigars), 1 liter (slightly more that 1 quart) of liquor or 2 liters of wine, 50 grams of perfume, 500 grams (1 pound) of coffee, and 100 grams (3 ounces) of tea; children are allowed only per-fume. You cannot bring currency in excess of 10,329€ ($12,395 at press time, though the dollar amount will depend on the conversion rate on the day you travel). See "Quick Concierge" in Appendix A for Customs regula-tions on what you can bring home. You can also find detailed information at the Italian Customs Web site (www.agenziadogane.it).

 As a foreigner, you're required to have your passport with you at all times, to prove both your identity and your legal status. We recommend you either carry it in a safe place on your person (such as a document pouch worn under your clothes), or leave the original in the safe at your hotel and carry a photocopy.

Getting oriented at Fiumicino/Leonardo da Vinci

Though officially named after Leonardo, everybody refers to this airport as Fiumicino (☎ 06-65951; www.adr.it), after the name of the nearby town. The airport is compact and very well organized (but ever expand-ing), with three terminals connected by a long corridor. Terminal A han-dles domestic travel; Terminal B handles domestic and internal flights to the Schengen European Community; and Terminal C manages all other international flights. If you're flying directly from a U.S. airport, Terminal C is your likely point of entry; it is connected to a newer set of gates by a cool monorail.

 Don't be concerned if you see police officers with submachine guns walking around — due to recent world tensions, it's now routine proce-dure. Be aware, though, that the security forces at Fiumicino have terror-ists in mind, not common thieves — that means you still have to watch your belongings like a hawk, and don't leave anything precious in your checked luggage.

After exiting passport control and Customs, you enter the main con-course, a long hall that connects all three terminals. Here's where you'll find ATMs (one per terminal), 24-hour currency exchange machines, and a *cambio* (exchange) office, open from 8:30 a.m. to 7:30 p.m. and located just outside Customs in the international arrivals area.

 If you're using traveler's checks, you may want to change them at the *cambio* office — its rates are usually the best in town.

On your way out to ground transportation, you'll find a very good **tourist information desk** (☎ 06-65956074) that provides information on Rome at one end and on the rest of Italy at the other. Nearby is a help desk for **last-minute hotel reservations** — the service, however, doesn't cover all hotels in Rome. Public transportation — including **taxis** and

Taxi fares in Rome

The meter starts at 2.33€ ($2.80). It adds 1.29€ ($1.55) for every kilometer (⅔ mile) if you're moving at up to 20kmph (12 mph), and for every 85.3m (280 feet) if you're going faster. This rate decreases within the urban limits (G.R.A. highway) to 0.78€ (95¢) for every kilometer (⅔ mile) if you're moving at up to 20kmph (12 mph), for every 141m (462 feet) if you're going faster, and for every 19.2 seconds if you're stuck in traffic. You'll pay a surcharge of 2.58€ ($3.10) at night (10 p.m.–7 a.m.), and of 1.03€ ($1.20) on Sundays and holidays. The luggage supplement is 1.04€ ($1.20) for each bag larger than 35×25×50 centimeters (14×9.8×20 inches).

car-rental shuttle buses — is just outside along the sidewalk; the **train station** is on the second floor of a building attached to the international terminal.

Getting from the Fiumicino airport to your hotel

Fiumicino lies about 30km (18 miles) from Rome and is well connected by highway, train, shuttle train, and bus.

The easiest way to get to your hotel is by taking a **taxi:** The line forms on the curb just outside the terminals and is marked by a sign. Expect to pay about 45€ ($54) for the 50-minute ride (well over an hour at rush hour) for three adult passengers (only some taxis will accept four).

 Beware of Gypsy cabdrivers who approach you as you exit the arrivals gate: They will easily charge you double the regulated cab rates. Regulation taxis are white with a checkered line on the sides, have a meter, and wait at the regular stand.

Taking the **shuttle train** into Rome is equally simple — and a lot faster during rush hour. If you have a lot of luggage, you can hire help at the baggage-claim area for 2€ ($2.40) per item; they'll take your bags to the train. The railroad terminal is connected to the air terminal through a corridor on the second floor, just outside arrivals (follow the sign marked TRENI). The best train is the **Leonardo Express,** a 35-minute shuttle ride to **Termini** (Rome's central rail station); it runs daily every 30 minutes from 6:37 a.m. to 11:37 p.m. and costs 9.50€ ($11). Trains pull in at a separate rail terminal inside Termini rail station, way at the back of the regular gates. It is quite a hike to the main concourse, but you don't really need to get there: A taxi stand is downstairs (there's an elevator) and to the left of your arrival gate. Otherwise, take the moving sidewalk located on the lower level, which connects the arrivals terminal with the main concourse of Termini rail station.

There also is a cheaper local **commuter train** (look for trains with the final destination Orte or Fara Sabina), which makes various stops along the way and within Rome but doesn't stop at Termini. It takes about 40 minutes, depending on your stop, and runs every 15 minutes Monday through Saturday and every 30 minutes on Sunday for about 5€ ($6). Get off at **Roma Ostiense** if your hotel is in the area of the Aventino or the Colosseum; **Roma Trastevere** if it is in the area of Trastevere, San Pietro, or Prati; and **Roma Tiburtina** if it is in the Porta Pia or Villa Borghese areas.

Tickets for both trains are sold at the ticket booth in the terminal. Remember to stamp your ticket at one of the small yellow validation boxes before you board the train.

If you're planning to use the commuter train from the airport and later use public transportation in Rome, buy a **day pass** or a **tourist three-day ticket** (see "Getting Around Rome," later in this chapter) at the tobacconist in the railroad terminal — the commuter-train ride (though not on the Leonardo Express) is included in both of those passes.

Whichever train you take, you'll find a taxi stand immediately outside each of the train stations upon your arrival. You'll also find ranks of public buses, with signs indicating their numbers and routes, in the area in front of train stations, while the subway is underneath.

Finally, you can take a **shuttle bus** into Rome. **Terravision** (☎ 06-79494572; www.terravision.it) runs a shuttle to Termini station and to Tiburtina station, with stops at a few major hotels. The fare is 9€ ($11) for adults and 5€ ($6) for children 2 to 12.

Arriving at Ciampino airport

A number of international charter flights, as well as some airlines that mainly serve Europe, arrive at **Ciampino** (☎ 06-794941 or 06-79340297), 16km (10 miles) from the center of Rome. This airport has few structures or services; it's almost like an American civil-aviation airport.

Taxis are by far the easiest way to get to town from Ciampino. Expect to pay about 35€ ($42) for the 45-minute trip (see earlier for details on rates). You can also take a **shuttle bus** — **Terravision** runs a shuttle service in concert with Ryanair flights, while **Schiaffini** runs a shuttle coinciding with EasyJet flights. Both take you to Termini station for 8€ ($9.60); tickets are sold at the Hotel Royal Santina or at the Hotel Stromboli on Via Marsala, just across from the Termini train station.

By train

Rome is a major railroad hub, offering service to every domestic and international destination. The national train service, **Trenitalia** (☎ 892021; www.trenitalia.it), is cheap, reliable, and frequent. No fewer than six railway stations are located in the center of Rome, but the most central and largest is **Termini** (☎ 800-431784; www.romatermini.it), while the second-busiest is **Tiburtina**. Trains usually stop at one or the other.

At Termini station, public toilets and luggage storage are at either end of the platform area. Exits located near platforms 1 and 22 lead to the main concourse, a long commercial gallery with a bar to the north and a pharmacy to the south; in between are many newsstands, a tobacconist, a travel agency, ATMs, and a *cambio* office, as well as information booths. One floor below, you'll find a mall complete with a large bookstore, supermarket, cosmetics store, shoe-repair shop, and ATMs; here is also the entrance to the subway (both lines cross here; see "Getting Around Rome," later in this chapter). If you stay on the main concourse level and continue in a straight line across the gallery, you'll reach the main hall, where train tickets are sold at the windows and at automatic machines. You can exit to the street at either end of the gallery (where you'll find small taxi stands) or from the main hall, which opens onto Piazza dei Cinquecento, the largest bus terminal in Rome. The main taxi stand is just outside the main hall near the metro sign on the right. For some mysterious reason, the line forms at the end farthest from the exit of the train station, so depending on how many people are waiting, you may have to walk a bit (see earlier for rates and a warning on Gypsy cabs).

Orienting Yourself in Rome

Rome started outgrowing its ancient Roman and medieval walls (some of which are still standing in places) only in the 20th century, but it has seen immense urban sprawl over the past two decades. From the older central body of the city, arms of newer urban development have formed along the main roads heading out of town, and lately, the space in between has been filled in with modern developments. As a result, Rome is quite large — in fact, it is Italy's largest city. It is divided by the river **Tevere** (Tiber), which meanders southward, leaving about a third of the city on its western bank and the rest on its eastern bank.

On the eastern bank of the Tevere is the political, cultural, commercial, and tourist heart of the city. About three millennia of consecutive layers of urban development have created a confused layout of streets, with tiny medieval roads crossed by larger and newer avenues. At the east end on **Piazza dei Cinquecento** is Termini, Rome's main train station and major public transportation hub. Leading out of Piazza dei Cinquecento is **Via Cavour,** heading toward the Colosseum. Branching out of Piazza della Repubblica are **Via Barberini,** which leads into Via Veneto and Via del Tritone; and **Via Nazionale,** which descends to Piazza Venezia and continues — as Via del Plebiscito, then Corso Vittorio Emanuele II — all the way to the River Tiber, and as Via della Conciliazione across it to St. Peter's and the Vatican. The major cross streets at Piazza Venezia are **Via del Corso** and **Via dei Fori Imperiali,** joining Piazza del Popolo at one end and the Colosseum at the other. Beyond the Colosseum begins **Via Appia,** the first highway created by the ancient Romans. A section of it has been transformed into an archaeological and natural park (see Chapter 12).

On the western bank of the Tevere, you'll find the **Gianicolo** hill over-looking the neighborhood of **Trastevere,** as well as the **Vatican** — the tiny city-state that is the base of the Catholic religion, with the pope as both a religious and administrative leader. The Vatican's major feature is the basilica of **San Pietro.** North of the Vatican is the largish area called **Prati,** crossed by the busy **Via Cola di Rienzo** and **Via Ottaviano.**

Introducing the neighborhoods

We have divided the historic center of Rome into several smaller neigh-borhoods; all are desirable places to stay, with lively nightlife, restau-rants, and cafes nearby. The neighborhoods are identified on the "Rome Orientation" map in this chapter.

Aventino

This elegant residential neighborhood is one of the original seven hills of Rome, where a number of monasteries were built in the Middle Ages. It has known very little urban development since, and it's now a unique island of quiet, where small restaurants and a few hotels are surrounded by greenery and peaceful streets. It is well connected via public trans-portation to all other destinations in Rome.

Campo de' Fiori

Along the left bank of the Tiber, this authentic neighborhood is mostly residential but is made very lively by the market square and the con-nected commercial strip of **Via dei Giubbonari.** You'll find plenty of restaurants and an active nightlife here. Among the attractions is the beautiful **Palazzo Farnese.**

Colosseo

The Colosseum was at the heart of ancient Rome, and the area around it is a romantic mix of residential buildings and ruins. The Colosseo is home to the most illustrious monuments of ancient Rome, including the **Palatino,** the **Roman Forum,** the **Campidoglio,** and, of course, the **Colosseum** itself. To the north, in an area sloping up along Via Cavour, is a very authentic and residential neighborhood. Although not elegant, it is experiencing new life with the opening of trendy restaurants, small hotels, and bars. To the east is another small, residential, and very Roman neighborhood, with a few hotels and some nice neighborhood restaurants.

Navona/Pantheon

On the southwestern side of the **Corso,** this lively neighborhood is a mix of elegant Renaissance and medieval buildings, including the beautiful palaces that house the government and the two chambers of the Italian Parliament (the **Parlamento** and **Senato**). Many hotels are in this area, and several nice restaurants and bars can be found along **Via del Governo Vecchio.** Some of Rome's best antiques shops line the **Via** dei Coronari. Graced by two of Rome's greatest attractions — **Piazza Navona** and the **Pantheon** — at its heart, this is one of the most desirable areas to stay; its popularity means that you have to put up with crowds, especially in summer.

Piazza del Popolo

Squeezed between the old city walls and the river, around one of the most beautiful squares of Rome, this lively neighborhood has a lot of trendy new restaurants and bars in the area extending west of the **Corso.**

Piazza di Spagna

On the east side of the **Corso,** this former residential neighborhood has been almost completely taken over by the fashion and tourist industries. It is the best shopping neighborhood in Rome, home to all the great names of Italian couture, plus a lot of other tony boutiques. It has many hotels, including some of the city's best. The shopping streets get a bit deserted at night, and if you're seeking some nightlife, you have to edge toward **Fontana di Trevi** or cross over the Corso.

Prati

This residential neighborhood on the western bank of the Tiber takes its name from the fields *(prati)* that still existed here at the end of the 19th century. It stretches north of the Vatican along the river. Reflecting its late-19th-century origins, streets are wide, straight, and lined with trees. The area is pleasant and only a bridge away from Piazza del Popolo; it has a relatively active, if subdued, nightlife, with restaurants, jazz clubs, and an important shopping area along **Via Cola di Rienzo.**

Repubblica

Piazza della Repubblica is a gorgeous square created over what was the main hall of Diocletian's thermal baths, a few steps west of Piazza dei Cinquecento and the Termini train station. The areas along Via Cernaia on one side of the square and Via Nazionale on the other are lively during the day because of the numerous shops and offices, but not particularly happening at night, when this turns into a quiet residential neighborhood with a few hotels and restaurants. Very convenient to most of Rome's attractions and very well connected by public transportation, this is a good alternative to the more glamorous and pricey areas nearby.

San Pietro

On the western bank of the Tiber, this area is mainly occupied by the walled city of the **Vatican** (seat of the Holy See and site of the Vatican Museums and the Sistine Chapel). It is dominated, of course, by the grandiose **St. Peter's Basilica** and **Castel Sant'Angelo.** Flanking the basilica are two ancient and picturesque residential neighborhoods that are home to a few hotels and restaurants.

Rome Orientation

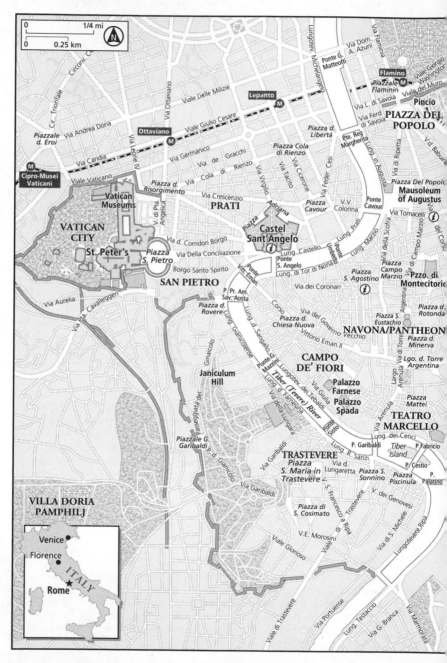

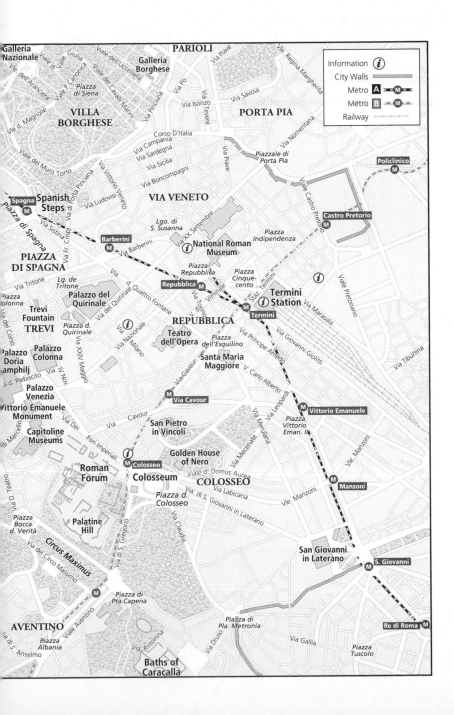

Teatro Marcello

This area covers what is still commonly referred to as the Ghetto, the old Jewish neighborhood at the edge of ancient Rome. It is among the most authentic of the historic neighborhoods and remains very residential. Some nice restaurants are tucked away in its small streets, along with pubs, local shops, and a few archaeological treasures.

Trastevere

Located on the western bank of the Tiber at the foot of the **Gianicolo** hill, this neighborhood is just across the river from the Aventino. Literally meaning "on the other side of the Tiber," during ancient Roman times, this was the traditional (and rather seedy) residence of poorer artisans and workers. Its character was preserved during the Middle Ages and the Renaissance, and to some extent up to the last century. In recent times, though, it has been largely transformed into an artsy, cultured neighborhood, famous for its restaurants, street life, and nightlife, and appealing to younger and not-so-young Romans and visitors.

Trevi

On the east side of the **Corso,** this neighborhood slopes up the Quirinale hill with the magnificent Renaissance presidential (formerly papal) residence as its centerpiece. Aside from the tourist hubbub around its famous fountain — always surrounded by a sea of humanity — it's a relatively unspoiled neighborhood with many small restaurants and shops.

Via Veneto

Made famous by Fellini as the heart of *La Dolce Vita,* this elegant street is lined by famous hotels and a few upscale stores. The environs are very quiet at night. There are a number of nice hotels on the side streets, but relatively few restaurants and nightspots. Well connected by public transportation, the areas behind the glitzy strip of Via Veneto are a good alternative to the glamorous and expensive areas nearby, especially if you go toward **Via XX Settembre** (at the southeastern edge of this neighborhood).

Finding information after you arrive

The visitor center is at Via Parigi 5, off Piazza della Repubblica (☎ 06-488991; www.romaturismo.it; Mon–Sat 9 a.m.–7 p.m.). You'll also find information desks at international arrivals in Terminal B of Fiumicino Airport (☎ 06-65956074; daily 8 a.m.–7 p.m.) and at several points around the city near major attractions (daily 9 a.m.–6 p.m.), including the following locations:

- ✔ **Castel Sant'Angelo,** Piazza Pia, to the west of the Castel Sant'Angelo (☎ 06-68809707; Metro: Ottaviano–San Pietro)

- ✔ **Fontana di Trevi,** Via Minghetti, off Via del Corso (☎ 06-6782988; Minibus: 117 or 119)

✔ **Fori Imperiali,** Piazza Tempio della Pace on Via dei Fori Imperiali (☎ 06-69924307; Metro: Colosseo)

✔ **Largo Goldoni,** on Via del Corso at Via Condotti (☎ 06-68136061; Metro: Piazza di Spagna)

✔ **Palazzo delle Esposizioni,** Via Nazionale (☎ 06-47824525; Bus: 64)

✔ **Piazza delle Cinque Lune,** off Piazza Navona to the north (☎ 06-68809240; Minibus: 116)

✔ **San Giovanni,** Piazza San Giovanni in Laterano (☎ 06-77203535; Metro: San Giovanni)

✔ **Santa Maria Maggiore,** Via dell'Olmata, on the southeastern side of the church (☎ 06-4740955; Metro: Termini)

✔ **Stazione Termini,** Piazza dei Cinquecento, in front of the railroad station (☎ 06-47825194; Metro: Termini)

✔ **Stazione Termini,** inside the gallery (☎ 06-48906300; Metro: Termini)

✔ **Trastevere,** Piazza Sonnino (☎ 06-58333457; Tram: 8)

Usually, the staff at the information points in or near Termini station are the most overwhelmed; elsewhere, you'll find people more available to assist you.

The **Holy See** maintains its own tourist office. It is located in Piazza San Pietro (☎ 06-69884466; Mon–Sat 8:30 a.m.–6 p.m.), just left of the entrance to the Basilica di San Pietro. The office has information on the Vatican and on its tourist attractions and religious events. You may also make reservations for a visit to the Vatican gardens or fill out the form to participate in a papal audience — but we recommend making reservations to do so before you leave home (see Chapter 12 for more information).

Getting Around Rome

Rome's historic hills are no myth: They are real — and sometimes even steep. The one myth is that there are only seven of them. Rome may look flat on a map, but it's very hilly — you'll soon understand why locals use mopeds (or cars, unfortunately) and public transportation, and why you see so few bicycles around. Remember also that the city is thousands of years old, meaning that much of it isn't designed for any mode of conveyance other than the human foot. There are times, however, when you'll welcome public transportation. Taxis, for example, are a great convenience at night when crossing large sections of the city.

By subway (metropolitana)

Although the *metropolitana,* or metro for short, has only two lines (work has just started on the third line), it is the best way to get around

Getting a ticket to ride

ATAC (☎ 800-431784 or 06-46952027; www.atac.roma.it), Rome's transport authority, runs all public transportation in the city, and the same ticket is valid for all. You need to buy tickets **before boarding** (although a few bus lines now have onboard vending machines, do not count on finding one — they are still quite rare), and you must **stamp** them upon boarding, or else they aren't valid (on subway and trains, the stamping machines — little yellow boxes — are at the entrance gates; on buses and trams, they're onboard). A regular *biglietto* (ticket) for the bus/metro is valid for 75 minutes and costs 1€ ($1.20). Within the 75 minutes of validity, you can take as many buses and trams as you want, but only one subway ride. You can also get a day pass called **BIG** that costs 4€ ($4.80), a three-day ticket called **BTI** for 11€ ($13), or a weekly pass called **CIS** for 16€ ($19). All passes give you unlimited rides on the bus, metro, and urban trains. You can buy tickets and passes at the metro ticket booths, the ATAC bus information booth in front of Stazione Termini (near Platform C), from vending machines at some major bus stops, and at many bars, tobacconist shops (signed TABACCHI or with a white *T* on a black background), and newsstands.

because the underground routes don't suffer from the terrible city traffic. In addition, the routes naturally stay the same — unlike the city bus system, which is under constant reorganization. **Line A Battistini–Anagnina** and **Line B Laurentina–Rebibbia** cross at the Termini station; a big red *M* marks all metro entrances. The metro runs Sunday through Friday from 5:30 a.m. to 11:30 p.m. and Saturday from 5:30 a.m. to 12:30 a.m.

The Colosseum, Circus Maximus, and Cavour stops on Line B don't offer full elevator/lift service and aren't accessible to the disabled. (For tips for travelers with disabilities, see Chapter 9.)

By bus and tram

Rome's bus system is large and under continuous improvement, yet the city's ancient layout resists any real modernization, so things don't always go smoothly: Buses are very crowded at rush hour, and traffic jams are endemic. Still, buses remain an excellent resource because they go absolutely everywhere in Rome. Especially useful are the diminutive **electric buses** that are the only vehicles allowed in the tiny, narrow streets of the historic heart of the city (**116** and **116T** from the Gianicolo hill to Villa Borghese; **117** from Piazza del Popolo to San Giovanni in Laterano; **118** from Piazzale Ostiense to Appia Antica; and **119** from Piazza del Popolo to Largo Argentina). Among the other bus lines, those that you are most likely to use are the **23** (Prati to Aventino), **62** (Castel Sant'Angelo to Repubblica), **64** (Termini to Vatican), **87** (Prati to Colosseum), **492** (Tiburtina railroad station to Vatican Museums), and **910** (Termini to Villa Borghese). Rome also has a few tram lines; they aren't as spectacular as the cable cars in San Francisco, but they're fun to ride. A line we like a lot is the **3,** which passes by the Basilica di San Giovanni and the Colosseum. Another line that you're likely to use is the **8,** from Largo Argentina to Trastevere. Most buses run daily from 5:30 a.m. to 12:30 a.m., but some stop at 8.30 p.m. A few night lines are marked with an *N* for *notturno* (night); they usually run every hour, leaving the ends of the line on the hour.

On foot

Walking is by far the best way to experience Rome — you'll get to see the most as you wander the curving streets that merge into others, narrow to almost shoulder width, change names, and meander among beautiful old buildings. Wear very comfortable shoes, and be ready to switch to another form of transportation — usually handy — when you get tired.

To enjoy Rome's delightful labyrinth, you'll need a good map. The free tourist-office map is quite good, but it doesn't have a *stradario* (street directory), which is essential for locating addresses. You can buy a detailed city map with a *stradario* at any newsstand and many bookstores.

By taxi

Taxi rates are reasonable in Rome (see earlier for details on fares), but taking a cab can be expensive during those busy times of day when you're stuck in traffic. Still, they're a great resource for getting to your hotel from the train station and for traveling around at night after the buses and metro stop running.

Taxis don't cruise the streets, as in most U.S. cities; they return to taxi stands and wait for a call. Hence, you usually cannot hail a taxi on the street unless you happen to find one that's returning to a stand. You'll find many taxi stands around, especially near major landmarks, including **Piazza Barberini** (at the foot of Via Veneto), **Piazza San Silvestro,** and **Piazza SS. Apostoli** (the latter two not far from the Trevi Fountain). You can identify taxi stands by a smallish telephone on a pole marked TAXI. But if you're starting from a place with a phone — like a hotel or restaurant — then asking the staff to call a taxi for you is easiest. For a **24-hour radio taxi,** call ☎ **06-88177,** 06-6645, or 06-4994.

Staying in Style

Finding a hotel in Rome has become easier than ever: Many properties have been recently refurbished, several new ones have opened, and hundreds of B&Bs are on the scene. On the flip side, prices have risen sharply in recent years. A weak dollar and poor exchange rate haven't helped. Rome is a capital city, and capital cities the world over are expensive. The off season has shrunk to a few weeks in January, February, August, and November (see Chapter 3 for more on seasons). In peak tourist season, you will find it difficult to find a decent room without paying through the nose. If you come to town without a reservation at all, you should be prepared to find a room only in the most expensive hotels, or in those outside the city center. The best way to get a deal is to plan in advance. See Chapter 8 for money-saving tips and advice on what to expect from your hotel: Globalization may be here, but cultural differences remain alive and well.

Below are our picks for our preferred hotels in Rome, followed by some acceptable alternatives if you have trouble booking a room in our top choices. Unless otherwise specified, all rooms in the hotels we recommend come with private bathrooms. Note that many of the hotels in historic areas are housed in ancient buildings and have relatively few rooms, so reserve well in advance.

If you arrive without a room reservation (something we do not recommend), remember that there's a hotel reservations desk at the airport as well as one at Termini station.

The top hotels

Albergo Cesàri Hotel
$$ Navona/Pantheon

You can't beat the location of this hotel: It lies between the Pantheon and the Corso, and the Trevi Fountain is not far away. The Cesàri has been a hotel since 1787 (it still has its original license from Pope Pius VI), and has been run by the same family since 1899. Guest rooms vary in size and décor — some are more modern, while others have beautiful hardwood reproduction beds and armoires. All have double-paneled windows, most have wooden floors with nice carpets, and many bathrooms have a tub and are good-sized. For families or small groups, inquire about the triple and quad rooms.

See map p. 116. Via di Pietra 89a, south of Piazza Colonna on the Corso. ☎ *06-6749701. Fax: 06-67497030.* www.albergocesari.it. *Bus: 60, 175, or 492 to the Corso; 116 to Via di Pietra. Rack rates: 220€ ($264) double; 265€ ($318) triple; 310€ ($372) quad. AE, DC, MC, V.*

Albergo del Senato
$$$$ Pantheon

This elegant hotel has an ideal location across from the Pantheon. Guest rooms are spacious — the suites are palatial — and beautifully furnished, with antiques and quality reproductions, marble-topped tables, and hardwood floors. The marble bathrooms are huge (for Rome) and nicely appointed. The terrace has a spectacular view and is perfect for enjoying Rome's sunsets. The hotel has been recently wired for Wi-Fi Internet access.

See map p. 116. Piazza della Rotonda 73. ☎ *06-6784343. Fax: 06-699-40297.* www.albergodelsenato.it. *Bus: 60, 175, or 492 to the Corso; 116 to Pantheon. Rack rates: 365€ ($438) double; 410€ ($492) triple; 440€ ($528) quad; suites 475€ ($570) and up. AE, DC, MC, V.*

Albergo Santa Chiara
$$$ Navona/Pantheon

Operated since 1838 by the Corteggiani family, this is our favorite moderately priced hotel in Rome. Inside is a chapel built in the room where St. Clare (St. Francis's spiritual sister) lived her last years. Located behind the Pantheon and a few steps from Piazza della Minerva, it's both functional and comfortable. From the entry hall, with its statuary and porphyry columns, to the skylit breakfast room, the Santa Chiara offers a feeling of elegance and simplicity. Guest rooms vary in shape and furnishings: Some are in a modern style, some have carpeting (while others have wood floors), and some feature beamed ceilings. All have good-sized bathrooms. There are also some triples and quads, plus three garret suites with private terraces.

See map p. 116. Via Santa Chiara 21. ☎ *06-6872979. Fax: 06-6873144.* www.albergo santachiara.com. *Bus: 116 to Pantheon or 64 or 70 to Largo Argentina, then walk north. Rack rates: 240€ ($288) double; 260€ ($312) triple; 320€ ($384) quad; 460€ ($552) suite. Rates include breakfast. AE, DC, MC, V.*

Bernini Bristol
$$$$ Via Veneto

We particularly appreciate this hotel for its great location — just at the foot of Via Veneto — and its impeccable service, provided at (relatively) moderate rates, particularly if you get one of the great Internet specials. Opened in 1874, it served as the background location for many scenes of Dan Brown's novel *Angels and Demons*. Most of its guest rooms are classically furnished, but a few have been redone in elegant modern style. All are outfitted with luxury fabrics and carpeting, fine linens, and elegant marble bathrooms. The best rooms open onto great views over Rome. From the splendid rooftop restaurant, the Olympus, you can enjoy a 360-degree vista; the hotel also has a spa and gym for its guests.

See map p. 116. Piazza Barberini 23. ☎ *06-488931. Fax: 06-4824266.* www.bernini bristol.com. *Metro: Line A to Barberini. Rack rates: 436€–499€ ($523–$599) double; suites 700€ ($840) and up. AE, DC, MC, V.*

Casa Valdese
$ Prati

Located on the Vatican side of the river, near Castel Sant'Angelo and the shopping district of Cola di Rienzo, this small hotel offers great value. The name "Valdese" refers to the Protestant group of Swiss origin, and the hotel reflects this in its simple but spotlessly clean and pleasant rooms. The very moderate prices and the excellent location — basically across the river from Piazza del Popolo — are other pluses. A half-board plan (including breakfast and dinner) is available.

See map p. 116. Via A. Farnese 18, off Via Cola di Rienzo. ☎ *06-3218222. Fax: 06-3211843.* www.casavaldeseroma.it. *Metro: Lepanto. Walk toward the river on Via Giulio Cesare and take the first right. Rack rates: 116€ ($139) double; 159€ ($191) triple; 189€ ($227) quad. Rates include breakfast. AE, V.*

Rome Accommodations and Dining

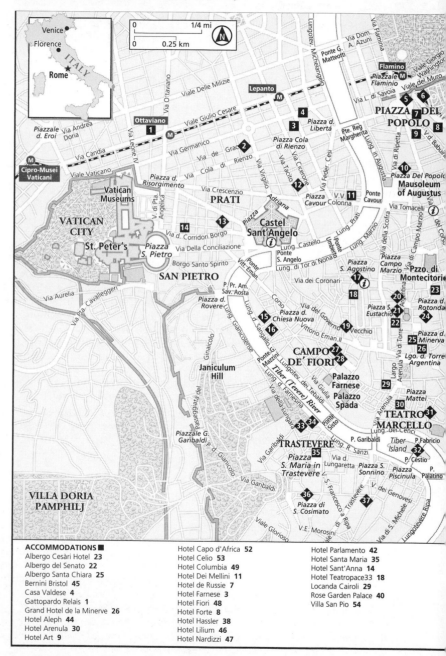

ACCOMMODATIONS ■

Albergo Cesàri Hotel **23**
Albergo del Senato **22**
Albergo Santa Chiara **25**
Bernini Bristol **45**
Casa Valdese **4**
Gattopardo Relais **1**
Grand Hotel de la Minerve **26**
Hotel Aleph **44**
Hotel Arenula **30**
Hotel Art **9**

Hotel Capo d'Africa **52**
Hotel Celio **53**
Hotel Columbia **49**
Hotel Dei Mellini **11**
Hotel de Russie **7**
Hotel Farnese **3**
Hotel Fiori **48**
Hotel Forte **8**
Hotel Hassler **38**
Hotel Lilium **46**
Hotel Nardizzi **47**

Hotel Parlamento **42**
Hotel Santa Maria **35**
Hotel Sant'Anna **14**
Hotel Teatropace33 **18**
Locanda Cairoli **29**
Rose Garden Palace **40**
Villa San Pio **54**

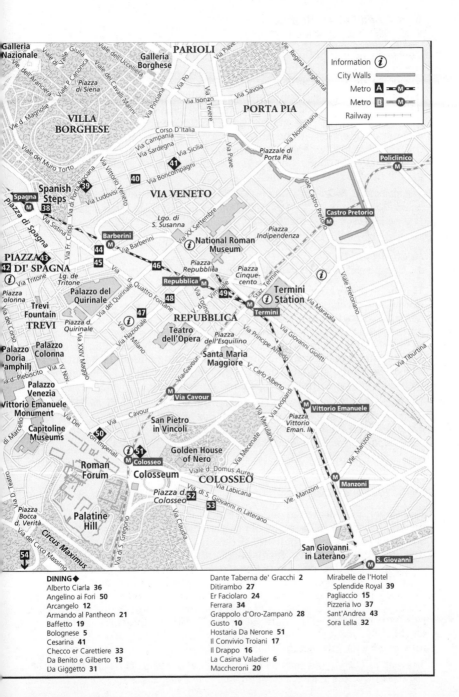

Information ⓘ
City Walls
Metro Ⓐ ═Ⓜ═
Metro Ⓑ ═Ⓜ═
Railway ┼───┼───┼

Galleria
Nazionale
Viale di Valle Giulia
Galleria
Borghese
PARIOLI
Via Piave
Vle Regina Margherita
Viale dell'Uccelliera
Viale dei Cavalli Marini
Viale P. Canonica
Piazza
di Siena
Via Pinciana
Via Po
Via Isonzo Tevere
Via Savoia
PORTA PIA
Vle. dell'Aranciera
Vle. d. Magnolie
VILLA
BORGHESE
Corso D'Italia
Via Campania
Via Sardegna
Via Sicilia
Via Nomentana
Viale del Muro Torto
Via Vittorio Veneto
41
Via Boncompagni
Piazzale di
Porta Pia
Via Piave
Policlinico Ⓜ
40
Spanish **39**
Spagna
Steps
Ⓜ
38
Via Ludovisi
VIA VENETO
Lgo. di
S. Susanna
Piazza
Indipendenza
Castro Pretorio Ⓜ
Piazza di Spagna
Via Sistina
Via Fr. Crispi
Barberini
44
Via Barberini
Via XX Settembre
ⓘ National Roman
Museum
PIAZZA **43**
42 DI' SPAGNA
ⓘ
45
Lg. de
Tritone
46
Repubblica Ⓜ
Piazza
Repubblica
Piazza
Cinque-
cento
ⓘ
Via Pretoriano
Viale Castro Pretorio
Via Tritone
Piazza
olonna
Trevi
Fountain
Palazzo del
Quirinale
d. Quattro Fontane
48
Via Nazionale
Staz. Termini
49
Termini Ⓜ
Termini ⓘ
Station
Via Marsala
Via Marsala
Palazzo
Colonna
TREVI
Piazza d.
Quirinale
ⓘ
47
REPUBBLICA
Via del Corso
Palazzo
Doria
amphilj
Palazzo
Colonna
Via IV Nov.
Via XXIV Maggio
Via Milano
Teatro
dell'Opera
Piazza
dell'Esquilino
Santa Maria
Maggiore
V. Carlo Alberto
Via Principe Amedeo
Via Giovanni Giolitti
Via Tiburtina
ia-d-Plebiscito
Palazzo
Venezia
Vittorio Emanuele
Monument
Via Dei
Via
Cavour
Via Cavour
Via Leopardi
Via Merulana
Piazza
Vittorio
Eman. II
Vittorio Emanuele Ⓜ
Vle. Manzoni
di Marcello
Capitoline
Museums
Fori Imperiali
50
San Pietro
in Vincoli
Golden House
of Nero
Via Mecenate
Via Labicana
Manzoni Ⓜ
ⓘ **51**
Ⓜ Colosseo
Roman
Forum
Colosseum
Vle d. Domus Aurea
COLOSSEO
Via Labicana
Vle. Manzoni
Via del Teatro
Piazza
Bocca
d. Verità
Palatine
Hill
Piazza d. **52**
Colosseo
53
Via di S. Giovanni in Laterano
Via Claudia
Via di S. Gregorio
Circus Maximus
San Giovanni
in Laterano
S. Giovanni Ⓜ
54
Via del Circo Massimo

DINING◆
Alberto Ciarla **36**
Angelino ai Fori **50**
Arcangelo **12**
Armando al Pantheon **21**
Baffetto **19**
Bolognese **5**
Cesarina **41**
Checco er Carettiere **33**
Da Benito e Gilberto **13**
Da Giggetto **31**

Dante Taberna de' Gracchi **2**
Ditirambo **27**
Er Faciolaro **24**
Ferrara **34**
Grappolo d'Oro-Zampanò **28**
Gusto **10**
Hostaria Da Nerone **51**
Il Convivio Troiani **17**
Il Drappo **16**
La Casina Valadier **6**
Maccheroni **20**

Mirabelle de l'Hotel
Splendide Royal **39**
Pagliaccio **15**
Pizzeria Ivo **37**
Sant'Andrea **43**
Sora Lella **32**

Grand Hotel de la Minerve
$$$$ Navona/Pantheon

This very elegant hotel is located in one of our preferred small squares in the center of Rome and offers magnificent accommodations and service to boot. Housed in a 17th-century palace, the spacious guest rooms are appointed with stylish contemporary furnishings that whisper of comfort and excellent taste; some of the rooms have beautifully decorated ceilings with fine moldings. The marble bathrooms are spacious and contain all manner of amenities. In the warm season, the hotel's restaurant moves to the roof garden, where you can enjoy a gorgeous view of the dome-studded skyline. There's live music in the bar every evening. A very nice gym is right on the premises.

See map p. 116. Piazza della Minerva 69. ☎ *06-695201. Fax: 06-6794165.* www.grand hoteldelaminerve.it. *Bus: 116 to Pantheon; 64 or 70 to Largo Argentina. Rack rates: 460€–600€ ($552–$720) double. AE, DC, MC, V.*

Hotel Arenula
$ Campo de' Fiori/Teatro Marcello

This hotel offers large and well-appointed guest rooms at moderate prices. Above all, you can't beat its location. Situated on the second floor of a nice *palazzo,* with a beautiful marble spiral staircase leading to it (no elevator), it lies within walking distance of many of the center's main attractions and to buses and trams that will take you to the others. Nearby Campo de' Fiori is busy with a market during the day, and dining and nightlife after dark. Guest rooms are spacious and bright, simply furnished but welcoming, with decent-size bathrooms and good amenities.

See map p. 116. Via Santa Maria de' Calderari 47, off Via Arenula. ☎ *06-6879454. Fax: 06-6896188.* www.hotelarenula.com. *Bus: 64, 70, 170, 492, or 40 to Largo Argentina. Walk south on Via Arenula; take the fourth street on your left. Rack rates: 125€ ($150) double. Rates include buffet breakfast. AE, DC, MC, V.*

Hotel Art
$$$$ Piazza di Spagna

This new hotel, located in one of the most desirable areas of Rome, edges beyond modern into the realm of postmodern. If you don't get a room here, stop by just to see the hall and the court, with its crystal staircase and designer contemporary furnishings, and the bar — created in the columned and frescoed chapel of a palace. These striking features illustrate the artistic "eclecticism" on which the hotel prides itself. Each floor is color-coordinated with the details of the rooms (even down to the stationery and pens), and much of the furniture is made of fine hardwoods. Hotel Art has the feel of boutique hotels found in all the great cities of the world. The accent here is on comfort, service, and, of course, style. Check its Web site for Internet specials.

See map p. 116. Via Margutta 56, next to via del Babuino. ☎ *06-328711. Fax: 06-36003995.* www.hotelart.it. *Metro: Piazza di Spagna. Walk on Via del Babuino;*

take the first right and then the first left. Rack rates: 429€–495€ ($515–$594) double. Rates include breakfast. AE, DC, MC, V.

Hotel Capo d'Africa
$$$ Colosseo

This elegant new hotel is set on an atmospheric street between the Colosseum and San Giovanni, close to most of the sights of ancient Rome. Run by the same owners as the Hotel Dei Mellini (see review later in this chapter) and known for its excellent service, the Capo d'Africa offers comfortable rooms furnished in a warm, modern-ethnic style. The marble bathrooms are a good size and nicely fitted out. The hotel also offers some suites and wheelchair-accessible rooms. Don't miss the roof terrace and its splendid views.

See map p. 116. Via Capo d'Africa 54. ☎ *06-772801. Fax: 06-77280801.* www.hotel capodafrica.com. *Metro: Colosseo. Walk southeast across Piazza del Colosseo to Via Capo d'Africa. Rack rates: 340€–380€ ($408–$456) double; suites 500€ ($600). Rates include buffet breakfast. AE, DC, MC, V.*

Hotel Celio
$$$ Colosseo

This small hotel is a real jewel, housed in an 1870 building just steps from some of the city's most famous monuments. Rooms are individually decorated in Renaissance and ancient Roman style, with mosaic floors and frescoed walls. The beautiful bathrooms are done in marble and mosaics. The decoration and the furnishings — fine modern reproductions and some antiques — are the essence of what people mean by "old-world charm." The roof terrace, where breakfast is served in fine weather, enjoys gorgeous views over ancient Rome — as do the three private terraces of the Pompeian suite.

See map p. 116. Via dei Santissimi Quattro 35/c. ☎ *06-70495333. Fax: 06-7096377.* www.hotelcelio.com. *Metro: Colosseo. Walk east across Piazza del Colosseo to Via dei Santissimi Quattro. Rack rates: 280€–330€ ($336–$396) double; 370€ ($444) triple; 400€ ($480) quad; 470€–570€ ($564–$684) suite. Rates include buffet breakfast. AE, DC, MC, V.*

Hotel Dei Mellini
$$$ Prati

Within walking distance of Piazza del Popolo and Castel Sant'Angelo, this new hotel has a sophisticated atmosphere, with a relaxing inner garden and a contemporary-art collection in the public areas. Guest rooms are pleasantly furnished in modern-classic style with marble bathrooms; some rooms have private terraces. Children up to 12 stay free in a parent's room. Check the Web site for Internet specials.

See map p. 116. Via Muzio Clementi 81, off Via Colonna. ☎ *06-324771. Fax: 06-32477801.* www.hotelmellini.com. *Bus: 30, 70, 81, 87, 186, or 492 to Via Colonna. Rack rates: 290€–320€ ($348–$384) double. AE, DC, MC, V.*

Hotel de Russie
$$$$ Piazza di Spagna

Making the lists of the world's top hotels ever since it opened in 2000, the Russie is the most elegant place to stay in Rome, offering superb location, service, and accommodations. If you stay here, you'll follow in the steps of the rich and famous — Bill and Chelsea Clinton, among others. Housed in a beautiful *palazzo* enclosing a delightful terrace garden, the hotel is furnished in extremely tasteful and classy contemporary Italian style. Guest rooms are huge and have all kinds of amenities. You'll also find a spa with sauna; a health club; and, amazingly enough, a swimming pool (all for an extra fee). The restaurant on the premises, Le Jardin du Russie, gets excellent reviews.

See map p. 116. Via del Babuino 9. ☎ *06-328881. Fax: 06-32888888.* www.hotelde russie.it. *Metro: Piazza di Spagna. Rack rates: 693€–737€ ($832–$884) double. AE, DC, MC, V.*

Hotel Farnese
$$$ Prati

Tucked behind Castel Sant'Angelo in a quiet neighborhood and across the Tiber from Piazza del Popolo, this hospitable choice occupies a 1906 patrician *palazzo*, which has been completely renovated. Quiet and off the beaten path, it is elegantly decorated and features spacious guest rooms — the largest ones geared for families. The bathrooms are particularly nice, clad in marble and tile and with new modern fixtures. The Farnese is steps from one of Rome's best shopping streets — Via Cola di Rienzo — and within walking distance of the Vatican and the historic center. The hotel also has a roof garden.

See map p. 116. Via Alessandro Farnese 30. ☎ *06-3212553. Fax: 06-3215129.* www. hotelfarnese.com. *Metro: Line A to Lepanto; then walk northeast on Via degli Scipioni to Via Farnese. Rack rates: 300€–370€ ($360–$444) double; 430€ ($516) triple; 420€ ($504) junior suite. Rates include buffet breakfast. AE, MC, V.*

Hotel Fiori
$$ Repubblica

This small budget hotel offers a central location and comfortable accommodations at a moderate (for Rome) price. Guest rooms are large and bright, with wooden or tiled floors, good-sized bathrooms and showers, and tasteful, high-quality furnishings in reproduction style.

See map p. 116. Via Nazionale 163. ☎ *06-6797212. Fax: 06-6795433.* www.hotel-fiori.com. *Minibus: 117. Bus: 40, 60, 64, 70, or 170 to Via Nazionale. Rack rates: 180€ ($216) double; 250€ ($300) triple; 300€ ($360) quad. AE, DC, MC, V.*

Hotel Forte
$$ **Piazza di Spagna**

This hotel is a good find — often booked solid — offering accommodations at a moderate price in the most glamorous area of the historic center. Guest rooms vary in size, but all are pleasant, with quality wooden furniture in streamlined classic style. Most have carpeted floors. Bathrooms are not huge, but are functional and come with all the usual comforts. Amenities include Wi-Fi Internet access.

See map p. 116. Via Margutta 16. ☎ *06-3207625. Fax: 06-3202707.* www.hotel forte.com. *Metro: Spagna. Cross Piazza di Spagna and take the second street on your left from Via del Corso. Rack rates: 232€ ($278) double. AE, DC, MC, V.*

Hotel Lilium
$$ **Via Veneto/Termini**

Hotel Lilium defines itself as both refined and cheap. It's a great addition for budget travelers, offering a convenient if not glamorous location, along with bright, clean, and welcoming accommodations. The smallish guest rooms are individually decorated with wooden furniture and charming hand-painted floral motifs. The best rooms have spacious bathrooms and small, delightful private balconies. Triples are also available. The hotel offers 24-hour free Internet access. ☎ *06-4741133. Fax: 06-23328387.* www. liliumhotel.it. *Metro: Repubblica. Rack rates: 170€–190€ ($204–$228) double; 230€–250€ ($276–$300) triple. Rates include breakfast. AE, DC, MC, V.*

See map p. 116. Via XX Settembre 58a.

Hotel Parlamento
$$ **Pantheon**

Located right in the heart of Rome, this hotel is housed in a 15th-century building and offers great accommodations at excellent prices (off-season prices can be half the rack rate). Rooms are bright and spacious, with tiled floors, large beds, and comfortable bathrooms (some with tubs). Weather permitting, breakfast is served on the pleasant roof terrace. Internet access is free, but air-conditioning costs an extra 12€ ($14) per day.

See map p. 116. Via delle Convertite 5, off Piazza San Silvestro. ☎ */fax: **06-69921000.*** www.hotelparlamento.it. *Bus: 492 or 116 to Piazza San Silvestro. Rack rates: 170€ ($204) double; 195€ ($234) triple; 230€ ($276) quad. Rates include breakfast. MC, V.*

Hotel Santa Maria
$$ **Trastevere**

This small hotel occupies a block of low buildings surrounding a romantic garden-courtyard lined by a portico. Most of the guest rooms are on the first floor and open directly onto the courtyard (except one garret suite on the second floor). Rooms are cozy and welcoming, decorated with terra-cotta–tiled floors, whitewashed walls, and dark-wood furniture; however, they can be a bit dark on rainy days, as all light naturally comes from the portico. The courtyard, though, is a pleasant place to take breakfast on a sunny morning; in the afternoon and early evening, guests can have a glass of wine at the wine bar. The suites are on two levels and are designed for families with children (up to six beds).

See map p. 116. Vicolo del Piede 2, off Piazza Santa Maria in Trastevere. ☎ *06-5894626. Fax: 06-5894815.* www.htlsantamaria.com. *Tram: 8 to Piazza Sonnino. Take Via della Lungaretta to Piazza Santa Maria in Trastevere; cross the square and turn right. Rack rates: 220€–250€ ($264–$300) double; 270€ ($324) triple; suites 330€ ($396) and up. Rates include buffet breakfast. AE, MC, V.*

Hotel Teatropace 33
$$ Navona/Pantheon

Opened in 2004, this hotel is a good find and a great addition to Rome's accommodations. With its romantic location — hidden on a narrow street behind Piazza Navona — it offers both atmospheric lodgings and excellent amenities. It is housed in a 17th-century *palazzo*, with a grand baroque marble staircase still the only way up (the hotel personnel will assist you with your luggage). Guest rooms are furnished with personality, featuring wooden floors and ceiling beams, quality furniture, and nicely done, good-sized bathrooms.

See map p. 116. Via del Teatro Pace 33, 1 block west of Piazza Navona. ☎ *06-6879075. Fax 06-68192364.* www.hotelteatropace.com. *Bus: 64 to Corso Vittorio Emanuele. Rack rates: 230€ double ($276). Rates include buffet breakfast. AE, DC, MC, V.*

Locanda Cairoli
$$$ Campo de' Fiori

This small hotel offers elegance and perfect service with a self-consciously clubby, British feeling. Guest rooms are furnished with antiques and original work by contemporary artists, creating refined yet warm and relaxing surroundings. You need to book well in advance to snag one of the 15 well-appointed rooms.

See map p. 116. Piazza Benedetto Cairoli 2, off Via Arenula. ☎ *06-68809278. Fax: 06-68892937.* www.locandacairoli.it. *Bus: 64, 70, 170, 492, or 40 to Largo Argentina; then walk south on Via Arenula. Rack rates: 240€ ($288) double. Rates include breakfast. AE, DC, MC, V.*

Rose Garden Palace
$$$–$$$$ Via Veneto

In the exclusive area around Via Veneto, you'll find this new hotel housed in a Liberty (Italian Art Nouveau) building from the beginning of the 20th century. The eponymous inner rose garden is perfect for a private stroll. Charm isn't the only thing you'll find here, however — the amenities are top-notch as well. The marble bathrooms have both showers and bathtubs; the rooms themselves are large; and the entire hotel is furnished with very sleek yet inviting modern décor. A new health club and even a swimming pool are on-site. Check the Web site for special Internet rates. *See map p. 116. Via Bonconpagni 19.* ☎ *06-421741. Fax: 06-4815608.* www.rose gardenpalace.com. *Bus: 116 to Via Boncompagni; then walk north 1 block. Rack rates: 300€–440€ ($360–$528) double. Rates include buffet breakfast. AE, DC, MC, V.*

Villa San Pio
$$$ Aventino

This is the best of a group of three beautifully located and family-run hotels on the Aventino. It is a peaceful spot, surrounded by a private garden, yet only steps from attractions and transportation. Guest rooms are large and elegantly decorated, with period furniture and delicate frescoes and moldings on the walls. Good-sized marble bathrooms add to the value. If this hotel is full, an employee will suggest that you reserve at one of the nearby sister hotels, which we also recommend. **Hotel Sant'Anselmo** is at Piazza Sant'Anselmo 2, while **Hotel Aventino** is at Via San Domenico 10; each has its own personality. *See map p. 116. Via Santa Melania 19.* ☎ *06-5745231. Fax: 06-5741112.* www. aventinohotels.com. *Tram: 3 to Piazza Albania; then take Via di Sant'Anselmo, and turn right. Metro: Circo Massimo; walk up Viale Aventino to Piazza Albania, and follow directions for Tram. Metro: Piramide. Rack rates: 240€ ($288) double; 260€ ($312) triple; 270€ ($324) quad. Rates include buffet breakfast. AE, DC, MC, V.*

Runner-up accommodations

Gattopardo Relais

$$ Prati   Conveniently located near the metro line and within walking distance of the Vatican, this very small hotel offers great value. Housed in a historic residence, its rooms are bright and elegantly appointed with wooden floors, stucco moldings, and period furniture; the marble bathrooms are good-sized. *See map p. 116. Viale Giulio Cesare 94, at Via Vespasiano.* ☎ *06-37358480. Fax: 06-37501019.* www.ilgattopardorelais.it.

Hotel Aleph

$$$$ Via Veneto   We love this hotel in Rome, for it is almost perfect: very stylish furnishings, elegant but not overwhelming or stuffy atmosphere, and ideal location. However, it is quite expensive — and some of the even more luxurious hotels sometimes offer better deals — hence its position in this section. *See map p. 116. Via di San Basilio 15, off Piazza del Tritone.* ☎ *06-422901. Fax: 06-42290000.* www.aleph.boscolohotels.com.

Hotel Columbia

$$ Termini This conveniently located, family-run hotel offers spacious and bright guest rooms, many with beamed ceilings, some with arched windows or Murano chandeliers. All rooms are individually furnished with some antiques and quality reproductions. The hotel also has a pleasant roof garden with a bar, where breakfast is served. *See map p. 116. Via Viminale 15.* ☎ *06-4744289. Fax: 06-4740209.* www.hotelcolumbia.com.

Hotel Hassler

$$$$ Piazza di Spagna If money is no object, this luxury hotel is the place to be in Rome, with its fantastic location up the Spanish Steps. The basic rooms may not have the charm of the deluxe rooms and suites, but the amenities are tops. The hotel also offers a nice gym, sauna, bicycles to take to nearby Villa Borghese, terraces, and a number of bars and restaurants. *See map p. 116. Piazza Trinita dei Monti 6.* ☎ *06-699340. Fax: 06-6789991.* www.hotelhasslerroma.com.

Hotel Nardizzi

$$ Repubblica This family-run hotel offers excellent value and a good location. Guest rooms are simply furnished, and some enjoy a good view, but the tiled bathrooms are a bit cramped. Triples and quads are available. The hotel has a roof terrace. Check online for its interesting Internet specials. *See map p. 116. Via Firenze 38, off Via Nazionale.* ☎ *06-48903916.* www.hotelnardizzi.it.

Hotel Sant'Anna

$$ San Pietro Housed in a 16th-century building that surrounds a garden-courtyard (where breakfast is served in nice weather), this hotel offers excellent value only a stone's throw from the Vatican. The large rooms contain elegant modern furnishings, carpeting, and good-sized marble bathrooms; a number of rooms have coffered ceilings. The vaulted breakfast room has bright fresco decorations. *See map p. 116. Via Borgo Pio 133.* ☎ *06-68801602. Fax: 06-68308717.* www.hotelsantanna.com.

Dining Out

It used to be said that Rome lacked a really good restaurant — but things have changed, and the capital now boasts some of the best restaurants in the country. Also, as hotel dining becomes more fashionable in Rome, more and more accommodations are making the special effort to hire great chefs and transform their previously nondescript restaurants into real winners. In addition to many elegant and trendy new restaurants, Rome offers a great number of simple, down-to-earth *trattorie* and *osterie* preparing excellent traditional Roman fare. Restaurants crowd the historic center, with the highest concentration in the area around Campo de' Fiori, in Trastevere, and in the Navona/Pantheon and Trevi areas, in that order. See Chapter 2 for more on Roman cuisine, eating hours, smoking rules, and dress codes.

Alberto Ciarla
$$$ Trastevere   ROMAN/SEAFOOD

This restaurant will satisfy both gourmands looking for creative dishes and those seeking traditional Roman cuisine. The chef claims to have invented the *crudo* ("raw" — as in raw fish) Italian style, and he keeps researching new flavors: The ever-changing menu may list a napoleon with local fish mousse in white-wine sauce or his version of the classic *zuppa di fagioli e frutti di mare* (bean and seafood stew). The tasting menus range from Roman traditional (50€/$59) to the chef's grand cuisine (84€/$101).

See map p. 116. Piazza San Cosimato 40. ☎ *06-5818668.* www.albertociarla. com. *Reservations recommended. Tram: 8. Secondi: 18€–31€ ($21–$37). AE, DC, MC, V. Open: Mon–Sat 8:30 p.m.–12:30 a.m. Closed 10 days in Jan and 10 days in Aug.*

Angelino ai Fori
$$ Colosseo   ROMAN/SEAFOOD/PIZZA

A local favorite, this is another stronghold of Roman cuisine that may appear like a tourist trap due to its perfect location across from the Roman Forum — but it's actually an authentic traditional restaurant. We definitely recommend the *bucatini all'amatriciana* (tomato-and-bacon sauce with pecorino cheese), the *saltimbocca alla romana* (sautéed veal with ham and sage), and — when on the menu — the *pollo alla Romana* (chicken stewed with red and yellow peppers). It also serves nice fish dishes that vary with market offerings (check the display by the entrance). The terrace is a great plus in nice weather, but service may get slow.

See map p. 116. Largo Corrado Ricci 40. @☎ *06-6791121. Reservations recommended. Metro: Colosseo. Secondi: 7€–18€ ($8.40–$22). AE, DC, MC, V. Open: Wed–Mon noon to 3:15 p.m. and 7–11 p.m. Closed Jan.*

Arcangelo
$$ Prati   ROMAN/INNOVATIVE ITALIAN/SEAFOOD

Arcangelo's chef is among those who've taken to the trend of enlivening Italian cuisine with new combinations that grandma never made. Here the experiments are subtle and delicious — though the more traditional offerings on the menu keep your options open. The Cucina Romana tasting menu is a great choice and may include *maccheroni all'amatriciana* (tomato-and-bacon sauce with pecorino cheese) or *saltimbocca*; less typical menu offerings may include spaghetti with garlic, olive oil, and local crayfish, or perhaps pasta with fresh tuna, marinated pumpkin, and lemon zest.

See map p. 116. Via G.G. Belli, 59, off Via Cicerone, 1 block from Piazza Cavour. ☎ *06-3210992. Reservations recommended. Bus: 30, 70, or 81. Secondi: 13€–21€ ($16–$25). AE, DC, V. Open: Mon–Fri 12:30–3 p.m.; Mon–Sat 7:30–10:30 p.m. Closed Aug.*

Lunch on the go in Rome

Pizza is a good choice for a quick and inexpensive meal — and to make the kids happy, if you have any with you. The best and most convenient pizza parlors are **Pizza** (Via del Leoncino 28; ☎ 06-6867757), **Pizza a Taglio** (Via della Frezza 40; ☎ 06-3227116), **Pizza** (Via della Penna 14; ☎ 06-7234596), **Pizza Rustica** (Via del Portico d'Ottavia, ☎ 06-6879262; and Via dei Pastini 116, ☎ 06-6782468), **Il Tempio del Buongustaio** (Piazza del Risorgimento 50; ☎ 06-6833709), **Pizza Al Taglio** (Via Cavour 307; ☎ 06-6784042), and **PizzaBuona** (Corso Vittorio Emanuele II 165; ☎ 06-6893229). **Pizza Forum** (Via San Giovanni in Laterano 34; ☎ 06-7002515) is a sit-down *pizzeria* with fast service.

Another good — and cheap — alternative is to grab a sandwich while standing up at a bar counter (you can also sit down if you prefer — and pay the table service sur-charge).

In nice weather, you can have great picnics in the Pincio Gardens, Villa Borghese, and Gianicolo (see Chapter 12). For supplies, try **Fattoria la Parrina** (Largo Toniolo 3, between Piazza Navona and the Pantheon; ☎ 06-68300111), which offers wonderful organic cheese, wine, and veggies; **L'Antico Forno di Piazza Trevi** (Via delle Muratte 8; ☎ 06-6792866), where you'll find superb focaccia and bread, as well as a variety of other items; and the savory and sweet baked goods at **Forno Food e Cafè**, with several small shops around the Pantheon (Via della Stelletta 2, ☎ 06 99705346; Piazza della Rotonda 4, ☎ 06 99705344; Via della Scrofa 33, ☎ 06 68307505) as well as one near Via Boncompagni at Via Quintino Sella 8 (☎ 06 47822926).

Armando al Pantheon
$$ Navona/Pantheon ROMAN

We like to come to this traditional *trattoria,* where kids are welcome and portions generous, to find some of the old Rome spirit, only steps from the Pantheon and its throngs of tourists. We recommend the specialties, all great classics of Roman cuisine — especially the *zuppa di farro* (spelt soup), the guinea hen with porcini mushroom and dark beer, and, for the most daring, the *trippa alla romana* (tripe Roman style).

See map p. 116. Via Salita De' Crescenzi 31. ☎ *06-68803034. Reservations required. Bus: 117 or 119. Secondi: 10€–19€ ($12–$23). AE, DC, MC, V. Open: Mon–Sat 12:30–3 p.m.; Mon–Fri 7–11 p.m. Closed Aug.*

Ar Montarozzo
$$ Appia Antica ROMAN

This is where we come when we go for a stroll in the Appia Antica Park. We like the old-fashioned atmosphere and the old Rome feeling in this huge restaurant, which has several rooms and an outdoor area that fill with fam-ilies of locals delighting in their traditional weekend lunch. We're partial to the *bucatini all'amatriciana* and the juicy roasted veal.

Via Appia Antica 4. ☎ *06-77208434.* www.armontarozzo.it. *Reservations required. Bus: Archeobus, 118, 218, or 360. Secondi: 8€–21€ ($10–$25). AE, DC, MC, V. Open: Tues–Sun 12:45–3 p.m. and 7:45–11 p.m. Closed Jan.*

Baffetto
$ **Navona/Pantheon   PIZZA**

This is our favorite *pizzeria* in Rome — an old-fashioned place that serves real Rome-style pizza, which is thinner and crunchier, and has more toppings, than its Neapolitan counterpart. Its two floors get filled to the brim with young and not-so-young customers; tourists usually sit at the few outside tables. Bruce is partial to the *rughetta e pomodori* (arugula and cherry tomatoes), Alessandra to the *capricciosa* (mushrooms, ham, and artichoke hearts), but we recommend them all.

See map p. 116. Via del Governo Vecchio 114. ☎ *06-6861617. Reservations not accepted. Bus: 42, 62, or 64. Pizza: 5€–9€ ($6–$11). No credit cards. Open: Daily 6:30 p.m.–1 a.m. Closed 2 last weeks in Aug.*

Bolognese
$$ **Piazza del Popolo   BOLOGNESE**

Elegant and hip, this restaurant serves well-prepared food at moderate prices in a nicely appointed dining room or, in good weather, on the outdoor terrace. Even Romans admit that Bologna has produced some good dishes, like the lasagna prepared so well here. The *tagliatelle alla Bolognese* (homemade pasta with tomato and meat sauce) and the *fritto di verdure e agnello* (tempura of vegetables and lamb tidbits) are mouthwatering. End with something from the unusually large selection of delicious desserts.

See map p. 116. Piazza del Popolo 1. ☎ *06-3611426. Reservations required. Bus: 117 or 119. Secondi: 10€–39€ ($12–$47). AE, DC, MC, V. Open: Tues–Sun 12:30–3 p.m. and 8:15 p.m. to midnight. Closed 3 weeks in Aug.*

Cesarina
$$$ **Via Veneto   ROMAN/BOLOGNESE**

Offering a nice selection of specialties from Rome and Bologna, this restaurant is an excellent choice in the residential area north of Via Veneto and away from the crowds. The food is wonderful — go for the tasting menu of homemade pastas or the choice of meat dishes. The *bollito misto* (variety of boiled meats) is delicious.

See map p. 116. Via Piemonte 109. ☎ *06-4880828. Reservations recommended. Metro: Line A to Barberini. Bus: 56 or 58 to Via Piemonte (the 4th street off Via Boncompagni coming from Via Veneto). Secondi: 12€–28€ ($14–$34). AE, DC, MC, V. Open: Mon–Sat 12:30–3 p.m. and 7:30–11 p.m.*

Looking for a *gelato* break?

Why waste your time — and calories — with industrial ice cream when you can have handmade *gelato?* Here are a few of the best (in our not-so-modest opinion) in Rome: **Giolitti,** Via Uffici del Vicario 40 (☎ 06-6991243; Minibus: 116), is the oldest *gelato* parlor in Rome and is reliably excellent. **Pica,** Via della Seggiola 12 (☎ 06-6880-3275; Tram: 8), near Campo de' Fiori, is another good address. Near Fontana di Trevi, head for **Gelateria Cecere,** Via del Lavatore 84 (☎ 06-679-2060; Bus: 116 or 492). In Trastevere, we love **Gelateria alla Scala,** Via della Scala 5 (☎ 06-5813174; Tram: 8), and in Prati, **Gelateria dei Gracchi,** Via dei Gracchi 272 (☎ 06-3216668; Metro: Lepanto).

Checco er Carettiere
$$ Trastevere   ROMAN

This traditional *trattoria* is still faithful to the old Italian-cuisine values of fresh ingredients and professional service. It even prepares the fish for you at your table. The *bombolotti all'amatriciana* is excellent, and so are the *abbacchi scottadito* (grilled lamb chops) and the *coda alla vaccinara* (oxtail stew). Homemade desserts round out the menu nicely.

See map p. 116. Via Benedetta 10, near Piazza Trilussa. ☎ 06-5800985. Reservations recommended. Bus: 23 or 115 to Piazza Trilussa. Secondi: 13€–18€ ($16–$22). AE, DC, MC, V. Open: Daily 12:30–3 p.m.; Mon–Sat 7:30–11:30 p.m. Closed Sun and Mon lunch in July and Aug.

Da Benito e Gilberto
$$ San Pietro   SEAFOOD

Don't expect a written menu and a lot of time to make up your mind in this informal restaurant — you'll have to listen to the daily offerings and recommendations of your waiter, but go for it. Don't worry; you won't regret it: The quality of the ingredients and the preparation of the food are outstanding. The *pasta e fagioli con frutti di mare* (bean and seafood soup) is warm and satisfying; the *tagliolini alla pescatora* (homemade pasta with seafood), delicate; and the *fritto di paranza* (fried small fish), delicious. Also try the grilled daily catch.

See map p. 116. Via del Falco 19, at Borgo Pio. ☎ 06-6867769. Reservations required several days in advance. Bus: 23 or 81 to Via S. Porcari. Secondi: 12€–18€ ($14–$22). AE, MC, V. Open: Tues–Sat 7:30–11:30 p.m. Closed Aug.

Da Giggetto
$$ Teatro Marcello   JEWISH ROMAN

For decades, this famous restaurant has drawn those who want to taste some of the specialties of Jewish Roman cuisine. Some say Giggetto is a little past its prime, but we think it's still a good place to sample *carciofi alla giudia* (crispy fried artichokes) as well as traditional Roman dishes such as *fettuccine all'amatriciana* and *saltimbocca alla romana.*

See map p. 116. Via del Portico d'Ottavia 21. ☎ 06-6861105. Reservations recommended. Bus: 63 or 23; then walk north behind the synagogue. Secondi: 12€–18€ ($14–$22). AE, DC, MC, V. Open: Tues–Sun 12:30 to 3 p.m.; Tues–Sat 7:30–11 p.m. Closed 2 weeks in Aug.

Dante Taberna de' Gracchi
$ San Pietro   ROMAN

This classic Roman restaurant comprises several small (and air-conditioned) dining rooms, often filled with local aficionados. Among the specialties are spaghetti with clams, veal cutlets sautéed in white wine, and a daily soup with choice of various *sfizi fritti* (fried tidbits).

See map p. 116. Via dei Gracchi 264, between Via M. Colonna and Via Ezio. ☎ 06-3213126. www.tabernagracchi.com. *Reservations required. Metro: Line A to Lepanto; walk on Via Colonna for 3 blocks, and turn right. Secondi: 12€–16€ ($14–$19). AE, DC, MC, V. Open: Mon–Sat 12:30–3:30 p.m. and 7:30–11:30 p.m. Closed Dec 24–27 and 3 weeks in Aug.*

Ditirambo
$ Campo de' Fiori   CREATIVE ROMAN

The success of this restaurant is due not only to the perfect location and moderate prices, but also to the quality of the food and the courtesy of the service. We like the seasonal menu with just the right touch of innovation — which may mean wild boar as well as fresh seafood. We also love the vegetarian menu and the large selection of wines by the half bottle.

See map p. 116. Piazza della Cancelleria 74. ☎ 06-6871626. www.ristorante ditirambo.it. *Reservations necessary. Bus: 64 to Corso Vittorio Emanuele. Secondi: 8€–18€ ($10–$25). MC, V. Open: Tues–Sun 12:30–3 p.m.; daily 7:30–11:30 p.m. Closed 3 weeks in Aug.*

Er Faciolaro
$ Pantheon   ROMAN

Here we come, as generations of Romans have done before us, for the sympathetic service and the homemade food, which includes some hard-to-find Roman classics. Our favorite pasta dishes are the *trofie cacio e pepe* (fresh pasta with pecorino cheese and black pepper) and the *spaghetti alla gricia,* but many come for the *trippa alla romana* and the *coda alla vaccinara* (ox-tail stew). Sit out on the terrace in good weather.

See map p. 116. Via dei Pastini 123. ☎ 06-6783896. Reservations recommended on weekends. Bus: 64 to Corso Vittorio Emanuele. Secondi: 8€–18€ ($10–$22). MC, V. Open: Tues–Sun 12:30–3 p.m.; daily 7:30 p.m.–1 a.m.

Ferrara
$$$ Trastevere   CREATIVE ITALIAN/WINERY

A seasonal menu with many interesting flavors, the warm and picturesque yet elegant surroundings, and one of the best wine cellars in Rome have made this restaurant a favorite in spite of steepish prices. If it's on offer, we recommend the *brandade di baccalà con uova di quaglia e fiori di zucca* (saltcod with quail eggs and zucchini flowers). Leave room for such desserts as white-chocolate mousse with local strawberries. Wine and food are also offered in the wine bar; the adjacent store sells wine and specialties.

See map p. 116. Piazza Trilussa 41, at Ponte Sisto. ☎ *06-58333920.* www.enoteca ferrara.it. *Reservations recommended. Bus: 23 or 115 to Piazza Trilussa. Secondi: 16€–28€ ($19–$34). DC, MC, V. Open: Daily 8 p.m. to midnight.*

Grappolo d'Oro — Zampanò
$ Campo de' Fiori   CREATIVE ITALIAN/PIZZA

Across from Ditirambo (see earlier), this is another very successful restaurant serving a well-rounded menu, homemade bread, and good pizza (except on Mon). The outdoor terrace is a pleasant plus. The seasonal menu may include *ravioli di parmigiano e scorza di limone con riduzione di basilico e pomodorini* (Parmesan and lemon-zest ravioli with reduction of basil and cherry tomatoes) or *carré d'agnello con spuma di sedano* (rack of lamb with celery mousse). Desserts are simple but tasty.

See map p. 116. Piazza della Cancelleria 80. ☎ *06-6897080. Reservations recommended. Bus: 64 to Corso Vittorio Emanuele. Secondi: 8€–18€ ($10–$22). AE, DC, MC, V. Open: Sat–Sun 12:30–3 p.m.; daily 7:30–11 p.m. Closed Aug.*

Gusto
$$ Piazza del Popolo   CREATIVE ITALIAN/PIZZA

If an establishment can be all things to all people, then this is it: a restaurant, an *enoteca* (wine bar), a *pizzeria,* a cigar club — and a kitchenware store. Always popular, especially at dinner and for the weekend buffet brunch, it serves a variety of tasty dishes ranging from *carbonara di maccheroncini con fave* (carbonara with homemade pasta and fava beans) to couscous, plus wok-prepared Asian dishes. As for the pizzas, we're partial to *cicoria e funghi* (with dandelion greens and mushrooms). The wine bar in back offers a large choice of drinks, whiskeys, and grappas (Italian brandy).

See map p. 116. Piazza Augusto Imperatore 9. ☎ *06-3226273.* www.gusto.it. *Reservations recommended for dinner. Bus: 117 or 119 from Piazza del Popolo to Via della Frezza/Piazza Augusto Imperatore. Secondi: 11€–21€ ($13–$25). AE, DC, MC, V. Open: Daily noon to 3 p.m. and 7 p.m. to midnight.*

Ethnic and other non-Italian dining

"When in Rome, do as Romans do," goes the adage, and indeed, you'll find that Rome's cosmopolitan population has mostly embraced the local culinary culture: Non-Italian restaurants are rare and often more expensive. At the ubiquitous Chinese restaurant — about one per neighborhood and none to write home about — you will spend the same as in the local *trattoria* or *pizzeria*. The others are pricier, fancier places where Romans go for something special or exotic. We love Japanese cuisine, which is available at **Hasekura** (Via dei Serpenti 27; ☎ 06-483648; open daily) and **Hamasei** (Via della Mercede 35; ☎ 06-6792134; closed Mon). For Indian, try the moderately priced **Il Guru** (Via Cimarra 4; ☎ 06-4744110; closed Sun) or the more upscale **Surya Mahal** (Piazza Trilussa 50; ☎ 06-5894554; closed Sun). A few other interesting choices are South American cuisine at **Baires** (Corso Rinascimento 1; ☎ 06-6861293; open daily), Caribbean at **Macondo** (Via Marianna Dionigi 37; ☎ 06-3212601; closed Sun), and French Colonial at **Eau Vive** (Via Monterone 86; ☎ 06-68801095; closed Sun). Not a restaurant at all but rather a fast-food place is **Oriental Express** (Via Calatafimi 7; ☎ 06-4818791; open daily lunch only), which serves excellent Arab fare.

You'll find more moderate prices among the European restaurants: **Bistrot d'Hubert** (Via Sardegna 135; ☎ 06-42013161) serves traditional French, while for a taste of Mitteleuropa, try **Birreria Viennese** (Via della Croce, 21, off Piazza di Spagna; ☎ 06-6795569; open daily) or **Cantina Tirolese** (Via Vitelleschi 23, off Castel Sant'Angelo to the west; ☎ 06-6869994; closed Mon). We also like **Charly's Saucière** (Via San Giovanni in Laterano 270; ☎ 06-70495666), the best Swiss restaurant in Rome. If you fancy Greek, head for **Ouzerie** (Via dei Salumi 2; ☎ 06-5816378; closed Sun; live music Fri–Sat). Finally, though it's not really an ethnic restaurant, **Naturist Club CMI** (Via della Vite 14 on the fifth floor; ☎ 06-6792509; closed Sun) offers organic vegetarian meals with a menu that changes daily.

Hostaria Da Nerone
$ Colosseum   ROMAN

We love this old family *trattoria,* conveniently located near the ruins of Nero's palace — but you don't need the budget of an emperor to enjoy the great view from the terrace (or the good food). We like it especially for the heartier Roman specialties, like *osso buco* (stewed veal shank) and even *trippa alla Romana* — an acquired taste.

See map p. 116. Via Terme di Tito 96, off Via Nicola Salvi uphill from the Colosseum. ☎ *06-4817952. Reservations necessary Sat only. Metro: Colosseo. Secondi: 9€–14€ ($11–$17). AE, MC, V. Open: Mon–Sat noon to 2:30 p.m. and 7–11 p.m.*

Il Convivio Troiani
$$$$ Navona/Pantheon   CREATIVE ROMAN

This is the best restaurant in Rome, provided that what you're after is excellent food and not superb views (which you get at La Pergola; see later in this chapter). The classic elegance of the dining rooms is the perfect background to the unforgettable food — and your bill will be about a third cheaper here. Chef Angelo Troiani concocts innovative renditions of great Roman dishes; you may find the much imitated *sorbetto di pomodoro* (tomato savory sherbet) and the superb ginger-and-honey-glazed tuna with green-apple salad. Leave room for dessert — they're really good. The wine list is extensive and well priced.

See map p. 116. Vicolo dei Soldati 31, steps from Piazza Navona to the north. ☎ 06-6869432. www.ilconviviotroiani.com. *Reservations recommended. Bus: 116 or 116T to Piazza di Ponte Umberto I. Secondi: 29€–31€ ($35–$37). DC. Open: Mon–Sat 8–11 p.m. Closed Jan and Aug.*

Il Drappo
$ Campo de' Fiori   SARDINIAN

The subdued atmosphere of Drappo is the perfect setting for serious cuisine at moderate prices. The *malloreddus con vongole pomodorini e basilico* (homemade pasta with clams, cherry tomatoes, and basil) and the *fettuccine con fiori di zucca* (homemade pasta with zucchini flowers) contain wonderful bursts of flavors. Other typical dishes are *maialino al mirto* (suckling pig) and *anatra alle mele* (duck with apples).

See map p. 116. Vicolo del Malpasso 9, off Via Giulia. ☎ 06-6877365. Reservations recommended. Bus: 116 or 117 to Lungotevere Sangallo. Secondi: 11€–16€ ($13–$19). AE, DC, MC, V. Open: Mon–Sat 12:30–3 p.m. and 7:30–11 p.m. Closed 4 weeks in Aug/Sept.

La Casina Valadier
$$$$ Piazza del Popolo   CREATIVE ROMAN

Beautifully located by the Pincio, one of the most romantic spots in Rome, this elegant restaurant offers great views, sophisticated service, and surprisingly good food. Closed for decades, this early-19th-century building opened its doors again after 23 months of restoration to an expectant Roman audience, which had grown up with memories of this chic hot spot of the era of *La Dolce Vita*. On the first floor, you'll find a wine bar opening onto the garden; above is the formal restaurant, with an exclusive dining room in the fourth-floor tower, affording good views. The menu does not reach the impressive heights of the other restaurants reviewed in this price range, but it's very satisfactory. You may find *fricelli alle erbe con ragout d'anatra e funghi porcini* (fresh green pasta with a duck ragout and porcini mushrooms), or perhaps *costolette d'agnello con purea di melanzane al timo* (lamb cutlets with thyme eggplant purée). For dessert, try the specialty sherbets.

See map p. 116. Piazza Bucarest, Villa Borghese. ☎ 06-69922090. Reservations required for dinner. Bus: 116 to Piazza del Popolo. Secondi: 18€–32€ ($22–$38). AE, DC, MC, V. Open: Tues–Sun 12:30–3 p.m.; Tues–Sat 8–11 p.m. Closed 10 days in Aug.

La Pergola of the Rome Cavalieri Hilton
$$$$ Monte Mario CREATIVE ITALIAN

No doubt about it: This restaurant, located inside the Rome Cavalieri Hilton on the Monte Mario (a steep hill overlooking Prati), is a hike. There's also no doubt that it's one of the most magical restaurants in Italy. The site is breathtaking, with all of Rome laid out before you, and the elegant furnishings and professional service only add to the experience. Chef Heinz Beck is known for concocting unexpected combinations, such as *tortellini verdi con vongole e calamaretti* (green tortellini with clams and squid) and *triglia su ragout di carciofi* (red mullet served over a ragout of artichokes). The tasting menu is a perfect way to sample it all. Finding your way here by public transportation would be impressive but laborious; take a taxi instead.

Via A. Cadlolo 101, up the Monte Mario hill. ☎ *06-35092152.* www.cavalieri-hilton.it. *Reservations necessary. Secondi: 36€–54€ ($43–$65). AE, DC, MC, V. Open: Tues–Sat 7:30–11 p.m. Closed Jan 1–23 and 2 weeks in Aug.*

Maccheroni
$ Pantheon ROMAN

This clean, bright, nouveau *trattoria* has great food, including excellent pastas and wines, and a wonderful location only steps from the Pantheon but out of the hubbub. The focus is on pasta, and the specialty is traditional Roman recipes, among which the *gricia* is queen. We recommend the *contorni* (vegetables) and the appetizers, including excellent cold cuts and cheese. The house wine is very good as well.

See map p. 116. Piazza delle Coppelle 44. ☎ *06-68307895. Bus: 64, 70, 75, or 116. Secondi: 9€–16€ ($11–$19). AE, MC, V. Open: Daily noon to 3 p.m. and 8–11:30 p.m.*

Mirabelle de l'Hotel Splendide Royal
$$$$ Via Veneto CREATIVE ITALIAN

This hotel restaurant offers the second-best dining with a view, after La Pergola (see earlier), but at much more affordable prices (ask for the terrace). The quality of the food is excellent and the service perfect. The menu includes both market offerings and traditional dishes. You may find napoleon of zucchini and eggplant, chickpea-and-seafood soup, or local fish with capers and olives.

See map p. 116. Via di Porta Pinciana 14. ☎ *06-42168838.* www.splendideroyal.com. *Reservations necessary. Secondi: 29€–32€ ($35–$38). AE, DC. Open: Daily noon to 2:30 p.m. and 7:30–11 p.m.*

Pagliaccio
$$$ Navona/Pantheon CREATIVE ROMAN

The two small dining rooms of this restaurant are popular with connoisseurs. From the ravioli of candied lemon, celery leaves, and ricotta to the delicate yet savory sautéed pigeon with almonds to the scrumptious desserts, you will not be disappointed. The menu also offers two tasting menus (45€/$54 and 65€/$78), but your whole party has to join in.

See map p. 116. Via dei Banchi Vecchi 129a. ☎ *06-68809595.* www.ristoranteil pagliaccio.it. *Reservations necessary. Secondi: 29€–32€ ($35–$38). AE, DC, MC, V. Open: Wed–Sun 12:30–3:30 p.m.; Tues–Sun 7:30–11 p.m.*

Pizzeria Ivo
$ Trastevere   PIZZA

One of Rome's most established *pizzerie,* Ivo is as popular with locals as it is with visitors. Luckily, the place is big! Here you can enjoy an entire range of *pizzeria* appetizers, pizzas, crostini, and calzones. All the pizzas are good, but we love the *capricciosa* (prosciutto, carciofini, and olives) and the seasonal one with *fiori di zucca* (zucchini flowers).

See map p. 116. Via di San Francesco a Ripa 158. ☎ *06-581-7082. Reservations not necessary. Tram: 8 to Via di San Francesco a Ripa (on the right off Viale Trastevere). Secondi: 8€–12€ ($10–$14). DC, MC, V. Open: Wed–Mon 12:30–3:30 p.m. and 7:30–11 p.m.*

Sant'Andrea
$$ Piazza di Spagna   ROMAN

We're always surprised to find that this restaurant, only a few steps from Piazza di Spagna, has not become a tourist trap. Instead, this small eatery — with a few tables outside in good weather — continues to be frequented by locals who come for the traditional Roman cuisine. We recommend the specialty, *coratella d'abbacchio con cipolla* (sautéed onions and lamb liver and organ meat), but you can also choose from the well-rounded menu.

See map p. 116. Via S. Andrea delle Fratte 9/13. ☎ *06-6793167. Reservations recommended. Metro: Piazza di Spagna. Secondi: 12€–21€ ($14–$25). AE, DC, MC, V. Open: Sun–Fri noon to 3 p.m. and 6–11 p.m. Closed Aug and Dec 25.*

Sora Lella
$$ Trastevere   ROMAN

This family-run restaurant — created by the sister of the famous Roman actor Aldo Fabrizi and run today by his son and grandsons — was already a Roman institution, but with the recent renovations both in the dining room and on the menu, it has won new admirers. The gnocchi are superb, as are the many new dishes, such as the delicious *polpettine al vino* (small meatballs in a wine sauce). Tasting menus and a vegetarian menu are available, and the traditional *contorni,* such as dandelion greens and artichokes, are exceptional.

See map p. 116. Via di Ponte Quattro Capi 16, on Isola Tiberina, in the river between the center and Trastevere. ☎ *06 6861601. Reservations recommended. Bus: 23, 63, or 115 to Isola Tiberina. Secondi: 14€–20€ ($17–$24). AE, DC, V. Open: Mon–Sat noon to 2 p.m. and 7–11 p.m. Closed Aug.*

Fast Facts: Rome

American Express

The office is at Piazza di Spagna 38 (☎ 06-67641; Metro: Line A to Spagna); open Monday through Friday from 9 a.m. to 5:30 p.m. and Saturday from 9 a.m. to 12:30 p.m.; closed major local holidays.

Area Code

The local area code is **06** (see "Telephone" in the "Fast Facts" section of Appendix A for more on calling to and from Italy).

ATMs

They're available everywhere in the city center, near hotels, and at many post offices.

Baby Sitters

Good agencies are Giorgi Tiziana (Via Cavour 295; ☎ 06-4742564) and GED (Via Sicilia 166/b; ☎ 06-42012495; www.ged online.it).

Camera Repair

A good shop is Dear Camera (Via G. Manno 3; ☎ 06-77073770; www.dearcamera. com; Metro: Furio Camillo).

Currency Exchange

You can find exchange bureaus (marked CAMBIO/CHANGE/WECHSEL) everywhere in the center of Rome and at points of entry such as major train stations.

Doctors and Dentists

Contact your embassy or consulate (see Appendix A) to get a list of English-speaking doctors and dentists.

Embassies and Consulates

See Appendix A.

Emergencies

For an ambulance, call ☎ **118**; for the fire department, call ☎ **115**; for road assistance, call ☎ **116**.

Hospitals

The major hospitals in the historic center are the Santo Spirito (Lungotevere in Sassia 1; ☎ 06-68351 or 06-68352241 for first aid) and the Fatebenefratelli on the Isola Tiberina (Piazza Fatebenefratelli 2; ☎ 06-68371 or 06-6837299 for first aid).

Information

The tourist information hot line at ☎ 06-82059127 can provide you with information in four languages, including English, from 9 a.m. to 7 p.m. See "Finding information after you arrive," earlier in this chapter, for locations of tourist info kiosks. For cultural events, the best resource is *The Happening City,* a free monthly publication (available in English) distributed at the information kiosks. For restaurants and nightlife, buy the magazine *Time Out Rome.* Also available at newsstands are *Roma C'è,* which has a section in English and comes out on Thursdays, and *Wanted In Rome,* an all-English publication.

Internet Access

The ever-expanding easyInternetcafé chain has 350 computers at Piazza Barberini 2, open 24 hours a day, seven days a week. Internet Train has several locations, including Via Pastini 125, near the Pantheon; Via delle Fornaci 3, near San Pietro; Via Merry del Val 20, in Trastevere; and Via in Arcione 103 by Fontana di Trevi. Netgate (www. thenetgate.it) has several locations around Rome, and more are on the way; the most central are Piazza Firenze 25 (☎ 06-6893445) and Via in Arcione 103 (☎ 06-69922320).

Maps

If you want something more detailed than the free tourist map, we recommend you buy a map with a *stradario* (street directory), available at newsstands.

Newspapers and Magazines

All the newspaper kiosks in the historic center sell the European issues of *Time, The Economist,* and the *Financial Times.* The kiosk on Via Veneto, off Piazza Barberini across from the U.S. Embassy, has a particularly large selection.

Pharmacies

Pharmacies are usually open Monday through Friday from 8:30 a.m. to 1 p.m. and again from 4 to 7:30 p.m. A few pharmacies are open all night: Piazza dei Cinquecento 49, at Termini Station (☎ 06-4880019); Via Cola di Rienzo 213 (☎ 06-3244476); Piazza Risorgimento 44 (☎ 06-39738166); Via Arenula 73 (☎ 06-68803278); Corso Rinascimento 50 (☎ 06-68803985); Piazza Barberini 49 (☎ 06-4871195); and Viale Trastevere 229 (☎ 06-5882273).

Police

There are two police forces in Italy; call either one. For the Polizia, dial ☎ 113; for the Carabinieri, dial ☎ 112.

Post Office

The main post office in the historic center is located at Piazza San Silvestro 19, not far from Piazza di Spagna. You'll also find post offices at Via di Porta Angelica 23, near San Pietro, and Viale Mazzini 101, in the Cola di Rienzo area. They're open Monday through Friday from 8:30 a.m. to 6:30 p.m. and Saturday from 8:30 a.m. to 1 p.m. For information, call ☎ 800-160000.

Restrooms

Public toilets are few and far between. You'll find some outside the Colosseum on the southeast side; halfway up the steps from Piazza del Popolo to the Pincio, on the left side; and facing San Pietro, under the colonnade on the right. Make sure you have some change to tip the attendant. Your best bet may be to go to a nice-looking cafe (though you'll have to buy something, like a cup of coffee, to use the restroom).

Safety

Rome is a very safe city except for pickpockets, who practice with great skill in tourist areas, on public transportation, and in any crowded place, including stations (Termini is notorious) and open-air markets. Someone will distract you by asking for information, and an affiliate will snap your unattended bag at your feet. Roving gangs of Gypsy children are now less common than they once were; they try to surround you, creating distraction and confusion, while an artful dodger picks your pocket.

Smoking

In 2005, Italy passed a law outlawing smoking in most public places. Smoking is allowed only where there is a separate, ventilated area for nonsmokers. If you want to smoke at your table, call beforehand to make sure the restaurant or cafe you'll be visiting offers a smoking area.

Taxes

See Chapter 5 for information on IVA (Value Added Tax).

Taxis

Walk to one of the numerous taxi stands — some of the most central include Termini rail station, Piazza della Repubblica, Piazza Barberini, Piazza Venezia, Via Zanardelli, Vicolo del Gallinaccio (Trevi fountain), Piazza della Cancelleria, Piazza Belli, and Piazza del Risorgimento — or call ☎ 06-3570, 06-88177, 06-6645, 06-4994, 06-5551, or 800-090214 for radio taxi service.

Transit Info

The local public transportation authority (for bus, tram, and subway) is ATAC (☎ 800-431784 or 06-46952027; www.atac.roma.it). For railroad information, call Trenitalia (☎ 892021; www.trenitalia.it).

Weather Updates

Your best bet is the news on TV and the Web: Try www.cnn.com. (There's no phone number for weather forecasts in Italy, as there is in the U.S.)

Chapter 12

Exploring Rome

In This Chapter

▶ Experiencing Rome's great attractions
▶ Checking out other fun things to see and do
▶ Going through Rome by guided tour
▶ Choosing from itineraries
▶ Finding Rome's hot shopping spots
▶ Discovering Roman nightlife

*T*he seven hills of Rome have been continuously inhabited for the
past 3,000 years or so. The Eternal City has lived through thousands
of years of history, and today about 2.6 million people live — and many
more work — in this place designed for chariots rather than cabs, with
city buses and hordes of *motorini* (mopeds and motor bikes) buzzing
around ancient sites. They walk on ruins from the days of Caesar, turn
along the same alleys trod by masters of the Renaissance, and thrill to
the same lighted fountains that were reflected in the eyes of Fellini's
beautiful debauchers. Rome also contains a city-state — the **Vatican,** the
official seat of the Catholic faith — whose vast complex of museums,
apartments, chapels, and gardens is filled with masterpieces and riches.
Rome wasn't built in a day, or even a millennium, so don't think you can
see it all in a day: Set aside several days to do the city right.

For a service fee of 1.50€ ($1.80), you can make reservations for a
number of attractions — and even buy your tickets online — by contacting **Pierreci** (☎ 06-39967700; www.pierreci.it), the official agency
that manages reservations for many Roman attractions. Pierreci will
send you a voucher by e-mail, and you pick up your tickets at a special
desk directly at the attraction entrance, thereby skipping the line.
Pierreci's hours are Monday through Saturday from 9 a.m. to 1:30 p.m.
and 2:30 to 5 p.m. The official agent for reservations and tickets for
other attractions — such as the Galleria Borghese — is **Ticketeria**
(☎ 06-32810; www.ticketeria.it). Just as with Pierreci, Ticketeria
sends you a voucher by e-mail, enabling you to pick up your tickets at a
special location at the attraction entrance.

The **Vatican** is a separate state, and you must make reservations for the
attractions there at its visitor office (see "Visiting the Vatican's Top
Attractions," later in this chapter).

Don't pass up these deals

If you're planning to do a lot of sightseeing in Rome, you may want to purchase discount cards offered by various museums and attractions.

The brand-new **Rome Pass** (☎ 06-82059127; www.comune.roma.it) is valid for three days, costs 18€ ($22), and includes admission to two major attractions, discounts on all others, and free public transportation. You can buy it at any tourist info desk and in all museums.

If you're planning an extensive visit of ancient Rome, the best deal is the seven-day **Roma Archeologia Card:** For 20€ ($24), you can access the **Colosseum, Palatine Hill,** all the sites of the **National Roman Museum** (Octagonal Hall, Palazzo Altemps, Palazzo Massimo, Terme di Diocleziano, and Cripta Balbi), **Caracalla Baths,** and the two sites of the **Park of the Appian Way** that charge admission (Mausoleum of Cecilia Metella and Villa of the Quintili). You can purchase the card at any of the participating sites (except for the Via Appia locations) or at the main visitor center of the Tourist Board of Rome (APT), at Via Parigi 5 (☎ 06-36004399).

The complex of the **Capitoline Museums** offers a combination ticket; it is valid for seven days and includes admission to the two Capitoline Museums, in addition to the Tabularium and the Centrale Montemartini (the postmodern annex created in a former power plant), for 8.50€ ($10) — a savings of 6.50€ ($7.80).

The **Appia Antica Card** costs 6€ ($7.20) and gets you into Caracalla Baths, the Mausoleum of Cecilia Metella, and Villa of the Quintili. The pass is valid for seven days and is available from any of the three sites.

 As everywhere in Italy, bare shoulders, halter tops, tank tops, shorts, or skirts above the knee will lead to your being turned away at the entrance of churches — no kidding, and no matter your age and sex (see Chapter 2).

Discovering Rome's Top Attractions

Rome's sights could keep you going for days, weeks, months, and even years. In this treasure-trove of possibilities, you have to make some decisions. The sights in this section comprise our roster of the most important Roman attractions.

Capitoline Museums
Teatro Marcello

These museums are housed in the two palaces — Palazzo Nuovo and Palazzo dei Conservatori — that open onto the beautiful **Piazza del Campidoglio,** designed by Michelangelo. The oldest public collection in

Rome Attractions

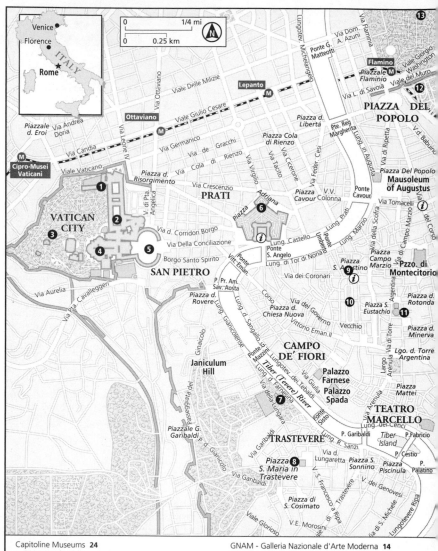

Capitoline Museums **24**
Caracalla Baths **31**
Castel Sant'Angelo **6**
Colosseum **27**
Domus Aurea **26**
Galleria Borghese **16**
Galleria Doria Pamphili **21**
Galleria Nazionale d'Arte Antica in
  Palazzo Barberini **19**

GNAM - Galleria Nazionale d'Arte Moderna **14**
National Etruscan Museum of Villa Giulia **13**
National Museum of Musical Instruments **30**
Palatine Hill **28**
Palazzo Altemps (National Roman Museum) **9**
Palazzo Braschi and Museo di Roma **10**
Palazzo Massimo alle Terme
  (National Roman Museum) **20**
Pantheon **11**

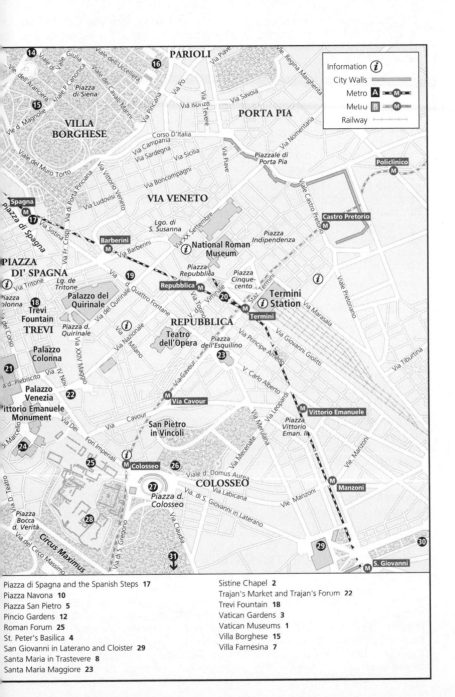

Piazza di Spagna and the Spanish Steps **17**

Piazza Navona **10**

Piazza San Pietro **5**

Pincio Gardens **12**

Roman Forum **25**

St. Peter's Basilica **4**

San Giovanni in Laterano and Cloister **29**

Santa Maria in Trastevere **8**

Santa Maria Maggiore **23**

Sistine Chapel **2**

Trajan's Market and Trajan's Forum **22**

Trevi Fountain **18**

Vatican Gardens **3**

Vatican Museums **1**

Villa Borghese **15**

Villa Farnesina **7**

the world, the museums hold a treasury of ancient sculpture and an important collection of European paintings from the 17th and 18th centuries. They also preserve the original second-century bronze **equestrian statue of Marcus Aurelius** (the one you see standing in the middle of the square is a copy). The statue was saved only because early Christians thought it was the first Christian emperor, Constantine.

In the Palazzo Nuovo, you will find famous sculptures such as the *Capitoline Venus* and the *Dying Gaul,* a Roman copy of a Greek original. The bulk of the sculpture collection, though, is now at the Centrale Montemartini annex (Via Ostiense 106; ☎ **06-5748038;** www.centrale montemartini.org). Entering Palazzo dei Conservatori, you will find the dismembered pieces of an ancient 40-foot **statue of Constantine II,** which you may have already seen in photographs: the huge head, hands, foot, kneecap, and so on. Also in this museum is the famous *Lupa Capitolina,* the wolf suckling Romulus and Remus, a fifth-century-B.C. bronze that is the symbol of Rome. On the top floor is the **Pinacoteca Capitolina** (picture gallery), a superb collection that includes such famous paintings as Caravaggio's *Fortune Teller* and *John the Baptist,* Titian's *Baptism of Christ,* and works by Veronese, Rubens, and others.

Between the Palazzo Nuovo and the Palazzo dei Conservatori, closing Piazza del Campidoglio to the south, is the **Senatorial Palace (Palazzo Senatorio).** This palace, used for administrative purposes until recently, was built in the Middle Ages over the **Tabularium,** an imposing Roman building that housed the public archives of the Roman Republic. The Tabularium was built of massive stone blocks with Doric columns in the facade. You can clearly see its remains from the Forum (3 of the original 11 arcades remain). It's now part of the museum complex, and its admission is included in the ticket. An in-depth visit will take about four hours, but you can see the highlights in about two hours.

See map p. 140. Piazza del Campidoglio 1, off Piazza Venezia. ☎ 06-67102475. www. museicapitolini.org. *Bus: Minibus 117. Admission: 6.50€ ($7.20); 1.50€ ($1.80) extra for special exhibits. Audio guides: 4€ ($4.80). Open: Tues–Sun 9 a.m.–8 p.m. Ticket booth closes 1 hour earlier. Closed Jan 1, May 1, Oct 28–29, and Dec 25.*

Caracalla Baths
Aventino

Built by the Roman emperor Caracalla, these baths were completed in A.D. 216 and operated until A.D. 537. They are the best preserved large thermal baths in Rome, and some of the internal decoration can still be seen, allowing the imagination to reconstruct what it must have been like: richly decorated with enormous marble columns, hundreds of statues, colored marble or mosaic floors, and more colored marble or stucco and frescoes on the walls. The baths in Roman times were much more than just a sauna; people came here to wash, but also to relax and exercise. After entering the building from the porticos on the northeast side, one would find the dressing rooms first and then move through the deep cleansing area, a sort of sauna similar to Turkish baths: starting with the *calidarium* (hot room) and then proceeding to the *tepidarium* (first cooling down), the *frigidarium* (complete cooling down), and *natatio* (swimming pool). Two *gymnasium* (exercise rooms) were also provided, with trainers on duty, as well as gardens for reading and relaxing. Plan to spend about an hour here.

See map p. 140. Via delle Terme di Caracalla 52. ☎ 06-39967700. www.pierreci. it. *Metro: Circo Massimo. Admission: 6€ ($7.20). Includes admission to Mausoleum of Cecilia Metella and Villa of the Quintili. Open: Mon 9 a.m.–2 p.m.; Tues–Sun 9 a.m. to 1 hour before sunset. Ticket booth closes 1 hour earlier. Closed Jan 1 and Dec 25.*

Castel Sant'Angelo
San Pietro

This "castle" is a perfect example of recycling, Roman style: It began as a mausoleum to hold the remains of Emperor Hadrian, was then transformed into a fortress, and is now a museum of arms and armor. Built in A.D. 123, it may have been incorporated into the city's defenses as early as 403 and was attacked by the Goths (one of the barbarian tribes who pillaged Rome in its decline) in 537. Later, the popes used it as a fortress and hide-out, and for convenience connected it to the Vatican palace by an elevated corridor — the *passetto* — which you can still see near Borgo Pio, stretching between St. Peter's and the castle. Besides the museum, you can also visit the elegant papal apartments from the Renaissance, as well as the horrible cells in which political prisoners were kept (among them sculptor Benvenuto Cellini). Count on about two hours for a full visit.

See map p. 140. Lungotevere Castello 50. ☎ 06-6819111. Bus: 62 or 64 to Lungotevere Vaticano. Admission: 5€ ($6). Audio guides: 4€ ($4.80). Open: Tues–Sun 9 a.m.–8 p.m. Ticket booth closes 1 hour earlier. Closed Jan 1 and Dec 25.

Catacombs of San Callisto
Park of Appia Antica

There are several places to visit the catacombs in Rome — including the catacombs of St. Sebastian, at Via Appia Antica 136 (☎ 06 7850350), and those of Ste. Domitilla, Via delle Sette Chiese 282 (☎ 06 5110342; www. catacombe.domitilla.it) — but the catacombs of St. Callisto are among the most impressive, with 20km (12½ miles) of tunnels and galleries underground, organized on several levels. (It's cold down there at 18m/60 ft., so bring a sweater.) The catacombs began as quarries outside ancient Rome where travertine marble and the soil used to make cement were dug. Early Christians, however, hid out, held mass, and buried their dead in the catacombs. The Catacombs of St. Callixtus (Callixtus III was an early pope, elected in 217) have four levels, including a crypt of several early popes and the tomb where St. Cecilia's remains were found. Some of the original paintings and decoration are still intact and show that Christian symbolism — doves, anchors, and fish — was already well developed. You can tour the catacombs in about one hour.

Via Appia Antica 110. ☎ 06-51301580. www.catacombe.roma.it. *Metro/Bus: Colli Albani (on Sun to Arco di Travertino); then Bus 660 to Via Appia Antica. Admission: 5€ ($6). Open: Thurs–Tues 8:30 a.m. to noon and 2:30–5 p.m. (in summer to 5:30 p.m.). Closed Feb.*

Colosseum
Colosseo

The Colosseum, along with St. Peter's Basilica, is Rome's most recognizable monument. However, "Colosseum" isn't its official name. Begun under the Flavian Emperor Vespasian, it was named the Amphiteatrum Flavium and was finished in A.D. 80. Its nickname came from the colossal statue of Nero that was erected nearby in the second century A.D. Estimates are that the Colosseum could accommodate up to 73,000 spectators. The entertainment included fights between gladiators and battles with wild animals. In the labyrinth of chambers beneath the original wooden floor of the Colosseum, deadly weapons, vicious beasts, and gladiators were prepared for mortal combat. (Contrary to popular belief, the routine feeding of Christians to lions is a legend.) The Colosseum was later damaged by fires and earthquakes, and eventually abandoned; it was then used as a marble quarry for the monuments of Christian Rome until Pope Benedict XV consecrated it in the 18th century. Today, the Colosseum houses special exhibitions as well as performances. Next to it is the **Arch of Constantine,** built in 315 to commemorate the emperor's victory over the pagan Maxentius in 312. Pieces from other monuments were reused, so Constantine's monument includes carvings honoring Marcus Aurelius, Trajan, and Hadrian.

We strongly recommend reserving your tickets in advance (by phone or online) to avoid the long lines. Plan to spend about an hour here.

See map p. 140. Via dei Fori Imperiali. ☎ *06-39967700.* www.pierreci.it. *Metro: Colosseo. Bus: Minibus 117. Admission: 8€ ($9.60) plus 2€ ($2.40) for exhibitions. Advance reservations 1.50€ ($1.80). Ticket price includes admission to the Palatine Hill. Audio guides: 4€ ($4.80). Open: Daily 9 a.m. to 1 hour before sunset. Ticket booth closes 1 hour earlier. Closed Jan 1 and Dec 25.*

Domus Aurea
Colosseo

The complex of Domus Aurea (literally "Golden House") was the brainchild of the infamous Emperor Nero. Built after the great fire of A.D. 64 (which is traditionally but perhaps incorrectly blamed on him), it once covered more than 200 acres, with buildings scattered over a park landscaped to look like romantic countryside with an artificial lake, pastures, and vineyards. The lavishly decorated main reception building — the Golden House itself — was abandoned after Nero's fall in 68 and buried under the thermal baths of the emperors Titus and Trajan. Completely forgotten, it was stumbled upon in the 18th century when Romans digging in the "hill" across from the Colosseum found caves that turned out to be ceilings of ancient rooms decorated with Roman frescoes. The site was excavated and open to the public in 2000. **Note:** The site is currently closed for restorations and is expected to reopen by the end of 2007.

See map p. 140. Viale della Domus Aurea 1, off Via dei Fori Imperiali. ☎ *06-39967700.* www.pierreci.it. *Metro: Colosseo. Bus: Minibus 117. Tram: 3. Admission: 5€ ($6), plus 1.50€ ($1.80) for required advance reservations. Audio guides: 2€ ($2.40). Open: Wed–Mon 9 a.m.–7:45 p.m. Ticket booth closes 1 hour earlier. Closed Jan 1, May 1, and Dec 25.*

Galleria Borghese
Villa Borghese

The Galleria Borghese is housed in the splendid building inside the Villa Borghese (now a large public park; see "Finding More Cool Things to See and Do," later in this chapter) that Cardinal Scipione Borghese created in 1613 for his art collection. The art inside is probably the most stunning smaller collection on view in Italy. The ground floor focuses on sculpture, including Canova's sensual reclining *Paulina Borghese as Venus Victrix* (Paulina was Napoleon's sister) and breathtaking marble carvings by the young Gian Lorenzo Bernini. His *David,* captured in the middle of a slingshot windup, is full of charmingly boyish concentration; *Apollo and Daphne* freezes in marble the moment when Daphne turns into a laurel tree, her fingers bursting into leaves and bark enveloping her legs. In the *Rape of Proserpine,* a sculpture Bernini executed in collaboration with his father, the god's fingers uncannily seem to press into her marble flesh. The extensive painting collection contains many masterpieces: Caravaggio's haunting self-portrait as *Bacchus* and his *St. Jerome Writing,* Antonello da Messina's subtle and mysterious *Portrait of a Man,* a young Raphael's *Deposition,* and Tiziano's *Sacred and Profane Love.* Andrea del Sarto, Coreggio, Lucas Cranach, Bronzino, Lorenzo Lotto, and many other artists are also represented in this dazzling display of genius.

 The Galleria Borghese can accommodate only so many people, so reservations are required for admission, and your visit must be limited to two hours. (The astounding number of true masterpieces will make you long for a second visit.)

See map p. 140. Piazzale del Museo Borghese. ☎ *06-8417645. Reservations required by calling* ☎ *06-328101 or going to* www.ticketeria.it. *Bus: 52, 53, or 910 to Via Pinciana behind the villa; 490 to Viale San Paolo del Brasile inside the park; or Minibus 116 to the Galleria Borghese. Metro: Line A to Spagna; take the Villa Borghese exit and walk up Viale del Museo Borghese. Admission: 6.50€ ($7.80), plus 2€ ($2.40) reservations fee. Open: Tues–Sun 9 a.m.–7 p.m.*

Galleria Nazionale d'Arte Antica in Palazzo Barberini
Via Veneto

Completed in 1633, the Palazzo Barberini is a magnificent example of a baroque Roman palace. Bernini decorated the rococo apartments in which the gallery is now housed, and they're certainly luxurious. Also preserved in the Palazzo Barberini is the wedding chamber of Princess Cornelia Costanza Barberini and Prince Giulio Cesare Colonna di Sciarra, exactly as it was centuries ago. Although the structure itself is an attraction, the collection of paintings that makes up the gallery is most impressive — it includes Caravaggio's *Narcissus,* Tiziano's *Venus and Adonis,* and Raphael's *La Fornarina,* a loving, informal portrait of the bakery girl who was his mistress (and the model for his Madonnas). Other artists represented are the great Sienese painters Il Sodoma and Simone Martini, as well as Filippo Lippi. The galleria's **decorative-arts collection** contains not only Italian pieces, but also fine imported objects, including some from

Japan. In addition to the permanent collections, the gallery regularly houses special exhibits. Two hours should be enough for a complete visit. *See map p. 140. Via Barberini 18.* ☎ *06-4824184. We recommend that you book the visit to the apartments in advance by calling* ☎ *06-328101. Metro: Barberini. Admission: 5€ ($6). Open: Tues–Sun 9 a.m.–7 p.m.*

GNAM — Galleria Nazionale d'Arte Moderna
Villa Borghese

Housed in the beautiful Liberty-style (Italian Art Nouveau) **Palazzo delle Belle Arti,** this important art museum preserves a rich collection of modern work from the 19th and 20th centuries. Italian artists are well represented, but the collection includes pieces by all sorts of great artists. The two sections dedicated to the 19th century hold a great selection of paintings by artists of the *Macchiaioli* movement and a number of works by French modern artists such as **Rodin, van Gogh,** and **Monet,** but the real riches are in the two sections dedicated to the 20th century, where you can admire a profusion of artwork by **De Chirico, Giorgio Morandi, Marino Marini, Lucio Fontana,** and **Giò Pomodoro,** to name some highlights. The collection also includes international names such as **Pollock, Calder,** and **Tápies,** among others. Schedule about two hours for your visit.

GNAM's new annex, MAXXI (Via Reni 2, off Piazza Apollodoro; ☎ 06-3202438; www.maxximuseo.org), is housed in the ex-Barracs Montello nearby; it holds the museum's 21st-century collection. Admission is free; hours are Tuesday through Sunday from 11 a.m. to 7 p.m.

See map p. 140. Viale delle Belle Arti 131. ☎ *06-322981, or 06-3234000 for reservations.* www.gnam.arti.beniculturali.it. *Tram: 3 or 19. Admission: 6.50€ ($7.80). Open: Tues–Sun 8:30 a.m.–7:30 p.m.*

National Etruscan Museum of Villa Giulia
Villa Borghese

This splendid papal villa, built by the most prominent architects of the 16th century, houses the world's most important Etruscan collection. Originally from Asia Minor, the Etruscans were a mysterious people who dominated Tuscany and Lazio, including Rome, up to the fifth century B.C. Many of the objects in this museum came from Cerveteri, an important Etruscan site northwest of Rome. One of the most spectacular objects is the **bride-and-bridegroom sarcophagus** from the sixth century B.C., upon which two enigmatic figures recline. You can also see a fairly well-preserved **chariot** and some impressive sculptures. Some of the most amazing works are the tiniest: The Etruscans made **intricate decorative objects** from woven gold. (Their goldsmithing techniques remain a mystery today.) In the summer, the garden is the site of musical events. Allow about two hours for a visit.

See map p. 140. Piazzale di Villa Giulia 9. ☎ *06 3226571.* www.ticketeria.it. *Tram: 3 or 19 to last stop, then walk down Viale delle Belle Arti to Piazzale di Villa Giulia; or 225 to Via di Villa Giulia. Admission: 4€ ($4.80). Open: Tues–Sun 8:30 a.m.–7:30 p.m. Closed Jan 1 and Dec 25.*

Palatine Hill
Colosseo

This is one of our preferred spots in Rome: Huge blocks of brick surrounded by trees and greenery testify to what was once an enormous residential complex of patrician houses and imperial palaces, built with the grandiose ambitions of the emperors. The throne room of the **Domus Flavia** was approximately 30m (100 ft.) wide by 39m (131 ft.) long. This hill is also where Romulus drew the original square for the foundation of Rome and the first houses were built: Excavations in the area uncovered remains that date back to the eighth century B.C. — **Casa di Livia (Livia's House)** is one of the best-preserved homes. During the Middle Ages, the site was transformed into a fortress, and during the Renaissance it again became the residence of the aristocracy, who built large villas (the **Horti Palatini,** built by the Farnese on top of the palaces of Tiberius and Caligula, for example).

Housed in what was the Palace of Caesar — later transformed into a convent — the **Palatine Museum** preserves the most precious artwork recovered from the archaeological excavations of the Palatino, including frescoes and sculptures (admission is included in your ticket).

The ruins here are impressive, but may be confusing if you're not on a guided tour; we definitely recommend taking one. Depending on your pace and whether you visit the museum, you should allow up to two and a half hours for your visit.

See map p. 140. Via di San Gregorio 30 or Piazza Santa Maria Nova 53, off Piazza del Colosseo. ☎ *06-39967700. Metro: Colosseo. Bus: Minibus 117. Admission: 8€ ($9.60); includes admission to the Colosseum. Guided tour 3.50€ ($4.20). Open: Daily 9 a.m. to 1 hour before sunset. Ticket booth closes 1 hour earlier. Closed Jan 1 and Dec 25.*

Palazzo Altemps (National Roman Museum)
Piazza Navona

Situated behind Piazza Navona, this *palazzo* was begun sometime before 1477 and finished by Marco Sittico Altemps, who enlarged it at the end of the 1500s. It was restored (in such a way that you can see the layers of medieval, Renaissance, and later decoration) to house the **Ludovisi Collection,** one of the world's most famous private art collections — particularly strong in Greek and Roman sculpture as well as Egyptian works. The most important piece is the **Trono Ludovisi,** a fifth-century-B.C. Greek masterpiece, finely carved to depict Aphrodite Urania rising from the waves on one side; a female figure offering incense on another; and a naked female playing a flute on yet another. The remarkable *Dying Gaul,* depicting a man apparently committing suicide with a sword, was commissioned by Julius Caesar and placed in his gardens to commemorate his victories in Gaul. The *Ares Ludovisi,* a statue restored by Bernini in 1622, is believed by art historians to be a Roman copy of an earlier Greek work and shows a warrior (possibly Achilles) at rest. The colossal **head of *Hera*** (also known as Juno) is one of the best-known Greek sculptures; Goethe wrote of it as his "first love" in Rome and said it was like "a canto of

Homer." It has been identified as an idealized portrait of Antonia Augusta, mother of Emperor Claudius. Plan to spend at least one hour here.

See map p. 140. Piazza Sant'Apollinare 46. ☎ 06-39967700. Bus: Minibus 116 to Via dei Coronari; then walk away from Piazza Navona. Admission: 7€ ($8.40); includes admission to Palazzo Massimo. Audio guides: 4€ ($4.80). Open: Tues–Sun 9 a.m.– 7:45 p.m. Ticket office closes 1 hour earlier. Closed Jan 1 and Dec 25.

Palazzo Massimo alle Terme (National Roman Museum)
Repubblica

This is our favorite museum of antiquity in Rome. The collection of ancient Roman art (from decades of excavations in Rome and the city's environs) is simply astounding — and includes, at the upper level, a magnificent collection of **floor mosaics** and **frescoes.** Entire rooms from the **Villa of Livia** on the Palatine Hill have been reconstructed here, so you can enjoy the frescoes as they were meant to be seen. (*Note:* You can visit the fresco collection by guided tour only — you can sign up when you enter, but it's best to book advance reservations.) On the lower floors, you'll find a huge sculpture collection that encompasses the striking **satyr pouring wine,** a Roman copy of the original by Greek sculptor Praxiteles; the *Daughter of Niobe,* from the Gardens of Sallust; and an *Apollo* copied from an original by Phidias, one of the greatest ancient Greek sculptors. We also enjoyed the interesting series of sculptures showing how the style of representation changed under various emperors, and even discussing the family resemblances of the Claudians, Flavians, and other dynasties.

Even the basement contains some fascinating things, such as a very well done **numismatic exhibit,** with coins dating from the eighth century B.C. through the 21st century and an explanation of the economy of ancient Rome and of Renaissance Italy. There's also the royal house of Savoy's collection of Roman jewelry, including many items from burial sites, such as a **rare Roman mummy** of a child buried with her most precious belongings. Allow a minimum of two hours for your visit, including the tour of the frescoes.

See map p. 140. Largo di Villa Peretti 1. ☎ 06-39967700. Metro: Line A or B to Termini. Bus: 64 or 70. Admission: 7€ ($8.40); includes admission to Palazzo Altemps. Audio guides: 4€ ($4.80). Open: Tues–Sun 9 a.m.–7:45 p.m. Ticket office closes 1 hour earlier. Closed Jan 1 and Dec 25.

Pantheon
Navona/Pantheon

Rome's best-preserved monument of antiquity, the imposing Pantheon was built by the emperor Hadrian in A.D. 125 as a temple for all the gods (from the ancient Greek *pan theon,* meaning "all gods"). It was eventually saved from destruction by being transformed into a Christian church in A.D. 609. The adjective that all descriptions of the Pantheon should contain is *perfect:* The building is 43m (142 ft.) wide and 43m (142 ft.) tall. The portico is supported by huge granite columns, all but three of which are original, and the bronze doors weigh 20 tons each. Inside, the empty niches surrounding the space once contained marble statues of Roman gods; most of the marble floor is also original. Animals were once sacrificed beneath the beautiful **coffered dome,** whose 5.4m (18-ft.) hole *(oculus)* lets in the light (and sometimes rain) of the Eternal City. An architectural marvel, this dome inspired Michelangelo when he was designing the dome of St. Peter's. Also inside are the tombs of the painter Raphael and of two of the kings of Italy.

Crowds always congregate out front on the **Piazza della Rotonda,** one of the nicest squares in Rome; it's lined with cafes and graced by a fountain by Giacomo della Porta. A half-hour should be enough to take in the highlights of the monument, plus another hour to soak up the atmosphere from the terrace of one of the cafes.

See map p. 140. Piazza della Rotonda. ☎ *06-68300230. Bus: Minibus 116. Admission: Free. Open: Mon–Sat 8:30 a.m.–7:30 p.m.; Sun 9 a.m.–6 p.m.; holidays 9 a.m.–1 p.m.*

Piazza di Spagna and the Spanish Steps
Piazza di Spagna

The Piazza and its famous steps are one of the favorite meeting places of Rome — in high season, it's packed with wall-to-wall tourists, lovers, backpackers, Roman youths, and so on. The atmosphere is festive and convivial, and especially romantic in spring, when the steps are decorated with colorful azaleas.

The *piazza's* name dates to the 16th century, when the Spanish ambassador made his residence here. In those days, the piazza was far less hospitable. (People passing through at night sometimes disappeared, because it was technically Spanish territory, and the unwary could be press-ganged into the Spanish army.) In more recent times, the area's most famous resident was English poet John Keats, who lived and died in the house to the right of the steps, which is now the **Keats–Shelley Memorial House** (☎ **06-6784235;** open Mon–Fri 9 a.m.–1 p.m. and 3–6 p.m., Sat 11 a.m.–2 p.m. and 3–6 p.m.; admission: 3€/$3.60). When you climb the steps, you'll find their real name: Scalinata della Trinità dei Monti, because they lead to the **Trinità dei Monti church,** whose towers loom above. At the foot of the steps, the **boat-shaped fountain** by Pietro Bernini, father of Gian Lorenzo, is one of the most famous in Rome.

See map p. 140. Via del Babuino and Via dei Condotti. Metro: Line A to Spagna. Bus: Minibus 117 or 119 to Piazza di Spagna.

Piazza Navona
Navona/Pantheon

Our favorite *piazza* in Rome, this is the most beautiful and also one of the most popular hangouts. Built on the ruins of the **Stadium of Domitian** from the first century A.D., where chariot races were held (note the oval track form), it has kept its public role to this day: Between the 17th and 19th centuries, the bottom of the square was flooded for float parades in the summer; now it is where the traditional Epiphany market is held during the Christmas period.

The *piazza* is dominated by the twin-towered facade of **Santa Agnese in Agone,** a baroque masterpiece by Borromini, who renovated and rebuilt the original church, which had been constructed on the site between the 8th and the 12th centuries. The interior was also redecorated in the 17th century, but on the lower level, you'll find vestiges of Domitian's stadium, with an ancient Roman mosaic floor. The square's other great baroque masterpiece is Bernini's **Fountain of the Four Rivers,** with massive figures representing the Nile, Danube, della Plata, and Ganges (the figure with the shrouded head is the Nile, as its source was unknown at the time). Built in 1651, it is crowned by an **obelisk,** a Roman copy from Domitian's time. This fountain came as a monumental addition to the two simple fountains already existing at each end of the square and created in 1576 by Giacomo della Porta. They were decorated with figures only later: Bernini designed the figures of the **Fountain of the Moor** at the *piazza's* south end (the tritons and other ornaments are 19th-century copies made to replace the originals, which were moved to the Villa Borghese lake garden), while the figures of the **Fountain of Neptune,** at the *piazza's* north end, were added in the 19th century for balance.

On the southeast side of the square is the famous **Palazzo Braschi,** which opened its doors in 2002 after being closed for 15 years. It houses the **Museo di Roma,** which covers the cultural, social, and artistic life of the city from the Middle Ages to the first half of the 20th century. The *palazzo* is an attraction in itself, a baroque palace with a grand staircase (Via di San Pantaleo 10; ☎ 06-67108346; www.museodiroma.comune.roma.it; open: Tues–Sun 9 a.m.–7 p.m.; admission: 6.20€/$7.40).

See map p. 140. Just off Corso Rinascimento. Bus: 70 or 116 to Piazza Navona.

Roman Forum
Colosseo

This was the heart of ancient Rome's public life, including markets, meeting places, and major religious and administrative buildings. Gradually expanded by the various emperors with the so-called Imperial Forums along Via dei Fori Imperiali, it joined the Capitoline hill — where the great Jupiter Temple was — and the Palatine hill, where the royal palace and those of other noble families were located, along a central street: the **Via Sacra** ("sacred way"), which you can still walk today. The oldest part of the forum is the **Cloaca Massima,** a huge drainage and sewage canal built under the forum to drain the existing marshes at the end of the seventh century B.C., and still in use today. The forum has many ruins (some, like the sanctuary of the sewer goddess Venus Cloaca, are just a mark on the ground) as well as a few standing buildings. The most important is the square **Curia,** where the Senate once met; most of the walls were heavily restored in 1937, but the marble-inlay floor inside is original, from the third century A.D. Also well preserved is the **Temple of Antoninus and Faustina** (the emperor Antoninus Pius, who succeeded Hadrian in A.D. 138), which was turned into a church and given a baroque facade (as the Chiesa di San Lorenzo in Miranda). Near the Curia is the **Arch of Septimius Severus,** built in A.D. 203 to commemorate his victories. The arch mentioned his two sons, Caracalla and Geta, but Caracalla had Geta's name removed after murdering him. At the other end of the forum is the **Arch of Titus,** who reigned as emperor from A.D. 79 to 81. Nearby is the hulking form of the fourth-century **Basilica of Constantine and Maxentius,** Rome's law courts.

 You can buy a map at the entrance to make sense of all the structures, but we recommend taking a guided tour. The tour in English is at 10:30 a.m. daily; it's best to make advance reservations. Allow about 45 minutes for a visit.

See map p. 140. Piazza Santa Maria Nova 53, off Piazza del Colosseo; and Largo Romolo e Remo 5, off Via dei Fori Imperiali. ☎ *06-39967700. Metro: Colosseo. Bus: Minibus 117. Admission: Free. Guided tours: 3.50€ ($4.20). Audio guides: 4€ ($4.80). Open: Daily 9 a.m. to 1 hour before sunset.*

San Giovanni in Laterano and Cloister
Colosseo

Built in A.D. 318 by Constantine, this is Rome's cathedral (St. Peter's is in the separate city-state of the Vatican). It suffered many indignities during its existence, including being sacked by the Vandals (a barbarian tribe whose name has given us the word *vandalism*), burned, and then damaged in an 896 earthquake. The basilica was restored and rebuilt at various times; the facade, designed and executed by Alessandro Galilei in 1735, is crowned by **15 giant statues** (7m/22 ft. tall) representing Christ, St. John the Baptist, John the Evangelist, and others; you can see them from many parts of Rome.

The interior of the basilica as you see it today was redesigned by Borromini in the 17th century. The **papal altar** — under a beautiful 14th-century *baldacchino* (canopy) — preserves an important relic: the wooden altar on which Peter and the other paleo-Christian popes after him are said to have celebrated mass in ancient Rome's catacombs. In the left transept is the altar of the **Santissimo Sacramento,** decorated with four giant gilded-bronze columns that are the only remains of the original basilica. Under the *baldacchino* of this altar is another important relic, said to be the table of Christ's Last Supper. The apse was redone during the 19th century, and its mosaics are copies of the original medieval mosaics. However, the fresco fragment depicting Pope Boniface VIII, who declared the first Papal Jubilee in 1300, is from the 14th century. The **Baptistery** was built by Constantine in the fourth century, which would make it the first of the Western world — except that only the walls are original, while the interior decoration was restored several times and last redesigned by Borromini (hence the title goes to the baptistery of the Duomo of Naples, still bearing its original mosaics; see Chapter 18).

From a side door, you can access the delightful 13th-century **cloister,** a showcase for carvings and other art pieces from the older basilica, including paleo-Christian inscriptions. Outside is an **Egyptian obelisk,** the tallest in Rome (32m/105 ft.), consecrated in the fourth century as a symbol of Christianity's victory over pagan cults. Set aside at least an hour for your visit here.

See map p. 140. Piazza di San Giovanni in Laterano. ☎ 06-69886433. Metro: San Giovanni. Bus: 81, 85, 850, or Minibus 117. Tram: 3. Admission: Basilica free; cloister 2€ ($2.40). Open: Daily Basilica 7 a.m.–6:45 p.m.; cloister 9 a.m.–7 p.m.; Baptistery 8 a.m.–12:30 p.m. and 3:30–7 p.m.

St. Peter's Basilica

See "Visiting the Vatican's Top Attractions," later in this chapter.

Trajan's Market and Trajan's Forum
Colosseo

Many Roman emperors added luxurious public constructions to the original Roman Forum (see listing earlier in this chapter), and each new forum was named after the emperor who built it. Emperor Trajan added the most splendid of them all, an elegant open space — **Trajan's Forum** — overlooked by a tall curved building — **Trajan's Market.** Unfortunately, many of the temples and decorations were dismantled during the Middle Ages and the Renaissance, when the marble was used for other construction, but the archaeological remains are still fascinating — plus you get to walk along an original ancient Roman alley lined with what is believed to have been small *osterie.* Walking north along the Via dei Fori Imperiali from the Colosseum, you can see the archaeological site from the outside (to your right), but a visit to the impressive brick complex itself affords an unforgettable experience. This second-century structure housed stalls and small boutiques — sort of an ancient mall — as well as meeting places.

Note: Most of the Imperial Fori were covered in the 1920s to build Via dei Fori Imperiali, a major transportation artery; today, the whole area is being dug up in the largest Roman archaeological excavation to date. The plan is to exhibit the findings in Trajan's Market. To accommodate the excavation, visitors are temporarily limited to Trajan's Forum and part of the semicircular building; the temporary entrance is from Trajan's Column off Piazza Venezia, and the reduced admission is 3.20€ ($3.80). Count on about 40 minutes for this reduced visit.

Via 4 Novembre 94. ☎ 06-6790048. Admission: 3.20€ ($3.80). Open: Tues–Sun 9 a.m.–4:30 p.m. winter; until 6:30 p.m. in summer.

A pocketful of change

In many of Rome's churches, fragile paintings are kept in semi-obscurity, but you will often find a light box nearby. When you insert a coin or two, a light pops on to illuminate a painting, fresco, or sculpture for a limited amount of time. Therefore, carrying a pocketful of coins is always a good idea.

Trevi Fountain
Trevi

The imposing Trevi Fountain, fronting its own little *piazza,* existed for centuries in relative obscurity before it became one of the must-see sights of Rome, thanks to the film *Three Coins in the Fountain.* Today, it seems that many of the thousands who clog the space in front of it don't take the time to *really* look at it — instead, they throw coins in it, have their pictures taken in front of it, and go on their way. If you want a tranquil moment to actually appreciate the artwork, you must visit late at night or early in the morning. The fountain was begun by Bernini and Pietro da Cortona, but there was a 100-year lapse before it was completed, in 1751, by Nicola Salvi. The central figure is Neptune, who guides a chariot pulled by plunging sea horses. *Tritons* (mythological sea dwellers) guide the horses, and the surrounding scene is one of wild nature and bare stone.

Of course, you still have to toss a coin in the Trevi, something all kids love to do. To do it properly (Romans are superstitious), hold the coin in your right hand, turn your back to the fountain, and toss the coin over your left shoulder. According to tradition, the spirit of the fountain will then see to it that you return to Rome one day.

See map p. 140. Piazza di Trevi. Bus: 62 or Minibus 116 or 119. Take Via Poli to the fountain.

Visiting the Vatican's Top Attractions

In 1929, the Lateran Treaty between Pope Pius XI and the Italian government recognized the independent state of the Holy See, with its physical seat in Vatican City (St. Peter's Basilica and adjacent buildings). Politically independent from Italy, the Vatican is the world's second-smallest sovereign state, with its own administration, post office, and tourist office. The Vatican comprises St. Peter's Basilica, the Vatican Museums, and the Vatican Gardens, all reviewed in this section.

Make your first stop the **Vatican Information Office** (☎ 06-69884466; open Mon–Sat 8:30 a.m.–7 p.m.) — it's just to the left of the entrance to St. Peter's. In the tourist office, you can get a plan of the basilica — very useful, given the sheer size of the thing — and make a reservation for a tour of the Vatican Gardens. You can also find the **Vatican Post Office** — with nice stamps and reliable service — and public restrooms.

Consider that at the Vatican, even the men wear ankle-length gowns, and the most popular color is black. Bare shoulders and thighs — this means halter tops, tank tops, shorts, and skirts above the knee — will *definitely* result in your being turned away from the basilica. This is, after all, the center of a world religion, not just a tourist extravaganza.

How to attend a papal audience

Many Catholics who come to Rome like to attend a papal audience, during which the pope addresses a small crowd of people gathered in the Vatican (of course, you don't have to be Catholic to attend). To do so (on Wed only; entrance between 10 and 10:30 a.m.), you must get free tickets from the **Prefecture of the Papal Household** (☎ **06-69883114**), at the bronze door under Piazza San Pietro's right-hand colonnade (Mon–Sat 9 a.m.–1 p.m.). To get tickets in advance, write to the Prefecture of the Papal Household, 00120 Città del Vaticano, indicating your language, the dates of your visit, the number of people in your party, and (if possible) the hotel in Rome to which the office should send your tickets the afternoon before the audience.

Piazza San Pietro
San Pietro

One of the world's greatest public spaces, this *piazza* was designed by Bernini. As you stand in the huge square (no cars allowed), you'll find yourself in the arms of an ellipse that's partly enclosed by a majestic Doric-pillared colonnade, atop which stand statues of some 140 saints. Straight ahead is the facade of **St. Peter's Basilica;** the two statues flanking the entrance represent St. Peter and St. Paul, Peter carrying the Keys to the Kingdom. To the right, above the colonnade, are the ocher buildings of the **papal apartments** and the **Vatican Museums.** In the center of the square is an **Egyptian obelisk,** brought from the ancient city of Heliopolis on the Nile delta. On either side are 17th-century **fountains** — the one on the right by Carlo Maderno, who designed the facade of St. Peter's, was placed here by Bernini himself; the one on the left is by Carlo Fontana. The *piazza* is particularly magical at night during the Christmas season, when a *presepio* (nativity scene) and a large tree take center stage.

See map p. 140. Bus: 62 or 64 to Via della Conciliazione; follow it to the end. Metro: Ottaviano/San Pietro; take Via di Porta Angelica and follow it to the end.

St. Peter's Basilica
San Pietro

In 324, Emperor Constantine commissioned a sanctuary to be built on the site of St. Peter's tomb. The first apostle was thought to have been buried here under a simple stone, and excavation and studies commissioned by the Vatican under the Basilica have confirmed that thesis. The original basilica stood for about 1,000 years, but with its accrued importance and stability, the papacy decided it was time for renovations. Work began in 1503, following designs by the architects Sangallo and Bramante. Then Michelangelo was appointed to finish the magnificent dome in 1547, but he died — in 1564 — before seeing the work completed, and his disciple Giacomo della Porta finished the job.

The inside of the basilica is almost too huge to take in — walking from one end to the other is a workout, and the opulence will overpower you. On the right as you enter is Michelangelo's exquisite *Pietà,* created when the master was in his early 20s. (Because of an act of vandalism in the 1970s, the statue is kept behind reinforced glass.) Dominating the central nave is Bernini's 29m-tall (96-ft.) **baldaquin,** supported by richly decorated twisting columns. Completed in 1633, it was criticized for being excessive and because the bronze was supposedly taken from the Pantheon. The canopy stands over the papal altar, which in turn stands over the symbolic tomb of St. Peter. A **bronze statue of St. Peter** (probably by Arnolfo di Cambio, 13th century) marks the tomb; its right foot has been worn away by the millions of pilgrims kissing it in the traditional devotional gesture to salute the pope. By the apse, above an altar, is the **bronze throne** sculpted by Bernini to house the remains of what is, according to legend, the chair of St. Peter.

 To visit **Michelangelo's dome** and marvel at the astounding view, you have to climb some 491 steps. Make sure that you're ready and willing to climb, however, because after you've started up, you're not allowed to turn around and go back down. If you want to take the elevator as far as it goes, it'll save you 171 steps. You must make a reservation for the elevator when you buy your ticket to enter the dome (you'll pay an additional 1€/$1.20). On busy days, expect to wait in line to get a lift.

Beneath the basilica are **grottoes,** extending under the central nave of the church. You can visit them and wander among the tombs of popes. The excavations proceed farther down, to the **paleo-Christian tombs** and **architectural fragments of the original basilica** that have been found here, but you need to apply in writing at least three weeks beforehand to arrange for a visit. Plan on at least two hours to see the entire basilica. *See map p. 140. Piazza San Pietro.* ☎ *06-69883712. Bus: 62 or 64 to Via della Conciliazione. Metro: Ottaviano/San Pietro. Take Viale Angelico to the Vatican. Admission: Basilica and grottoes free; dome 4€ ($4.80), with elevator 5€ ($6). Open: Oct–Mar basilica daily 7 a.m.–6 p.m., dome daily 8 a.m.–4:45 p.m.; Apr–Sept basilica daily 7 a.m.–7 p.m., dome daily 8 a.m.–5:45 p.m.; grottoes daily 8 a.m.–5 p.m.*

Vatican Gardens
San Pietro

People often think the Vatican is made up of only the basilica and the museums, but behind those walls lies a busy town surrounding a huge — and splendid — park. You can catch a glimpse of the park from the windows of the Vatican Museums, revealing groomed grounds, fountains, and elegant Renaissance buildings. Although normally you need a special permit to enter the Vatican grounds, you can sign up for a special guided tour that takes small numbers of visitors to the gardens. These tours last two hours and start by bus. If you've forgotten to make a reservation in advance (by phone or fax), try to sign up directly at the Vatican Information Office (see contact information at the beginning of this section) — it may be able to fit you in on an upcoming tour.

See map p. 140. Piazza San Pietro. ☎ *06-69884466. Fax: 06-69885100. Bus: 62 or 64 to Via della Conciliazione. Metro: Ottaviano/San Pietro. Take Viale Angelico to the Vatican. Admission: 10€ ($12). Guided tours: Tues, Thurs, and Fri 10 a.m.*

Vatican Museums and Sistine Chapel
San Pietro

This enormous complex of museums could swallow up your entire vacation, with its tons of Egyptian, Etruscan, Greek, Roman, paleo-Christian, and Renaissance art. Among the several museums, the **Gregorian Egyptian Museum** holds a fantastic collection of Egyptian artifacts; the **Gregorian Etruscan Museum,** a beautiful collection of Etruscan art and jewelry; the **Ethnological Missionary Museum,** a large collection of artifacts from every continent, including superb African, Asian, and Australian art; and the **Pinacoteca (Picture Gallery)** — the most famous of the Vatican Museums — contains works by medieval and Renaissance masters. In Room 9 of the Pinacoteca is Leonardo da Vinci's *St. Jerome,* which has been pieced back together — one piece had ended up as a stool seat in a shoemaker's shop; the other, as a tabletop in an antiques shop. In Room 2 is Giotto's luminous *Stefaneschi Triptych;* in Room 8, Raphael's *Transfiguration.* Other highlights include works by Beato Angelico, Perugino, Bernini, and Caravaggio (a single but great painting, the *Deposition from the Cross*).

Also part of the museums are the **Stanze di Raffaello,** which translates as **Raphael's Rooms,** although they are in fact the private apartments of Pope Julius II, which were frescoed by the artist. The largest of the four rooms is that of **Constantine,** painted between 1517 and 1524, which illustrates key moments in the life of the first Christian emperor, including his triumph over Maxentius and his vision of the cross. Along the way, you'll come across the **Borgia Apartments,** designed for Pope Alexander VI (the infamous Borgia pope), and the **Chapel of Nicola V,** with floor-to-ceiling frescoes by Fra Angelico.

Of course, it's the **Sistine Chapel,** Michelangelo's masterpiece, that is the crowning glory of the museums. Years after their restoration, conflict continues over whether too much paint was removed, flattening the figures. On the other hand, the brilliant color has been restored. Whether you like the colors of the drapery or not, Michelangelo's modeling of the human form is incredible. The most famous scenes are the *Creation of Adam* and the temptation and fall of Adam and Eve. Michelangelo also painted a terrifying and powerful *Last Judgment* on the end wall.

Binoculars or even a hand mirror will help you appreciate the Sistine ceiling better; your neck will tire long before you can take it all in. Just think how poor Michelangelo must have felt while painting it flat on his back atop a tower of scaffolding!

Visiting the whole museum complex in one day is impossible. If you don't want to take a guided tour, you can follow one of the **four color-coded itineraries** (A, B, C, or D), taking you to the highlights of the museums. They range from one and a half to five hours, and all end at the Sistine Chapel.

The Vatican Museums

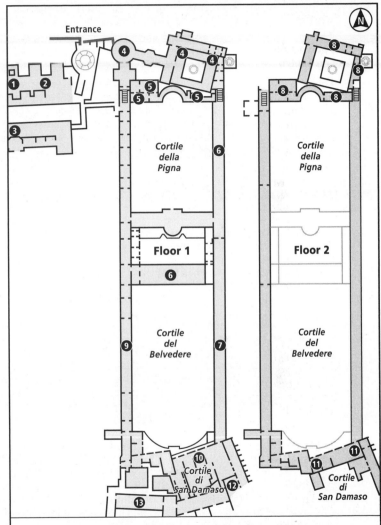

Entrance

Cortile della Pigna

Cortile della Pigna

Floor 1

Floor 2

Cortile del Belvedere

Cortile del Belvedere

Cortile di San Damaso

Cortile di San Damaso

Borgia Apartments **10**	Gregorian Etruscan Museum **8**
Chapel of Nicholas V **12**	Gregorian Roman
Chiaramonti Museum (Antiquity) **6**	and Greek collection **2**
Epigraphy **7**	Pio-Clementino Museum (Antiquity) **4**
Ethnological Missionary Museum **1**	Picture Gallery (Pinacoteca) **3**
Gallery of Candelabra (Antiquity) **9**	Raphael's Rooms (Stanze di Raffaello) **11**
Gregorian Egyptian Museum **5**	Sistine Chapel **13**

Whatever you do, we recommend the audio guide (rental: 5.50€/$6.60) to avoid the "Stendhal syndrome" of sensory overload (see "Seeing Rome by Guided Tour," later in this chapter). The guide discusses over 300 artworks; select what you want to hear by pressing a work's labeled number.

The museums are free the last Sunday of each month — and everyone knows it. Be prepared for huge mobs — or pay your way at another time.

See map p. 157. Viale Vaticano, to the northeast of St. Peter's basilica. ☎ *06-69884947. Reservations for guided tours 06-69884676.* www.vatican.va. *Admission: 12€ ($14) adults, 8€ ($9.60) children; free last Sun of each month. Open: Jan 2–Feb 28 and Nov 2–Dec 31 Mon–Sat 8:45 a.m.–1:45 p.m.; Mar 1–Oct 30 Mon–Fri 8:45 a.m.–4:45 p.m. and Sat 8:45 a.m.–1:45 p.m. Entrance closes 85 minutes earlier. Closed Jan 1 and 6; Feb 11; Mar 19; Easter Mon; May 1; June 29; Aug 14–15; Nov 1; Dec 8, 25, and 26 and other religious holidays.*

Finding More Cool Things to See and Do

Once you've covered all of Rome's musts — and there are plenty — you'll still have plenty to choose from. Below are a few more of our favorite attractions. For more, see our *Rome For Dummies*.

✔ Behind Caracalla Baths (see earlier in this chapter) starts the beautiful **Archaeological Park of the Appian Way** (☎ 06-5130682; www.parcoappiaantica.org; Bus: Archeobus, 118, 218, or 360; free admission). Here, you can walk over an original section of what the ancient Romans called the **Regina Viarum (Queen of Roads)**. Started in 312 B.C. as the highway to Capua, the road was progressively extended to reach Benevento (233km/146 miles to the southeast), then Taranto (an extra 281km/176 miles), and finally all the way to Brindisi (another 70km/40 miles). It was on this road that St. Peter, in flight from Rome, had his vision of Jesus and turned back toward his martyrdom. The street is still paved with the original large, flat basalt stones and lined with the remains of villas, tombs, and monuments against the background of the beautiful countryside. Besides the Catacombs of San Callisto (see earlier in this chapter), we think the most interesting attractions are the **Mausoleum of Cecilia Metella** (Via Appia Antica 161) and the impressive **Villa dei Quintili** (Via Appia Nuova 1092). All archaeological sites (☎ 06-39967700; Admission: 6€/$7.20; includes admission to Caracalla Baths, Villa dei Quintili, and Mausoleum of Cecilia Metella) are open Tuesday through Sunday from 9 a.m. to one hour before sunset. The best way to visit this park's attractions is via the hop-on/hop-off **Archeobus** (see "Seeing Rome by Guided Tour," later in this chapter) or by renting bicycles at the park visitor center, **Cartiera Latina** (Via Appia Antica 42), or at the **Bar Caffè dell'Appia Antica** (Via Appia Antica 175). Bikes rent for 3€ ($3.60) per hour or 10€ ($12) for the whole day.

✔ Surrounding the Galleria Borghese (see earlier in this chapter), you'll find **Villa Borghese,** one of Rome's most beautiful parks, dotted with pretty pavilions and graced by a romantic small lake where you can rent rowboats. Inside the park is also the **Piazza di Siena,** a picturesque oval track surrounded by tall pines, used for horse races and for Rome's international horse-jumping event, the **Concorso Ippico Internazionale di Roma,** in May (see Chapter 3). The park connects to the south to the famous **Pincio Gardens,** with their panoramic terrace overlooking **Piazza del Popolo** — another one of Rome's wonderful *piazze* — and offering one of the best views of the city, particularly striking at sunset.

✔ A wonderful way to experience Rome is by sailing down the Tiber on a **boat tour** with the **Compagnia di Navigazione Ponte San Angelo** (☎ **06-6789361;** www.battellidiroma.it); it offers day and evening cruises leaving from the pier at Ponte Umberto I, off Via Zanardelli, east of Castel Sant'Angelo. Prices range from 12€ ($14) for a day cruise to 53€ ($64) for the candlelight dinner cruise. If you're feeling cheap or need a way to amuse the kids, there's also regular boat service with stops at the following bridges: **Risorgimento, Cavour, Sant'Angelo, Sisto, Isola Tiberina,** and **Ripa Grande.** A single fare is only 1€ ($1.20); you can get a daily pass for 3€ ($3.60).

✔ Opening onto a *piazza* graced by an early baroque fountain, **Santa Maria in Trastevere** (Piazza Santa Maria in Trastevere; ☎ **06-5814802;** Bus: 23; Tram: 8; Admission: Free; Open: Daily 8 a.m.– 12:30 p.m. and 4 p.m.–7:30 p.m.) is believed to be the first Roman church to be officially opened to the public in the third century A.D. The stars of the show are the beautifully preserved original **mosaics** decorating the apse. Over the main altar is another famous work: the *Madonna della Clemenza,* a unique painting from the sixth century.

✔ The Doria Pamphili family still live in their 18th-century Roman *palazzo,* but you're welcome to visit their picture gallery and historic apartments. A bit worn and dusty, the **Galleria Doria Pamphili** (Piazza del Collegio Romano 1/A; ☎ **06-6797323;** www.doria pamphilj.it; Bus: Minibus 62, 116, 117, or 119) nonetheless houses some superb artwork, including paintings by Filippo Lippi, Raphael, Caravaggio, Tiziano, and our favorite: Velázquez's portrait of Pope Innocent X. The gallery is open Friday through Wednesday from 10 a.m. to 5 p.m.; closed on major holidays. It is also open on some evenings for classical concerts, which you can combine with a visit to the galleries. Admission is 8€ ($9.60), or 12€ ($14) with the concert.

✔ Even if you aren't a musician, you'll love the incredible variety of instruments — some of them true works of art — housed in the **National Museum of Musical Instruments** (Piazza Santa Croce in Gerusalemme 9a; ☎ **06-7014796;** www.museostrumentimusicali. it). Begun with the private collection of famous Italian tenor Evan Gorga (he was the first Rodolfo in Puccini's *Boheme,* back in 1896), it now counts over 3,000 pieces stretching from antiquity to the 19th century. Admission is 2€ ($2.40), more for special exhibits; it's open Tuesday through Sunday from 8:30 a.m. to 7:30 p.m.

✔ The church of **Santa Maria Maggiore** (Piazza di Santa Maria Maggiore; ☎ 06-483195; Metro: Termini; Bus: 70; Admission: Free; Open: Daily 7 a.m.–6:45 p.m.) is one of Rome's four great basilicas. Started in the fourth century A.D., it was later given a baroque facade. Inside are the original Byzantine mosaics (apse and side walls), the 12th-century Cosmatesque-style (mosaic in marble and colored stones) floors, and the 15th-century coffered wooden ceiling, richly decorated with gold (said to be the first gold brought back from the New World and donated by the Spanish queen). To the right of the altar is the **tomb of Gian Lorenzo Bernini**, Italy's most important baroque sculptor/architect.

✔ Not exactly a picture gallery, the elegant early-16th-century **Villa Farnesina** (Via della Lungara 230; ☎ 06-68027268; www.lincei.it; Bus: 23; Tram: 8; Admission: 5€/$6; Open: Mon–Sat 9 a.m.–1 p.m.) was frescoed by **Raphael** and other artists. Built as a noble residence for the Chigi and then the Farnese family, it is today the seat of the Accademia dei Lincei, a major Italian cultural institute, and of the National Print Gallery, the largest print collection in Italy.

✔ Only a few metro stops away from the center of Rome, the ruins of **Ostia Antica** (Viale dei Romagnoli 717, off Via Ostiense; ☎ 06-56358099; www.itnw.roma.it/ostia/scavi; Admission: 4€/$4.80; Open: Tues–Sun 8:30 a.m.–4 p.m. in winter, 9 a.m.–6 p.m. in summer), ancient Rome's seaport and shipyard, are less preserved than Pompeii — they weren't buried under a volcanic eruption, after all — but the site is still impressive. You'll walk on Roman roads and see the theater (where shows are held in summer; see "Living It Up After Dark," later in this chapter), temples, and homes. We recommend signing up for an official guided tour of the archaeological area. You can reach the site by subway or by boat (see later in this chapter for boat tours on the Tiber).

✔ One of the locals' preferred destinations is the small town of **Tivoli**, only 40 minutes away by train (frequent departures from Tiburtina rail station) or coach (from Rebibbia metro stop). You can visit two interesting villas here: the splendid remains of **Ancient Roman Emperor Hadrian's Villa** (Via di Villa Adriana, 5km/3½ miles from the center of Tivoli; ☎ 0774-530203; Bus: 4 or 4X from Largo Garibaldi, Tivoli's main square; Admission: 6.50€/$7.80; Open: Daily 9 a.m.–sunset; ticket booth closes 90 minutes earlier), maybe the most beautiful Roman villa that ever was; and the elegant Renaissance **Villa d'Este** (Piazza Trento, west of Largo Garibaldi, Tivoli's main square; ☎ 199-766166 within Italy and 0424-600460 from abroad; www.villadestetivoli.info; Admission: 6.50€/$7.80; Open: Tues–Sun 8:30 a.m. to one hour before sunset; ticket booth closes one hour earlier), with a unique garden full of fountains that are an engineering marvel — and a wonderfully cool place to be on a hot afternoon. Dining is also a major draw, as the local restaurants have a good reputation for traditional dishes — such as the tasty *cannelloni.* Try the **Albergo Ristorante Adriano** (Via di Villa Adriana 194, near the ticket booth to Villa Adriana; ☎ **0774-382235;** Open: Lunch daily, dinner Mon–Sat).

Seeing Rome by Guided Tour

The French writer Stendhal once wrote, "As soon as you enter Rome, get in a carriage and ask to be brought to the Coliseum [sic] or to St. Peter's. If you try to get there on foot, you will never arrive: Too many marvelous things will stop you along the way."

Once you arrive in Rome, taking an introductory bus tour of this complicated city is still an excellent idea. Doing so will help you get a general feel for the place and give you an idea of what you'd like to see in depth.

Bus tours

We like the hop-on/hop-off formula: You can stay on to take the complete tour and listen to the guide, and then start again and get off at the various stops. Here are the best in Rome:

✔ The **110 Open** (☎ 800-281281 in Italy, or 06-46952252; www.tram bus.com) double-decker buses leave from Piazza dei Cinquecento (across from Termini train station) every 20 minutes between 8:40 a.m. and 8:20 p.m. and make ten stops at Rome's major attractions. At the same spot, you can also get on the **Archeobus,** which stops at 15 archaeological sites including the **Park of the Via Appia** (see earlier in this chapter). The 16-seat electric buses leave daily every 40 minutes between 9:45 a.m. and 4:45 p.m. Tickets — sold on board — cost 13€ ($16) for the 110 Open and 8€ ($9.60) for the Archeobus (children under six ride free) and are valid for one day; you can also get a 20€ ($24) combination ticket valid on both bus tours.

✔ Leaving from a stop nearby are the **Roma Cristiana** (☎ 06-68809625; e-mail: roma.cristiana@serviziroma.com) double-decker buses, a similar operation run by the Vatican. The tour makes 16 stops at all of the most important Roman churches and basilicas; buses run daily with departures every 30 minutes between 8:30 a.m. and 7:30 p.m. Tickets cost 13€ ($16) and are valid 24 hours.

If you prefer a more traditional bus tour, several options are available. Tours usually depart around 9 a.m., 3 p.m., and 8 p.m. — with possible pickup from your hotel included. A three-hour tour will cost about 28€ ($34). The best operators are: **Appian Line** (Piazza dell'Esquilino 6; ☎ 06-487861; www.appianline.it), **Green Line** (Via Farini 5/A; ☎ 06-483787; www.greenlinetours.com), and **Vastours** (Via Piemonte 34; ☎ 06-4814309; www.vastours.it).

Walking tours

Enjoy Rome (Via Varese 39, 3 blocks north off the side of Stazione Termini; ☎ 06-4451843; www.enjoyrome.com; Metro: Termini) offers a variety of three-hour walking tours, including a night tour that takes you through the historic center, plus a tour of Trastevere and the Jewish Ghetto. All tours cost 21€ ($25) for adults and 15€ ($18) for those under 26, which includes admission to some attractions. The office is open Monday through Friday from 8:30 a.m. to 2 p.m. and 3:30 to 6:30 p.m., Saturday from 8:30 a.m. to 2 p.m. Enjoy Rome also organizes bike tours with English-speaking guides.

Boat tours

You can enjoy a simple ride down the Tiber or sign up for a special cruise with **Compagnia di Navigazione Ponte San Angelo** (see "Finding More Cool Things to See and Do," earlier in this chapter). Our favorite is the special cruise to **Ostia Antica,** which includes a two-hour stop at the archaeological area. It leaves Friday through Sunday from Ponte Marconi (Bus: 170) at 9:15 a.m. and returns at 4 p.m. (but check with the company, as schedules vary). The cost is 13€ ($16) for adults, 7€ ($8.40) for children 6 to 12, and free for children under six; you can also skip the return and take the metro, if you're pressed for time, but the one-way price is just 1€ ($1.20) less. You'll need to make reservations in advance for this tour.

Suggested One-, Two-, and Three-Day Itineraries

So much to see, so little time. In the following three itineraries, we make recommendations on how best to spend your time in Rome.

Rome in one day

It's a tall order to try to see the Eternal City in what amounts to the blink of an eye. But if you don't have more time, then here it is: Head to the Termini train station early in the morning and take the **110 Open Stop & Go bus tour.** Get off at the **Colosseum** for a visit; then walk through the **Roman Forum.** Hop on the bus again and get off at the stop near **Piazza Navona** to visit this famous square. Afterward, stroll to the nearby **Pantheon** and have lunch at **Maccheroni.** Enjoy some shopping in the area before getting back on your bus. Head to **St. Peter's Basilica,** where you'll get off to visit the church. After your visit, climb back on the bus and continue to the stop near **Fontana di Trevi** for a visit to the world's most famous fountain. Then head toward **Piazza di Spagna** and the **Spanish Steps,** enjoying a bit of shopping on your way. Have a special dinner at **La Pergola** (see Chapter 11).

Rome in two days

If you have two days in Rome, you can spend time absorbing the sights rather than just seeing them and moving on. You also don't have to make as many painful choices.

Day 1

You can begin as in the "Rome in one day" itinerary, above, but spend more time visiting the archaeological area, including the **Colosseum, Roman Forum,** and **Palatine Hill.** Have lunch at **Pizza Forum** (see Chapter 11). In the afternoon, head for **Galleria Borghese,** where you have made reservations in advance. After your visit, stroll down through the **Pincio Gardens** overlooking **Piazza del Popolo,** if possible at sunset. Have your *aperitivo* here at **La Casina Valadier.**

Day 2

Get up early and head for the **Vatican Museums** to see the **Sistine Chapel,** and continue your visit with **St. Peter's Basilica.** You'll then be ready for a good lunch at **Dante Taberna de' Gracchi** (see Chapter 11). Take a peek at **Piazza Navona** and the **Pantheon** on your way to the **Spanish Steps** and **Piazza di Spagna.** Stroll to the **Trevi Fountain** and have your last dinner in Rome at **La Pergola** (see Chapter 11).

Rome in three days

Day 1

Head to Termini train station and take the **110 Open Stop & Go bus tour**: an excellent way to orient yourself in Rome as well as a means of transportation between attractions. Stop at the **Colosseum** and spend your morning imbibing in ancient Rome, visiting the **Roman Forum** and **Palatine Hill** as well. After a nice lunch at **Hostaria Nerone,** get back on your bus and finish the tour (it's a loop) to scope out the rest of the city. Get off at the stop near **Piazza Navona** to visit this famous square; then stroll over to the **Pantheon** for a visit. Have dinner at **Maccheroni** or **Il Convivio Troiani,** depending on your budget (see Chapter 11).

Day 2

Get up early and head for the **Vatican Museums** to see the **Sistine Chapel,** and continue your visit with **St. Peter's Basilica.** You'll then be ready for a good lunch at **Dante Taberna de' Gracchi** (see Chapter 11). In the afternoon, see **Castel Sant'Angelo** and cross the river **Tiber** over **Ponte Sant'Angelo.** You can then walk north along the river and turn right at Via del Clementino toward the **Spanish Steps** and **Piazza di Spagna.** Head over to the **Trevi Fountain** and have dinner at **Presidente.**

Day 3

In the morning, explore the funky medieval neighborhood of **Trastevere,** on the south side of the river Tiber, visiting the **Villa Farnesina** and

Santa Maria in Trastevere. In the afternoon, head for **Galleria Borghese**, where you have made reservations in advance. After your visit, stroll down through the **Pincio Gardens** overlooking **Piazza del Popolo**, if possible at sunset. Have your *aperitivo* here at **La Casina Valadier**, and then head to **La Pergola** for your last dinner in Rome.

Shopping the Local Stores

People say Rome isn't good for shopping, at least not compared to Milan (the fashion capital of Italy). That may be true, but there is certainly a vast array of goods for sale in the capital city, not to mention a selection of some items — antique prints, for instance — that other Italian cities cannot match. You'll also find bargains here if you know where to look — and you'll have a great time browsing in the process!

In terms of crafts, Rome isn't as rich as it was in ages past. Alas, very few workshops still practice traditional arts. On the other hand, Rome is the capital of the country, so you can find basically everything here — including specialties from places that you may not have time to visit.

Best shopping areas

The best shopping area in Rome is the triangle of medieval and Renaissance streets running between Piazza del Popolo, Piazza Venezia, and Piazza di Spagna. On the exclusive **Via Frattina** and **Via dei Condotti**, you'll find the showrooms of all the **big names** of Italian fashion, from **Armani** to **Valentino**. You'll also see a lot of small shops specializing in everything from stylish Italian housewares to antiques. The area's main artery, **Via del Corso** — now restricted to pedestrians (except for buses and taxis) — is lined with shops ranging from fashionable to tacky and selling everything from clothing to shoes to CDs. **La Rinascente** (Piazza Colonna; ☎ 06-6784209) is an elegant department store carrying mainly clothes and accessories; across the street is the **Galleria Alberto Sordi,** a shopping gallery with many nice shops and two bars.

The maze of medieval streets on the west side of the Corso, around the Pantheon and Piazza Navona, hides a great trove of elegant and original boutiques, along with some of the oldest establishments in Rome. The area contains a huge variety of goods, from old prints to exclusive fashions, books to antique furniture. The foot traffic is often lighter here than on the Corso, which on major shopping days and holidays looks like New York's Fifth Avenue around Christmastime. You'll find old craftsmen shops on Via degli Sediari and Via Orsini; elegant men's apparel at **Davide Cenci** (Via Campo Marzio 1–7; ☎ 06-6990681; Bus: Minibus 116 to Pantheon), which is popular with locals; and, just a stone's throw away, handsome clothes and shoes for women and men at **Tombolini** (Via della Maddalena 31–38; ☎ 06-69200342), which emphasizes timelessly classic styling rather than chic. If you really want to make your friends green with envy, have a pair of shoes custom-made by **Listo** (Via della Croce 76; ☎ 06-6784567) or stop by Rome's most special source of intoxicants: **Ai Monasteri** (Corso Rinascimento 72; ☎ 06-68802783; Bus: Minibus 116), off the east side of Piazza Navona, selling liqueurs, elixirs, and other alcoholic concoctions that Italian monks have been making since the Middle Ages.

Another excellent shopping area is along **Via Cola di Rienzo,** in the Prati neighborhood. This area is best for clothes and is also excellent for shoes, with shops catering to every level of price and style. Stores line both sides of **Via Ottaviano** and **Via Cola di Rienzo.**

For a dip into romantic medieval Rome and an interesting mix of artists' workshops, crafts showrooms, and small shops selling anything from mystic art to traditional food, head for **Trastevere.** Some of the shops have been here for decades, while others are new ventures. **Via della Scala** is the best, lined almost wall-to-wall with showrooms and workshops. One interesting shop is **Pandora** (Piazza Santa Maria in Trastevere 6; ☎ 06-5895658), which carries a great selection of Murano glass and Italian designer goods; others are **Modi e Materie** (Vicolo del Cinque; ☎ 06-5885280), with ceramics from the island of Sardinia; **Ciliegia** (Via della Scala 5; ☎ 06-5818149), specializing in fashions from Positano, from handmade sandals and dresses to curios; and **Guaytamelli** (Via del Moro 59; ☎ 06-5880704), which sells sundials and other ancient time-measuring instruments.

What to look for and where to find it

Shopping hours are generally Monday through Saturday from 9 or 9:30 a.m. (later for boutiques) to about 1 or 1:30 p.m., and then from 3:30 or 4 to 7:30 p.m.; most apparel boutiques are closed Monday mornings, while food shops are closed Thursday afternoons. In the historic center, however, many shops choose to stay open at lunchtime and on Sundays.

Antiques

Rome is famous for its number of reputable antiques shops, and some of the best — and priciest — in town are on **Via del Babuino** and **Via Margutta** (a reputable shop here is **Dr. Sensi,** Via Margutta 86; ☎ 06-3207643). Don't miss **Via dei Coronari,** which is literally lined with antiques shops: Whether it's furniture, glass, lamps, or paintings, you'll find it here (a good shop among many is **Dr. De Sanctis,** Via dei Coronari 219; ☎ 06-68801254). The fun continues on the more elegant **Via Giulia;** for more casual shopping, try **Via del Pellegrino.**

Artwork and prints

If you had a euro for every picture that's been drawn of the Forum over the years, you could buy your own villa. Rome has been a magnet for artists for centuries, and views of the city's ancient and baroque monuments are endlessly reproduced. For high-quality prints, two well-known shops are **Nardecchia** (Piazza Navona 25; ☎ **06-6869318;** Bus: Minibus 116) and **Alinari** (Via Alibert 16/a; ☎ **06-6792923;** Metro: Line A to Spagna). On the upscale Via del Babuino is **Fava** (Via del Babuino 180; ☎ **06-3610807;** Metro: Line A to Spagna), specializing in Neapolitan scenes. **Antiquarius** (Corso Rinascimento 63; ☎ **06-68802941;** Bus: Minibus 116) is also worth a stop. If you're not after museum-quality prints, the nearby **antiquarian book and print market,** on Piazza Fontanella Borghese (Bus: 81 or Minibus 117 or 119 to the Corso at Via Tomacelli), is a great place to browse. If you know your stuff, you may find some treasures — otherwise, *caveat emptor* (let the buyer beware), to use a Roman (or at least Latin) phrase.

Books and magazines

Of course, it's not always the case that you're looking for something Italian; the **English Bookshop** (Via di Ripetta 248; ☎ **06-3203301;** Bus: Minibus 117 or 119 to Piazza del Popolo) stocks a wide variety of books in — you guessed it — English, as does **The Corner Bookshop** (Via del Moro 48; ☎ **06-5836942**), in Trastevere. The **Libreria Babele** (Via dei Banchi Vecchi 116; ☎ **06-6876628;** Bus: Minibus 116 to Via dei Banchi) is Rome's most central gay/lesbian bookstore. In addition, many of the larger newsstands in the *centro* have English-language newspapers and magazines as well as fiction bestsellers and some classics.

Clothing

Italian fashion is world famous. Around Piazza di Spagna, you'll find all the established names, including **Fendi** (Via Borgognona 39; ☎ **06-696661**), **Valentino** (Via dei Condotti 13; ☎ **06-6739420**), **Gucci** (Via Condotti 8; ☎ **06-6793888**), **Armani** (Via dei Condotti 77; ☎ **06-6991460**), and **Emporio Armani** (Via del Babuino 140; ☎ **06-36002197**), as well as **Battistoni** (Via dei Condotti 61/a; ☎ **06-697611**) and **Testa** (Via Frattina 104; ☎ **06-6791294**) — both men's clothing specialists. For some emerging dressmakers, try **Scala Magica** (Via della Scala 66; ☎ **06-5894098**) and **Scala 14** (Via della Scala 14; ☎ **06-5883580**), in Trastevere.

Crafts

Rome has an old tradition of crafts ranging from *vimini* (basketry) to ironwork, plasterwork to mosaics (including reproductions of Roman and Pompeian mosaics), pottery to jewelry and embroidery. For beautiful ceramic work, try **Ceramica Sarti** (Via Santa Dorotea 21; ☎ **06-5882079**) or the **Compagnia del Corallo** (Via del Corallo 27; ☎ **06-6833697**). For elegant wrought iron, head to **Nicola Arduini** (Via degli Specchi 12; ☎ **06-68805537**). For plasterwork, including reproductions of antique designs (some objects are small enough to take home; others can be shipped), visit the **Laboratorio Marani** (Via Monte Giordano 27; ☎ **06-68307866**). For handmade lace, go to **Ricami Italia Garipoli** (Borgo Vittorio 91; ☎ **06-68802196**). You'll find woodcarving at **Laboratorio Ilaria Miani** (Via degli Orti di Alibert 13/A; ☎ **06-6861366**). Handmade stringed instruments are featured at **Mohesen** (Vicolo del Cedro 33; ☎ 06-5882484).

Jewelry

Rome has an old tradition of handmade, high-quality jewelry and gold-smith work, which has been rediscovered in recent times. For some excellent jewelry, check out the **Bottega Mortet** (Via dei Portoghesi 18; ☎ 06-6861629), **Elisabeth Frolet** (Via della Pelliccia 30; ☎ 06-5816614), or **Carini** (Piazza dell'Unitá 9; ☎ 06-3210715), as well as the goldsmiths **Massimo Langosco di Langosco** (Via della Scala 77; ☎ 06-5896375) and **Ferrone** (Via della Scala 76; ☎ 06-5803801).

Leather clothing and accessories

Although Florence is more the place for leather clothing, you can find some nice stores on Rome's **Via Nazionale**. For leather accessories, the two best areas are **Via dei Condotti** (near Piazza di Spagna) and **Via Cola di Rienzo** (in the Vatican area). If money isn't an issue, check out the leather bags and wallets at **Bottega Veneta** (Piazza San Lorenzo in Lucina 9; ☎ 06-68210024; Bus: 81 or Minibus 116 to Piazza San Lorenzo), famous for its beautiful woven leather designs, often in rich and startling colors; and **Prada** (Via dei Condotti 88–90; ☎ 06-6790897; Metro: Line A to Spagna), another famous store.

Religious art and crafts

The tradition of religious objects and attire goes back to the Middle Ages; naturally, many shops specializing in such fare are located in the Vatican area. Although you probably don't want to buy a cardinal's outfit, you may want to browse the huge selection of figurines, bronzes, candleholders, paintings, crèches, and other religious objects, some of high artistic quality. Two good stores are **Ghezzi** (Via de Cestari 32; ☎ 06-6869744) and **Salustri** (Via de Cestai 11; ☎ 06-6791587), near Piazza Navona. **Savelli,** near the Vatican, has two locations: one special-izing in mosaics at Via Paolo VI 27 (☎ 06-68307437), another right off Piazza San Pietro with a huge variety of other objects (Piazza Pio XII; ☎ 06-68806383).

Shoes

Among the top names are **Dominici** (Via del Corso 14; ☎ 06-3610591), **Ferragamo** (Via dei Condotti 73–74; ☎ 06-6798402), and **Ferragamo Uomo** (Via dei Condotti 75; ☎ 06-6781130). You can get custom-made shoes at **Listo** (Via della Croce 76; ☎ 06-678-4567).

Stationery

Paper in various forms — colored, marbled, deckle-edged — is an Italian specialty and can be found all over Rome. This is one of the most popu-lar, portable, and affordable gifts for the folks back home. For especially refined stationery, go to **Pineider,** founded in 1774, with one location at Via Fontanella Borghese 22 (☎ 06-6878369; Bus: Minibus 117 or 119 to the Corso at Via Tomacelli) and another at Via dei Due Macelli 68 (☎ 06-6795884; Bus: Minibus 116, 117, or 119 to Via Due Macelli). **Officina della Carta** (Via Benedetta 26; ☎ 06-5895557) also sells paper and leather goods in the best Italian tradition.

Living It Up After Dark

The cheapest and most popular nighttime activity in Rome is a *passeggiata:* a stroll through the historic center, enjoying the magical tableau created by the illuminated monuments, from ancient Roman ruins to Renaissance and baroque buildings. Don't miss a walk through the Roman *piazze* by night, perhaps sampling a tasty gelato (see the sidebar in Chapter 11) — or you can sit on the outdoor terrace of a famous cafe and watch the pageant as you sip an espresso or a glass of local wine.

The Estate Romana Festival

From June through September — during the off season of many venues in Rome — Roman nights come alive with a series of musical, theatrical, and other cultural events. Many are free, while others require advance reservations; ticket prices vary widely, but are rarely higher than 20€ ($24). Performances often take place in some of the most picturesque locations and monuments in Rome, lit up especially for the event, which transforms the show into a multidimensional treat; venues range from the **Colosseum** to the **Theater of Caracalla Baths** (Viale delle Terme di Caracalla 52; ☎ 06-48160255 for information), where the **Teatro dell'Opera** holds some of its summer season. One of the best theater companies is **The Miracle Players** (☎ 06-70393427; www.miracleplayers.org), which performs in English at the **Roman Forum** (Via dei Fori Imperiali; ☎ 06-70393427). At the **Toti Globe Theatre** in **Villa Borghese** (Largo Aqua Felix, entrance at Piazzale delle Ginestre; ☎ 06-82077304; www.globe theatreroma.com) — a perfect replica of the 16th-century Globe Theatre in London — you can enjoy Shakespeare as well as other productions. Latin American jazz is featured at **Fiesta!** (Ippodromo delle Capannelle, Via Appia Nuova 1245; ☎ 06-7182139). You can delight in both the music and the setting at the concerts of **Villa Celimontana** (Via della Navicella; ☎ 06-7182139). And **Gay Village** (☎ 340-5423008; www.gayvillage.it) includes music and theater performances, as well as disco and other entertainment particularly geared to gays and lesbians. Other venues during the festival include **Castel Sant'Angelo** (Lungotevere Castello 50; ☎ 06-32869 or 06-32861) and the **Roman Theater of Ostia Antica** (Viale dei Romagnoli 717, Ostia Antica; ☎ 06-56352850). You can find details on the festival by going to www.estate romana.comune.roma.it (also in English) or calling ☎ 06-68809505 Monday through Saturday between 10 a.m. and 5 p.m.

You'll find a very lively cultural life in Rome: Italy's capital and a major art city with a long cultural tradition and international visibility, it attracts all kinds of world-famous artists and performers. For a schedule of events in the city, pick up or download a copy of *The Happening City,* an excellent monthly review published by Rome's tourist board; it's available online at www.romaturismo.it.

The opera, classical concerts, and ballet always call for elegant dress, as do the most famous theaters and even the best jazz clubs. People dress up to go out, even just for drinks. More-casual attire is okay for other venues and shows.

The performing arts

Rome offers splendid opportunities for lovers of the performing arts. Concerts, theater, dance, ballet, and opera are scheduled throughout the year. Expect to pay between 10€ and 120€ ($12–$144) depending on the venue, the performer, and the quality of the seat. Free or very inexpensive concerts are also often available. You can get a full schedule of events from the tourist office. To make reservations and buy tickets in advance, try a ticket service such as the Italian **TicketOne** (☎ 02-392261 for an English-speaking operator; www.ticketone.it) or the British **Global Edwards & Edwards** (☎ 800-223-6108 in the U.S.), or go directly to the Web sites of the following venues:

✔ **Parco della Musica** (Viale Coubertin 34; ☎ 06-8082058; www.auditorium.com; Bus: M from Piazza del Popolo), with three concert halls as well as other structures, including **La Cavea,** a 3,000-seat outdoor concert space reminiscent of a classical amphitheater. In addition to classical, pop, and contemporary music, you can see theater and dance performances here as well. Restaurants, stores, lecture halls, and a host of other activities and services are located on-site.

✔ **Teatro dell'Opera** (Piazza Beniamino Gigli 1, just off Via Nazionale; ☎ 06-48160255; www.opera.roma.it; Metro: Line A to Repubblica; Bus: Minibus 116 to Via A. Depretis), a beautiful venue built at the end of the 19th century, hosts opera as well as ballet and classical concerts.

✔ **Teatro Olimpico** (Piazza Gentile da Fabriano; ☎ 06-3265991; www.teatroolimpico.it; Tram: 225 from Piazzale Flaminio), another great space, hosts musical performances of all kinds.

Keep in mind that the curtain is usually right on time, and if you miss yours, you'll usually have to wait until intermission to get to your seat. It's also customary to give a small tip to your usher.

All that jazz and more

Romans love jazz, and the city is home to many first-rate jazz venues featuring excellent local musicians as well as all the big names of the international scene. Most clubs are in Trastevere and in Prati. They open their doors around 10 p.m. and close around 3 a.m. Cover charges vary depending on the event and the club, but usually range from 7€ ($8.40) for a regular night all the way up to 30€ ($36) for special concerts. Reservations are recommended at all the top venues.

The most famous jazz clubs are the **Alexanderplatz** (Via Ostia 9, just off the Musei Vaticani; ☎ **06-39742171;** www.alexanderplatz.it; Metro: Line A to Ottaviano/San Pietro; Bus: 23 to Via Leone IV); **Big Mama** (Vicolo San Francesco a Ripa 18 in Trastevere; ☎ **06-5812551;** www.bigmama.it; Metro: Piramide; Tram: 8); and the **Fonclea** (Via Crescenzio 82/a, behind Castel Sant'Angelo; ☎ **06-6896302;** www.fonclea.it; Bus: 23 to Via Crescenzio), which also has some excellent ethnic and other concerts.

In addition to jazz and contemporary music, you may hear traditional Italian songs at **Arciliuto** (Piazza Montevecchio 5; ☎ **06-6879419;** Bus: 62 or 64 to Corso Vittorio Emanuele), located in the maze of streets behind Piazza Navona.

The **Centrale RistoTheatre** (Via Celsa 6, off Piazza del Gesu; ☎ **06-6780501;** www.centraleristotheatre.com) is an ultramodern restaurant–cabaret–theater hall presenting musical and theatrical performances that you can enjoy over an *aperitivo* or full dinner. The dinner is at 7:30 p.m.; the live show is at 10:30 p.m.

Historic cafes

Rome boasts some famous cafes that haven't lost their glamour since first opening in the 18th century. Although some are protected historic sites, they still operate as regular Italian-style bars (see Chapter 2 for more about bars in Italy), opening early in the morning — usually by 8 a.m. — and closing around 9 or 10 p.m. All are in the historic center.

The **Antico Caffè della Pace** (Via della Pace 3–7; ☎ **06-6861216;** Bus: Minibus 116 to Piazza Navona) is one of the most popular cafes in the city — folks here linger at outdoor tables opening onto a romantic little square. Another sought-after spot is the beautifully furnished **Caffè Greco** (Via Condotti 84; ☎ **06-6791700;** Metro: Line A to Spagna); among its customers were famous writers like Stendhal, Goethe, and Keats. Also noteworthy is the **Caffè Rosati** (Piazza del Popolo 4–5; ☎ **06-3225859;** Bus: Minibus 117 or 119), which retains its 1920s Art Nouveau décor.

Wine bars and pubs

Rome has many a fine *enoteca* (wine shop), a very popular hangout for young and not-so-young Romans. Some of them are regular wine shops that turn into a wine bar–cum–restaurant after 8 p.m. (and sometimes also at lunch, between 1 and 3 p.m.). Others are wine bars that open exclusively in the evening, usually from 8 p.m. to 1 a.m. They're scattered everywhere in Rome, with some of the most popular located in the *centro*, In particular the Pantheon/Navona, Colosseo, Trastevere, and Campo de' Fiori areas.

The granddaddy of Roman wine stores, **Trimani** (Via Goito 20; ☎ 06-4469661; www.trimani.com; Bus: 60 or 62; closed Sun and Aug), has been run by the same family since 1821. Its happening wine bar is set in the old residential neighborhood behind the Terme di Diocleziano. Across town, the exceedingly popular but old-fashioned wine bar called **Vineria** (Campo de' Fiori 15; ☎ 06-68803268) still holds its own amid the nightly crowds swarming this trendy *piazza*, popular with all age groups. For something calmer, try the intimate wine bar at **Gusto** (see Chapter 11).

For something less Italian, head to **Drunken Ship** (Campo de' Fiori 20; ☎ 06-68300535), an American-style bar with a DJ, often jammed with people; **The Albert** (Via del Traforo 132, off Via del Tritone, before the tunnel; ☎ 06-4818795), a real English pub imported from the old country; or one of the many Irish pubs around. Of the latter, we think the nicest ones are **Mad Jack** (Via Arenula 20, off Largo Argentina; ☎ 06-68808223), with live music on Wednesday and Thursday; and **Abbey Theatre Irish Pub** (Via del Governo Vecchio 51–53, near Piazza Navona; ☎ 06-6861341).

Dance clubs

Romans, especially the younger set, love dancing, and clubs abound. Cover charges hover between 10€ and 20€ ($12–$24) for the hippest venues. They usually open around 10:30 p.m. and close around 4 a.m.

Alpheus (Via del Commercio 36, near Via Ostiense; ☎ 06-5747826; Bus: 23, but best to take a cab) has several halls offering different kinds of music, from jazz to Latin to straight-ahead rock. **Alien** (Via Velletri 13–19; ☎ 06-8412212; www.aliendisco.it; Bus: 490 to Piazza Fiume) is Rome's clubbiest club — with mirrors, strobe lights, and a New York–style atmosphere appealing to a frenetic 20-something crowd. Not to be outdone is **Gilda** (Via Mario de Fiori 97; ☎ 06-6797396; www.gilda discoclub.it; Metro: Line A to Spagna), which caters to an older crowd and plays classic rock as well as some newer stuff.

Gay and lesbian bars

Rome has a lively gay scene with gay clubs scattered around the city (although the area between San Giovanni and the Colosseo has been developing as a small gay enclave). They observe the same hours as other clubs and discos in town. The cover usually runs about 10€ ($12).

Trends change quickly, but at press time, **Alibi** (Via di Monte Testaccio 40–44; ☎ 06-5743448; www.alibionline.it; Bus: 23; Tram: 3, though taking a cab is best), followed by **Angelo Azzurro** (Via Cardinale Merry del Val 13 in Trastevere; ☎ 06-5800472; Tram: 8 to Viale Trastevere at Piazza Mastai) were the hot gay clubs, while **The Frequency** (Viale Odoardo Beccari 10; ☎ 06-7851504) was the trendiest cruising bar. The leading lesbian club was **New Joli Coeur** (Via Sirte 5; ☎ 06-86215827; Bus: 56 or 88 to Piazza Sant'Emerenziana).

Part IV
Florence and the Best of Tuscany and Umbria

The 5th Wave   By Rich Tennant

In this part . . .

Tuscany is the most visited region in Italy, and its concentration of attractions — sights, scenery, food, and wine — is beyond compare. Practically every hill town offers something interesting to visit. (This is true of all of Italy, but you'll find so many more hills in Tuscany!) Tuscany has proud traditions and a unique character and flavor, including the regional delicacies that each part of Italy seems to offer. Umbria follows close behind, with a more dramatic landscape, a great number of art towns, and a delicious cuisine. Perugia, a city on a hill (of course) with a rich artistic patrimony, is Umbria's capital. In the following chapters, we give you the top of the top, the not-to-be-missed things to see and do in these regions.

Chapter 13 is dedicated to the beautiful city of Florence. Chapter 14 covers the northern Tuscan towns of Lucca and Pisa and detours to the Italian Riviera for a glimpse of the Cinque Terre, the five fishing villages of Monterosso al Mare, Vernazza, Corniglia, Manarola, and Riomaggiore. In Chapter 15, we take you to southern Tuscany to explore Siena, San Gimignano, and the rest of the Chianti region, as well as to Umbrian cities such as Assisi, Perugia, and Spoleto.

Chapter 13

Florence

● ●

In This Chapter

▶ Finding your way to and around Florence

▶ Discovering the best neighborhoods, hotels, and restaurants

▶ Exploring the magnificent sights of Florence

▶ Getting the scoop on the best shopping areas and nightlife

● ●

*F*lorence maintains its compact medieval scale and Renaissance core, and at the same time feels like a real place; the city is also one of the world's most incredible repositories of art and architecture, home to such treasures as the paintings by Botticelli and Leonardo in the Galleria degli Uffizi, Michelangelo's *David* in the Galleria dell'Accademia, Brunelleschi's dome crowning the Duomo (Santa Maria del Fiore), Giotto's Campanile (bell tower), Ghiberti's "Gates of Paradise" on the Baptistery (Battistero di San Giovanni), and the Ponte Vecchio over the Arno River. These treasures have made Florence into one of the paramount tourist stops in Italy, starting back in the 18th century with the Grand Tour (the cultural trip that educated people took through Europe). Tourism has exploded in recent years — this relatively small town is now crammed with six million visitors annually.

Florence has much to see, but it's small. Three days are enough to do everything, but you can hit the highlights in less time, especially if you have children with you — younger ones will rapidly succumb to "museum overload."

Getting There

By air

Florence is served by its own airport, the **Aeroporto Amerigo Vespucci (Peretola)**, and by Pisa's nearby **Aeroporto Galileo Galilei** (see Chapter 14). There are no direct flights from the United States to Florence or

Pisa, but connecting flights are available from a number of European and Italian cities. Below are tips for getting through the airport and to your hotel:

✔ **Getting oriented at the airport:** Both airports are small (Pisa's is the larger of the two) and easy to get around. ATMs, currency-exchange booths, and tourist information desks can be found at both airports in the arrivals concourse.

✔ **Navigating your way through passport control and Customs:** As these are not major international airports, most of the flights originate from within the European Union. Only those flights from countries outside the Schengen European Community are subject to passport control. In most cases, you'll go directly to baggage claim and then through Customs, where you'll find two gates: one for those who have something to declare (beyond the standard allowance), and one for those who don't.

✔ **Getting from Florence's airport to your hotel:** Locally referred to as **Peretola** after the name of the village nearby, the **Aeroporto Amerigo Vespucci** (☎ 055-3061300; www.aeroporto.firenze.it) is only 4km (2½ miles) outside of Florence, a few minutes away by public transportation. You'll find everything just outside the arrivals concourse on your right. A **taxi** will take about 15 minutes and cost about 20€ ($24). The **Volainbus shuttle bus** (SITA: ☎ 800-373760; ATAF: ☎ 800-424500; www.ataf.net) costs 4€ ($4.80); you can buy tickets on board. Shuttles leave for the 25-minute trip every 20 minutes between 5:30 a.m. and 8:30 p.m. and hourly later on, arriving at Florence's SITA bus terminal, just behind the central rail station of Santa Maria Novella. You can also get into town by taking the regular **city bus no. 62,** which takes about half an hour and also arrives at Santa Maria Novella; the fare is 0.80€ (90¢).

✔ **Getting from Pisa's airport to your hotel:** The **Aeroporto Galileo Galilei** (☎ 050-849111; www.pisa-airport.com) is 80km (50 miles) west of Florence. The easiest way to get into town is to board the dedicated **shuttle train** (☎ 892021; www.trenitalia.it) from the airport's terminal; it arrives at Florence's air terminal inside Santa Maria Novella rail station. The shuttle makes ten runs a day, takes about an hour, and costs about 4.95€ ($5.90).

By train

If you aren't flying, the train (☎ 892021; www.trenitalia.it) is the best way to get to Florence: Frequent and fast service exists from all major Italian towns. It will take you only about two hours from Rome and three from Venice, depending on the kind of train (intercity or the faster Eurostar). Trains arrive at Florence's main station, Santa Maria Novella, often abbreviated **SMN Firenze** (☎ 055-288765); you'll find a luggage check at the head of Track 16. Also at the station are a last-minute hotel-reservations desk and a tourist information desk that distributes a free city map; this is where you can pick up your reserved tickets for the

Uffizi or the Accademia (see the tip under "Exploring Florence," later in this chapter). Public transportation is just outside the station: You'll see a taxi stand and a bus terminal with lines to basically anywhere in town. The station is also within walking distance of a number of attractions.

By car

Florence lies on *autostrada* A1, in a good central position, only 277km (172 miles) north of Rome and 298km (185 miles) south of Milan.

 If you're planning a driving tour of smaller towns in Tuscany, schedule it before or after your stay in Florence; that way, you can either drop off the car when you arrive or pick it up when you're ready to leave. You'll spare yourself a few headaches, as Florence's center is closed to traffic. Parking lots are to the north of the historic district, under the SMN train station and under Piazza Libertà, north of Fortezza da Basso.

Orienting Yourself in Florence

Florence developed beyond its medieval perimeter only toward the end of the 19th century, and the new areas have little historic interest. The old part of town is quite small and has a relatively simple layout, bisected east–west by the river Arno. The heart of the historic center is on the north — or right — bank of the river. To the north of the center lies the **Santa Maria Novella train station** and **Fortezza da Basso**, a fortress and armory now transformed into an exposition hall. The top attractions are mostly clustered on this bank, around **Piazza del Duomo, Piazza della Repubblica**, and **Piazza della Signoria**. North–south streets run toward the river, **Via dei Calzaiuoli** and **Via Ricasoli** being the most central. Four bridges cross the Arno within the historic center, but chances are that you'll use only two of them: the famous **Ponte Vecchio**, the most central, and **Ponte Santa Trinità**, the next bridge west. The left bank of the Arno river is **Oltrarno**, literally meaning "on the other side of the Arno"; its main hubs are **Piazza del Carmine** and **Piazza Santo Spirito**.

Introducing the neighborhoods

Here we highlight the neighborhoods in Florence where you'll spend most of your time as a visitor: all are equally safe, but each has its own character which will make it more or less appealing to you.

Accademia

At the northeast corner of the historic district, this neighborhood develops around **Piazza San Marco**, where many bus lines cross. The main attraction here is the **Accademia**, with Michelangelo's famous *David.* This is a quiet and accessible neighborhood with many picturesque streets and what we feel is Florence's prettiest *piazza* (Santissima Annunziata).

Florence Orientation

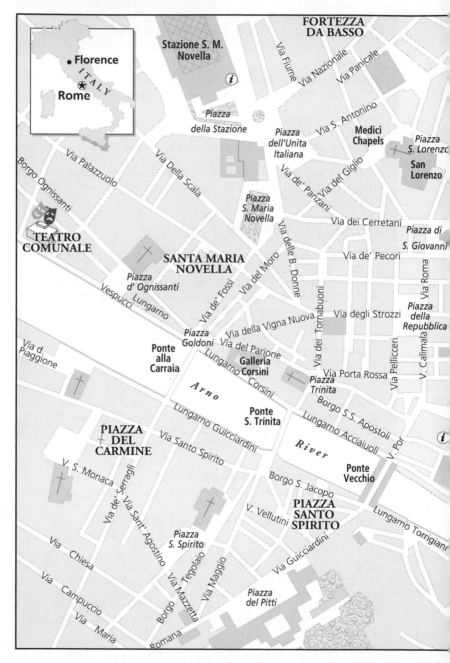

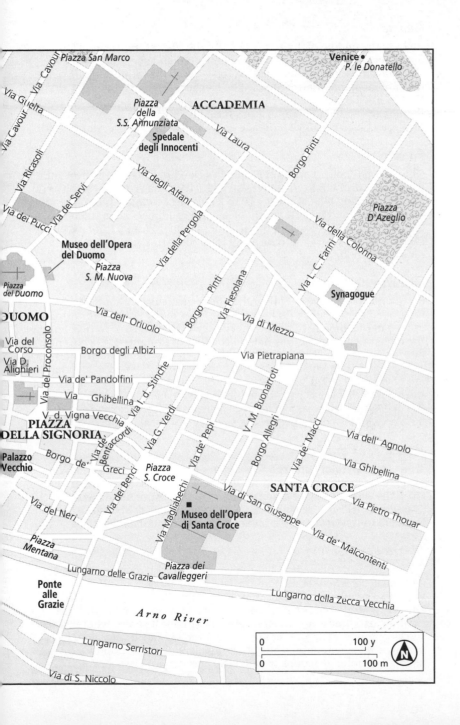

Piazza San Marco

Venice•
P. le Donatello

Via Cavour

Via Cavour

Via Guelfa

Via Cavour

Via Ricasoli

Piazza della S.S. Annunziata

ACCADEMIA

Via Laura

Borgo Pinti

Spedale degli Innocenti

Via degli Alfani

Via dei Servi

Via dei Pucci

Via della Pergola

Via della Colonna

Piazza D'Azeglio

Via L. C. Farini

Museo dell'Opera del Duomo

Piazza S. M. Nuova

Piazza del Duomo

Pinti

Via Fiesolana

Synagogue

DUOMO

Via dell' Oriuolo

Borgo

Via di Mezzo

Via del Corso

Via D. Alighieri

Borgo degli Albizi

Via Pietrapiana

Via del Proconsolo

Via de' Pandolfini

Via Ghibellina

Via I. d. Stinche

V. d. Vigna Vecchia

Via de' Benci

PIAZZA DELLA SIGNORIA

Via di Bentaccordi

Via G. Verdi

Via de' Pepi

Borgo Allegri

Via de' Macci

Via dell' Agnolo

Palazzo Vecchio

Borgo de' Greci

Piazza S. Croce

V. M. Buonarroti

Via Ghibellina

Via del Neri

Via dei Benci

Via Maglabechi

Via di San Giuseppe

SANTA CROCE

Via Pietro Thouar

■ **Museo dell'Opera di Santa Croce**

Via de' Malcontenti

Piazza Mentana

Lungarno delle Grazie

Piazza dei Cavalleggeri

Lungarno della Zecca Vecchia

Ponte alle Grazie

Arno River

Lungarno Serristori

Via di S. Niccolo

0	100 y
0	100 m

N

Duomo

Right in the middle of it all, this neighborhood centers around Florence's magnificent **Duomo.** It is very well connected and serviced, with all kinds of shops, restaurants, and hotels — plus it's within walking distance of most major attractions. The elegant commercial district along **Via dei Tornabuoni** is nearby, as is the business area near Piazza della Repubblica and Via Roma. Visitors based here will feel in touch with the everyday business life of Florence as well as with its more touristy side.

Fiesole

Only 4.5km (3 miles) north of Florence's Duomo, **Fiesole** is a pleasant small town on a hill from which you get marvelous views of the city and the surrounding hills. It is only 10 to 20 minutes away by bus, depending on the traffic, and is particularly pleasant in summer, when it offers a cool, welcoming break from the stuffiness below. Fiesole is an excellent place to stay if you want to be away from the crowds; it also makes a nice dinner outing.

Fortezza da Basso

On the northeast side of SMN rail station, this neighborhood has grown up around the **Fortezza da Basso.** It includes many hotels and restaurants catering mostly to businesspeople working in the area or attending the commercial expositions held in the Centro Congressi (Expo Centre) inside the fortress. Within walking distance of the *centro storico* and very well connected, it offers an excellent compromise: The hotel standards are high here, but the prices aren't marked up because this is away from the main tourist area. The downside to staying here is that it's outside the pedestrian zone, so you'll have to deal with car noise and exhaust. It's also a bit less picturesque, but you get more real-life surroundings.

Piazza del Carmine

The western half of **Oltrarno** was included within the walls of Florence "only" in 1173. With many restaurants opening in the streets near the river, the whole area has taken on some of the characteristics of Trastevere in Rome — especially the old popular neighborhood of San Frediano to the west, once a bit seedy and today bohemian.

Piazza della Signoria

This is the heart of medieval Florence. Packed with monuments and museums, it's where you'll find the **Uffizi,** the **Bargello,** and **Ponte Vecchio.** Completely closed to traffic — public buses and electric *navettes* (shuttle buses) excluded — it is a visitor's heaven, with many exciting restaurants and most of the best hotels. It is also where you'll see all of the tourists who come to town, which may bother you. Its narrow streets and hidden alleys, though, are delightful, and we love having our hotel just steps from all the best art in Florence. You'll also see locals, who come here all the time to shop and dine in the many fine restaurants.

Piazza Santo Spirito

Also included within the walls of Florence in 1173, the eastern part of **Oltrarno** was and still is a quiet and elegant residential area. This is where the rulers of Florence decided to build their last palace: **Palazzo Pitti.** You'll find fewer attractions here, yet the magic of the medieval city is still present, with the great advantage of reduced crowds and a more real neighborhood. The **Ponte Vecchio** is only steps away.

Santa Croce

At the southeast corner of the historic district, this neighborhood is one of our favorites: It's within walking distance of all the major attractions, yet enough out of the way so it's not overcrowded with tourists — and still residential enough to feel like a real place. However, it is less accessible than other areas and has fewer restaurants and hotels. It's centered around the beautiful church of **Santa Croce.**

Santa Maria Novella

At the northwest corner of the historic district, this neighborhood is situated around the church of **Santa Maria Novella** — one of the key attractions here, together with the church of **San Lorenzo.** It is the best connected of all — SMN train and bus stations are just around the corner — and has all the services you might need: hotels, restaurants, shops, and a good share of attractions.

Teatro Comunale

Stretching around the theater that houses the **Maggio Fiorentino Festival** (see "Finding more cool things to see and do," later in this chapter), this residential area west of Santa Maria Novella is quiet and historic — and a very pleasant place to stay. Although it is part of medieval walled Florence, it is not completely closed to traffic and is well connected by public transportation. Hotels are cheaper than in the more central districts because they are not right by the Duomo or the Uffizi, but those attractions are only a short walk away. We definitely recommend it.

Finding information after you arrive

The tourist office maintains three information desks in town; you can get maps and brochures at each of them, but the last two are the best:

- ✔ **Santa Maria Novella** (Piazza Stazione 4/a; ☎ **055-212245**) at SMN rail station; open Monday through Saturday from 9 a.m. to 7 p.m. and Sunday from 8:30 a.m. to 2 p.m.

- ✔ **Via Cavour 1r** (☎ **055-290832** or 055-290833), about 3 blocks north of the Duomo; open Monday through Saturday from 8:30 a.m. to 6:30 p.m. and Sunday from 8:30 a.m. to 1:30 p.m.

> ✔ **Borgo Santa Croce 29r** (☎ 055-2340444), behind Piazza Santa
> Croce; open Monday through Saturday from 9 a.m. to 7 p.m. and
> Sunday from 8:30 a.m. to 2 p.m.

Getting Around Florence

Florence is very safe, but the major crime — especially in the historic
districts — is pickpocketing, an activity that traditionally occurs in
crowded areas (mostly train station, buses, and outdoor markets).

The free **tourist office map** is completely adequate for most visitors,
especially if you combine it with the free bus map you can get from the
ATAF information booth at the SMN train station. But if you're an ambitious explorer, you can buy a *cartina con stradario* (map with street
directory) at any newsstand for about 6€ ($7.20).

On foot

Since the historic district is closed to all traffic except for public buses —
no cars, no taxis, and no mopeds — and attractions lie relatively close to
one another, walking is the best way to enjoy the town. The walk from the
Accademia to Palazzo Pitti — probably the two farthest attractions from
each other within the historic center — will take you about one hour at
an average pace; you'll also pass most of the major sights in town along
the way.

By bus

Florence's bus system is well organized and easy to use. For the most
part, you'll probably use the electric minibuses — identified by the letters
A, B, C, and D — which are allowed within the *centro storico* (historic district). These minibuses do come in handy when your feet ache after a long
day at the Uffizi or shopping on Via Tornabuoni! Regular buses are a great
way to get quickly back and forth between **Oltrarno** and the center of
town (nos. 36 and 37), as well as to reach some out-of-the-way attractions
such as **Fiesole** (no. 7) or **San Miniato** (nos. 12 and 13).

You can buy bus tickets at most bars, tobacconist shops (signed *tabacchi* or by a white *T* on a black background), and newsstands; a single
ticket (a *biglietto*) costs 1€ ($1.20) in advance or 1.50€ ($1.80) on
board. It's valid for one hour on as many buses as you want. You can
save a bit if you get a **Carta Agile** — an electronic card worth 12 single
tickets for the price of 10 (10€/$12), or 25 tickets for the price of 20
(20€/$24), which can be used by more than one person if you're travel-
ing together (just pass it in front of the magnetic eye of the machine on
board the bus as many times as you have passengers in your group; if
you want to know how much money you have left on the card, press the
button on the machine marked *info* and swipe your card). You can also

Street numbering, Florence style

Florence's tradition of independence is probably behind the town's peculiar way of marking street addresses: Restaurant, office, and shop doors are numbered independently from residential and hotel doors. The first set of numbers is usually painted in red and always marked with the letter *r* appended to the number (for *rosso*, "red"); the second is painted in black or blue. Therefore it can easily happen that no. 1r (office or business) and no. 1 (private residence — or hotel — this is where it gets confusing) are in different buildings, and maybe a few door numbers apart.

get unlimited-ride passes: a **24-hour pass** costs 4.50€ ($5.40); a **two-day pass** is 7.60€ ($9.10); and a **three-day pass** goes for 9.60€ ($12).

Another option if you're in town for a few days is the **Iris pass** (23€/$28 for adults, 12€/$14 for youths under 15), valid until 1 p.m. of the fourth day: It gives access to all public transportation — including trains — within the province of Florence and Prato, plus a 20 percent discount on attractions.

Bus drivers don't make change: Always have the exact fare with you. Also remember that tickets need to be stamped upon boarding; unlimited-ride passes need to be stamped only once on your first trip.

Staying in Style

As Florence is a major tourist destination, the choice of accommodations is large and varied. Still, it may be hard to secure a nice room at a decent price during high season (May–June and Sept–Oct); depending on your budget, you might have to settle for a less central location, or else make sure you reserve well in advance (see Chapter 8 for more on hotel booking).

The **Firenze4you card** gives you four nights for the price of three (at participating hotels, listed on the Web site), plus a 10 to 20 percent discount at participating restaurants. You'll get your card when you check in at your hotel.

If you arrive in Florence without a hotel reservation, your best bet is the room-finding service run by the tourist info desk at the **Santa Maria Novella rail station.** If you're driving, there are similar services at the tourist info desks in the **Area di Servizio AGIP Peretola** (rest area) on Highway A11 (☎ 055-4211800) and in the **Area di Servizio Chianti Est** on Highway A1 (☎ 055-621349).

Florence Accommodations and Dining

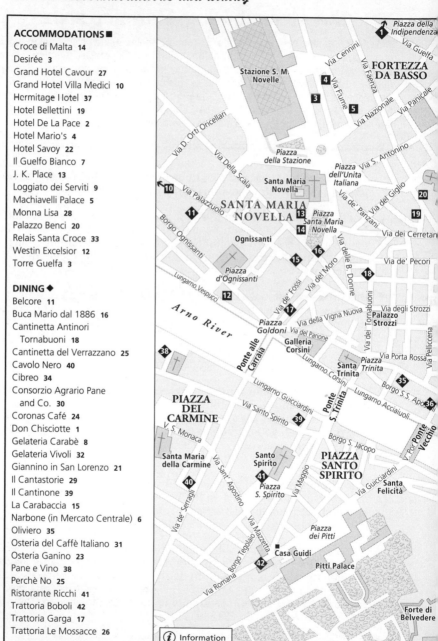

ACCOMMODATIONS ■

Croce di Malta 14
Desirée 3
Grand Hotel Cavour 27
Grand Hotel Villa Medici 10
Hermitage Hotel 37
Hotel Bellettini 19
Hotel De La Pace 2
Hotel Mario's 4
Hotel Savoy 22
Il Guelfo Bianco 7
J. K. Place 13
Loggiato dei Serviti 9
Machiavelli Palace 5
Monna Lisa 28
Palazzo Benci 20
Relais Santa Croce 33
Westin Excelsior 12
Torre Guelfa 3

DINING ◆

Belcore 11
Buca Mario dal 1886 16
Cantinetta Antinori
  Tornabuoni 18
Cantinetta del Verrazzano 25
Cavolo Nero 40
Cibreo 34
Consorzio Agrario Pane
  and Co. 30
Coronas Café 24
Don Chisciotte 1
Gelateria Carabè 8
Gelateria Vivoli 32
Giannino in San Lorenzo 21
Il Cantastorie 29
Il Cantinone 39
La Carabaccia 15
Narbone (in Mercato Centrale) 6
Oliviero 35
Osteria del Caffè Italiano 31
Osteria Ganino 23
Pane e Vino 38
Perchè No 25
Ristorante Ricchi 41
Trattoria Boboli 42
Trattoria Garga 17
Trattoria Le Mossacce 26

(i) Information

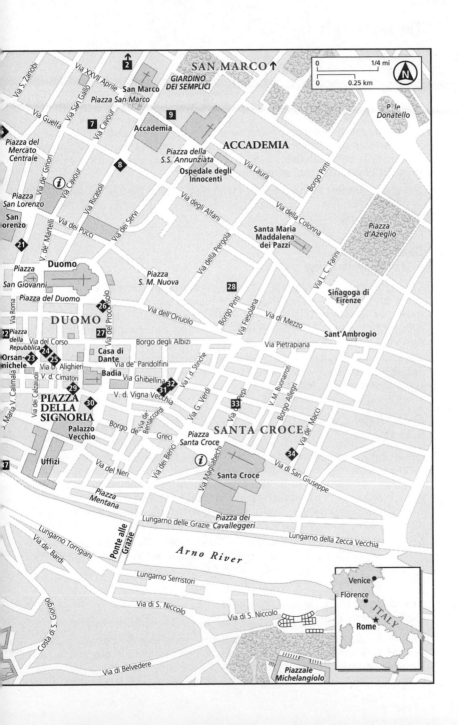

The top hotels

Croce di Malta
$$$ Santa Maria Novella

This elegant hotel offers large, nicely appointed guest rooms — furnished with modern but classic handcrafted furniture — and a garden with a small pool, plus a roof terrace where you can have breakfast or a drink and enjoy the lovely view. Venetian plaster walls in warm tones and quality carpeting give each room an individual ambience; many of the upper-floor guest rooms have small balconies as well. The hotel is accessible for people with disabilities and the staff is extremely helpful.

See map p. 184. Via della Scala 7, at Piazza Santa Maria Novella. ☎ *055-2611870. Fax: 055-287121.* www.crocedimalta.it. *Bus: A, 11, 36, or 37. Rack rates: 297€ ($356) double. AE, DC, MC, V.*

Desirée
$ Fortezza da Basso

This Liberty-style (Italian Art Nouveau) hotel boasts stained-glass windows by Polloni, rare floral-decorated floors, and welcoming accommodations that are outfitted with painted wood or iron bedsteads. Some rooms offer views of the dome of San Lorenzo. Bathrooms are a good size and very well kept.

See map p. 184. Via Fiume 20, off Via Nazionale, near the train station. ☎ *055-2382382. Fax: 055-291439.* www.desireehotel.com. *Bus: 4, 12, or 25. Rack rates: 135€ ($162) double. AE, DC, MC, V.*

Grand Hotel Cavour
$$$ Duomo

Grand public spaces with marble floors welcome you to this centrally located hotel. The beautifully appointed guest rooms are of a good size, with fine furniture and rich carpeting. Bathrooms are new. The hotel's roof garden, where you'll find the restaurant and breakfast buffet, affords wonderful views. The rooms overlooking the street are a bit noisy despite the double-paned windows. The hotel is accessible to those with disabilities.

See map p. 184. Via del Proconsolo 3, at Via del Corso. ☎ *055-2662701. Fax: 055-218955.* www.albergocavour.it. *Bus: A. Rack rates: 230€–300€ ($276–$360) double. Rates include buffet breakfast. AE, DC, MC, V.*

Grand Hotel Villa Medici
$$$$ Teatro Comunale

This is the best of the luxury hotels if you're visiting Florence in summer: While the beautiful 18th-century *palazzo* is welcoming in any season, the large garden and swimming pool will feel absolutely heavenly in the town's heat — a unique plus for a centrally located hotel. The large, individually decorated guest rooms are tasteful, if a bit old-fashioned. All have beautiful bathrooms done in Carrara marble. Rooms on the higher floors have small terraces and panoramic views of the city.

See map p. 184. Via il Prato 42, at Via Rucellai and Via Palestro. ☎ *800-273226 or 055-2381331. Fax: 055-2381336.* www.villamedicihotel.com. *Bus: D or 1. Rack rates: 520€–570€ ($624–$684) double. AE, DC, MC, V.*

Hotel Bellettini
$$ Duomo

This reliable, moderately priced hotel is run by two sisters who are very friendly and helpful. Housed in a 14th-century *palazzo* just steps from the Duomo, it is pleasantly old-fashioned and offers simple, clean guest rooms — some with fantastic views — and one of the best breakfasts in town for the price, with a buffet that includes ham and fresh fruit. You can get cheaper rates if you choose a shared bathroom, or you can splurge on one of the superior rooms in the new annex. The latter are more spacious and come with Carrara marble bathrooms.

See map p. 184. Via de' Conti 7, steps from the Duomo. ☎ *055-213561. Fax: 055-283551.* www.hotelbellettini.com. *Bus: 1, 6, or 11 to Martelli; take Via de' Cerretani and turn right on Via de' Conti. Rack rates: 140€–170€ ($168–$204) double; 180€–200€ ($216–$240) triple. Rates include buffet breakfast. AE, DC, MC, V.*

Hotel De La Pace
$$ Accademia

Aptly named (*pace* means peace in Italian), this hotel exudes feelings of quiet and relaxation. The good-sized guest rooms are decorated in warm tones, with terra-cotta floors and fine fabrics; many have balconies. Furnishings are modern but elegant. There's complimentary pickup at the station on request.

See map p. 184. Via Lamarmora 28, at Via Venezia, north of Piazza San Marco. ☎ *055-577343. Fax: 055-577576.* www.hoteldelapace.it. *Bus: 1 or 7. Rack rates: 195€ ($234) double. Rates include breakfast. AE, DC, MC, V.*

Hotel Savoy
$$$$ Piazza della Signoria

In-depth renovations have brought modernity to this landmark hotel — which opened in 1896 — while respecting the original architecture. The spacious guest rooms are luxuriously appointed and done in a refined Italian style: clean and elegant, but also warm and welcoming. One of the Savoy's big draws is its special attention to children, with games, gifts, and child-sized everything, including slippers and bathrobes in the rooms.

See map p. 184. Piazza della Repubblica 7. ☎ *055-27351. Fax: 055-2735888.* www.hotelsavoy.it. *Bus: 36 or 37. Rack rates: 520€–720€ ($624–$864) double. AE, DC, MC, V.*

Il Guelfo Bianco
$$ Accademia

This hotel occupies a 15th-century *palazzo* and its neighboring 17th-century *palazzo*. The guest rooms in the former are pleasantly furnished and come with beautiful bathrooms; many overlook the inner garden and courtyard. The rooms in the other building boast ceiling frescoes. All are large and individually decorated with some antique furniture and modern art. And you need not worry about noise, even in rooms overlooking the street — the new windows are triple-paned!

See map p. 184. Via Cavour 57r, at Via Guelfa. ☎ *055-288330. Fax: 055-295203.* www. ilguelfobianco.it. *Bus: 1 or 6 to Cavour 02 or 1, 6, 7, 10, or 11 to San Marco 01. Rack rates: 180€–235€ ($216–$282) double. Rates include breakfast. AE, DC, MC, V.*

J. K. Place
$$$ Santa Maria Novella

A nice addition to the Florence hotel scene, this small lodging is a mix of charm and modernity. The public spaces are welcoming, with glowing fireplaces in winter and a pleasant rooftop terrace in good weather. Guest rooms are spacious and uniquely decorated: The four-poster beds, fireplaces, antiques, and stylish modern furniture make you feel like an aristocrat from this century — a rare opportunity. Bathrooms are modern and comfortable.

See map p. 184. Piazza Santa Maria Novella 7. ☎ *055-2645181. Fax: 055-2658387.* www.jkplace.com. *Bus: 14 or 23. Rack rates: 330€–470€ ($396–$564) double. Rates include buffet breakfast. AE, DC, MC, V.*

Loggiato dei Serviti
$$ Accademia

Set in the beautiful *piazza* near the Accademia Gallery — some say the most beautiful square in Florence — this hotel offers guest rooms done in a rich Florentine baroque style, with beautiful wood or terra-cotta floors, fine drapes, and canopied beds in most units. The hotel occupies a landmark 16th-century building designed by Antonio da Sangallo il Vecchio (the Elder) to match the twin buildings of the Ospedale degli Innocenti across the square. Originally a monastery, it was transformed into a hotel early in the 20th century and has been restored to its simple Renaissance beauty.

See map p. 184. Piazza Santissima Annunziata 3, steps from Piazza San Marco. ☎ *055-289592. Fax: 055-289595.* www.loggiatodeiservitihotel.it. *Bus: C. Rack rates: 205€ ($246) double. Rates include breakfast. AE, DC, MC, V.*

Machiavelli Palace
$$ Fortezza da Basso

Housed in an early-18th-century palace that was once a convent, this hotel boasts frescoes and coffered ceilings, as well as very nice guest rooms with pastel walls and elegant bedsteads. A full buffet with cold cuts and cheese is served in the frescoed refectory of the old convent. Rooms overlooking the street are somewhat noisy, however.

See map p. 184. Via Nazionale 10, at Via Faenza. ☎ *055-216622. Fax: 055-214106.* www. hotelmachiavelli.it. *Bus: 12 or 35. Rack rates: 160€–180€ ($192–$216) double. Rates include buffet breakfast. AE, DC, MC, V.*

Monna Lisa
$$$$ Santa Croce

If you stay here, you'll feel like a guest in a private collector's home. The rooms of this beautiful 14th-century *palazzo,* once home to the Neri family, vary in style and size. The antique furnishings, original coffered ceilings, inner garden and patio, modern bathrooms (some with Jacuzzis), and important artwork make this a very desirable choice. The hotel is accessible for people with disabilities.

See map p. 184. Borgo Pinti 27, off Via dell'Oriuolo. ☎ *055-2479751. Fax: 055-2479755.* www.monnalisa.it. *Bus: A, 14, or 23 to Salvemini. Rack rates: 299€–360€ ($359–$432) double. Rates include breakfast. AE, DC, MC, V.*

Palazzo Benci
$$ Duomo

Recently opened west of the Duomo, this hotel occupies a lovingly restored 16th-century *palazzo,* the Renaissance residence of the Benci family. The common spaces are absolutely gorgeous, with richly stuccoed walls, and the breakfast room boasts coffered wooden ceilings. The guest rooms are simple but tasteful; many open onto the delightful courtyard garden, affording a little peace and quiet.

See map p. 184. Piazza Madonna degli Aldobrandini 3, off Via del Giglio, behind San Lorenzo. ☎ *055-213848. Fax: 055-288308.* www.palazzobenci.com. *Bus: 1, 6, or 11 to Martelli; walk west on Via dei Gori, then across Piazza San Lorenzo and around the church on Corso Tonelli into Piazza Madonna degli Aldobrandini. Rack rates: 192€ ($230) double. Rates include breakfast. AE, DC, V.*

Relais Santa Croce
$$$$ Santa Croce

This small luxury hotel in the heart of the historic district offers the comfort level of the top hotels in Florence, with a warm atmosphere and unique style — no dusty old elegance or stuffiness here. The 18th-century Ciofi-Jacometti *palazzo* combines antique furnishings and period architectural details — the original frescoes are magnificent — with contemporary Italian design. Precious fabrics, elegant wood panels, and marble bathrooms — all with separate shower and tub — complete the picture.

See map p. 184. Via Ghibellina 87, at Via de' Pepi. ☎ *055-2342230. Fax: 055-2341195.* www.relaissantacroce.it. *Bus: A. Rack rates: 460€–490€ ($552–$588) double. Rates include breakfast. AE, DC, MC, V.*

Runner-up accommodations

Hermitage Hotel

$$$ **Piazza della Signoria** This hotel is right off the Ponte Vecchio, nearer the Uffizi. Many rooms have views of the river; all have antique furniture and premium bathrooms. The rooftop garden is a real plus. *See map p. 184. Vicolo Marzio 1.* ☎ *055-287216. Fax: 055-212208.* www.hermitagehotel. com.

Hotel Mario's

$$ **Fortezza da Basso** Recently renovated, this hotel offers bright, pleasant guest rooms with pastel walls and beamed ceilings. *See map p. 184. Via Faenza 89.* ☎ *055-218801. Fax: 055-212039.* www.hotelmarios.com.

Torre Guelfa

$$$ **Piazza della Signoria** Near the Ponte Vecchio and the Uffizi, the Torre Guelfa offers richly decorated rooms, good service, and a breathtaking view from its 13th-century tower. *See map p. 184. Borgo Santi Apostoli 8.* ☎ *055-2396338. Fax: 055-2398577.* www.hoteltorreguelfa.com.

Westin Excelsior

$$$$ **Duomo** This is the best luxury hotel in the *centro storico,* with outstanding Florentine baroque décor, including stained-glass windows, rich carved and painted ceilings, and marble columns. Check the Web site for Internet specials. *See map p. 184. Piazza Ognissanti 3.* ☎ *888-6255144 in the U.S. and Canada, or 055-27151. Fax: 055-210278.* www.westin.com/excelsior florence.

Dining Out

The best dining in Florence is in the area between Santa Croce and Piazza della Signoria, and also around Piazza del Carmine in Oltrarno — the popular area of San Frediano. You'll have to compete with locals for a table at the most popular restaurants, especially on weekends, thus we always recommend you make reservations — even if it's just calling earlier on the same day. Tuscans are very proud of their cuisine (see Chapter 2), and it is difficult to find a good restaurant serving anything but Tuscan fare. Expect lots of grilled meats and hearty soups — such as *pappa al pomodoro* (tomato and bread soup) and the famous *ribollita.*

Belcore

$$ **Santa Maria Novella CREATIVE SEAFOOD/VEGETARIAN**

At this elegant gourmet restaurant, you'll be pleased with the kind service, welcoming atmosphere, and intriguing dishes on the seasonal menu (which also has a vegetarian section). You might find such choices as artichoke flan with Stilton cheese sauce, Parmesan and fresh thyme risotto with spinach and calamari sauce, and seafood fondue for two.

Tuscan pride

Tuscans love to remind those who admire French cuisine that many typical French dishes are actually descended from Tuscan specialties imported to France by the gourmet queen Caterina de' Medici in the 16th century. Not trusting northern barbarians to cook food to her liking, she brought her own cooks with her when she married Henri II of France. For example, French crêpes are derived from Florentine *crespelle,* and *omelette* is nothing else but *frittata.*

See map p. 184. Via dell'Albero 28. ☎ 055-211198. www.ristorantebelcore.it. *Reservations recommended. Bus: A, 36, or 37 to Piazza Santa Maria Novella. Secondi: 18€–28€ ($22–$34). AE, DC, MC, V. Open: Thurs–Mon 12:30–3 p.m.; Wed–Mon 7:30–10 p.m.*

Buca Mario dal 1886
$$$ Santa Maria Novella   FLORENTINE

This historic restaurant serves traditional Tuscan cuisine in a friendly atmosphere. It's housed in a cellar (*buca* in Florentine), with vaulted and whitewashed dining rooms decorated with dark-wood paneling (the décor is original). Everything is well prepared, though it doesn't come cheap. We liked the classic *ribollita* and the *osso buco,* as well as the *coniglio fritto* (fried rabbit), a Tuscan delicacy!

See map p. 184. Piazza degli Ottaviani 16r, just south of Santa Maria Novella. ☎ 055-214179. www.bucamario.it. *Reservations recommended. Bus: A, 36, or 37 to Piazza Santa Maria Novella. Secondi: 18€–28€ ($22–$34). AE, MC, V. Open: Fri–Tues 12:30–3 p.m.; Thurs–Tues 7:30–10 p.m. Closed Aug.*

Cantinetta Antinori Tornabuoni
$$$ Santa Maria Novella   FLORENTINE/ITALIAN

Antinori is the family name of the oldest and one of the best producers of wine in Italy. In this restaurant, typical Tuscan dishes and many specialties from the Antinori farms are served to accompany the wine. The *cantinetta* (small wine cellar) occupies the 15th-century *palazzo* of this noble family and serves as their winery in town. You can sample the vintages at the counter, or sit at a table and have a full meal. The *pappa al pomodoro* is delicious, as is the risotto with prawns.

See map p. 184. Piazza Antinori 3r, off the north end of Via de' Tornabuoni. ☎ 055-292234. Reservations recommended. Bus: A, 6, 11, 36, or 37 to Piazza Antinori. Secondi: 14€–25€ ($17–$30). AE, DC, MC, V. Open: Mon–Fri 12:30–3 p.m. and 7:30–10 p.m. Closed 1 week at Christmas and 1 week in Aug.

Cavolo Nero
$$ Piazza del Carmine   FLORENTINE

Cavolo Nero serves great food, prepared with enthusiasm and creativity. The name of the restaurant refers to the black cabbage (similar to kale) that is typical of Tuscan cooking. The menu isn't very extensive, but its offerings are delicious. We enjoyed the homemade gnocchi with broccoli and wild fennel, as well as the bass filet rolled in eggplant and served over a yellow-pepper purée.

See map p. 184. Via d'Ardiglione 22, off Via de' Serragli. ☎ *055-294744.* www.cavolo nero.it. *Reservations recommended. Bus: D, 11, 36, or 37 to Via de' Serragli. Secondi: 10€–16€ ($12–$19). AE, DC, MC, V. Open: Mon–Sat 7:30–10 p.m. Closed 3 weeks in Aug.*

Cibreo
$$$ Santa Croce   FLORENTINE

Renowned chef-owner Fabio Picchi changes his menu daily, depending on the market and his imagination. The backbone of the menu is historic Tuscan, with some recipes that go back to the Renaissance — but they're presented here in a modern way. One hallmark of the place is that you won't find pasta of any kind; the other is that dinner is at 7:30 or 9 p.m., and if you choose the first service, you'll have to be out by 9 p.m. On the menu, you'll find soufflés, polenta, roasted and stuffed birds — such as the superb pigeon stuffed with a traditional fruit preparation — and the much imitated *pomodoro in gelatina* (tomato aspic). For a more informal atmosphere and lower prices, you can try the **trattoria** next door (Via de'Macci 122r) or the **Caffè Cibreo** across the street.

See map p. 184. Restaurant: Via Andrea del Verrocchio 8r. ☎ *055-2341100.* cibreo. fi@tin.it. *Reservations required for the restaurant; not accepted for the trattoria. Bus: A to Piazza Sant'Ambrogio (outdoor vegetable market). Secondi: 35€ ($42). AE, DC, MC, V. Open: Tues–Sat 7:30–9 p.m. Trattoria also open for lunch. Closed first week in Jan and Aug.*

Don Chisciotte
$$$ Fortezza da Basso   FLORENTINE/SEAFOOD

This small restaurant is rightfully known for its imaginative fish dishes, served in a friendly but classy atmosphere. Just north of the main tourist area, it gets quite busy, especially on weekends. The dining room is on the second floor of a typical *palazzo*. We liked the tagliatelle with asparagus and prawns, along with the tuna steak with cooked greens.

See map p. 184. Via C. Ridolfi 4r, off Via Nazionale. ☎ *055-475430. Reservations recommended. Best to get here by taxi. Secondi: 15€–21€ ($18–$25). AE, DC, MC, V. Open: Daily 12:30–2:30 p.m. and 7:30–10 p.m. Closed Aug.*

Fast food, Florence style

For a cheap but delicious meal, drop by an *alimentari* (grocery shop) for picnic fixings. Our favorite is **Consorzio Agrario Pane and Co.**, Piazza San Firenze 5r, at Via Condotta (☎ 055-213063; Bus: A to Condotta), where you'll find local cheeses and cured meats, including the excellent *cinghiale* (wild boar), plus mineral water, wine, and all the rest. You can also get a nice fruit tart or some other pastries.

Or head for the colorful and noisy **Mercato Centrale**, near Piazza San Lorenzo (entrance on Via dell'Ariento), where you'll find stalls selling all kinds of edibles and nonedibles, from fruits and vegetables to fragrant Tuscan bread. For a quick Florentine-style bite, you can try the centuries-old fare served at **Narbone** (stand no. 292 on the ground floor; Open: Mon–Sat 7 a.m.–2 p.m.), a counter with a few tables. We recommend the *panino col bollito* (boiled beef sandwich) and, if you're up to it, the *trippa alla Fiorentina* (tripe with tomato sauce and Parmesan). At the other end of the spectrum, the elegant **Cantinetta del Verrazzano** (Via dei Tavolini 18r; ☎ 055-268590; Open: Mon–Sat 8 a.m.–4 p.m., in winter until 9 p.m.) sells focaccia hot from the oven and wine by the glass, plus it has a small self-service lunch counter.

Giannino in San Lorenzo
$$ Duomo FLORENTINE

Serving roasted meats since 1920, this informal restaurant prides itself on its *fiorentina* (grilled porterhouse steak of local beef). Under the vaulted ceilings of a 17th-century shopping gallery, you can relax and have excellent Tuscan food at moderate prices. You may enjoy the *crostini* (toasted bread with savory toppings), *ribollita,* and famous *salsicce toscane alla griglia con cannellini* (grilled local sausages with Tuscan white beans). And for the wine, you can visit the wine steward in the wine cellar to help you make your selection.

See map p. 184. Via Borgo San Lorenzo 35/37r. ☎ *055-212206.* www.gianninoin florence.com. *Reservations recommended Fri–Sat. Bus: 1, 6, 7, 10, or 11 to Duomo. Secondi: 8.50€–18€ ($10–$22). AE, MC, V. Open: Daily 12:30–3 p.m. and 7:30–10 p.m.*

Il Cantastorie
$ Piazza della Signoria TUSCAN

With a good singer performing every night, excellent wine, and hearty food, Il Cantastorie is always a lively spot. Defining itself as a bit of Tuscan countryside in the heart of Florence, this pleasant *trattoria* is decorated in the Tuscan tradition of terra-cotta floors and wooden tables. You'll find all the typical Tuscan specialties and some of the best Chianti you've ever had. *Ribollita, salsiccia e bietola* (pork sausages and green chard), *crostoni* (larger version of *crostini*), and *sottoli* (vegetables preserved in herbs and olive oil) are some of the choices you may find on a menu that changes daily. The same management runs Il Cantinone (reviewed later).

See map p. 184. Via della Condotta 7/9r, just east of Piazza della Signoria. ☎ 055-2396804. Reservations recommended on Sat. Bus: A to Ghibellina. Secondi: 8€–16€ ($9.60–$19). MC, V. Open: Wed–Mon 12:30–3 p.m. and 7:30–10 p.m.

Il Cantinone
$$ Piazza Santo Spirito   FLORENTINE

Il Cantinone combines a convivial atmosphere and good traditional Florentine cuisine in a setting of low arched ceilings and long wooden tables. It's a real *enoteca del Chianti Classico* — a winery specializing in Chianti Classico, the heart of the DOCG Chianti (which means it's denomination controlled and guaranteed). To accompany the wine, try the excellent soups — *ribollita, pappa al pomodoro, pasta e fagioli* (pasta and beans) — or the *salsicce* (grilled pork sausages). The prix-fixe menu *degustazione* for two includes a different wine with each serving.

See map p. 184. Via Santo Spirito 6R. ☎ 055-218898. Reservations recommended on Sat. Bus: 11, 36, or 37 to Sauro or Frescobaldi; walk south to Via Santo Spirito, a block south of the river, off Ponte Santa Trinita and Ponte alla Carraia. Secondi: 8€–18€ ($9.60–$22). MC, V. Open: Tues–Sun 12:30–3 p.m. and 7:30–10 p.m.

La Carabaccia
$$ Santa MariaNovella   FLORENTINE

The name of this restaurant refers both to a traditional working boat that once plied the Arno and to *zuppa carabaccia,* a hearty onion soup favored by the Medicis during the Renaissance. The menu features daily choices of pasta, fresh vegetables, and fish, depending on what caught the chef's eye in the market that morning, plus a variety of homemade breads.

See map p. 184. Via Palazzuolo 190r. ☎ 055-213203. Reservations recommended on Sat. Bus: A to Moro; turn left from Via del Moro into Via Palazzuolo, west of Via de' Tornabuoni. Secondi: 9.50€–21€ ($11–$25). AE, MC, V. Open: Tues–Sat 12:30–3 p.m.; Mon–Sat 7:30–10 p.m. Closed 2 weeks in Aug.

Oliviero
$$ Piazza della Signoria   CREATIVE FLORENTINE

We love this elegant restaurant, where the service is always impeccable and the cuisine superb — and the prices remain moderate. The first courses might include an excellent *zuppa di cicerchie con mazzancolle* (local legume soup with local prawns) or perhaps artichoke ravioli with prawns, followed by a second course of delicious guinea fowl in a Chianti sauce. Both the dessert and the wine menus are very satisfactory.

See map p. 184. Via delle Terme 51r. ☎ 055-212421. www.ristorante-oliviero.it. Reservations recommended. Bus: 14 or 23 to Tornabuoni. Secondi: 7€–15€ ($8.40–$18). DC, MC, V. Open: Mon–Sat 7:30–10 p.m. Closed Aug.

Looking for a *gelato* break?

Ice cream is certainly one of the best treats in Italy, and Florence is famous for its *gelato*. Of a different school from the Venetian, the Roman, or the Sicilian *gelati*, Florentine ice cream was invented — as were many other Tuscan gastronomic specialties — to gratify the palates of the Medicis. Alas, to our taste at least (one of us is from Rome, you know), the Medici family had a very big sweet tooth, judging from the result: Florentine ice cream is extremely sugary. You'll find some of the best in town at **Gelateria Vivoli** (Via Isola delle Stinche 7r, between the Bargello and Santa Croce; ☎ 055-292334; Bus: A to Piazza Santa Croce), which is truly a marvel for its zillions of flavors, but also at **Coronas Café** (Via Calzaiuoli 72r; ☎ 055-2396139; Bus: A to Orsanmichele) and **Perchè No** (Via dei Tavolini 19r, just off Via Calzaiuoli; ☎ 055-2398969; Bus: A to Orsanmichele), one of the oldest Florentine *gelaterie*. For excellent Sicilian *gelato* that's been rated among the best in Italy, stop by **Gelateria Carabè** (Via Ricasoli 60r, near the Accademia; ☎ 055-289476; Bus: C or 6, to Santissima [SS] Annunziata), where the owner has the ingredients — lemons, almonds, pistachios — shipped from Sicily.

Osteria del Caffè Italiano
$$ **Santa Croce** **FLORENTINE**

This is our favorite place in Florence: serving genuine Tuscan food all day long until late at night, with some of the best Tuscan wines by the glass. And it's no wonder: This *osteria* is the urban outpost of Tuscany's ten best vineyards, which send a selection of their finest products here regularly. Featuring both a more formal dining room and a casual tavern, this place allows you to choose between a complete meal or light fare; lunch is also available in either room. *Ribollita, farinata al cavolo nero* (thick black cabbage soup), *cinghiale in salmì* (wild-boar stew), and a great choice of Tuscan cold cuts will more than satisfy.

See map p. 184. Via Isola delle Stinche 11–13r. ☎ *055-289020.* www.caffe italiano.it. *Reservations recommended on Sat. Bus: A or 14 to Piazza Santa Croce. Secondi: 9€–19€ ($11–$23). AE, DC, MC, V. Open: Tues–Sun noon to 11 p.m.*

Osteria Ganino
$$ **Piazza della Signoria** **FLORENTINE**

At this cozy, centrally located *trattoria*, you'll find ubiquitous Florentine specialties like *bistecca alla fiorentina* and tagliatelle with truffle sauce, served on polished stone tables covered in paper. Though prices may seem a bit high for this simple setting, the food is nicely prepared and served by an attentive staff; you'll welcome the offering of mortadella before you order. Sit out on the small terrace in good weather.

See map p. 184. Piazza dei Cimatori 4r. ☎ *055-214125. Reservations recommended. Bus: A to Condotta or Cimatori; Via dei Cimatori is 2 short blocks north of Piazza della*

Signoria. Secondi: 9€–18€ ($11–$22). AE, DC, MC, V. Open: Mon–Sat 12:30–3 p.m. and 7:30–10 p.m.

Pane e Vino
$ **Piazza della Signoria   CREATIVE FLORENTINE**

In the comfortably modern dining room of this *trattoria,* you'll find a wide choice of dishes, ranging from simple countryside "snacks" — such as a variety of rare local cheeses served with sweet fruit preparations — to elaborate main courses. We liked the pasta with a pork and wild-fennel *ragù,* as well as the *saltimbocca di rana pescatrice con ratatouille di zucchine* (sautéed fish and bacon bites with zucchini stew). The restaurant also offers a tasting menu (30€/$36) and many wines by the glass.

See map p. 184. Piazza di Cestello 3r. ☎ *055-2476956. Reservations recommended. Bus: 14 or 23 to Proconsolo. Secondi: 7€–15€ ($8.40–$18). DC, MC, V. Open: Mon–Sat 7:30–10 p.m. Closed 2 weeks in Aug.*

Ristorante Ricchi
$$$ **Piazza Santo Spirito   TUSCAN/SEAFOOD**

While you decide what to order, you'll welcome a glass of prosecco and a little something to eat at this friendly seafood restaurant. The white-washed walls and beamed ceilings are a perfect complement to the well-prepared food. We loved the fried zucchini flowers with crabmeat; also excellent were the *carpaccio di branzino,* the squid-ink risotto, and the grilled fish. The cafe next door also serves light fare in the evening.

See map p. 184. Piazza Santo Spirito 8/9r. ☎ *055-215864.* www.caffericchi.it. *Reservations recommended. Bus: D, 11, 36, or 37 to Piazza Santo Spirito. Secondi: 18€–24€ ($22–$29). AE, DC, MC, V. Open: Mon–Sat 7:30–10 p.m.*

Trattoria Boboli
$$ **Piazza Santo Spirito   FLORENTINE**

Near the Palazzo Pitti and the entrance to Boboli Gardens, this is a real mom-and-pop operation where you'll find a lot of warmth and all the specialties of Tuscan cuisine. The dining room is small, but the food is good. They make a good *ribollita* and *pappa al pomodoro,* as well as an excellent *osso buco.*

See map p. 184. Via Romana 45r. ☎ *055-2336401.* www.paginegialle.it/ bobolitratt. *Reservations recommended. Bus: D, 6, 11, 36, or 37 to Via Romana. Secondi: 8€–19€ ($9.60–$23). AE, MC, V. Open: Thurs–Tues 12:30–2:30 p.m. and 7:30–10:30 p.m.*

Trattoria Garga
$$$ **Santa Maria Novella   TUSCAN/CREATIVE**

The ebullient personality of the chef-owner, Garga, has overflowed onto the walls, which he has personally decorated with his own frescoes.

Elegant yet laid-back, this restaurant isn't cheap. The extravagant atmosphere pairs perfectly with his interpretations of Tuscan fundamentals. Try the famous *taglierini alla Magnifico* (angel-hair pasta with a mint-cream sauce flavored with lemon and orange rind and Parmesan cheese).

See map p. 184. Via del Moro 50r. ☎ *055-2398898.* www.fol.it. *Reservations required. Bus: A to Via del Moro. Secondi: 21€–23€ ($25–$28). AE, DC, MC, V. Open: Tues–Sun 7:30–10 p.m.*

Trattoria Le Mossacce
$ Duomo   FLORENTINE

This small, cheap, historic *trattoria* offers home-style Florentine food. Listen up to the daily offerings from the waiter and make your pick among the choice of Tuscan specialties such as *crespelle* (eggy crepes, served lasagna-style or rolled and filled) and *ribollita* as well as spaghetti with clams. Among the *secondi,* try the *involtini* (rolled and filled veal scaloppine cooked in tomato sauce).

See map p. 184. Via del Proconsolo 55r, near the Duomo. ☎ *055-294361. Reservations recommended. Bus: 14 or 23 to Proconsolo. Secondi: 8€–12€ ($9.60–$14). AE, MC, V. Open: Mon–Fri 12:30–3 p.m. and 7:30–10 p.m.*

Exploring Florence

Florence offers precious little in the way of bargains. You might consider the **Iris pass** (see "Getting Around Florence," earlier in this chapter), which gives you a 20 percent discount on most attractions.

We highly recommend that you **reserve your tickets in advance** for the Galleria degli Uffizi and the Galleria degli Accademia (☎ **055-294883;** Fax: 055-264406; www.firenzemusei.it; Mon–Fri 8:30 a.m.–6:30 p.m., Sat 8:30 a.m.–12:30 p.m) in order to save literally hours of waiting in line. There is a reservations fee of 3€ ($3.60) per ticket. Upon arrival in Florence, you will then pick up your tickets at the tourist office inside the SMN train station. You can always make last-minute reservations and buy your tickets at the information booth inside the Uffizi, but you'll run the risk of all time slots being sold out.

Discovering the top attractions

Baptistery of St. John
Duomo

Part of the tricolored marble trio on Piazza del Duomo (see also the Duomo and Giotto's Bell Tower, in this section), the octagonal Baptistery is a beautiful example of the Florentine Romanesque style. It was probably built on the site of a Roman palace and splendidly decorated. Glittering

Florence Attractions

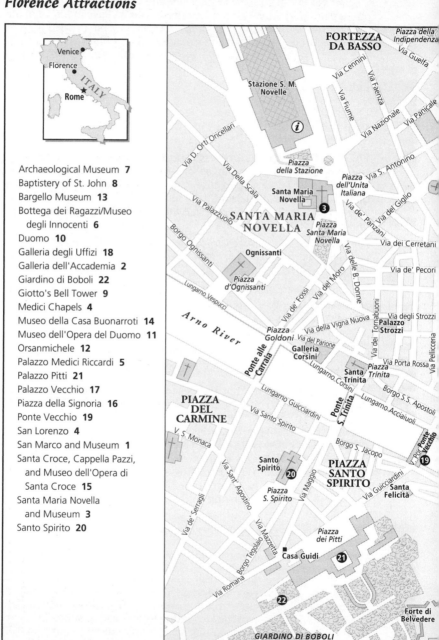

Archaeological Museum **7**
Baptistery of St. John **8**
Bargello Museum **13**
Bottega dei Ragazzi/Museo
  degli Innocenti **6**
Duomo **10**
Galleria degli Uffizi **18**
Galleria dell'Accademia **2**
Giardino di Boboli **22**
Giotto's Bell Tower **9**
Medici Chapels **4**
Museo della Casa Buonarroti **14**
Museo dell'Opera del Duomo **11**
Orsanmichele **12**
Palazzo Medici Riccardi **5**
Palazzo Pitti **21**
Palazzo Vecchio **17**
Piazza della Signoria **16**
Ponte Vecchio **19**
San Lorenzo **4**
San Marco and Museum **1**
Santa Croce, Cappella Pazzi,
  and Museo dell'Opera di
  Santa Croce **15**
Santa Maria Novella
  and Museum **3**
Santo Spirito **20**

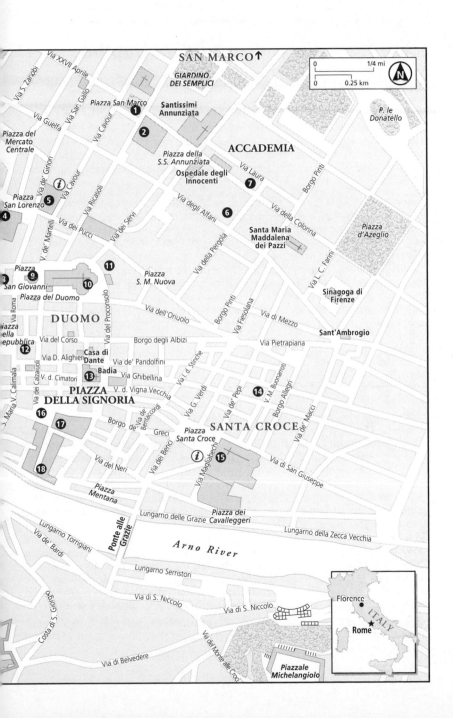

From small village to Italy's capital

With a splendid location by the Arno river, the small town of Fiesole, on the hill over-looking what was to become Florence, began thriving in the ninth century B.C. and became an important Etruscan center. Florence was born in Roman times, a flourishing but small village. It remained so until medieval times, when it grew to be a great banking center, dominating the European credit market. The town's wealth encouraged the development of the arts and of a lively culture: Dante was born here in 1265, and so was the painter Cimabue (Giotto's teacher). The Renaissance blossomed here in the 1300s, despite difficulties that deterred it elsewhere: a flood, the black plague, and political upheaval.

The 15th century brought the rule of Lorenzo the Magnificent, head of the powerful Medici clan, when the town reached its apogee. By this point, Florence had become the leading city-state in central Italy, overcoming the competition of nearby Siena and Pisa. During this, Florence's greatest period, the artists Leonardo, Michelangelo, and Raphael produced amazing works. After a brief restoration of the republic, in 1537, the Medici family returned to power in the person of Cosimo I, but it was the end of the Renaissance: The Inquisition began in 1542, suffocating cultural life, while Italy became the appetizing booty of the succession wars among royal families in Europe. Florence Gran Duchy resisted as such and passed to the Lorraine house, which main-tained its power and independence through the 17th and 18th centuries, passing then to the Bourbon. In 1860, the population rebelled and was able to join the burgeoning Italian kingdom. Florence was then made the capital of Italy from 1865 to 1870, when the capital finally moved to Rome.

13th-century mosaics cover the interior. The Baptistery's north and east doors — the life's work of Lorenzo Ghiberti — are the key attractions here. He began working on the beautiful bronze reliefs adorning the north doors in 1401, when he was 20, and finished them more than two decades later. They are now considered one of the world's most important pieces of Renaissance sculpture; see, for instance, how they depict Isaac's sacrifice with marvelous detail. The east doors, completed shortly before the artist's death, are even more beautiful: known as the **Gates of Paradise** (when he saw them, Michelangelo supposedly said, "These doors are fit to stand at the gates of Paradise," and the name stuck), the ten panels show stunning scenes from the Old Testament. The panels presently in place are copies of the originals, which have been moved to the **Museo dell'Opera del Duomo** (see later in this section) for safekeeping. The south doors were created by Andrea Pisano in the mid–14th century and show a more static Gothic style than Ghiberti's revolutionary work.

See map p. 198. Piazza San Giovanni. ☎ 055-2302885. Bus: 1, 6, 7, 10, 11, or A. Admission: 3€ ($3.60). Open: Mon–Sat noon to 7 p.m.; Sun 8:30 a.m.–2 p.m. Last entry 30 minutes earlier. Closed 1 week in Feb.

Bargello Museum
Signoria

If you like sculpture, we think visiting this museum instead of the Galleria dell'Accademia (see later in this section) is a better use of your time: The Bargello hides a treasury of Renaissance sculpture, with two *Davids* by Donatello (one in marble, the other in bronze) and another *David* by Michelangelo (it may also be Apollo). In addition, you'll find several other works by Michelangelo, including a **bust of Brutus** and the famous drunken *Bacchus* (which he executed when he was only 22). You'll also find the **bust of Cosimo I** by Benvenuto Cellini. Compare the two bronze panels depicting the *Sacrifice of Isaac,* one by Brunelleschi and one by Ghiberti, which were submitted in the famous contest to see who'd get to do the Baptistery doors (see earlier in this section).

The museum is housed in the Palazzo del Capitano del Popolo, which dates back to 1255. This is the oldest seat of Florence's government and was the official residence of the Podestà (governor) until 1502; it then became the seat of the Justice and Police Council. Hence the name *bargello,* which meant "cop" in local parlance, and was used to refer to the chief of police. The prisons here were used until the 19th century; it was only in 1886 that the Bargello was transformed into the sculpture museum of Florence.

See map p. 198. Via del Proconsolo 4, between Via Ghibellina and Via della Vigna Vecchia. ☎ *055-2388606.* www.polomuseale.firenze.it. *Bus: A. Admission: 4€ ($4.80), 7€ ($8.40) for special exhibits. Open: Daily 8:15 a.m.–6 p.m. Closed second and fourth Mon each month and May 1; ticket booth closes 40 minutes earlier.*

Duomo (Basilica di Santa Maria del Fiore)
Duomo

The Duomo's famous red-tiled dome, a masterpiece of great Renaissance architect Filippo Brunelleschi, is the symbol of Florence (the church facade, in contrast, is a much later addition in neo-Gothic style). The largest in the world at the time it was built, the dome is 45m (150 ft.) wide and 104m (300 ft.) high from the drum to the distinctive lantern at the top of the cupola. Brunelleschi had to take over the project when the previous builders left off, unsure of how to complete the building without having it collapse; his ingenious solution was to construct the dome in two layers enclosing a space inside, and to have each layer become progressively thinner toward the top, thus reducing the weight. If you're up to it, you can climb the 463 spiraling steps hidden in the space between the layers to see this architectural marvel from the inside.

The dome was frescoed by Giorgio Vasari and Federico Zuccari, while the rest of the interior was frescoed by Paolo Uccello in the 1430s and 1440s. Take notice of the memorial to Sir John Hawkwood, an English mercenary hired by the Florentines, who promised him a statue but gave him a fresco of a statue instead. The bronze doors of the **New Sacristy,** by Luca della Robbia, are the best work of art inside the Duomo.

Under the Duomo, you can visit the remains of **Santa Reparata,** the former Duomo, torn down in 1375 to build the new cathedral. Excavations, begun in 1966, uncovered a rich trove of material dating back over centuries, including walls of Roman houses and Roman ceramic, glass, and metalwork, as well as paleo-Christian and medieval objects (Brunelleschi's tombstone was also discovered here). Free tours are given Monday through Saturday, every 40 minutes from 10:30 a.m. to noon and 3 to 4:20 p.m.

See map p. 198. Piazza Duomo. ☎ 055-2302885. Bus: A, 1, 6, 7, 10, or 11. Admission: Cathedral free; cupola 6€ ($7.20); Santa Reparata 3€ ($3.60); 5 and under free. Open: Mon–Wed and Fri 10 a.m.–5 p.m., Thurs and first Sat of each month 10 a.m.–3:30 p.m., other Sat 10 a.m.–4:45 p.m., Sun and holidays 1:30–4:45 p.m. (open Sun morning for services only); Cupola: Mon–Fri 8:30 a.m.–7 p.m., Sat 8:30 a.m.–5:40 p.m., except first Sat of month 8:30 a.m.–4 p.m. Last ascent to the cupola 40 minutes earlier.

Galleria degli Uffizi
Piazza della Signoria

Occupying a Renaissance *palazzo* built by Vasari to house the administrative offices (*uffizi* means "offices") of the Tuscan Duchy, the gallery houses a mind-blowing collection of work. Here you pictorially experience the birth of the Renaissance, seeing how the changing ideas about the nature of humanity (the new humanism) were translated into visual form. Medieval artists weren't bad painters — their work just reflected a holistically Christian viewpoint, with no concept of "nature" as something separate from the divine — but the new humanism changed all this. You can witness this shift if you start your visit with Cimabue's great *Crucifixion,* still inspired by the flat forms and ritualized expressions of Byzantine art. Follow with the work of his student Giotto, where the human figure begins to take on greater realism. The work of Sandro Botticelli — including his *Birth of Venus* (the goddess emerging from the waves on a shell) and *Primavera* (an ambiguous allegory of spring) — show how the revival of classical (pagan) myth opened a new range of expression and subject. Across from Botticelli's *Venus,* don't miss the spectacular **triptych of Hugo**

Lorenzo's hiding spot

The New Sacristy in Florence's Duomo is where Lorenzo de' Medici hid out after he and his brother (who was murdered) were ambushed during mass by some of their rivals in one of Florence's endless power struggles.

Mass at the Duomo is still full of surprises: At the end of Easter Sunday mass, a mechanical dove flies down from the Duomo's top (sliding along a wire) and falls on a cart laden with flowers and led by white oxen. If all runs smoothly, the cart explodes when the hundreds of fireworks hidden beneath the flowers are ignited by the fuse inside the dove.

van der Goes, whose humanism emerges in the intensity of expression and powerful realism of his poor peasants (also look for the fanciful monster lurking in the right panel). **Piero della Francesca's diptych** features full-profile portraits of Federico da Montefeltro and his wife, painted in the third quarter of the 15th century; note how he brings his subjects to life with luminosity and incredible detail, warts and all. You can then delight in the full explosion of the Renaissance, with Masaccio's *Madonna and Child with St. Anne,* Leonardo's *Adoration of the Magi* and *Annunciation,* several **Raphaels,** Michelangelo's *Holy Family,* Caravaggio's *Bacchus* . . . there's so much at the Uffizi that you should really come twice to absorb it all.

See map p. 198. Piazzale degli Uffizi 6, off Piazza della Signoria. ☎ *055-2388651 or 055-294883 for reservations. Bus: B. Admission: 6.50€ ($7.80); reservation additional 3€ ($3.60). Open: Tues–Sun 8:15 a.m.–6:50 p.m. Last admission 45 minutes earlier. Closed Jan 1, May 1, and Dec 25.*

Galleria dell'Accademia (Michelangelo's David)
Accademia

The Accademia's undisputed star is Michelangelo's *David,* set on a pedestal at the heart of the museum. Michelangelo was just 29 when he took a 5.1m (17-ft.) column of white Carrara marble abandoned by another sculptor and produced the masculine perfection of *Il Gigante (The Giant),* as *David* is nicknamed. The statue stands beneath a rotunda built expressly for it in 1873, when it was moved here from Piazza della Signoria (a copy stands in its place on the square). In 1991, *David* was attacked by a lunatic with a hammer, so you now have to view him through a reinforced-glass shield (like the *Pietà* in Vatican City). The gallery's other remarkable works include Michelangelo's *St. Matthew* and his interesting series of *Slaves* (which are either unfinished or were poetically left partly formed from the original hunks of stone). Among the paintings, you'll find Perugino's *Assumption* and *Descent from the Cross* (the latter done in collaboration with Filippino Lippi); *The Virgin of the Sea,* attributed to Botticelli; and Pontormo's *Venus and Cupid.*

See map p. 198. Via Ricasoli 60, at Via Guelfa. ☎ *055-2388609.* www.sbas. firenze.it/accademia. *Bus: 1, 6, 7, 10, or 11 to Via Guelfa, then walk 1 block east; C to Piazza San Marco, then walk 1 block south. Admission: 6.50€ ($7.80), 9.50 € ($11) for special exhibits. Open: Tues–Sun 8:15 a.m.–6:50 p.m. Ticket booth closes 45 minutes earlier. Closed Jan 1, May 1, and Dec 25.*

Giotto's Bell Tower
Duomo

Giotto was known as a painter and not an architect — but shortly before the end of his life, he designed this beautiful, soaring 84m (276-ft.) bell tower banded with pink, green, and white marble. Giotto had completed only the first two levels by his death in 1337, and the replacement architect had to correct the mistakes Giotto had made — such as not making

The Uffizi Gallery

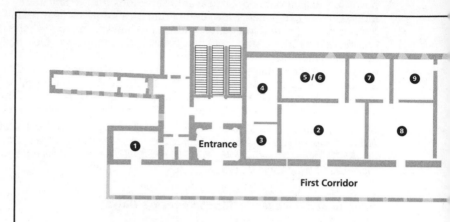

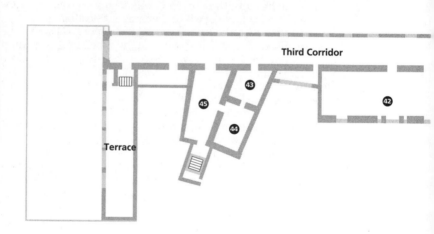

1 Archaeological Room
2 Giotto & 13th-Century Paintings
3 Sienese Paintings (14th Century)
4 Florentine Paintings (14th Century)
5/6 International Gothic
7 Early Renaissance
8 Filippo Lippi
9 Antonio del Pollaiolo
10/14 Botticelli & Ghirlandaio

15 Leonardo da Vinci
16 Geographic Maps
17 Ermafrodito
18 The Tribune
19 Perugino & Signorelli
20 Dürer & German Artists
21 Giovanni Bellini & Giorgione
22 Flemish & German Paintings
23 Mantegna & Correggio

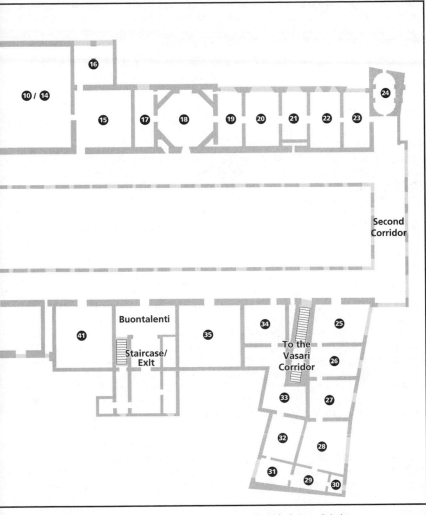

24 Miniatures
25 Michelangelo & Florentine Artists
26 Raphael & Andrea del Sarto
27 Pontormo & Rosso Fiorentino
28 Tiziano & Sebastiano del Piombo
29 Parmigianino & Dosso Dossi
30 Emilian Paintings
31 Veronese
32 Tintoretto

33 16th-Century Paintings
34 Lombard School
35 Barocci
41 Rubens & Flemish Paintings
42 Niobe
43 Caravaggio
44 Rembrandt
45 18th-Century Paintings

the walls thick enough to support the structure. Some of the artwork that originally graced the tower — by Donatello, Francesco Talenti, Luca della Robbia, and Andrea Pisano — are now housed in the **Museo dell'Opera del Duomo** (see later in this section), so copies have taken their place. If you're up to it, climbing the 414 steps to the top affords excellent views of the city and especially of the Duomo next door.

See map p. 198. Piazza Duomo. ☎ 055-2302885. Bus: A, 1, 6, 7, 10, or 11. Admission: 6€ ($7.20). Open: Daily 8:30 a.m.–7:30 p.m. Last admission 20 minutes earlier.

Medici Chapels
Duomo

With a separate entrance to the back of the church of San Lorenzo, these chapels are part of the same structure; the burial place of the Medici family, they are more a tribute to Michelangelo than to the people who bankrolled the Renaissance. While the octagonal **Chapel of the Princes** is a gaudy baroque affair, decorated with marble and semiprecious stones and containing monumental tombs of Medici grand dukes, the **New Sacristy,** begun by Michelangelo and finished by the artist/author Vasari, is somber and impressive. The design reflects some of the elements of the Old Sacristy inside San Lorenzo (see later in this section), but with bold innovations so that it became one of the founding works of the Mannerist style. Michelangelo's funerary sculptures are brilliant: The **Monument to Lorenzo Duca d'Urbino** represents the seated duke flanked by *Aurora* (Dawn) and *Crepuscolo* (Dusk); the **Monument to Giuliano Duca di Nemours** (the son of Lorenzo the Magnificent) is shown rising, with the figures of *Giorno* (Day) and *Notte* (Night) at his sides. In front of the sacristy's altar is Michelangelo's *Madonna and Child;* Lorenzo the Magnificent is buried under this sculpture. Ironically, because Michelangelo didn't live to complete his plan (he died in 1564), Lorenzo got a much less magnificent tomb than some of the lesser Medicis. To the left of the altar is a small subterranean chamber containing some drawings attributed to Michelangelo; you can see them by making an appointment when you enter.

See map p. 198. Piazza Madonna degli Aldobrandini, behind the church of San Lorenzo. ☎ 055-2388602. Bus: 1 or 6 to Martelli 02. Admission: 6€ ($7.20). Open: Daily 8:15 a.m.–5 p.m. Ticket booth closes 30 minutes earlier. Closed second and fourth Sun of each month; first, third, and fifth Mon of each month; Jan 1, May 1, and Dec 25.

Museo dell'Opera del Duomo
Duomo

We definitely recommend visiting this museum: It's where you'll find all of the original Renaissance works that decorated the Duomo, its Bell Tower, and its Baptistery (see earlier in this section) — they were removed from their settings to avoid damage from pollution and hammer-wielding maniacs. You'll see Ghiberti's breathtaking bronze **Gates of Paradise** panels from the Baptistery; Donatello's highly realistic **sculpture of Habbakuk** and his *Mary Magdalen* in polychromed wood from Giotto's Bell Tower; one of Michelangelo's *Pietà;* and Luca della Robbia's **cantoria** (choir loft) facing a similar work by Donatello, offering an example of the diversity of Renaissance styles.

See map p. 198. Piazza Duomo 9, behind the Duomo. ☎ *055-2302885.* www.opera duomo.firenze.it. *Bus: 1, 6, 7, 10, 11, or A. Admission: 6€ ($7.20); 10€ ($12) for special exhibits. Open: Daily 9 a.m.–7:30 p.m. Last admission 40 minutes earlier.*

Orsanmichele
Piazza della Signoria

Born as a granary and warehouse, this building was transformed into a church in the 14th century, when it was the site of a miracle — an image of the Madonna supposedly appeared here. The new church was decorated by the best artists of the time, including Donatello, Ghiberti, Verrocchio, and others. Inside, you'll find vaulted Gothic arches, 500-year-old frescoes, and a stone-encrusted 14th-century tabernacle by Andrea Orcagna protecting a 1348 *Madonna and Child* by Bernardo Daddi. The art — including the originals from the church facade (those there now are copies) — is in the attached museum, accessible from the Palazzo della Lana of the powerful wool merchants' guild (wool is *lana* in Italian), built in 1308. This was still closed at press time, but it is scheduled to open soon.

See map p. 198. Via Arte della Lana, off Via Orsanmichele. ☎ *055-284944. Bus: A to Orsanmichele. Admission: Free. Open: Mon–Fri 9 a.m. to noon and 4–6 p.m.; Sat, Sun, and holidays 9 a.m.–1 p.m. and 4–6 p.m. Closed the first and last Mon of each month.*

Palazzo Pitti and Giardino di Boboli
Piazza Santo Spirito

Begun in 1458 by the textile merchant/banker Luca Pitti, the *palazzo* was finished by the Medici family in 1549 (they tripled its size and added the Boboli Gardens). It houses a superb painting collection in the **Galleria Palatina:** several works by **Raphael,** including his *Madonna of the Chair* and the famous *La Fornarina* (modeled on the features of his Roman mistress); what is perhaps the largest single collection of works by moody psychological painter **Andrea del Sarto;** and several famous portraits by **Titian, Veronese,** and **Tintoretto.** Well worth a visit are the **Royal Apartments,** where three ruling families once resided (the Medici, Lorena, and finally Savoy), now adorned with furnishings and rich decorations from the Renaissance to Rinascimento. The beautifully frescoed and decorated halls of the first floor and mezzanine house the **Museo degli Argenti** — a collection of objects in precious metals, ivory, and crystal — where we recommend you see the splendid vases of Lorenzo de' Medici in semiprecious stone, as well as the cameos and carved precious stones of the Medici collection. Also worth visiting is the **Modern Art Gallery,** which holds several famous paintings of the Macchiaioli movement (the Italian counterpart to the French Impressionists); most notable are those by Giovanni Fattori and Telemaco Signorini. If you're interested in

The birth of opera

The story goes that in 1589, the Medici organized a wedding reception in the Giardino di Boboli and, of course, wanted something grand. They hired the best local composers of the time — Jacopo Peri and Ottavio Rinuccini — to provide musical entertainment. The pair came up with the idea of setting a classical story to music and having actors sing the whole thing, as in a modern musical. The show was a great success and the Medici added another feather to their caps: the birth of opera.

Renaissance clothing, do not miss the historical clothing collection in the **Galleria del Costume.**

But if your time is limited, after you see the Galleria Palatina and the Royal Apartments, run behind the *palazzo* to visit the **Boboli Gardens.** This is the world's most grandiose example of Italianate gardens. The expanse of 45,000 sq. m (11 acres) was designed in the 16th century and expanded in the 18th and 19th centuries. Take the **Viottolone** (literally "large lane") — lined with laurels, cypresses, and pines and punctuated by statues — to the **Piazzale dell'Isolotto,** with the beautiful **Fontana dell'Oceano (Ocean Fountain).** You'll also see several pavilions, such as the 18th-century neo-classical **Palazzina della Meridiana** as well as the elegant **Casino del Cavaliere** — built in the 17th century as a retreat for the Granduca and dominating the whole park from the top of the hill. It houses the **Porcelain Museum,** which includes Sèvres, Chantilly, and Meissen pieces, as they were used at the tables of the three reigning families that resided in the palace.

See map p. 198. Piazza de' Pitti, just steps from the Ponte Vecchio. ☎ *055-294883. www.polomuseale.firenze.it. Bus: D. Admission: Combination ticket for all the museums and Giardino di Boboli 11€ ($13). Galleria Palatina, Royal Apartments, and Modern Art Gallery 8.50€ ($10). Museo degli Argenti, Porcelain Museum, Galleria del Costume, and Giardino di Boboli 8€ ($9.60). Open: Galleria Palatina, Royal Apartments, and Modern Art Gallery Tues–Sun 8:15 a.m.–6:50 p.m. Closed Jan 1, May 1, and Dec 25. Royal Apartments closed Jan. Museo degli Argenti, Porcelain Museum, Galleria del Costume, and Giardino di Boboli daily 8:15 a.m. to 1 hour before sunset. Last admission 1 hour earlier (30 minutes for Museo degli Argenti). Closed Jan 1, May 1, and Dec 25.*

Palazzo Vecchio
Piazza della Signoria

Built in 1299, this *palazzo* housed the Signoria — Florence's government — during its first period and was taken over by Cosimo de' Medici and his family in the 16th century, before they moved to Palazzo Pitti. They are responsible for the grandiose redecoration. The highlight is the **Hall of the 500 (Sala dei Cinquecento),** where the 500-member council met when Florence was still a republic and before the Medicis' rule; here you'll find Michelangelo's *Genius of Victory* statue. On the upper floor are the private apartments of the Grand Duc, including the private chapel of Eleonora di Toledo (wife of Cosimo), masterfully frescoed by **Bronzino,** along with several elegant halls.

See map p. 198. Piazza della Signoria. ☎ *055-2768465. Bus: B. Admission: 6€ ($7.20). Open: Fri–Wed 9 a.m.–7 p.m., Thurs 9 a.m.–2 p.m. Ticket booth closes 30 minutes earlier.*

Piazza della Signoria
Piazza della Signoria

Signoria is the name of the political system that governed the city during medieval times — the Medicis were the *signori* (lords) — and this was the political heart of Florence. A beautiful example of medieval architecture, the L-shaped square is flanked by the **Palazzo Vecchio** (see earlier) on the east side and the famous **Loggia della Signoria** on the south. This elegant Gothic structure is also called Loggia dei Lanzi (after the *Lanzichenecchi* soldiers who camped here in the 16th century) or Loggia dell'Orcagna — after Andrea di Cione, called Orcagna, the supposed architect (in fact, it was built by Benci Cione and Simone Talenti). Once used for political ceremonies, it later became a sculpture workshop.

Several sculptures still decorate it, including the ***Rape of the Sabines*** — an essay in three-dimensional Mannerism — and ***Hercules with Nessus the Centaur,*** both by Giambologna. He's also the creator of the bronze equestrian statue of **Cosimo de' Medici** in the middle of the square. Also in the Loggia are Benvenuto Cellini's famous ***Perseus,*** holding up the severed head of Medusa; a copy of Michelangelo's ***David*** (the original was moved to the Galleria dell'Accademia in the 19th century); and a ***Heracles*** by Baccio Bandinelli. At the corner of Palazzo Vecchio is the much criticized **Fountain of Neptune,** built by the architect Ammannati in 1575 and disparaged by Michelangelo as well; Florentines used to mock it as *Il Biancone* ("Big Whitey").

See map p. 198. Off Via dei Calzaiuoli. Bus: B.

Savonarola was here

Another famous town resident was the passionate reformer Girolamo Savonarola. He was the prior of the Dominican monastery of San Marco (see later in this section) and devoted his life to the purification of the Catholic church and the Florentines. He directed the burning of jewels, books, riches, and art pieces judged too "pagan" on pyres erected in Piazza della Signoria. His sermons against worldly corruption gave him increasingly more political power, but eventually brought him into conflict with Pope Alexander VI (who had four illegitimate children, including Cesare and Lucrezia Borgia). Excommunicated and betrayed by the Florentines who at one time supported him, he was condemned as a heretic and burned on Piazza della Signoria in 1498. The small disk in the ground near the Fountain of Neptune marks the spot where he was executed.

Ponte Vecchio
Piazza della Signoria

This is the only surviving medieval bridge in Florence. Many lovely ones spanned the Arno until the 20th century, but the Germans blew them all up during their retreat from Italy toward the end of World War II (they've since been replaced). Today, this symbol of the city of Florence offers beautiful views and thrives with shops selling leather goods, jewelry, and other items. If you look up, you'll see the famous **Vasari Corridor:** After the completion of the Palazzo Pitti in the 16th century, Cosimo de' Medici commissioned Vasari to build an aboveground "tunnel" running along the Ponte Vecchio rooftops and linking the Palazzo degli Uffizi with the new *palazzo*. Inside, the corridor is richly decorated with art (visits are scheduled on specific days; make reservations at the Galleria degli Uffizi).

See map p. 198. At the end of Via Por Santa Maria. Bus: B.

San Lorenzo
Duomo

San Lorenzo, founded in the fourth century, was the parish church of the powerful Medici family, some of whom are buried in the **Medici Chapels** (see earlier in this section). Behind its unfinished facade, it hides a treasure-trove of artwork: The counter-facade was decorated by Michelangelo, while the interior was designed by Brunelleschi; the monument to the left of the Sacristy's entrance is a masterpiece Verrocchio created for Giovanni and Piero de' Medici. The **Old Sacristy** itself is a tour de force of Renaissance architecture, designed by Brunelleschi and then decorated by Donatello, who executed the cherubs all around the cupola; he might also be the author of the bronze pulpits and the terra-cotta bust of San Lorenzo — or they could be by Desiderio da Settignano. From the pretty cloister on the left of the basilica facade, you can reach — via an elaborate stone staircase — another of Michelangelo's works: Also designed in 1524, the **Biblioteca Laurenziana** houses the Medicis' fabulous collection of manuscripts, some of which are on display.

See map p. 198. Piazza San Lorenzo, off Borgo San Lorenzo. ☎ *055-216634. Bus: 1, 6, 7, 10, or 11 to Martelli 02. Admission: 2.50€ ($3). Open: Mon–Sat 10 a.m.–5 p.m.*

San Marco and Museum
Accademia

The main reason for a visit to this Dominican monastery is to see the early Renaissance masterpieces by the incomparable **Fra' Beato Angelico** — vividly painted, exceptionally human works. The dormitory contains his famous *Annunciation,* while the part of the structure that's now a museum contains panel paintings and altar pieces, including the *Crucifixion.* Another notable work here is the *Last Supper* by **Ghirlandaio.** The church itself is decorated with works by Fra Bartolomeo and other artists.

See map p. 198. Piazza San Marco 1. ☎ 055-2388608. Bus: C, 1, 6, 7, 10, or 11. Admission: 4€ ($4.80). Open: Mon–Fri 8:15 a.m.–1:50 p.m.; Sat 8:15 a.m.–6:50 p.m.; Sun 8:15 a.m.–7 p.m. Ticket booth closes 30 minutes earlier. Closed first, third, and fifth Sun and second and fourth Mon of each month, Jan 1, May 1, and Dec 25.

Santa Croce, Cappella Pazzi, and Museo dell'Opera di Santa Croce
Santa Croce

This is the world's largest Franciscan church, begun in 1294 by Arnolfo di Cambio, the first architect of Florence's Duomo, and a magnificent example of Italian Gothic. Many notable Renaissance figures have found their final resting place in this church: Over 270 tombstones pave the floor, and monumental tombs line its walls. Michelangelo, Galileo, Rossini, and Machiavelli are all buried here; Dante's tomb is just a *cenotaph* (an empty burial monument) because he died in exile in Ravenna and was buried there. The convent compound's key attraction are not Giotto's frescoes in the church — which are not very well preserved — but the 15th-century **Cappella de' Pazzi**, a wonderful example of early Renaissance architecture by Brunelleschi.

Don't miss the **Museo dell'Opera di Santa Croce,** which houses art taken from the church and the cloisters, including a splendid sculpture of San Ludovico da Tolosa by **Donatello**. The famous *Crucifixion* by **Cimabue** is also on display, although restoration of the artwork was not able to undo the great damage caused by the flood of 1966.

See map p. 198. Piazza Santa Croce. ☎ 055-2466105. Bus: C. Admission: 4€ ($4.80) includes admission to the Museo dell'Opera di Santa Croce. Open: Mon–Sat 9:30 a.m.–5:30 p.m.; Sun and holidays 1–5:30 p.m.

Santa Maria Novella and Museum
Santa Maria Novella

This splendid example of Italian Gothic was built as a Dominican church between 1246 and 1360; it is decorated with frescoes by such great artists as Domenico Ghirlandaio and Filippino Lippi, but the star of the show is the *Trinità* by Masaccio. The other star is Giotto's *Crucifix,* gracing the main nave. Adjoining the church is the entry to the museum, which occupies the cloisters of the church, including the splendid **Green Cloister,** named for the beautiful coloration of its frescoes (some by Paolo Uccello). The **Cappellone degli Spagnoli** (Chapel of the Spaniards) is worth a visit: It was frescoed by Andrea di Buonaito between 1367 and 1369 with scenes from the lives of Christ and St. Peter as well as two famous Triumphs, that of St. Thomas and that of the Dominicans. (Cosimo de' Medici's wife, Eleonora, was from Toledo, Spain, hence the name of the chapel.)

See map p. 198. Piazza Santa Maria Novella. ☎ 055-215918. Bus: 6, 11, 36, 37, or A. Admission: 2.70€ ($3.20). Open: Mon–Thurs and Sat 9:30 a.m.–5 p.m.; Sun and holidays 9 a.m.–2 p.m. Closed Sun in Aug.

Santo Spirito
Piazza Santo Spirito

Behind the 18th-century facade of this church, you'll discover an architectural jewel. Built between 1444 and 1488, the interior was designed by **Brunelleschi** and is divided into three naves separated by elegant arches; the sacristy was designed by **Sangallo,** while the handsome bell tower on the left of the facade was designed by Baccio d'Agnolo. Inside, you'll find frescoes and paintings from various artists. Do not miss the beautiful *Madonna col Bambino e santi* by Filippino Lippi.

See map p. 198. Piazza Santo Spirito. ☎ *055-210030. Admission: Free. Open: Mon–Tues and Thurs–Fri 10 a.m. to noon and 4–5:30 p.m.; Wed 10 a.m. to noon; Sat–Sun 4–5:30 p.m.*

Finding more cool things to see and do

After you've exhausted all the "musts" on your list, here are a few more worthwhile sights and activities:

- ✔ The **Museo della Casa Buonarroti** (Via Ghibellina 70; ☎ 055-241-752; Bus: A; Admission: 6.50€/$7.80; Open: Wed–Mon 9:30 a.m.–2 p.m.) may never have had Michelangelo as a tenant, but he and his heirs did own it. Some of the museum's holdings are very interesting — they include a few of the master's earliest works, such as the *Madonna of the Steps,* which he did when only in his mid-teens.

- ✔ Florence finally has an attraction specifically designed for the young ones: The **Bottega dei Ragazzi (Youth Workshop)** inside the **Museo degli Innocenti** (Via dei Fibbiai 2; ☎ 055-2478386; www.istitutodeglinnocenti.it; Open: Mon–Sat 9 a.m.–1 p.m. and 3–7 p.m.) has just opened its doors. This large space inside a beautiful Renaissance building (another of Brunelleschi's works beside the famous dome in the Duomo) includes playrooms, workshops, and an auditorium where children and teens can get their hands on typical Renaissance techniques and crafts.

- ✔ The **Palazzo Medici Riccardi** (Via Cavour 3; ☎ 055-2760340; Bus: 1, 6, 7, 10, or 11; Open: Thurs–Tues 9 a.m.–7 p.m.; Admission: 4€/$4.80) is where Cosimo de' Medici and his family lived before they took over the Palazzo Vecchio. It was built by Michelozzo in 1444 and has a lighter feel than later *palazzi,* such as the Pitti. Benozzo Gozzoli, a student of Fra Angelico's, decorated the chapel — **Cappella dei Magi** — with marvelous frescoes. The *palazzo* gives a good idea of what upper-class Florentine life was like during the Renaissance.

- ✔ During the **Maggio Musicale Fiorentino** (see "Living It Up After Dark," later in this chapter), the town organizes a variety of events, including special museum exhibits, street performances, musical performances in bars and boutiques, and even a golf tournament! A prize is awarded for the best shop-window decorations following the Maggio Fiorentino theme. Ask your hotel or the tourist office

for the special program that's published and distributed for the
occasion.

✔ If you have the time and disposition for another museum, the
Archaeological Museum (Via della Colonna 38; ☎ 055-23575; Bus:
6; Admission: 4€ ($4.80); Open: Mon 2–7 p.m., Tues and Thurs
8:30 a.m.–7 p.m., Wed and Fri–Sun 8:30 a.m.–2 p.m.) is a good
choice. Housed inside the elegant 17th-century Palazzo della
Crocetta, near the beautiful Piazza Santissima Annunziata, it contains stunning Etruscan pieces and a very good collection of
Egyptian art. The core of the collection was put together by the
Medici and Lorena families who ruled Florence. Exhibited in the
Uffizi until 1888, it was then moved into its present location and
further expanded.

✔ If you're in town toward the end of June, do not miss the tournament of Renaissance soccer, the **Gioco di Calcio Storico Fiorentino**
(☎ 055-290832) in which two sets of 27 players confront each
other. This rather rough play takes place on the 16th, 24th, and
30th of June to mark the feast of St. John, Florence's patron saint.
Each day culminates with fireworks on the river Arno.

✔ The little hill town of **Fiesole,** 4.5km (3 miles) north of Florence,
makes a wonderful excursion. It's just an easy bus ride away (take
no. 7 from SMN train station or Piazza San Marco). Fiesole existed
well before Florence — it started as an Etruscan settlement in the
sixth century B.C. — and retains the character of a small town and
its independence as a municipality. In summer, it hosts music,
theater, and other cultural events. Be sure to visit the **Duomo
(Cattedrale di San Romolo)** on the main square, Piazza Mino da
Fiesole, which was built in 1028. The archaeological area includes
Roman and Etruscan ruins: **Teatro Romano and Museo Civico** (Via
Partigiani 1; ☎ 055-59477; www.fiesolemusei.it; Open: winter
Wed–Mon 9:30 a.m.–5 p.m., summer daily 9:30 a.m.–7 p.m.). The
theater, built in the first century B.C., is the site of outdoor concerts
in summer. The **Museo Bandini,** near the Duomo, features 13th- to
15th-century Tuscan art. A combination ticket, **Biglietto Fiesole
Musei,** includes round-trip bus fare from Florence and admission to
the archaeological area with the Roman theater, the archaeological
museum, the Museo Bandini, and the Cappella San Jacopo — all for
7.20€ ($8.60). The *biglietto* is sold at the ATAF information booth at
the SMN train station and in bars and newsstands displaying a
sticker advertising it.

Seeing Florence by guided tour

The guided **walking tours** arranged through the tourist office (see "Finding information after you arrive," earlier in this chapter) are extremely
well organized and a great way to explore Florence's pedestrian-only
historic center. If you contact the **Ufficio Guide Turistiche** (Viale Gramsci
9a; ☎ 055-247-8188), you can organize a guided tour tailored to your
specific needs.

We like the hop-on/hop-off bus tour run by **Florence City Sightseeing** (☎ 800-424500), which offers two itineraries; tickets are valid for 24 hours and cost 20€ ($24) for adults and 10€ ($12) for children three to ten. **Line A** departs the SMN train station every 30 minutes — in winter from 9 a.m. to 7 p.m., in summer until 11 p.m. — and tours the *centro storico,* making 15 stops. **Line B** runs every 60 minutes — in winter from 9 a.m. to 6 p.m., in summer until 10 p.m. — between Porta San Frediano in Oltrarno all the way to Fiesole, making 23 stops.

Suggested one-, two-, and three-day itineraries

You could easily spend a week in Florence and not tire of it, especially if you take day trips to the destinations highlighted in the next two chapters. But if your time is limited, you'll need to make choices. Here's what we would do:

Florence in one day

If you only have one day in Florence, you'll have to start bright and early. Head to the **Galleria dell'Accademia** (where you've made advance reservations), strolling on your way through Piazza Santissima Annunziata — one of Florence's nicest squares — and maybe stopping for a *gelato* at **Carabé** (see "Looking for a *gelato* break?" earlier in this chapter). For those who are not as keen on the *David,* we recommend the **Bargello Museum,** near Piazza della Signoria, Florence's best sculpture museum. Head later for the **Duomo,** enjoying the sight of the cathedral and of **Giotto's Bell Tower,** but linger only in the **Baptistery,** since you're short on time. After your visit, lunch on a sampling of cheeses and cured meats from the Tuscan countryside at **Consorzio Agrario Pane and Co.** (see "Fast food, Florence style," earlier in this chapter) while you wait for your timed entry to the **Galleria degli Uffizi,** where you've also made advance reservations. Once you are oversaturated with Renaissance paintings, walk around **Piazza della Signoria,** taking in **Palazzo Vecchio;** then head for **Ponte Vecchio** on Via Por Santa Maria, and cross over to **Oltrarno.** Check out some of the shops on your way, such as **C.O.I.** for gold, **Cirri** for embroidered linen, **Madova Gloves** for, well, gloves, and **Giulio Giannini & Figlio** for marbleized paper (see "Shopping the Local Stores," later in this chapter). After a nice stroll along the Arno, it is now time for *aperitivo,* and what better opportunity to try the Florentine invention *Negroni?* Try it at the **Negroni Florence Bar** (see "Bars, pubs, and clubs," later in this chapter). For dinner, treat yourself at **Cibreo** (see "Dining Out," earlier in this chapter).

Florence in two days

Two days are a lot better than one — you'll be able to see most of the highlights in town.

Day 1

Dedicate the morning to sculpture: the **Galleria dell'Accademia,** if you absolutely want to see the *David,* and the **Museo del Bargello,** for

Florence's best sculpture museum. Near the Accademia, stroll to Piazza Santissima Annunziata for a peek at one of Florence's nicest squares and a stop for *gelato* at **Carabé** (see "Looking for a *gelato* break?" earlier in this chapter). Later on, pick up the makings of a tasty picnic at **Consorzio Agrario Pane and Co.**, or have a full lunch at **Osteria Ganino** or **Pane e Vino** (see "Dining Out," earlier in this chapter). Continue your day with the **Galleria degli Uffizi,** where you have made advance reservations. After your visit, spend the rest of your afternoon and evening exploring **Ponte Vecchio, Palazzo Vecchio,** and **Piazza della Signoria.**

Day 2

Start your day with an exploration of the **Duomo,** with **Giotto's Bell Tower** and the **Baptistery.** Continue with the **Museo dell'Opera del Duomo.** Have lunch at **Le Mossacce** (see "Dining Out," earlier in this chapter). In the afternoon, head for the church of **San Lorenzo,** and visit the **Medici Chapels** behind it as well. You can also stroll through the **Mercato San Lorenzo** for some shopping (see later in this chapter) before heading for the church of **Santa Maria Novella** and its splendid cloisters. Have your *Negroni aperitivo* at the cafe that invented it, **Giacosa** (see "Bars, pubs, and clubs," later in this chapter). For dinner, treat yourself at **Cibreo** (see "Dining Out," earlier in this chapter).

Florence in three days

Three days is a good amount: You'll be able to see all the best the town has to offer, without feeling pressed for time.

Day 1 and 2

Follow Day 1 and 2 in "Florence in two days," earlier in this chapter.

Day 3

Head for the **Basilica Santa Croce,** and visit the **Cappella Pazzi** and the **Museo dell'Opera di Santa Croce.** Outside the convent compound, don't forget to take a look at the leather goods of the **Scuola del Cuoio di Santa Croce** (see "Shopping the Local Stores," later in this chapter). Have lunch at the **Osteria del Caffè Italiano** (see "Dining Out," earlier in this chapter). In the afternoon, head for **Palazzo Pitti** and the **Giardino di Boboli.** End your day with a stroll and dinner in Oltrarno, perhaps at **Cavolo Nero** (see "Dining Out," earlier in this chapter).

Shopping the Local Stores

With a long tradition of crafts, Florence offers some very nice specialty products, such as leather, fine woven straw, jewelry, embroidered linens and lace, and quality paper products. It's also a center for casual fashion. Many of these goodies are still available at the historic outdoor markets, which are fun even if you don't intend to buy anything.

The outdoor markets of Florence

There are two famous markets in Florence: the leather market **San Lorenzo** (Piazza del Mercato Centrale, 1 block north of the Basilica of San Lorenzo) and the straw market **Mercato della Paglia** (Via Por Santa Maria, off Ponte Vecchio), which sells traditional straw goods (hats, chairs, bags) of unique quality — plus a lot of cheap things mixed in. Both markets are open from 7:30 a.m. to 6 p.m. daily in summer, Tuesday through Saturday in winter. They're good places to shop for T-shirts and small gifts. Good buys can be had, but don't expect to pay peanuts: Try to have a fair idea in your mind of what things are worth and be suspicious of prices that seem too low (the quality might not be what you think). The leather market of San Lorenzo is held around the building of the Mercato Centrale, which houses a great food market (see "Fast food, Florence style," earlier in this chapter).

Remember that all crowded areas, including the outdoor markets, are the preferred hunting ground for pickpockets and purse-snatchers. Don't display your cash too liberally, and keep an eye on your pockets and purse.

Best shopping areas

For elegant shopping, the place to go is **Via de' Tornabuoni,** in the *centro storico* near Santa Maria Novella (between Piazzetta degli Antinori and Piazza di Santa Trinità). This street is at the heart of the ritzy shopping district that includes **Via Strozzi** and **Via della Vigna Nuova** (both off Via de' Tornabuoni); you'll find all the big names of Italian fashion here, such as **Ferragamo** (Via Tornabuoni 16), **Loro Piano** (Via della Vigna Nuova 37r), and **Giorgio Armani** (Via della Vigna Nuova 51r), plus a selection of reliable but expensive boutiques. Other stylish boutiques line the **Lungarno Corsini** (take a left from Via della Vigna Nuova and continue along the river); here you'll find the luxury linen purveyor **Pratesi** (see later in this section), among other nice smaller shops. This shopping district extends east, all the way to **Via Roma, Piazza della Repubblica, Via del Corso, Via dei Calzaiuoli,** and **Via Calimala** off the Ponte Vecchio. You'll see lots of real-life stores here, including the Italian-style department stores **La Rinascente** (Piazza della Repubblica 1; ☎ 055-219113), which sells mostly clothes and housewares, and **COIN** (Via dei Calzaiuoli 56r; ☎ 055-280531).

What to look for and where to find it

Retail shops are generally open Monday from 4 to 7:30 p.m., Tuesday through Saturday from 9 or 10 a.m. to 1 p.m. and 4 to 7:30 p.m. As in all Italian cities, many shops shut down for the month of August, but department stores don't — and are sometimes open during the lunch break as well. During high season, a few stores might be open on Monday mornings and Sundays.

Embroidery and linens

Cirri (Via Por Santa Maria; ☎ 055-2396593; Bus: B to Ponte Vecchio) is a good place for Florentine embroideries, but they don't come cheap. **Pratesi** (Lungarno Corsini 32–34r; ☎ 055-211327; www.pratesi.com; Bus: D) is the place to go for beautifully crafted luxury linens of all kinds.

Housewares and accessories

Controluce (Via della Vigna Nuova 89r; ☎ 055-2398871; Bus: 6, 11, 36, or 37 to Tornabuoni) has a beautiful assortment of designer lamps and accessories. **Emporium** (Via Guicciardini 122r; ☎ 055-212646; Bus: D to Pitti) is good for a variety of stylish accessories. **Viceversa** (Via Ricasoli 53r; ☎ 055-2398281; Bus: C or 6 to Santissima Annunziata) is a great place for browsing and discovering neat gift ideas.

Jewelry

Befani e Tai (Via delle Terme 9; ☎ 055-287825; Bus: B) is a reputable goldsmith shop that sells both antiques and special-order jewelry.

Leather products

Beltrami (Via de' Tornabuoni 48r; ☎ 055-287779; Bus 6, 11, 36, or 37 to Tornabuoni) is the place to go for beautiful leather accessories, including shoes, bags, and luggage. The **Beltrami Outlet** (Via de' Panzani 1r, near the church of Santa Maria Novella; ☎ 055-212661; Bus: A, 1, 6, 11, 36, or 37 to SMN) offers last season's inventory at a discount. For gloves, head straight to **Madova Gloves** (Via Guicciardini 1r; ☎ 055-2396526; www.madova.com; Bus: D to Pitti), which is actually a traditional glove-maker's workshop. **Scuola del Cuoio di Santa Croce (Santa Croce's Leather School)** (Piazza Santa Croce, enter from the church's right transept; ☎ 055-244533; www.leatherschool.it; Bus: A to Piazza Santa Croce) is your best bet if you want to know about the ancient art of leather embossing. The beautifully crafted goods don't come cheap, though.

Ponte Vecchio's gold

It is commonly assumed that Ponte Vecchio is the place to go for gold jewelry: Indeed, in this area, you will find one jewelry shop after the next, but all with pretty much the same merchandise. The prices are no longer great and it's difficult to find something original — perhaps after 500 years and a trillion tourists, the street has gotten a tad stale.

Mosaic "stone painting"

Le Pietre nell'Arte (Piazza Duomo 36r; ☎ 055-212587; Bus: A) is the showroom of a talented father-and-son duo turning out collector-quality items. **Pitti Mosaici** (Piazza Pitti 23r; ☎ 055-282127; Bus: D to Pitti) is one of the few traditional craftsmen left in Florence who specialize in this art form.

Stationery and paper goods

Giulio Giannini & Figlio (Piazza Pitti 37r; ☎ 055-212621; Bus: D to Pitti) is a historic paper provider that has specialized in marbleized goods since the 19th century. You'll find an excellent choice of stationery here. **J. Pineider** (Piazza della Signoria 13r; ☎ 055-284655; Bus: B; also at Via de' Tornabuoni 76; ☎ 055-211605; Bus: 6, 11, 36, or 37), opened in 1774, has supplied paper to many royal figures.

Living It Up After Dark

Nightlife in Florence usually means hanging out in a pub with friends, going for a drink at a trendy bar, or taking a stroll and enjoying some *gelato* in the historic center. Younger crowds like to go dancing at one of the popular discos out of town.

The free monthly *Informacittà* pamphlet, distributed free at tourist offices, gives information on events, exhibits, and concerts.

The performing arts

Several churches in town present evening **concerts,** mainly in the fall. For listings, pick up a free copy of *Welcome to Florence* from the tourist office. The most popular are the concerts of the **Florentine Chamber Orchestra** (☎ 055-783374; www.orcafi.it) in the Orsanmichele church. The season runs March through October; tickets are available at the box office (Via Luigi Alamanni 39, by Fortezza de Basso; ☎ 055-210804) or online at www.boxol.it.

In May, Florence blossoms with music — it's the month of Italy's oldest music festival, **Maggio Musicale Fiorentino** (☎ 800-112211 or 055-213535; Fax: 055-2779410; reservations accepted starting in Sept). Tickets are also sold online at www.maggiofiorentino.com; they range from 20€ to 155€ ($24–$186). Continuing until the end of June, this concert and dance series includes famous performers and world premieres. The final concert, held in the Giardino di Boboli, is a magical experience. At the center of the festival is the **Teatro Comunale** (Corso Italia 16; ☎ 055-213535; Tues–Fri 10 a.m.–4:30 p.m., Sat 10 a.m.–1 p.m.), which also has a regular program of ballet and opera at other times of the year.

Teatro Verdi (Via Ghibellina 99; ☎ 055-212320), a small theater, also offers prestigious dance and classical music performances.

Bars, pubs, and clubs

The oldest *caffè* in town is **Gilli** (Piazza della Repubblica 39r/Via Roma 1r; ☎ 055-213896; Bus: A to Orsanmichele), which dates back to the 18th century and boasts both a great location and elegant décor. **Giacosa** (Via de' Tornabuoni 83r; ☎ 055-2396226; Bus: 6, 11, 36, or 37 to Tornabuoni; closed Sun) is known for its drinks, particularly the Negroni (the ancestor of the Italian pre-dinner *aperitivo*), which apparently was invented here by Mr. Negroni and his barman. Named in honor of that drink, the **Negroni Florence Bar** (Via de'Renai 17r, off Ponte delle Grazie in Oltrarno; ☎ 055-243647) becomes a lively spot in the evening, with music almost every night; it stays open until 2 a.m.

The chef-owner of the popular restaurant Cibreo has opened **Teatro del Sale** (Via de' Macci 111r; ☎ 055-2001492; Open: Tues–Sat 9 p.m. to midnight), a pleasant club offering a tasty buffet-dinner-and-show combination; performances range from jazz to poetry readings. The historic **Jazz Club** (Via Nuova de' Caccini 3; ☎ 055-2479700; Open: Mon–Sat 9 p.m.– 2 a.m.) features live music every night.

Florence has been swept up in a passion for Irish pubs. The beer is original, but the atmosphere a little less so. Try the **Fiddler's Elbow** (Piazza Santa Maria Novella 7r; ☎ 055-215056; Bus: A, 1, 6, 11, 36, or 37), a successful branch of the Italian chain, or the **Dublin Pub** (Via Faenza 27r; ☎ 055-293049; Bus: A to Orsanmichele).

Hot with the elegant crowds are the restaurants and bars of many hotels in the city, such as the **Savoy** (Piazza della Repubblica 7; ☎ 055-27351), the **Donatello Bar** at the **Westin-Excelsior** (Piazza Ognissanti 3; ☎ 055-264201), the **Lungarno** (Borgo San Jacopo 14r; ☎ 055-27261), and the **Fusion Bar** (Gallery Hotel, Vicolo dell'Oro 5; ☎ 055-27263).

Discos

Yab (Via Sassetti 5r; ☎ 055-215160) is open October through May, Monday and Thursday through Saturday from 7:30 p.m. to 4 a.m.; it also serves dinner. **Universale** (Via Pisana 77r, Oltrarno, between Via di Monte Oliveto and Viale B. Gozzoli; ☎ 055-221122; www.universale firenze.it; Bus: 6) is open September through May only, Thursday through Sunday nights. The cover ranges from 11€ to 18€ ($13–$22). Another hot spot is **Jaragua** (Via Erta Canina 12r, Oltrarno, off Viale Michelangiolo; ☎ 055-2343600), a disco and tropical bar with plenty of Caribbean and Latin music, free dance classes, and more. It's open daily from 9:30 p.m. to 3 a.m.; no cover.

Gay and lesbian bars

Tabasco (Piazza Santa Cecilia 3r, by Piazza della Signoria; ☎ 055-213000; Bus: B) is Florence's — and Italy's — oldest gay dance club, housed in a 15th-century building near Piazza della Signoria. The crowd is mostly men in their 20s and 30s. The dance floor is downstairs, while a small video room and piano bar are on the upper level. Open Tuesday through Saturday from 10 p.m. to 3 a.m.; the cover is 8€ to 16€ ($9.60–$19). Tabasco owns two other venues in town: **Silver Stud** (Via della Fornace 9; ☎ 055-688466), a cruising bar, and **Florence Baths** (Via Guelfa 93r; ☎ 055-216050), a gay sauna.

Crisco (Via San Egidio 43r; ☎ 055-2480580) is the leading gay bar in town; it also owns the **Tin Box Club** (Via dell'Oriuolo 19r; ☎ 055-2466387).

In summer at **Discoteca Flamingo** (Via del Pandolfini 26r, near Piazza Santa Croce; ☎ 055-243356; Bus: A), the crowd is international. Thursday through Saturday nights, it's a mixed gay/lesbian party; the rest of the week, it's men only. Open Sunday through Thursday from 10 p.m. to 4 a.m., Friday and Saturday from 10 p.m. to 6 a.m. The bar is open year-round; the disco September through June only. Cover, including the first drink, is 6.20€ ($7.40) Sunday through Thursday; 8€ to 10€ ($9.60–$12) Friday and Saturday.

Fast Facts: Florence

American Express

The office is at Via Dante Alighieri 22R (☎ 055-50981; Bus: A to Condotta); open Monday through Friday from 9 a.m. to 5:30 p.m. and Saturday from 9 a.m. to 12:30 p.m.

Area Code

The local area code is **055** (see "Telephone" in the "Fast Facts" section of Appendix A for more on calling to and from Italy).

ATMs

Numerous banks and exchange offices are located along Via dei Calzaiuoli, between the Duomo and the Palazzo Vecchio.

Doctors and Dentists

Call your consulate or the American Express office for an up-to-date list of English-speaking doctors and dentists. The Tourist Medical Service (Via Lorenzo il Magnifico 59; ☎ 055-475-411; Bus: 8 or 80 to Lavagnini, 12 to Poliziano) is open 24 hours.

Embassies and Consulates

The consulate of the United States is at Lungarno Amerigo Vespucci 38, near the intersection with Via Palestro (☎ 055-266951; Bus: 12 to Palestro). The consulate of the United Kingdom is at Lungarno Corsini 2 (☎ 055-284133; Bus: 11, 36, or 37 to Lungarno Corsini). All embassies are in Rome (see Appendix A).

Emergencies

For an ambulance, call ☎ 118; for the fire department, call ☎ 115.

Hospitals

The main hospital is on Piazza Santa Maria Nuova, 1 block northeast from the Duomo (☎ 055-27581). Pronto Soccorso (First Aid) Careggi is at Viale Pieraccini 17 (☎ 055-7949644).

Information

The tourist office, APT (Via A. Manzoni 16, 50121 Firenze; ☎ 055-23320; Fax: 055-2346286; www.firenzeturismo.it), maintains three info desks in town: at Via Cavour 1r (☎ 055-290832; Open: Mon–Sat 8:30 a.m.–6:30 p.m., Sun 8:30 a.m.–1:30 p.m.); at SMN rail station (Piazza Stazione 4/a; ☎ 055-212245; Open: Mon–Sat 9 a.m.–7 p.m., Sun 8:30 a.m.–2 p.m.); and at Borgo Santa Croce 29r (☎ 055-2340444; Open: Mon–Sat 9 a.m.–7 p.m., Sun 8:30 a.m.–2 p.m.)

Internet Access

The Caironet chain has several locations, the most convenient being Via de' Ginori 59r, off Via Guelfa (☎ 055-2399376), and Via Faenza 49r, near SMN train station (☎ 055-2645560). The easyInternetcafé chain has a branch near the Duomo inside Libreria Martelli (Via Martelli 22; ☎ 055-2657603; Open: Daily 9 a.m.–8 p.m.).

Maps

Any newsstand, especially those near the train station, will have a good selection of local maps.

Pharmacies

There are many pharmacies in Florence, but the Farmacia Molteni, Via Calzaiuoli 7r (☎ 055-289490; Bus: A to Orsanmichele), is open 24 hours, as are the Farmacia Comunale, inside the Santa Maria Novella train station (☎ 055-289435), and All'insegna del Moro, Piazza San Giovanni 20r (☎ 055-211343).

Police

There are two police forces in Italy; call either one. For the Polizia, dial ☎ 113; for the Carabinieri, dial ☎ 112.

Post Office

The main post office is the *ufficio postale* at Via Pellicceria 3, off Piazza della Repubblica

(☎ 055-2736481; Open: Mon–Fri 9 a.m.–6 p.m., Sat 9 a.m.–2 p.m.).

Restrooms

You'll find a few public restrooms at strategic points — the SMN train station, Mercato Centrale (market) — as well as others that are open only in high season. Your best bet is to go to a cafe displaying the "Courtesy Point" logo; these have an agreement with the city to offer such service. Better yet, because Florence is full of museums, use one while you're inside. Also a good bet are department stores, such as the Rinascente in Piazza della Repubblica.

Safety

Florence is quite safe; your only major worries are pickpockets and purse-snatchers due to the huge concentration of tourists. Avoid deserted areas after dark (such as behind the train station and the Cascine Park) and exercise normal urban caution.

Smoking

In 2005, Italy passed a law outlawing smoking in most public places. Smoking is allowed only where there is a separate, ventilated area for nonsmokers. If you want to smoke at your table, call beforehand to make sure the restaurant or cafe you'll be visiting offers a smoking area.

Taxes

See Chapter 5 for information on IVA (Value Added Tax).

Taxi

For a radio taxi, call ☎ 055-4390, 055-4798, 055-4242, or 055-4499.

Transit Info

For air travel, call the airport at ☎ 055-373498 or 050-500707. For city buses, call ☎ 800 424500 in Italy or 055-56501, or go online to www.ataf.net. For out-of-town buses, call SITA (☎ 800-373760). For trains, contact Trenitalia (☎ 892021; www.trenitalia.it).

Weather Updates

Your best bet is the news on TV. (There's no phone number for weather forecasts in Italy, as there is in the U.S.)

Chapter 14

Northern Tuscany and the Cinque Terre

. . . .

In This Chapter
▶ Exploring city ramparts in Lucca
▶ Gaping at the Leaning Tower in Pisa
▶ Discovering fishing villages in the Cinque Terre

. . . .

*N*orthern Tuscany is an area rich in history and natural beauty. Near the Tyrrhenian Sea, you'll find **Pisa,** with its justly famous Leaning Tower; a little farther inland is **Lucca,** one of Italy's most delightful medieval walled cities. No trip to the area could be complete without a glimpse of the Italian Riviera, especially as it is experienced in the national park of the **Cinque Terre,** a group of five picturesque villages clinging to abrupt cliffs and surrounded by a protected marine area.

You'll need a minimum of a day each for these destinations, but if you have the time and the disposition, this region could naturally justify a longer stay. Pisa makes an excellent base for exploring this area; it's not only central but also a pleasant city to visit, with a selection of moderately priced hotels. Alternatively, you can easily visit any of the destinations in this area as a day trip from Florence.

Lucca

The English poet Percy Bysshe Shelley passed through here and wrote "The Baths of Lucca," celebrating the unspoiled medieval town surrounded by powerful red ramparts. Lucca may have expanded a bit beyond its ramparts, but the effect is still unchanged.

Lucca is an easy side trip from Florence, and a day will be enough for a full visit. If you have time, it's also a wonderful place to spend a couple of days leisurely strolling the walls and enjoying an opera or a concert, especially during the September festival (see "More cool things to see and do," later in this section).

Tuscany and Umbria

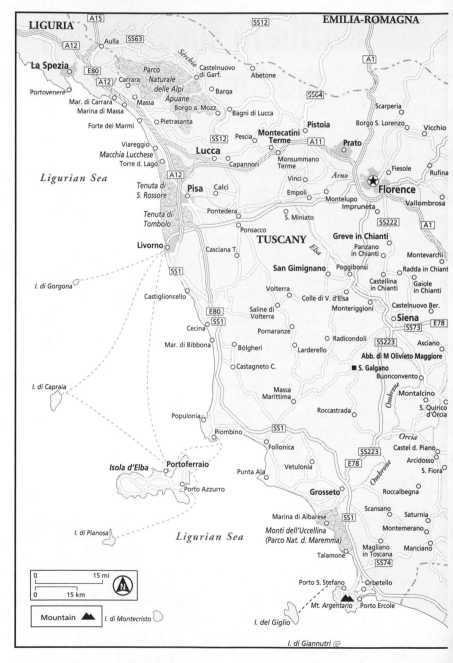

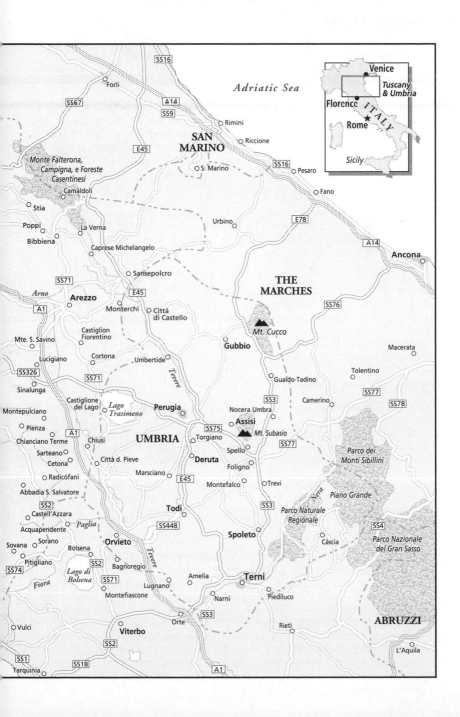

Getting there

Lucca is 64km (40 miles) west of Florence and just 22km (14 miles) north of Pisa. If you are arriving by **plane** at Pisa's airport (see later in this chapter), you can get the direct shuttle to Lucca that leaves every hour between 6 a.m. and 8 p.m.

The area is well served by **train** (☎ 892021; www.trenitalia.it). Trains for Lucca leave Florence every hour; the one-hour trip costs about 4.55€ ($5.50). Trains from Pisa travel as frequently, but the trip is only 20 to 30 minutes and costs 2.05€ ($2.50). Lucca's **train station** (☎ 0583-467013) is on Piazzale Ricasoli, off Porta San Pietro (St. Peter's Gate) on the south side of the walls, within walking distance from the center of town.

You can also get a **bus** to Lucca. **Lazzi** (☎ 055-363041; www.lazzi.it) runs regular service from both Pisa and Florence. The trip takes about an hour from Florence (for 4.70€/$5.60), about 30 minutes from Pisa (for 2.20€/$2.60). The bus terminal is in Piazzale Verdi, within Lucca's walls, on the west side.

If you're coming by **car,** get on *autostrada* A11 from Florence and exit at Lucca. From Pisa, take the local road SS12 to Lucca. Parking lots are located near most of the six city gates — only locals are allowed to drive inside — and town buses connect each of them as well as the rail station to the center of town. Bus tickets are for sale at most tobacconists and newstands for 0.60€ (72¢) for a single ride, 6€ ($7.20) for 12.

Spending the night

Besides the suggestions below, you may want to consider staying at one of Tuscany's most elegant hotels, **Locanda L'Elisa** (Via Nuova per Pisa 1952, off SS12; ☎ 0583-379737; www.locandalelisa.it), a Relais & Châteaux member located only 3km (2 miles) south of the town walls, with splendid accommodations and unique grounds. Another option is its neighbor across the street, **Villa La Principessa** (Via Nuova per Pisa 1616, off SS12; ☎ 0583-370037; www.hotelprincipessa.com).

Hotel Ilaria
$$ **Via Santa Croce**

Tasteful guest rooms, breakfast on a quiet terrace overlooking a beautiful park, free use of bicycles, a parking garage on the premises — all right in the center of Lucca. What else do you want, discounted prices at the best restaurants in town? You got it: The management of Hotel Ilaria has an agreement with three establishments, including the well-recommended Giglio and Buca di Sant'Antonio (see "Dining locally," later in this chapter). Beautifully renovated, this elegant hotel is housed in the former stables of the Villa Bottini and overlooks the villa's park — a quiet setting near the canal that crosses the city toward the east. Accommodations are spacious, with modern furniture and good-sized bathrooms. Some rooms are accessible to people with disabilities.

Lucca

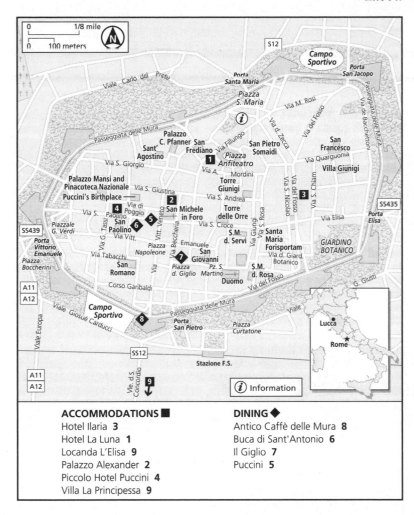

ACCOMMODATIONS ■
Hotel Ilaria **3**
Hotel La Luna **1**
Locanda L'Elisa **9**
Palazzo Alexander **2**
Piccolo Hotel Puccini **4**
Villa La Principessa **9**

DINING ◆
Antico Caffè delle Mura **8**
Buca di Sant'Antonio **6**
Il Giglio **7**
Puccini **5**

See map above. Via del Fosso 26, off Via Santa Croce. ☎ *0583-47-615. Fax: 0583-991-961.* www.hotelilaria.com. *Free parking. Rack rates: 230€ ($276) double. Rates include buffet breakfast. AE, DC, MC, V.*

Palazzo Alexander
$$ Piazza San Michele

This hotel, which opened in 2000, offers luxurious accommodations right in the center of town. The 12th-century palace was restored according to the style of the original furnishings and decorations. Guest rooms are quite magnificent, done in what the management refers to as *stile nobile Lucchese* (Luccan aristocratic style) — featuring much gilded furniture, stuccoes, and damask fabrics. The bathrooms are outfitted with marble and other local stones; some have Jacuzzis as well.

See map p. 227. Via Santa Giustina 48, near Piazza San Michele. ☎ *0583-583571. Fax: 0583-583-610.* www.palazzo-alexander.it. *Free valet parking. Rack rates: 170€ ($204) double. AE, DC, MC, V.*

Piccolo Hotel Puccini
$ Piazza San Michele

In the heart of the historic center is this romantic hotel, offering moderate-sized, cozily furnished rooms at low rates. Situated just across from the house where Puccini was born, it is based in a small 15th-century *palazzo*. All of the bathrooms were being completely renovated at press time. This popular spot is always full, so book well in advance. Note that this hotel lacks an elevator and air-conditioning.

See map p. 227. Via di Poggio 9, off Piazza San Michele. ☎ *0583-55-421. Fax: 0583-53-487.* www.hotelpuccini.com. *Parking: 15€ ($18) in nearby garage. Rack rates: 83€ ($100) double. AE, DC, MC, V.*

Dining locally

There are fewer good restaurants in Lucca than you would expect, but most provide a decent meal — you are in Tuscany, after all — although sometimes it's overpriced. Those listed below are the best spots in town. See Chapter 2 for more on Tuscan cuisine.

Antico Caffè delle Mura
$$ City Ramparts   LUCCAN/TUSCAN

With its fantastic location atop the city walls, this elegant restaurant tries to revive 19th-century atmosphere. After being seated in a paneled formal dining room or, in good weather, the garden out back, you will be able to choose from traditional Luccan dishes and other Tuscan favorites, such as homemade fresh pasta and delectable rabbit, duck, and lamb.

See map p. 227. Piazza Vittorio Emanuele, at Baluardo Santa Maria. ☎ *0583-47962. Reservations necessary. Secondi: 14€–18€ ($17–$22). AE, DC, MC, V. Open: Wed–Mon noon to 3 p.m. and 7:30–11 p.m. Closed 3 weeks in Jan.*

Buca di Sant'Antonio
$ Piazza San Michele   LUCCAN

Lucca's best restaurant boasts excellent food at very reasonable prices. The cuisine is strictly traditional — you wouldn't expect any less from a place that's been around since 1782. The *capretto garfagnino allo spiedo* (spit-roasted baby goat from the Garfagnana area) is a classic, as are the *tortelli lucchesi al sugo* (ravioli with a meat sauce). The remarkable atmosphere is characterized by a labyrinthine succession of small rooms decorated with musical instruments and copper pots.

See map p. 227. Via della Cervia 3, near Piazza San Michele. ☎ *0583-55881. Reservations necessary. Secondi: 13€–14€ ($15–$16). AE, DC, MC, V. Open: Tues–Sun 12:30–3:30 p.m., Tues–Sat 7:30–11 p.m. Closed 3 weeks in July.*

Il Giglio
$ Piazza Napoleone   LUCCAN

Less formal than Antico Caffè delle Mura (reviewed above), Il Giglio offers excellent Luccan specialties and a friendly atmosphere. Dine indoors or, in pleasant weather, alfresco. Try the famed *zuppa di farro* (thick spelt soup) or the homemade *tortelli al ragù*. The *secondi* are also very tasty; you can never go wrong with the rabbit or the roasted lamb.

See map p. 227. Piazza del Giglio 3, near Piazza Napoleone. ☎ *0583-494058. Reservations recommended. Secondi: 14€–16€ ($17–$19). AE, DC, MC, V. Open: Thurs–Tues 12:30–3 p.m.; Thurs–Mon 7:30–10:30 p.m. Closed 2 weeks in Feb.*

Puccini
$$ Piazza San Michele   FISH/LUCCAN

You'll always get a fine seafood meal here — but you may not receive the service to match. The cuisine mixes tradition with innovation, and the offerings vary with the daily catch. More creative dishes such as *tortelloni neri di crostacei con asparagi e pomodorini* (black round seafood ravioli with asparagus and cherry tomatoes) and marinated salmon in a pink-pepper sauce are offered side by side with the classics, like the excellent *frittura di paranza* (fried small fish) — one of our favorites. A special children's menu offers simpler dishes with fewer spices.

See map p. 227. Corte San Lorenzo 1/2, near Piazza San Michele. ☎ *0583-316116. Reservations necessary. Secondi: 16€–21€ ($19–$25). AE, DC, V. Open: Thurs–Mon noon to 2:30 p.m.; Wed–Mon 7:30–10:30 p.m. Closed Jan–Feb.*

Exploring Lucca

To fully enjoy the medieval flavor of the town, the best way to explore is on foot. **Cityphone Guided Tour** is a recorded tour — available in Italian, English, French, Spanish, and German — that offers explanations of all of Lucca's sights. Rent one Cityphone for 9€ ($11), two for 14€ ($17), and each additional one for 7€ ($8.40). Together with the **free city map,** it's all you need to explore Lucca. Both are available at the tourist office in Piazzale Verdi (see "Fast Facts: Lucca," later in this chapter).

You can buy a **combination ticket** that includes the Duomo, with its sacristy and museum, and the church and baptistery of Santi Giovanni e Reparata, for 5€ ($6). Another combination ticket includes the Museo Nazionale Palazzo Mansi and the Villa Guinigi for 6.50€ ($7.80).

The red ramparts of Lucca

Lucca's architecture speaks of its past glory: An important city under the Romans, it later became a republic, fighting for its independence against Pisa (see Chapter 2). It was — and still is — famous for the works produced in its music school, founded in A.D. 787. A famous student of the school was Giacomo Puccini, who gave the world some of its greatest operas, such as *Madame Butterfly* and *Tosca*.

The top attractions

Duomo (Cattedrale di San Martino)
Piazza San Martino

Gracing a pretty medieval square, this cathedral is a perfect example of Luccan-Pisan Romanesque architecture. Striped with green and white marble, the facade is decorated with three tiers of polychromed columns. Walk behind the church to admire the imposing apse, surrounded by a small park. The interior is Gothic, divided into three naves, and contains several fine pieces, such as Tintoretto's *Last Supper* over the altar in the third chapel to the right, and a famous relic: the **Volto Santo,** a wooden crucifix showing the real face of Christ, said to have been miraculously carved (the marble housing is by Matteo Civitali, the best 15th-century Luccan artist). The most important art is in the **sacristy:** Ghirlandaio's *Madonna with Saints* and Jacopo della Quercia's **funeral monument to Ilaria del Carretto Guinigi,** one of the finest examples of 15th-century Italian sculpture. Ilaria was the first wife of Paolo Guinigi, ruler of Lucca, and he had the monument built to commemorate her death (she died at 26 after only two years of marriage). The adjacent **museum** contains art once housed in the cathedral, such as Matteo Civitali's masterly carved choir. Count on about an hour for your visit, including sacristy and museum.

See map p. 227. Piazza San Martino. ☎ *0583-957068. Admission: Duomo free; sacristy 2€ ($2.40); museum 4€ ($4.80). Open: Duomo and sacristy Mon–Fri 9:30 a.m.–4:45 p.m., Sat 9:30 a.m.–6:45 p.m., Sun 11:20–11:50 a.m. and 1–4:30 p.m., summer also 5–6 p.m.; museum Nov–Mar Mon–Fri 10 a.m.–2 p.m., Sat–Sun 10 a.m.–5 p.m., Apr–Oct daily 10 a.m.–6 p.m.*

Palazzo Mansi and Pinacoteca Nazionale
Porta San Donato

This lavish 17th-century palace built for the Mansi, a powerful Luccan family, is decorated with some of its original furnishings and frescoes. Of special note are the **Music Room (Salone della Musica)** and **Nuptial Room (Camera degli Sposi).** The collection in the *pinacoteca* (picture gallery) includes Italian and foreign artists from the Renaissance to the 18th century, such as Pontormo, Andrea del Sarto, Veronese, and Domenichino. Allow about an hour here.

See map p. 227. Via Galli Tassi 43. ☎ 0583-55570. Admission: 4€ ($4.80). Open: Tues–Sat 8:30 a.m.–7:30 p.m.; Sun 8:30 a.m.–1:30 p.m. Ticket booth closes 30 minutes earlier.

San Frediano
Piazza Anfiteatro

Built in the early 12th century, this church has a simple facade decorated with a beautiful Byzantine-style mosaic depicting the ascension of Christ, as well as a soaring bell tower. Inside are noteworthy Jacopo della Quercia **carvings** in the left nave's last chapel, a 12th- and 13th-century **mosaic floor** around the main altar, and a beautifully carved **Romanesque font** at the right nave's entrance. Allow about 30 minutes here.

See map p. 227. Piazza San Frediano. ☎ 0583-493627. Admission: Free. Open: Mon–Sat 8:30 a.m. to noon and 3–5 p.m.; Sun 9–11:30 a.m. and 3–6 p.m.

San Giovanni church and archaeological excavations
Piazza San Martino

The 12th-century church of Santi Giovanni e Reparata was partly rebuilt in the 17th century. Together with the adjacent baptistery, adorned with a Gothic dome, they are a lovely sight. However, the real attraction here is the excavations under the church that take you back in time. Underneath the later constructions, you can see the remains of a previous basilica, beneath which are the remains of a paleo-Christian church, itself built over a Roman temple, which was built atop a more ancient Roman house. The excavations are accessible to the public via guided tour; it's best to make a reservation in advance. Expect to spend about 40 minutes here.

See map p. 227. Piazza San Giovanni. ☎ 0583-490-530 for reservations. Admission: 2.50€ ($3). Open: Nov–Mar Sat–Sun 10 a.m.–5 p.m.; Mar–Oct daily 10 a.m.–6 p.m.

San Michele in Foro
Piazza San Michele

Probably one of the greatest examples of Luccan-Pisan Romanesque architecture, the church of San Michele was built between the 12th and 14th centuries. It derives its name from the fact that it was built over the ancient Roman city's **Forum.** The facade is graced by four tiers of small columns and is decorated with different colors of marble, while the apse powerfully illustrates the Pisan influence. Inside is a beautiful **Filippino Lippi** painting, representing the saints Sebastian, Jerome, Helen, and Roch. Piazza San Michele, which surrounds this wonderful church, is itself lovely. Allow about 30 minutes for your visit.

See map p. 227. Piazza San Michele. ☎ 0583-48459. Admission: Free. Open: Daily winter 9 a.m. to noon and 3–6 p.m.; summer 7:40 a.m. to noon and 3–6 p.m.

Villa Guinigi
Porta Elisa

Formerly the residence of the Guinigi family — Lucca's rulers during the Renaissance — this elegant villa has been transformed into a museum. You can see some of the original furnishings dating back to the Renaissance as well as an interesting collection of Lucchese artwork, including paintings and sculptures from the 13th to the 18th centuries, along with some ancient Roman and Etruscan artifacts. Allow 40 minutes here.

See map p. 227. Via della Quarquonia. ☎ 0583-496003. Admission: 4€ ($4.80). Open: Tues–Sat 8:30 a.m.–7:30 p.m. Ticket booth closes 30 minutes earlier.

More cool things to see and do

Lucca is more than just churches and palaces. Herewith, more to explore:

- ✔ Lucca is a city of music, and you'll find that one musical festival or another is going on almost throughout the year. October through February is the opera season at the historic **Teatro del Giglio** (☎ 0583-46531 or 0583-467521 for tickets; www.teatrodelgiglio.it), where Puccini performed his works. If you're in town between April and December, you can enjoy the concerts of the **Lucca in Musica** festival, held in the Basilica of San Frediano and in the Auditorium di San Romano. A good time to visit is during the **Settembre Lucchese,** when a variety of events liven the city, including many concerts. Another great musical event is the **Sagra Musicale Lucchese** (organized by Cappella Musicale Santa Cecilia; ☎ 0583-48421), which takes place between April and June, when concerts of religious and classical music are performed in several of the city's churches. For a schedule of concerts, check with the tourist office (see "Fast Facts: Lucca," later in this chapter).

- ✔ Overlooking the whole city, the **Passeggiata delle Mura** — the promenade built on top of the city walls — is one attraction enjoyed by visitors and Luccans alike. Erected between 1544 and 1650, this is the third and final set of city walls built by the independent Republic of Lucca (the first set was built in Roman times in the second or third century A.D., the second between the 11th and 13th century). In fact, they're Europe's only practically undamaged set of defense ramparts from the Renaissance — perhaps thanks to their monumental scale, measuring 35m (115 ft.) thick at the base and soaring 12m (40 ft.) high, and with *baluardi* (projecting defense works) at 11 different points. The tops of the walls were transformed into a tree-lined 4.2km (2½-mile) public promenade in the early 19th century, with access ramps at 9 of the 11 *baluardi*. Do as the Luccans do and **rent a bike** at the city-run stand (Casermetta San Donato, near the city walls in Piazzale Verdi; ☎ 0583-583150). Prices range from about 6€ ($7.20) per hour to about 20€ ($24) per day.

- ✔ Though not as numerous as the ones in San Gimignano, Lucca's medieval towers are still quite special: A full garden with real trees tops **Torre Guinigi** (Via Sant' Andrea, off Via Guinigi; ☎ 0583-316846;

Admission: 4€/$4.80; Open: Nov–Feb 9:30 a.m.–5:40 p.m., Mar 9:30 a.m.–6 p.m., Apr–May 9 a.m.–8 p.m., June–Oct 9 a.m. to midnight.). The **Torre delle Ore** (Via Fillungo, between Vicolo San Carlo and Via Sant'Andrea; ☎ **0583-316846**; Admission: 3.50€/$4.20; Open: Nov and Jan–Feb Sat–Sun 10:30 a.m.–4 p.m., Dec daily 10:30 a.m.–4 p.m., Mar 10 a.m.–6 p.m., Apr–Oct 10 a.m.–7 p.m.) has marked the passing of time since the 14th century. You can buy a 5€ ($6) combination ticket for both towers.

✔ The birthplace of musician Giacomo Puccini has been turned into a museum: **Casa Natale di Giacomo Puccini** (Corte San Lorenzo 9, off Via di Poggio; ☎ **0583-584028**; Admission: 3€/$3.60; Open: Oct–Dec and Mar–May Tues–Sun 10 a.m.–1 p.m. and 3–6 p.m.; June–Sept daily 10 a.m.–6 p.m.).

Fast Facts: Lucca

Area Code

The local area code is **0538** (see "Telephone" in the "Fast Facts" section of Appendix A for more on calling to and from Italy).

ATMs

There are many banks in town, including several in Piazza San Michele, Piazza San Martino, and Via Vittorio Veneto, where you can find ATMs and change money. There's also a *cambio* (exchange office) in the rail station as well as one near the tourist office on Piazzale Verdi, plus others around town.

Emergencies

For an ambulance, call ☎ **118**; for the fire department, call ☎ **115**; for road assistance, call ☎ **116**.

Hospitals

The Ospedale Generale Provinciale Campo di Marte is on Via dell'Ospedale (☎ 800-869143 or 0583-9701).

Information

The APT office is at Piazza Santa Maria 35 (☎ 0583-919931; www.luccaturismo. it; Open: Daily Apr–Oct 9 a.m.–8 p.m.,

Nov–Mar 9 a.m.–1 p.m. and 3–6 p.m.) and Piazza Napoleone (Open: Apr–Oct Mon–Sat 10 a.m.–6 p.m., Nov–Mar 10 a.m.–1 p.m.). Other tourist information offices are inside Porta Sant'Anna on Piazzale Verdi (☎ 0583-442944; Open: Daily 9:30 a.m.–6:30 p.m., to 3:30 p.m. in winter) and at Porta Elisa (☎ 0583-462-377; Open: Daily 9:30 a.m.–6:30 p.m. Apr–Oct).

Police

There are two police forces in Italy; call either one. For the Polizia, dial ☎ **113**; for the Carabinieri, dial ☎ **112**.

Post Office

The post office *(ufficio postale)* is at Via Vallisneri Antonio 2, behind Piazza San Martino and near Via Guinigi (☎ 0583-492-991).

Taxis

There are stands at the rail station on Piazzale Ricasoli (☎ 0583-494989); at Piazza Napoleone (☎ 0583-492691); at Piazza Santa Maria (☎ 0583-494190); and at Piazzale Verdi (☎ 0583-581305).

Pisa

Pisa is much more than its famous Leaning Tower: Its medieval alleys and buildings overlooking the curving Arno are little visited, yet offer some of Italy's nicest riverside views.

You will not need more than three or four hours to visit Pisa's most famous attractions, and you can easily do so on a day trip from Florence, but you would miss much: Pisa deserves exploration and knows how to reward its visitors. If you have the time, we recommend spending at least one night. Pisa also makes an excellent base for exploring the many other destinations in northern Tuscany, since it has a good selection of moderately priced hotels and restaurants and a lively cultural life.

Getting there

Only 3km (2 miles) south of town, Pisa's **Aeroporto Galileo Galilei** (☎ 050-849111; www.pisa-airport.com) is Tuscany's main airport, with daily flights from most major towns in Italy and the rest of Europe. From the airport, you can take a taxi to the center of town; it will cost you about 5€ to 7€ ($6–$8.40) and take about ten minutes. You can also take the train to Pisa Centrale rail station, a five-minute ride for 1€ ($1.20); trains depart the airport about every hour. If you're driving, rental-car counters are at arrivals, inside the airport. Once you have your car, just follow the signs for PISA CENTRO.

From other points in Italy, the **train** (☎ 892021; www.trenitalia.it) is an excellent way to get to Pisa. The station, **Pisa Centrale** (☎ 050-41385), is about an hour from Florence and three and a half hours from Rome. Trains run about every half-hour from Florence and every hour from Rome; the trip costs about 5€ ($6) and 24€ ($29), respectively. From the station, take shuttle bus A across the Arno to the Leaning Tower.

If you're arriving by **car,** you'll be able to drive the 96km (60 miles) from Florence in about an hour or less. From Florence, take *autostrada* A11 to Lucca and follow the signs for A12 toward Livorno; watch for the exit for Pisa shortly after the junction with A12 South. From Florence, you can also follow the signs for Empoli-Livorno to reach Pisa by the more direct but slower *superstrada* (small highway). Three large free parking lots are located near the center of Pisa, just north of the town's walls; each is linked to the center by bus service (electric or otherwise), which costs 0.80€ (90¢) per ticket. The lots are on **Via Pietrasantina,** only a few hundred yards from the Duomo (Bus: A); **Via di Pratale,** a few hundred yards from the Via del Brennero (Bus: 7); and **Via del Brennero,** near Via Paparelli and Porta Zeno, 1km (⅔ mile) from the Duomo (Bus: E); this last lot is closed on Wednesday and Saturday from 7 a.m. to 4 p.m. because of an open-air market. Paid parking can be found at **Piazza dei Miracoli** and in a lot on **Via Cammeo** for 1.50€ ($1.80) per hour, the same rate as metered street parking.

Spending the night

Hotel Leonardo
$ Piazza dei Cavalieri

Within walking distance of both Campo dei Miracoli and the Arno river, this new hotel offers quiet accommodations at a moderate price. It's housed in a historic building — nothing less than the study of Galileo Galilei. Today, the completely renovated hotel has pleasant guest rooms, with whitewashed walls, vibrant fabrics, and simple yet stylish furnishings. Some of the rooms boast a view of Pisa and the Leaning Tower.

See map p. 236. Via Tavoleria 17. ☎ *050-579946. Fax: 050-598969.* www.hotel leonardopisa.it. *Free street parking with hotel permit. Rack rates: 115€ ($138) double. Rates include continental breakfast. AE, DC, MC, V.*

Hotel Relais dell'Orologio
$$$ Duomo

Steps from Campo dei Miracoli, this medieval mansion — built in the 13th century — was restored in 2004 and transformed into a hotel. Guest rooms are decorated with a subdued elegance that enhances the arched window frames and beamed ceilings typical of this style of building. Bedrooms and bathrooms alike are large and comfortable. The garden is the perfect place to have breakfast in nice weather. Ask about specials when you make your reservation.

See map p. 236. Via della Faggiola 12–14. ☎ *050-830361. Fax: 050-551869.* www. hotelrelaisorologio.com. *Free parking. Rack rates: 326€ ($391) double. Rates include breakfast. AE, DC, MC, V.*

Royal Victoria
$ Lungarno–Ponte di Mezzo

This hotel, right on the Arno and within walking distance of major attractions, is about old-fashioned elegance, romantic views, and friendly service. Opened in 1839 as Pisa's first hotel, it is still run by the same family. It occupies several medieval buildings, including the remains of a tenth-century tower; as a result, guest rooms differ greatly from one another — some have frescoed ceilings, while others are more simply decorated — but all are furnished with antiques and kept extremely clean. If you're planning to use the garage, you must reserve that ahead of time as well.

See map p. 236. Lungarno Pacinotti 12. ☎ *050-940111. Fax: 050-940-180.* www.royal victoria.it. *Parking: 18€ ($22). Rack rates: 125€ ($150) double. Rates include breakfast. AE, DC, MC, V.*

Villa Kinzica
$ Duomo

Located just across from the Leaning Tower, the Villa Kinzica is an excellent value. It has bright, clean guest rooms, most of which afford a glimpse

Pisa

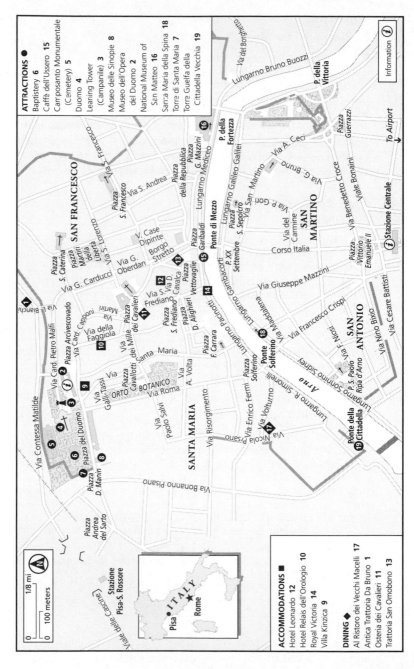

ATTRACTIONS ●
Baptistery **6**
Caffè dell'Ussero **15**
Camposanto Monumentale (Cemetery) **5**
Duomo **4**
Leaning Tower (Campanile) **3**
Museo delle Sinopie **8**
Museo dell'Opera del Duomo **2**
National Museum of San Matteo **16**
Santa Maria della Spina **18**
Torre di Santa Maria **7**
Torre Guelfa della Cittadella Vecchia **19**

Information ⓘ

ACCOMMODATIONS ■
Hotel Leonardo **12**
Hotel Relais dell'Orologio **10**
Royal Victoria **14**
Villa Kinzica **9**

DINING ◆
Al Ristoro dei Vecchi Macelli **17**
Antica Trattoria Da Bruno **1**
Osteria dei Cavalieri **11**
Trattoria San Omobono **13**

of the famous monument. They're done up with simple yet tasteful furnishings, whitewashed walls, and small bathrooms. The hotel name comes from a Pisan heroine who saved the city from the Saracens. A nice touch is the homemade rolls for breakfast.

See map p. 236. Piazza Arcivescovado 2. ☎ *050-560419. Fax: 050-551204.* www. hotelvillakinzica.it. *Free street parking with hotel permit. Rack rates: 108€ ($130) double. Rates include breakfast. AE, DC, MC, V.*

Dining locally

It is very difficult to have a bad meal here: Restaurants and *trattorie* are plentiful and excellent. Food in Pisa includes typical Tuscan fare (see Chapter 2), such as *ribollita* (here called *zuppa pisana,* or Pisan soup — old rivalries die hard) and, because the sea is nearby, lots of seafood.

Al Ristoro dei Vecchi Macelli
$$ **Piazza Solferino PISAN/SEAFOOD**

Near the edge of the historic district is Pisa's best traditional restaurant and a local favorite. Housed in a 15th-century slaughterhouse *(macello)*, it nonetheless offers a cozy atmosphere, with beamed ceilings and dark wood floors. This family-run place serves up traditional Pisan recipes that are reinterpreted with genius to produce delectable results: homemade ravioli stuffed with fish and served with a shrimp sauce; delicious gnocchi with pesto and shrimp; stuffed rabbit with creamy truffle sauce; sea bass with onion sauce . . . we can't wait to go back!

See map p. 236. Via Volturno 49, off Piazza Solferino. ☎ *050-20424. Reservations necessary. Secondi: 10€–18€ ($12–$22). AE, DC. Open: Thurs–Tues noon to 3 p.m. and 7:30–11 p.m. Closed 2 weeks in Aug.*

Antica Trattoria Da Bruno
$ **Duomo PISAN**

Within walking distance of the Duomo and just outside the city walls, this *trattoria* offers traditional homemade food in a warm atmosphere. You can sit in one of the various dining rooms, including a small "private" room that's the quietest; all have beamed ceilings and whitewashed walls decorated with photographs and copper utensils. The menu is based on the traditional local cuisine. We definitely recommend the homemade pappardelle with hare sauce, the *baccalà coi porri* (codfish with fresh tomatoes and leeks), and the wild-boar stew.

See map p. 236. Via Luigi Bianchi 12, 3 blocks east of Piazza dei Miracoli. ☎ *050-560818. Reservations recommended. Secondi: 8€–15€ ($9.60–$18). AE, DC, MC, V. Open: Wed–Mon 12:15–2:30 p.m.; Wed–Sun 7:15–10:30 p.m.*

A picnic in Pisa

The **food market** on **Piazza delle Vettovaglie,** a few steps north of Ponte di Mezzo, is a wonderful sight. Located here since the Middle Ages, it is a lively affair held Monday through Saturday from 7 a.m. to 1:30 p.m. Food producers from the countryside offer their specialties for sale — fresh vegetables and fruits, Tuscan bread, cured meats, and all the fixings — so you can get the makings of a great picnic to enjoy along the riverbank.

Osteria dei Cavalieri
$ Piazza dei Cavalieri   PISAN

One of the liveliest restaurants in Pisa, this *osteria* offers simple and tasty fare at moderate prices. The two small, bright dining rooms are a perfect background for the food, which delicately mixes tradition with innovation. We loved the gnocchi with zucchini flowers and pistachio nuts, the *zuppa Pisana,* and the *tagliata di manzo ai funghi pioppini con cannellini,* a perfect steak served with wild local mushrooms and white beans.

See map p. 236. Via San Frediano 16, off Piazza dei Cavalieri. ☎ *050-580858. Reservations recommended. Secondi: 8€–12€ ($9.60–$14). AE, DC, MC, V. Open: Mon–Fri 12:30–2:30 p.m.; Mon–Sat 7:30–10:30 p.m. Closed 4 weeks in Aug.*

Trattoria San Omobono
$ Ponte di Mezzo   PISAN

Near the food market of Piazza delle Vettovaglie, this *trattoria* offers traditional Pisan fare at moderate prices. To experience real Pisan cuisine, try the homemade pasta or have the typical *zuppa Pisana.* Among the tasty *secondi,* we enjoyed the *baccalà alla livornese* (codfish with onion and fresh tomatoes) and a melt-in-your-mouth roasted pork.

See map p. 236. Piazza San Omobono 6. ☎ *050-540847. Reservations recommended. Secondi: 10€ ($12). No credit cards. Open: Mon–Sat 12:30–2:30 p.m. and 7:30–11 p.m. Closed 2 weeks in Aug.*

Exploring Pisa

If you're in town between March and October, the **biglietto unico** is a great deal: Valid for eight days and priced at 13€ ($16), it includes admission to the ten top attractions in Pisa, except the Leaning Tower (Duomo, Cemetery, Baptistery, Museo delle Sinopie, Museo dell'Opera del Duomo, Museo Nazionale di San Matteo, Museo Nazionale di Palazzo Reale, Santa Maria della Spina, Torre di Santa Maria and town walls, and Torre Guelfa). It can be purchased at the ticket booth of one of the four participating museums and at Santa Maria della Spina.

If you're feeling less ambitious, you can get a combination ticket for your choice of two (6€/$7.20) or three (8€/$9.60) of the museums and monuments in Campo dei Miracoli; again, your options do not include the Leaning Tower.

To see Pisa via guided tour from Florence, contact **American Express** (☎ **055-50981**) or **SitaSightseeing** (☎ **055-214721**) in Florence. Both offer tours of Pisa for about 26€ ($31).

The top attractions

Campo dei Miracoli, also called Piazza del Duomo, is Pisa's monumental *piazza.* Built in medieval times abutting the city walls, it is carpeted with perfect green grass — an ideal background for the carved marble masterpieces in the monumental compound.

Baptistery
Campo dei Miracoli

Standing across from the Duomo, the Baptistery was built between the 12th and 14th centuries, and its architecture reflects the passage from the Romanesque to the Gothic style during those years. It is the largest baptistery in Italy and is actually taller — counting the statue on top — than the famous Leaning Tower. The richly decorated exterior was once further embellished with statues by the local artist Giovanni Pisano, but many have been removed to the Museo dell'Opera del Duomo (see later) for safekeeping. Inside is a unique **hexagonal pulpit,** carved by Nicola Pisano (father of Giovanni) between 1255 and 1260, and a **baptismal font,** carved and inlaid by Guido Bigarelli da Como. Allow about 30 minutes for your visit.

See map p. 236. Piazza del Duomo. ☎ *050-560547.* www.opapisa.it. *Admission: 5€ ($6). Open: Daily Nov–Feb 10 a.m.–5 p.m.; Mar 9 a.m.–6 p.m.; Apr–Sept 8 a.m.– 8 p.m.; Oct 9 a.m.–7 p.m. Last admission 30 minutes earlier.*

Camposanto Monumentale (Cemetery)
Campo dei Miracoli

On the edge of Piazza del Duomo stands the elegantly decorated wall of what must have been the world's most beautiful cemetery. Designed by Giovanni di Simone and built in 1278, it was filled with holy dirt from Golgotha (Calvary) in Palestine — where Christ was crucified — that was brought back by ship after a Crusade. Decorated with splendid frescoes inside, it was the burial ground for Pisa's constables, who had their tombs richly decorated with sarcophagi, statues, and marble bas-reliefs. During the 1944 U.S. bombing of Pisa to dislodge the Nazis, the cemetery's loggia roof caught fire, and most of the magnificent frescoes were destroyed. Parts of the frescoes that were salvaged are exhibited inside, along with photos showing the Camposanto before the destruction. The Museo delle Sinopie nearby (see later in this section) holds the preliminary frescoes. Allow at least 20 minutes for your visit.

See map p. 236. Piazza del Duomo. ☎ *050-560-547.* www.opapisa.it. *Admission: 5€ ($6). Open: Daily Nov–Feb 10 a.m.–5 p.m.; Mar 9 a.m.–6 p.m.; Apr–Sept 8 a.m.–8 p.m.; Oct 9 a.m.–7 p.m. Last admission 30 minutes earlier.*

Duomo (Cattedrale di Santa Maria Assunta)
Campo dei Miracoli

The center of Campo dei Miracoli is occupied by the magnificent cathedral, Pisa's Duomo, built by Buschetto in the 11th century. The facade, with four layers of open-air arches diminishing in size as they ascend, is actually from the 13th century. In 1595, the cathedral was heavily damaged by a fire that destroyed three of the four bronze exterior doors and much of the art inside. The cathedral was restored during the 16th century, integrating some baroque elements. Still original is the **monumental bronze door** at the south entrance (Porta San Ranieri), cast by Bonanno Pisano in 1180; the Andrea del Sarto painting of *Sant'Agnese* at the choir entrance; the 13th-century mosaic of *Christ Pantocrator;* and the Cimabue *San Giovanni Evangelista* in the apse. The **polygonal pulpit** carved by Giovanni Pisano was restored in 1926 when the original pieces were found; they had been put in storage after the fire in the 16th century. Plan to spend about 40 minutes here.

See map p. 236. Piazza del Duomo. ☎ *050-560547.* www.opapisa.it. *Admission: 2€ ($2.40). Open: Daily Nov–Feb 10 a.m.–1 p.m. and 2–5 p.m.; Mar 10 a.m.–6 p.m.; Apr–Sept 10 a.m.–8 p.m.; Oct 10 a.m.–7 p.m. Sun and holidays open for service only until 1 p.m. Last admission 30 minutes earlier.*

The maritime republic of Pisa

The origins of Pisa as a powerful entity in the Mediterranean stretch back to Roman times, when the Italic settlement that had existed since 1000 B.C. was transformed into a commercial harbor (in the second century B.C.). The harbor thrived, but the city's maritime power was realized only in the 11th century, when Pisa became one of the four powerful Italian maritime republics, ruling the Mediterranean along with Venice, Amalfi, and Genoa. These rival ports developed far-flung mercantile empires. Pisa controlled Corsica, Sardinia, and the Balearic Islands, competing with Genoa for commerce with the Arabs. Later, the city lost its water access (the river silted up) and its power: In 1284, Genoa finally won its struggle against Pisa, whose fleet was destroyed. Genoa became the dominant power in the Tyrrhenian Sea, while Pisa, after severe battles, shrank to a possession of Florence. During the three centuries of its splendor, however, the wealth coming from far-flung commerce funded the construction of the monumental town that you can still admire today.

Leaning Tower (Campanile)
Campo dei Miracoli

Behind the Duomo is the famous tower, actually built as the Duomo's campanile (bell tower). Started in 1173 by the architect Bonnano, this beautiful eight-story carved masterpiece, with open-air arches matching those on the Duomo, was finally finished in 1360. It took so long to build because it started leaning almost from the beginning, so the Pisans stopped construction in 1185. In 1275, they started again and built up to the belfry, cleverly curving the structure as they went to compensate for the lean. The construction stopped again, until 1360, when the belfry was added. Later architects and engineers studied the problem — the shifting alluvial subsoil, saturated with water — but couldn't devise a solution (one attempt to fix it made it lean more). In 1990, the lean became so bad — 4.5m (15 ft.) out of plumb — that the tower was closed to the public. Two years later, a belt of steel cables was placed around the base, and in 1993, it was decided to stop using the bells in the belfry to prevent vibrations from shaking the tower. Finally, after a $24-million restoration, engineers succeeded in reducing the tower's lean by 38cm (15 in.). It reopened in December 2001.

The visit is guided and tours start every 30 minutes; your ticket is valid only for the time stamped on it. You can make reservations ahead of time by going to www.opapisa.it a minimum of 15 days in advance for an additional cost of 2€ ($2.40) per ticket; you must pick up your printed voucher from the ticket office at least an hour before your reserved slot.

 There are no elevators in the tower, and access is through the original — and very narrow — staircase. It's 300 steps to the top and it's impossible to stop or turn around, making the climb physically and psychologically taxing. Anybody suffering from vertigo or claustrophobia should not attempt it. Children under 8 are not allowed in the tower.

See map p. 236. Piazza del Duomo. ☎ *050-560547.* www.opapisa.it. *Admission: 15€ ($18). Open: Daily Nov–Feb 9:30 a.m.–5 p.m.; Mar 1–13 9 a.m.–6 p.m.; Mar 14–20 9 a.m.–7 p.m.; Mar 21–June 13 and Sept 5–30 8:30 a.m.–8:30 p.m.; June 14–Sept 4 8:30 a.m.–11 p.m.; Oct 9 a.m.–7 p.m.*

Museo delle Sinopie
Campo dei Miracoli

On the other side of Piazza del Duomo, across from the Camposanto, this museum houses the *sinopie* (preparatory sketches for frescoes) found under the charred remains of the frescoes in the Camposanto after the fire that destroyed most of them. Each *sinopia* faces an engraving that shows what the Camposanto frescoes looked like before their destruction. It is very well done, allowing visitors to re-experience what the magnificent Camposanto must have looked like before 1944. More reproductions are in the Museo dell'Opera (see below). Allow about 30 minutes for your visit. Note that the museum was temporarily closed at press time, but should be open again by the time of your visit.

Galileo Galilei

Born in Pisa in 1564, Galileo was an astronomer, astrologer, and philosopher, and earned his status as one of the fathers of modern physics. Much of his visible activity involved watching pendulums and dropping balls of differing weights off the Leaning Tower to prove that they would hit the ground at the same time. Many people thought he was nuts, and the church excommunicated (and nearly executed) him for the blasphemy of suggesting that the universe did not revolve around the earth, but instead the earth revolved around the sun. In the scientific world, he is considered the father of modern science, together with Francis Bacon. Among his achievements are several improvements on the telescope and the discovery of the first and second laws of motion.

See map p. 236. Piazza del Duomo. ☎ 050-560547. Admission: 5€ ($6). Open: Daily Nov–Feb 10 a.m.–5 p.m.; Mar 9 a.m.–6 p.m.; Apr–Sept 8 a.m.–8 p.m.; Oct 9 a.m.–7 p.m. Last admission 30 minutes earlier.

Museo dell'Opera del Duomo
Campo dei Miracoli

Located on the south side of the Leaning Tower, this museum is a show-case for all the original artworks that were removed from the Duomo and the other monuments on the Campo dei Miracoli for preservation, includ-ing the statues by Giovanni Pisano from the Baptistery (see earlier in this section). Particularly notable are the 11th-century Islamic bronze of a **griffin** — booty from a Crusade — that decorated the Duomo's cupola before being replaced by a copy, and Giovanni Pisano's *Madonna col Bambino,* carved from an ivory tusk. Also interesting are the **etchings** that were prepared in the 19th century by Carlo Lasinio for the restoration of the frescoes in the Camposanto (see earlier in this section): Colored by Lasinio's son, they're the best existing record of the frescoes. The museum also holds the original plans of the Duomo, as well as a collection of ancient artifacts found on the site when the Duomo was built. Allow about an hour for your visit.

See map p. 236. Piazza del Duomo. ☎ 050-560547. Admission: 5€ ($6). Open: Daily Nov–Feb 10 a.m.–5 p.m.; Mar 9 a.m.–6 p.m.; Apr–Sept 8 a.m.–8 p.m.; Oct 9 a.m.–7 p.m. Last admission 30 minutes earlier.

National Museum of San Matteo
Piazza Mazzini

The monuments on Campo dei Miracoli steal the show in Pisa, but this important museum should not be overlooked if you are interested in Italian Renaissance art. Its collection of paintings from the 12th to the 15th centuries is one of the best in the world, and its sculpture gallery — including works from the Middle Ages to the 16th century — is very rich.

Some of the works come from nearby churches, particularly from Santa Maria della Spina (see later), while others are from ecclesiastical buildings farther away in the town's territory. Important masterpieces include the 1426 painting *San Paolo* by **Masaccio,** two paintings of the *Madonna con i Santi* by **Ghirlandaio,** the sculpture of the *Madonna del Latte* by **Andrea** and **Nino Pisano,** and sculptures by **Donatello.** Consider spending one or two hours at this museum.

See map p. 236. Lungarno Mediceo-Piazza San Matteo, near Piazza Mazzini. ☎ *050-541865. Admission: 5€ ($6). Open: Tues–Sat 9 a.m.–7 p.m.; Sun 9 a.m.–2 p.m. Closed Jan 1, May 1, Aug 15, and Dec 25.*

Santa Maria della Spina
Ponte Solferino

This small church, which has survived in spite of its dangerous location on unstable ground near the river bed, is a treasure-trove of marble carvings. Built on the river shore in 1230 as an oratory near a bridge that was destroyed in the 15th century, the church was enlarged during the 14th century and decorated by some of the town's best artists of the time. Its foundation was reinforced several times over the centuries, and in 1871, as a final drastic effort to consolidate the ground on which the church was built, the entire structure was taken apart and rebuilt on a 1.2m-high (4-ft.) base. During this process, many of the original sculptures were moved to the Museo Nazionale di San Matteo and replaced with copies, and the entire sacristy was destroyed. Although this loss somewhat ruined the proportions of the building, it remains one of the most delightful examples of Tuscan Gothic architecture. The many delicate carvings on the external walls, as well as the elegant arches and windows and the simple interior, make a wonderful setting for the sculptural masterpiece by Andrea and Nino Pisano, the *Madonna Della Rosa* (1345–48). Plan to spend about a half-hour here.

See map p. 236. Lungarno Gambacorti, near Ponte Solferino. ☎ *055-321-5446. Admission: 1.50€ ($1.80). Open: Nov–Feb Tues–Sun 10 a.m.–2 p.m., second Sun of the month 10 a.m.–1 p.m. and 2:30–5 p.m.; Mar–Oct Tues–Fri 10 a.m.–1:30 p.m. and 2:30–5 p.m., Sat–Sun 10 a.m.–7 p.m.*

More cool things to see and do

✔ Some of the town celebrations are great fun: A traditional event is the **Gioco del Ponte,** held on the last Sunday in June, when teams from the north and south sides of the Arno fight each other. Wearing Renaissance costumes, the teams use a decorated 6,300-kilogram (7-ton) cart to push each other off the Ponte di Mezzo, the Roman bridge at the center of Pisa. Another celebration is the **Festa di San Ranieri,** on June 16th and 17th, held in honor of Pisa's patron saint. The Arno is lit with torches all along its length, which makes for quite a beautiful sight. Contact the tourist office for more info (see "Fast Facts: Pisa," later in this chapter).

✔ To get a different perspective on the town, you can visit one, or both, of Pisa's medieval towers. The **Torre di Santa Maria** (Piazza del Duomo; ☎ 050-560547; Admission: 2€/$2.40, free for children under 10; Open: Daily Mar–Oct 11 a.m.–2 p.m. and 3–6 p.m.; Closed: Nov–Feb) overlooks the Campo dei Miracoli; the visit includes the parapet of the town's medieval walls. The **Torre Guelfa della Cittadella Vecchia** (Piazza Tersanaia; ☎ 055-3215446; Admission: 2€/$2.40, free for children under 10; Open: Mar–Oct Fri–Sun 3–7 p.m., Nov–Feb Sat–Sun 2–5 p.m., second Sun of month 10 a.m.–1 p.m. and 3–5 p.m.) affords great views of the Arno and surrounding countryside.

✔ The best way to fully savor the medieval flavor of Pisa is to take the **Tour Lungarno cruise** along the urban portion of the Arno, operated by the **Cooperativa il Navicello** (Lungarno Galilei 7; ☎ 050-540162 or 338-9808867; www.ilnavicello.it). Boats leave from San Paolo a Ripa d'Arno toward the west edge of the historic district, April through November on Saturday, Sunday, and holidays at 11 a.m., noon, 4 p.m., and 5 p.m. (May–Sept also Tues–Sat 3, 4, and 5 p.m.). Tours are by reservation only, the trip lasts about an hour, and tickets are 5€ ($6) per person.

✔ Pisa has a long tradition of intellectual life — local circles played an important role during the Risorgimento, the movement that led to the unification of Italy in the 19th century (see Chapter 2). The **Caffè dell'Ussero** (Largo Pacinotti 27; ☎ 050-581100) is where Pisa's intellectuals and their famous visitors met and mingled. Housed in the 15th-century Palazzo Agostini and still decorated with some of the original furnishings, it makes a delicious ice cream that you can savor on the terrace by the Arno river or as you stroll along the promenade.

Fast Facts: Pisa

Area Code

The local area code is **050** (see "Telephone" in the "Fast Facts" section of Appendix A for more on calling to and from Italy).

ATMs

There are many banks in town with ATMs, particularly on Corso Italia and Via G. Mazzini. There's a *cambio* (exchange office) at the airport and several in town, including one on Piazza del Duomo.

Emergencies

For an ambulance, call ☎ 118; for the fire department, call ☎ 115; for road assistance, call ☎ 116.

Hospitals

The Ospedale Santa Chiara is at Via Roma 67, near the Duomo (☎ 050-554433).

Information

The tourist office (☎ 050-929777; Fax: 050-929764) maintains three information booths: one outside Pisa Centrale, just to the left when you exit (☎ 050-42-291; Open: Mon–Sat 9 a.m.–7 p.m., Sun 9:30 a.m.–3:30 p.m.); one near the Duomo at Via Cammeo 2 (☎ 050-560464; Open: Mon–Sat 9 a.m.– 6 p.m., Sun 10:30 a.m.–4:30 p.m.); and one at the airport (☎ 050 503700; Open: Daily 10:30 a.m.–4:30 p.m. and 6–10 p.m.).

Internet Access

Internet Surf is at Via Carducci 5, west of the Duomo, by Piazza Martiri della Libertà (☎ 050-830-800; www.internetsurf. it; Open: Mon–Fri 10 a.m.–11 p.m., Sat 10:30 a.m.–11 p.m., Sun 3–11 p.m.).

Police

There are two police forces in Italy; call either one. For the Polizia, dial ☎ **113**; for the Carabinieri, dial ☎ **112**.

Post Office

The central post office is at Piazza Vittorio Emanuele II 7/8 (☎ 050-519-41), near the rail station of Pisa Centrale.

Taxi

There are taxi stands at Piazza della Stazione (for info, call the station at ☎ 050-41252) and at Piazza del Duomo (☎ 050-561878). For a radio taxi, call ☎ 050-541600.

The Cinque Terre

If you push on a bit farther along the coast, you'll enter the eastern part of the Italian Riviera, the Riviera di Levante. Nestled here at the water's edge, and insulated from the areas farther inland by towering promontories, are five small towns: **Monterosso al Mare, Vernazza, Corniglia, Manarola,** and **Riomaggiore,** defining a fishing and agricultural area of great natural beauty. Generally called **Cinque Terre** (literally "five lands"), they were declared a national park a few years back — the first example of a national park created to protect a man-made environment. In addition, the sea surrounding them is now a national marine park.

 The Cinque Terre region is a great place to spend time with your kids. The breathtaking views, the sea, and the swimming and hiking provide a great respite from the usual cultural attractions.

While it is possible to "do" the Cinque Terre in a day, the area is definitely worth more time if you can spare it — especially if you're into hiking and swimming.

Getting there

Auto traffic within the park is limited to residents, but each of the villages is served by **train.** Contact **Trenitalia** (☎ **892021**; www. trenitalia.it) for details. There is direct service from Pisa to Riomaggiore and to Monterosso; from all other towns, you'll have to switch in La Spezia to the local line for Levanto, stopping at each of the five village stations (some runs go only to Riomaggiore and Monterosso). Don't expect a scenic ride, though, as the route has been carved into the cliff and most of the trip is inside a tunnel. It will cost about 5€ ($6) from Pisa for the 30-minute trip. Electric minibuses connect each train station with the village harbors, trail heads, and other destinations in the park.

The Cinque Terre

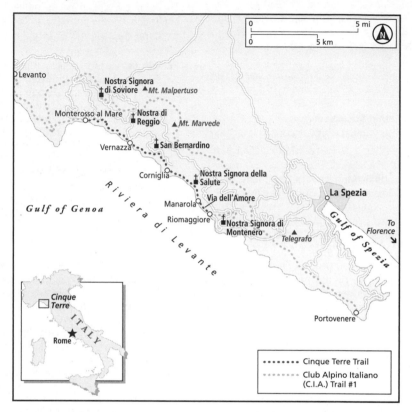

You can also take a **boat** from La Spezia, a magnificent experience affording superb views (see later in this section). Regular boat service (Consorzio Marittimo Golfo dei Poeti; ☎ 0187-732987; www. navigazionegolfodeipoeti.it) runs between Monterosso and Riomaggiore, with stops in Vernazza and, every other trip, also in Manarola. Service starts at 9:20 a.m. in Riomaggiore and 10 a.m. in Monterosso; boats run about every hour. The last boat leaves Riomaggiore at 5:25 p.m. and Monterosso at 6 p.m. A one-way ticket between Monterosso and Manarola is 3€ ($3.60); a day pass costs 12€ ($14) for adults and 6.50€ ($7.80) for children 6 to 11.

If you have a **car,** you'll have to park it. Your best bet is the **ACIPARK lot** in La Spezia (Via Crispi 73; ☎ 0187-510545), which will cost you only 4€ ($4.40) for the day. There is also a **parking lot** in Monterosso al Mare (☎ 0187-802050) that gets very crowded in high season and costs about 8.30€ ($10) per day. From there, you can get a taxi to town for about 7€ ($8.40) or take the shuttle bus (fare included in the Cinque Terre Card; see sidebar in this section).

The gulf of the poets

This idyllic stretch of coast, the eastern section of the Italian Riviera, has gained its romantic nickname for being the favorite destination — and, at times, abode — of famous poets and artists. The name actually refers to the bay of La Spezia (the major town in the region), but extends to the Cinque Terre, which lie on the western shore of the promontory closing the gulf to the west. From the Latin poet Polibio to Dante, Petrarch, and Montesquieu, the charms of this coast have inspired many a writer. The most famous of all were probably Mary Shelley, the author of *Frankenstein,* and her husband, Percy Bysshe Shelley — who met his death in these beautiful waters — but other famous visitors have included Lord Byron, Virginia Woolf, and D. H. Lawrence.

Spending the night

Ca' d'Andrean
$ Manarola

This pleasant hotel has a beautiful garden where you can relax after a day exploring or basking in the sun. Guest rooms are well appointed, simply but pleasantly furnished, with tiled floors and spacious bathrooms. Some have a private balcony. The seaside is a short walk away.

Via Discovolo 101. ☎ ***0187-920040.*** *Fax: 0187-920452.* www.cadandrean.it. *Rack rates: 90€ ($108) double. Rates include buffet breakfast. AE, MC, V. Closed 5 weeks in Nov/Dec.*

Hotel Marina Piccola
$ Manarola

Come here for small, bright rooms with a beautiful view at moderate prices. This hotel is the way to go if you want to keep a lid on expenses and can do without air-conditioning or an elevator. The ironwork beds and whitewashed walls give a very Mediterranean feel to the rooms; bathrooms are quite small, however. The hotel restaurant is excellent.

Via Birolli 120. ☎*/fax:* ***0187-920103.*** www.hotelmarinapiccola.com. *Rack rates: 105€ ($126) double. Rates include continental breakfast. AE, DC, MC, V. Closed Jan.*

Hotel Porto Roca
$$$ Monterosso

This luxury hotel offers spectacular views from its cliff location above town. The luminous guest rooms have whitewashed walls and wooden furniture with some antiques; most have large balconies and full bathrooms. The hotel's amenities include a welcoming bar, a restaurant with an extensive cellar of Italian wines, a private beach, a garden terrace, and free parking — a rarity in this area. The hotel also provides free car service to the train station. Book early during high season.

Via Corone 1. ☎ *0187-817502. Fax: 0187-817692.* www.portoroca.it. *Free parking. Rack rates: 195€–280€ ($234–$336) double. Rates include buffet breakfast and use of beach chairs and umbrellas. AE, DC, MC, V. Closed Nov–Mar.*

Il Vigneto
$ **Manarola/Riomaggiore**

If you don't need to stay right on the beach, this bed-and-breakfast — surrounded by lush gardens and located up high in the promontory overlooking the sea — is one of our favorite places in the area. The friendly hosts will welcome you to one of the nicely appointed guest rooms, with whitewashed walls and vaguely mission-style furniture. The terrace, where breakfast is served in good weather, offers a breathtaking view that sweeps over the sea. There is no air-conditioning, but the mountain air will keep you cool. The minibus to the center of town and to the rail station stops right by.

Via Pasubio 64 in Volastra, a small village above Riomaggiore and Manarola. ☎ *0187-762053. Fax: 0187-762173.* www.ilvigneto5terre.com. *Rack rates: 75€–120€ ($90–$144) double. Rates include breakfast. AE, MC, V.*

Dining locally
The cuisine of the Cinque Terre is one of the attractions of the park. Based on local seafood, it uses plenty of fresh herbs — such as the basil for the pesto sauce, now famous around the world (see Chapter 2). Here are our favorite options besides the very good restaurant in the **Hotel Marina Piccola** (see earlier in this section).

Cappun Magru in Casa di Marin
$$ **Groppo   CREATIVE LIGURIAN**

You'll have to climb up the cliff to enjoy the superb cuisine at this gourmet hide-out. The restaurant is small and delightful, and the menu spins tradition with flair for the best combinations. We highly recommend the dish that gives its name to this restaurant, the *cappon magro* (a rich fish and vegetable layered salad), as well as the gnocchi with prawns and a delicious Gorgonzola and Calvados sauce. Leave room for the scrumptious chocolate mousse with stewed cherries.

Via Volastra 19, in the hamlet of Groppo. ☎ *0187-920563. Reservations recommended. Secondi: 14€–23€ ($17–$28). AE, MC, V. Open: Wed–Sat 7:30–10:30 p.m.; Sun 12:30–3 p.m. Closed 8 weeks Dec/Feb.*

Gambero Rosso
$$ **Vernazza   LIGURIAN**

Set in the picturesque square at the heart of town, this is one of the best fish restaurants around, offering some of the less common local dishes accompanied by friendly yet professional service. The *spaghetti alle vongole* is truly excellent, but if you want to try something more typical, go for the *tian*, the local specialty of oven-roasted anchovies, potatoes, tomatoes, and rosemary. You will also enjoy the complimentary glass of *Sciacchetrà* at the end of the meal — it's the famous local (and rare) *passito*, a sweet wine.

Piazza Marconi 7. ☎ *0187-811265. Reservations recommended. Secondi: 14€–27€ ($17–$32). AE, DC, MC, V. Open: Tues–Sun 12:30–3 p.m. and 7:30–10:30 p.m. Closed Nov–Feb.*

Ripa del Sole
$$ Riomaggiore   LIGURIAN

This new restaurant offers cooking that's true to the best local traditions with a menu that's certified organic. The yellow walls, wood accents, and beautiful linens and real crystal on the tables create a sunny atmosphere. The terrace — open in peak season — is high above the sea, with a breathtaking view. We definitely recommend the *antipasto* platter, with all the Cinque Terre fish specialties: stuffed mussels and anchovies, marinated octopus and anchovies, and *baccalà* (codfish) dumplings.

Via de Gasperi 282, on the mountain side of the village. ☎ *0187-920-143.* www. ripadelsole.it. *Reservations recommended. Secondi: 8€–21€ ($9.60–$25). AE, MC, V. Open: Summer, lunch and dinner daily; winter, lunch and dinner Tues–Sun. Closed Nov.*

Trattoria Gianni Franzi
$$ Vernazza   LIGURIAN

Tradition is the key word at Gianni's, where the recipes of Ligurian cuisine are prepared with care and served in refined surroundings. From late spring to mid-fall, you can dine alfresco and enjoy gorgeous sunsets by the sea. You will find all the classics prepared with local fish, herbs, and vegetables; our favorites include a fantastic *zuppa di pesce* and excellent *troffie al pesto* (the linguine is made from chestnut flour). The *ravioli di*

The Cinque Terre Card

Available at any of the tourist info desks inside the rail stations of La Spezia, Riomaggiore, Manarola, Vernazza, Corniglia, and Monterosso (see "Fast Facts: The Cinque Terre," later in this chapter), the Cinque Terre Card (www.parconazionale5 terre.it) is the best deal in the park: The pass gives you unlimited rides on trains between La Spezia and each of the villages in the Cinque Terre, and on the minibuses within the park, as well as free access to the trails and all the structures of the park (picnic areas, nature observation centers, and so on). You also get free maps and discounts on the boat pass, mountain-bike rentals, and horse and carriages rides. The daily card costs 5.40€ ($6.50) for adults and 2.70€ ($3.25) for children 5 to 12. Three- and seven-day cards are also available.

pesce (fish ravioli) are very good, as are the local anchovies, stuffed or marinated. Gianni's also rents rooms in town.

Piazza Marconi 5. ☎ *0187-821003. Reservations recommended. Secondi: 10€–20€ ($12–$24). MC, V. Open: Thurs–Tues 12:30–3 p.m. and 7:30–10:30 p.m. Closed Jan–Mar.*

Exploring the Cinque Terre

To fully enjoy this magnificent land that slopes steeply to the sea, we recommend taking a **boat tour:** Viewing the Cinque Terre from the water is part of the magic that shouldn't be missed. The **Consorzio Marittimo Turistico 5 Terre** *Golfo dei Poeti* (☎ 0187-732987; www.navigazione golfodeipoeti.it) runs half- and full-day cruises during the season (Mar 27–Nov 1), leaving from Molo Italia (dock Italia) in La Spezia. Boats leave at 9:15 a.m. and 10 a.m. for the full-day excursion, or 2:15 p.m. for the afternoon trip, and return by 6:30 p.m. The cost is 21€ ($25) for the whole day and 16€ ($19) for the afternoon only; children 6 to 11 pay 12€ ($14) for either cruise. You're free to hop on and off between the villages as you please using the local boat service, as your ticket also includes unlimited rides for that.

 Purchasing the **Cinque Terre Card** (see sidebar earlier) will give you unlimited access to all the trails of the park and to public transportation, including trains between the villages and — more important — the electric minibuses running up and down along the cliff and connecting all the attractions.

The top attractions

The cliffs surrounding the villages are the real attraction of the National Park of the Cinque Terre, which was recently declared a World Heritage Site by UNESCO. Amazingly steep, they have been cultivated for centuries, with narrow terraces built using dry stone walling — over 7,000m (21,000 ft.) of it. Vineyards are planted all the way down to the edge of the sea, together with luscious lemon and olive trees. During the harvest, farmers secure themselves with ropes to keep from falling. Progress has come to the area, however, so here and there you may notice small lifts that look something like monorails.

Corniglia

The only inland village of the Cinque Terre — though you can reach the sea by way of an old flight of steps — it is also the most agricultural of them all. The cobblestone streets of Corniglia wind from door to door and to its church, **San Pietro.** Built in 1334 above a chapel from the 11th century, the church was redone during the baroque period, but the Romanic facade was preserved. The whole town is like a step back in time, with several medieval buildings of interest — such as the arched Gothic building made of black stone, believed to have been the postal station of the Fieschi family. The town's agricultural tradition goes back millennia: Corniglia was already exporting wine to Pompeii during the Roman period.

Manarola

Manarola, a lovely sight from a distance with its gaily colored houses, is a real fishermen's village, still dependent on the sea. It's enclosed in a gorge opening onto a small harbor between two rocky cliffs. Manarola contains the 14th-century Romanic church of **San Lorenzo,** highlighted by a splendid rose window. From Manarola starts — or ends — the famous **Via dell'Amore** (Love Trail), the easiest of the trails joining the villages (see "More cool things to see and do," later in this chapter).

Monterosso al Mare

This is the largest of the five villages that comprise the Cinque Terre; it's also the only one with a nice sandy beach, giving Monterosso the feeling of an old-fashioned seaside resort. It's wonderful for swimming, even though most of the beach is divided into private swaths for the hotels lining the beachfront. This is also the busiest of the villages, and some say the least authentic. In reality, it's just different: Because high cliffs don't surround it on all sides, the old town has seen the growth of a modern section toward the rail station and the beach, called Fegina.

But the heart of Monterosso is still beautiful and unspoiled. The **medieval tower Aurora** separates the modern town from the old; it's where you'll find the late-Romanic church **San Giovanni Battista,** with a beautiful rosette on the facade and an elegant portico in back. Farther up, you'll climb to the other church in town, **San Francesco,** within the complex of the **convent of the Capuchins.** Built in 1619, it is a nice example of Tuscan/Ligurian Gothic in green-and-white-striped marble. Inside, you can admire a fine crucifixion attributed to Van Dyck.

Riomaggiore

Like Manarola, fishing is still an important industry in this village. Noteworthy attractions include the church of **San Giovanni Battista,** a fine example of late-Romanic architecture with two beautiful lateral portals from the 14th century. Uniting this village with Manarola is the most famous section of the coastal path: the **Via dell'Amore** (Love Trail) — a trail that was excavated in the cliff and offers fabulous views. It was closed for more than five years after a landslide blocked it, but it is now fully accessible again.

Vernazza

Vernazza is a very tiny fishing village with a strong medieval flavor. Dominated by its castle, it was founded around the year 1000. Overlooking the village is the Gothic church of **Santa Margherita di Antiochia,** built right on the water with an unusual octagonal bell tower. The fishing harbor offers a fine view over the rest of the bay.

More cool things to see and do

✔ If you are here to hike, you can tackle the **Cinque Terre Trail** (difficulty level: easy; Admission: one section 3.50€/$4.20, unlimited with Cinque Terre Card, described earlier in this chapter) between Riomaggiore and Monterosso al Mare: It will take you about five hours, but you need an iron will not to stop and linger in any of the villages or the beaches along the way. To everybody else, we recommend instead the easy — and fairly flat — section of the trail known as the **Via dell'Amore** between Riomaggiore and Manarola: You'll get the full Cinque Terre experience without exhausting yourself. The walk takes only about 30 minutes. If you're more ambitious, add the two sections from Manarola to Corniglia and Corniglia to Vernazza, each taking about 45 minutes. The last section of the trail — from Vernazza to Monterosso — is quite different, with winding ups and downs, and a precipitous descent into Monterosso. We don't recommend it, except for those fit travelers who specifically want to hike; allow about one and a half hours. Always hike with at least one companion, bring at least a quart of water per person (especially in summer, when it gets *very* hot), and wear sturdy walking shoes. The trail is along a cliff, and landslides are not uncommon. If you're lucky, during your walk you may see a local farmer standing where you'd think only goats can perch, lovingly tending to one of his plants.

✔ Only a few sandy **beaches** can be found along this rocky coast: The largest is in **Monterosso al Mare,** where you can even rent a beach chair — but it gets extremely crowded, as it is right in town. Between Corniglia and Vernazza, you can climb down — via a steep path off the Cinque Terre Trail (see above for admission prices) — to the romantic small pebble-and-sand beach of **Guvano,** where you can dive into the clean waters of the park in the nude, if you wish (it's a favorite nudist spot). Easier access is through the tunnel starting north of Corniglia train station (ring the bell at the gate for access). You'll also find a tiny but pretty beach in **Riomaggiore** at the south of the harbor, down a flight of steps.

✔ More trails connect each of the villages with its **Sanctuary** (church dedicated to the Madonna) up the cliff. The trails were the traditional paths used by the villagers before the local road — SS370 — was built to reach the churches and the hamlets in between, but nowadays you can also use public transportation (taxis and minibuses). The destination of religious processions, these Romanesque and early Gothic churches dominate the surrounding countryside high above the sea — fantastic stages for breathtaking views. Some are more interesting than others: **Nostra Signora di Soviore,** overlooking Monterosso, sports the oldest campanile in Liguria, dating back to the eighth century, while its simple 14th-century facade is ornamented with a beautiful rose window and portal. The area in front of the church offers awe-inspiring views and serves as venue for classical concerts during high season (ask the local information office for a schedule). **Nostra Signora di Montenero** overlooks Riomaggiore 340m (1,120 ft.) above sea level; the church was built in 1335, perhaps over an eighth-century chapel, and the monastery now houses a good and atmospheric restaurant, **Ca' de Cian** (☎ 0187-920992; cadecian.tsx.org; reservations necessary; prix-fixe lunch or dinner: 20€/$24; Open: Thurs–Sun 12:30–2:30 p.m. and 7:30–9:30 p.m.; Closed: Nov–Mar). **Nostra Signora della Salute,** in Volastra, also has a simple facade enlivened by a superb carved portal and a delicate Gothic double-arched window.

✔ Hiking is not the only way to explore the park: you can go **mountain biking** or **horseback riding,** or even relax on a horse-drawn **carriage ride** along the many trails in the area. You can rent mountain bikes for just 4€ ($4.80) per day or book a carriage ride or a horseback ride (or even a class) at any of the tourist information desks inside the rail stations in the park (also in La Spezia for the horse and carriage rides; see "Fast Facts: The Cinque Terre," later in this chapter). Prices for horse and carriage rides depend on the number of hours and participants; consider about 16€ ($19) per hour per person for a horse ride and about 25€ ($30) per hour per person for a carriage ride.

✔ The sea along the national park is a protected **marine park** which can be best enjoyed via snorkeling and scuba-diving excursions. **Daiwing 5 Terre Immersioni,** in Riomaggiore (Via San Giacomo 1; ☎ 0187-920011), is a licensed dive center offering guided excursions and equipment rentals. Excursions cost about 22€ ($26) per person; equipment rental is an extra 18€ ($22).

Fast Facts: The Cinque Terre

Area Code

The local area code is **0187** (see "Telephone" in the "Fast Facts" section of Appendix A for more on calling to and from Italy).

ATMs

You can exchange money at the Pro loco office in Monterosso (see "Information," below); there are also ATMs in the banks of Monterosso and Vernazza.

Emergencies

For an ambulance, dial ☎ **118** — or in Riomaggiore, ☎ **0187-920-777;** in Manarola,

☎ **0187-920-766;** in Monterosso, ☎ **0187-817-475;** and in Vernazza, ☎ **0187-821-078.** For the fire department, call ☎ **115;** for road assistance, call ☎ **116.**

Hospital

The nearest hospital is San Nicolo Levanto, in the town of Levanto, just west of Monterosso al Mare (☎ **0187-800-409**); there is also a larger hospital in La Spezia (☎ **0187-5331**).

Information

You'll find a small tourist office inside each of the train stations within the park:

Monterosso (☎ 0187-817059), Corniglia (☎ 0187-812523), Vernazza (☎ 0187-812533), Manarola (☎ 0187-760511), and Riomaggiore (☎ 0187-920633); as well as in the train station of La Spezia (☎ 0187-743500). You'll also find small tourist offices in Monterosso al Mare at Via Figena 38 (☎ 0187-817506; Open: Mon–Sat 10 a.m. to noon and 5–7:30 p.m., Sun 10 a.m. to noon) and on Via del Molo (☎ 0187-817204; Open: June–Sept, same hours).

Internet Access

In Monterosso, go to The Net (Via Vittorio Emanuele 55; ☎ 0187-817288; e-mail: info@monterossonet.com).

Police

Call ☎ 113.

Post Office

The main post office for the area is in Monterosso al Mare, on Piazza Garibaldi, in the center of town.

Chapter 15

Southern Tuscany and Umbria

. . . .

In This Chapter

▶ Checking out medieval towers in San Gimignano
▶ Exploring medieval Siena
▶ Discovering medieval Perugia and sweet Baci
▶ Visiting saints and monasteries in Assisi
▶ Thrilling to the music festivals in Spoleto

. . . .

*T*he beauty of the landscape and the rich culture of this area make this part of Italy the most beloved both by Italians and foreigners. While this may be where the wealthy dream to have their countryside homes, all visitors can enjoy the riches of this area, where a castle or walled city seems to top each hill. Perhaps the most famous of all is **San Gimignano,** with its beautiful towers — a perfectly preserved medieval town of considerable commercial importance back then, and delightfully romantic now. Continuing southeast across the **Chianti region,** famous for its flavorful ruby-red wine, you arrive at **Siena,** Italy's most beautiful medieval town — and our favorite. We love it all, from the **Palio delle Contrade** (a furiously contested horse race that has been held in the city's main square, the Piazza del Campo, since medieval times) to its streets and many monuments. Continuing southeast, you'll enter **Umbria** with its deep-green hills. **Perugia,** the region's capital, is a wonderful and lively university town, rich in art and historic sights. Not far to the east is **Assisi,** hometown of San Francesco (St. Francis), Italy's patron saint, and Santa Chiara (St. Clare). **Spoleto** is famous for its music and art festivals — the **Festival di Spoleto** and the **Stagione Lirica** — but it's also a delightful small medieval town offering beautiful vistas and interesting monuments.

If you have the time to explore the charms of the countryside, we definitely recommend renting a car (especially if you want to cover a lot of ground) — you're then free to base yourself outside the major towns.

You will not need your car within the towns, however, since each is small enough to be easily seen on foot (even Perugia, which is the largest of all). So, if your time is limited, you can do quite well using public transportation between the major destinations. Siena and Perugia both make good bases for exploring the region, as they offer lots of services as well as gorgeous surroundings. To see the scope of the entire Tuscan and Umbrian landscape, see the "Tuscany and Umbria" map in Chapter 14.

San Gimignano

This is one of southern Tuscany's most famous destinations, and with good reason: It is a perfectly preserved medieval town with a picturesque skyline of towers.

San Gimignano makes an easy day trip from Siena or even Florence, but it can also be a romantic place to spend the night, with its view of the twinkling lights of other Tuscan hill towns. You can explore the town's major attractions in about four hours.

Getting there

The easiest way to reach San Gimignano is by **bus** from Siena; **TRA-IN** (☎ 0577-204246; www.trainspa.it) offers regular service. The trip takes about 50 minutes and costs 4€ ($4.80). From all other locales, you need to first reach the nearby town of **Poggibonsi,** well served by both **train** (☎ 892021; www.trenitalia.it) and bus, and from there switch to the local bus to San Gimignano — it's doable, but laborious. To avoid the hassle, it would be easier to join a guided tour from Florence (see later in this section) or to rent a car.

To reach San Gimignano by **car,** get on the *autostrada* Florence–Pisa and take either the COLLE DI VAL D'ELSA exit (which takes you along picturesque small roads through the countryside) or the much faster POGGIBONSI exit, through a busy industrial area. The sign on the highway doesn't say San Gimignano, but after you exit, you will see signs for San Gimignano on SS324. The trip takes about 1½ hours from Florence and slightly less time from Siena. Once you arrive, you'll need to park outside the town's walls, as San Gimignano is closed to private traffic. You can drive to your hotel to deposit your luggage, but you need to have the authorization arranged by the hotel in advance. None of the hotels inside the town walls have parking, but you can use the lots outside the walls for 16€ ($19) per day.

Spending the night

In the low season between November and March, the major hotels in town take turns staying open, so there is always a place to stay.

San Gimignano

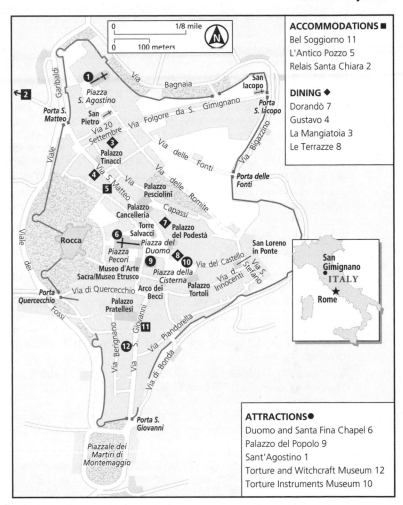

ACCOMMODATIONS ■
Bel Soggiorno 11
L'Antico Pozzo 5
Relais Santa Chiara 2

DINING ♦
Dorandò 7
Gustavo 4
La Mangiatoia 3
Le Terrazze 8

ATTRACTIONS●
Duomo and Santa Fina Chapel 6
Palazzo del Popolo 9
Sant'Agostino 1
Torture and Witchcraft Museum 12
Torture Instruments Museum 10

Bel Soggiorno
$ Duomo

This historic hotel is the second best inside the town walls, offering simple, quiet accommodations with great views. Guest rooms are spacious and comfortable; bathrooms are modern and well kept. The public spaces are cozy and inviting. The hotel restaurant is good, with a panoramic terrace and a wine bar.

See map p. 257. Via San Giovanni 91. ☎ *0577-940375. Fax: 0577-907521.* www.hotel belsoggiorno.it. *Rack rates: 120€ ($144) double. AE, DC, MC, V. Closed Jan 6–Feb 28.*

L'Antico Pozzo
$$ Duomo

This is our favorite hotel within the town walls: Housed in a 15th-century *palazzo*, it balances an elegant historical atmosphere with modern amenities (including Internet access). Guest rooms are large — some with frescoed ceilings, others with beamed ceilings — and some afford nice views of the city. All are furnished with antiques, mostly from the 19th century. In good weather, breakfast is served on the hotel's panoramic terrace.

See map p. 257. Via San Matteo 87. ☎ *0577-942014. Fax: 0577-942117.* www.antico pozzo.com. *Rack rates: 130€ ($156) double; 160€ ($192) junior suite. Rates include buffet breakfast. AE, DC, MC, V. Closed a variable period between Nov and Mar.*

Relais Santa Chiara
$$ Outside town walls

This is our favorite hotel here — if you don't mind a ten-minute walk outside the town walls. Actually a resort overlooking the luscious countryside and surrounded by a private park with a pool and Jacuzzi, it's the grand way to see San Gimignano, and yet it isn't really that expensive — especially if you take advantage of its special rates or stay in one of the smaller rooms. All rooms are beautifully decorated; some have private terraces.

See map p. 257. Via Matteotti 15. ☎ *0577-940701. Fax: 0577-942096.* www.rsc.it. *Free parking. Rack rates: 225€ ($270) double. Rates include buffet breakfast. AE, DC, MC, V. Closed Nov 20–Mar 11.*

Dining locally

The area is known for its wines, and the best place to sample them is at **Gustavo** (Via San Matteo 29; ☎ 0577-940057), perhaps accompanied by the excellent selection of local cured meats, cheese, and *fett'unta* (toasted bread with extra-virgin olive oil and veggie toppings). Another wine bar is attached to the restaurant of the **Bel Soggiorno** hotel (see earlier).

Dorandò
$$ Duomo   SIENESE/CREATIVE

On a tiny street near the Duomo, this excellent restaurant is popular with both locals and Italian gourmands. The food has a classic Tuscan base, with seasonal themes and some variations on local specialties. You'll find perfect *pici* (fresh homemade local pasta), maybe seasoned with a rabbit ragout, and excellent stewed local lamb. Note that the *secondi* here always include a side dish.

Rise and fall of a small town

San Gimignano was a dormant small village for centuries after it was established by the Etruscans in the third century B.C. It was only when the main route from Italy to France went right through the village in the Middle Ages that San Gimignano's fortunes changed. Thanks also to a flourishing saffron industry, the local merchants became rich and marked their increasing pride by building *palazzi*. Towers, the symbol of the *palazzo* owner's wealth, went up like crazy during the town's period of great economic success in the 13th century. So much competition existed in tower-building — always higher and higher — that the government made a law forbidding any tower taller than the one on the Palazzo del Popolo, the seat of the government. The economic boom was suddenly wiped out by the plague (which hit San Gimignano several times between the 14th and 17th centuries), a disaster that ultimately preserved the town, allowing it to remain basically intact as a typical walled medieval village with no modern additions.

See map p. 257. Vicolo dell'Oro 2, off Piazza del Duomo; turn right at the beginning of Via San Matteo. ☎ **0577-941862.** www.ristorantedorando.it. *Reservations required. Secondi: 18€–20€ ($22–$24). AE, MC, V. Open: Tues–Sun 12:30–2:30 p.m. and 7:30–9:30 p.m.; Easter–Oct daily same hours.*

La Mangiatoia
$ Duomo   SIENESE

This is the best deal in San Gimignano: You can try all the traditional favorites at a moderate price, while dining in an elegant yet rustic atmosphere beneath whitewashed brick arched passageways. The medieval-inspired cuisine is strong on wild game: We recommend the *pappardelle* with wild-boar sauce, the wild boar with walnut sauce, and the duck with truffle sauce.

See map p. 257. Via Mainardi 5. ☎ **0577-941528.** *Reservations recommended. Secondi: 12€–16€ ($14–$19). MC, V. Wed–Mon 12:15–2:30 p.m. and 7:30–9:30 p.m. (July and Aug same hours but Mon–Sat). Closed 4 weeks Nov/Dec.*

Le Terrazze
$ Duomo   TUSCAN

This restaurant is the classiest place to dine in San Gimignano, yet it's still very affordable. It opens onto the village's most picturesque square and features two dining rooms, one with a breathtaking view of the surrounding valley, and the other — original from the 13th century — with medieval beamed ceilings and wooden furniture. The food is classic countryside fare, starting from the excellent *crostini* to the mouthwatering grilled meat and game *ragù*.

See map p. 257. Piazza della Cisterna 24. ☎ **0577-940328.** www.hotelcisterna. it. *Reservations recommended. Secondi: 13€–21€ ($16–$25). AE, DC, MC, V. Open:*

Thurs–Mon 12:30–2:30 p.m. and Wed–Mon 7:30–10 p.m. Closed for a period between Nov and Mar.

Exploring San Gimignano

You can book a **guided tour** or pick up an audio guide (5€/$6) at the tourist office (ProLoco; Piazza Duomo 1; ☎ **0577-940008;** www. sangimignano.com). You can also book a **bus tour** from Florence; the best are organized by **American Express** (☎ **055-50981**) and **SITA** (☎ **055-214721;** www.sita-on-line.it), which both charge about 50€ ($60).

 The **Civic Museums combination ticket** includes admission to Palazzo del Popolo, Pinacoteca, Torre Grossa, Santa Fina Apothecary, and Archaeological Museum; it costs 7.50€ ($9). Another combination ticket includes admission to the Duomo and the Museum of Religious Art for 5.50€ ($6.60).

The top attractions

The town itself is the attraction here, and walking through its medieval alleys is quite magical. Of the original 72 or so **medieval towers** which are the symbol of town, only 15 remain today, including the tallest: the one on the Palazzo del Popolo (see later in this chapter). **Piazza della Cisterna,** at the heart of town, is the most attractive in San Gimignano and an elegant example of medieval architecture: Triangular in shape and beautifully paved with bricks, it is lined with some of the town's most important *palazzi,* such as the Palazzo Tortoli-Treccani at no. 22, with its double row of *bifore* (double lancet windows). The center of the square is graced by a picturesque well: It gives access to an underlying cistern, which held the town's water supply in case of siege. The main street — **Via San Matteo** — is a section of the medieval highway to France which brought wealth and renown to town. Besides its historical interest — it was the most important route between northern and southern Europe — it's a beautiful section of medieval San Gimignano, lined with palaces and towers.

Duomo (Basilica di S. Maria Assunta) and Santa Fina Chapel

Still called the Duomo by locals — although according to the Catholic church's administration, it technically doesn't deserve the title (the town has no bishop and its cathedral should be called a Collegiata) — the basilica was built in the 12th century. Its facade is very plain, but once inside you'll discover a gorgeously decorated Romanesque interior with tiger-striped arches and a galaxy of gold stars. Among the treasures are the wooden statues of *Gabriele* and *Annunziata* by Jacopo della Quercia and the 14th-century frescoes decorating the naves. The right nave's last chapel is the **Chapel of Santa Fina,** one of the most beautiful from the Tuscan Renaissance. Designed by Giuliano and Benedetto da Maiano — Benedetto also carved the panel of the altar — its glorious cycle of frescoes by

Domenico Ghirlandaio describes the life of a local girl named Fina, who became the town's patron saint.

See map p. 257. Piazza del Duomo. ☎ *0577-940316. Admission: 3.50€ ($4.20). Open: Feb 1–Mar 31, Nov 1–15 and Jan 2–15 Mon–Sat 9:30 a.m.–4:40 p.m., Sun and holidays 12:30–4:40 p.m.; Apr 1–Oct 31 Mon–Fri 9:30 a.m.–7:10 p.m., Sat 9:30 a.m.–5 p.m., Sun and holidays 12:30–5:10 p.m.; Nov 16–30 and Jan 16–30 open only for mass. Closed Jan 1, Jan 31, Mar 12, Dec 25, and first Sun in Aug.*

Palazzo del Popolo

Built between 1288 and 1323 (except for its crenellations, which were a 19th-century addition), this was the government headquarters. Its tower, the **Torre Grossa,** was added in 1311 and is the tallest in town, 53m (177 ft.) high. We recommend climbing the tower to get a superb view over the town. The interior of the palace is decorated with great frescoes and furnishings from the 14th and 15th centuries. It also houses the **Civic Museum,** where you'll find the *Sala di Dante* (Dante's Room), decorated with splendid frescoes by Lippo Memmi (his *Maestà* is considered a masterpiece).

See map p. 257. Piazza del Duomo 1. ☎ *0577-990312. Admission: 5€ ($6). Open: Daily Mar 1–Oct 31 9:30 a.m.–7 p.m.; Nov 1–Feb 28 10 a.m.–5:30 p.m. Closes at 1:30 p.m. Dec 24, 5 p.m. Dec 25 and 31. Closed Jan 31.*

More cool things to see and do

If you have the time, you may want to explore more of the village's medieval delights. Here are a few additional options:

✔ A pleasant and easy excursion is the 15-minute walk out of town from Porta delle Fonti to the **medieval fountain.** You'll follow in the footsteps of medieval town dwellers: This fountain provided San Gimignano with running water and was where locals did their laundry. The 14th-century arched construction hides the 9th-century Longobard fountain inside.

✔ **Sant'Agostino** (Piazza Sant'Agostino; ☎ 0577-940383) is a beautiful 13th-century Romanesque-Gothic church. Its plain facade hides a superb cycle of frescoes on the life of St. Augustine, done by Benozzo Gozzoli; also interesting is his fresco of St. Sebastian on the third altar to the left. The church is open daily from 7 a.m. to noon and 3 to 6 p.m. (Jan and Feb reopens at 4 p.m.; Apr 1–Oct 31 closes at 7 p.m.). Admission is free.

✔ To explore the dark side of San Gimignano, you can visit the **Torture Instruments Museum** (Via del Castello 1, off Piazza della Cisterna; ☎ 0577-942243; Admission: 8€/$9.60; Open: daily 10 a.m.–5 p.m., later on weekends and in summer), appropriately housed in the so-called Devil's Tower; and the smaller **Torture and Witchcraft Museum** (Via San Giovanni, ☎ 0577-940526; Admission: 4€/$4.80; Open: daily 9 a.m.–7 p.m.). *Note:* These museums may be appropriate for teenagers, but not for young children.

Fast Facts: San Gimignano

Area Code

The local area code is **0577** (see "Telephone" in the "Fast Facts" section of Appendix A for more on calling to and from Italy).

ATMs

You'll find ATMs inside the banks in town. You can exchange money at the tourist office (see "Information," later in this section) and the Protur booth (Piazza San Domenico; ☎ 0577-288-084; open Mon–Sat 9 a.m.–7 p.m. in winter and until 8 p.m. in summer).

Emergencies

For an ambulance, call ☎ **118**; for the fire department, call ☎ **115**. For road assistance (ACI, the Italian Automobile Club), call ☎ **116**.

Hospitals

The nearest hospital is the Ospedale Poggibonsi (Via Pisana 2; ☎ 0577-915555).

Information

The Pro Loco tourist office is at Piazza Duomo 1 (☎ 0577-940008; www. sangimignano.com). Summer hours are daily from 9 a.m. to 1 p.m. and 3 to 7 p.m. Winter hours are daily from 9 a.m. to 1 p.m. and 2 to 6 p.m.

Police

Call ☎ **113**.

Post Office

The post office (ufficio postale) is at Piazza delle Erbe 8 (☎ 0577-941983).

Siena

This is our favorite town in Tuscany. With its rich orange tones and myriad tiled roofs baking in the strong sun, Siena is a sculpture in its own right. It is a magnificent medieval city surrounded by sun-drenched countryside, but Siena is far from being a museum piece. Passion pervades Sienese life — and you can experience the love the residents have for their town and their traditions during their time-honored Palio horse race (see later in this section).

To do justice to Siena, you should spend the night in town. But if you don't have the time, one day is enough to see the highlights; you can also visit as a day trip from Florence, which is better than nothing.

Getting there

Only 62km (37 miles) south of Florence, Siena is best reached by **bus,** either from Florence or Rome. The bus station is in Piazza Gramsci, off the La Lizza pedestrian gallery only steps from the town center. **TRA-IN** (☎ 0577-204246; www.trainspa.it) and SITA (☎ 800-373760; www.sita-on-line.it) offer regular service from Florence (from the SITA bus station near the SMN train station); the trip takes 1¼ hours and costs about 5€ ($6), with buses leaving every half-hour. **SENA** (☎ **800-930960** or 0577-283203; www.sena.it) runs seven daily buses from

The Chianti Region

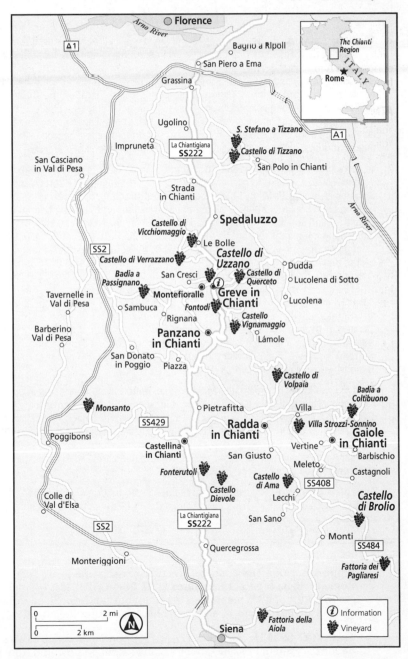

The Chianti

This gorgeous region between Florence and Siena has it all: velvety hills, tiny medieval towns, and acres of vineyards and olive groves. An agricultural area of uncommon beauty, the soft slopes of its hills bloom with magnificent colors in every season. The tallest hills are topped by medieval walled towns and *pieve* (fortified churches). Break our rule about driving in Italy and put the pedal to the metal on the **Chiantigiana** (SS222), the local road linking Florence to Siena (or at least take a bus tour; see later in this chapter). This winding 66km (41-mile) road was established as the route for collecting wine from each vineyard in the region and bringing it to Florence — so it's perfect for tourists, as it passes through each of the major points of interest in the area.

If you're pressed for time, head to **Greve in Chianti,** the area's main village. It has a delightful *piazza* and an excellent restaurant/hotel, the **Giovanni da Verrazzano** (Piazza Giacomo Matteotti 28; ☎ **055-853189;** closed Wed and Sun). Good restaurants, hotels, resorts, and vineyards abound, of course, as it is difficult to have a bad meal in the Chianti — and impossible to have a bad glass of wine, provided you stick to the local red. Among the places to stay, we recommend the **Castello di Spaltenna,** in Gaiole in Chianti (Via Spaltenna 13; ☎ **0577-749483;** www.spaltenna.com), a real medieval castle; and the much more modest but delightful **Villa Rosa di Boscorotondo,** in Panzano (Via San Leolino 59, 5km/3 miles south of Greve on SS222; ☎ **055-852577;** www.resortvillarosa.it). In Spedaluzzo, **La Cantinetta** (Via Mugnano 93, 2.3km/1½ miles north of Greve on SS222; ☎ **055-8572000;** closed Mon) is a superb restaurant housed in a two-centuries-old farmhouse. Worth a visit is the 11th-century **Castello di Uzzano** (☎ **055-854032;** Open: Apr–Oct daily 8:30 a.m.–6 p.m., winter, by reservation only), a beautiful vineyard located on a side road 5km (3 miles) northeast of Greve in Chianti. You can visit the cellars (admission: 5€/$6) and tour the famous gardens (admission: 6€/$7.20).

Head of the Chianti League in the Middle Ages, **Radda in Chianti** also makes a good destination. Nearby (about 11km/7 miles southeast of Radda), you can visit the **Castello di Brolio** (☎ **0577-749066;** www.ricasoli.it), one of the region's oldest wine-producing estates and the birthplace of the Chianti Classico we know today. Visitors can explore part of the spectacular grounds and gardens (Admission: 3€/$3.60; Open: summer 9 a.m. to noon and 3–6 p.m.; winter 9 a.m. to noon and 2–5 p.m.) and take a tour of the cellars (by appointment) for 23€ ($28).

If you don't care for driving, we recommend the day tours organized by **SITA** (☎ **055-214721;** www.sita-on-line.it). They cost 32€ ($38) and are offered daily from Florence.

Rome's Stazione Tiburtina for 17€ ($20); reservations are required from Rome to Siena (contact **Eurolines** at ☎ **06-44252461;** it will deliver tickets to your hotel via messenger service), but not from Siena to Rome. SENA also makes runs to and from Milan and other Italian cities.

Trains (☎ **892021;** www.trenitalia.it) pull in at Siena's **rail station,** on Piazza Fratelli Rosselli, about 2.5km (1½ miles) downhill from the town center (☎ 0577-280115). You then have to take a taxi or a minibus (no. C to Piazza Gramsci). You'll find direct train service from Florence (and the nearby towns of Empoli and Chiusi), but from most other destinations, you'll have to change trains at one of the above stations. The trip from Rome takes about 3 hours and costs about 17€ ($20); from Venice, it takes about 5 hours and costs about 28€ ($34). Florence is about 1½ hours away and costs about 6€ ($7.20).

If you're renting a **car,** it is easy enough to drive here (via the Florence/ Siena highway or by taking exit VAL DI CHIANA from the A1 highway, and then following SS326), but keep in mind that the town center is pedestrian-only. When you arrive in Siena, you will need to leave your car for the duration of your stay at one of the parking lots (Siena Parcheggi; ☎ 0577-228711; www.sienaparcheggi.com) at the various gates of town; they charge 1.50€ ($1.80) per hour, which adds up to 36€ ($43) per day. Don't even dream of parking for free outside the town walls if you don't want your car broken into or stolen. From the parking lots, you can then use the public minibus to reach the center of town; the buses run daily from 6 a.m. to 9 p.m. One ticket, valid one hour, costs 0.90€ ($1); a daily pass is 3.50€ ($4.20).

Spending the night

It used to be that all hotels in Siena's historic district were modest properties offering basic accommodations, and if you wanted modern amenities you had to head for the modern part of town — but this has changed, and you'll now find hotels for all tastes and budgets, including a luxury five-star: the recently opened **Grand Hotel Continental** (Banchi di Sopra 85; ☎ 0577-56011; www.grandhotelcontinentalsiena.it), housed in a beautifully frescoed historic *palazzo.*

Garden Hotel
$$ North of the town's medieval walls

This elegant 1700 villa is only 1.5km (1 mile) north of the city walls, up a hill among vineyards, olive groves, and a park full of oak trees. (The walk downhill to town is very pleasant, but take a bus or taxi on your way back.) Guest rooms are divided among the villa itself and three annexes; are all large and tastefully furnished. We prefer those in the Belvedere annex (decorated in period style with some antiques) and the Poggiarello annex (luminous and modern in décor). Guests have access to a tennis court and a large outdoor pool, and the terrace affords panoramic views of Siena and the countryside. The restaurant is elegant but has a warm atmosphere.

See map p. 266. Via Custoza 2. ☎ *0577-47056. Fax: 0577-46050.* www.garden hotel.it. *Free parking. Rack rates: 190€ ($228) double. Rates include breakfast. AE, DC, MC, V.*

Siena

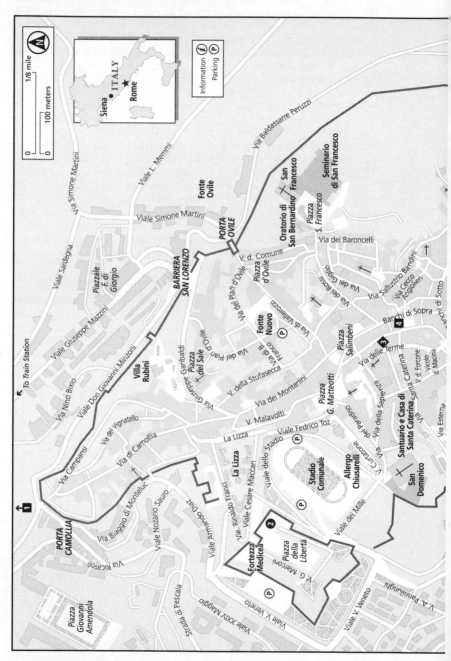

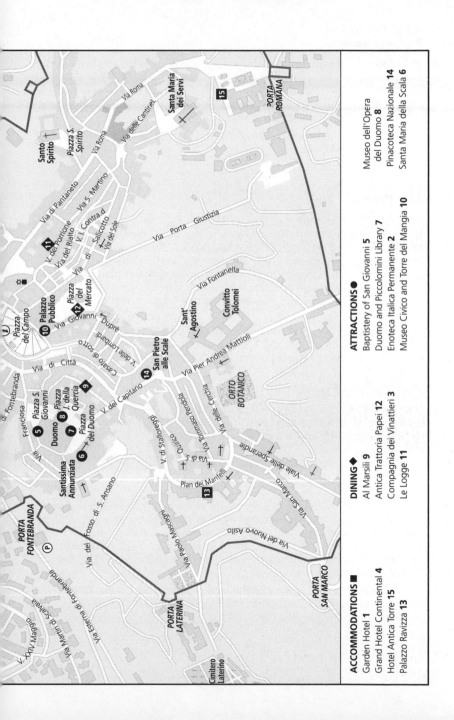

ACCOMMODATIONS ■
Garden Hotel **1**
Grand Hotel Continental **4**
Hotel Antica Torre **15**
Palazzo Ravizza **13**

DINING ◆
Al Marsili **9**
Antica Trattoria Papei **12**
Compagnia dei Vinattieri **3**
Le Logge **11**

ATTRACTIONS ●
Baptistery of San Giovanni **5**
Duomo and Piccolomini Library **7**
Enoteca Italica Permanente **2**
Museo Civico and Torre del Mangia **10**

Museo dell'Opera
del Duomo **8**
Pinacoteca Nazionale **14**
Santa Maria della Scala **6**

Hotel Antica Torre
$ Porta Romana

This small, family-run hotel has only eight rooms, but they're in a real 16th-century tower *(torre)*, romantically appointed with marble floors and antique furniture. The two rooms on the top floors offer views of Siena and the countryside. Because it's a tower, however, don't expect huge rooms, air-conditioning, or an elevator.

See map p. 266. Via di Fieravecchia 7. ☎ *and Fax: 0577-222255. Rack rates: 120€ ($144) double. AE, MC, V.*

Palazzo Ravizza
$$$ Duomo

The lengthy renovations of this 17th-century family palace have finally brought this hotel to its full potential: The beautiful architectural details — vaulted ceilings, checked tiled floors, hardwood parquet — have now been completely restored. Guest rooms are bright, with plaster walls and some with frescoed ceilings. The garden, which has beautiful views, is the setting for a typical American breakfast in the high season, as well as dinner, should you decide to take advantage of the hotel's perfectly adequate restaurant.

See map p. 266. Pian dei Mantellini 34. ☎ *0577-280462. Fax: 0577-211-597.* www. palazzoravizza.it. *Parking: Free in a garage nearby. Rack rates: 270€ ($324) double. Rates include buffet breakfast. AE, DC, MC, V.*

Dining locally
Sienese cuisine is a variety of Tuscan cooking (see Chapter 2), with a few specialties such as the *pici* (hand-rolled spaghetti), usually prepared with bread crumbs and tomato sauce.

Al Marsili
$$ Duomo SIENESE

If you've come to Siena for a romantic getaway, Al Marsili is the perfect choice. It lives up to its reputation by offering excellent service, an elegant but warm atmosphere, and superb food. You can find staples of Sienese cuisine here, such as delicious homemade *pici,* as well as specialties like *faraona alla Medici* (guinea hen with pine nuts, almonds, and prunes) and an excellent selection of wines.

See map p. 266. Via del Castoro 3, between Via di Città and the Duomo. ☎ *0577-47154. Reservations recommended. Secondi: 12€–18€ ($14–$22). AE, DC, MC, V. Open: Tues–Sun 12:30–2:30 p.m. and 7:30–10:30 p.m.*

Antica Trattoria Papei
$ Piazza del Mercato   SIENESE

This charming *trattoria*, close to Piazza del Campo, is a favorite with the Sienese. The food is good, sometimes remarkable. Try the duck stewed with tomatoes, the Sienese favorite *pici alla Cardinale* (homemade spaghetti with hot tomato sauce), or the pappardelle with wild-boar sauce. The place welcomes families with kids and provides a selection of half-portion dishes for the younger ones.

See map p. 266. Piazza del Mercato 6, behind the Palazzo Pubblico. ☎ *0577-280894. Reservations suggested. Secondi: 7€–12€ ($8–$14). AE, MC, V. Open: Tues–Sun 12:15–2:30 p.m. and 7:15–10 p.m.*

Compagnia dei Vinattieri
$ Santa Caterina   SIENESE/WINE BAR

The excellent cuisine here is a fine match for the wonderful cellar with over a thousand wines. The menu offers lighter choices for lunch and heartier ones at dinner — all made with local ingredients. We recommend the *ravioli maremmani* (ravioli with a sauce of goat cheese and basil) and the rabbit with olives. If you come during a lull, you can even ask for a tour of the cellars, which are housed in part of a medieval aqueduct running under the building.

See map p. 266. Via delle Terme 79, at Via dei Pittori. ☎ *0577-236568.* www. vinattieri.net. *Reservations recommended. Secondi: 9€–21€ ($11–$25). AE, DC, MC, V. Open: Daily 12:30–3 p.m. and 7:30–10:30 p.m.*

Le Logge
$$ Duomo   CREATIVE SIENESE

This is a popular, old-fashioned gourmet restaurant where creative Tuscan cuisine is paired with selections from a notable wine cellar, all served in historic dining rooms full of character. The seasonal menu includes both traditional and more sophisticated dishes: from the simpler *pappa al pomodoro* (tomato and bread soup) and *pici* (homemade spaghetti) to the *ravioli di coniglio pecorino e menta* (hare, local pecorino cheese, and fresh mint ravioli) and rabbit cutlets with eggplant and polenta.

See map p. 266. Via del Porrione 33. ☎ *0577-48013. Reservations recommended. Secondi: 14€–20€ ($17–$24). AE, DC, MC, V. Open: Mon–Sat 12:30–2:30 p.m. and 7:30–10:30 p.m. Closed 4 weeks Jan/Feb.*

Exploring Siena

The **Centro Guide-Associazione Guide Turistiche** (☎ 0577-43273; www. guidesiena.it) organizes tours of the town's highlights, which leave from the tourist office in Piazza del Campo, as well as custom-designed tours, such as a visit to Siena's museums. Prices vary according to the type of tour. For a bus tour from Florence, call **American Express** (☎ 055-50981) or the bus company **SITA** (☎ 055-214-721; www.sita-on-line.it); both offer tours for about 50€ ($60).

You can purchase admission tickets in advance through **Siena's town office** (Comune di Siena, ☎ **0577-41169;** Fax: 0577-226265; biglietteria.sienastore.com): This way, you'll avoid the lines and get a discount of 1€ ($1.20) or 0.50€ (60¢), depending on the attraction. They'll send you a confirmation and an account number for a bank transfer; once that has cleared, they will send you a receipt. Pick up your tickets at the attraction's entrance at the time of your visit.

 If you're planning to see everything in town, the **Siena Itinerari d'Arte (SIA) Pass** is the ticket for you: It exists in a winter (Nov 2–Feb 28 for 13€/$16) and summer (Mar 1–Nov 1 for16€/$19) version and is valid for seven days.

Those who are less ambitious, or have less time, can take advantage of the **Biglietto Cumulativo Musei Comunali,** which includes entrance to Museo Civico, Palazzo delle Papesse, and Santa Maria della Scala for 10€ ($12) and is valid for two days, or the **Biglietto Cumulativo Opera Duomo,** which also costs 10€ ($12), is valid for three days, and includes admission to the Duomo and Museo dell'Opera, Baptistery, and Oratorio di San Bernardino with Museum.

The top attractions

The medieval town is an attraction unto itself: Built over three hills, it is divided into *terza* (districts that cover a third of town each). North, along Via Banchi di Sopra, is the **Terza di Camollia;** southwest, along Via di Città, is the **Terza di Città** (with the Duomo); and southeast, along Via del Porrione, is the **Terza di San Martino.** The three terza meet at **Piazza del Campo.**

Baptistery of San Giovanni

Built in the 14th century, its unfinished Gothic facade is by Domenico di Agostino; inside, it is a succession of lavish frescoes, most of which depict the lives of Christ and St. Anthony and were painted in the 15th century. At the center of it all is the baptismal font, a splendid masterpiece of monumental proportions made of six bronze panels depicting scenes of the life of St. John the Baptist, divided by figurines representing the virtues, each carved by one of the best artists of the time. The *Feast of Herod* and the figurines of *Faith* and *Hope* are by Donatello; Lorenzo Ghiberti carved the *Baptism of Christ* and the *Arrest of the Baptist;* Giovanni di Turino did the *Preaching of the Baptist* and, with Turino di Sano, the *Birth of the Baptist.* Crowning the font is the marble ciborium with the statue of St. John the Baptist carved by Jacopo della Quercia. The angels are by Donatello and Giovanni di Turino.

See map p. 266. Piazza San Giovanni, behind the Duomo. ☎ *0577-283048.* www. operaduomo.siena.it. *Admission: 3€ ($3.60). Open: Daily Nov 2–Feb 28 10 a.m.–5 p.m.; Mar 1–May 31 and Sept 1–Nov 1 9:30 a.m.–7 p.m.; June 1–Aug 31 9:30 a.m.–8 p.m. Closed Jan 1 and Dec 25.*

Duomo and Piccolomini Library

Some consider this Romanesque-Gothic cathedral the most beautiful in Italy: Decorated with contrasting colored marble both inside and out, it was built during the first half of the 13th century in Romanesque and Gothic styles. It contains many works of art, including a superb **13th-century pulpit** carved by Nicola Pisano — the artist who crafted the magnificent pulpit in Pisa's Baptistery and the father of Giovanni Pisano (who carved the pulpit in Pisa's Duomo). The cathedral pavement is another work of art upon which many famous artists of the time worked. Unfortunately, in order to protect it, it is visible only between August 23 and October 27, in honor of the Palio. Another masterpiece inside the Duomo is the **Piccolomini Library,** built by Cardinal Francesco Piccolomini (later Pius III) to honor his uncle, Pope Pius II. The library was beautifully frescoed by Pinturicchio with scenes from the life of the pope and contains the *Three Graces,* an exquisite Roman sculpture of the third century B.C. designed after a Greek model.

See map p. 266. Piazza del Duomo. ☎ *0577-283048.* www.operaduomo.siena.it. *Admission: 3€ ($3.60); during the exposure of the floor 6€ ($7.20). Open: Mar 1–May 31 and Sept 1–Nov 1 Mon–Sat 10:30 a.m.–7:30 p.m., Sun and holidays 1:30–5:30 p.m.; June 1–Aug 31 Mon–Sat 10:30 a.m.–8 p.m., Sun and holidays 1:30–6 p.m.; Nov 2–Feb 28 Mon–Sat 10:30 a.m.–6:30 p.m., Sun and holidays 1:30–5:30 p.m.*

Museo Civico and Torre del Mangia

The Museo Civico is housed in the beautiful 13th-century **Palazzo Pubblico,** the seat of the government in Siena's republican period and today its town hall. Its richly frescoed rooms host some of Siena's important artwork. On the second floor, the loggia is the showcase for the eroded panels from the masterpiece fountain that decorated Piazza del Campo — the 14th-century **Fonte Gaia** was carved by Jacopo della Quercia and replaced by a replica in the 19th century. In the **Sala del Mappamondo (Globe Room),** just off the chapel, are two important pieces by 14th-century Sienese painter Simone Martini: the *Maestà* and the magnificent fresco of *Guidoriccio da Fogliano,* captain of the Sienese army (though there's been debate about the attribution of the latter work to Martini). In the **Sala della Pace (Peace Room)** — the meeting room of the Council of Nine that governed Siena — is a famous series of frescoes by another 14th-century Sienese painter, Ambrogio Lorenzetti: the secular medieval *Allegory of the Good and Bad Government and Its Effects on the City and the Countryside.* From the *palazzo's* 14th-century **Torre del Mangia** — accessible from the courtyard — is a breathtaking view of the town and the surrounding hills (if you're up to climbing the 503 steps, that is). At 100m (335 ft.), the Torre del Mangia is the second-tallest medieval tower in Italy (the tower in Cremona is taller).

See map p. 266. Piazza del Campo. ☎ *0577-292226. Admission: Museo 7€ ($8.40), 6€ ($7.20 with reservation); Tower 6€ ($7.20); Both: 10€ ($12). Open: Museum daily, Mar 16–Oct 31 10 a.m.–7 p.m.; Nov 1–26, Dec 23–Jan6, and Feb 16–Mar 15 10 a.m.–6:30 p.m.; Nov 26–Dec 22 and Jan 7–Feb 15 10 a.m.–5:30 p.m. Jan 1 noon to 4 p.m. Tower daily, Mar 16–Oct 31 10 a.m.–7 p.m.; Nov 1–Mar 15 10 a.m.–4 p.m. Jan 1 noon to 4 p.m. Both closed Dec 25.*

The Palio day by day

The Palio is organized by the town government and strictly regulated. Only 10 of the 17 *contrade* (town neighborhoods) participate in each of the two races: the seven that didn't run the previous year in the same race plus three that are drawn from the remaining ten. The drawing, which takes place at least 20 days before each race, signals the beginning of the competition, but the official opening of the festivities occurs three days before the race and is marked by the ceremony of the drawing of the horse — when each of the ten chosen animals is assigned to a *contrada* — and the first of six trial runs on Piazza del Campo; other trial runs take place during each of the three days before the Palio. At 3 p.m. on the day of the Palio, each horse is blessed in the church of its *contrada,* and then is led to join the historic cortege. After the cortege has assembled, it tours the town before convening with the other horses in Piazza del Campo around 5 p.m. for the race. The alignment of the horses for the start is also decided by a drawing, and the last horse starts on the run from the back: When he moves the rope at the front, it is hastily lowered and the race begins. After the race, the colors of the winning *contrada* are brought triumphantly around town in a lively parade. The winning contrada will celebrate all night — and indeed until the next year. The victory dinner for the whole contrada — with thousands of participants — takes place around the end of September.

Museo dell'Opera del Duomo

This museum occupies a part of the originally projected Duomo, which was never built. The ambitious plan was to create a cathedral of such huge proportions that the current Duomo would have been just the transept, but it never happened because of engineering problems and the plague of 1348. Today, the space has been turned into a museum; the gallery contains all the original artwork that was removed from the Duomo for safekeeping and to prevent further decay, such as the splendid statues that Giovanni Pisano carved for the facade. The rich collection also includes a number of painting masterpieces, such as Duccio di Buoninsegna's *Maestà,* depicting the Virgin Mary, and Pietro Lorenzetti's beautiful triptych the *Birth of the Virgin.*

See map p. 266. Piazza Jacopo della Quercia, adjacent to Duomo. ☎ *0577-283048.* www.operaduomo.siena.it. *Admission: 6€ ($7.20). Open: Daily, Mar 1–May 31 and Sept 1–Nov 1 9:30 a.m.–7 p.m.; June 1–Aug 31 9:30 a.m.–8 p.m.; Nov 2–Feb 28 10 a.m.–5 p.m. Closed Jan 1 and Dec 25.*

Palio delle Contrade
Piazza del Campo

We love coming to Siena for these famous events that have been lighting the locals afire with passion since at least the Middle Ages (the origin of the Palio is uncertain and could even go back to the Etruscans, but the first written document mentioning the race is from 1238). Far from just a tourist attraction, the Palio is a deeply felt and hotly contested competition among the city's 17 districts *(contrade)* — trust us, the Super Bowl doesn't incite as much passion as this medieval-style derby. This is the world's most difficult horse race, run bareback on Piazza del Campo, which is temporarily filled with dirt for the occasion. The horses run around the square three times while riders hit the horses — and each other — with a short whip. It's a *horse* race: The horse that arrives first wins, even if it has thrown his rider! Before the 17th century, the Palio was run in the streets, a bit in the style of the Monte Carlo car race, making it even more dangerous and brutal — even today, injuries aren't uncommon. The two Palio competitions are run in July and August; all the races are breathtaking, but we also love the colorful parades of medieval costumes — each *contrada* has its own colors — that take place on the side, and particularly the flag juggling, a difficult and skillful art which has been passed on since time immemorial. The pageantry shows are competitive as well, and at the end of the Palio, the contrada with the best behavior, costumes, and skills wins the *Masgalano,* traditionally a silver bowl weighing at least 1 kilogram (2¼ pounds) and decorated with Palio scenes, though it could be a different work of art.

 If you want to attend the Palio, you don't need to buy expensive tickets, unless you really want to see the horse racing up close. Standing in the center of the square is free — and a lot of fun. Note, though, that if you do seat yourself in the middle, you won't be able to get out until the race is over. Wherever you sit, bring lots of refreshments and a hat, as the sun gets very strong, and get there early, as the square quickly fills to capacity.

Piazza del Campo. www.comune.siena.it. *Tickets for a seat in the grandstands or at a window of one of the buildings surrounding the piazza are controlled by the building owners and the shops in front of which the stands are set up.* **Palio Viaggi** *(Piazza La Lizza 12;* ☎ *0577-280828; Fax: 0577-289114) can help you score a seat. Seats can cost anywhere from 200€ to over 1,000€ ($240 to over $1,200) and need to be reserved as far as 6 months in advance. Final races: July 2 and Aug 16. Trials start June 29 and Aug 13.*

Pinacoteca Nazionale

This picture gallery, housed in the 15th-century Palazzo Buonsignori, contains an expansive collection of art showing the unique Sienese Renaissance style, which retained Greek and Byzantine influences long after realism came into play elsewhere (notably Florence), and also emphasized rich coloration. It includes works from the 12th century to the first half of the 17th century. **Guido da Siena,** an early developer of the Sienese school, is well represented, along with the more famous **Duccio di Buoninsegna,** the real founder of the style; his painting of the Virgin is a marvel of delicacy and pathos. Also represented is **Giovanni di Paolo** — don't miss his beautiful little painting of the Virgin.

See map p. 266. Via San Pietro 29. ☎ *0577-46052.* www.ticketeria.it. *Admission: 4€ ($4.80). Open: Tues–Sat 8 a.m.–7:15 p.m., Sun–Mon 8:15 a.m.–1:15 p.m. Closed Jan 1 and Dec 25.*

Santa Maria della Scala

Housed in the former Hospital of Siena, this huge complex of buildings has been recently opened to the public. Many of its rooms were lavishly decorated with frescoes during the Renaissance and later periods, and almost all the great Sienese artists worked for the hospital at one time or another. One of the most surprising rooms is the **Pellegrinaio,** which held hospital beds until only a few years ago. Built in the 14th century, it saw its original wooden ceiling replaced in the 15th century by a beautiful vaulted ceiling decorated with frescoes narrating the history of the hospital — note that the last vault by the window was added in the 16th century. The **Cappella del Sacro Chiodo** — or *Sagrestia Vecchia* (Old Sacristy) — was also built in 1444, to hold the relics and reliquaries bought by the Spedale from the imperial palace of Byzantium. It was frescoed by Lorenzo Vecchietta with a cycle on the New and Old Testaments. The chapel also holds the famous fresco by Domenico di Bartolo, *Madonna della Misericordia,* painted in 1444 in the Cappella del Manto, but moved to its present location in 1610.

See map p. 266. Piazza Duomo 2. ☎ 0577-224828. www.santamaria.comune. siena.it. *Admission: 6€ ($7.20), 5.50€ ($6.60) with reservations. Open: Daily, Nov 1–Dec 24 and Jan 7–Mar 15 10:30 a.m.–4:30 p.m., Dec 25–Jan 6 10 a.m.–6 p.m., Mar 16–Oct 31 10:30 a.m.–6:30 p.m. Ticket booth closes 30 minutes earlier.*

More cool things to see and do

✔ For a wonderful outing, we highly recommend a ride on the **Treno Natura** (Ferrovia della Val d'Orcia; ☎ 0577-207413; www.ferrovie turistiche.it) — and not only for families. When the local train line closed a few years ago, a group of volunteers, in cooperation with the Italian Railroads Company, decided that it was too bad to let this scenic ride go to waste. They restored some antique engines and carriages and reopened the line. It's a hit, and kids love it, too. Antique carriages trailed by a diesel engine run on Sundays at 8:30 a.m., 11:15 a.m., and 3:45 p.m., but there are a number of special steam-engine tours that are scheduled only on special dates and require advance reservations. Diesel-engine runs cost 15€ ($18), steam-engine runs cost 25€ ($30), and children under 10 ride for free. Reservations are required; call the APT tourist office in Siena (☎ 0577-280551).

✔ If you have some room left in your head for more Renaissance paintings, the **Oratorio di San Bernardino and Museo Diocesano di Arte Sacra** (Piazza San Francesco 10; ☎ 0577-283048; www. operaduomo.siena.it) is worth a visit. San Bernardino's lower chapel was frescoed by the best Sienese painters of the 17th century, while the upper one is a beautiful example of the Italian Renaissance. Next door, the museum holds works collected from churches and convents in the area. Admission is 3€ ($3.60). Open: March through October, daily from 10:30 a.m. to 1:30 p.m. and 3 to 5:30 p.m.

✔ You may want to visit the **Home-Sanctuary of Saint Caterina** (Via Costa di Sant'Antonio 6; ☎ 0577-288175; www.caterinati.org), the Sienese saint's house and the sanctuary (which includes several works of art) that was built around in it in 1464, when she was sanctified. Caterina Benincasa was born here in 1347, the daughter of a fabric dyer and launderer and one of 26 children (!); she fought for peace and for the papacy to come back to Rome from its exile in Avignon — at a time when women had little say in political questions. Admission is free; the site is open daily from 9:30 a.m. to 7 p.m.

✔ Siena is a town with a lively cultural life, much of which is centered on sampling the wonderful local wine in one of the many *enoteche* — wine shops that turn into wine bars at night. The best of all is the **Enoteca Italica Permanente** (Fortezza Medicea, Via Camollia 72; ☎ 0577-288811; www.enoteca-italiana.it; Open: Mon noon to 8 p.m., Tues–Sat noon to 1 a.m.), housed in the cellars of a 16th-century fortress. It's actually an official institution, preserving the best vintages from all over Italy.

Shopping for local treasures

Among the city's specialties are, of course, the wine and spirits of the surrounding hills — the Chianti. If you intend to bring some home, note that *grappa* (clear Italian brandy) travels better than wine, which "bruises" and has to be left to sit for months after being carried on a plane. One of the best places to buy is the **Enoteca San Domenico** (Via del Paradiso 56; ☎ 0577-271181), which offers a good selection of local wines as well as an assortment of specialty foods. The **Antica Drogheria Manganelli** (Via di Città 71–73; ☎ 0577-280002) sells high-quality local products — including oils, vinegars, and cured meats — and has been making its own *panforte* (the typical Sienese honey-and-almond fruitcake) since 1879.

Local products include embroidery and fine fabrics. You can find a variety of hand-embroidered goods at **Siena Ricama** (Via di Città 61; ☎ 0577-288339), where you can also place an order for custom-made items fashioned after Renaissance patterns. **Antiche Dimore** (Via di Città 115; ☎ 0577-45337) carries beautiful fabric, both sold by the yard and made into embroidered linens for the home. Also interesting is **Ceramiche Santa Caterina** (Via di Città 51, 74, and 76; ☎ 0577-283098), the showroom of local master ceramicist Marcello Neri.

Fast Facts: Siena

Area Code

The local area code is **0577** (see "Telephone" in the "Fast Facts" section of Appendix A for more on calling to and from Italy).

ATMs

Exchange offices and banks with ATMs can be found on Via di Città and by the pedestrian underpass La Lizza.

Emergencies

For an ambulance, dial ☎ **118**; for the fire department, dial ☎ **115**; for road assistance (ACI, the Italian Automobile Club), dial ☎ **116**.

Hospitals

The Policlinico Le Scotte is at Viale Bracci Mario 16 (☎ 0577-585111).

Information

APT Siena (Piazza del Campo 56; ☎ 0577-280-551; Fax: 0577-281-041; www.terre siena.it) is open Monday through Saturday from 8:30 a.m. to 7:30 p.m. in summer, and Monday through Friday from 8:30 a.m. to 1 p.m. and 3:30 to 6:30 p.m. and Saturday from 8:30 a.m. to 1 p.m. in winter.

Internet Access

The Internet Train chain has branches at Via Pantaneto 54, near Piazza del Campo (☎ 0577-247460), and at Via di Città 121 (☎ 0577-226366).

Police

Call ☎ **113**.

Post Office

The main post office is at Piazza Matteotti 37 (☎ 0577-42178).

Taxi

Go to the taxi stand in Piazza Matteotti (☎ 0577-289350), or call ☎ 0577-49222 for pickup.

Perugia

The capital of Umbria, this splendid town is renowned for its art, stretching from Etruscan to modern times; its universities (including a popular university for foreigners); and its chocolate! It's the home of the chocolate house of Perugina, which makes the delicious *Baci.*

You can visit its major attractions in a day, but we recommend you stay the night to partake of the lively local culture, atmosphere, and excellent cuisine.

Getting there

Perugia is connected by **train** (☎ 892021; www.trenitalia.it) with all major destinations, although you sometimes have to change in Foligno or Terontola. Rome is only 2¼ hours away; the ticket will cost about 17€ ($20). Florence is 2 hours away, a ride that costs about 8€ ($9.60). Perugia's **train station,** on Piazza Vittorio Veneto (☎ **075-5006865**), is about 10 minutes by taxi or 15 minutes by bus to Piazza Italia, in the town center.

Coaches arrive in Perugia in Piazza Partigiani, an escalator ride from Piazza Italia at the center of town, making the **bus** quite convenient from most destinations in Italy. SULGA (☎ **800-099661** or 075-5009641; www.sulga.it) has three daily bus runs from Rome and one from Florence; the ride from Rome takes 2½ hours and costs 23€ ($28) round-trip, while the one from Florence is 1¾ hours and costs about 16€ ($19) round-trip. SITA (☎ **055-214721;** www.sita-on-line.it) also makes one daily run to and from Florence for about the same price. SENA

(☎ **800-930960** in Italy; www.sena.it) travels to and from Siena; the one-hour trip costs 11€ ($13). Perugia's Transit Authority, **APM** (☎ **800-512141** or 075-506781; www.apmperugia.it), connects Perugia with Assisi on a daily basis for 2.80€ ($3.35); it also serves other cities in Umbria.

If you have a **car,** Perugia is on the E45, an easy 180km (115 miles) from Rome and 150km (94 miles) from Florence. From the A1 highway, take the exit TERNI if you're coming from Rome or the exit VAL DI CHIANA BETTOLLE-SINALUNGA from Florence. The center of the historic town is at the top of a steep hill and is restricted to traffic. You'll have to leave your car in one of the numerous parking lots — a convenient one is Piazza Partigiani's underground lot, just south of the historic center. All parking lots are linked to the center by elevators or escalators.

Spending the night

Castello dell'Oscano
$$ **Localita Cenerente**

Seven kilometers (4⅓ miles) from the center of Perugia, this is a fantastic place to stay in full luxury. It's a real castle — crenellated towers and all — that's been beautifully restored, right down to the frescoed ceilings and terra-cotta floors. The rooms are large and nicely appointed. The castle has a lovely garden and a big pool; the **Turandot** is a popular gourmet restaurant. There are also rooms in a villa on the property — Villa Ada — but these are a lot more ordinary.

Strada della Forcella 37, Localita Cenerente. ☎ *075-584371. Fax: 075-690666.* www.oscano.com. *Free parking. Rack rates: 230€ ($276) double. Rates include buffet breakfast. AE, DC, MC, V.*

Hotel Brufani Palace
$$$ **Piazza Italia**

This is the best hotel in Perugia, providing luxury accommodations right in the heart of town. You'll tread in the steps of the rich and famous, as this has been the choice hotel for the visiting aristocracy since its opening in 1884. Guest rooms have been updated since then, however, and now offer all kinds of amenities such as Wi-Fi; they are spacious and elegantly furnished in classic style. Some have delightful views over Perugia's rooftops.

See map p. 279. Piazza Italia 12. ☎ *075-5731541. Fax 075-5720210.* www.brufanipalace.com. *Rack rates: 320€ ($384) double. AE, DC, MC, V.*

Hotel La Rosetta
$$ **Piazza Italia**

This pleasant, old-fashioned hotel is a good moderately priced choice in town. Its location is very convenient, and the service professional and welcoming. It even boasts a national historical landmark in one of its guest rooms (Suite 55, which is richly decorated with frescoes). Accommodations vary in size and furnishings, but all are well kept. The hotel's **restaurant** is popular for its reliable rendition of local cuisine.

See map p. 279. Piazza Italia 19. ☎*/fax: 075-5720841. E-mail:* larosetta@perugia online.com. *Parking: 20€ ($24). Rack rates: 135€ ($162) double. Rates include buffet breakfast. AE, DC.*

Locanda della Posta
$$ Corso Vannucci

Locanda della Posta, right on the busiest (pedestrian) street in the heart of town, is an excellent value. Its traditions date back to the 18th century — Goethe stayed here, as did Frederick II of Prussia — when this delightful *palazzo* of a marquis eventually became the first and only lodging in town. Today, the hotel offers guest rooms that vary in size and décor — some luxurious with gilded moldings and fine details, others plainer but full of charm. Bathrooms are modern and nicely decorated with hand-painted tiles.

See map p. 279. Corso Vannucci 97. ☎ *075-5728925. Fax: 075-5732562. Rack rates: 170€ ($204) double. Rates include buffet breakfast. AE, DC, MC, V.*

Dining locally

A university town, Perugia has a lot of *pizzerie* and cheap *trattorie* where you can have a bite in a lively, casual atmosphere, as well as some really nice gourmet restaurants. The food is typically Umbrian (see Chapter 2 for more on this cuisine) and relies heavily on *tartufi* (truffles) and *porcini* mushrooms. Consider also **La Rosetta,** in the hotel by the same name (see earlier in this chapter).

Il Falchetto
$$$ UMBRIAN

With a real medieval atmosphere (one dining room is from the 14th century) and a traditional menu, Falchetto is an excellent place for discovering Umbrian cuisine — especially if you're in the mood to splurge. The homemade fettuccine is exceptional, and the meat dishes are all excellent: Try the hare with olives or the *torello alla Perugina* (beef with homemade game pâté). The terrace is particularly in demand during the summer Umbria Jazz Festival.

See map p. 279. Via Bartolo 20. ☎ *075-5731775. Reservations recommended. Secondi: 15€–30€ ($18–$36). AE, DC, MC, V. Open: Tues–Sun 12:30–3 p.m. and 7:30–10:30 p.m. Closed Jan.*

La Taverna
$$ UMBRIAN/CREATIVE

This lively restaurant, located in a historic palace, offers regional specialties and some tasty innovations. If you're in luck, the seasonal menu may

Perugia

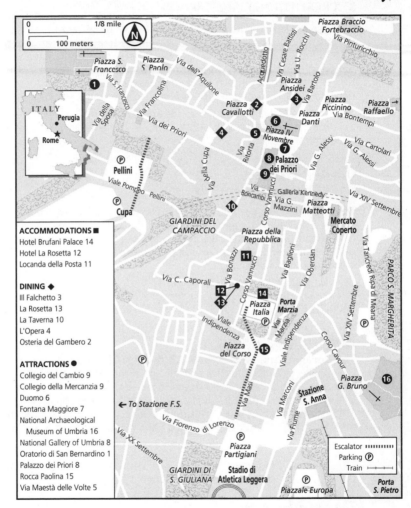

0 ———— 1/8 mile

0 ———— 100 meters

Piazza S. Francesco

Piazza S. Paolo

ITALY
Perugia
Rome

Via dell'Aquilone

Piazza Braccio Fortebraccio

Via Pinturicchio

Via Cesare Battisti

Via U. Rocchi

Piazza Ansidei

Via Bartolo

Via Francolina

Piazza Cavallotti ❷

❸

Piazza Piccinino

Piazza Danti

Via Bontempi

Piazza Raffaello →

Via dei Priori

❹ ❺ Piazza IV Novembre

❻

Via Ritorta

❼

❽ Palazzo dei Priori

❾

Via G. Alessi

Via Cartolari

Via G. Alessi

Ⓟ Pellini

Via della Cupa

Viale Pompeo Pellini

Ⓟ Cupa

Via Boncambi

Via G. Mazzini

Galleria Kennedy

Piazza Matteotti

Via XIV Settembre

GIARDINI DEL CAMPACCIO

Piazza della Repubblica

Mercato Coperto

Corso Vannucci

ACCOMMODATIONS ■
Hotel Brufani Palace 14
Hotel La Rosetta 12
Locanda della Posta 11

Via C. Caporali

❶❶

Via Bonazzi

Via Baglioni

Via Oberdan

Via Tancredi Ripa di Meana

PARCO S. MARGHERITA

DINING ◆
Ill Falchetto 3
La Rosetta 13
La Taverna 10
L'Opera 4
Osteria del Gambero 2

❶❷
❶❸

Corso Vannucci

Piazza Italia

❶❹ Porta Marzia

Via Indipendenza

Viale Indipendenza

Corso Cavour

Via XIV Settembre

ATTRACTIONS ●
Collegio del Cambio 9
Collegio della Mercanzia 9
Duomo 6
Fontana Maggiore 7
National Archaeological
  Museum of Umbria 16
National Gallery of Umbria 8
Oratorio di San Bernardino 1
Palazzo dei Priori 8
Rocca Paolina 15
Via Maestà delle Volte 5

Ⓟ

← To Stazione F.S.

Piazza del Corso ❶❺

Via Masi

Via Marconi

Stazione S. Anna

Piazza G. Bruno ❶❻

Via Fiorenzo di Lorenzo

Ⓟ

Via Fiume

Ⓟ

Via XX Settembre

Piazza Partigiani

GIARDINI DI S. GIULIANA

Stadio di Atletica Leggera

Ⓟ

Piazzale Europa

Escalator
Parking Ⓟ
Train

Porta S. Pietro

include *crostini al tartufo* (an Umbrian version of the Tuscan variety), *lasagnette al tartufo* (small lasagna with truffles), or beef medallions with truffles. Should you not like truffles, try the delicious roasted lamb.

*See above map. Via delle Streghe 8. ☎ **075-5724128**. Reservations recommended. Secondi: 10€–18€ ($12–$22). AE, DC, MC, V. Open: Tues–Sun 12:30–2:30 p.m. and 7:30–11 p.m.*

L'Opera
$ CREATIVE UMBRIAN/SEAFOOD

Come to the historic heart of town to delight in perfect homemade pastas, breads, and desserts here. Foodies will be happy to see quite a few creative offerings on the seasonal menu, mostly centered on seafood. We recommend the *umbricelli* (fresh local pasta) with the sauce of the day: We had it with duck speck, fresh tomatoes, and *pecorino di fossa,* a special hard cheese. The wine list includes many choices by the glass.

See map p. 279. Via della Stella 6. ☎ 075-5724286. Reservations recommended. Secondi: 10€–18€ ($12–$22). AE, DC, MC, V. Open: Daily 12:30–3 p.m. and 7:30–10:30 p.m.

Osteria del Gambero
$ CREATIVE UMBRIAN/WINE BAR

This elegant country-style restaurant is just the place to come for a special dinner. The menu changes seasonally, but may feature excellent duck-meat ravioli with fresh herbs and deep-fried sage, or perhaps red grouse with herbs, almonds, and peach coulis. The wine list is well-rounded and offers some moderate choices.

See map p. 279. Via Baldeschi 17. ☎ 075-5735461. www.osteriadelgambero.it. Reservations recommended. Secondi: 8€–21€ ($9.60–$25). AE, DC, MC, V. Open: Mon–Sat 12:30–3 p.m. and 7:30–10:30 p.m. Closed Jan 10–25 and May 16–30.

Exploring Perugia

The **Perugia Città Museo card** (☎ 800-697616 in Italy; www.comune.perugia.it) is just the ticket if you're visiting more than one museum or monument in Perugia: It comes in a one-day version for 7€ ($8.40); a three-day version for 12€ ($14); and a family or group version for 35€ ($42) that's valid for one year and gives access to a maximum of four people. You can purchase the card at any of the sites and avoid lines thereafter.

The **Museum Pass** is a combination ticket to Collegio del Cambio and Collegio della Mercanzia; it costs 3.10€ ($3.70).

The top attractions

Collegio del Cambio
On the Palazzo dei Priori's ground floor (see later in this section), this was the town's Goods Exchange in Renaissance times. The interesting architecture of the three halls is enlivened by magnificent frescoed ceilings: Those of the **Sala dell'Udienza (Audience Hall)** are by Perugino and his assistants — one of whom was Raphael — and illustrate the life of Christ; there's also a self-portrait of Perugino himself. The splendid wooden carvings of the **Legist Chamber** are by Giampiero Zuccari; the adjacent **Chapel**

A bit of history

Etruscan in origin, Perugia developed as an important urban center during the Middle Ages. Further expanding during the Renaissance, the city-state became infamous for its fierce battles and attempts at maintaining its independence, particularly from the Roman Church State. The town was finally subjugated by the popes in 1540, who imposed a few hundred years of steady rule, building the Rocca Paolina fortress. Perugia was also the hometown of painter Pietro Vannucci, who brought fame to himself and his town under the name "Il Perugino."

of Saint John the Baptist is frescoed by Giannicola di Paolo, a pupil of Perugino. Half an hour will suffice for your visit.

See map p. 279. Corso Vannucci 25. ☎ 075-5728599. Admission: 2.60€ ($3.10). Open: Mon–Sat 9 a.m.–12:30 p.m. and 2:30–5:30 p.m.; Sun and holidays 9 a.m.–1 p.m.

Collegio della Mercanzia

This was the medieval **Merchants' Guild;** it is a small attraction that you can visit in just 15 minutes, but it's definitely worth the time. As you enter, you'll find yourself in the 13th-century Audience Hall, decorated with intricately carved wood paneling and beautiful vaulted ceilings. Look around to admire all the wonderful details.

See map p. 279. Corso Vannucci 15. ☎ 075-5730366. Admission: 1€ ($1.20). Open: Mar 1–Oct 30 and Dec 20–Jan 6 Tues–Sat 9 a.m.–1 p.m. and 2:30–5:30 p.m., Sun and holidays 9 a.m.–1 p.m.; Nov 1–Dec 19 and Jan 7–Feb 28 Tues, Thurs, and Fri 8 a.m.– 2 p.m., Wed and Sat 8 a.m.–4:30 p.m., Sun 9 a.m.–1 p.m.

Duomo (Cathedral of San Lorenzo) and cloisters

Opening onto the beautiful Piazza IV Novembre, this church presents a simple, unfinished facade. Begun in the tenth century, the church was consecrated only in 1569; the Gothic interior was decorated in the 18th century and holds some earlier art, including a beautiful 15th-century carved wooden choir, miraculously preserved with only minimal damage from a fire that developed in the Duomo in 1985. From the elegant **cloisters,** you can access the **Museo Capitolare,** which has an important collection of illuminated manuscripts and 15th-century art, including the famous *Madonna Enthroned* by **Luca Signorelli** (a pupil of Piero della Francesca). Allow about 45 minutes for your visit.

See map p. 279. Piazza IV Novembre ☎ 075-5723832. Admission: Duomo free; Museum 3.50€ ($4.20). Open: Duomo Mon–Sat 7 a.m.–12:45 p.m. and 4–7:45 p.m., Sun 7 a.m.–1 p.m. and 4–7 p.m.; Museum Tues–Sun 10 a.m.–1 p.m. and 2:30–5:30 p.m. Closed Jan 1 and 6; Aug 15; Nov 1; and Dec 8 and 25.

National Gallery of Umbria

Housed on the third floor of Palazzo dei Priori (see later in this section), this gallery holds a splendid and rich collection of Umbrian art stretching from the 13th to the 19th centuries. In our opinion the most enjoyable of all Italian museums, it is strong in late-medieval/early-Renaissance art, documenting the important phase during which Giotto and Cimabue revolutionized painting techniques. The treasures are too numerous to list here: five unique 13th-century sculptures by **Arnolfo di Cambio**, several paintings by **Perugino**, a *Madonna and Child* by **Gentile da Fabriano**, the *Polyptych of San Dominico* masterpiece of **Beato Angelico**, the famous (and stunning) **Piero della Francesca** *Polyptych of Sant'Antonio*, and much more. Set aside about two hours for your visit.

See map p. 279. Palazzo dei Priori, Corso Vannucci 19. ☎ *075-5721009.* www. gallerianazionaleumbria.it. *Admission: 6.50€ ($7.80). Open: Tues–Sun 8:30 a.m.–7:30 p.m. Closed Jan 1 and Dec 25.*

Oratorio di San Bernardino

Built in 1452 and designed by Agostino di Duccio, this shrine is a delightful Renaissance masterpiece. The facade is a delicate carving of multicolored marble, with intricate reliefs illustrating the life of the saint. A paleo-Christian sarcophagus (fourth century) was recycled as the altar. Allow 30 to 45 minutes for your visit.

See map p. 279. Piazza San Francesco al Prato, at the end of Via dei Priori. Admission: Free. Open: Daily 8 a.m.–12:30 p.m. and 3–6 p.m.

Palazzo dei Priori and Fontana Maggiore

This is one of the finest examples of Gothic architecture in Italy, a striking travertine building with white-and-red marble inlays. Built between 1298 and 1353, this *palazzo* was created as the seat of the government. The main portal — accessible by a wide semicircular staircase — is off-center in the facade; it leads to the spacious **Hall of the Notables (Sala dei Notari),** a Romanesque architectural marvel supported by 12 arches. The two bronzes over the door represent a griffin and a lion, the symbols of Perugia. You can visit the *palazzo's* many frescoed rooms, some of which house the National Gallery of Umbria (see earlier in this section).

The building opens onto the elegant **Piazza IV Novembre;** once a Roman reservoir, it is graced by the splendid **Fontana Maggiore,** a Gothic masterpiece carved by the famous Pisan sculptors Nicola and Giovanni Pisano. Carved from white and pink marble, it has been called the most beautiful fountain in the world. Its 24 sides bear allegorical panels representing each month of the year and the signs of the zodiac; the elegant carvings are now visible after a difficult restoration that lasted several years. Departing from the *piazza* is a typical medieval street, **Via Maestà delle Volte,** a uniquely atmospheric vaulted covered passage. Consider a couple of hours to take it all in.

See map p. 279. Piazza IV Novembre. ☎ *075-5772339. Admission: Free. Open: Summer daily 9 a.m.–1 p.m. and 3–7 p.m.; winter Tues–Sun 9 a.m.–1 p.m. and 3–7 p.m.*

More cool things to see and do

✔ The **Rocca Paolina** (Piazza Italia and Via Masi; ☎ 075-5725778; Admission: free; Daily 8 a.m.–7 p.m.) was a grandiose fortress designed by the famous architect Antonio da Sangallo the Younger, and built in 1540 by Pope Paul III (hence the name) on top of medieval and earlier structures. (You can still see an arch from the original Etruscan city walls, the **Porta Marzia** from the second century B.C.). The upper part of the Rocca was demolished in 1860, but the lower sections were preserved, and the archaeological site has now been excavated. By a series of escalators, you can see the inside, viewing the fortification's huge walls, parts of dwellings and ancient streets, and even fragments of the ancient stadium where a forerunner of soccer was played. Free guided tours — occasionally offered in English — bring it all to life; reservations are required.

✔ The imposing complex of the **church and convent of San Domenico** was begun in the 13th century and progressively enlarged over the following two centuries. In the 18th century, the monastery was turned into an archaeology museum — now the **National Archaeological Museum of Umbria** (Piazza Giordano Bruno 10; ☎ 075-5727141; www.archeopg.arti.beniculturali.it; Admission: 4€/$4.80; Open: Mon 2:30–7:30 p.m.; Tues–Sun 8:30 a.m.– 7:30 p.m.; Closed: Jan 1 and Dec 25). Its findings include a travertine stone with the longest inscription in the Etruscan language ever found. The Etruscan-Roman section also includes jewelry, funerary urns, statues, and other objects. The visit will take you about an hour.

✔ Chosen as the seat of the **Eurochocolate** fair in October, Perugia is famous for its chocolate manufacturers. King of all is **Perugina,** the creator of world-famous Baci ("kisses") — the hazelnut-and-chocolate bonbons wrapped in silver-and-blue foil. You can take a free tour at the **Perugina Factory Museum** (San Sisto, 6km/3 miles west of the city center; ☎ 075-52761, or ☎ 075-5276796 for reservations; www.perugina.it; Admission: free; Open: Mon–Fri 9 a.m.– 1 p.m. and 2–5:30 p.m., Mar–Sept also Sat). In town, you can buy some of the most delicious chocolates at **Talmone** (Via Maestà delle Volte 10; ☎ 075-5725744).

✔ Perugia is positively afire during the world-famous **Umbria Jazz Festival** (☎ 075-5721003 or 800-462311 in Italy; www.umbriajazz.com). The concerts, featuring some of the best international names, take place during two weeks in July. You'll need to make reservations well in advance for the most popular performances. You can even participate in special jazz clinics organized during the event.

✔ Come dusk, all Perugia meets along **Corso Vannucci** for a stroll, a *gelato,* an *aperitivo,* and later for a visit to one of the *osterie* and clubs dotting the narrow alleys nearby. One of the most popular is the **Zibaldone** (Via Cesare Battisti 4; ☎ 075-5735567; www.zibaldone.org), with several rooms including a cocktail bar, a restaurant, and even a small Liberty-style theater featuring live music, from chamber to jazz. The club opens at 7 p.m.

Fast Facts: Perugia

Area Code

The local area code is **075** (see "Telephone" in the "Fast Facts" section of Appendix A for more on calling to and from Italy).

ATMs

You will find many banks and ATMs, especially along Corso Vannucci and Piazza Italia. You can also exchange money at the F.S. rail station, on Piazza Vittorio Veneto, or at Genefin, Via Pinturicchio 14–16.

Emergencies

For an ambulance, call ☎ **118**; for the fire department, call ☎ **115**; for road assistance, call ☎ **116**.

Hospitals

The Ospedale Monteluce is on Piazza Monteluce (☎ 075-5781).

Information

Perugia's main tourist office, APT, is at Via Mazzini 21 (☎ 075-5723327). Once in town,

you can visit the tourist booth just off the stairs of the Palazzo dei Priori at Piazza IV November 3 (☎ 075-573-6458; e-mail: info@iat.perugia.it), open daily from 8:30 a.m. to 1:30 p.m. and 2:30 to 6:30 p.m.

Internet Access

A branch of the chain Internet Train is located at Via Ulisse Rocchi 30, near the cathedral (☎ 075-5720107).

Police

Call ☎ **113**.

Post Office

The *ufficio postale* is on Piazza Matteotti.

Taxi

You'll find stands on Piazza Italia and Corso Vannucci; for a radio taxi, call ☎ 075-5004888.

Assisi

The hometown of St. Francis, Assisi is famous around the world for its art and religious monuments. Many of its visitors are actually pilgrims who come to honor the humble man who was said to speak to animals and who created the Franciscan order. Indeed, visiting Assisi is somewhat of a mystical experience. The small town is remarkably beautiful, built in pink stone on the top of a steep hill, and sparklingly clean now that all has been restored after the severe damage of the 1997 earthquake (at press time, the repaving of the side streets was nearing completion). Luckily, the town's monuments and most of its masterpieces were spared, although some of the frescoes were irreplaceably lost.

Assisi is only a small town of about 3,000 souls, though millions flock here every year. You can easily visit it on a day trip from Florence or Rome, but if you have the time to stay overnight, you will not regret it.

Getting there

Taking a **bus** is the easiest way to get to Assisi: The bus station is in Piazza Matteotti, only steps from the Duomo and the center of town. **APM** (☎ 800-512141 or 075-506781; www.apmperugia.it) runs regular service from Perugia (Piazza Partigiani) for 2.80€ ($3.40); **Sulga** (☎ 800-099661 or 075-5009641; www.sulga.it) operates buses from Rome (a 3-hour trip) and Florence (a 2½-hour trip) for about 18€ ($22) round-trip.

Having your own **car** will allow you to visit the attractions outside town without having to walk or use the shuttle bus, but since Assisi is mostly closed to traffic (you can drive through some of the streets, but not park there), you'll have to leave your car in one of the two parking lots at either end of town (about 11€/$13 per day; open 7 a.m.–9 p.m.). Note that these lots fill quickly with cars and tourist buses; in high season, you may have to park all the way back in Santa Maria degli Angeli — a village 6km (3¾ miles) from Assisi — and take a shuttle bus. Assisi is only 27km (17 miles) from Perugia on SS3; from either Florence or Rome, pass through Perugia (see directions earlier in this chapter) and then follow the Assisi signs, which are very well marked.

The nearest **train** station to Assisi is in Santa Maria degli Angeli, well connected to Assisi by taxis and a shuttle bus that departs every half-hour. Train service (☎ 892021; www.trenitalia.it) is frequent from all major destinations. It's a direct 25-minute trip from Perugia or Spoleto, though you may need to change trains if you're coming from Rome or Florence; the trip takes less than 3 hours from either destination and costs about 13€ ($16).

Spending the night

It used to be that if you wanted a modern room, you had to stay in the new but charmless hotels of Santa Maria degli Angeli. While that remains a good option — since many hotels in Assisi are still cheap accommodations catering to bus tours of pilgrims — you can now find more than a few comfortable choices right in town. Book early if you're planning to come for the Feast of St. Francis (Oct 3–4) or the Calendimaggio (first weekend after May 1).

Fontebella Hotel
$$ Piazza San Francesco/Piazza del Comune

Located midway between Assisi's major attractions, this is a great new hotel — family run with efficiency and modern spirit. Housed in a historic building, it offers pleasant public spaces with red marble floors and arched ceilings, along with spacious guest rooms of all different configurations. There are even a few rooms with a loft, good for families. Bathrooms are modern and generally good-sized (some with tubs and others with showers), but a couple are tiny. Most rooms have grand views, as does the romantic **Il Frantoio,** the highly recommended restaurant here (daily noon to 2:15 p.m. and 7–9:15 p.m.).

See map p. 287. Via Fontebella 25. ☎ *075-812883. Fax 075-812941.* www.
fontebella.com. *Rack rates: 185€ ($222) double; 230€ ($276) family rooms. Rates
include buffet breakfast. Closed Jan 8–Feb23. AE, DC, MC, V.*

Hotel Subasio
$$ Piazza San Francesco

For a long time, this was the only good hotel in Assisi, and it remains the
best for the exceptional service, elegance, and unique location: It is housed
in a 16th-century *palazzo* practically attached to St. Francis Basilica. The
grand public spaces include terraces and a windowed restaurant/break-
fast room with a garden terrace offering excellent views. Guest rooms vary
in size, but all are tastefully and individually decorated — some with a few
antiques — and all have renovated bathrooms. Rooms overlooking the ter-
races have absolutely breathtaking views, and some have their own bal-
conies. In high season, the hotel's excellent **restaurant** is open daily from
7 to 9:30 p.m., plus weekends from noon to 2:30 p.m.

See map p. 287. Via Frate Elia 2. ☎ *075-812206. Fax: 075-816691.* www.hotel
subasio.com. *Rack rates: 233€ ($280) double. Rates include buffet breakfast.
Closed Jan–Feb. AE, DC, MC, V.*

Hotel Umbra
$ Piazza del Comune

As you enter this charming, family-run hotel, you'll feel miles away from
the busy main street. Its historic *palazzo* is graced with a private walled
garden that is a delight to look at (only part of it is accessible to guests).
The welcoming rooms are uniquely decorated and configured; some have
Deruta tiles on the floors, others have carpeting, and all have a view (and
sometimes a balcony) — either of the garden or of the surrounding hills.
Bathrooms are all new and good-sized, though some have only smallish
showers. The Umbra's **restaurant** is particularly good; it's popular with
locals as well as visitors, especially in summer when a few tables are put
in the garden (open Mon–Sat 7:15–9:30 p.m.).

See map p. 287. Via degli Archi 6, just off Piazza del Comune (west side). ☎ *075-
812240. Fax: 075-813653.* www.hotelumbra.it. *Parking: 11€ ($13). Rack rates: 123€
($148) double. Rates include breakfast. Closed mid-Jan to mid-Mar. AE, DC, MC, V.*

Dining locally

We highly recommend the restaurants of our favorite hotels: the splen-
did and delicious **Subasio,** the pleasant **Umbra,** and the romantic **Il
Frantoio** of the **Fontebella Hotel** (see earlier in this chapter).

Buca di San Francesco
$$ Piazza del Comune   UMBRIAN

In the center of town, this restaurant is set in a medieval building with a
cellar that goes back to Roman times. The seasonal menu focuses on local

Assisi

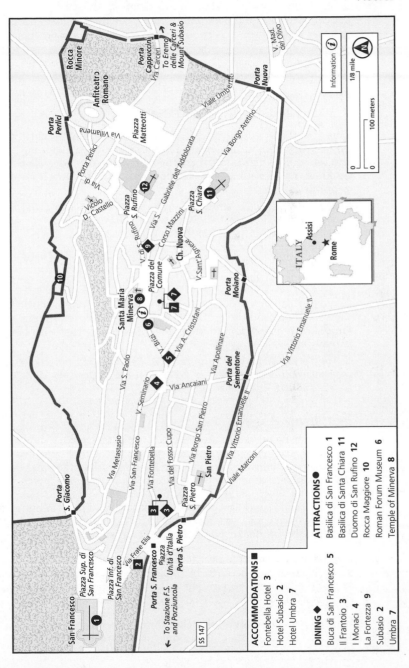

ACCOMMODATIONS ■
Fontebella Hotel **3**
Hotel Subasio **2**
Hotel Umbra **7**

DINING ◆
Buca di San Francesco **5**
Il Frantoio **3**
I Monaci **4**
La Fortezza **9**
Subasio **2**
Umbra **7**

ATTRACTIONS ●
Basilica di San Francesco **1**
Basilica di Santa Chiara **11**
Duomo di San Rufino **12**
Rocca Maggiore **10**
Roman Forum Museum **6**
Temple of Minerva **8**

Information (*i*)

1/8 mile

100 meters

ITALY

Assisi
Rome

traditions, including such hard-to-find specialties as the *piccione all'Assisana* (slow-roasted pigeon with herbs, olives, and capers). The wine list is excellent and the garden terrace provides pleasant outdoor dining.

See map p. 287. Via Brizi 1. ☎ *075-812204. Reservations recommended. Secondi: 7€–16€ ($8.40–$19). AE, DC, MC, V. Open: Tues–Sun noon to 2:30 p.m. and 7–10:30 p.m. Closed July.*

I Monaci
$ **Piazza del Comune UMBRIAN/PIZZA**

This is a really good pizzeria, run by Naples expats who cook perfect pizzas in a wood-burning oven. The variety is huge, including both tomato and tomatoless pizzas (we recommend the one with local sausages). You'll also find a full menu with pasta dishes and *secondi* to satisfy everyone in your party.

See map p. 287. Via Scalette, off Piazzetta Verdi. ☎ *075-812512. Reservations recommended. Secondi: 7€–15€ ($8.40–$18). Pizza: 5€–8€ ($6–$9.60). AE, DC, MC, V. Open: Thurs–Tues noon to 2:30 p.m. and 7–10:30 p.m.*

La Fortezza
$ **Piazza del Comune UMBRIAN**

Come to this family-run spot for good food at moderate prices. We liked the *cannelloni* and the local grilled meats, but if you're into truffles, the *faraona in crosta al tartufo nero* (guinea hen in a crust with black truffles) is really special.

See map p. 279. Vicolo della Fortezza, off via San Rufino. ☎ *075-812418. Reservations recommended. Secondi: 7€–12€ ($8.40–$14). MC, V. Open: Fri–Wed 7:30–9:30 p.m.; Sat–Sun also 12:30–2:30 p.m. Closed Feb and 1 week in July.*

Exploring Assisi

The Franciscan order in town gives tours of the major Franciscan sites in Assisi (also in English), including parts of the St. Francis Basilica and of the Eremo delle Carceri; you can sign up at the office just outside the entrance to the lower basilica on the left, in Piazza Inferiore di San Francesco (☎ **075-8190084;** Fax: 075-8155208; www.sanfrancesco assisi.org). Tours last about an hour and take place Monday through Saturday from 9 a.m. to noon and 2 to 5:30 p.m. (winter to 4:30 p.m.). They're free, but make a donation since the order exists only on alms.

If you'd like a more complete tour, contact the **Tourist Guide Association,** at Via Dono Doni 18b (☎ **075-815228;** Fax: 075-815229; www.assoguide. it), or the **Guides Cooperative** at the Infotourist Point in Perugia (Piazza Partigiani 3b; ☎ **075-5757;** Fax: 075-5727235; www.guideinumbria.com).

You can buy a **combination ticket** for the Rocca and the Roman Forum Museum (and one other attraction) for €4.50 ($5.40), valid for seven days.

St. Francis and St. Clare

San Francesco was born in 1182 to a wealthy merchant family and died in 1226 in a simple hut. How he traversed the social scale and caused a revolution in Christianity is a remarkable story. In 1209, after a reckless youth and even imprisonment, Francis experienced visions that led him to sell his father's cloth and give away the proceeds. He tried to follow the Bible literally and live the life of Christ, publicly renouncing his inheritance and rejecting wealth absolutely (this didn't endear him to the rich medieval church hierarchy). Two years before his death, he received the stigmata on a mountaintop — this and other scenes from his life were popular subjects for painters of the late medieval period and the Renaissance. Santa Chiara was his mystic sister who followed his teachings. Canonized in 1255, she was the founder of the order of the Poor Clares, with strict rules of simplicity similar to the Franciscan order. Chiara left her family to follow St. Francis, abandoning wealth and worldly pretensions as he did and cutting off her hair to symbolize her renunciation of the world. A number of miracles are attributed to her, one of which, a vision, led to her being proclaimed the patron saint of TV (saints don't get asked whether they want these honors).

 Some of Assisi's streets are quite steep: Wear good shoes and be prepared to use the shuttle bus or a taxi if you cannot walk long distances or if you get tired easily.

The top attractions

Basilica di San Francesco

Begun in 1228 to house the bones of St. Francis, the basilica is actually two churches, one on top of the other, and a truly majestic sight. You access the **Lower Basilica** from a splendid Gothic portal and enter the main nave with the first cycle of frescoes on Francis's life; off the sides open several chapels, among them the **Cappella della Maddalena** (third on the right), frescoed by Giotto and his helpers. You'll find more of his work in the apse and the right transept. The left transept is all decorated by the Sienese master Pietro Lorenzetti, including his beautiful *Crucifixion* and *Deposition.* A set of stairs descends to the crypt, where St. Francis's coffin is exposed ever since being rediscovered in the 19th century. The **Upper Basilica** contains Cimabue's work, including his dramatic *Crucifixion* in the left transept, and Giotto's celebrated cycle of frescoes on the life of the saint in the main nave (now believed to have been painted by several artists), including *St. Francis Preaching to the Birds.* The 1997 earthquake endangered the very structure of the church and monastery, and destroyed some frescoes beyond repair (in the Upper Basilica), but through the generosity of donors all over the world, the ambitious schedule of repairs was completed in time for the Papal Jubilee in 2000. Most of the damaged frescoes were reassembled from the immense puzzles of thousands of pieces (pretty amazing, given that one fresco was in 50,000 pieces).

See map p. 287. Piazza Superiorie di San Francesco/Piazza Inferiore di San Francesco.
☎ *075-819001.* www.sanfrancescoassisi.org. *Admission: By donation. Open: Lower Basilica daily 6 a.m.–6 p.m.; Upper Basilica daily 8:30 a.m.–6 p.m.; during daylight saving time, both close at 6:45 p.m.*

Basilica di Santa Chiara

Simple, powerful, and full of grace, this basilica is a beautiful building in alternating stripes of pink and white stone, with a huge rose window on its facade. Inside, it is divided in two: To the right is the **Chapel of the Crucifix**, with the crucifix that miraculously spoke to St. Francis and led him to start on his difficult path in the face of family, church, and society. To the left is the main church, with another 14th-century crucifix over the altar. On the left wall is a gate closing off the **Chapel of the Saint Sacrament;** you can still look through it to admire the beautiful stained-glass windows. Stairs lead to the lower church, built in the 19th century in neo-Gothic style to honor the remains of the saint. Only some of the church's original frescoes remain, but those are beautiful, particularly in the apse of the main nave.

See map p. 287. Piazza di Santa Chiara. ☎ *075-812282. Admission: By donation. Open: Daily 6:30 a.m. to noon and 2–7 p.m. (winter only to 6 p.m.)*

Duomo di San Rufino

Overshadowed by the other attractions in town, this cathedral has a splendid **Romanesque facade** — we highly recommend seeing at least this — with three portals and delicate carvings and decorations. The interior was redone in the 16th century and is richly decorated with paintings, frescoes, and sculptures. In the apse is a magnificent wooden carved choir. More artwork — mostly detached from the cathedral during the various renovations — is kept in the **museum,** while the **crypt** holds some ancient Roman and early Christian artifacts. The superb Romanesque **bell tower** outside was built over an ancient **Roman cistern,** which you can visit from inside the church and museum.

See map p. 287. Piazza San Rufino. ☎ *075-812283.* www.assisimuseo cattedrale.com. *Admission: Duomo free; museum and Crypt 3€ ($3.60). Open: Duomo Oct 16–Mar 15 daily 7 a.m.–1 p.m. and 2:30–6 p.m.; Mar 16–Oct 15 Mon–Fri 7 a.m.–1 p.m. and 3–7 p.m., Sat–Sun 7 a.m.–7 p.m. Museum and crypt Mar 16–Oct 15 daily 10 a.m.–1 p.m. and 3–6 p.m.; Oct 16–Mar 15 Thurs–Tues 10 a.m.–1 p.m. and 2:30–5:30 p.m. Museum and crypt closed Jan 1 and Dec 25.*

Piazza del Comune

This is the heart of Assisi civil life and a wonderful example of medieval and ancient Roman architecture (with so much religious art around, few realize Assisi was a thriving Roman town). The medieval buildings that surround the *piazza* were built over the Roman ones (this was the town's Forum at Roman times), and you can still see the powerful Corinthian columns of the **Temple of Minerva,** from the first century B.C. Probably the best-preserved Roman temple in Italy after the Pantheon, it was converted into a church by early Christians and eventually given a baroque

interior (Admission: free; Open: Mon–Tues and Thurs–Sat 7:15 a.m.–
7:30 p.m.; Wed 7:15 a.m.–2 p.m. and 5:15–7:30 p.m.; Sun 8 a.m.–7:15 p.m.).
Adjoining the temple is the 13th-century tower built by the Ghibellines.
From the nearby **Roman Forum Museum** (Via Portica 2, off Piazza del
Comune; ☎ **075-813053;** www.sistemamuseo.it; Admission: 3.50€/$4.20),
you can access the archaeological excavations under the *piazza.* The site is
open daily 10 a.m.–1 p.m.; Mar–May and Sept Oct also 2:30–6 p.m.; Nov–Feb
also 2–5 p.m.; and June–Aug also 2:30–7 p.m.; closed Jan 1 and Dec 25.

See map p. 287. Corso Mazzini, Via San Rufino, and Via Portica.

Rocca Maggiore

Rebuilt by Cardinal Albornoz in the 14th century, when the papacy subdued Assisi and brought the area under Vatican rule, this is an impressive
fortress dominating the town. Recently restored — it survived the 1997
quake, only to be damaged by lightning in 2000 — it is well worth the climb
(you can also drive here from outside the town walls) to enjoy the fabulous
views of the walls, the town, and the surrounding valley. The foundations
go back to Etruscan and Roman times, and you can visit the corridors and
main halls inside.

See map p. 287. Via della Rocca, from Via Porta Perlici, off Piazza San Rufino. ☎ 075-
812033. www.sistemamuseo.it. *Admission: 2€ ($2.40). Open: Daily Sept–May*
10 a.m.–sunset; June–Aug 9 a.m.–sunset; closed Jan 1 and Dec 25.

More cool things to see and do

✔ In nearby Santa Maria degli Angeli (6km/3.5 miles from Assisi), the
Basilica della Porziuncola (☎ 075-8051430; www.porziuncola.
org; Open: Thurs–Sat and Mon–Tues 9 a.m. to noon and 3–6 p.m.)
is a grandiose structure, built between 1569 and 1679 and graced
by a superb cupola. The basilica was built around the **Porziuncola,**
the first Franciscan church where Santa Chiara was ordered by San
Francesco in 1211 and where he died in 1226. The church and the
museum have a collection of frescoes and paintings from the 14th
to the 18th centuries. Admission is by voluntary donation.

✔ If you want to partake of the silence of **Mount Subasio** and visit the
hermitage where St. Francis retired to meditate and pray, we recommend the pleasant walk (4km/2½ miles east of Assisi, out from
Porta Cappuccini) to the **Eremo delle Carceri** (☎ 075-812301;
www.assisiofm.org). Several of his miracles occurred here, and
you can still see the sites — such as the ancient tree believed to be
the one where he preached his sermon to the birds and the dried-
out stream he quieted because its noise was interrupting his
prayers. Even if you are not a believer, the walk in the **selva** (free
admission; open June–Aug 9:30–12:30 and 3:30–6:30) is uplifting.
Alternatively, you can choose to go for a stroll or a hike on the
marked trails in the park. You can also reach the Eremo by taxi or
minibus. Admission to the Eremo is by donation; it's open daily
6:30 a.m.–6 p.m. (during daylight saving time, closes at 7:15 p.m.).
Access to the park is free.

Fast Facts: Assisi

Area Code

The local area code is **075** (see "Telephone" in the "Fast Facts" section of Appendix A for more on calling to and from Italy).

ATMs

You can change money in the ticket office at the rail station in Santa Maria degli Angeli, the small town nearby, which also has banks and ATMs.

Emergencies

For an ambulance, call ☎ **118**; for the fire department, call ☎ **115**. For road assistance (ACI, the Italian Automobile Club), call ☎ **116**.

Hospitals

The Ospedale di Assisi is just outside town in the direction of San Damiano (☎ 075-81391).

Information

The main tourist office is at Piazza del Comune 27 (☎ 075-812450; www.umbria 2000.it). It's open in summer, daily from

8 a.m. to 6:30 p.m.; in winter, Monday through Saturday from 8 a.m. to 2 p.m. and 3:30 to 6:30 p.m., Sunday from 9 a.m. to 1 p.m.

Internet Access

You can get online at the Bar Caffè Duomo (Piazza S. Rufino 5; ☎ 075-813-794) and at the bar at Via Portica 29/B.

Police

Call ☎ 113.

Post Office

The *ufficio postale* is at Largo Properzio 4 (☎ 075-812355).

Taxi

You'll find taxi stands in Piazza Santa Chiara, Piazza del Comune, Porta Nuova, and Piazza Unita d'Italia, where cabs wait for their fares. For a radio taxi, call ☎ 075-813100.

Spoleto

This is one of the most picturesque towns in Umbria, built in the shadow of an imposing fortress. The town was founded by the local population of the Umbri in pre-Roman times; during the Roman period, Spoleto valiantly resisted the advances of Hannibal and later became a summer resort for wealthy Romans. Devastated by the black plague and an earthquake in the Middle Ages, Spoleto remained a coveted prize fought over by Perugia and the papacy. Today, this jewel set among the Umbrian hills is known the world over as a town of music and culture.

Spoleto is surrounded by the countryside that has made Umbria famous: olive groves, green hills, and beautiful mountains. Small enough to be visited as a day trip from Rome, Florence, or a neighboring town (four to five hours will suffice to see the sights), it's also a wonderful place to spend some days of leisure, especially during one of its art and music festivals.

Getting there

Spoleto is well connected by **train** (☎ 892021; www.trenitalia.it) to all major destinations. There's direct and frequent service from Assisi and Perugia, whereas you may need to change trains if you're coming from Rome (a 1½-hour trip, about 15€/$18) and Florence (a three-hour trip, about 19€/$23). Trains arrive at Spoleto's **Stazione FS,** on Piazza Polvani (☎ 0743-48516), across the river Tessino to the north of the city's center. The station is well connected to the town by bus (line A, B, C, or D).

You can also get here by **bus** from Perugia. **SIT** (☎ 0743-212211) has two daily runs; the 90-minute trip costs about 7€ ($8.40).

If you're coming by **car,** Spoleto lies about 130km (80 miles) from Rome on the Flaminia (SS3), the scenic but narrow consular road heading north from Rome. A faster possibility is the A1; you exit at Orte and take the *superstrada* for Terni (follow the directions for Terni). The *super-strada* merges back into SS3 right after Terni; then just follow the directions for Spoleto.

Spending the night

Note that hotel reservations for the **Spoleto Festival** are made as much as a year in advance, so plan ahead if you'd like to attend.

Hotel Gattapone
$$ Rocca

Named after the architect who built the Rocca Albornoz (see "More cool things to see and do," later in this section), this hotel is one of our favorites in Spoleto. Its two 17th-century buildings dominate the town from a splen-did location on the side of the Rocca, a short (uphill) distance from the center. The well-appointed guest rooms are spacious, all with views and modern bathrooms.

See map p. 295. Via del Ponte 6. ☎ *0743-223447. Fax: 0743-223-448.* www.hotel gattapone.it. *Free parking. Rack rates: 170€–230€ ($204–$276) double. Rates include breakfast. AE, DC, MC, V.*

Hotel San Luca
$$ Centro

This is Spoleto's best hotel deal: a wonderfully restored 19th-century build-ing with a delightful courtyard garden. This small, family-run hotel offers rooms that are moderate in size, but decorated with quality furniture and elegant plasterwork; some have terraces. The family is justly proud of their bathrooms, which are modern, spacious, and done in beautiful Carrara marble.

See map p. 295. Via Interna delle Mura 21, inside the south side of the town walls. ☎ *0743-223399. Fax: 0743-223800* www.hotelsanluca.com. *Parking: 13€ ($16) in* *hotel garage. Rack rates: 150€–240€ ($180–$288) double. Rates include buffet break-fast. AE, DC, MC, V.*

Palazzo Dragoni
$$$ Centro

This is your most elegant choice in town. Housed in a 15th-century *palazzo* built over older structures (in the basement you can see the remains of tenth-century houses), it is very atmospheric, to say the least. From its magnificent lobby, you ascend to the guest rooms, which are elegantly appointed with antiques, wooden floors, and plaster walls. Some have balconies overlooking the Duomo and a panoramic view of the valley. Book early — the hotel has only 15 rooms.

See map p. 295. Via del Duomo 13. ☎ 0743-222220. Fax: 0743-225225. www.palazzo dragoni.it. *Free parking in nearby piazza. Rack rates: 250€ ($300) double. Rates include buffet breakfast. AE, DC, MC, V.*

Dining locally

Of course, as in other parts of Italy, Umbria has its own traditional cuisine and two food specialties: *tartufi* (truffles) and *porcini* mushrooms. Spoleto offers a number of good places to sample both.

Apollinare
$ Teatro Romano   CREATIVE UMBRIAN

One of the best restaurants in town, the Apollinare is situated underneath the hotel Aurora, across the square from the Sant'Agata monastery. The excellent food includes traditional Umbrian dishes as well as imaginative interpretations of the classics. You may find *stringozzi al tartufo* (local fresh pasta with truffles) and guinea fowl with artichokes. Be prepared for the crowds, especially on weekends.

See map p. 295. Via Sant'Agata 14. ☎ 0743-223256. Reservations required. Secondi: 11€–18€ ($13–$22). AE, DC, MC, V. Open: Nov–Mar Wed–Mon 1–3 p.m. and 7–10:45 p.m.; Apr–Oct daily same hours. Closed 2 weeks in Jan or Feb and in Aug.

Caffè della Signoria
$ Piazza della Signoria   UMBRIAN

Particularly pleasant in summer, when you can enjoy the view of the garden and the surrounding countryside, this small restaurant offers simple cuisine true to Umbrian tradition. Excellent choices include the *torte di verdure* (savory greens pie), the *crespelle al forno* (crepes filled with ricotta and spinach and baked with tomato sauce and cheese), and the local sausages.

See map p. 295. Piazza della Signoria, 5b. ☎ 0743-46333. Reservations recommended. Secondi: 8€–14€ ($9.60–$17). DC, MC, V. Open: Thurs–Tues 12:15–3 p.m. and 7–10:45 p.m. Closed 2 weeks in Jan.

Spoleto

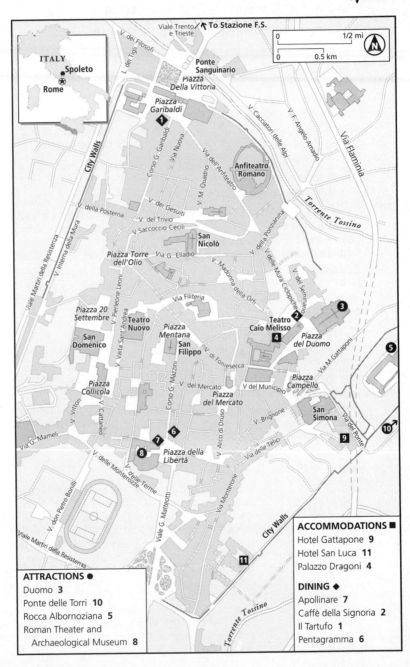

ITALY
Spoleto
Rome

Viale Trento e Trieste / To Stazione F.S.

V. dei Filosofi
L. dei Tigli

Ponte Sanguinario
Piazza Della Vittoria

Piazza Garibaldi ❶

City Walls

Corso G. Garibaldi
Via Nuova
Via dell'Anfiteatro
V. M. Quadrio

V. Cacciatori delle Alpi
V. F. Angelo Amado

Anfiteatro Romano

Via Flaminia

Torrente Tossino

V. della Posterna
V. dei Gesuiti
V. del Trivio
V. Saccoccio Cecili

San Nicolò

Via G. Elladio
V. della Pommanina
V. delle Mura Ciclopiche
V. del Seminario

Piazza Torre dell'Olio

Via Filiteria

V. Interna della Mura
Viale Martiri della Resistenza
V. Pietrone Leoni
V. Vaita Sant'Andrea

Piazza 20 Settembre
Teatro Nuovo
Piazza Mentana
San Filippo

Teatro Caio Melisso ❷ ❸

Piazza del Duomo ❹ ❺

San Domenico

V. di Foniesecca

Via M. Gattaponi

Piazza Collicola

Corso G. Mazzini
V. del Mercato
Piazza del Mercato
V. del Municipio
V. Arco di Druso

Piazza Campello

San Simona ❾ ❿

V. Vittori
V. Cattaneo

Via G. Mameli
V. delle Monterozze
V. delle Telici
V. Brignone

❼ ❻

Piazza della Libertà ❽

V. delle Terme
Viale G. Matteotti
Via Monterone

V. don Pietro Bonilli
Viale Martiri della Resistenza

City Walls

❶❶

Torrente Tossino

ACCOMMODATIONS ■
Hotel Gattapone **9**
Hotel San Luca **11**
Palazzo Dragoni **4**

ATTRACTIONS ●
Duomo **3**
Ponte delle Torri **10**
Rocca Albornoziana **5**
Roman Theater and
  Archaeological Museum **8**

DINING ◆
Apollinare **7**
Caffè della Signoria **2**
Il Tartufo **1**
Pentagramma **6**

0 — 1/2 mi
0 — 0.5 km

Il Tartufo
$$ Piazza Garibaldi   UMBRIAN/CREATIVE

Il Tartufo, as its name suggests, specializes in dishes based on truffles, but its culinary offerings go well beyond that, including homemade bread, delicious *grissini* (breadsticks), and simple yet uncommonly good pasta dishes and desserts. This is traditional Umbrian cuisine at its best, with a modern twist. Try the truffle and cod ravioli or the homemade pasta with broccoli, lentils, and sausages. We definitely recommend the tasting menus.

See map p. 295. Piazza Garibaldi 24. ☎ *0743-40236. Reservations required. Secondi: 12€–20€ ($14–$24). AE, DC, MC, V. Open: Tues–Sun noon to 3 p.m.; Tues–Sat 7:30–10:30 p.m. Closed 2 weeks in Jan/Feb and 10 days in summer.*

Pentagramma
$ Teatro Romano   UMBRIAN

Pentagramma specializes in pasta dishes served with a variety of tasty sauces — we love the ones with truffles or porcini mushrooms, fresh when in season. In addition, it serves a variety of soups, such as the hearty *zuppa di farro* (spelt soup), and a delicious *risotto al radicchio.*

See map p. 295. Via Martani 4. ☎ *0743-223141. Reservations recommended. Secondi: 10€–15€ ($12–$18). DC, MC, V. Open: Thurs–Tues 12:30–2:30 p.m. and 7:30–10:45 p.m. Closed Aug and 2 weeks in Jan/Feb.*

Exploring Spoleto

The two-week long **Festival di Spoleto** is immensely popular, but there's much more to explore in this picturesque town.

The top attractions

A medieval town built over a Roman one, Spoleto is a uniquely picturesque sight in itself. Strolling its atmospheric — and steep — alleys lined with *palazzi* and churches would be enough to fill your visit.

Duomo (Santa Maria Assunta)

This 12th-century Romanesque cathedral has a majestic facade, graced by a 1207 mosaic by Solsterno depicting Christ in typical Byzantine style. Because of the position of the church on the slope of the hill, you can get a spectacular view looking down on the Duomo and its *piazza.* The **bell tower** was pieced together using stone looted from Roman temples. The church's interior, refurbished in the 17th century, still has the original mosaic floor in the central nave. In a niche at the entrance is the bronze bust of Urban VIII by Gian Lorenzo Bernini. Among all the treasures inside, the most important are in the **apse,** which was decorated in the 15th century with great Filippo Lippi frescoes, including the brooding and powerful *Morte della Vergine (Death of the Virgin Mary).* The final concert of the Spoleto Festival is held every year in the *piazza* in front of the Duomo.

See map p. 295. Piazza del Duomo. Admission: Free. Open: Summer daily 8 a.m.– 1 p.m. and 3–6:30 p.m.; winter daily 8 a.m.–1 p.m. and 3–5:30 p.m.

Roman Theater and Archaeological Museum

This theater dates back to the first years of the Roman Empire and is one of numerous vestiges of ancient Roman Spoleto that are still visible. It was uncovered by a local archaeologist under Piazza della Libertà at the end of the 19th century and excavated in the 1950s, revealing some well-preserved structures. The museum has interesting archaeological findings from the area, including some sculptures and the famous *Lex Spoletina* (set of tablets bearing the carved law protecting the sacred wood of Monteluco nearby). East of the theater is the first-century **Arco di Druso (Via Arco di Druso),** once the monumental arched entry to the Forum (now Piazza del Mercato). The impressive **fountain** in the *piazza* is a baroque addition.

See map p. 295. Via Sant'Agata 18, Piazza della Libertà. ☎ *0743-223277.* www. archeopg.arti.beniculturali.it. *Admission: 4€ ($4.80). Open: Daily 8:30 a.m.–7:30 p.m.*

Spoleto Festival

Also known as the **Festival dei Due Mondi** (Festival of Two Worlds), the Spoleto Festival was created by Gian Carlo Menotti in 1958 as a way to bring together the best of "two worlds," Europe and America. Now a two-week festival from late June to early July, it attracts major performing-arts figures from around the world in a variety of disciplines, including theater, dance, music, and even cinema (Spoletocinema). Performances are held all over town, but the most important are held outdoors in the **Teatro Romano** (Piazza della Libertà; ☎ 0743-223419), the **Rocca,** and the scenic **Piazza del Duomo;** and indoors in the **Teatro Nuovo** (Via Filetteria 1; ☎ 0743-223419) and the **Teatro Caio Melisso** (Piazza del Duomo; ☎ 0743-222209).

Box office: Piazza del Duomo 8, or buy tickets online. ☎ *800-565600 in Italy, or 0743-220-320. Fax: 0743-220-321.* www.spoletofestival.it. *Once in Spoleto, you can also get tickets at the Teatro Nuovo. Tickets: 8€–50€ ($9.20–$60), depending on the event.*

More cool things to see and do

If you have a bit more time and the steep streets have not tired you out, here are a few more choices.

✔ If you stroll along Via del Ponte out of town, you'll rapidly reach the famous **Ponte delle Torri,** an impressive bridge and aqueduct over a deep gorge dating probably from the 13th century. Its ten elegant arches — 76m (250 ft.) high — are a unique sight.

✔ Dominating the town, the powerful fortress **Rocca Albornoziana** (Piazza Campello 1; ☎ 0743-43707; www.spoletopermusei.it; Admission 6.50€/$7.80; Open: Sept 15–Nov 1 and Apr 1–June 10

Mon–Fri 10 a.m.–1 p.m. and 3–7 p.m., Sat–Sun 10 a.m.–7 p.m.; June 11–Sept 15 daily 10 a.m.–8 p.m.; Nov 1–Mar 31 Mon–Fri 10 a.m.–12:30 p.m. and 3–5 p.m., Sat–Sun 10 a.m.–5 p.m.) was built in the 14th century, transformed into a prison in 1817, and used as such until 1983! After lengthy restorations, the Rocca is now open to the public and houses the **National Museum of Spoleto** — exhibiting artwork from a number of collections in town — as well as an exhibition hall and a theater.

✔ Among the several pleasant small churches in town, the fifth-century **Chiesa di San Pietro** is well worth the detour for its Romanesque facade decorated with splendid bas-reliefs.

Fast Facts: Spoleto

Area Code

The local area code is **0743** (see "Telephone" in the "Fast Facts" section of Appendix A for more on calling to and from Italy).

ATMs

You can exchange money at the Banca Popolare di Spoleto, Piazza Pianciani 5, by the Duomo (☎ 075-230126).

Emergencies

For an ambulance, call ☎ **118**; for the fire department, call ☎ **115**. For road assistance (ACI, the Italian Automobile Club), call ☎ **116**.

Hospitals

There's an Ospedale on Via Loreto (☎ 0743-2101).

Information

The tourist office is on Piazza della Libertà (☎ 0743-220311; www.comune.spoleto.pg.it). Summer hours are Monday through Friday from 9 a.m. to 1 p.m. and 4 to 7 p.m., Saturday and Sunday from 10 a.m. to 1 p.m. and 4 to 7 p.m.; winter hours are Monday through Saturday from 9 a.m. to 1 p.m. and 3:30 to 6:30 p.m., Sunday from 10 a.m. to 1 p.m.

Police

Call ☎ **113**.

Post Office

The central post office is on Piazza della Libertà (☎ 0743-40231).

Part V

Venice and the Best of the Pianura Padana

The 5th Wave By Rich Tennant

"Funny I just assumed it would be Carreras too."

In this part . . .

You'll have heard this before: "Venice isn't like any other place." Well, once you're here, you'll see how true this is — and how difficult it can be to find words to fully describe this unique destination. Venice, arguably the world's most romantic city, is a city of water — beguiling, mesmerizing, relaxing — where you'll never hear an automobile (though the growling diesel motors of boats are never very far away). The artistic and cultural influence of Venice has also spread to the surrounding region of the Pianura Padana, whose towns offer many splendid sights.

In Chapter 16, we take you through the watery roads and alleys of Venice and the most interesting of the nearby lagoon islands. In Chapter 17, we introduce you to the Pianura Padana's other three important art cities: Padua and Verona, with their rich endowment of beauties and treasures, and Milan, the business and industrial capital of Italy.

Chapter 16

Venice

In This Chapter

▶ Making your way to Venice and getting around without getting your feet wet
▶ Finding the best lodging and food in the city
▶ Experiencing the sights, smells, and tastes of Venice
▶ Getting the scoop on the best shopping areas and nightlife attractions

*A*s soon as you arrive in Venice, you'll realize this city goes beyond all you have imagined or seen. The elegant private *palazzi* lining the canals bear witness to a past of tremendous wealth, power, and culture. It's truly a magnificent human achievement. And yet people have been calling Venice a dead city for a century and a half. Henry James wrote, "She exists only as a battered peep-show and bazaar." Only 70,000 people actually live in Venice, but if you're ever alone anywhere for more than five minutes, consider yourself lucky. The crowds are unbelievable: Everywhere you go, someone is already there.

And yet . . . Canal Grande after sunset, Piazza San Marco early in the morning, the Gallerie dell'Accademia, the Lagoon, the Canaletto skies, and the stillness beneath the hubbub are sights you just have to experience to understand. And Venice's famous serenity (the republic was called *La Serenissima,* the "serene one") is as seductive as ever. Cranky Henry James and many other famous travelers have succumbed to Venice before you. James conceded that "the only way to care for Venice as she deserves it is to give her a chance to touch you often — to linger and remain and return."

If you could stay a week in Venice, it would be time well spent, but you can see the highlights in two days.

Getting There

 Regardless of how you arrive, remember to pack light: Unless your hotel has water access, you'll have to carry your luggage from the closest waterway to the door of your accommodations.

By air

Small but not too small, Venice's **Aeroporto Marco Polo** (☎ 041-2609260; www.veniceairport.it), 10km (6¼ miles) north of the town center, receives daily flights from most Italian and other European destinations. Below are tips for getting through the airport and to your hotel:

✔ **Getting oriented at the airport:** The airport is well organized and very easy to get around, as there's only one terminal. You will find an ATM, a currency-exchange counter, and a tourist information desk in the main concourse of the arrivals area.

✔ **Navigating your way through passport control and Customs:** You'll probably arrive in Venice via a connecting flight from another Italian or European airport, which means that you've already cleared Customs in the city where you changed flights. If your connecting flight originated in a country outside the Schengen European Community, then you'll have to line up for passport control before going to baggage claim. After picking up your checked bags, you'll go through Customs. Here you'll find two gates: one for those who have something to declare (above the standard allowance), and one for those who don't.

✔ **Getting from the airport to your hotel:** From the airport, you can reach the city by either bus or water. Though romantic and convenient, a **water taxi** (☎ 041-5415084) will cost a whopping 70€ ($84) on average for two to four persons. The *motoscafo* (shuttle boat) run by **Cooperativa San Marco/Alilaguna** (☎ 041-5235775; www.alilaguna.it) is a cheaper option: It takes about 50 minutes to Piazza San Marco, with stops at Murano and Lido, and costs 10€ ($12) per person. The **ATVO shuttle bus** (☎ 041-5205530; www.atvo.it) is an even cheaper option; it runs every hour to Piazzale Roma (Venice's car terminal on the mainland) and costs 3€ ($3.60) per person. The trip takes about 20 minutes. From there, you can take a *vaporetto* (the local water bus, described later in this chapter) or a water taxi to your hotel.

By train

Venice is well connected by rail (☎ 892021; www.trenitalia.it). The fastest trains get you to Venice in about 4½ hours from Rome, in just under 3 hours from Florence, and in 3½ hours from Milan. A one-way ticket from Rome costs about 40€ ($48), depending on the category of train you choose.

Venice's train station is called **Santa Lucia;** its mainland rail hub is **Mestre.** Choose a direct train to Santa Lucia if you want to avoid switching in Mestre to a local shuttle train for the ten-minute trip to Santa Lucia. Just outside Santa Lucia rail station, you'll find the ticket booth for the *vaporetto* (water bus, described later in this chapter), as well as water taxis.

By car

Venice is off *autostrada* A4; the distance is 530km (327 miles) from Rome, 266km (165 miles) from Milan, and 243km (151 miles) from Florence. After the exit, take SS11, always following signs for VENEZIA; you'll pass over the scenic bridge — Ponte della Libertà — connecting Mestre and the mainland to Piazzale Roma, Venice's car terminal. No cars can enter Venice, so you'll have to park here. Expect to pay 20€ to 28€ ($24–$34), depending on the size of your car. The **ASM Garage** (☎ 041-2727211; www.asmvenezia.it) and the **Garage San Marco** (☎ 041-5232213; www.garagesanmarco.it) are convenient to boat stops. A cheaper alternative is on the island of Tronchetto, just before Piazzale Roma to your right, where the **COMPARK** (☎ 041-5207555; www.venice parking.it) costs about 15€ ($18) per day.

Leaving your car on the mainland, in **Mestre,** may be a better (and cheaper) idea in high season and on weekends, when monstrous traffic jams are likely around Piazzale Roma. You can try the parking lot at the **Mestre train station** (☎ 041-938021; www.garagestazione.it), **Garage Serenissima** (☎ 041-938021), or **Crivellari** (☎ 041-929225).

By ship

Traditionally, Venice was accessible only by water — the bridge to the mainland was not built until 1846. You can still get to Venice by ship, and it is a unique experience indeed to be welcomed by the town. But pleasant as it is, it's also rare. Although several international lines offer cruises to Venice — your travel agent can help you sort through the options — it's a long way here from most international ports of call, usually a minimum of a month (most travelers don't have that kind of time). If you do come by ship, you'll arrive at the **Marine Terminal (Stazione Marittima)** in Santa Croce, in the heart of Venice. From there, the regular city transportation is at your disposal.

Orienting Yourself in Venice

The city of Venice comprises three major areas: the **historic district,** a cluster of several islands linked by numerous bridges; the **Terraferma,** a modern development on the mainland which includes **Mestre** — where a large part of the city's population actually lives; and the *Laguna* **(Lagoon),** stretching from the Adriatic Sea to the mainland and including the larger islands of **Lido** and **Murano,** among others.

Made up of more than 100 islands linked by 354 bridges over 177 canals, the historic district can be quite confusing to the uninitiated. It is divided into *sestieri* (a *sestiere* is a sixth of the city), each made up of several small islands, divided by canals — Venice's "streets" — crossed by small bridges. The central canal — **Canal Grande** — divides the city with its reversed "S" shape, leaving three sestieri on each side: **San Marco, Cannaregio,** and **Castello** *de citra* ("this side" of the canal); and

Dorsoduro, San Polo, and **Santa Croce** *de ultra* ("the far side"). This was the city's major thoroughfare and is still lined by elegant *palazzi,* which belonged to the most important and wealthiest families and merchant groups. It is crossed by three bridges: the **Ponte dell'Accademia** between San Marco and Dorsoduro; the famous **Ponte di Rialto** between San Marco and San Polo, and the **Ponte degli Scalzi** between Santa Lucia train station and Santa Croce. San Marco is in the center; to the north, you'll find first San Polo, then Santa Croce, and finally Cannaregio; to the east is Castello, and to the west and south, Dorsoduro. The **Santa Lucia train station,** the car terminal in **Piazzale Roma,** and the **Marine Terminal** are to the northwest, each on its own small island connected to the mainland through Ponte della Libertà.

Introducing the neighborhoods

There's no "bad neighborhood" in the historic district, and each sestiere has its individual flavor. But if you're after a more authentic or romantic Venice, you'll have to know where to look.

Cannaregio

This is an authentic neighborhood where locals still live and work; it gets a bit crowded in the high season only where it borders San Marco and around **Santa Lucia train station.** The painter Tintoretto was born here, near the **Madonna dell'Orto** church, not far from the **Ghetto.** Along Canal Grande, you'll find the **Ca' d'Oro;** on the lagoon side, the **Fondamenta Nuove** *vaporetto* station, where boats depart for the islands of **Murano, Burano,** and **Torcello.** This area is home to no-frills restaurants, a bit of nightlife (toward the Canal Grande), and a number of moderately priced hotels.

Castello

This is our favorite sestiere in Venice, as you don't need to go far to escape the crowds. Behind the grandiose promenade of **Riva degli Schiavoni** (in high season, crawling with tourists), with its unique views of the bay of San Marco and its expensive hotels and restaurants, you'll find the development of an authentic working district. It's crossed by **Via Garibaldi,** one of the few real streets in town (actually a paved-over canal), lined with neighborhood shops, *osterie,* and an outdoor market. You'll also find the **Basilica dei Santi Giovanni e Paolo** and the **Arsenale (Naval Armory).** Farther to the east are the **Giardini Pubblici** — very nice public gardens with a playground — which every other year play host to the **International Film Festival** and the famous international art show, the **Biennale di Venezia.**

Dorsoduro

This artsy neighborhood is where the university is located, together with some famous attractions — **Gallerie dell'Accademia, Ca' Rezzonico,** the **Peggy Guggenheim Collection, Santa Maria della Salute** — and many interesting small restaurants, along with a few simpler hotels. Crowds

Venice Orientation

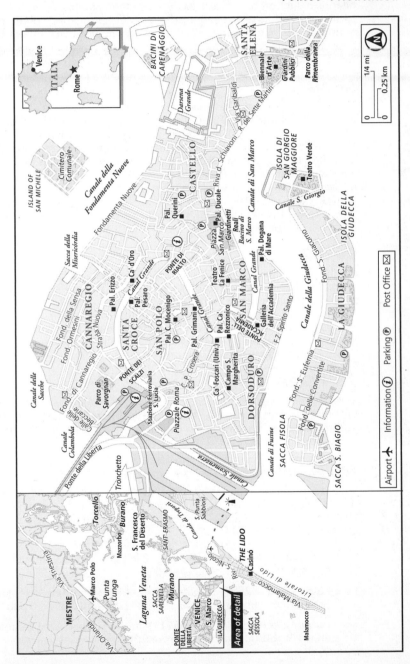

cluster around the Accademia in high season and on weekends, but all in all, this neighborhood is far less crowded than San Marco. In the evening, locals and visitors alike head for the beautiful promenade of the **Zattere,** famous for its outdoor cafes. This area also includes **La Giudecca,** a long and skinny cluster of islands separated from the rest of the sestiere by the **Canale della Giudecca** (second in importance after Canal Grande).

San Marco

Named after the famous Basilica, this is the heart of the historic district and the main tourist destination, as it contains some of the major attractions in Venice: **St. Mark's Basilica, Palazzo Ducale, Ponte dei Sospiri, Correr Museum, Palazzo Grassi, Teatro La Fenice,** and the **Ponte di Rialto.** Here you'll find lots of hotels (including some of the most expensive in the city), several fabulous shops, and a few administrative offices — but not many locals live here. The many restaurants tend to be "touristy," and the streets overcrowded. To appreciate its picturesque side, explore the area at night, when the crowds have receded, or come in the off season.

San Polo

On the other side of Canal Grande from San Marco, this was the main market in Venice back when Rialto was the marine terminal of the medieval city. It is still a commercial neighborhood with many shops, some simple restaurants, and just a few hotels. Its major attractions are the **Scuola Grande di San Rocco,** the **Basilica dei Frari,** and **Ponte di Rialto.** It gets crowded — especially around the Rialto during shopping hours — but mostly in high season and on weekends

Santa Croce

This small borough is the least visited part of Venice, as its few interesting churches and the pretty **Riva di Basio** promenade are little known. To the west are the islands with the marine and car terminals; hotels and restaurants are rare here.

Finding information after you arrive

Stop at one of these tourist information desks in town, if only to get the current opening hours of churches and museums — they keep changing — and, if you need wheelchair access, to get the special maps available:

- ✔ **Aeroporto Marco Polo** (☎ 041-5298711), arrivals main concourse; open daily from 9:30 a.m. to 7:30 p.m.

- ✔ **Lido** (☎ 041-5265711), *vaporetto* station; open June through September, daily from 9 a.m. to 12:30 p.m. and 3:30 to 6 p.m.

- ✔ **Piazzale Roma** (☎ 041-5298711), in the **Garage ASM (Azienda Sevizi Mobilità);** open daily from 9:30 a.m. to 6:30 p.m.

✔ **San Marco all'Ascensione** (☎ 041-5298711), at San Marco 71/F; open daily from 9 a.m. to 3:30 p.m.

✔ **Santa Lucia Train Station** (☎ 041-5298711); open daily from 8 a.m. to 6:30 p.m.

✔ **Venice Pavillion** (San Marco Ex Giardini Reali; ☎ 041-5298711); open daily from 10 a.m. to 6 p.m.

Getting Around Venice

Venice is very safe — the only real dangers are being served a bad meal at a touristy restaurant and being overcharged for your purchases. No matter how deserted and run-down a *calle* (street) may be, you can stroll anywhere, even at night. That shouldn't induce you, though, to do foolish things such as display large quantities of cash or leave your expensive camera unattended: Plenty of pickpockets are still around to take advantage of distracted tourists in crowded areas.

Think of Venice's canals as its streets: These waterways are the main means of access to the houses, which is why the facades of buildings are on the canals. The easiest and best way to get around is by boat, and you'll see plenty of small motorboats put-putting along the canals.

No book-sized map can give full details of the narrow *calli* and bridges. If you're planning to do some major exploring, we recommend picking up a good map — such as the smartly folded **Falk map** — at most bookstores and newsstands.

On foot

Behind Venice's canals are narrow streets that divide one building from another. Crossing these canals are small bridges with steps up and down — a major difficulty for anything on wheels (just imagine how difficult loading and unloading for shops must be). We've seen many a visitor, unprepared for the rigors of walking Venice, slumped in dismay in front of the steps of yet another bridge. Yet, after having your own boat, walking is the best way to visit Venice, and you'll be doing a lot of it. The only things you need to remember are: Keep to your right — yes, even walking; do not stop and block traffic on narrow bridges (a major breach of local etiquette); and wear comfortable shoes.

Although it may appear daunting and mazelike, you can't get lost in Venice as you would in a regular city. There are very few streets, and you'll always run into a canal — so at worst, you'll have to backtrack and then try the next turn. Don't feel shy about exploring, no matter how deserted a calle may look: You are never very far from a crowded spot where you can ask for directions.

As you wander, look for the ubiquitous signs with arrows (sometimes a little old, but still readable) that direct you toward major landmarks, such as **Ferrovia** (the train station), **Piazzale Roma** (the car terminal), **Vaporetto** (the nearest *vaporetto* stop), **Rialto** (the bridge), **Piazza San Marco**, **Accademia** (the bridge), and so on.

The famous *acqua alta* (high tides) shouldn't be a concern. They occur only occasionally between November and March, and there is no need to pack your waders (unless you want to wander in the smallest or most out-of-the-way streets at high tide): Wooden platforms are placed along the major routes. The best hotels actually lend their guests plastic boots in an ample choice of sizes. Particularly high tides are announced by a siren.

By vaporetto

Public transportation in Venice (☎ 041-2722111; www.actv.it) is by boat: The *vaporetto* is a water bus — something between a small barge and a ferry — and can be great fun. One must-do experience is the ride down the Canal Grande early in the day or by night (see "Exploring Venice," later in this chapter). With rush-hour crowds, remember to put your backpack down when you're standing: It'll also be less exposed to pickpockets. A simple ride along the Canal Grande costs 2€ ($2.40), whereas a 60-minute ticket valid on all lines is 5€ ($6).

If you plan to use the *vaporetto* a lot, go for a **24-hour pass** for 12€ ($14), or a **72-hour pass** for 25€ ($30); they give you access to the whole public transportation system, including the lines crossing the Lagoon to Murano, Burano, and Lido. Another option is the **Venice Card Blue**, which includes unlimited *vaporetto* rides plus free access to the city-run public bathrooms. A day card costs 17€ ($20) for adults and 15€ ($18) for youths 4 to 29; a three-day card is 34€ ($41) and 30€ ($36), and a seven-day card 52€ ($62) and 47€ ($56), respectively. Finally, with the

---

How to get around if you're wheelchair-bound

Although the city has made big efforts, Venice still isn't easy for visitors in wheelchairs. The only real problem is the bridges over the canals, all with steps up and down to allow boat passage underneath. But this is an issue only if you want to explore the little streets, as all the main attractions are accessible by water — and *vaporetti* are boarded by gangways, which have no steps. A few bridges have been equipped with motorized lifts (alas, we saw a number that were inoperable): You'll need to pick up a key at a tourist info desk, which can also provide you with a special **city map with wheelchair-accessible itineraries.** You can also get the latest info online at www.comune.venezia.it/handicap.

Street names and numbers in Venice

Even street addresses are different in Venice: There are no street numbers, only postal addresses, therefore "2534 San Marco" and "2536 San Marco" may well be on two different streets (the post office has a map of buildings). That's why all hotels and restaurants have small maps printed on the back of their business cards and why even Venetians call for directions before going to an address they haven't been to before. Always make sure you have the name of the *sestiere* (borough): Venice has many streets of the same name! You'll also notice that there are very few "Via"; streets here are called *calle* (pronounced with a hard *l*) — or *salizzada* or *calle larga* if they are larger — but also *rio terà* (a canal that was filled in to make a street), *sottoportico* (passage under a building), and *fondamenta* (promenade running alongside a canal). There's only one *piazza* in Venice, and that's **Piazza San Marco** — all the others are *campo* or *campiello*.

Rolling Venice Card (see "Exploring Venice," later in this chapter) you'll get a three-day transportation pass for 15€ ($18).

 See the Cheat Sheet at the front of this guide for a map of Venice's *vaporetto* system.

By traghetto (ferry skiff)

Many people don't know that a traditional type of boat similar to the *gondola* is still used as public transportation: the *traghetto*. It's moved by two rowers instead of one and is much simpler in its decoration. These operate along the Canal Grande, providing additional crossing — only three bridges span this long canal — for a mere 0.50€ (46¢) per person. The eight traghetto stations are San Tomà, Santa Maria del Giglio, Dogana, Ferrovia, Rialto, San Marcuola, San Samuele, and Santa Sofia. The operating hours vary for each traghetto; all start between 7 and 8 a.m., but only those of Santa Maria del Giglio, San Tomà, and Santa Sofia run in the afternoon (until between 7 and 9 p.m.); the others stop at 1 to 2 p.m. To take it, walk down to the small wooden dock indicated by the sign TRAGHETTO (the street leading to the dock is often called Calle del Traghetto) and wait for the boat to come. You'll notice that Venetians ride *traghetti* standing, proudly displaying their sea legs — but don't try to imitate them, as the water in the Canal Grande is none too clean!

By water taxi

Though a little expensive, water taxis are the perfect way to get to and from your hotel with your luggage — and to have a taste of luxury. You can get one by walking to a taxi stand — at San Marco, the rail station, or Rialto — or by calling for pickup (see "Fast Facts: Venice," at the end of this chapter). The fare for up to four people starts at 8.70€ ($10), plus 1.30€ ($1.60) for every 60 seconds and 1.50€ ($1.80) for each piece of luggage larger than 50 centimeters (20 inches) per side; there's also a 6€ ($7.20) call surcharge and a 5.50€ ($6.60) night or 5.90€ ($7) holiday surcharge. Remember that even water taxis can't reach certain locations — and hotels — in which case you'll have to walk the rest of the way.

Be aware of "Gypsy" water taxis that will offer you a ride. Official taxis do not cruise around looking for passengers.

Staying in Style

You'll find plenty of accommodations in Venice for every budget, but if you're looking for a spacious and bright room in a hotel with an elevator in the historic district in high season, you'll have to pay full price or book way in advance — up to a year for the most sought-after spots. Low season is short — from mid-November to mid-December, the beginning of January to mid-February, July, and August; at all other times, you'll have to compete with literally hundreds of thousands of fellow tourists from around the world. On the other hand, during low season, prices will literally drop by half. In this section, we have selected the hotels that provide the best quality-to-price ratio and that are accessible either by water or a short walk (and whenever possible without crossing bridges).

If you arrive without a reservation, the **Hotel Association of Venice** (AVA; ☎ **800-843006** in Italy, or 041-5222264; www.veneziasi.it) offers a free reservations service; it maintains booths at the train station, at Piazzale Roma, at the airport, and at the tourist info desks at the end of the highway on the mainland.

The top hotels

Antica Locanda Sturion
$$ **San Polo**

The oldest hotel in Venice — it was commissioned by the *doges* as a guest-house back in 1290 — this is still a charming place to stay. It was turned into a private house and then back into a hotel, now with modern amenities (except for, alas, an elevator). The medium-sized guest rooms have been redone to contemporary standards, but have retained some of the antique flavor thanks to the ornate Venetian-style furnishings, parquet floors, and damask upholstery. Bathrooms are modern with all the necessary amenities. The cozy breakfast room overlooks the canal.

See map p. 312. Calle del Storione, 679 San Polo. ☎ *041-5236243. Fax: 041-5228378. www.locandasturion.com. Vaporetto: 1 to San Silvestro; walk up along Fondamenta San Silvestro/Fondamenta del Vin and take the third left. Rack rates: 250€–310€ ($300–$372) double; 300€–360€ ($360–$432) triple; 340€–380 ($408–$456) quad. Rates include buffet breakfast. AE, DC, MC, V.*

Cipriani and Palazzi
$$$$ Dorsoduro

At the tip of La Giudecca — a few minutes from San Marco by free shuttle boat — this hotel offers one of the most romantic experiences in Venice and some of the highest rates in Europe. Housed in a 16th-century monastery overlooking the water on three sides, and complete with cloisters, it offers individually decorated rooms that are sumptuous but not overly ornate. All are spacious and feature elegant furnishings, quality linens, large bathrooms, and views. Public spaces include gardens and a private pool. With a ratio of two staff members for each room, the service here is perfect. The **Fortuny** is one of the best restaurants in Italy. For those desiring extra privacy, the two annexes — Palazzo Vendramin and Palazzo Nani-Barbaro — are 15th-century, all-suite gems connected to the main building by flowery courtyards.

See map p. 312. Isola della Giudecca 10. ☎ *041-5207744. Fax: 041-5207745.* www. hotelcipriani.com. *Vaporetto: 41, 42, or 82 to Zitelle. Rack rates: 815€–1,330€ ($978–$1,596) double; suites 1,730€ ($2,074) and up. Rates include full American breakfast. Children 12 and under stay free in parent's room. AE, DC, MC, V.*

Hotel Campiello
$$$ Castello

This pink 15th-century building, once a convent, is a bargain for the area. The location is nearly perfect, just off Riva degli Schiavoni but somewhat quieter. Guest rooms are decorated in either Liberty (Art Nouveau) or 19th-century style, and all have new bathrooms. The triples and quads are great for families. Run by two sisters, this hotel offers friendly and expert service. The substantial buffet breakfast is served in a rather glitzy hall.

See map p. 312. Campiello del Vin, 4647 Castello. ☎ *041-239682. Fax: 041-5205798.* www.hotelcampiello.it. *Vaporetto: 1, 5, 41, 42, 51, 52, or 82 to San Zaccaria; walk up Calle del Vin. Rack rates: 250€ ($300) double; 270€ ($324) triple; 300€ ($360) quad. Rates include buffet breakfast. AE, MC, V.*

Hotel Colombina
$$ Castello

This elegant hotel is a great addition to Venice hotel scene, only steps away from St. Mark's Basilica. Once inside, you'll feel miles away from the crowds outside. Guest rooms are spacious and nicely done in Venetian style, with fine fabrics and quality reproductions. The staff is attentive and friendly. Note that Internet specials may bring rates down by as much as 40 percent.

See map p. 312. Calle del Remedio 4416 Castello. ☎ *041-2770525. Fax: 041-2776044.* www.hotelcolombina.com. *Vaporetto: 82 to San Zaccaria; walk up Calle Rasse, turn left and immediately right on Calle Sagrestia, turn left at Campo San Zani and continue on to Calle Remedio to the left. Rack rates: 295€–440€ ($354–$528) double. Rates include buffet breakfast. AE, DC, MC, V.*

Venice Accommodations and Dining

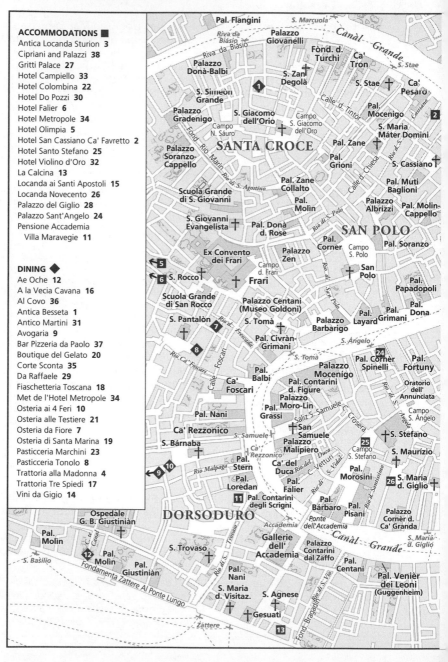

ACCOMMODATIONS ■
Antica Locanda Sturion **3**
Cipriani and Palazzi **38**
Gritti Palace **27**
Hotel Campiello **33**
Hotel Colombina **22**
Hotel Do Pozzi **30**
Hotel Falier **6**
Hotel Metropole **34**
Hotel Olimpia **5**
Hotel San Cassiano Ca' Favretto **2**
Hotel Santo Stefano **25**
Hotel Violino d'Oro **32**
La Calcina **13**
Locanda ai Santi Apostoli **15**
Locanda Novecento **26**
Palazzo del Giglio **28**
Palazzo Sant'Angelo **24**
Pensione Accademia
    Villa Maravegie **11**

DINING ◆
Ae Oche **12**
A la Vecia Cavana **16**
Al Covo **36**
Antica Besseta **1**
Antico Martini **31**
Avogaria **9**
Bar Pizzeria da Paolo **37**
Boutique del Gelato **20**
Corte Sconta **35**
Da Raffaele **29**
Fiaschetteria Toscana **18**
Met de l'Hotel Metropole **34**
Osteria ai 4 Feri **10**
Osteria alle Testiere **21**
Osteria di Fiore **7**
Osteria di Santa Marina **19**
Pasticceria Marchini **23**
Pasticceria Tonolo **8**
Trattoria alla Madonna **4**
Trattoria Tre Spiedi **17**
Vini da Gigio **14**

Hotel Metropole
$$$$ Castello

One of the few posh hotels that's still family run (the others have been bought by American chains), this romantic property includes the chapel where Vivaldi composed the *Four Seasons*. From its elegant canalside entrance to the opulent Venetian baroque interior, from the peaceful courtyard garden to the kindness of the staff, this hotel sets itself apart. Each guest room is spacious and individually furnished with quality fabrics and some antiques. The suites are palatial — nos. 401 and 403 have an *altana* (sort of a widow's walk), while the Angels Suite is beautifully frescoed — and the good-sized bathrooms (all with tubs) are done in marble or mosaic. The restaurant is one of the best in Italy (see later in this chapter), and the beautiful Mirror Hall features afternoon tea with homemade pastries.

See map p. 312. Riva degli Schiavoni, 4149 Castello. ☎ *041-5205044. Fax: 041-5223679.* www.hotelmetropole.com. *Vaporetto: 1, 5, 41, 42, 51, 52, or 82 to San Zaccaria; walk right. Rack rates: 500€–650€ ($600–$780) double; suite 700€ ($840) and up. Rates include buffet breakfast. AE, DC, MC, V.*

Hotel San Cassiano Ca' Favretto
$$$ Santa Croce

This is your chance to stay in a gorgeous 14th-century *palazzo* on the Canal Grande without spending a fortune. Located across from the Ca' d'Oro and left of the Ca' Corner della Regina, the hotel has been carefully renovated, so all guest rooms now have quality dark-wood furniture, brightly colored wallpaper, and large windows. Many have views of the Ca' d'Oro or the smaller canal on the side. The hotel also has a beautiful terrace overlooking the canals.

See map p. 312. Calle della Rosa, 2232 Santa Croce. ☎ *041-5241768. Fax: 041-721033.* www.sancassiano.it. *Vaporetto: 1 to San Stae; walk to the left of Campo San Stae, cross the canal and turn right on Fondamenta Rimpetto Mocenigo, then left on Calle del Forner, cross the bridge, continue on Calle del Ravano, cross the bridge, and turn left on Calle della Rosa. Rack rates: 270€–390€ ($324–468) double. Rates include breakfast. AE, V.*

Hotel Santo Stefano
$$$ San Marco

This charming small hotel offers excellent value. Housed in the 15th-century watchtower of a convent on the beautiful Campo Santo Stefano, it features lushly decorated accommodations and a nice terrace. Guest rooms are individually furnished and may come with coffered ceilings, Murano chandeliers, and antiques. All are equipped with comfortable Poltrona Frau beds (the best Italian maker of modern beds and sofas), quality Venetian-style reproductions, and marble and mosaic bathrooms.

See map p. 312. Campo S. Stefano, 2957 San Marco. ☎ *041-5200166. Fax: 041-5224460.* www.hotelsantostefanovenezia.com. *Vaporetto: 3, 4, or 82 to*

S. Samuele stop; walk to Salizzada S. Samuele and turn right on Calle Crosera. Rack rates: 310€–360€ ($372–$432) double. Rates include buffet breakfast. AE, DC, MC, V.

Hotel Violino d'Oro
$$$ San Marco

This family-run boutique hotel has an excellent location, very close to San Marco. Housed in the 18th-century Palazzo Barozzi, it overlooks the canal Rio San Moisè. Guest rooms are brightly decorated with fine fabrics and Venetian-style furniture. Some of the rooms are larger than others, but all have Murano chandeliers and marble bathrooms (only a few with tubs). A nice roof terrace and an attentive staff round out the perks. Internet specials can bring down rates by over half.

See map p. 312. Campiello Barozzi, 2091 San Marco. ☎ 041-2770841. Fax: 041-2771001. www.violinodoro.com. *Vaporetto: 1, 3, 4, or 82 to San Marco/Vallaresso stop; walk up Calle Vallaresso, turn left on Salita San Moisè, and cross the bridge over the canal. Rack rates: 300€ ($360) double. Rates include breakfast. AE, DC, MC, V.*

La Calcina
$$ Dorsoduro

This historic *pensione* has been renovated to respect its simple original style and refitted with antique furniture. This is where Victorian writer John Ruskin stayed in 1876 when he wrote *The Stones of Venice*. The location overlooking the Canale della Giudecca is both beautiful and less hectic than the area around San Marco. The good-sized guest rooms have parquet floors and sometimes beamed ceilings. In warm weather, a buffet breakfast is served on the terrace. The hotel also has a solarium (roof terrace). Be forewarned that this desirable, moderately priced hotel fills up fast: You'll need to reserve up to six months in advance for high season.

See map p. 312. Zattere ai Gesuati, 780 Dorsoduro. ☎ 041-5206466. Fax: 041-5227045. Vaporetto: 51, 52, 61, 62, or 82 to Zattere; turn right along the Canale della Giudecca to the Rio di San Vio. www.lacalcina.com. *Rack rates: 182€ ($218) double. Rates include buffet breakfast. AE, DC, MC, V.*

Locanda ai Santi Apostoli
$$ Cannaregio

This small family-run hotel offers cozy accommodations and charming details. Set on the top floor of a 14th-century *palazzo* overlooking the Canal Grande, the guest rooms are quite large and individually decorated with a mix of modern furnishings and period reproductions, along with a few antiques. Bathrooms are small, but come with all the amenities. Two of the rooms have views of the canal, and many are large enough to accommodate families.

See map p. 312. Strada Nuova, 4391a Cannaregio. ☎ 041-5212612. Fax: 041-5212611. www.locandasantiapostoli.com. *Vaporetto: 1 to Ca' d'Oro; walk up Calle ca' d'Oro and turn right. Rack rates: 230€–330€ ($276–$396) double. Rates include buffet breakfast. AE, DC, MC, V.*

Locanda Novecento
$$ San Marco

Only a few steps from St. Mark's and Accademia is this delightful new family-run boutique hotel, which offers individual and attentive service. The theme of the hotel is in its name — "1900" — and the décor of both the public spaces and the sumptuous guest rooms was inspired by the famous Spanish artist Mariano Fortuny, who worked and lived in Venice in the first half of the 20th century. The small garden — used for breakfast in good weather — is a delight.

See map p. 312. Campo San Maurizio, Calle del Dose, 2694 San Marco. ☎ *041-2413765. Fax: 041-5212145.* www.novecento.biz. *Vaporetto: 1 to Giglio; walk up to Campo Santa Maria del Giglio, make a right, and cross two bridges. Rack rates: 260€ ($312) double. Rates include buffet breakfast. AE, DC, MC, V.*

Palazzo del Giglio
$$ San Marco

Next door to the Gritti Palace, this was formerly part of that famous hotel, but is now independent. Housed in a charming pink-colored *palazzo*, it offers plush accommodations and excellent service. Guest rooms — mostly suites — are nicely furnished in a restrained palette, with some antique pieces and some reproductions. Bathrooms are above average in size and appointments: Dressed in Carrara marble, they all have tubs with hydromassage. Breakfast is served in your room. Most of the suites are equipped with a kitchenette for long-term business travelers, but they are also a great resource for families.

See map p. 312. Campo Santa Maria del Giglio, 2462 San Marco. ☎ *041-2719111. Fax: 041-5205158.* www.hotelgiglio.com. *Vaporetto: 1 to Giglio. Rack rates: 225€–240€ ($270–$388) double; suite 310€ ($372) and up. Rates include breakfast. AE, DC, MC, V.*

Palazzo Sant'Angelo
$$$$ San Marco

The first hotel to open on the Canal Grande in over a century, this is a welcome addition to the Venice luxury options. Housed in Palazzo Corner-Spinelli, it offers a perfect location, with a private entrance on the Canal Grande and a *vaporetto* stop next door, in one of the few quiet corners of the San Marco neighborhood. The public spaces are gorgeous — the living room has its original Palladian marble floors — and the guest rooms are sumptuous. The spacious bathrooms, done in green-and-white marble, have hydromassage bathtubs. The rooms overlooking the Canal Grande are the most beautiful.

See map p. 312. 3488 San Marco. ☎ *041-2411452. Fax: 041-2411557.* www.palazzo santangelo.com. *Vaporetto: 1 to Sant'Angelo. Rack rates: 495€–660€ ($594–$792) double. Rates include buffet breakfast. AE, DC, MC, V.*

Pensione Accademia Villa Maravegie
$$$ Dorsoduro

In a beautiful location two steps from the Accademia, this hotel occupies a 17th-century villa with a garden, and the whole place has a wonderfully old-fashioned feel. The guest rooms feature 19th-century furnishings and decent-sized bathrooms. It's very popular, so reserve well in advance to secure a room with a view of the garden. *See map p. 312. Fondamenta Bollani, 1058 Dorsoduro.* ☎ *041-5210188. Fax: 041-5239152.* www.pensioneaccademia.it. *Vaporetto: 1, 3, 4, or 82 to Accademia; turn right on Calle Corfù, left on Fondamenta Priuli, right on the first bridge, and then right again on Fondamenta Bollani. Rack rates: 275€ ($330) double. Rates include breakfast. AE, DC, MC, V.*

Runner-up accommodations

Gritti Palace

$$$$ San Marco If you can afford it, a stay at this ornate 16th-century palace offers an experience of Venice at its most serene. Guest rooms are spacious and decorated with antique paintings and Venetian-style furniture. *See map p. 312. Campo Santa Maria del Giglio, San Marco 2467.* ☎ *800-3253535 in the U.S. and Canada, or 041-794611. Fax: 041-5200942.* www.starwood.com/italy.

Hotel Do Pozzi

$$ San Marco The Hotel Do Pozzi occupies a strategic position between St. Mark's Square and the Teatro La Fenice. Most rooms are furnished in antique style. Guests receive a 10 percent discount at the Ristorante Da Raffaele (see "Dining Out," later in this chapter). *See map p. 312. Corte dei Do Pozzi, 2373 San Marco.* ☎ *041-5207855. Fax: 041-5229413.* www.hoteldopozzi.it.

Hotel Falier

$$ Santa Croce A great moderate choice, the Falier's rooms have been furnished with taste and care; they're decorated with lace curtains and bright bedspreads. *See map p. 312. Salizada S. Pantalon, 130 S. Croce.* ☎ *041-710882. Fax: 041-5206554.* www.hotelfalier.com.

Hotel Olimpia

$$$ Santa Croce The good-sized rooms here are decorated with ornate furniture in Venetian style, and some units overlook the hotel's pleasant private garden. *See map p. 312. Fondamenta delle Burchielle 395 Santa Croce.* ☎ *041-711041. Fax: 041-524-6777.* www.hotel-olimpia.com.

Dining Out

Venice is a tricky place to eat. That's not because the local cuisine isn't good — it is delicious, especially if you like seafood, which is used in abundance — but because so many eateries in the city are such tourist traps. Venice is small enough that restaurants and *trattorie* are basically everywhere, but good ones are hard to find. When you find the right place, though, it can be heavenly: The staples of Venetian cuisine are fish and shellfish from the lagoon and the Adriatic, served on rice, pasta, or *polenta* (cornmeal) — and wine is an important part of the meal (see Chapter 2 for more details). Note that restaurants here are rather expensive, and all will add to your bill a *coperto* (cover) charge of between 1.50€ and 5€ ($1.80–$6) and 10 to 15 percent service.

There is no fishing on Sundays, thus the fish market is closed on Mondays and the seafood you'll eat is from the Saturday before. On Mondays, have meat or a pizza instead.

Ae Oche
$ Dorsoduro   PIZZA

This loftlike restaurant — housed in a former storage building — is a branch of a local restaurant focusing on quality and speed of service. The décor combines modern touches with respect for ancient beauty — note the beamed roof and Murano chandeliers — while the menu includes 100 different pizzas and a choice of beers on tap, plus an extensive salad selection and a few meat and pasta dishes. The original restaurant is at Campo San Giacomo dall'Orio, at Calle de le Oche (Santa Croce 1552; ☎ 041-5241161).

See map p. 312. Fondamenta Zattere, 1414 Dorsoduro. ☎ *041-5223812.* www. aeoche.it. *Reservations recommended. Vaporetto: 61 or 82 to San Basilio; walk right. Secondi: 8€–15€ ($9.60–$17); Pizza: 4.50€–9€ ($5.40–$11). AE, MC, V. Open: Daily noon to 3 p.m. and 6:30–11 p.m.*

A la Vecia Cavana
$$$ Cannaregio   VENETIAN

This renowned restaurant is housed in a 17th-century boathouse (*gondole* were repaired and stationed here), completely restored and decorated in bright colors. The cuisine is typically Venetian, with many "turf" options beside the "surf" ones. The oven-roasted crab is an excellent *antipasto*, as are the *baccalà mantecato* (creamed cod) and the savory sardines. Also very good is the risotto with basil and scallops, along with the *frittura mista* (fried calamari and small fish).

See map p. 312. Rio Terà Santi Apostoli, 4624 Cannaregio. ☎ *041-5287106.* www. veciacavana.it. *Reservations recommended. Vaporetto: 1 to Ca' d'Oro; walk straight ahead to Strada Nuova, turn right, and bear left at Campo dei Apóstoli. Secondi: 13€–24€ ($16–$29). AE, DC, MC, V. Open: Tues–Sun noon to 2:30 p.m. and 7–10:30 p.m. Closed 2 weeks in July.*

Lunch on the go in Venice

Eating in Venice is very expensive — your wallet will welcome a little picnic break now and then. You'll find many bars selling sandwiches, but we like making our own. You'll find local specialties, fresh bread, and scrumptious sweets at the bakeries and grocery shops lining **Strada Nuova** in Cannaregio; nearby, on Rio Terà Santi Apostoli (4612 Cannaregio), you'll find a **Coop** (a supermarket with mainland prices). Two other excellent places are **Via Garibaldi** in Castello — where you'll see another **Coop** supermarket — and around **Campo Rialto Nuovo** in San Polo, where you'll discover the lively and colorful fish, produce, and flower markets. Remember that Piazza San Marco is an open-air museum and, as such, eating on the premises is forbidden.

Al Covo
$$$ Castello   VENETIAN

This elegant restaurant is a highlight of the Venice dining scene, offering reliable and tasty cuisine. Only the best ingredients make it to your table here, and the service in the two small dining rooms is impeccable. The menu is strictly seasonal, but you will always find our favorite: the *gran fritto di pesce* (great seafood fry). We also recommend the daily seafood risotto and the mussel stew with polenta. A tasting menu is available for 65€ ($78).

See map p. 312. Campiello della Pescaria, 3968 Castello. ☎ *041-5223812. Reservations recommended. Vaporetto: 1, 41, or 42 to Arsenale; walk west along Riva degli Schiavoni and turn right after the first bridge. Secondi: 29€–39€ ($35–$47). AE, MC, V. Open: Fri–Tues 12:45–2:15 p.m. and 7:30–10 p.m. Closed Jan 6–Feb 6.*

Antica Besseta
$$ Santa Croce   VENETIAN/SEAFOOD

Located well away from the tourist areas, this small *trattoria* from 1700 is very popular with locals — and no wonder, as the food is very good and moderately priced (reservations are a good idea). The seasonal menu includes many excellent *risotti* — such as a well prepared squid-ink risotto. The fish *secondi* vary, but all are delicious renditions of traditional Venetian dishes.

See map p. 312. Salizada de Ca' Zusto, 1395 Santa Croce. ☎ *041-721687. Reservations recommended. Vaporetto: 1, 51, or 52 to Riva de Biasio; walk up Calle Zen, turn left, and make an immediate right on Salizada de Ca' Zusto. Secondi: 16€–22€ ($19–$25). AE, MC, V. Open: Thurs–Mon noon to 2:15 p.m.; Wed–Mon 7–10:30 p.m.*

Antico Martini
$$$$ San Marco VENETIAN/CREATIVE

This elegant restaurant, on the site of an 18th-century cafe, is one of the city's best — and as such comes with a high price. Under gilded frames and chandeliers — and on the delightful terrace in fine weather — you can sample Venetian specialties such as the excellent veal liver with onions, as well as innovative dishes like a wonderful torte of young artichokes and prawns. This gourmet spot is also famous for its *involtini di salmone al caviale* (rolled salmon and caviar).

See map p. 312. Campo San Fantin, 1983 San Marco. ☎ *041-5224121.* www.antico martini.com. *Reservations required. Vaporetto: 1 to Giglio; walk up Calle Gritti, turn right on Calle delle Ostreghe, continue onto Calle Larga XXII Marzo, turn left on Calle delle Veste, and follow it to Campo San Fantin. Secondi: 25€–56€ ($30–$67). AE, DC, MC, V. Open: Thurs–Mon noon to 2:30 p.m.; Wed–Mon 7–11:30 p.m.*

Avogaria
$$ Dorsoduro CREATIVE ITALIAN

This stylish restaurant/lounge is where local youths come for a nice evening out. The setting is the perfect background for the food and music. The menu always includes a choice of surf or turf made with first-rate ingredients; we loved the *trofie alla ricotta* (homemade fresh pasta with a ricotta-based sauce) and the stuffed squid. The small courtyard is delightful on summer evenings.

See map p. 312. Calle dell'Avogaria, 1629 Dorsoduro. ☎ *041-2960491.* www. avogaria.com. *Reservations recommended. Vaporetto: 61, 62, or 82 to San Basilio; follow Fondamenta San Basilio and turn right at San Sebastian. Secondi: 15€–25€ ($18–$30). MC, V. Open: Wed–Mon 12:30–3 p.m. and 7:30 p.m. to midnight.*

Bar Pizzeria da Paolo
$ Castello PIZZA/VENETIAN

This local hangout has a good location across from the Arsenale, plus cozy dining rooms and a pleasant décor. The pizza is good, as are the local dishes. If you dine outside, the small *campo* with the Arsenale and its canal in the background are especially quiet and picturesque at night.

See map p. 312. Campo Arsenale, 2389 Castello. ☎ *041-5210660. Reservations not necessary. Vaporetto: 1, 41, or 42 to Arsenale; follow Calle dei Forni to its end, turn left on Calle di Pegola, and turn right into Campo Arsenale. Secondi: 8€–15€ ($9.60–$18). MC, V. Open: Tues–Sat noon to 3 p.m.; Mon–Sat 6–11 p.m.*

Corte Sconta
$$ Castello VENETIAN/SEAFOOD

This simple yet elegant restaurant offers quality cuisine in a quiet neighborhood — and it has a pleasant courtyard for dining alfresco. The menu is all seasonal seafood; you should find the superb sardines marinated with onions, and perhaps the marinated anchovies with a caper sauce, along with homemade fresh pasta with seafood. Polenta often accompanies the elaborately prepared daily catches, such as a splendid artichoke-stuffed calamari.

See map p. 312. Calle del Pedestrin, 3886 Castello. ☎ *041 5227024. Reservations recommended. Vaporetto: 1, 41, or 42 to Arsenale; walk west along Riva degli Schiavoni, cross the bridge, turn right on Calle del Forno, and bear right. Secondi: 18€–25€ ($22–$30). MC, V. Open: Tues–Sat 12:30–2 p.m. and 7–9:30 p.m. Closed Jan 7–Feb 6 and July 15–Aug 15.*

Da Raffaele
$$ San Marco VENETIAN

Go to this canalside restaurant for excellent fish and other specialties. If you're tired of seafood, try the tasty pastas and grilled meats. Everything is reliable — which is why this place has been a major tourist magnet for years (make a reservation). A nice plus is the terrace dining in summer.

See map p. 312. Ponte delle Ostreghe, 2347 San Marco. ☎ *041-5232317. Reservations recommended. Vaporetto: 1 or 82 to Vallaresso; walk up Calle Vallaresso, turn left on Salizzada San Moisè, and continue to Calle Larga XXII Marzo and Calle delle Ostreghe. Secondi: 18€–31€ ($22–$37). AE, DC, MC, V. Open: Fri–Wed 11:30 a.m.– 2:30 p.m. and 6:30–10 p.m. Closed Dec 10–Feb.*

Fiaschetteria Toscana
$$$ Cannaregio VENETIAN

The Venetian-Tuscan marriage gave birth here to a refined cuisine, making this one of Venice's best restaurants. You can still get steaks in true Tuscan style, but the traditional Venetian cuisine has taken over much of the menu. Excellent choices include the *bigoli in salsa* and the *spaghetti al cartoccio ai frutti di mare* (spaghetti with seafood cooked in a pouch), as well as the *frittura della Serenissima* (deep-fried seafood and vegetables). Leave room for dessert, as they are homemade and delicious.

See map p. 312. Salizzada San Giovanni Crisostomo, 2347 Cannaregio. ☎ *041-5285281.* www.fiaschetteriatoscana.it. *Reservations required. Vaporetto: 1, 4, or 82 to Rialto; walk along Canal Grande, turn right past the Ponte di Rialto, then immediately left onto Salizzada San Giovanni Crisostomo. Secondi: 16€–30€ ($19–$36). AE, DC, MC, V. Open: Wed–Sun 12:30–2:30 p.m.; Wed–Mon 7:30–10:30 p.m. Closed July.*

Met de l'Hotel Metropole
$$$ Castello CREATIVE VENETIAN

You'll get heavenly treatment in the cozy and luxurious dining room of the charming Hotel Metropole (see earlier in this chapter), overlooking the bay of San Marco. The menu is strictly seasonal and offers many delights: pheasant ravioli with cheese flan and vegetables, a superb slow-roasted

Taking a sweet break

Venetians definitely have a sweet tooth and make delicious pastries; you can sample typical delights at **Pasticceria Tonolo** (San Pantalon, 3764 Dorsoduro; Vaporetto: San Tomà) or **Pasticceria Marchini** (Spadaria, 2769 San Marco; ☎ 041-5229109). Good *gelato* (ice cream) is more difficult to find: Industrial and pretend-homemade ice cream is sold at every corner, but it is a pale imitation of what you can have in Rome, Naples, or heavenly Sicily. One of the best places is the hole-in-the-wall **Boutique del Gelato** (Salizzada San Lio, 5727 Castello; ☎ 041-5223283), where everything is made fresh on the premises.

baby pig with apples and thyme, and local fish cooked in almond milk with savory eggplant and mushroom stew. Desserts are superb as well.

See map p. 312. Riva degli Schiavoni, 4149 Castello. ☎ *041-5205044.* www.hotel metropole.com. *Reservations recommended. Vaporetto: 1, 5, 41, 42, 51, 52, or 82 to San Zaccaria. Secondi: 25€–32€ ($30–$38). AE, DC, MC, V. Open: Tues–Sun 12:30–2:30 p.m. and 7:30–10:30 p.m.*

Osteria ai 4 Feri
$ Dorsoduro VENETIAN

This modest *osteria* is one of those traditional, charming restaurants that are rapidly disappearing from Venice. A real local hangout, it dishes up simple food in an old-fashioned setting. We recommend the excellent spaghetti with clams and the grilled fish sold by the weight, a tasty treat.

See map p. 312. Calle Lunga San Barnaba, 2754 Dorsoduro. ☎ *041-5206978. Reservations recommended in the evening. Vaporetto: 1 to Ca' Rezzonico; follow Calle Traghetto and cross Campo San Barnaba. Secondi: 9€–17€ ($11–$20). MC, V. Open: Mon–Sat 12:30–3 p.m. and 7:30–11 p.m.*

Osteria alle Testiere
$$$ Castello CREATIVE VENETIAN/SEAFOOD

This tiny *osteria* is unassuming, but serves delicious food in a simple and friendly atmosphere. The chef creates masterly variations on traditional recipes using the best offerings from the local fish market. We recommend the spaghetti with clams and saffron, the asparagus and ricotta ravioli served with scallops, and the fish filet with herbs and citrus sauce.

See map p. 312. Corte del Mondo Novo, off Salizada San Lio, 5801 Castello. ☎ *041-5227220. Reservations required. Vaporetto: 1, 4, or 82 to Rialto stop; walk to Campiello San Bartolomeo and across to your left up Calle Bissa, cross the bridge, continue on Calle San Antonio and across Campo San Lio to Salizzada San Lio. Secondi: 24€–25€ ($29–$30). MC, V. Open: Tues–Sat noon to 2 p.m. and 7–10 p.m. Closed 3 weeks Dec/Jan and 4 weeks July–Aug.*

Osteria da Fiore
$$$$ San Polo VENETIAN/SEAFOOD

One of the most exclusive restaurants in Venice, this is also the best. The well-prepared dishes are made with only the freshest ingredients and are carefully served in the subdued elegance of the two dining rooms. Excellent choices include the *spaghetti al cartoccio* (cooked in a pouch); the prawns with a lemon, tomato, and celery sauce; and the many seasonal seafood *antipasti*.

See map p. 312. Calle del Scaleter, 2202/A San Polo. ☎ 041-721308. Reservations required. Vaporetto: 1 or 82 to San Tomà; walk straight ahead to Campo San Tomà, continue straight on Calle larga Prima toward Santa Maria dei Frari and the Scuola di San Rocco, and a block before the Scuola and behind the Frari, turn right on Calle del Scaleter. Secondi: 25€–43€ ($30–$52). AE, DC, MC, V. Open: Tues–Sat 12:30–2:30 p.m. and 7:30–10 p.m. Closed Dec 25–Jan 15 and 10 days around Aug 15.

Osteria di Santa Marina
$$ Castello CREATIVE VENETIAN

This is a special restaurant in Venice, favored by local and other Italian gourmets. Served in a warm atmosphere, the menu includes updates of traditional dishes — such as the splendid risotto with scallops and local shellfish — and innovative creations like the Mediterranean squid with onion and orange peel. If it's on the menu, end your meal with the frozen eggnog soufflé with raspberry coulis. The three tasting menus (40€–70€/ $48–$84) are an excellent way to go.

See map p. 312. Campo Santa Marina, 5911 Castello. ☎ 041-5285239. www.osteria disantamarina.it. Reservations recommended. Vaporetto: 1, 4, or 82 to Rialto; walk up Salizzada Pio X, continue on Calle dello Zocco, turn left and immediately right over the bridge of Calle Bissa, then left at Campo San Lio, over 1 bridge and straight. Secondi: 22€–24€ ($26–$29). MC, V. Open: Tues–Sat 12:30–2:30 p.m.; Mon–Sat 7:30–9:30 p.m. Closed second half of Jan and 2 weeks in Aug.

Trattoria alla Madonna
$ San Polo VENETIAN/SEAFOOD

Seafood and more seafood! In this local *trattoria,* you'll find all the bounty the Adriatic has to offer — including some existing only in the Venetian lagoon — masterly prepared according to tradition. The market offerings are grilled, roasted, fried, or served with pasta, risotto, or polenta. The moderate prices attract crowds, so be prepared for a wait.

See map p. 312. Calle della Madonna, 594 San Polo. ☎ 041-5223824. Reservations accepted only for large parties. Vaporetto: 1, 4, or 82 to Rialto; cross the bridge, turn left on Riva del Vin along the Canal Grande, and turn right onto Calle della Madonna. Secondi: 12€–18€ ($14–$22). AE, MC, V. Open: Thurs–Tues noon to 3 p.m. and 7:15–10 p.m. Closed Dec 24–Jan and 1 week around Aug 15.

Trattoria Tre Spiedi
$$ Cannaregio   VENETIAN

This friendly *trattoria* is a favorite with local families; it's also a convenient choice in the touristy area near Ponte di Rialto. The traditional cuisine features a lot of fresh fish. The many spaghetti *primi* are excellent; for *secondo*, try the veal liver sautéed with onions or the eel stew, both served with polenta.

See map p. 312. Salizada San Canciano, 5906 Cannaregio. ☎ *041-5208035. Reservations not accepted. Vaporetto: 1, 4, or 82 to Rialto; walk up and turn left on Salizada S. Giovanni Grisostomo, cross the bridge, continue and turn right on Salizada San Canciano. Secondi: 11€–18€ ($13–$22). AE, MC, V. Open: Tues–Sat 9 a.m.–2:45 p.m. and 6–9:45 p.m.; Sun 12:30–3:30 p.m.*

Vini da Gigio
$$ Cannaregio   VENETIAN/WINE BAR

The restaurant attached to this traditional *enoteca* (wine bar) — still one of the best in town — has become a favorite for both the excellent service and the tasty food. The menu is based on traditional fare: We loved the pasta with squid and the grilled eel. Leave room for the homemade desserts.

See map p. 312. Fondamenta della Chiesa, 3628a Cannaregio. ☎ *041-5285140.* www. vinidagigio.com. *Reservatons recommended. Vaporetto: 1 to Ca d'Oro; walk up to Strada Nova and turn left; pass the bridge and turn right. Secondi 12€–18 ($14–$22). DC, MC, V. Wed–Sun 12:15–2:30 p.m. and 7:15–10:30 p.m. Closed 3 weeks Jan/Feb.*

Exploring Venice

It is of paramount importance during high season, and a good idea at all times, to make advance reservations for **Palazzo Ducale** and the **Gallerie dell'Accademia** — thereby avoiding the long lines.

Venice offers a number of interesting passes and discount cards:

>   ✔ The **Venice Card Orange** (☎ 041-2424; www.venicecard.it) is the most comprehensive: It gives you access to all public transportation, public bathrooms, city-run museums (the equivalent of a Museum Pass, described below), and the Venice Casinò (adult version only). It also grants discounts at participating shops, restaurants, and attractions. It comes in one-day (29€/$35 adults; 22€/$26 youths under 29), three-day (54€/$65 adults; 45€/$54 youths), and seven-day (76€/$91 adults; 67€/$80 youths) versions. The card is free for children under 4. For an additional fee, you can include the airport shuttle boat or parking at the ASM Garage at Piazzale Roma (you need to pay this online when you reserve). Cards must be reserved at least 48 hours in advance (also online).

After you arrive in Venice, you can pick up your card at ticket booths at Piazzale Roma, Tronchetto, the Santa Lucia train station, and the Marco Polo airport. The **Venice Card Blue** does not include city-run museums (see "Getting Around Venice," earlier in this chapter).

✔ If you're between the ages of 14 and 29, the **Rolling Venice Card** (☎ 041-2413908; www.comune.venezia.it) is a great deal: It gives you substantial discounts — from 10 to 40 percent — on hotels, restaurants, museums, public transportation (see earlier in this chapter), and shops. If you decide to get the Venice Card (see earlier in this chapter), the Rolling Venice discounts are on top of those. It costs 3€ ($3.60) and you need to register with a photo ID at one of the Rolling Venice information kiosks, the most convenient being the one inside the **Santa Lucia train station** (☎ 041-5242852; open daily 8 a.m–8 p.m. July–Oct); they'll give you your card plus a map of Venice charting the location of all the participating hotels, restaurants, clubs, and shops, as well as a special guidebook with interesting facts and smart itineraries.

✔ The **Museum Pass** for 18€ ($22) gives you admission to Palazzo Ducale, Correr Museum, Libreria Marciana, Ca' Rezzonico, the Glass Museum in Murano, and the Lace Museum in Burano, plus a few others.

✔ A **combination ticket** for the Ca' d'Oro, Museo Orientale in Ca' Pesaro, and Gallerie dell'Accademia is available for 11€ ($13); you can purchase it at the ticket booth of any of the three museums.

✔ If you already have the Venice Card (see earlier in this chapter) and you're staying a few days, you can get a free **Chorus Card** (☎ 041-2740462; www.chorusvenezia.org), giving you access to 15 of the best churches in Venice (including Santa Maria Gloriosa dei Frari and the Chiesa del Redentore) with audio guide; without the Venice Card, the pass costs 8€ ($9.60). A family version, for two adults and two children 11 to 18, goes for 16€ ($19). The pass is valid for one year and is for sale at all participating churches except Santa Maria Gloriosa dei Frari.

 As everywhere else in Italy, bare shoulders, halter tops, tank tops, shorts, and skirts above the knee will lead to your being turned away at church entrances — no kidding, and no matter what your age and sex (see Chapter 2).

Discovering the top attractions

Ca' d'Oro
Cannaregio

The Ca' d'Oro (Gold House), as its name suggests, was once richly decorated with gold, now worn away to reveal the marble beneath. Begun in 1422, it's one of the most beautiful of the *palazzi* fronting the Canal Grande.

Venice Attractions

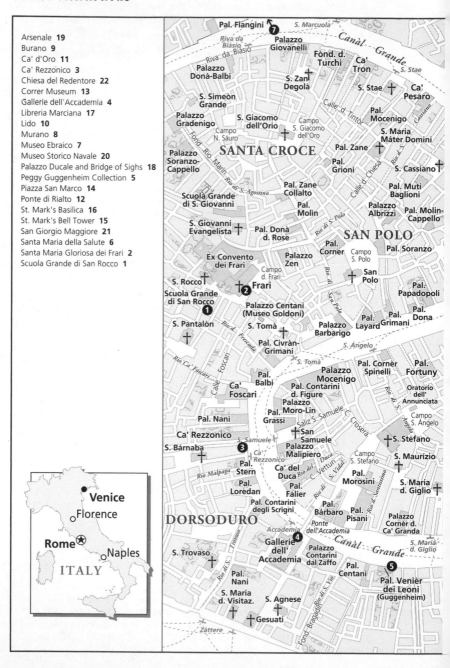

Arsenale **19**
Burano **9**
Ca' d'Oro **11**
Ca' Rezzonico **3**
Chiesa del Redentore **22**
Correr Museum **13**
Gallerie dell'Accademia **4**
Libreria Marciana **17**
Lido **10**
Murano **8**
Museo Ebraico **7**
Museo Storico Navale **20**
Palazzo Ducale and Bridge of Sighs **18**
Peggy Guggenheim Collection **5**
Piazza San Marco **14**
Ponte di Rialto **12**
St. Mark's Basilica **16**
St. Mark's Bell Tower **15**
San Giorgio Maggiore **21**
Santa Maria della Salute **6**
Santa Maria Gloriosa dei Frari **2**
Scuola Grande di San Rocco **1**

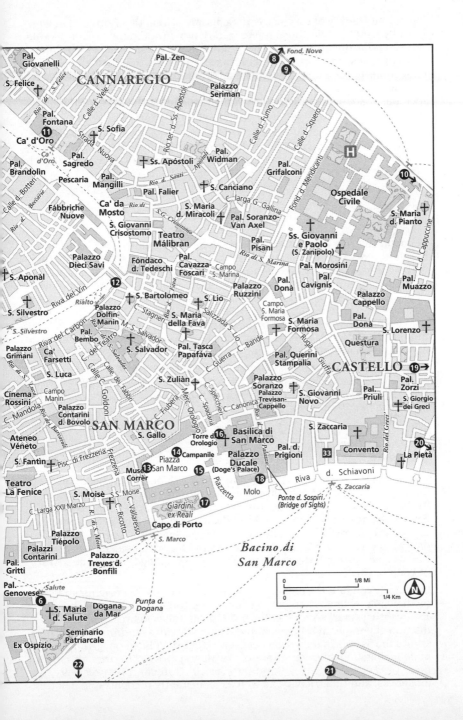

Its elegant tracery of carvings is the epitome of Venetian Gothic, that wonderfully ornate style that's never gaudy nor broodingly morbid like its northern European cousin. The building was bought in 1895 by musician/art collector Giorgio Franchetti, who donated the Ca' d'Oro and his collections to the public in 1916. Besides antique furniture, tapestries, and **Venetian ceramics** from as far back as the 12th century, the collection includes many works by the best Italian masters. The stars of the show are Mantegna's *San Sebastian* and Titian's *Venus at the Mirror.*

See map p. 326. Calle Ca' d'Oro. ☎ 041-5238790. www.cadoro.org. *Vaporetto: 1 to Ca' d'Oro. Admission: 5€ ($6); children under 12 free. Open: Mon 8:15 a.m.–2 p.m., Tues–Sun 8:15 a.m.–7:15 p.m.; ticket booth closes 30 minutes earlier; closed Jan 1, May 1, and Dec 25.*

Ca' Rezzonico
Dorsoduro

Begun in 1649 for the Bon, an important Venetian family, it was acquired a hundred years later by the Rezzonico family, who completed the structure, making it into one of the most magnificent *palazzi* on the Canal Grande. The most famous resident was the English poet Robert Browning, who died here in 1889. The Ca' Rezzonico contains the **Museum of the 18th Century in Venice,** and among its elegant rooms is the Throne Room, whose ceilings were painted by **Giovanni Battista Tiepolo.** You can step out onto the balcony and gaze down the Canal Grande like a brooding poet and get a feel for the life of a Venetian aristocrat.

See map p. 326. Fondamenta Rezzonico 3136. ☎ 041-2410100. www.musei civiciveneziani.it. *Vaporetto: 1 to Ca' Rezzonico. Admission: 6.50€ ($7.80). Open: Wed–Mon, Apr–Oct 10 a.m.–6 p.m., Nov–Mar 10 a.m.–5 p.m.; closed Jan 1, May 1, and Dec 25.*

Gallerie dell'Accademia
Dorsoduro

Rivaling Florence's Uffizi Gallery and Rome's Galleria Borghese, this is a fantastic collection of paintings from the 13th through the 18th centuries. Its 24 rooms are housed in a former church and attached monastery, the **Scuola Grande di Santa Maria della Carità,** one of Venice's religious associations. The complex also houses Venice's **Academy of Fine Arts.** You can follow the development of art from the medieval period to the Renaissance through the galleries, while also walking through the history of Venetian art.

In room 1, you find the luminous, influential works of Veneziano, still very medieval in feeling. Then you pass into the totally different world of the 15th century, marked by greater naturalism, fuller figures, and the introduction of perspective. For example, Jacopo Bellini's *Madonna and Child* shows the figures in three-quarter view rather than head-on, giving an intimate feeling. In succeeding rooms are Mantegna's *St. George* and examples of Tintoretto's revolutionary work (radical postures, greater looseness, and theatricality, as well as an instantly recognizable palette).

Sinking beauty

Venice has weathered wars, dictators, and conspiracies, and enjoyed more than a thousand years of democracy. But its most treacherous foe may be the very ground beneath it. The increase in the sea levels registered all over the planet in recent years has had especially dramatic consequences for Venice — the city is literally sinking into the muddy lagoon on which it was built. In spite of advice from experts all over the world, cement injections, and the ongoing work of restoration and solidification of the canals, the city continues to sink. The search for ways to save one of the most beautiful and extraordinary cities ever built continues.

There's too much in the Accademia to even give an adequate summary, but don't miss Lorenzo Lotto's striking **portrait of a young man** watched by a small lizard on a table; Giorgione's haunting **portrait of an old woman;** and the Tiepolo **ceiling paintings** rescued from a now-destroyed building. One of the most famous works is Veronese's incredible, enormous *Last Supper.* Its frenzied energy and party atmosphere (with wine flowing and dwarf figures in the foreground) brought a charge of heresy (and a hasty change of title to *The Banquet in the House of Levi*). At the end of room 15 is Palladio's gravity-defying **staircase.** Room 20 contains a fascinating series of paintings by Carpaccio, Bellini, and others, all commissioned to illustrate miracles of the True Cross, a fragment of which was brought to Venice in 1369, but also illustrating Venice as it once was.

See map p. 326. Campo della Carità, at the foot of the Accademia Bridge. ☎ *041-5222247 or 041-5200345 for reservations.* www.gallerieaccademia.org. *Vaporetto: 1 or 82 to Accademia. Admission: 6.50€ ($7.80); advance reservation 1€ ($1.20). Open: Mon 8:15 a.m.–2 p.m., Tues–Sun 8:15 a.m.–7:15 p.m.; ticket booth closes 30 minutes earlier; closed Jan 1, May 1, and Dec 25.*

Palazzo Ducale and Bridge of Sighs
San Marco

Shimmering after a lengthy restoration, the pink-and-white marble facade of Venice's most beautiful *palazzo* has been returned to view. Pause to take in the delicate decorations, the expressive carvings, and the splendid bas-reliefs of its columns before entering. Once the private home of the *doges* (the *doge* was leader of the republic, elected for life), as well as the seat of government and the court of law, the Palazzo Ducale was the heart of the republic. In Gothic-Renaissance style, it was begun in 1173, integrating the walls and towers of the previously existing A.D. 810 castle. The *palazzo* was enlarged in 1340 with the addition of the new wing housing the **Great Council Room,** a marvel of architecture for the size of the unsupported ceilings (decorated by Tintoretto's *Paradise*). On the left side of the courtyard is the **Staircase of the Giants,** guarded by two giant stone figures and a Renaissance masterpiece. At the top of these steps, you enter the loggia, from which departs the famous **Scala d'Oro (Golden Staircase)** leading to the *doge's* **apartments** and the **government chambers.** These were splendidly decorated by the major artists of the 16th century, including **Titian, Tintoretto, Veronese,** and **Tiepolo.** A little-known part of the palace's collection is a group of paintings bequeathed by a bishop, including interesting works by **Hieronymus Bosch.**

From the *palazzo,* continue your visit on the famous **Bridge of Sighs,** which didn't get its name from the lovers who met under it: The bridge was built in the 17th century to connect the *palazzo* — and the Courts of Justice — to the prisons, and those condemned to death passed over this bridge (supposedly sighing heavily) both on their way into the prison and eventually on their way out to be executed in Piazzetta San Marco. The two red columns on the facade of Palazzo Ducale mark the place where the death sentences were read out. You can visit both the 16th-century **New Prisons,** built when the palace's limited facilities became insufficient, and the **Old Prisons;** these were also called *pozzi,* literally "wells," but "pits" would be a better translation, as they were at and below the ground level — which, in Venice, means they flooded at high tide.

If you're interested in the dark history of these ages, you'll love the special guided tour **"Secret Itineraries,"** which takes you into the *doges'* hidden apartments and the **Courts of Justice,** where the most important decisions were made. You'll also visit the famous **Piombi** (literally "leads"), the prisons under the lead roof of the palace: Horribly hot in summer and cold in winter, this is where **Casanova** was held and from where he made his illustrious escape. The tour is offered in several languages and costs an extra 4€ ($4.80) (reserve at least 48 hours in advance).

The Palazzo Ducale is huge, especially when you count the labyrinthine prison next door. You can easily spend four hours inside, especially if you take one of the special tours.

See map p. 326. Piazza San Marco; the entrance to the palace is from the Porta del Frumento on the water side. ☎ *041-2715911. Vaporetto: 1 or 82 to San Marco. Admission: 12€ ($14); includes Correr Museum and Libreria Marciana. Audio guide: 5.50€ ($6.60). Open: Daily Apr–Oct 9 a.m.–7 p.m., Nov–Mar 9 a.m.–5 p.m.; ticket booth closes 60 minutes earlier. Closed Jan 1, May 1, and Dec 25.*

Peggy Guggenheim Collection
Dorsoduro

Housed in the elegant Palazzo Venier dei Leoni on the Canal Grande, this museum holds one of Italy's most important collections of avant-garde art. The reason the building looks so short is that it's the ground floor of a 1749 *palazzo* that was never completed. American expatriate collector Peggy Guggenheim lived here for 30 years; after her death in 1979, the building and collection became the property of New York's Guggenheim Foundation. Peggy G.'s protégés included Jackson Pollock, represented by ten paintings, and Max Ernst, whom she married. From dada and surrealism to abstract expressionism, the collection is rich and diverse, with works by Klee, Magritte, Mondrian, De Chirico, Dalí, Kandinsky, Picasso, and others. The sculpture garden includes works by Giacometti.

See map p. 331. Calle San Cristoforo 701. ☎ 041-2405411. www.guggenheim venice.it. *Vaporetto: 1 or 82 to Accademia; walk left past the Accademia, turn right on Rio Terà A. Foscarini, turn left on Calle Nuova Sant'Agnese, continue on Piscina Former, cross the bridge, continue on Calle della Chiesa and then Fondamenta Venier along the small canal, and turn left on Calle San. Cristoforo. Admission: 10€ ($12); children under 12 free. Open: Wed–Mon 10 a.m.–6 p.m.; closed Dec 25.*

Piazza San Marco
San Marco

Possibly the world's most famous *piazza,* this beautiful space was created in the 11th century. Lined on one side by St. Mark's Basilica (see later in this section) and on the three others by the porticos and loggias of the Procuratie buildings, it was and is the heart of Venice, site of ceremonies, celebrations, and, at one time, tournaments. The buildings on the north side are the **Procuratie Vecchie,** built in the Renaissance as offices for the city's magistrature; facing it to the south are the **Procuratie Nuove,** built to house more offices and, after the fall of the Venetian Republic at the hands of Napoleon, turned into the Royal Palace. The wing enclosing the *piazza* to the west was added by Napoleon, after demolishing the church that was once there. This last building now houses the **Correr Museum** (☎ 041-2405211; Admission: 12€/$14, which includes Palazzo Ducale and Libreria Marciana; Open: Daily Apr–Oct 9 a.m.–7 p.m., Nov–Mar 9 a.m.–5 p.m.), whose interesting collection includes some remarkable artwork, such as Canova's **bas-reliefs;** the famous painting by Carpaccio called *Two Venetian Ladies;* a strange Lucas Cranach, with Christ rising from the tomb and two bearded soldiers looking trollish; and Hugo van der Goes's small but strikingly emotional *Crucifixion.* Part of the building contains the Risorgimento museum — with mementos and documents from that period — and an eclectic collection of items that make up a history of daily Venetian life. From the Correr, you can also access the **Archaeological Museum,** with its rich collection of Greek sculptures.

To the north of the *piazza,* adjacent to St. Mark's Basilica, is the **Torre dell'Orologio** (☎ 041-5209070; www.museiciviciveneziani.it), a clock tower built in 1496. The clock has two huge quadrants, the one below indicating the phases of the moon and signs of the zodiac. The one above is the clock with a complicated mechanism propelling wooden statues of the Magi (the three kings bringing offerings to Jesus) guided by an angel to come out at the striking of the hour and pass in front of the Virgin and Child. Above this, yet another mechanism propels two bronze Moors to strike a bell on the hour. A gruesome legend has it that when the clock was completed, it was such a wonder that the workman who designed and built it was blinded so he could never duplicate it anywhere else. The whole thing has been under restoration for years; we hope you'll find the clock back in place and the tower reopened when you get to Venice.

To the south, **St. Mark's Bell Tower** (☎ 041-5224064; Admission: 6€/$7.20; Open: Daily Nov–Mar 9:30 a.m.–4:15 p.m.; Apr–June and Sept–Oct 9 a.m.–7 p.m.; July–Aug 9 a.m.–9 p.m.) dominates the *piazza.* Used as a lighthouse by approaching boats, this tall belfry — 97m (324 ft.) high — was originally built in the ninth century. It suddenly collapsed in 1902, but was faithfully rebuilt using most of the same materials. From atop, you can admire a 360-degree panorama of the city and the famous *piazza* below — and you can do so without climbing hundreds of steps, as there's an elevator!

Attached to Piazza San Marco is Piazzetta San Marco, a smaller space opening onto the bay and lined on one side by the **Palazzo Ducale** (see earlier in this section) and on the other by the **Libreria Marciana** (☎ 041-2405211; Admission: 12€ ($14), which includes Palazzo Ducale and Correr Museum; Open: Daily Apr–Oct 9 a.m.–7 p.m., Nov–Mar 9 a.m.– 5 p.m.). Also called **Libreria Sansoviniana (Sansovino Library),** after the name of its architect, Jacopo Sansovino, this elegant building was erected between 1537 and 1560 to house the republic's collection of Greek and ancient Roman manuscripts. Those are made available only to scholars, but everybody is allowed to see the beautifully decorated rooms and works of art. We recommend the library's free guided tour, available at press time on Saturdays and Sundays at 10 a.m., noon, 2 p.m., and 4 p.m.

Outside, two granite columns — brought from the east in the 12th century — decorate the *piazzetta*. They are topped by Venetian-Byzantine capitals: one supporting the lion symbol of St. Mark, and the other San Teodoro, the city's patron saint before the body of St. Mark was brought back to Venice. This was the setting for capital executions and cruel, extraordinary punishments for which the Serene Republic was notorious.

 Don't eat or drink while visiting Piazza San Marco and its surroundings: It is considered an open-air museum and you will be fined if caught eating, drinking, or littering outside the authorized areas.

See map p. 326. Off Riva degli Schiavoni. Vaporetto: 1 or 82 to San Marco–Vallaresso.

Ponte di Rialto
San Marco/San Polo

When the original wooden bridge here started rotting away, the citizens of Venice decided, in 1588, to replace it with the current stone-and-brick marvel. The bridge opens onto the Rialto district in San Polo, Venice's main merchant area since the Middle Ages. Ships arrived here after stopping at the *Dogana* **(Customs House),** at the tip of Dorsoduro, and discharged their merchandise in the large warehouses. Goods were then sold at the general market surrounding the warehouses. The fish and produce wholesale markets were moved to the new merchant and marine terminal across from Santa Lucia rail station only in 1998, but the retail markets have survived, retaining their picturesque flavor. Lined with shops on both sides and busy with crowds of tourists, it is difficult to truly enjoy this splendid bridge's architectural beauty during the day; for the best view, try early in the morning or late in the evening.

See map p. 326. Across the Canal Grande, between Riva del Vin and Riva del Carbon. Vaporetto: 1 or 82 to Rialto.

Piazza San Marco

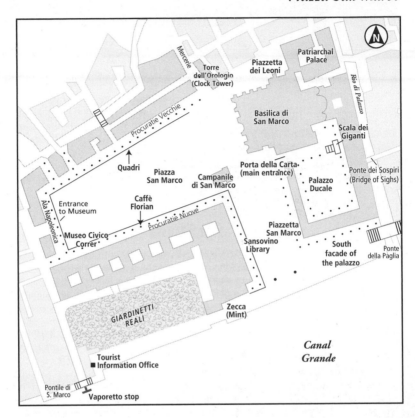

Santa Maria della Salute
Dorsoduro

Built after the 1630 black-plague epidemic as an *ex-voto* (thanks offering to God), the octagonal St. Mary of Good Health is an enduring baroque landmark at the end of Dorsoduro, almost across from Piazza San Marco. On the main altar is a 13th-century **Byzantine icon** and Titian's *Descent of the Holy Spirit;* in the Sacristy are three Titian **ceiling paintings** as well as Tintoretto's wonderful *Wedding at Cana.* If you happen to be in town on November 21, you can see the feast of the Madonna della Salute, a centuries-old commemorative pageant in which a pontoon bridge is constructed across the Canal Grande, linking La Salute with the San Marco side.

See map p. 326. Campo della Salute. ☎ *041-5225558. Vaporetto: 1 to Salute. Admission: Church voluntary offering; Sacristy 1.50€ ($1.80). Open: Daily 9 a.m. to noon and 3–6 p.m.; open only for mass Sun 11 a.m.–12:30 p.m.*

La Serenissima

After the fall of the Western Roman Empire in 475 A.D., barbarians overran Italy's peninsula, prompting some in the region to flee to where no sane barbarian could attack: the middle of the water. Although the Venetian lagoon was populated with fishing communities, Venice rapidly built itself up as a commercial seafaring powerhouse under the protection of Bisance (Constantinople, the capital of the Eastern Roman Empire). A thriving commercial harbor and shipyard, it detached itself and became independent in the eighth century A.D. with its first *doge* (the head of the government elected by the town's citizen) — the word *doge* is the Venetian mutation of the Latin word *dux* ("leader"). Venice became a harbor of international importance in the tenth century, when the Republic started regulating commerce between Europe and the Orient. The city we know today started developing around St. Mark's Basilica (Basilica di San Marco), constructed to house the relics of the saint. The group of islands in the lagoon was built up, the canals drained, and their edges reinforced. The city had begun its metamorphosis.

The Venetian Republic was a great experiment in government. Over the centuries, a complicated network of institutions and checks and balances was built to limit the power of the *doge* and all the other political institutions that governed the city-state. At the heart was the *Maggior Consiglio* (Great Council), which elected the *doge*. Originally elective, membership to the Maggior Consiglio became hereditary in 1297. The smaller Council of Ten was established in 1310 to judge conspirators in a failed plot, but it became permanent (the *doge* and his counselors were also members). It became so powerful that the Maggior Consiglio passed legislation to limit its powers in 1582, 1628, and 1762. Most powerful of all, perhaps, was the Grand Chancellor, who, as the head of the secret police, knew all the dark secrets of the nobility, so other institutions were established to limit his power. The experiment was successful: Venice remained a republic until May 12, 1797, when Napoleon invaded northern Italy and established a new European order. After Napoleon's fall, the Austro-Hungarian empire took over Venice, and it was only in 1866 that they were chased away and Venice became part of the newly created Italian kingdom.

Santa Maria Gloriosa dei Frari
San Polo

This church is a magnificent example of the Venetian Gothic, built in the first half of the 14th century and enlarged in the 15th. Beside it is the original 14th-century **bell tower.** We single out this church not only for its architecture, but also for the exquisite artwork it contains, none more so than Titian's **Pala Pesaro (Pesaro Altarpiece)** and his **Assumption** over the main altar. Another star here is Donatello's **St. John the Baptist,** a rare sculpture in wood. Be sure to visit the original wooden choir, where monks participated in mass — this is the only extant choir of its kind in Venice. The triangular marble monument dedicated to sculptor Antonio Canova was actually designed by Canova to be a monument to Titian (Canova's followers appropriated the design for their master after he died in 1822).

A bit of trivia: If you look carefully at the walls near the monument, you can see an **Austrian bomb** that was dropped on the church during World War I but miraculously failed to explode.

See map p. 326. Campo dei Frari. ☎ 041-5222637. Vaporetto: 1 or 82 to San Tomà; walk up to Calle Campaniel, turn right, turn left on Campo San Tomà, continue onto Calle larga Prima, and turn right. Admission: 2.50€ ($3); audio guide 0.50€ (60¢). Open: Mon–Sat 9 a.m.–6 p.m.; Sept–June Sun 1–6 p.m. Closed Jan 1, Easter, Aug 15, and Dec 25.

St. Mark's Basilica
San Marco

The symbol of Venice, it was built in A.D. 829 to house the remains of San Marco, one of the four evangelists, martyred by the Turks in Alexandria of Egypt, and the city's patron saint. The original church was rebuilt after it burned down in 932, and again in 1063, taking its present shape. Five domes — originally gilded — top the five portals, while an elegant **loggia** opens in between: This is where the *doge* presided over the public functions held in the square (multilingual audio boxes up here give a brief description of the sites you can see around the *piazza*). The bronze doors of the Basilica's main portal are booty from the Fourth Crusade from Constantinople. Above the entrance hall is the **gallery,** from which you can have a close-up view of the rich mosaic decorations of the portals. Only one of the mosaics above the doorways is original — the one in the first doorway to the left. The others are 17th- and 18th-century reproductions. The rooms above house the **Museo Marciano,** which holds the original horses of the *Triumphal Quadriga:* the famous gilded bronze horses (the ones outside gracing the loggia are copies) which were brought back from Constantinople in 1204 after the Fourth Crusade. Experts have estimated that the horses are Greek sculptures from the fourth century B.C. The museum also has a collection of mosaics, altarpieces, and sculptures that decorated the basilica at one time or another. You can access the loggia, as well as the gallery and the museum, from a long and steep flight of stone steps inside the basilica entrance on the right.

Entering the portal, you may be overwhelmed by the luxury of the decorations: gold mosaics and colored inlaid marble everywhere. The lower part of the basilica is decorated in Byzantine and Venetian style and the second story in Flamboyant Gothic. The atrium's ceiling mosaics date from 1225 to 1275 and depict Old Testament scenes. The floors are in geometric marble mosaics of typical Byzantine style from the 11th and 12th centuries. The inner basilica mosaics, depicting scenes from the New Testament, were begun in the 12th century and finished in the 13th. The **treasury** holds the basilica's rich collection of relics and art, including loot from Constantinople and the Crusades. Behind the main altar is the famous **Pala d'Oro,** a magnificent altarpiece in gold and enamel started in the 10th century and further decorated in the 14th and 15th centuries. Finely chiseled in Byzantine-Venetian style, it is encrusted with over 2,000 precious stones.

Due to the crowds, the visit to the basilica is limited to ten minutes; you can make a free reservation for your time slot at least 48 hours in advance by going to www.alata.it.

See map p. 326. Piazza San Marco. ☎ 041-5225205. Vaporetto: 1 or 82 to San Marco–Vallaresso. Admission: Basilica free; Pala d'Oro 1.50€ ($1.80); Treasury 2€ ($2.40); Galleria and Museo Marciano 3€ ($3.60). Audio guides: 5.50€ ($6.60). Open: Mon–Sat Nov–Mar 9:45 a.m.–4:30 p.m.; Apr–Oct 9:45 a.m.–5:30 p.m.; Sun and holidays 2–4 p.m.

Scuola Grande di San Rocco
San Polo

San Rocco is Jacopo Tintoretto's Sistine Chapel. From 1564 to 1587, **Tintoretto,** a brother of the school, decorated the **Sala dell'Albergo,** the **lower hall,** and the **upper hall** with a series of incredibly beautiful paintings depicting biblical and Christian subjects. There are 21 paintings on the upper-hall ceiling alone (mirrors are available so you don't have to strain your neck). The most impressive is his *Crucifixion,* a painting of almost overpowering emotion and incredible detail (the tools used to make the cross are strewn in the foreground); the painter shows the moment when one of the two thieves' crosses is raised. The upper hall is also decorated with a fascinating collection of **wood sculptures** carved by Francesco Pianta in the 17th century; some depict artisans and the tools of their trade with an amazing realism.

See map p. 326. Campo San Rocco 3058. ☎ 041-5234864. www.scuolagrande sanrocco.it. Vaporetto: 1 or 82 to San Tomà; walk up to Calle Campaniel, turn right, turn left on Campo San Tomà, continue onto Calle Larga Prima and Salizzada San Rocco, and turn left. Admission: 7€ ($8.40). Open: Daily Apr–Oct 9 a.m.–5:30 p.m.; Nov–Mar 10 a.m.–4 p.m. Closed Jan 1, Easter, and Dec 25.

Finding more cool things to see and do

 ✔ Yes, we know, gondolas are for, ahem, *tourists* . . . but really, what can be more romantic than being rowed in a gondola along off-the-beaten-path canals? These historic crafts built of wood and iron are conducted according to the strictest traditional rules, and require enormous skill (not to mention expensive maintenance). A gondola ride is the best way to admire the city's Venetian Gothic and Renaissance architecture. The *palazzi* on the canals were once the residences of Venice's wealthiest families, but many have been transformed into museums or hotels, while others are still lived in (lucky tenants!); a few seem forlorn and abandoned. The official rates (set by Ente Gondola; ☎ 041-5285075; www.gondola venezia.it) are 73€ ($88) during the day and 91€ ($109) from 8 p.m. to 8 a.m. for 50 minutes, with a maximum of six people; each additional 25 minutes will cost 37€ ($56) during the day and 47€ ($56) at night. All gondola stations in Venice are about equal, but make sure you use only authorized gondolas — and establish the price and time in advance, before you get in the boat, to avoid unpleasant surprises. You'll find gondola stations at San Marco

(☎ 041-5200685), San Tomà (☎ 041-5205275), Rialto (Riva del Carbon; ☎ 041-5224904), Santa Maria del Giglio (☎ 041-5222073), Campo San Moisé off Calle Larga 22 Marzo (☎ 041-5231837), and Riva Schiavoni (across from Danieli; ☎ 041-5222254).

✔ You may want to take your tour at high tide — to be more level with the pavement, instead of the rather scummy canal sidewalls. You'll also want to avoid the Canal Grande, except maybe in the wee hours: It is so large and busy that it gets very noisy and choppy and can therefore be quite unpleasant in a small boat.

✔ Built in the 12th century, the **Arsenale** (Vaporetto: 1, 41, or 42 to Arsenale; follow Calle dei Forni to its end, turn left on Calle di Pegola, and turn right into Campo Arsenale) was the Venetian Republic's shipyard — the name comes from the Arab word *darsina'a* (shipyard) — the largest in the world for centuries. At its heyday, when there were as many as 100 galleons ready to sail, crews could assemble a vessel from prefab timbers in a single day — and a crew at that time could number as many as 16,000! The Arsenale is still part of the Italian Navy, but is now open to the public for special exhibits, such as **Navalis** — the wooden boat show — and the **Biennale di Venezia,** the international art show that takes place in odd-numbered years. We recommend taking *vaporetto* no. 51 or 52 to enjoy the daunting view from the water. Nearby is the **Museo Storico Navale** (Campo San Biagio, 2148 Castello; ☎ 041-5200276; Admission: 1.60€/$1.90; Open: Mon–Fri 8:45 a.m.–1:30 p.m., Sat 8:45 a.m.–1 p.m.), housed in the 15th-century Granary of the Venetian Republic and in part of the Arsenale. It is the largest in Italy and includes a beautiful collection of historical boats and models.

✔ The word *ghetto* has been used to name the neighborhood once set apart for Jews in European cities, but the **Venetian Ghetto (Ghetto Novo)** was Europe's first. It was established in 1516 on a small island accessible by only one bridge, which was closed at night. In 1541, when Jews from Germany, Poland, Spain, and Portugal fled to Venice, the government allowed the community to expand into the **Old Ghetto (Ghetto Vecchio),** the area between the Ghetto Novo and the Rio di Cannaregio, which has the two largest places of worship — **Scola Levantina** and **Scola Spagnola** (the Levantine and Spanish synagogues). To accommodate the growing population, buildings were made taller and taller, which is why this area has some of the tallest buildings in Venice. Every hour beginning at 10:30 a.m. daily, guided tours of the Ghetto (6.20€/$7.40) start at the **Museo Ebraico** (Campo del Ghetto Novo; ☎ 041-715359; Vaporetto: 1 or 82 to San Marcuola; Open: Daily Oct–May 10 a.m.–5:30 p.m., June–Sept 10 a.m.–7 p.m.; closed Jan 1, May 1, and Dec 25). Admission is 3€ ($3.60) for the museum and 8.50€ ($10) for the tour, which includes the synagogues (25 percent discount with the Venice Card).

✔ A visit to Venice isn't complete without a trip to the **Lagoon.** The closest and largest island is **Murano** (Vaporetto: 41 or 42) — actually a cluster of islands. It feels like a smaller, much quieter replica of Venice, down to its main canal meandering across it. Known as the island of the glassmakers, an industry that was created here centuries ago, it's still famous as ever for the unique quality of its artistic glass work. This community of more than 6,000 contains about 70 glass factories, some of which allow you to sit and watch glass being blown (most only in the morning). You'll find many shops selling glass of all kinds — from cheap trinkets to million-dollar chandeliers — and several good seafood restaurants. We recommend the moderately priced **Ostaria ai Vetrai** (Fondamenta Manin 29; ☎ 041-739293; Open: Wed–Sun noon to 3 p.m.), with a pleasant canalside terrace serving excellent seafood. At the **Glass Museum** (Fondamenta Giustinian; ☎ 041-739586; Admission: 6€/$7.20; Open: Thurs–Tues Apr–Oct 10 a.m.–5 p.m.; Nov–Mar 10 a.m.–4 p.m.), you can see a number of splendid antique masterpieces. Founded in the 7th century and rebuilt in the 12th in Venetian Byzantine style, the church of **Santa Maria e Donato** is really one of the wonders of the whole Venetian region: The floor is decorated with a mosaic of birds and animals in semiprecious stone, dating from 1140 — it's a marvel unto itself.

✔ The farthest island from Venice — about half an hour by *vaporetto* LN from Fondamenta Nove — is **Burano,** a fishing village renowned for its lacemaking. The houses on Burano are famous for their bright colors, ranging from purple to bright yellow. The town itself is almost wholly given up to lace shops, not necessarily selling the real thing. But the **Lace School** and the attached **Lace Museum** (Piazza Baldassarre Galuppi 187; ☎ 041-730034; Admission: 4€/$4.80; Open: Wed–Mon Apr–Oct 10 a.m.–5 p.m., Nov–Mar 10 a.m.–4 p.m.) — a world-renowned center — are the repository of ancient techniques and skills. In the museum, you can delight in the amazing creations at leisure, without salespeople pressing you to buy. The **Duomo,** with its tilting campanile, is just across the street and features a Tiepolo *Crucifixion;* it's open daily from 9 a.m. to 12:30 p.m. and 3 to 6 p.m.

✔ **Lido** (Vaporetto: 1, 6, 51, 52, or 82) is the long barrier island that protects the lagoon from the open sea. Inhabited since ancient times, it bloomed at the end of the 19th century with the development of an elegant Art Nouveau resort. Its name means "beach," so it's no surprise that its huge **beach** is where Venetians come to take their seaside vacations. It feels a bit like California, with a lot of green spaces and a beach atmosphere (cars can circulate here). The Lido is also the site of some of the most elegant hotels from the early 1900s, such as the **Hotel des Bains** (Lungomare Marconi 17; ☎ **800-3253535** in the U.S., or 041-5265921; www.starwood italy.com; closed Nov to mid-Mar), restored by Starwood to its Art Nouveau splendor (Thomas Mann's *Death in Venice* was set here). Many visitors stay at one of Lido's numerous hotels because it's only a short *vaporetto* ride from San Marco — and you get much more for your money. You can spend a decadent evening at the elegant historic **casino** (still functioning in summer), ride a bike around this barrier island (which extends for 11km/7 miles), or play golf. If you choose to bike, you can rent one not far from the ferry station at **Gardin Anna Vallè** (Piazzale Santa Maria Elisabetta 2/a, ☎ 041-2760005).

✔ The period before Lent — known as Mardi Gras in New Orleans — is celebrated as **Carnevale** all over Italy, and Venice's celebrations are spectacular, culminating the week before Ash Wednesday (usually in Feb) and on the last day, *Martedi Grasso* (Fat Tuesday). In 1797, Napoleon suppressed Carnevale, which had grown into a month-long bacchanal, but this festive holiday was revived in 1980 and is a big deal in Venice. The city is famous for its elaborate costumes and masks, which are historical and elegant rather than Halloween-ish. Musical events take place at all times, and big crowds surge all over. Some of the events are reserved only for those who are in disguise, such as the Gran Ballo in Piazza San Marco. Other events include a daily Children's Carnevale on Piazza San Polo, a cortege of decorated boats on the Canal Grande, and a market of Venetian costumes at Santo Stefano (see "Shopping the Local Stores" later for other sources of authentic Venetian getups). Costumes are for rent at **Tragicomica di Gualtiero dell'Osto** (Campiello dei Meloni, 2800 San Polo; ☎ 041-721101; Vaporetto: 1 to San Stae).

✔ If you love the work of Palladio, the famous architect of so many elegant villas along the Brenta river (see Padua in Chapter 17), you should not miss some of his best churches here in Venice. The **Chiesa del Redentore** (Campo del Redentore on the Giudecca island; Vaporetto: 82 to Redentore; Admission: 2.50€/$3; Open: Mon–Sat 10 a.m.–5 p.m.) is the largest, built in the 16th century to celebrate the end of yet another spell of the black death; huge yet perfectly proportioned, the monument was decorated by important artists including Tintoretto and Veronese. We prefer the smaller but still imposing — and much less visited — **San Giorgio Maggiore** (Vaporetto: 82 to San Giorgio; free admission; Open: Mon–Sat 9:30 a.m.–12:30 p.m. and daily 2:30–4:30 p.m., till 6:30 pm. in summer), on the small San Giorgio island across from Riva degli Schiavoni. Palladio died before its completion, but he would have been proud of the result; the interior is decorated with works by great artists, including Tintoretto, who left two of his masterpieces here: the *Last Supper* and the *Fall of the Manna*, both in the presbytery. Sunday mass at 11 a.m. is chanted Gregorian style.

Seeing Venice by guided tour

If you'd like your own personal guided tour, take advantage of the **PlanetAudio guide** (☎ 041-5285051; www.planetaudioguide.com), the first outdoor audio tour in Italy, automatically activated by your walking, thanks to the complex GPS technology. You'll find it at the tourist info desks (10 percent discount with the Venice Card). The best traditional guided tours are offered by **American Express** (Salizzada San Moisè, 1471 San Marco; ☎ 041-5200844; Vaporetto: 1 or 82 to San Marco–Vallaresso), for about 27€ ($32) for a two-hour tour and 40€ ($48) for a full day.

Suggested one-, two-, and three-day itineraries

Time in Venice always seems to fly. Here are a few suggestions on how to schedule your visit:

Venice in one day

If you have only one day in Venice, you definitely want to make the most of it with an early start. Begin your day on **Piazza San Marco** with a visit to the **Basilica,** including the climb to the **loggia** upstairs, where the light is at its most beautiful in the morning. You should then have a little time left for the **Doge's Palace.** Have a *caffè* or *cappuccino* on the terrace of one of the two historic cafes — **Caffè Florian** and **Caffè Quadri** (see "Living It Up After Dark," later in this chapter) — on the *piazza:* expensive, but oh so romantic. Afterward, have a look at the beautiful Murano glass — and maybe even buy some — in **Venini** and **Pauly & C.** or at the more affordable **Marco Polo** (see "Shopping the Local Stores," later in this chapter). Then walk toward the Accademia, taking the footbridge over the Canal Grande and having lunch in the lively area nearby at **Osteria da Fiore.** If you just want a sweet snack, the **Pasticceria Tonolo** is wonderful (see "Dining Out," earlier in this chapter). After you've had a bite to eat, visit the **Gallerie dell'Accademia** for a tour of several hundred years of Venetian art. You'll then be in the mood for a Venetian *aperitivo* — a *cicchetto* (a glass of dry wine accompanied by some savory tidbits) — in one of the small bars near the Accademia, or across the Canal Grande at the **Antico Martini.** Treat yourself to dinner at **Met** in the Hotel Metropole. Take a post-dinner **gondola ride** if you can afford it or settle for a slow ride down the **Canal Grande** on *vaporetto* line no. 1. Bask in that magical atmosphere, the glorious facades of the *palazzi* lining the canal, and the romantic **Ponte di Rialto** as you pass beneath it.

Venice in two days

Two days in Venice are better than one, but you still don't have time to waste. Here is what we would do:

Day 1

Start off by following our one-day itinerary, above, in the morning, but dedicate more time to **St. Mark's Basilica.** In the afternoon, take a tour of the **Doge's Palace** and the **Bridge of Sighs.** After your visits, head to **Antico Martini** for a well deserved *aperitivo* and possibly dinner. Afterward, stroll to the **Ponte di Rialto.**

Day 2

Devote your morning to the **Gallerie dell'Accademia.** Have lunch at **Osteria da Fiore** and, after you eat, visit the **Basilica de' Frari** and the **Scuola Grande di San Rocco.** Follow our dinner and after-dinner recommendations in "Venice in one day" itinerary, above.

Venice in three days

On Day 1 and 2, follow our "Venice in two days" itinerary, above. Dedicate your third day to the Lagoon, visiting first **Murano,** with its **Glass Museum** and the showrooms of the most famous glassmakers, and then **Burano,** with its **Lace Museum.** End the day with a bike ride on the island of **Lido;** if it's high season, take a swim and grab drinks at the **Casino.** Alternatively, you can visit the other top churches in Venice: **Santa Maria della Salute** and Palladio's masterpieces, **Chiesa del Redentore** and **San Giorgio Maggiore.**

Shopping the Local Stores

Venice's most renowned wares reflect the city's aura of delicate, shimmering beauty. Where else would you find exquisite goblets tinged with gold, or lace as fine as snowflakes? Where else would fine paper be fashioned from molds from the 18th century? The good stuff is definitely here, but so is the not-so-good: Be careful to buy only from reputable merchants.

Best shopping areas

In Venice, you may feel like a bull in a china shop — there's glass here, there, and everywhere. You'll be tempted to buy some as a souvenir. For a real Murano art object, the best bets are the — usually expensive — showrooms of Murano's big names of glassmaking, as well as galleries carrying a selection of works by several glass artists. Another option, of course, is to go to **Murano** itself and shop around; a huge array of glass shops and showrooms lines both sides of the **Rio dei Vetrai** (see "Finding more cool things to see and do," earlier in this chapter). Prices will be the same as in town, but the selection will be larger.

If your thing is lace, you should be even more careful than with glass: You may find local handmade lace, or local but not handmade, or not handmade at all and actually produced thousands of miles away. **Burano** (see "Finding more cool things to see and do," earlier in this chapter) has become an outdoor market selling everything from machine-made stuff from Singapore to genuine handmade local lace. Again, if you know your linens and laces, you can tell what you're getting. If not, going to a reputable shop in Venice may be better.

For general shopping, the best streets are the **Mercerie** (the zigzag route from the Piazza San Marco clock tower to the Ponte di Rialto) and the path leading from Piazza San Marco to Campo Santo Stefano, including

Calle Larga XXII Marzo. Here you can find big-name Italian stores specializing in everything from shoes to housewares to clothing.

What to look for and where to find it

Venice is known for its exquisite blown glass, lace, fine paper, and the incredibly beautiful Carnevale costumes; lesser-known items include lovely hand-worked metal (both iron and brass) and blown-glass lanterns.

Generally, shopping hours are daily from 9 a.m. to 1 p.m. and 3:30 to 7:30 p.m. In Venice, only local neighborhood shops close on Sundays.

Cast iron

Murano chandeliers are gorgeous, but lanterns are also very beautiful and affordable. At **De Rossi** (showroom at Strada Nuova, 4311 Cannaregio; ☎ 041-5222436; workshop at Fondamenta Nuove, 5045 Cannaregio; ☎ 041-5200077), you'll find a large collection of Venetian lanterns, the glass blown directly inside the handmade iron fittings, plus a variety of other iron and brass work.

Glass

Founded in the early 1920s, **Venini** (Piazzetta dei Leoncini, just to the left of St. Mark's Basilica, 314 San Marco; ☎ 041-5224045; Vaporetto: 1 or 82 to San Marco-Vallaresso; and at Fondamenta Vetrai, Murano 47/50; ☎ 041-2737211; www.venini.com) is world renowned. Prices are what you'd expect for works of art; one drinking glass could cost up to $1,000.

Pauly & C. (Palazzo Trevisan Cappello, Ponte dei Consorzi 4391/A San Marco, off Calle Larga San Marco; ☎ 041-5209899; www.paulyglass factory.com) has three nice boutiques in Piazza San Marco (Piazza San Marco 73, ☎ 041-5235484; Piazza San Marco 77, ☎ 041-277-0279; and Piazza San Marco 316, ☎ 041-523-5575). If you have the time, though, visit the company headquarters on Rio di Palazzo, where you'll see a large collection of antiques and high-quality copies of ancient models.

Barovier & Toso (Fondamenta Vetrai, Murano 28; ☎ 041-739049; www.barovier.com) has been a family business since the 13th century. You can visit its showroom as well as a small but rich museum with its historic pieces, both housed in a 17th-century *palazzo* in Murano.

L'Isola (Campo San Moise, 1468 San Marco; ☎ 041-5231973; Vaporetto: 1 or 82 to San Marco–Vallaresso) is the showroom of Carlo Moretti, one of Murano's great names.

The gallery **Murano Collezioni** (Fondamenta Manin, Murano 1CD; ☎ 041-736272) has a selection of works by the three biggest names in Venetian glass — Barovier & Toso, Venini, and Carlo Moretti — and makes for good one-stop shopping if you're short on time.

Lace

Jesurum (Mercerie del Capitello, 4857 San Marco; ☎ 041-5206177; www. jesurum.it; Vaporetto: 1 or 82 to San Marco–Vallaresso) is a reliable lace shop that's been in business since the 1870s. High quality is expensive, but the range of items, from cocktail napkins to bed linens, means that you stand a good chance of finding something within your budget.

Another good choice is **Martinuzzi** (Piazza San Marco, 67/A San Marco; ☎ 041-5225068), with an extensive selection of beautiful lace and embroidered linen.

Masks and costumes

If you're in town to enjoy Carnevale and you didn't pack your 18th-century finery, you're going to need a mask, at the very least. The **Laboratorio Artigianale Maschere,** just a short way from SS. Giovanni e Paolo (Barbaria delle Tole, 6657 Castello; ☎ 041-522310; Vaporetto: 41, 42, 51, or 52 to Ospedale), has some of the most beautiful costumes.

Another option is the more affordable **Mondonovo** (Rio Terà Canal, 3063 Dorsoduro; ☎ 041-5287344; Vaporetto: 1 or 82 to Accademia). Still, expect to pay 16€ ($19) for a basic mask; for the most beautiful and artistic masks, prices run much higher.

Paper

Handmade marbleized paper is a specialty of Venice, and **Piazzesi** (Campiello della Feltrina, just off Santa Maria del Giglio, 2511 San Marco; ☎ 041-5221202; Vaporetto: 1 to Giglio) is said to be one of the oldest in the business — founded in 1900.

Living It Up After Dark

As is often the case in Italy, nightlife for the locals means visiting pubs, sitting at the outdoor terraces of well-placed cafes, going to concerts, and (for the younger crowd) dancing at discos. Nightlife ends early in Venice and you'll be hard-pressed to find a place that stays open much past midnight. For the big discos, you have to go to Lido or the Terraferma.

The performing arts

Many Venice churches and *palazzi* become venues for concerts — mostly classical — throughout the year. You'll find a schedule of events in the free brochure *Un Ospite a Venezia,* distributed by the tourist office. The **Teatro Goldoni** (Calle Goldoni, 4650/B San Marco; ☎ 041-2402011; Vaporetto: 1 or 82 to Rialto) is one of Venice's premier theaters and one of the oldest, dating back to the 17th century. Venice's largest opera theater, the **Teatro La Fenice** (Campo San Fantin, 1965 San Marco; ☎ 041-786511; www.teatrolafenice.it) is perhaps the most elegant in Italy. True to its mythological name, it was reborn from its ashes twice, after the fire of 1836 and the more recent one of 1996. Tickets are about 12€ to 50€ ($14–$60).

Bars, pubs, and clubs

Since Hemingway's days in Venice, one of the classic things for visitors to do is head to **Harry's Bar** (Calle Vallaresso, 1323 San Marco; ☎ 041-528-5777; Vaporetto: 1 to San Marco–Vallaresso) for a martini or a Bellini (made with proscceo, a champagne-like white wine, and the juice of white peaches). The **Devil's Forest Pub** (Calle Stagneri, 5185 San Marco; ☎ 041-5200623; Vaporetto: 1 or 82 to Rialto) is often crowded. Another popular spot, with younger crowds as well, is the wine bar **VinoVino** (Ponte della Veste, San Marco 2007a; ☎ 041-2417688; closed Tues), which offers a choice of over 350 wines. Attached to the Antico Martini restaurant is the **Martini Scala** (Campo San Fantin, 1980 San Marco, left of Teatro La Fenice; ☎ 041-522-4121; closed Tues), open until 3:30 a.m. with a good live piano bar. **Bacaro Jazz** (Rialto, San Marco 5546; ☎ 041-5285249) is a wine bar with good music. At **Il Piccolo Mondo** (Calle Contarini Corfu, Dorsoduro 1056a; ☎ 041-5200371), near Accademia, you'll find younger crowds; the action goes on often until 4 a.m.

You won't find any gay or lesbian bars in Venice, but as someone once said, every bar in Venice is a gay bar if you look in the right corner.

Cafes

Right on St. Mark's Square are two packed restaurant-cafes that square off (sorry!) against each other with classical music ensembles. They've been here forever: **Caffè Florian** (☎ 041-5205641; www.caffeflorian.com) since 1720 and **Caffè Quadri** (☎ 041-5222105; www.quadrivenice.com) since 1638. If you want something a little more authentic, **Le Cafe** (Campo Santo Stefano, 2797 San Marco; ☎ 041-5237201; Vaporetto: 1 or 82 to Accademia, then cross the bridge) serves a large assortment of drinks, good coffee, and salads at its outdoor tables.

Venice's Casino

The historic **Palazzo Vendramin-Calergi** (Campo San Marcuola, Cannaregio 2079; ☎ 041-5297111; www.casinovenezia.it; Vaporetto: 1 or 82 to San Marcuola) — the great composer Richard Wagner died here in 1883 — hosts Venice's casino from October through May. You'll need to be at least 18, and wearing a jacket and tie, to enter this elegant venue offering roulette, card games, and a few slot machines. In summer, the action moves to the island of Lido, where the **Municipal Casino** (Lungomare Marconi 4; ☎ 041-5297132; dedicated shuttle boat from Ferrovia, Piazzale Roma, and San Marco) welcomes its guests in a grand, if a bit stiff, atmosphere. It also offers dining and live shows.

Fast Facts: Venice

American Express

The office is at Salizzada San Moisè, 1471 San Marco (☎ 041-520-0844; Vaporetto: 1 or 82 to San Marco Vallaresso). Summer hours are Monday through Saturday from 8 a.m. to 8 p.m. for currency exchange, 8 a.m. to 5:30 p.m. for everything else; winter hours are Monday through Friday from 9 a.m. to 5:30 p.m., Saturday from 9 a.m. to 12:30 p.m.

Area Code

The local area code is **041** (see "Telephone" in the "Fast Facts" section of Appendix A for more on calling to and from Italy).

ATMs

You'll find banks with ATMs along Mercerie, Campo Santo Stefano, Calle Larga XXII Marzo, and Strada Nuova.

Doctors

The U.K. consulate and the American Express office keep a list of English-speaking doctors and dentists.

Embassies and Consulates

The consulate of the United Kingdom is at Piazzale Donatori di Sangue 2, Mestre (☎ 041-5055990); all others are in Rome and Milan.

Emergencies

For an ambulance, call ☎ **118;** for the fire department, call ☎ **115;** for first aid *(pronto soccorso),* call ☎ **041-5203222.**

Hospitals

The Ospedali Civili Riuniti di Venezia (Campo SS. Giovanni e Paolo; ☎ 041-260711; Vaporetto: 41, 42, 51, or 52 to Ospedale) has English-speaking doctors.

Information

The APT (Fondamenta San Lorenzo, Castello 5050, 30122 Venezia; ☎ **041-5298700;** www.venicetouristboard.com and www.turismovenezia.it) maintains tourist info desks at the airport (☎ 041-5298711; open daily 9:30 a.m.–7:30 p.m.); Piazzale Roma (☎ 041-5298711; open daily 9:30 a.m.–6:30 p.m.); Santa Lucia train station (☎ 041-5298711; open daily 8 a.m.–6:30 p.m.); Lido (☎ 041-5265711; open daily June–Sept 9 a.m.–12:30 p.m. and 3:30–6 p.m.); San Marco all'Ascensione (☎ 041-5298711; open daily 9 a.m.–3:30 p.m.); and Venice Pavillion off the San Marco *vaporetto* stop (San Marco Ex Giardini Reali; ☎ 041-5298711; open daily 10 a.m.–6 p.m.)

Internet Access

Venetian Navigator (Calle della Casselleria, 5300 Castello; ☎ 041-2771056; www.venetiannavigator.com; open 10 a.m.–10 p.m. in summer, 10 a.m.–8.30 p.m. in winter) is only steps behind St. Mark's.

Maps

One of the best maps is by Falk, but many other maps are available at most bookstores and newsstands around town.

Newspapers and Magazines

Most newsstands in town sell English-language papers. One of the largest is in the Santa Lucia train station. A helpful small publication, available in all major hotels, is *Un Ospite a Venezia,* a guide on everything from public transportation to special events.

Pharmacies

A centrally located one is the International Pharmacy (Calle Larga XXII Marzo, 2067 San Marco; ☎ 041-5222311; Vaporetto: 1 or

82 to San Marco–Vallaresso). If you need a pharmacy after-hours, ask your hotel or call ☎ 192 to get a list of those open near you.

Police

Call ☎ 113.

Post Office

You can find many post offices around town, but the central one is the *ufficio postale* near Ponte di Rialto (Fontego dei Tedeschi, 5550 San Marco; ☎ 041-271-7111).

Restrooms

The town maintains a number of well-kept public toilets — disabled accessible — available for a fee (free with the Venice Card; see "Exploring Venice," earlier in this chapter). The most centrally located are at the Giardini Reali and at the Diurno off Piazza San Marco, at San Bartolomeo near Ponte di Rialto; at Rialto Novo in San Polo; by the Accademia in Dorsoduro; and at San Leonardo in Cannaregio. They are well marked by signs on the walls and are open daily from 8 a.m. to 8 p.m.

Safety

Venice is very safe, even in solitary, off-the-beaten-path areas. The only real danger are pickpockets, always plentiful in areas with lots of tourists. Watch your bag and

camera, and don't display wads of cash or jewelry.

Smoking

In 2005, Italy passed a law outlawing smoking in most public places. Smoking is allowed only where there is a separate, ventilated area for nonsmokers. If smoking at your table is important to you, call beforehand to make sure the restaurant or cafe you'll be visiting offers a smoking area.

Taxes

See Chapter 5 for information on IVA (Value Added Tax).

Taxis

Walk to, or call for pickup at, one of the water-taxi docks around the city: San Marco (☎ 041-5229750); Ferrovia (☎ 041-716286); and Piazzale Roma (☎ 041-716922); Rialto (☎ 041-723112). Or call one of the taxi firms: Cooperativa Veneziana (☎ 041-716124) in Cannaregio; Cooperativa Serenissima (☎ 041-5221265) in Castello; or Cooperativa San Marco (☎ 041-5222303).

Weather Updates

Your best bet is the news on TV. (There's no phone number for weather forecasts in Italy, as there is in the U.S.)

Chapter 17

Padua, Verona, and Milan

. . . .

In This Chapter

▶ Discovering Padua and the famous Giotto frescoes

▶ Thrilling to Verona, the setting for the legend of Romeo and Juliet

▶ Shopping 'til you drop in bustling Milan

. . . .

*W*ith its art and unique setting, Venice towers over all other cities in northern Italy, shadowing many real gems. A little farther inland from Venice is **Padua,** with its wealth of churches and museums. Moving farther to the west is pleasant **Verona,** drawing visitors from all over the world to see the **House of Juliet** — which they like to believe was once the home of Shakespeare's tragic heroine — and the city's ancient Roman and Renaissance architecture. Finally, there's **Milan,** which is such an important business center — renowned for both its sizzling fashion and incredible shopping opportunities — that one forgets its art: **Leonardo da Vinci's** *Last Supper* and Milan's grandiose Gothic **Duomo,** for example, seem all but trifles.

Padua and Verona make easy day trips from Venice (Padua also makes an excellent base) — you can see the highlights of each in a few hours. Milan is farther west and a much larger city; if you want to see both its sides — the art and the shopping — we recommend you spend the night.

Padua: Home of Giotto's Fabulous Frescoes

Padua (Padova) is a small but bustling, elegant yet modern city, as well as the Veneto's economic heart. The historic district is delightful and full of artistic surprises, beyond Giotto's justly famous frescoes in the **Cappella degli Scrovegni,** so breathtaking that they dwarf the other worthy attractions in town. From its canals to its churches, Padua will not disappoint you.

You can easily see the highlights in one day, but spending the night will allow you to fully enjoy the town. In high season, or if you're on a budget, Padua also makes an excellent base for visiting Venice and the rest of the region, as it has less expensive and much less crowded hotels.

Getting there

On the main **train** route from Rome to the northeast, Padua enjoys excellent rail connections (☎ **892021;** www.trenitalia.it). The city is only 30 minutes from Venice, with trains running as frequently as every few minutes during rush hour; the fare is about 8€ ($10). The trip from Rome lasts four and a half hours and costs about 45€ ($54). The Padua **train station** is on Piazza Stazione (☎ **049-8751800**), a 10- to 15-minute walk from the town's major attractions. If you don't feel like walking, though, you can use the excellent bus service; a 75-minute ticket costs 1€ ($1.20). Get a bus map from the tourist office in the train station.

If you're getting here by **car,** Padua lies at the convergence of the *autostrada* A4 (east–west) and A13 (north–south); you can easily reach it by car from any direction. Traffic in the historic district is restricted, so park in one of the town-run lots: APS parking on **Prato della Valle,** at the **train station,** and on **Via Fra' Paolo Sarpi.**

Spending the night

You'd expect to find plenty of delightful hotels tucked away in the heart of Padua's romantic historic district — but the few that there are tend to be old-fashioned and lack style; the service is professional and kind, but the décor is always a bit drab. That said, below is our selection of the best hotels within walking distance of the major attractions.

Hotel Grand'Italia
$$ Train Station

Housed in a beautiful late-19th-century Liberty (Italian Art Nouveau) building that's been completely restored, this hotel offers excellent service — including baby sitting — and a very central location, which, together with the historic setting, makes it our preferred choice in town. The public spaces have been carefully decorated with fine antiques and carpets. The large and bright guest rooms are appointed with fine fabrics and contemporary furnishings.

See map p. 350. Via P. Bronzetti 62, across from the train station. ☎ 049-8761111. Fax: 049-8750850. www.hotelgranditalia.it. *Parking: 15€ ($18). Rack rates: 210€ ($252) double. Rates include buffet breakfast. AE, DC, MC, V.*

Hotel Plaza
$$ Center

The most popular hotel in town with businesspeople, the Plaza offers accommodations in line with international standards — large, carpeted rooms decorated with modern European furniture, as well as stylish public areas — but is housed in a nondescript modern building. The nearby annex offers nicely appointed suites and mini-apartments. Amenities include Wi-Fi and a gym.

The Pianura Padana and Milan

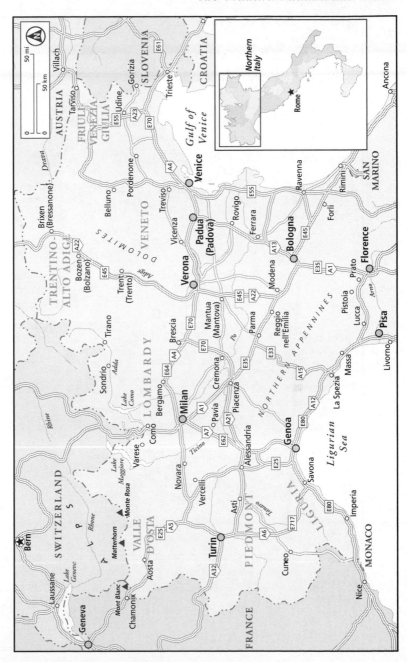

Padua

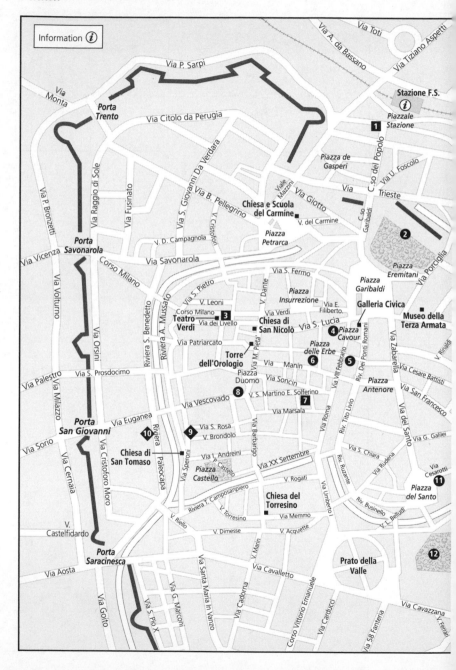

Information ⓘ

Via Toti

Via A. da Bassano

Via P. Sarpi

Via Tiziano Aspetti

Via Monta

Porta Trento

Via Citolo da Perugia

Stazione F.S.
ⓘ
Piazzale Stazione
1

Via P. Bronzetti

Via Raggio di Sole

Via Fusinato

Via S. Giovanni Da Verdara

Via B. Pellegrino

V. Cristofori

Piazza de Gasperi

C.so del Popolo

Via U. Foscolo

Via Giotto

Via

C.so Garibaldi

Trieste

Chiesa e Scuola del Carmine

V. del Carmine

Piazza Petrarca

2

Porta Savonarola

Via Vicenza

V. D. Campagnola

Via Savonarola

Corso Milano

Via S. Fermo

Piazza Eremitani

Via Porciglia

Via Volturno

Via S. Pietro

V. Leoni

Corso Milano

Via dei Livello

Via Patriarcato

Via Dante

Piazza Insurrezione

Piazza Garibaldi

Via E. Filiberto.

Via Verdi

Teatro Verdi **3**

Chiesa di San Nicolò

Via S. Lucia

Galleria Civica

Museo della Terza Armata

Riviera S. Benedetto

Riviera A. Mussato

V. M. Pietà

4 Piazza Cavour

Riv. Dei Ponti Romani

Via Zabarella

V. Rinaldi

Torre dell'Orologio

Via Manin

Piazza delle Erbe **6**

5

Via III Febbraio

Via Cesare Battisti

Via S. Prosdocimo

Piazza Duomo **8**

Via Soncin

V. S. Martino E. Solferino

7

Piazza Antenore

Riv. Tito Livio

Via San Francesco

Via Palestro

Via Milazzo

Via Orsini

Porta San Giovanni

Via Euganea **10**

Via Vescovado

Via Marsala

Via Roma

Via del Santo

Via Sorio

Via Cernaia

Via Cristoforo Moro

Riviera Paleocapa

9

Via S. Rosa

V. Brondolo

Via Barbarigo

Via XX Settembre

Riv. Ruzante

Via S. Chiara

Riv. Rudena

Via G. Galilei

Chiesa di San Tomaso

Via Speroni

A. Castello

Via I. Andreini

Piazza Castello

V. Rogati

Via Umberto I

Via Cesarotti

Piazza del Santo **11**

V. Castelfidardo

Riviera T. Camposanpiero

V. Torresino

Chiesa del Torresino

Via Memmo

Riv. Businello

V. E. Belludi

Porta Saracinesca

Via Aosta

V. Riello

V. Marin

V. Dimesse

V. Acquette

Prato della Valle

12

Via Cavazzana

V. Ferari

Via Goito

Via Santa Maria in Vanzo

Via G. Marconi

Via S. Pio X

V. Cadorna

Via Cavalletto

Corso Vittorio Emanuele

Via Carducci

Via S8 Fanteria

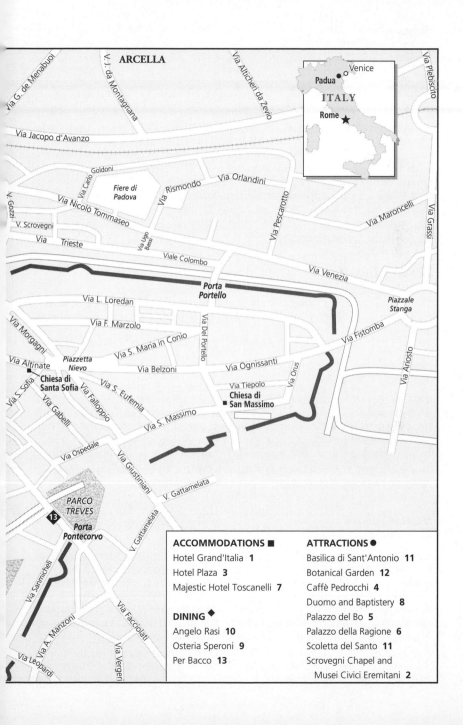

ARCELLA

V.-J.-da Montagnana

V.-J.-da Altichieri da Zevio

Via G. de Menabuoi

Via Plebiscito

Venice

Padua

ITALY

Rome

Via Jacopo d'Avanzo

Goldoni

Fiere di Padova

Rismondo

Via Orlandini

Via Carlo

V. Gozzi

Via Nicolò Tommaseo

V. Scrovegni

Via Pescarotto

Via Maroncelli

Via Grassi

Via Trieste

Via Ugo Bassi

Viale Colombo

Via Venezia

Porta Portello

Via L. Loredan

Piazzale Stanga

Via Morgagni

Via F. Marzolo

Via Del Portello

Via S. Maria in Conio

Via Fistomba

Via Altinate

Piazzetta Nievo

Via Belzoni

Via Ognissanti

Via Orus

Via Ariosto

Chiesa di Santa Sofia

Via S. Sofia

Via S. Eufemia

Via Falloppio

Via Tiepolo

Chiesa di San Massimo

Via Gabelli

Via S. Massimo

Via Ospedale

Via Giustiniani

V. Gattamelata

PARCO TREVES

13

Porta Pontecorvo

Via Gattamelata

V. Gattamelata

Via Sanmicheli

Via A. Manzoni

Via Facciolati

Via Leopardi

Via Vergeri

ACCOMMODATIONS ■

Hotel Grand'Italia **1**

Hotel Plaza **3**

Majestic Hotel Toscanelli **7**

DINING ◆

Angelo Rasi **10**

Osteria Speroni **9**

Per Bacco **13**

ATTRACTIONS ●

Basilica di Sant'Antonio **11**

Botanical Garden **12**

Caffè Pedrocchi **4**

Duomo and Baptistery **8**

Palazzo del Bo **5**

Palazzo della Ragione **6**

Scoletta del Santo **11**

Scrovegni Chapel and
    Musei Civici Eremitani **2**

See map p. 350. Corso Milano 40. ☎ *049-656822.* Fax: 049-661117. www.plaza
padova.it. Parking: 15€ ($18) in hotel garage. Rack rates: 200€ ($240) double.
Rates include buffet breakfast. AE, DC, MC, V.

Majestic Hotel Toscanelli
$$ Center

Just off an old market square, this is one of the best hotels in town and a
charming place to stay. The staff is helpful and the service excellent —
there's even baby sitting — while the public spaces are elegantly outfitted
with marble floors and fine furnishings. The guest rooms have been
renovated — some in Venetian baroque and others in Victorian style. You
won't lack for atmosphere, comfort, or amenities (including Wi-Fi).

See map p. 350. Via dell'Arco 2. ☎ *049-663244.* Fax: 049-8760025. www.toscanelli.
com. Parking: 19€ ($23) valet in hotel garage. Rack rates: 172€ ($206) double. Rates
include buffet breakfast. AE, DC, MC, V.

Dining locally

Padua's cuisine is typically Italian, with a Venetian influence. As a univer-
sity town, it offers a variety of cheap lunch spots, particularly on Piazza
Cavour and along Via Matteotti, with everything from pasta and pizza to
sandwiches.

Angelo Rasi
$ Centro PADUAN

This moderately priced *osteria* is famous for its excellent cuisine and
friendly service. In summer, you can dine in the pretty garden, which chil-
dren seem to enjoy. Good choices include ravioli with fresh herbs and *bac-
calà mantecato* (creamed cod), as well as a variety of surf or turf *secondi;*
half-portions are available for the little ones. The wine list is excellent.

See map p. 350. Riviera Paleocapa 7. ☎ *049-8719797.* Reservations recommended.
Secondi: 11€–15€ ($13–$18). MC, V. Open: Tues–Sun 7:30–10 p.m.

Osteria Speroni
$$ Centro PADUAN/SEAFOOD

Down the street from the Basilica di Sant'Antonio, this moderately priced
restaurant offers welcoming dining rooms and good cuisine. The menu
includes regional dishes from coastal Veneto, with an accent on seafood;
some of the specialties are *capitone* (a local kind of eel), when it's in
season, and fresh whole fish cooked in a salt crust. We also recommend
the superb antipasto buffet that can be a meal into itself; it includes a variety of preparations, from fried calamari to marinated zucchini.

See map p. 350. Via Speroni 36. ☎ *049-8753370.* Reservations recommended.
Secondi: 12€–20€ ($14–$24). AE, MC, V. Open: Mon–Sat 12:30–2:30 p.m. and
8–10:30 p.m. Closed 3 weeks in Aug.

Per Bacco
$$ Centro CREATIVE/ENOTECA

True to its name, this is a temple to good wine, with a wine list that includes hundreds of labels by the glass — all of it accompanied by excellent cuisine. The *ravioli di ricotta alla crema* (ricotta ravioli with a cream sauce) are delicious; we recommend following them with *composizione Per Bacco*, a tasting of three different meat dishes, which may include the excellent stuffed quail on a bed of zucchini, mint, and green apple, or the rabbit with pears.

See map p. 350. Piazzale Pontecorvo 10. ☎ *049-8754664.* www.per-bacco.it. *Reservations recommended. Secondi: 11€–21€ ($13–$25). AE, DC, MC, V. Open: Tues–Sun noon to 2:30 p.m. and 7:30–11 p.m. Closed 1 week in Jan and 2 weeks in Aug.*

Exploring Padua

Although Padua isn't very large and you can easily explore it on foot, you may like the new hop-on/hop-off tour offered by **City Sightseeing** (www.padova.city-sightseeing.it) from May through September. Buses depart from Basilica di Sant'Antonio every 20 to 30 minutes between 9 a.m. and 6 p.m. The route lasts one hour if you stay on board. Tickets — for sale on the bus and valid 24 hours — cost 13€ ($16) for adults and 6.50€ ($7.80) for children 5 to 15.

If you visit in high season, we recommend taking a **boat tour** of the historic network of urban canals; these inner waterways have been used for centuries and afford a very special view of Padua (see "More cool things to see and do," later in this section).

Associazione Guide Turistiche (☎ 049-8209741; www.guidepadova.it) offers a variety of walking tours — with classical, religious, scientific, and other themes — and will even custom-design a tour for you. Prices vary, depending on the number of persons and the length of the tour.

For 14€ ($17), the **Padova Card** (☎ 049-8767927; www.apt.padova.it) is an excellent deal, granting one adult (and one child under 12) free public transportation, parking in the APS lots, and admission to the major museums in town (except the 1€/$1.20 reservations fee for the Scrovegni Chapel). It also gives discounts on boat tours, City Sightseeing tours, and other guided tours (see later in this section). It's valid for 48 hours and is available at tourist info desks and at each participating attraction, including the parking lots.

The top attractions

Basilica di Sant'Antonio

Built in the 13th century, this basilica houses the remains of St. Anthony of Padua (including his tongue, still amazingly undecayed). The construction's distinctive Romanesque-Gothic style reveals Eastern influences, most visible in the eight round domes and the several *campanili* (bell towers) that are vaguely reminiscent of minarets. In front of the church is one of Donatello's masterpieces, the **equestrian statue of Gattamelata,** with a true-to-life horse and rider. Several prominent Renaissance artists worked on the church interior: Donatello sculpted the **bronze crucifix, reliefs,** and **statues** on the high altar (1444–48), whereas the **frescoes** are by 14th-century artists Altichiero and Giusto de' Menabuoi. From the basilica cloisters, you can access the **Museo Antoniano,** with a collection of works of art from the basilica; the stars are a fresco by **Mantegna** and a painting by **Tiepolo.** Attached to the basilica is the 14th-century **Oratory of San Giorgio** (ring the gatekeeper in the adjacent building if it's not open), decorated with a fine cycle of frescoes by Altichiero da Zevio, restored in 2000. Next door to the right is the **Scoletta del Santo,** a chapel and guild house in the style of the Venetian *Scole* built in the 15th century. The second floor was added at the beginning of the 16th century and decorated with sculptures and paintings by various artists — among them **Titian,** who left three beautiful frescoes.

See map p. 350. Piazza del Santo 11. Basilica: ☎ *049-8789722. Museum: 049-8225656.* www.santantonio.org. *Admission: Basilica free; Oratorio di San Giorgio 1.50€ ($1.80); Scoletta 1.55€ ($1.90); Museo Antoniano 2.50€ ($3). Open: Basilica summer daily 6:20 a.m.–7:45 p.m., winter daily 6:20 a.m.–7 p.m.; Oratorio and Scoletta summer daily 9 a.m.–12:30 p.m. and 2:30–7 p.m., winter daily 9 a.m.–12:30 p.m. and 2:30–5 p.m.; Museo Antoniano daily 9 a.m.–1 p.m. and 2–6 p.m.*

Duomo and Baptistery

Built between the 16th and 18th centuries, Padua's Duomo was partly designed by Michelangelo. Behind the unfinished facade, the two points of interest are the paintings in the **Sacristy** and the statues by Florentine artist Giuliano Vangi in the new **Presbytery.** Attached to the Duomo is a remarkable **Baptistery** dating from 1075 and recently restored; its interior is a 14th-century masterpiece, completely decorated with beautiful frescoes by Giusto de' Menabuoi that illustrate scenes from the lives of John the Baptist and Christ. A vision of paradise is gloriously depicted on the domed ceiling.

See map p. 350. Piazza Duomo. ☎ *049-656914. Admission: Duomo free; Baptistery 2.50€ ($3), free with Padova Card. Open: Duomo Mon–Sat 7:30 a.m. to noon and 3:45–7:30 p.m., Sun 7:45 a.m.–1 p.m. and 3:45–8:30 p.m.; Baptistery daily 10 a.m.–6 p.m. Closed Jan 1, Easter, and Dec 25.*

Palazzo della Ragione

Opening onto **Piazza delle Erbe** on one side and **Piazza della Frutta** on the other, this was the heart of medieval and Renaissance Padua. Open-air markets — a fresh produce market on one side, a fruit and dry-goods market on the other — were held then as today, and are still lively and colorful affairs. The ground floor, an elegantly colonnaded structure, was built in 1218, and it served as the seat of the city's courts of law and its assembly hall. The upper level, known as the *salone* (Great Hall), was added in

1306; it is a fine example of medieval architecture and one of the largest of its kind in the world: one huge open hall measuring 81m x 27m x 27m high (265 ft. x 89 ft. x 89 ft.) and topped with a beautifully crafted wooden vaulted roof. The rich wall frescoes, illustrating religious and astrological themes, date from the 15th century; they replaced the original 13th-century frescoes by Giotto and his school, which were unfortunately destroyed by fire. The *palazzo's* biggest conversation piece is a giant wooden horse built for a jousting event in 1466. Today, after a complete restoration that ended in 2002, the building houses special exhibitions.

See map p. 350. Via VIII Febbraio, between Piazza delle Erbe and Piazza della Frutta. ☎ *049-8205006. Admission: 8€ ($10); free with Padova Card. Open: Tues–Sun 9 a.m.–7 p.m.*

 Scrovegni Chapel and Musei Civici Eremitani (Civic Museums)

Construction of the **chapel** began in 1303 by banker Enrico Scrovegni, partly as an act of contrition because of his family's ill-gotten wealth (his father was an usurer). The idea had been developed by Dante in his *Inferno*, which would have put Enrico's father, Reginaldo, in the circle of hell reserved for usurers. (Ironically, the jewel that the chapel became under Giotto's hands led local monks to complain about the excessive luxury of the Scrovegni family — sometimes you just can't win.) The chapel is an early example of a complex project that reflects the vision of a single artist. The unusual design — windows on one side but not the other, no internal architectural decorations — made it a perfect canvas for Giotto's work, and the frescoes he executed are absolute masterpieces. The stories that he depicts move from left to right: The top row or band contains scenes from the life of Joachim and Anna, parents of the Virgin Mary; the middle and lower levels of the chapel contain scenes from the life of Jesus. Giotto also painted allegorical figures representing six virtues and six vices. The frescoes broke with tradition in a number of striking ways: His composition is dramatic rather than static, as in Byzantine art; he chose scenes that weren't usually depicted; and, above all, he repre-sented human beings with greater psychological realism, which a glance at these beautiful faces shows. On the altar are a beautiful Madonna with child and two angels by the sculptor Giovanni Pisano.

A special access gate — filtering the air and controlling humidity and other factors — protects the invaluable frescoes, as does the severely restricted number of visitors and the length of their stay (only 25 people every 30 minutes); you will need to make a reservation for a precise time slot. Note that reservations are also required for children under 6, even though they enter for free.

The chapel is surrounded by the archaeological remains of the **Roman Arena** — hence its other name, Cappella dell'Arena — and is accessible from the courtyard of the **museums**. Housed in the monastery attached to the chapel, these museums include a picture gallery upstairs — a rich col-lection of paintings by Venetian masters from the 15th to the 19th cen-turies, including important artists such as Giorgione, Titian, Veronese, and Tintoretto — and an archaeological museum downstairs, where you can see a collection of artifacts documenting the history of Padua from its pre-historic times.

See map p. 350. Piazza Eremitani 8, off Corso Garibaldi. ☎ 049-2010020. www. cappelladegliscrovegni.it. *Admission: 12€ ($14) adults; free with Padova Card; children under 6 free. Mandatory reservations fee 1€ ($1.20) per person. Open: Daily 9 a.m.–7 p.m. Closed Jan 1, Dec 25 and 26.*

More cool things to see and do

✔ Founded in 1222, the University of Padua is Italy's second oldest and counted among its scholars Galileo Galilei. It was moved to the **Palazzo del Bo** (Via VIII Febbraio, just off Piazza delle Erbe; ☎ **049-8273044** or 049-8273047 for reservations; www.unipd.it; Admission: 3€/$3.60) in the 16th century and later expanded to other buildings in town. It was the first university in the world to have an **Anatomy Theater,** an architectural masterpiece by G. Fabrici d'Acquapendente, built in 1594. Here medical students observed dissections of cadavers (sometimes in secret, for it was long forbidden by the church) in order to learn about the human body. You can visit only by guided tour; call for reservations or go at one of the set visiting times: Monday, Wednesday, and Friday at 3:15 p.m., 4:15 p.m., and 5:15 p.m.; and Tuesday, Thursday, and Saturday at 9:15 a.m., 10:15 a.m., and 11:15 a.m.

✔ Like Venice, Padua is also a town of water, crossed by many canals — these link Padua to the Brenta river and, farther away, to Venice and its Lagoon. During the Renaissance, rich Venetians had their country "houses" built along this river; many of these splendid villas were designed by Palladio, one of the greatest architects of all time, noted for the grace and balance of his designs. The **Consorzio Battellieri di Padova e Riviera del Brenta** (Passeggio de Gasperi 3; ☎ **049-8209825;** www.padovanavigazione.it) offers several boat tours, all very interesting, but we particularly recommend the **Urban Tour** of Padua's historic district (about 40 minutes) along the town's canals, as well as the tour of the villas along the **Riviera del Brenta,** which starts in Padua and brings you to Venice (a great way to get into Venice). A number of other companies offer similar cruises at comparable rates, so check with the tourist office to see which works best for you (see "Information" under "Fast Facts: Padua," later in this chapter). Boats run from March to October.

✔ **Caffè Pedrocchi** (Piazza Pedrocchi, off Piazza Cavour; ☎ **049-8205007** or 049-8781231; www.caffepedrocchi.it) has been the main intellectual gathering spot for the city's intelligentsia since its opening in 1831. At that time, Padua was under Austrian rule, and the cafe became a meeting place for patriotic and political groups; it maintained this role through the years, and as late as 1943 was the scene of a student uprising against the fascist regime. Completely restored to its elegant 19th-century glory, the cafe is open daily from 9 a.m. to 9 p.m. (until midnight Thurs–Sat) for regular business and live music — mostly jazz — in the evening. The upper floor, Piano Nobile, retains its elegant 19th-century original furniture and houses the **Museo del Risorgimento** (Admission: 3€/$3.60; free with Padova Card; Open: Daily 9:30 a.m.–12:30 p.m. and 3:30–8 p.m.), a collection of memorabilia from the political movement that led to Italy's unification. Closed two weeks in August.

✔ Padua boasts the world's first **Botanical Garden** (Via San Michele, behind the Basilica di Sant'Antonio; ☎ **049-8272119;** www.orto botanico.unipd.it; Admission: 4€/$4.80, free with Padova Card; Open: Mon–Sat 9 a.m.–1 p.m., summer also 3–6 p.m.), founded in 1545 as the garden for the university's faculty of medicine, where medicinal plants and herbs were grown. A pleasant and interesting sight, it offers a unique collection of rare plants as well as the university's original library and collection of botanical specimens, but there's nothing dusty and academic about it: It's organized like a Renaissance garden and makes for a very pleasant stroll.

Fast Facts: Padua

Area Code

The local area code is **049** (see "Telephone" in the "Fast Facts" section of Appendix A for more on calling to and from Italy).

ATMs

You'll find a number of banks with ATMs on Via Trieste, Via Santa Lucia, and Piazza Duomo. You can also change money at the train station (Open: Mon–Sat 8 a.m.–8 p.m.), as well as in the exchange office at Via L. Belludi 15 (☎ 049-660504).

Emergencies

For an ambulance, call ☎ **118;** for the fire department, call ☎ **115;** for first aid *(pronto soccorso),* call ☎ **049-8212856;** for road assistance, call ☎ **116.**

Hospitals

The Ospedale Civile is at Via Giustiniani 1 (☎ 049-8211111).

Information

The tourist board (www.turismopadova. it) maintains three info desks in town, one at the train station (☎ 049-8752077; Open: Mon–Sat 9:15 a.m.–7 p.m., Sun 9 a.m. to noon); one in the Galleria Pedrocchi, off Piazza Cavour (☎ 049-8767927; Open: Mon–Sat 9 a.m.–1:30 p.m. and 3–7 p.m.); and one at Piazza del Santo (☎ 049-8753087; Open: Mar–Oct daily 9 a.m.–5 p.m.).

Police

Call ☎ **113.**

Post Office

The main post office is at Corso Garibaldi 33 (☎ 049-8772111).

Taxi

Walk to Piazzale Stazione, in front of the rail station, or Piazza Garibaldi (south of the Scrovegni Chapel), or call ☎ 049-651333.

Verona: City of Juliet and Romeo

A town with ancient origins, as its famous **Roman theater** attests, Verona is today a major economic hub for the region. Its pretty historic center — rich in Romanesque churches, beautiful squares, and attractive Renaissance architecture — is now surrounded by a bustling, modern urban area, which contributes to a lively cultural life without spoiling the unique spirit of this beautiful medieval town.

You can easily visit the sights in a day, but if you're fond of opera and you're visiting during the Arena opera season, we recommend you spend the night and catch a show (see later in this section).

Getting there

The **train** (☎ **892021;** www.trenitalia.it) to Verona takes about 80 minutes from Venice and four and a half hours from Rome. The fare is approximately 11€ ($13) from Venice and 40€ ($48) from Rome. Trains arrive at the **Stazione Porta Nuova,** on Piazza XXV Aprile (☎ **045-590688**).

Verona's **Aeroporto Valerio Catullo,** in Villa Franca (☎ **045-8095666;** www.aeroportoverona.it), receives flights from most major destinations in Europe and Italy. **Meridiana** (☎ **892928** in Italy, or 0789-52682 from abroad; www.meridiana.it) offers daily hour-long flights from Rome for as low as 70€ ($84) round-trip. The airport is compact; in the arrivals lounge, you'll find a bank with ATM and a tourist info desk. The airport is 16km (10 miles) from the center of town, a 15-minute drive by taxi (you'll find a stand outside the airport). It's about 20 minutes away by **Aerobus,** the bus link to Verona's train station; tickets costs 4.50€ ($5.40) and buses leave every 20 minutes.

If you're coming by **car,** Verona lies on *autostrada* A4. From Rome, it will take you about six hours to cover the 505km (315 miles); from Venice, about two hours for the 110km (68-mile) drive. Verona's historic district is closed to private cars, so you'll have to park — the main parking lot is **Arsenale** (Piazza Arsenale 8; ☎ **045-8303281**).

Spending the night

Hotel Aurora
$ **Piazza delle Erbe**

Recently renovated, this hotel is housed in a 15th-century building and offers nicely appointed guest rooms and a great location. Public spaces feature exposed beams and terra-cotta tiled floors. Some of the guest rooms offer views over the famous *piazza* — the one on the top floor even has a balcony — and the bathrooms are of a decent size.

Verona

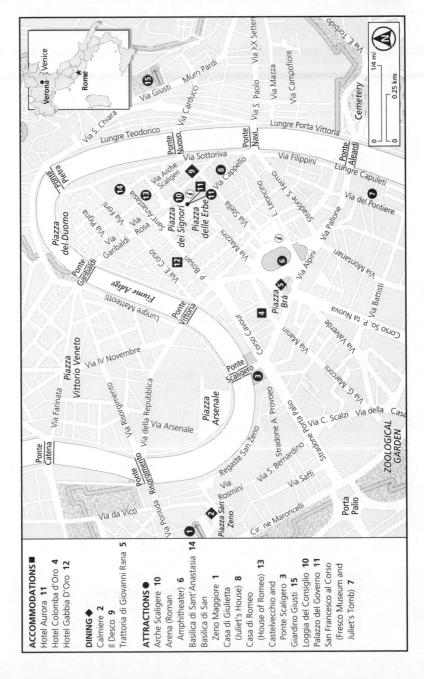

ACCOMMODATIONS ■
Hotel Aurora **11**
Hotel Colomba d'Oro **4**
Hotel Gabbia D'Oro **12**

DINING ◆
Calmiere **2**
Il Desco **9**
Trattoria di Giovanni Rana **5**

ATTRACTIONS ●
Arche Scaligere **10**
Arena (Roman
   Amphitheater) **6**
Basilica di Sant'Anastasia **14**
Basilica di San
   Zeno Maggiore **1**
Casa di Giulietta
   (Juliet's House) **8**
Casa di Romeo
   (House of Romeo) **13**
Castelvecchio and
   Ponte Scaligero **3**
Giardino Giusti **15**
Loggia del Consiglio **10**
Palazzo del Governo **11**
San Francesco al Corso
   (Fresco Museum and
   Juliet's Tomb) **7**

See map p. 359. Piazzetta XIV Novembre 2, off Piazza delle Erbe. ☎ *045-594717. Fax: 045-8010860.* www.hotelaurora.biz. *Parking: 10€ ($12). Rack rates: 135€ ($162) double. Rates include buffet breakfast. AE, DC, MC, V.*

Hotel Colomba d'Oro
$$ **Arena**

A couple of steps from the Roman Arena, this elegant yet moderately priced historic hotel — which has been an inn since the 19th century — occupies what was once a monastery. The hall is decorated with original 15th-century frescoes, and the good-sized guest rooms are furnished in style, with some antiques and a careful attention to detail. Bathrooms have all the comforts you'd expect; some are done in marble.

See map p. 359. Via Carlo Cattaneo 10. ☎ *045-595300. Fax: 045-594974.* www. colombahotel.com. *Parking: 20€ ($24). Rack rates: 214€ ($257) double. AE, MC, V.*

Hotel Gabbia D'Oro
$$$$ **Center**

This small luxury hotel is very centrally located. Housed in a charming 18th-century building, it opens onto a delightful year-round garden. Both the public spaces and the accommodations are very well kept, with a keen attention to detail. The elegant guest rooms are all individually decorated and have a lot of character: some with exposed brick walls and wooden beams, others with canopied beds or private balconies. The hotel is accessible to people with disabilities.

See map p. 359. Corso Porta Borsari 4/a. ☎ *045-8003060. Fax: 045-590293.* www. hotelgabbiadoro.it. *Parking: 28€–($34) valet. Rack rates: 352€–370€ ($422–$444) double. Rates include buffet breakfast. AE, DC, MC, V.*

Dining locally

Besides the suggestions below, consider also the **Osteria del Duca,** highlighted in "More cool things to see and do," later in this section.

Calmiere
$ **San Zeno** **VERONESE**

Opening onto what is arguably the most beautiful square in Verona, this restaurant offers excellent food — true to the best Veronese traditions — in a friendly and welcoming atmosphere. Try the pike served with polenta or the *carrello dei bolliti* (assortment of boiled meats and sausages served with several sauces).

See map p. 359. Piazza San Zeno 10. ☎ *045-8030765.* www.calmiere.com. *Reservations recommended. Secondi: 10€–13€ ($12–$16). AE, DC, MC, V. Open: Fri–Wed 12:30–2:30 p.m.; Fri–Tues 7:30–10:30 p.m. Closed 2 weeks around Christmas.*

Il Desco
$$$$ Center **CREATIVE VERONESE**

Il Desco doesn't come cheap, but it is heavenly. The menu changes with the seasons and the whims of the chef/owner, with such creations as foie gras with pears and a local wine sauce, breast of guinea hen with Jerusalem artichokes and a chocolate and balsamic vinegar sauce, and *tortelli di baccalà mantecato con pomodori e capperi* (large ravioli filled with cod in a tomato-and-capers sauce). Each fantastic dessert concoction is a perfect balance of flavor and texture. The tasting menu for 115€ ($138) is a gourmet celebration.

See map p. 359. Via Dietro San Sebastiano 7. ☎ *045-595358. Reservations recommended. Secondi: 28€–36€ ($34–$43). AE, DC, MC, V. Open: Tues–Sat 12:30–2:30 p.m. and 7:30–10 p.m. Closed 2 weeks in June and 2 weeks around Christmas.*

Trattoria di Giovanni Rana — Tre Corone
$$$ Center **NORTHERN ITALIAN**

In its large and elegant dining room, decorated with Murano chandeliers and marble floors, you will taste the best of the local culinary traditions. The menu is seasonal, but you will always find the classics: lasagna, tortellini in a butter and sage sauce, deep-fried veal cutlet, and *baccalà alla vicentina* (cod in a tomato sauce). In good weather, the terrace is very pleasant.

See map p. 359. Piazza Bra 16. ☎ *045-8002462. Secondi: 14€–22€ ($17–$26). AE, DC, MC, V. Open: Tues–Sun noon to 2:30 p.m.; Tues–Sat 7:30–10:30 p.m. (July–Aug also Sun).*

Exploring Verona

In peak season, you can take the **Bus Romeo** (☎ 045-8401207; e-mail: romeo@amt.it for reservations), a 90-minute guided tour that's accompanied by an audio guide (available in several languages). Tours depart from Piazza Bra and are offered from June to September, Tuesday through Sunday, four times a day (10 a.m., 11:30 a.m., 1 p.m., and 3:30 p.m.). You can make reservations up to one hour before departure by phone, through your hotel's reception desk, or at one of the two tobacconist shops on Piazza Bra (nos. 6b and 26). Tickets are 15€ ($18) for adults, 7€ ($8.40) for youths 5 to 18. The last run on Saturday has a live guide — in Italian and English, depending on the audience — and costs 5€ ($6) extra.

The **Verona Card** (☎ 045-8077774; www.verona.com) is a great deal, offering unlimited public transportation and free access to all major attractions in town. It comes in two versions: a 8€ ($10) one-day pass and a 12€ ($14) three-day pass, which you can purchase at any of the participating sites, a number of hotels in town, several tobacconist shops, or online.

If you spend at least three nights in any hotel — or even camping — in the province of Verona, you will receive the **Welcome Card,** granting discounts on many attractions, guided tours, public transportation, and even some shops and restaurants. Ask for it upon check-in should your host forget to give it to you.

You can get a **combination ticket** for the five most interesting churches in town — San Zeno, Duomo, Sant'Anastasia, San Lorenzo, and San Fermo — for 5€ ($6) per person. The ticket can be purchased at any of the participating churches (☎ 045-592813; www.chieseverona.it).

The top attractions

Arche Scaligere

These are the monumental tombs of the Scaligeri princes, enclosed in their private cemetery adjoining the Romanesque church of **Santa Maria Antica.** The wrought-iron gates bear the representation of ladders, the family's heraldic symbol. The grandest of the monuments is that of Cangrande I (he was certainly top dog — his name means "Big Dog"), which stands over the portal of the church and is crowned by his equestrian statue (a copy — the original is at the Castelvecchio; see later in this section). The two other major monuments are for Cansignorio (more or less "Sir Dog") and Mastino II ("Mastiff"). All richly decorated, the monuments are sculptural masterpieces. The church — originally built in the 8th century, but rebuilt in the 12th century after it was severely damaged by the earthquake of 1117 — still contains part of a mosaic floor believed to belong to the original 8th-century church. Tickets are sold at the booth by the Torre dei Lamberti (see Piazza dei Signori, later in this section).

See map p. 359. Via Arche Scaligere, off Via Sant'Anastasia and Via P. Bosari, near Piazza dei Signori. ☎ 045-8032726. Admission: 2.50€ ($3); includes Torre dei Lamberti. Open: June–Sept Mon 1:45–7:30 p.m.; Tues–Sun 9:30 a.m.–7:30 p.m. Closed Oct–May.

Arena (Roman Amphitheater)

This famous elliptical Roman arena dates from the reign of Diocletian (it was built around A.D. 290) and remains in surprisingly good condition. The inner ring is basically intact, though a 12th-century earthquake destroyed most of the outer ring (only four of the arches remain). This was Italy's third-largest Roman amphitheater and the second most important to have survived (after Rome's Colosseum). The amphitheater's overall length was 152m (499 ft.) and its height 32m (105 ft.); its 44 rows of seats could originally hold as many as 20,000 spectators, who watched gladiators and animals sparring. These days, however, the arena hosts more civilized entertainment: One of the greatest experiences in Verona is attending an opera or a ballet here. The season spans only the months of July and August. Ticket prices are 20€ to 160€ ($24–$192); for a schedule and reservations, call ☎ 045-8005151 or visit www.arena.it.

See map p. 359. Piazza Brà. ☎ 045-8003204. www.arena.it. Admission: 3.50€ ($4.20), 1€ ($1.20) first Sun of every month. Open: Tues–Sun 8:30 a.m.–7:30 p.m.; Mon

1:45–7:30 p.m. Ticket booth closes 45 minutes earlier. During the performance season (June–Aug), arena closes at 3:30 p.m.

Basilica di San Zeno Maggiore

A wonderful example of the Romanesque style and the most beautiful in northern Italy, this church and campanile were built between the 9th and 12th centuries above the tomb of Verona's patron saint (the original church dates from the 4th and 5th centuries). The fascinating 11th- and 12th-century **bronze door panels** illustrate San Zeno's miracles; like other works in this part of Italy (notably Venice), they reflect a mix of Byzantine, Gothic, and Turkish influences. Over the entrance is the famous **Ruota della Fortuna (Wheel of Fortune),** a beautiful rose window from the early 12th century. Inside, the church is decorated with graceful Romanesque capitals on the columns and frescoes (dating from the 12th to 14th centuries). The **timbered roof** is still the original 14th-century one. At the north end of the church, you can access the peaceful Romanesque **cloister.**

See map p. 359. Piazza San Zeno, just west of the Arena. ☎ 045-800-4325 or -6120. Admission: 2.50€ ($3). Open: Mar–Oct Mon–Sat 8:30 a.m.–6 p.m., Sun and holidays 1–6 p.m.; Nov–Feb Tues–Sat 10 a.m.–1 p.m. and 1:30–4 p.m., Sun and holidays 1–5 p.m. Ticket booth closes 15 minutes earlier.

Castelvecchio and Ponte Scaligero

The 14th-century **Castelvecchio,** perched over the Adige river, was the fortress and residence of the Scaligeri family, set to defend the famous bridge **Ponte Scaligero.** Built between 1355 and 1375, the bridge was destroyed by the Nazis during their retreat at the end of World War II, but was painstakingly rebuilt like an enormous puzzle, using the pieces that remained in the river. Today, this castle, complete with crenellated towers and walls, houses the **Museo Civico d'Arte,** a rich picture gallery containing paintings by great local artist **Paolo Veronese** and his school, as well as Venetian artists like **Tiepolo** and **Tintoretto.** The castle itself is worth a visit for its labyrinthine passageways and its tower, from which you can enjoy sweeping vistas of the city and its environs. In the courtyard is the **equestrian statue** of Cangrande I.

See map p. 359. Corso Castelvecchio 2, at the western end of Corso Cavour. ☎ 045-594734. www.comune.verona.it/Castelvecchio/cvsito. Admission: 4€ ($4.80), free the first Sun of each month. Audio guide 3.60€ ($4.30). Open: Mon 1:45–7:30 p.m.; Tues–Sun 8:30 a.m.–7:30 p.m. Ticket booth closes at 6:45 p.m.

Piazza dei Signori

One of northern Italy's most beautiful *piazze,* surrounded by equally beautiful palaces, this square was the center of Verona's government during its heyday. The **Palazzo del Governo** is where Cangrande della Scala (one of the first Scaligeri) extended the shelter of his hearth and home to the fleeing Florentine poet Dante Alighieri. A marble statue of Dante stands in the center of the square in memory. The **Palazzo della Ragione,** on the south side of the *piazza,* was built in 1123 but underwent changes many times in later centuries, including receiving a Renaissance facade in 1524. From its courtyard rises a medieval tower, the majestic **Torre dei Lamberti** (84m/277 ft.), also called the Torre del Comune. An elevator takes you to the top, where the views are magnificent. On the north side of the *piazza* is the 15th-century **Loggia del Consiglio,** which was the town council's meeting place; it's surmounted by five statues of famous Veronese citizens, and five arches lead into Piazza dei Signori.

See map p. 359. Torre dei Lamberti: Cortile Mercato Vecchio. ☎ *045-8032726. Admission: Oct–May1.50€ ($1.80), elevator 0.60€ (72¢); June–Sept 2.10€ ($2.50) and includes Arche Scaligere, elevator 0.50€ (60¢). Open: Tues–Sun 9:30 a.m.–7:30 p.m.; Mon 1:45–7:30 p.m. Ticket booth closes 30 minutes earlier.*

Piazza delle Erbe

This has been the seat of the market since Roman times — it was built on top of the Forum — and today, Veronese shoppers and vendors still mill about, surrounded by Renaissance palaces. The lively market should not distract you from the beauty of this *piazza,* graced in the center by the **Berlina** — a canopy supported by four columns where the election of the town's *signore* (elected prince) and the *podestà* (the governor) took place — and surrounded by medieval *palazzi:* the early-14th-century **Casa dei Mercanti (House of the Merchants),** restructured in 1870 to restore its original 1301 form; the baroque **Palazzo Maffei;** the adjacent **Torre del Gardello,** a tower built in 1370; and the **Casa Mazzanti,** another Scaligeri *palazzo,* decorated with frescoes. On the north side is a 14th-century **fountain** flanked by the venerated *Madonna Verona,* which is actually a restored Roman statue.

See map p. 359. Intersection of Via Mazzini and Via Cappello.

More cool things to see and do

✔ The small **Casa di Giulietta (Juliet's House),** at Via Cappello 23 (☎ 045-8034303; Admission: 3.50€/$4.20; Open: Tues–Sun 8:30 a.m.– 7:30 p.m., Mon 1:30–7:30 p.m.), is an original 12th-century house that the city bought in 1905 and turned into a tourist attraction (the famous balcony was added in 1935). Shakespeare's Capulets and Montagues (from his play *Romeo and Juliet*) were indeed versions of two historical Veronese families, the Capuleti (or Cappello) and the Montecchi. No proof exists that a family of Capulets ever lived in this house, but that doesn't stop people from flocking here to see the balcony where Juliet would have stood, if she'd been here at all. Tradition calls for you to rub the right breast of the bronze statue of Juliet for good luck. Of course, you can't have a Juliet without a Romeo, and there's a so-called **Casa di Romeo (House of Romeo)** at Via Arche Scaligere 2 (east of Piazza dei Signori), a 13th-century house that is said to have been the home of the Montecchi family. It now contains a small, cute restaurant, the **Osteria del Duca** (☎ 045-594474), serving excellent Veronese fare for lunch and dinner

Monday through Saturday. Reservations are not accepted; a prix-fixe menu is available for 13€ ($16).

✔ The **Fresco Museum** and **Juliet's Tomb** are housed in the 13th-century complex of **San Francesco al Corso** (Via Shakespeare; ☎ 045-8000361). It was inaugurated in 1935 with the display of a sarcophagus that, according to legend, holds the bodies of Romeo and Juliet. The museum displays an interesting collection of frescoes from a number of buildings in Verona, as well as 19th-century sculptures. The church of San Francesco has several paintings from the 15th, 16th, and 17th centuries and a large collection of Roman amphoras in the vaults. The complex is open Monday from 1:45 to 7:30 p.m., Tuesday through Sunday from 8:30 a.m. to 7:30 p.m. Admission is 3€ ($3.60) per person; free the first Sunday of each month.

✔ The **Basilica di Sant'Anastasia** (Piazza Sant'Anastasia; ☎ 045-8004325; Admission: 2.50€/$3; Open: Mar–Oct Mon–Sat 9 a.m.–6 p.m., Sun and holidays 1–6 p.m., Nov–Feb Tues–Sat 10 a.m.–1 p.m. and 1:30–4 p.m., Sun and holidays 1–5 p.m.) is Verona's largest church. Built between 1290 and 1481, it is graced by an unfinished Gothic facade adorned by a beautiful arched portal and an ornate campanile. Although the architecture (rather than the contents of the church) is its noblest feature, the **Cappella Giusti** does contain a Pisanello fresco of San Giorgio pictured with a princess, while the **Cappella Pellegrini** has terra-cotta works by Michele da Firenze.

✔ If you've ever wondered what an Italian garden should really look like, visit the **Giardino Giusti** (Via Giardino Giusti 2; ☎ 045-8034029). Built in the 14th century and given its current layout in the 16th, this Renaissance garden has survived more or less intact over centuries, and is now one of the most famous in Italy. Crossed by a main alley lined with cypress trees, the garden is embellished with grottoes, statues, and fountains. From a balcony at one end of the garden, you can enjoy a panoramic view of the city. It's open daily in summer, from 9 a.m. to 8 p.m., and until sunset in winter; admission is 5€ ($6).

Fast Facts: Verona

Area Code

The local area code is **045** (see "Telephone" in the "Fast Facts" section of Appendix A for more on calling to and from Italy).

ATMs

You can change currency inside the train station or at numerous banks around town (on Corso Cavour, for example, where you can also find ATMs).

Emergencies

For an ambulance, call ☎ **118**; for the fire department, call ☎ **115**; for first aid (pronto soccorso), call ☎ **045-807-2120**; for road assistance, call ☎ **116**.

Hospitals

The Ospedale Civile Maggiore Borgo Trento is at Piazzale Stefani 1 (☎ 045-8071111). At night and on weekends and holidays, you can reach a doctor by calling ☎ 045-8075627.

Information

Verona's tourist board (www.tourism.verona.it) maintains three tourist info desks: at Piazza Bra (Via degli Alpini 9; ☎ 045-8068680), at the Porta Nuova train station (Piazza XXV Aprile; ☎ 045-8000861), and at airport "V. Catullo" (☎ 045-8619163).

Police

Call ☎ 113.

Post Office

The post office *(ufficio postale)* is at Piazza Viviani 7 (☎ 045-8051111).

Taxi

You can walk to one of the taxi stands in town — the most central are Piazza Bra, Piazza delle Erbe, Piazza San Zeno, and the Porta Nuova train station — or call for a radio taxi at ☎ 045-532666.

Milan: Italy's Business and Fashion Center

As the economic heart of northern Italy — Italy's main industrial and manufacturing region — the city's charm as a tourist destination is tarnished by its fast-paced modern Milanese lifestyle and its inclement weather, which includes much fog in winter and steamy heat in summer. Still, Milan is a city of art, with deep historical roots, and it's home to several gems — including one of the best art galleries in Italy — making it well worth a detour. You can see the highlights in one day, but we recommend spending the night if you can spare the time.

Getting there

Milan's international airport of **Malpensa** (☎ 02-74852200), located 50km (31 miles) north of the city, has the dubious distinction of being called "the worst airport in Europe," but that's mainly due to the frequent fog that causes significant delays. In winter, Italians try to avoid flying to this airport. If you do land here, you can take the frequent (every 30 minutes) **Malpensa Express Train** to the **Cadorna train station,** a 40-minute ride, or the **shuttle bus** (every 40 minutes) to the **Milano Centrale train station,** a 50-minute ride. Count on spending over 70€ ($84) for a taxi ride, which, depending on traffic, could take you over an hour.

The smaller **Linate Airport** (☎ 02-74852200) is only 10km (6¼ miles) east of the city and has far fewer delays; it handles some European and most domestic flights. From here, it's a 15-minute taxi ride to the center of town. If you have no luggage, you can take the frequent (every ten minutes) **city bus** (no. 73) to the M1 subway line.

Milan is easy to reach by **train** (☎ 892021; www.trenitalia.it): The trip from Rome lasts about five hours — or four hours on the faster business train that makes two trips daily — and costs about 40€ ($48). Most long-distance trains arrive at **Milano Centrale,** on Piazza Duca d'Aosta.

We do not recommend driving to Milan: Although plenty of *autostrade* lead to the city, it's an absolute nightmare of traffic at most times, and safe parking garages are expensive (do not leave your car on the street for lengthy stays). If you need to, take the exit MILANO CENTRO for the historic district — and good luck.

Getting around

Milan's historic district is not huge, but it's still quite large, and you'll have to use some form of transportation to visit the attractions. Besides **taxis,** which are as good as in any other busy city, you'll want to use **buses** and **trams** — convenient, but slow in traffic — or the **metro (subway),** which is the fastest and simplest means of getting around. Buses, trams, and subways use the same tickets, which are sold at newsstands, tobacconists, and bars. A 75-minute ticket costs 1€ ($1.20), but you can also buy a carnet of ten tickets for 9.20€ ($11), a one-day travel card for 3€ ($3.60), or a two-day travel card for 5.50€ ($6.60). Pick up a public transportation map from the transportation authority's information booth inside the Duomo subway station (☎ **800-808181;** www. atm-mi.it; open Mon–Sat 8:30 a.m.–8 p.m.).

Spending the night

As Italy's business center, Milan has many hotels. Mostly geared toward business travelers, they tend to offer good weekend deals.

Antica Locanda Leonardo
$$ Center

This is a gem: a small, family-run hotel where you'll get individual attention and great accommodations at moderate rates, right in the center of it all. Housed in a 19th-century building overlooking a courtyard garden — perfect for a relaxing moment, especially in spring when the wisteria is in flower — it offers guest rooms done in classic style with period themes ranging from Liberty to rococo to modern. You'll find two computers with Internet access for hotel guests' use. Make sure you reserve in advance, as this hotel is not so secret anymore.

See map p. 368. Corso Magenta 78. ☎ *02-48014197. Fax 02-48019012* www.leoloc. com. *Parking: 25€ ($30) in nearby garage. Rack rates: 150€–205€ ($180–$246) double. AE, DC, MC, V. Closed 1 week in Jan and 3 weeks in Aug.*

Four Seasons
$$$$ Center

This is the kingdom of elegance and whispered luxury. Housed in a 15th-century convent, whose columned cloister now forms an inner courtyard, it boasts frescoes, marble floors, and convenient proximity to the chic shopping area of Via Montenapoleone — it isn't far from Brera and the Duomo, either. The rooms are large and tastefully decorated, with modern and antique details and state-of-the-art marble bathrooms. The service is

Milan

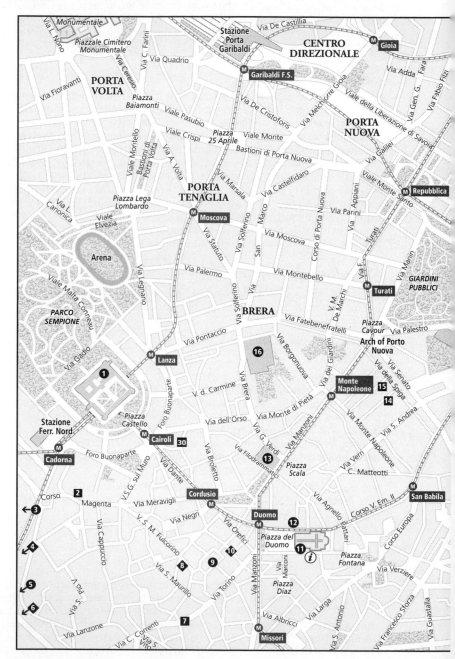

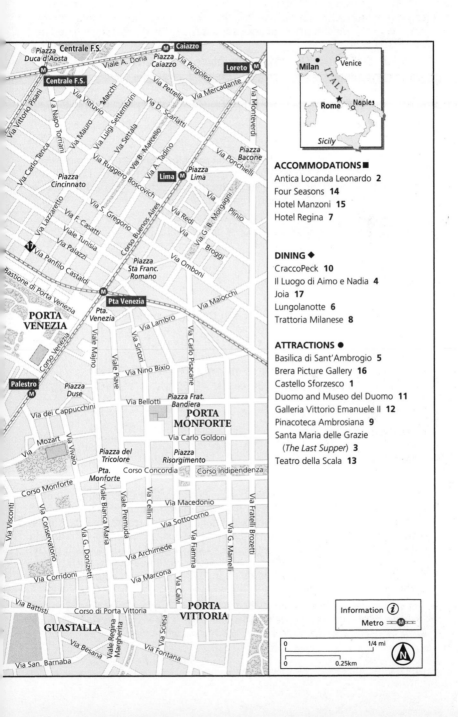

ACCOMMODATIONS ■
Antica Locanda Leonardo **2**
Four Seasons **14**
Hotel Manzoni **15**
Hotel Regina **7**

DINING ◆
CraccoPeck **10**
Il Luogo di Aimo e Nadia **4**
Joia **17**
Lungolanotte **6**
Trattoria Milanese **8**

ATTRACTIONS ●
Basilica di Sant'Ambrogio **5**
Brera Picture Gallery **16**
Castello Sforzesco **1**
Duomo and Museo del Duomo **11**
Galleria Vittorio Emanuele II **12**
Pinacoteca Ambrosiana **9**
Santa Maria delle Grazie
  (*The Last Supper*) **3**
Teatro della Scala **13**

Information ⓘ
Metro ▭M▭

top-notch, and children receive special attention (milk and cookies, video games). It comes at a price, of course, but the hotel does run weekend and other specials.

See map p. 368. Via Gesù 8, off Via Montenapoleone. ☎ *02-77088. Fax: 02-77085000.* www.fourseasons.com. *Parking: 51€ ($61) valet. Rack rates: 640€–800€ ($768–$960) double. AE, DC, MC, V.*

Hotel Manzoni
$$ Center

In a good central location, the Manzoni is an affordable choice in an expensive city. Housed in a modern postwar building, it offers comfortable guest rooms with tasteful modern or reproduction furniture. The bathrooms are unusually large by Italian standards.

See map p. 368. Via Santo Spirito 20. ☎ *02-76005700. Fax: 02-784212.* www.hotel manzoni.com. *Rack rates: 195€ ($234) double. AE, DC, MC, V. Closed Aug and Christmas.*

Hotel Regina
$$$ Center

Hotel Regina is an excellent choice in this price range. Housed in an elegant 18th-century *palazzo* in the heart of the historic center, it offers excellent service, a private garden courtyard, and spacious guest rooms with hardwood floors.

See map p. 368. Via C. Correnti 13. ☎ *02-58106913. Fax 02-58107033.* www.hotel regina.it. *Rack rates: 320€ ($384) double. AE, DC, MC, V. Closed Jan 1, Aug, and Dec 25.*

Dining locally

CraccoPeck
$$$$ Duomo CREATIVE MILANESE

Attached to the gourmet shop and cellar Peck, serving discerning Milanese since the 19th century, this is not only a gourmet temple but also one of the best restaurants in Italy. The chef delights in revisiting traditional classics — witness his perfect saffron risotto and superb roasted meats — but also in creating new dishes with a unique mix of flavors and textures, such as the *midollo alla piastra con fave e cioccolato* (grilled bone-marrow with chocolate and fava beans). The offerings change often; you can also choose one of the two tasting menus.

See map p. 368. Via Victor Hugo 4. ☎ *02-876774. Reservations required. Secondi: 28€–40€ ($34–$48). Tasting menus 95€ and 125€ ($114 and $150). AE, DC, MC, V. Open: Mon–Fri 12:30–2 p.m.; Mon–Sat 7:30–10 p.m. June–Aug closed Sat.*

Il Luogo di Aimo e Nadia
$$$$ Center   CREATIVE ITALIAN

This wonderful place is one of the best restaurants in Milan: Using simple yet excellent ingredients (personally chosen by the chef from small local producers throughout Italy), the chef prepares dishes that vary with the seasons and his own whims. We loved the *ricottine mantecate agli asparagi* (baby ricotta sautéed with asparagus), the *zuppa etrusca profumata al finocchio selvatico* (vegetable and legume soup with wild fennel), and the *trio di pesce con tortino di melanzane* (triglia, gallinella, and prawns with eggplant torte). The small lunch tasting menu is 35€ ($42), while the seven-course dinner tasting menu is 98€ ($118).

See map p. 368. Via Montecuccoli 6. ☎ *02-416886.* www.aimoenadia.com. *Reservations recommended. Secondi: 28€–55€ ($34–$66). AE, DC, MC, V. Open: Mon–Fri 12:30–2:15 p.m.; Mon–Sat 8–10:15 p.m. Closed Aug and 10 days in Jan.*

Joia
$$ Repubblica   CREATIVE VEGETARIAN/SEAFOOD

The Swiss chef Pietro Leeman is on a mission: to promote his love for gourmet vegetarian cuisine. He succeeds very well with this restaurant, as well as with his classes and other special events. The menu is seasonal and varied, including such concoctions as "the apparent egg and its taste": two pretend-eggs, one of white truffle and zucchini, the other of almonds and nutmeg. We definitely recommend the tasting menus, which come in three sizes: 13 courses for 95€ ($114), eight courses for 60€ ($72), and five courses for 50€ ($60).

See map p. 368. Via P. Castaldi 18. ☎ *02-29522124.* www.joia.it. *Reservations required 1 week in advance. Secondi: 16€–25€ ($19–$30). AE, DC, MC, V. Open: Mon–Fri 12:30–2:30 p.m.; Mon–Sat 7:30–11:30 p.m. Closed Dec 24–Jan 6 and Aug.*

Lungolanotte
$ Navigli   CREATIVE MILANESE

If you don't mind stepping a bit out of the historic district to get to an area popular with locals for nightlife (Navigli is a sort of small Venice, with canals that have been mostly covered over), you'll find a small and moderately priced gourmet hide-out. The menu changes often, but you will always find the *antipasto misto* — a great selection of local cured meats and marinated vegetables — and superb risotto (the one with artichokes and mascarpone is excellent), accompanied by a good choice of wines by the glass.

See map p. 368. Via Lodovico il Moro 133. ☎ *02-89120361. Reservations recommended. Secondi: 11€–18€ ($13–$22). DC, MC, V. Open: Mon–Fri noon to 2:30 p.m.; Mon–Sat 7–10:30 p.m. Closed 1 week in Jan and 3 weeks in Aug.*

Trattoria Milanese
$$$ Duomo   MILANESE

This traditional *trattoria* offers a choice of typical Milanese dishes in a pleasantly old-fashioned atmosphere. The *risotto alla Milanese* (with saffron and bone marrow) is excellent. For a *secondo*, try the perfect deep-fried beef cutlet or the juicy *osso buco*.

See map p. 368. Via Santa Marta 11. ☎ 02-86451991. Metro: M1 to Cordusio. Reservations recommended. Secondi: 9€–18€ ($11–$22). AE, DC, MC, V. Open: Wed–Mon noon to 3 p.m. and 7 p.m.–1 a.m. Closed July 15–Aug 31 and Dec 24–Jan 10.

Exploring Milan
The **Tram Turistico** (☎ 02-33910794; www.autostradale.it) is a guided tour using historic street cars from the 1920s; technically it's a hop-on/hop-off tour, but plan your stops well, as there are only two or three runs a day. Tickets are valid for one day and cost 20€ ($24) per person; rides start in Piazza Castello April through October, daily at 11 a.m., 1 p.m., and 3 p.m.; and November through March, Saturday, Sunday, and holidays only at 11 a.m. and 1 p.m. Trams don't operate January 1, May 1, December 25, December 31, and the second and third weeks in August. You can buy tickets at the tourist office in Piazza Duomo.

The **Centro Guide Turistiche Milano** (Via Marconi 1; www.centroguide milano.net) offers basic three-hour walking tours as well as other specialized options.

The top attractions

Brera Picture Gallery
Open since 1809 and housed in a beautiful 18th-century palace, this art museum was started by the Austrian Hapsburgs in the late 18th century as a small collection for the use of the students at the attached Art Academy. During the Napoleonic period, however, it was vastly enlarged with artwork confiscated by the French from museums as well as from the churches and monasteries that were shut down all over northern Italy. This already-rich art collection was further expanded with the addition of two private collections of modern art. The gallery includes paintings by famous masters from the 14th to the 18th centuries — such as the famous *Pala di Urbino,* by **Piero della Francesca;** *Sposalizio della Vergine,* by **Raffaello;** *Cristo Morto,* by **Andrea Mantegna;** and *Cena di Emmaus,* by **Caravaggio** — as well as important 19th- and 20th-century paintings by artists such as Carrà and Morandi. The loggias and other halls of the palace also hide an important collection of sculpture and artifacts.

See map p. 368. Via Brera 28. ☎ 02-722631. www.brera.beniculturali.it. Metro: M2 to Lanza. Admission: 5€ ($6). Open: Tues–Sun 8:30 a.m.–7:30 p.m. Last admission 6:45 p.m.

Castello Sforzesco

This castle embraces centuries of Milanese history and ruling clans, from small defensive *rocca,* built by the Visconti family in the 14th century, to its enlargement as a palace by the Sforza family, who dominated Milan during the Renaissance, and finally to its military development under the Austrian domination of the Hapsburg. Badly damaged during the Italian wars for Independence in the 19th century, the castle seemed doomed, but the powers that be finally decided to restore it to its original Renaissance glory. Kids will love the storybook crenellated walls, the underground passages, and the towers.

The *castello* houses several museums. The **Sculpture Museum,** located in the ducal public apartments, has a large collection ranging from Roman times to the Renaissance, including the famous **Pietà Rondanini** by **Michelangelo,** his last — and unfinished — work, finally visible again after a lengthy restoration and cleaning. The **Picture Gallery,** located in the ducal private apartments, holds a collection of Italian art from the 13th to the 18th centuries, including the *Madonna in Gloria con Santi,* by **Andrea Mantegna,** and the *San Benedetto,* by **Antonello da Messina.** Also on the premises is a great collection of arms and armor, along with a museum of musical instruments dating from the 15th to the 19th centuries. Underground is the **archaeological collection.**

See map p. 368. Porta Umberto. ☎ *02-88463651.* www.milanocastello.it. *Metro: M1 Cairoli or M2 Lanza/Cadorna. Admission: Castle free; museums 3€ ($3.60). Open: Castle Tues–Sun summer 7 a.m.–7 p.m., winter 7 a.m.–6 p.m.; museums daily 9 a.m.–5:30 p.m.*

Duomo and Museo del Duomo

This grandiose cathedral — second in Italy only to St. Peter's — covers about 10,034 sq. m (108,000 sq. ft.) and is 107m (356 ft.) high. Its construction lasted for centuries: Founded in 1386, the facade was completed at the beginning of the 19th century, and the last bronze portal was done in 1965. Its exterior is decorated with about 3,400 statues and 135 marble spires; its 1,394 sq. m (15,000 sq. ft.) of windows feature around 3,600 different characters. Some of the best artists of all periods participated in the project, a history illustrated by the very interesting collection in the **Museo del Duomo.** The museum is on the first floor of the **Royal Palace,** by the cathedral, and houses a huge collection of artwork assembled over the centuries of construction and ongoing restoration, including *Gesù al Tempio,* by **Tintoretto.** An important sculpture collection is organized chronologically and offers a unique panorama of Italian work from the late 14th to the 19th centuries. There is also a fascinating array of stained-glass windows. The baptistery is from the fourth century.

See map p. 368. Cathedral Piazza Duomo; Museum Piazza Duomo 14 (inside Palazzo Reale). ☎ *02-860358. Metro: M1 or M3 to Duomo. Admission: Cathedral free; crypt 1.55€ ($1.85); Baptistery 1.55€ ($1.85); roof 3.50€ ($4.20) and 5€ ($6) with elevator; museum 6€ ($7.20). Open: Cathedral daily 7 a.m.–7 p.m.; crypt daily 9 a.m. to noon and 2:30–6 p.m.; Baptistery Tues–Sun 10 a.m. to noon and 3–5 p.m.; roof daily 7 a.m.– 7 p.m.; Museum Tues–Sun 9:30 a.m.–12:30 p.m. and 3–6 p.m.*

Santa Maria delle Grazie and Leonardo's Last Supper

Built in the 15th century, this church was supposed to be the burial place of Ludovico il Moro and his descendants; the beautiful sculpted cover for the tomb is still here. But it's not tombs that draw tourists from all over the world: In the refectory of the church is the famous *Ultima Cena,* or *Last Supper,* by **Leonardo da Vinci.** It was painted by the master with an experimental technique (tempera over a plaster preparation) over four years of work between 1494 and 1498. The fresco was already looking quite bad by the end of the 16th century, so it required continuous repainting and restoration during the following centuries. The most recent restoration lasted 20 years and was completed in 1999; it removed the many previous restorations, revealing Leonardo's original work. Unfortunately, there are many gaps, but what remains is still a wonderful example of artistic achievement. Audio guides are available. *Note:* You need to reserve entry at least 24 hours in advance; you can do so by going to the Web site listed below.

See map p. 368. Piazza S. Maria delle Grazie 2, off Corso Magenta. ☎ 02-89421146. www.cenacolovinciano.it. Metro: M1 Conciliazione. Admission: 6.50€ ($7.80), plus 1.50€ ($1.80) mandatory reservations fee. Open: Tues–Sun 8:15 a.m.–7 p.m. Last admission 6:45 p.m.

More cool things to see and do

✔ Originally built in 386 by the Roman Magistrate Ambrogio on the burial site of two martyrs, Gervaso and Protaso, the **Basilica di Sant'Ambrogio** is the church of Milan's patron saint and an interesting example of Romanesque church (Piazza S. Ambrogio 15; ☎ 02-86450895; Metro: M2 S. Ambrogio; Admission: Church free, museum 2€/$2.40; Open: Church daily 9 a.m.–12:30 p.m. and 3:30–5 p.m.; museum Wed–Sun 10 a.m. to noon and 3–5 p.m.; closed Aug). Under the main altar is a ninth-century masterpiece housing the church's relics and decorated with scenes from the life of Jesus in gold, toward the front, and the life of St. Ambrose in silver, toward the back. You can still view the remains of the two martyrs, along with those of Ambrogio. The **chapel of San Vittore in Ciel d'Oro,** in the apse, is the only visible part of the church that dates from the fifth century. The **Museum of the Basilica,** recently reopened after a complete overhaul, is also worth a visit. Of particular interest is the **Urna degli Innocenti,** a jewelry masterpiece from the 15th century, and a **stucco portrait of Saint Ambrose** from the 11th century.

✔ Among the many other museums of Milan, you may enjoy visiting the **Pinacoteca Ambrosiana** (Piazza Pio XI; ☎ 02-806921; www.ambrosiana.it; Metro: M1 or M3 to Duomo), the oldest museum in town (opened in 1618). The art collection here includes the *Canestra,* by **Caravaggio;** *Madonna del Padiglione,* by **Botticelli;** and *Musico,* by **Leonardo** — although this last attribution is under debate. It's open Tuesday through Sunday from 10 a.m. to 5:30 p.m. (last entrance one hour earlier); admission is 7.50€ ($9).

✔ The famous **Teatro della Scala** (see "Living it up after dark," later in this section) is a landmark in the history of Milan and of Italian opera. If you love theater and opera, you shouldn't miss the interesting **Museo Teatrale della Scala,** in Palazzo Busca, near Leonardo's *Last Supper* (Corso Magenta 71; ☎ 02-4691528; Metro: M1 Conciliazione or M2 Cadorna). It's open daily from 9 a.m. to 6 p.m.; admission is 5€ ($6).

✔ Take a stroll under the **Galleria Vittorio Emanuele II** (off Piazza Duomo), a beautiful construction of wrought iron and glass covering four streets, built in the 1870s. Under the elegant canopy, you'll find a number of shops, cafes, and small boutiques.

Shopping the local stores

The heart of Italy's fashion industry, Milan means *prêt-à-porter* galore. The most famous shopping street for clothing and accessories is the world-renowned **Via Montenapoleone,** the fashion heart of Milan. Also worthy are the nearby streets of **Via della Spiga** and **Via Sant'Andrea.** Here, you'll find all kinds of shops and boutiques along with some of the top names of Italian fashion (**Valentino** and **Versace** are on Via Montenapoleone, **Dolce & Gabbana** is on nearby Corso Venezia, and **Armani** is on Via Manzoni). The shopping district, which now contains more down-to-earth retail as well, has spilled over all the way to **Piazza Duomo.**

If you aren't interested in haute couture, another excellent shopping area is the **Brera** district. In its back streets — **Via Solferino, Via Madonnina, Via Fiori Chiari,** and so on — you'll find elegant boutiques, with many designer names (including the young and trendy); antiques and bric-a-brac stores; and open-air market stalls. On the third Saturday of each month, the stretch of Via Brera near La Scala houses a large open-air market of antiques and knickknacks.

Finally, if you have the time and you're a keen shopper, you can head for **Corso Buenos Aires,** off **Piazza Oberdan,** for everything from designer clothes to scuba equipment.

Outlets, please

If you aren't visiting during sale periods (Jan and July), you may want to hit a few discount stores or outlets. Such places often sell the previous season's looks and items that have been worn on the runways. The discounts are excellent, though, and the atmosphere often competitive. **D Magazine Outlet** is right on Via Montenapoleone, at no. 26 (☎ 02-76006027). Others are a bit farther away, such as **Biffi** (Corso Ganova 6; ☎ 02-8311601; Metro: San Ambrogio), which specializes in women's wear in the main store and men's across the street. Another recommended shop — far from a secret anymore, unfortunately — is **Il Salvagente** (Via Bronzetti 16; ☎ 02-76110328), with a large array of women clothes. There's also a small children's section at Via Balzaretti 28 (☎ 02-26680764; Metro: San Babila).

Living it up after dark

For opera fans, attending a performance at the grand **Teatro della Scala** (Piazza della Scala; ☎ 02-72003744; www.teatroallascala.org) is an unforgettable experience. After three years of renovations, this grand theater reopened its doors in 2004 and is now better than ever: with wonderful acoustics, movable high-tech stages, and 200 additional seats. You'll need to reserve tickets well in advance. Prices range from 10€ to 90€ ($12–$108).

Fine classical music can be heard at the **Conservatorio** (Via del Conservatorio 12; ☎ 02-7621102); ticket prices range from 15€ to 35€ ($18–$42).

For a simpler evening out, head for one of the two major nightlife destinations in Milan. The more elegant **Brera** district gives a taste of trendy "Old Milan," with narrow streets and alleys. It used to be the artsy neighborhood of Milan, but of late it has become much more classy and established; expect sleek joints and stylish restaurants. The more casual **Ticinese/Navigli** district is a charming neighborhood of narrow streets and canals (although most of them have been paved over), lying to the southwest of the city center. Places here are open late and attract a more mixed crowd, with lots of trendy bars, small restaurants, clubs with live music, and hangouts for young people.

Enoteche (wine bars) abound in Milan. You can drink a glass — or a bottle — of excellent wine and accompany it with a tasty bite to eat. One of the most elegant is **Sadler Wine & Food** (Via Monte Bianco 2A; ☎ 02-4814677; Metro: Amendola Fiera). Our favorites include **Cotti** (Via Solferino 42; ☎ 02-29001096; open until the wee hours); **Ronchi** (Via S. Vincenzo 12; ☎ 02-89402627), which also has a wine museum; and **Enoteca Wine & Chocolate** (Foro Buonaparte 63; ☎ 02-862626), which features chocolate tastings as well.

Club Due (Via Formentini 2; ☎ 02-86464807; Metro: Lanza; Open: Daily) has a pleasant piano bar upstairs and a disco in the basement. If dance clubs are your thing, also try **Hollywood** (Corso Como; ☎ 02-6598996; Metro: Garibaldi or Moscova; Open: Tues–Sun) for some of the hottest sounds in town. For an elegant nostalgic atmosphere, head to **Gimmi's** (Via Cellini 2; ☎ 02-55188069; Open: Thurs–Tues), where after-dinner dancing is to tunes from the 1960s and '70s (jacket required).

Milan is also the center of Italy's gay scene. The most established gay disco is **Nuova Idea International** (Via de Castillia 31; ☎ 02-69007959; Metro Garibaldi; closed Mon). A popular disco and restaurant — with straight folks as well — is the mostly lesbian **After Line** (Via Sammartini 25; ☎ 02-6692130; Open: Daily). The **G-lounge** (Via Larga 8; ☎ 02-805-3042) is a trendy disco/bar with quality music.

Fast Facts: Milan

Area Code

The local area code is **02** (see "Telephone" in the "Fast Facts" section of Appendix A for more on calling to and from Italy).

ATMs

Currency-exchange bureaus can be found at the airport and inside Stazione Milano Centrale (the main train station); other exchange offices and banks with ATMs are scattered all around town and concentrated in the historic district.

Consulates

Australia: Via Borgogna 2 (☎ 02-777041); Canada: Via Pisani 19 (☎ 02-67581); United Kingdom: Via San Paolo 7 (☎ 02-723001); Ireland: Piazza S. Pietro In Gessate 2 (☎ 02-86464285); United States: Via Principe Amedeo 2 (☎ 02-290351); New Zealand: Via Guido D'Arezzo 6 (☎ 02-48012544).

Emergencies

For an ambulance, call ☎ **118**; for the fire department, call ☎ **115**; for first aid *(pronto soccorso)*, call ☎ **02-55033209**; for the Red Cross (Croce Rossa), call ☎ **3883**; for road assistance, call ☎ **116**.

Hospitals

The Ospedale Policlinico is at Via Francesco Sforza 35 (☎ 02-5503-3209), near the Duomo.

Information

The Milan tourist board (Piazza Duomo; ☎ **02-72524301;** www.milanoinfo tourist.com; Open: Mon–Fri 8:45 a.m.– 8 p.m., Sat 9 a.m.–1 p.m. and 2–7 p.m., Sun until 5 p.m.) maintains a tourist info desk inside Stazione Milano Centrale, near the Gran Bar (☎ 02-72524360; Open: Mon–Fri 8 a.m.–7 p.m., Sat 9 a.m.–6 p.m., Sun 9 a.m.– 12:30 p.m. and 1:30–6 p.m.).

Internet Access

There is an easyInternetcafé branch at Piazza Duomo 8 (www.easyinternet cafe.it), open daily from 10 a.m. to midnight.

Police

Call ☎ **113**.

Post Office

One of many post offices is at Via Orefici 15 (☎ 02-855-0081), off the Piazza Mercanti steps from the Duomo.

Taxi

For a radio taxi, call ☎ 02-8585, 02-4040, 02-5353, 02-8383, or 02-6767.

Part VI
Naples, Pompeii, and the Amalfi Coast

The 5th Wave   By Rich Tennant

" He had it made after our trip to Italy. I give you Fontana di Clifford."

In this part . . .

Naples is the capital of Campania, the beautiful region south of Rome. Campania is in many ways the heart of Italy — warm, welcoming, and mysterious. Its natural beauty has been famous since antiquity, and its history has made it a treasure-trove of fine art.

Chapter 18 covers the best of Naples, a city that borrows some of its character from Mount Vesuvius — the unpredictable volcano in whose shadow the city lies — and is ebullient with cultural happenings and treasures. Naples opens onto the most beautiful gulf in Italy: Chapter 19 guides you to excursions along these shores and beyond, including the splendid Royal Palace of Caserta, the picturesque Greek and Roman ruins in the Campi Flegrei, and Vesuvius, with its ring of ancient Roman towns that were violently and instantly destroyed by the volcanic eruption in A.D. 79. Finally, in Chapter 20, we explore the most beautiful area of all: the Sorrento Peninsula, with the mythical isle of Capri at its tip, and the most celebrated stretch of Italian coast, the justly renowned Amalfi Coast. All have entranced the artistic and well-to-do since the Roman Emperor Tiberius rioted in Capri with his playthings.

Chapter 18

Naples

● ●

In This Chapter

▶ Finding your way to and around Naples

▶ Choosing where to stay and where to eat

▶ Discovering art treasures and unique views

▶ Soaking up the Neapolitan atmosphere and activities

● ●

*I*f you look past the daunting traffic and noise of Naples, you'll find a seductive place — rich in art, churches, historic sites, and character — and one of the most vital cities anywhere. In a sense, if you haven't seen Naples, you haven't seen Italy. After the cultural renaissance begun in the 1990s, the historic district of Naples welcomes its visitors as never before, revealing again to our astounded eyes its many treasures. Refurbished monuments and areas reclaimed for pedestrians make it a very enjoyable destination.

Try not to visit Naples as a day trip: It's possible to see the highlights in a day, but if you can, take the time to explore this vivid, intense city by spending a couple of nights. Naples is also an excellent starting point for exploring other nearby sites (see Chapters 19 and 20) and a perfect jumping-off point for Sicily (see Chapters 21 and 22).

Getting There

Naples may feel a world apart from Rome or Florence, but logistically it is easily reached by rail, air, sea, or road.

By air

The small but well-run **Aeroporto Capodichino** (☎ 081-7896259; www. gesac.it) receives daily flights from Italian and other European destinations, including connecting flights from the United States. Here are a few tips for getting through the airport and to your hotel:

> ✔ **Getting oriented at the airport:** Capodichino is easy to navigate. You'll find a bank with ATM, a currency-exchange booth, and a tourist information desk in the arrivals concourse.

✔ **Navigating your way through passport control and Customs:** As most flights to Naples originate from within the European Union, you probably will have passed through passport control at your intermediate stop, in which case you'll go directly to baggage claim here and then go through Customs.

✔ **Getting from the airport to your hotel:** The airport is about 7km (4 miles) from the city center, only 15 minutes away. The easiest way to get into town is by taking a **taxi** directly to your hotel; the flat rate is 20€ ($23), plus gratuities. You can also arrange for a limousine pickup through your hotel, but you'll have to pay about 35€ ($42). A cheaper alternative is the **shuttle bus** (☎ 800-639525; www.anm.it), which costs 3€ ($3.60). It stops on Corso Garibaldi near the Napoli Centrale train station, as well as in Piazza Municipio, at the heart of the historic district. Departures are every 30 minutes.

By train

If you take one of the four daily high-speed trains from Rome, you'll be in Naples in only 87 minutes; other trains take about two and a half hours (☎ 892021; www.trenitalia.it). Trains from Rome to Naples depart often — nearly every hour — and cost about 20€ ($24). The trip from Florence takes about four and a half hours and costs about 35€ ($42), while the trip from Venice takes seven and a half hours and costs 50€ ($60). Trains arrive at **Napoli Centrale,** also known as **Stazione Centrale** (Piazza Garibaldi; ☎ 081-5543188), on the northeastern edge of the historic district. Outside the station, you'll find taxis and public transportation.

By ferry or ship

Naples's harbor is the major port of central Italy, with ferries and cruise ships stopping on their way to and from Capri and Sicily (see Chapters 20 and 21 for rates and schedules) and other Italian islands, as well as international destinations in the Mediterranean and beyond. Arriving by water is the best way to approach Naples: You will get the full effect of the magical beauty of the bay, and you will arrive in the heart of town, where most of the attractions lie. Most ships and ferries arrive at the **Stazione Marittima** seaport, off Via Cristoforo Colombo in the heart of the historic district. Other ferries and most hydrofoils arrive at the **Terminal Aliscafi** in **Mergellina,** to the west of the historic district. You'll see taxis and public transportation right outside the terminal.

By car

The aggressive driving style in Naples makes taking a car into town challenging, even for Italians, and we do not recommend it. Also, Naples is infamous for car theft, including from guarded parking lots. If you think you need a car to explore farther destinations such as the Amalfi Coast, think again — and see Chapter 20 for better options.

The Gulf of Naples and Salerno

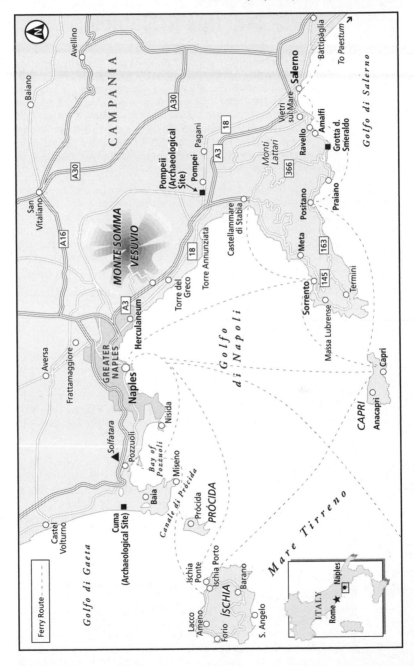

Taxi tips in Naples

Neapolitans get a bad rap for trying to rip off tourists whenever the occasion presents itself, and Gypsy cabs are largely to blame for it. Always and only use official taxis: They're white (the old yellow ones have mostly disappeared) and marked on the outside, while inside you'll see a meter and a town license bearing the code number, as well as a card with rates and a list of flat-rate destinations (20€/$23 from Capodichino airport to hotels in the historic district; 9.50€/$11 from Piazza Municipio to Museo di Capodimonte, and so on). If your ride is a flat-rate one, the meter will be turned off. Regular rates are 4.15€ ($5) minimum charge, 2.60€ ($3.10) initial charge, plus .05€ (6¢) for every 250 feet or 15 seconds. A 10 to 15 percent gratuity is expected, especially since these rates have not gone up since 2002.

Although most licensed taxi drivers are honest, you can always happen upon a bad apple who pretends his meter is broken in order to charge a little more. If this happens to you, take another cab. If you're picked up at your hotel or at a restaurant, ask your concierge or waiter for an estimate of what a reasonable fare may be to your destination, and get a quote from the taxi driver before boarding: If it is not extravagant, it is probably correct; if it doesn't seem right, demand an explanation in order to avoid surprises.

Orienting Yourself in Naples

Historically and geographically turned toward the sea — its high cliffs surrounding a perfect harbor — Naples developed like a crescent around its bay. Up the cliff is **Vomero,** and farther away to the northeast is **Capodimonte.** Down by the sea is the historic district, with the *città antica* (old city) at the heart, stretching from **Piazza Garibaldi** and the **Stazione Centrale** train station to the east, to **Via Toledo** — the main north–south street, lined with elegant palaces and fashionable shops, and continuing with different names all the way up to Capodimonte — to the west. To the south is the seaside artery Via Cristoforo Colombo, leading to the **Stazione Marittima (Seaport).** A main east–west street is **Via Benedetto Croce,** which, along with its continuation **Via Biagio dei Librai,** Neapolitans call **Spacca Napoli** ("Divide Naples") — as these divide the old city in two. Parallel to the north is **Via dei Tribunali,** while parallel to the south runs **Corso Umberto I** — a major and noisy shopping street.

West of Via Toledo is the **Quartieri Spagnoli.** To the south lies the civic heart of Naples, with the town hall in **Piazza Municipio** and the two former royal palaces: **Castel Nuovo** — built by the Angevins as the center for their two-century-long kingdom — and **Palazzo Reale,** the Royal Palace built for the Spanish rulers. Closed to traffic, **Piazza del Plebiscito** (by Palazzo Reale and at the end of Via Toledo) is at the heart of it all. West of the Stazione Marittima starts the fashionable waterfront, with the neighborhoods of **Santa Lucia** and **Chiaia**, followed by **Posillipo** and **Mergellina** — two nice suburbs of Naples.

Introducing the neighborhoods

Capodimonte

Overlooking the bay from a separate hill, **Capodimonte** is a middle- and lower-class residential neighborhood that developed to the west and north of its major landmarks: the royal palace housing the **Museo di Capodimonte**, with its park, and the nearby **Catacombs**, which are the only reasons to come to this otherwise uninteresting area.

Chiaia

Stretching along Naples's fashionable seafront, behind the pleasant green of the beautiful **Villa Comunale** gardens, this elegant residential area stretches up the slope toward the Vomero hill. Only a short distance from the historic district, it is a major destination for chic shopping as well as nightlife, especially along **Via Chiaia** and **Piazza dei Martiri**. Hotels are few, and restaurants tend to cluster in the eastern area.

Città antica

Today the embodiment of "Neapolitanness" — laundry drying at windows, mammas screaming at their kids down in the street, motor scooters rushing past, and so on — together with the Quartieri Spagnoli (later in this chapter), this is the city's heart. Along these streets are concentrated some of the most important attractions in Naples, particularly the churches — **Duomo, Santa Chiara, Sant'Anna dei Lombardi, San Lorenzo Maggiore** — as well as the university, which attracts a lively nightlife scene and rich cultural activity. Hotels tend to be on the southern edge of the area, whereas restaurants and small shops abound.

Piazza del Plebiscito

The most beautiful *piazza* in Naples, this is where Neapolitans, young and old, like to meet, especially in the evening. Called *il salotto* — the living room — it is a short distance from everything important in the city: the Stazione Marittima, **Teatro San Carlo,** the administrative and political offices of Piazza Municipio, and the restaurants and nightlife of Quartieri Spagnoli, *città antica,* Chiaia (Piazza dei Martiri is only steps away), and Santa Lucia. Off the *piazza* itself are a few cafes.

Piazza Garibaldi

At the eastern edge of the *città antica,* this is a huge square that's the major transportation hub: **Napoli Centrale** train station is here, as well as many bus lines, the subway, and, nearby, the Circumvesuviana railroad to Pompeii and other destinations (see Chapter 19). Very busy with locals and visitors, it is only a short distance from some major attractions and offers hotels, restaurants, and many shops. It gets a bit seedy at night, however.

Naples

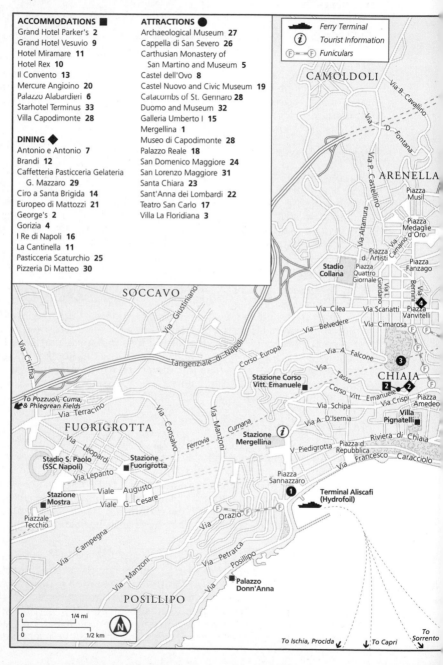

ACCOMMODATIONS ■
Grand Hotel Parker's **2**
Grand Hotel Vesuvio **9**
Hotel Miramare **11**
Hotel Rex **10**
Il Convento **13**
Mercure Angioino **20**
Palazzo Alabardieri **6**
Starhotel Terminus **33**
Villa Capodimonte **28**

DINING ◆
Antonio e Antonio **7**
Brandi **12**
Caffetteria Pasticceria Gelateria
   G. Mazzaro **29**
Ciro a Santa Brigida **14**
Europeo di Mattozzi **21**
George's **2**
Gorizia **4**
I Re di Napoli **16**
La Cantinella **11**
Pasticceria Scaturchio **25**
Pizzeria Di Matteo **30**

ATTRACTIONS ●
Archaeological Museum **27**
Cappella di San Severo **26**
Carthusian Monastery of
   San Martino and Museum **5**
Castel dell'Ovo **8**
Castel Nuovo and Civic Museum **19**
Catacombs of St. Gennaro **28**
Duomo and Museum **32**
Galleria Umberto I **15**
Mergellina **1**
Museo di Capodimonte **28**
Palazzo Reale **18**
San Domenico Maggiore **24**
San Lorenzo Maggiore **31**
Santa Chiara **23**
Sant'Anna dei Lombardi **22**
Teatro San Carlo **17**
Villa La Floridiana **3**

🚢 *Ferry Terminal*
ⓘ *Tourist Information*
Ⓕ═══Ⓕ *Funiculars*

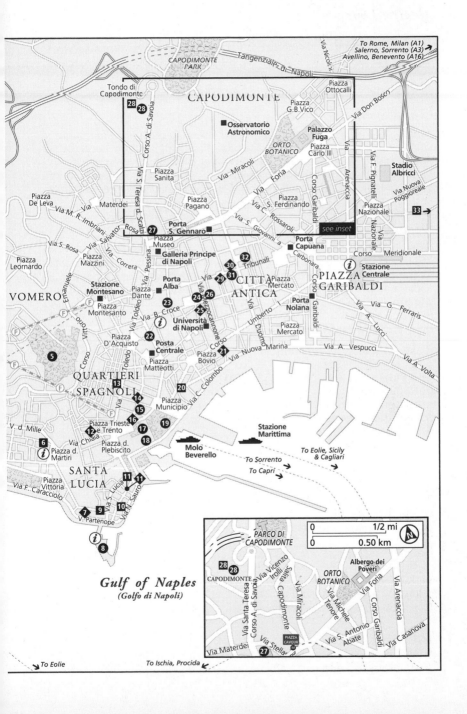

To Rome, Milan (A1)
Salerno, Sorrento (A3)
Avellino, Benevento (A16)

Via Nicola

CAPODIMONTE PARK

Tangenziale di Napoli

Piazza Ottocalli

Tondo di Capodimonte

CAPODIMONTE

Piazza G.B. Vico

28 28

Osservatorio Astronomico

Palazzo Fuga

Piazza Carlo III

ORTO BOTANICO

Via F. Pignatelli

Stadio Albricci

Piazza Sanita

Via Miracoli

Via Foria

Corso Garibaldi

Via Nuova Poggioreale

Piazza De Leva

Via M. R. Imbriani

Via Materdei

Via S. Teresa d. Scalzi

Piazza Pagano

Via S. Ferdinando

Via C. Rossaroli

Piazza Nazionale

33

Via Nazionale

Porta S. Gennaro 27

Via S. Giovanni a

Piazza Museo

Porta Capuana

Corso Meridionale

Piazza Leonardo

Piazza Mazzini

Galleria Principe di Napoli

32

Tribunali

Carbonara

Stazione Centrale

VOMERO

Stazione Montesano

Porta Alba

30 29 31

CITTA ANTICA

PIAZZA GARIBALDI

Piazza Dante

Piazza Montesanto

23

24 26

Piazza Mercato

Porta Nolana

Via G. Ferraris

Via A. Lucci

25

Università di Napoli

Piazza Mercato

Via A. Vespucci

Via A. Volta

Piazza D'Acquisto

22

Posta Centrale

Piazza Bovio

21

Via Nuova Marina

QUARTIERI SPAGNOLI

Piazza Matteotti

13

20

Piazza Municipio

14

15

16

Piazza Trieste e Trento

12 17 19

18

Stazione Marittima

V. d. Mille

6

Via Chiaia

Piazza d. Plebiscito

Molo Beverello

To Eolie, Sicily & Cagliari

Piazza d. Martiri

To Sorrento

SANTA LUCIA

11 11

To Capri

Piazza Vittoria

Via F. Caracciolo

7 9 10

V. Partenope

8

Gulf of Naples
(Golfo di Napoli)

PARCO DI CAPODIMONTE

0   1/2 mi
0   0.50 km

28 28

CAPODIMONTE

Via Santa Teresa

Corso A. di Savoia

Via Vincenzo Irollo

Salita Capodimonte

Via Miracoli

Via Michele Tenore

Albergo dei Poveri

ORTO BOTANICO

Via Foria

Via Arenaccia

Via Materdei

Via Stella

27

Via S. Antonio Abate

Corso Garibaldi

Via Casanova

To Eolie

To Ischia, Procida

Quartieri Spagnoli

A tight grid of narrow streets built by the Spanish in the 16th century to house their troops, this picturesque neighborhood lies along the west side of **Via Toledo,** the main street in the heart of Naples. It offers an excellent location near all major attractions, as well as a few very nice restaurants and hotels.

Santa Lucia

Famous for its elegant hotels along the promenade of **Via Partenope** and the picturesque view over the bay, this small neighborhood feels a bit secluded from the rest of Naples — yet it's only steps from everything. Its landmark is the city's most famous sight, **Castel dell'Ovo,** the fortress built on a small island at the end of a causeway and stretching into the bay.

Vomero

The hill of the **Vomero** is an elegant, middle- and upper-class residential neighborhood. The fresher air and the views attract visitors, especially in the summer, and you'll find some good shopping and limited nightlife. Its landmarks are the famous **Castel Sant'Elmo** and the **Certosa di San Martino,** as well as the lesser known but splendid **Villa La Floridiana.**

Finding information after you arrive

The best tourist information offices in town are at **Via San Carlo** (Via San Carlo 9, off Piazza del Plebiscito; ☎ 081-402394; www.inaples.it) and **Piazza del Gesù** (☎ 081-5512701), both open Monday through Saturday from 9 a.m. to 1:30 p.m. and 2:30 to 7 p.m. You'll also find a small tourist info desk inside **Stazione Centrale** (Piazza Garibaldi; ☎ 081-268799; Open: Mon–Sat 9 a.m.–7 p.m.), but it tends to have limited material.

Getting Around Naples

Naples is a large, bustling city, and although you won't be interested in the suburbs, you'll welcome some form of transportation to get from one attraction to the next.

The historic district of Naples is safe, but you will want to watch your purse and your belongings carefully, especially in crowded situations: pickpockets and purse-snatchers are a sad — and abundant — reality. At night, avoid poorly lit and deserted streets; muggers are rare, but unfortunately do exist.

On foot

You can cover a lot of ground on foot, and Naples offers beautiful walks, particularly in Santa Lucia, Chiaia, and in the *città antica,* where some sections have been reserved for pedestrians only. The free map from the tourist office is good enough for most visitors, but if you want more detail, get a map with a *stradario* (street directory) from any newsstand; personally, we like the wallet sized **Mini-City map,** sold at the bookshop of Palazzo Reale and other museums in town.

By subway, bus, funicular, and tram

Public transportation in Naples (☎ 800-482644 in Italy; www.ctpn.it) is good and extensive, but gets rather crowded at rush hour. You can choose between two **metropolitana (subway)** lines — the faster one runs daily from 5 a.m. to 11:30 p.m. There are also three *funivia* (funicular, or cable car) lines that go up and over the hills: **Montesanto,** which runs daily from 7 a.m. to 10 p.m.; **Chiaia,** at Piazza Amedeo, Monday through Thursday from 7 a.m. to 9 p.m. and Friday through Sunday from 7 a.m. to 1 a.m.; and **Centrale,** at Via Toledo, daily from 6 a.m. to 1 a.m. You can also take advantage of the several **bus** and **tram** lines. Trams fare a bit better against city traffic, but they're still the slowest from of transportation; also, after 8:30 p.m. many lines run only hourly, if at all. The most convenient are the special "tourist" bus lines marked *R,* which stop at major attractions (daily 5:30 a.m. to midnight), and the electric minibuses serving the *città antica.*

All public transportation uses the same tickets: the regular *biglietto* (ticket), valid for unlimited travel for 90 minutes at a cost of 1€ ($1.20); and the *giornaliero* (day pass), valid for unlimited travel for one day at a cost of 3€ ($3.60). You can buy them at bars, tobacconists, and newsstands around town.

By taxi

Taxis are a great resource: You may have to put up with colorful language and reckless driving to avoid traffic jams, but at least you'll be comfortably seated. Taxis do not cruise around as in New York, though, so you'll have to walk to a taxi stand to find one, or else call for pickup (see "Fast Facts: Naples," at the end of this chapter). Refer to the sidebar "Taxi tips in Naples," earlier in this chapter, for rates.

Staying in Style

Naples is a cheaper destination than Rome, Florence, or Venice, so you will be able to treat yourself to a higher caliber of hotel — which is a good thing, as some of the hotels are still quite old-fashioned. Overall, though, the lodging choices here are getting up to par with international standards.

The top hotels

Grand Hotel Parker's
$$$$ Chiaia

In competition with the Grand Hotel Vesuvio, below, for the title of best in Naples, this hotel offers a superb vantage point — on the slopes above Riviera di Chiaia — and a unique charm: Dating from 1870, its neoclassical interior and ornate Liberty (Italian Art Nouveau) plasterwork and decorations have been completely preserved and restored. The large, elegant guest rooms are decorated in period furniture — several with original pieces — and the best units afford grand views of the beautiful bay. The elegant marble bathrooms offer all the amenities you would expect. The roof garden houses **George's** (see "Dining Out," later in this chapter).

See map p. 386. Corso Vittorio Emanuele 135. ☎ *081-7612474. Fax: 081-663527.* www. grandhotelparkers.com. *Metro: Piazza Amedeo. Bus: C24 or C27 to Via Tasso. Parking: 16€ ($19). Rack rates: 325€–360€ ($390–$432) double. Rates include buffet breakfast. AE, DC, MC, V.*

Grand Hotel Vesuvio
$$$$ Santa Lucia

The best in town and the most renowned, this elegant historic hotel offers attentive, professional service and splendid views of Mount Vesuvius or the bay of Naples, with Castel dell'Ovo in the foreground. The bright and spacious guest rooms are individually decorated, some with antiques, others with stylish modern furniture, and still others with a mix of antiques and good-quality reproductions. All have large marble bathrooms with Jacuzzi tubs. The suites and the most expensive doubles have balconies — but you can enjoy the same breathtaking view from the excellent roof-garden restaurant, **Caruso.**

See map p. 386. Via Partenope 45. ☎ *081-7640044. Fax: 081-7644483.* www.vesuvio. it. *Bus: 152, 140, or C25 to Santa Lucia. Parking: 22€ ($26). Rack rates: 410€ ($492) double. Rates include buffet breakfast. AE, DC, MC, V.*

Hotel Miramare
$$ Santa Lucia

Built in 1914 as a private villa, this charming hotel right on the water offers bright guest rooms with beautiful bathrooms, decorated with quality modern furniture — and many with views of the sea. Recently renovated, this villa was the American consulate before being converted into a hotel. The public areas are still decorated in the original Liberty style. Breakfast is served on a terrace overlooking the bay, while a second panoramic terrace is used as a solarium. Guests here receive a 10 percent discount at the nearby **La Cantinella** restaurant (see "Dining Out," later in this chapter).

See map p. 386. Via Nazario Sauro 24. ☎ *081-764-7589. Fax: 081-764-0775.* www. hotelmiramare.com. *Bus/Tram: Bus R3 or tram 4 to Via Acton. Parking: 22€ ($26). Rack rates: 190€ ($228) double. Rates include buffet breakfast. AE, DC, MC, V.*

Hotel Rex
$ Santa Lucia

The Rex is well known (read: reserve well in advance) as a moderately priced hotel in the waterside neighborhood of Santa Lucia. It offers simply but carefully decorated guest rooms, some with a view of the harbor or Vesuvio, and all with private balconies. Housed in a 19th-century palace, most rooms and bathrooms are good-sized; in contrast to its lavish exterior, the furnishings are simple (many rooms are decorated in a 1960s style) but in good repair. A very nice breakfast is served in your room.

See map p. 386. Via Palepoli 12. ☎ *081-7649389. Fax: 081-764-9227. Bus/Tram: Bus R3 or tram 4 to Via Acton. Parking: 22€ ($26). Rack rates: 100€ ($120) double. Rates include breakfast. AE, V.*

Il Convento
$ Quartieri Spagnoli

Housed in a 17th-century palace in the heart of Naples, this hotel offers carefully restored guest rooms and public spaces at a moderate price. Guest rooms have pastel plaster walls and quality modern furniture. Some rooms have wooden beams, while others have arches or private roof gardens; the two family rooms are duplexes with a loft.

See map p. 386. Via Speranzella 137/a. ☎ *081-403-977. Fax: 081-400332.* www.hotel ilconvento.it. *Bus: R2 to Piazza Municipio. Parking: 16€ ($19). Rack rates: 130€ ($156) double. Rates include breakfast. AE, DC, MC, V.*

Palazzo Alabardieri
$$ Chiaia

A great addition to the Naples lodging scene, this hotel is housed in an elegant 19th-century *palazzo* with an inner courtyard garden and elegant marble floors in the public spaces. Guest rooms are spacious and done up with all the amenities, including hardwood floors and stylish furnishings mixed with period pieces. The good-sized bathrooms are clad in marble.

See map p. 386. Via Alabardieri 38. ☎ *081-415278. Fax: 081-19722010.* www.palazzo alabardieri.it. *Metro: Piazza Amedeo. Parking: 20€ ($24). Rack rates: 220€ ($264) double. Rates include buffet breakfast. AE, DC, MC, V.*

Runner-up accommodations

Mercure Angioino
$$ Città Antica   Located between the university and the harbor, this recently opened hotel is within sight of the Angioino castle. Housed in a beautiful restored 19th-century building, the Mercure is both modern and convenient, offering simple rooms with large beds and carpeting; one floor is nonsmoking. *See map p. 386. Via Depretis 123.* ☎ *081-552-9500. Fax: 081-552-9509. E-mail:* mercure.napoliangioino@@accor-hotels.it.

Starhotel Terminus

$$ Piazza Garibaldi After a complete overhaul, this elegant hotel near Napoli Centrale train station has become one of the most attractive in town, offering commodious rooms with all the comforts. Accommodations are modern, with carpeting, wood accents, and stylish furniture. Bathrooms are good-sized. The roof-garden bar is popular for drinks among elegant Neapolitans and visitors alike. *See map p. 386. Piazza Garibaldi 91.* ☎ *081-7793111. Fax: 081-206689.* www.starhotels.it.

Villa Capodimonte

$$ Capodimonte The appeal of this hotel is the great location near the Museo di Capodimonte, the beautiful views, and the private garden, which make it well insulated from the surrounding neighborhood. Guest rooms are large and furnished in classic style, with wooden floors and good-sized modern bathrooms. All open onto a terrace or the hotel's garden, making this a great choice if you have children. *See map p. 386. Via Moiariello 66.* ☎ *081-459000. Fax: 081-299344.* www.villacapodimonte.it.

Dining Out

We love the food in Naples — it is as sunny as the city and its people (see Chapter 2 for more on Neapolitan cuisine). You'll find plenty of both traditional and trendy restaurants here. The best places to browse for yourself are Via Partenope, in Santa Lucia, and the narrow streets around Piazza dei Martiri, in Chiaia.

Antonio e Antonio
$$ Santa Lucia NEAPOLITAN/PIZZA

The location is perfect, right along Via Partenope overlooking the picturesque Borgo Marinari, in the shadow of Castel dell'Ovo. The food is equally good at this popular restaurant. You'll find everything from seafood to meat to pizza (40 different varieties) on the seasonal menu. Everything is freshly made: We particularly recommend the buffet of appetizers, the *scialatielli ai frutti di mare* (fresh pasta with seafood), and the *polipetti in cassuola* (small squid stewed with tomatoes).

See map p. 386. Via Partenope 24. ☎ *081-2451987. Reservations recommended. Bus: C25, 140, 152. Secondi: 6€–17€ ($7.20–$20). AE, DC, MC, V. Open: Daily 12:30–3:30 p.m. and 7:30–11:30 p.m.*

Brandi
$ Quartieri Spagnoli PIZZA

Literally fit for a queen, this *pizzeria* opened in the 19th century and is the place where *pizza margherita* was invented. It takes its name from Margherita di Savoia, first queen of Italy, who graciously accepted having a pizza named after her (how many sovereigns can say that?). Her namesake pizza comes with tomato, basil, and mozzarella — red, green, and white, not coincidentally the colors of the united Italy. Brandi's menu includes a few appetizers — such as an excellent *impepata di cozze* (mussels stewed with black pepper) — as well as pizza. *See map p. 386. Salita Sant'Anna di Palazzo 1. ☎ 081-416928. Reservations recommended. Bus: R2 or R3 to Piazza Trieste e Trento. Pizza: 7€–18€ ($8.40–$22). No credit cards accepted. Open: Tues–Sun 12:30–3:30 p.m. and 7:30 p.m. to midnight.*

Ciro a Santa Brigida
$$ Città Antica NEAPOLITAN

This famous historic restaurant offers excellent food and professional service. The extensive menu — accompanied by an equally extensive wine list — includes the best dishes of the Neapolitan region, all prepared with attention to detail and the freshest ingredients. In addition to its homemade pastas and daily fish dishes, this place is known for its *fritti* (deep-fried specialties) and for the quality and variety of traditional vegetable *contorni*. It also serves excellent pizza and a large selection of desserts. *See map p. 386. Via Santa Brigida 71, off Via Toledo and the Galleria Umberto I. ☎ 081-5524072. Reservations required. Bus: R2 or R3 to Piazza Trieste e Trento. Secondi: 7.50€–15€ ($9–$17). AE, DC, MC, V. Open: Mon–Sat noon to 3:30 p.m. and 7–11:30 p.m.*

Europeo di Mattozzi
$$$ Città Antica NEAPOLITAN/SEAFOOD

In the welcoming atmosphere of this historic dining room, the chef offers tasty choices inspired by local traditions. We recommend the *zuppa di cannellini e cozze* (bean and mussel soup) and the *pasta e patate con provola* (pasta and potatoes with melted local cheese), as well as the *scorfano all' acquapazza* (scorpion-fish in a light herbed broth). The pizzas are also very good. Leave room for the great traditional desserts such as the *babà* (like a liquor-soaked brioche with a dollop of pastry cream) and the *pastiera* (tart filled with a creamy wheat-berry and candied-fruit mixture). *See map p. 386. Via Marchese Campodisola 4. ☎ 081-5521323. Reservations required. Bus: R2 or R3 to Piazza Trieste e Trento. Secondi: 11€–16€ ($13–$19). AE, DC, MC, V. Open: Mon–Sat noon to 3:30 p.m.; Thurs–Sat 7:30–11 p.m.; in summer dinner Thurs–Fri only. Closed 2 weeks in Aug.*

George's
$$$$ Chiaia CREATIVE NEAPOLITAN

Housed on the Art Nouveau Grand Hotel Parker's roof terrace, this is the best and most elegant restaurant in Naples. Come here to enjoy creative regional cuisine and magnificent views — while being pampered in sheer luxury. The menu is seasonal, and the acclaimed Chef Baciot (Vincenzo Bacioterracino) adds his creative touches to the simplest — and best — traditional ingredients. We loved the zucchini napoleon and the grilled

Sweet breaks

If you have a sweet tooth, try the local specialties (see Chapter 2 for details) at the **Pasticceria Scaturchio** (Piazza San Domenico Maggiore 19; ☎ 081-5516944; Bus: R2), one of the oldest pastry shops in town, established in 1903. Besides wonderful pastries, you may also want to sample the *Ministeriale*, a medallion of dark chocolate with a liqueur cream filling. Another excellent spot is **Caffetteria Pasticceria Gelateria G. Mazzaro** (Via Tribunali 359; ☎ 081-459248; www.pasticceriamazzaro.it), which serves not only splendid pastries but also excellent *gelato*.

calamari, as well as the delicious offerings on the special diet menu, based on the principles of French herbalist Marc Messegué.

See map p. 386. Corso Vittorio Emanuele 135. ☎ *081-7612474.* www.grandhotel parkers.com. *Reservations required. Metro: Piazza Amedeo. Bus: C24 or C27 to Via Tasso. Secondi: 22€–25€ ($26–$30). AE, DC, MC, V. Open: Daily 12:30–2:30 p.m. and 8–10:30 p.m.*

Gorizia
$$ Vomero   NEAPOLITAN/PIZZA

This excellent neighborhood spot serves typical local food prepared with a true love for cooking and good ingredients. The pizza is some of the best you'll taste in Naples, the dough prepared according to a century-old family secret recipe, but we also recommend the other dishes on the menu. The soup changes daily and is always tasty, as are the pasta dishes — such as splendid spaghetti with zucchini, tomatoes, and olives.

See map p. 386. Via Bernini 31, off Piazza Vanvitelli. ☎ *081-5782248. Reservations recommended in the evening. Funivia to Vomero. Bus: V1. Secondi: 5€–18€ ($6–$22). AE, DC, MC, V. Open: Tues–Sun 12:30–4 p.m. and 6 p.m.–1 a.m.*

1 Re di Napoli
$ Piazza del Plebiscito   NEAPOLITAN/PIZZA

With a view of the grand buildings of the Piazza Plebescito, and with outdoor dining in good weather, this is a nice place to sample the city's greatest culinary contribution at moderate prices. In addition to fine brick-oven pizza, the menu includes a full range of *antipasti* and vegetable dishes served buffet-style. There's a second location near the archaeological museum (Piazza Dante 16, off Via Toledo), which is also open from lunchtime until 1 a.m.

See map p. 386. Piazza Trieste e Trento 7. ☎ *081-423013. Reservations recommended on weekends. Bus/Tram: Bus R3 or R2 to Piazza Trieste e Trento. Pizza: 5€–9€ ($6–$11). AE, DC, MC, V. Open: Daily 11:30 a.m.–1 a.m.*

La Cantinella
$$$$ Santa Lucia   NEAPOLITAN/CREATIVE/FISH

One of the best and most-loved restaurants in Naples, this waterfront spot has plenty of style. It feels like a 1930s nightclub or something out of a movie, but the food is pure Neapolitan, with excellent *antipasto* and grilled seafood. Try the *pappardelle "sotto il cielo di Napoli"* (homemade pasta with zucchini, prawns, and green tomatoes) and the excellent *fritto misto* (deep-fried calamari, small fish, and shrimp). Do not forget the wine — the selection is excellent — or the dessert (if you have the patience for the lengthy preparation, choose the fantastic soufflé).

See map p. 386. Via Cuma 42, off Via Nazario Sauro. ☎ 081-7648684. Reservations required. Bus: C25, 140, or 152. Secondi: 19€–30€ ($23–$36). AE, DC, MC, V. Open: Mon–Sat 12:30–3:30 p.m. and 7:30 p.m. to midnight. Closed 1 week in Jan and 3 weeks in Aug.

Pizzeria Di Matteo
$ Città Antica   PIZZA

At this hole-in-the-wall restaurant, you'll find some of the most authentic pizza in Naples. The place is far from elegant — the dining room upstairs looks like a cafeteria — and the service minimal (you'd better make up your mind fast, and don't expect a menu), but the pizza is superb. It comes in only a few basic styles, but all are good. We recommend the *pizza fritta,* a Neapolitan traditional specialty: Two rounds of dough are filled with tomatoes, ham, and cheese, and then deep-fried in a special copper skillet (you'll see it downstairs as you enter).

See map p. 386. Via dei Tribunali 94, at Vico Giganti. ☎ 081-455262. Reservations not accepted. Bus: R2 to Duomo. Pizza: 3€–8€ ($3.60–$10). No credit cards accepted. Open: Mon–Sat 9 a.m.–3 p.m.

Exploring Naples

If you plan to do some extensive sightseeing, we recommend the **artecard** (☎ **800-600601** in Italy, or 06-39967650; www.campaniartecard.it). This pass is a really good deal, granting unlimited public transportation, free admission to two attractions, and a 50 percent discount at all other attractions on an extensive list that includes the major museums. It also gives discounts at participating shops and entertainment venues. The artecard comes in two versions: The 13€ ($16) **"3 days Naples and Campi Flegrei"** is limited to the area of Naples and the Campi Flegrei (including the dedicated Archeobus; see Chapter 19); while the 25€ ($30) **"3 days all sites"** covers the whole region, including Pompeii, Herculaneum, and Paestum (see Chapters 19 and 20). The card is for sale at all participating sites, as well as at the Capodichino airport, the *molo beverello* (harbor), the train station of Napoli Centrale, major hotels, and some news kiosks.

Discovering the top attractions

Declared a World Heritage Site by UNESCO in 1995, the historic district of Naples is one of the richest art destinations in Italy.

Archaeological Museum
Città Antica

If you want to visit just one archaeological museum in Italy, make it this one. Established in the 17th century, it is one of the world's oldest antiquity museums and one of the richest. Part of the astonishing collection is actually embedded in the walls and floors of the *palazzo,* as that was the style in the 17th century: Roman sculptures embellish the facade and superb ancient Roman mosaics decorate the floors, all originals from Pompeii, Herculaneum, and other archaeological excavations in the region. The collection of **Roman sculptures** on the first floor is superb, with many Roman copies of original Greek masterpieces such as the ***Ercole Farnese*** — a statue of Hercules copied from an original in bronze by Lisippo from the fourth century B.C., which greatly influenced the artists of the Renaissance — and the ***Toro Romano,*** a dramatic scene come to life in marble that stands over 4m (13 ft.) high; it depicts the punishment of the queen of Beotia from a Greek original of the second century B.C.

The mezzanine is dedicated to ancient **Roman mosaics,** the most wonderful of all the huge one depicting the **victory of Alexander the Great over the Persians** and found in the House of the Faun in Pompeii (see Chapter 19). But the best is on the second floor, where you'll find a unique collection of ancient **Roman paintings and frescoes** — entire rooms from Pompeii, Herculaneum, and other nearby sites have been reconstructed here with the original frescoes (we love room 77, with a series of landscapes and the portrait of Saffo, a young girl). Famous already back in Goethe's day is the so-called **Gabinetto Segreto (Secret Room):** a collection of Roman erotica originals documenting the attitude toward sexuality in Roman times (guilt-free and frank, to say the least). If you wish, you can sign up for a guided tour at the ticket booth. Allow a couple of hours for your visit; we recommend renting an audio guide (in English).

See map p. 386. Piazza Museo Nazionale 19. ☎ *081-440166. Metro: Museo or Piazza Cavour. Admission: 6.50€ ($7.80). Included on the artecard list. Audio guide: 4€ ($4.80). Open: Wed–Mon 9 a.m.–8 p.m. Ticket booth closes 1 hour earlier. Closed Jan 1 and Dec 25.*

Carthusian Monastery of San Martino and Museum
Vomero

This wonderful monastery provides the perfect excuse to take the funicular and visit the Vomero neighborhood. Built in the 14th century and enlarged in the 17th, it occupies a natural terrace at the edge of the cliff. Its **church** is considered the most beautiful baroque church in Naples, decorated with gorgeous marble floors and works of art. Now turned into a **museum,** you can visit the **Quarto del Priore,** the elegant apartments where the prior received the VIPs of the time; among the artwork here is a Madonna by Pietro Bernini, the father of the great Gian Lorenzo. The monastery centers around two beautiful cloisters, the imposing **Chiostro Grande** — with a cemetery enclosure decorated with carvings of skulls — and the smaller **Chiostro dei Procuratori.** From here, you can enter the *presepi* **(manger scenes)** collection, a typical Neapolitan art form that reached its peak in the 18th and 19th century but is still alive today (see "Shopping the Local Stores," later in this chapter). This collection includes the most famous historic *presepio,* the **Cuciniello** created in 1879 using figures and accessories by famous sculptors and architects from the 18th century. The upper floors display a collection of artwork with Naples as a subject, whereas the Gothic cellars contain the sculpture section.

Your admission includes the nearby **Castel Sant'Elmo** (Via Tito Angelini 20; ☎ **081-5784030;** Tues–Sun 8:30 a.m.–7:30 p.m.), the star-shaped 14th-century fortress looking over the city (its daunting walls are visible from everywhere downtown). Restored in the 16th century, it's now open to visitors who'd like to see its dungeons, halls, and terraces, affording 360-degree views of the city and bay.

See map p. 386. Largo San Martino. ☎ 081-5781769. Funivia to Vomero, then bus V1. Admission: 6€ ($7.20); includes Castel Sant'Elmo. Included on the artecard list. Open: Tues–Sun 8:30 a.m.–7:30 p.m.

Castel dell'Ovo
Santa Lucia

This is the most famous landmark in Naples, a picturesque fortress built on a small promontory projecting into the beautiful harbor. In Roman times, the celebrated gourmand Lucullus had his villa in this idyllic spot. The villa was fortified during the Middle Ages, and from those times comes the legend that Virgil (the poet author of the *Aeneid* and a reputed magician) placed a magic egg under the castle's foundations to protect it, hence the name (*ovo* means "egg"). When he took over the city, Frederick II transformed it into his castle, and his successors, the Angevins, later enlarged it. The castle is a fortified citadel, and from its walls you can enjoy a superb view of the city and the surrounding bay. Today, it houses the **Museum of Ethno-History** (☎ 081-2400055; admission varies, depending on the exhibit; 10 percent discount with artecard; Mon–Sat 8:30 a.m.–5 p.m., Sun 8:30 a.m.–2 p.m.), but at press time it was open only for special exhibits. If you get to enter, do not miss the **Sala delle Colonne (Hall of the Columns)** and the **Loggiato,** two architectural gems. Otherwise, limit your visit to the picturesque **Borgo Marinari** — a fishermen's hamlet that is now mostly taken over by restaurants — and enjoy the view of the castle from the beautiful promenade of **Via Partenope.**

See map p. 386. Off Via Partenope. Bus/Tram: C25, 140, or 152 to Santa Lucia.

Castel Nuovo and Civic Museum
Piazza Plebiscito

Built in the 13th century by Carlo d'Angió (Angevin dynasty) as the new royal residence — the Castel dell'Ovo didn't fit the needs of the new kingdom — this castle was renovated in the 15th century by Alfonso I of Aragona, who also added the grandiose **Triumphal Arch** over the inland entrance to commemorate the expulsion of the Angevins at his hands in 1443. A splendid example of early Renaissance architecture, this is the work of Francesco Laurana, the gifted Neapolitan sculptor. Inside, beyond the courtyard and up the staircase, you'll find the **Sala dei Baroni (Barons' Hall),** a monumental room with a star-shaped ceiling that was once decorated by Giotto (his frescoes have been lost, however). Most of the sculptures that decorated the room were destroyed by fire in 1919. Today, the hall is the seat of the Municipal Council.

The castle also houses the **Civic Museum,** through which you can visit the **Cappella Palatina,** the chapel opening onto the castle's courtyard and dedicated to Santa Barbara. The church was built in 1307 — only the carved portal and rose window are from the 15th century, replacing the originals which were destroyed by an earthquake — and was also completely decorated by Giotto, but only a few fragments remain. The chapel houses part of the museum's collection: a series of 14th-century frescoes from nearby churches and 15th-century sculptures, including Domenico Gagini's altarpiece of Madonna and child (Gagini was a pupil of Donatello and Brunelleschi) and two Madonnas by Francesco Laurana. The museum's second and third floors contain the picture gallery — stretching from the 15th to the 20th century — with works by Luca Giordano and Francesco Solimena, among many others.

See map p. 386. Piazza Municipio. ☎ *081-7955877. Bus: R1 or R4. Admission: 5€ ($6). Included on the artecard list. Open: Mon–Sat 9 a.m.–7 p.m.; Sun 9 a.m.–2 p.m.*

 Duomo and Museum
Città Antica

This grandiose church — also known as the Cathedral of Santa Maria Assunta — hides a treasure-trove of artwork inside. The monumental central body, built in the 13th century, is supported by 110 ancient granite columns; in the right transept you'll find **Perugino's** *Assunta* and the **Cappella Minutolo,** a Gothic marvel decorated with a mosaic floor and frescoes. In the crypt below is the **Cappella Carafa** (also called *Succorpo*), probably designed by the great Renaissance architect **Bramante,** and a marvel of architectural elegance. To the right of the Duomo's atrium opens the **Cappella di San Gennaro:** A church more than a chapel, it is lavishly decorated with marble and gold leaf — an apotheosis of Neapolitan baroque — and a dome with a cycle of frescoes by **Domenichino.** If you happen to visit on September 19th, on the first Sunday in May, or on December 16th, you'll see on display, over the main altar, the famous reliquary containing the skull and the vial with the blood of San Gennaro (patron saint of Naples), which is said to miraculously liquefy on these dates — it's a sign of great misfortune for the whole town if the miracle doesn't take place. To the left of the Duomo's atrium, you can access what's left of **Santa Restituta,** a paleo-Christian basilica from the sixth century that was incorporated into the Duomo when this was built. Redone in the 17th century, only one of its chapels is still decorated with the original Renaissance artwork, the sixth to the left. The real attraction, though, is its **baptistery** (entrance at the end of the nave to the right), which dates back to the fourth century; it's the world's oldest Western baptistery and is still decorated with beautiful fifth-century mosaics.

Attached to the Duomo is the entrance to the **museum,** which holds the **Treasure of San Gennaro,** a stunning collection of precious artwork donated to the saint throughout the centuries. The collection is so rich that the museum has to show it on a rotating basis, changing the display every year. From the museum, you can also visit the **sacristy,** with its beautiful frescoes by Luca Giordano and paintings by Domenichino. Should you find the doors to Santa Restituta and to the Cappella Minutolo closed, ask here to arrange for a visit.

See map p. 386. Via Duomo 147. Duomo: ☎ 081-449097; museum: ☎ 081-421609. Metro: Piazza Cavour. Admission: Duomo free; museum 2.60€ ($3.10), 25 percent discount with artecard. Open: Duomo Mon–Sat 8 a.m.–12:30 p.m. and 4:30 p.m.–7 p.m., Sun and holidays 8 a.m.–1:30 p.m. and 5–7:30 p.m.; museum Tues–Sat 9 a.m.–6:30 p.m., Sun and holidays 9 a.m.–7 p.m.

Museo di Capodimonte
Capodimonte

Built in the 18th century as the king's hunting lodge and private museum, this splendid *palazzo* was situated to afford beautiful views of the city and bay. Recently restored and reorganized, the museum holds a first-class painting collection. The Farnese collection alone includes Masaccio's *Crucifixion,* Perugino's *Madonna and Child,* Bruegel's *Misanthrope,*

Neapolis

Born from two Greek colonies — Partenope, established in the seventh century B.C. on the promontory behind Piazza del Plebiscito, and Neapolis, established 200 years later in the area now called *città antica* — the city grew and thrived. First taken over by the Sannites, it was annexed by the Romans by the third century B.C. The cultural melting pot gave birth to the unique personality we can still witness today. Always coveted for its splendid position, Naples passed under many rulers, first the Byzantines and the Longobards, then the Normans and the Angevins (house of Anjou), then the Spanish and finally the Bourbons. Made capital of the Southern Kingdom in 1266, it remained so until it became part of the new Italian Kingdom in 1860, and was enriched with artistic monuments by each of its rulers. It then knew a period of decadence that culminated in the 1980s, when most of its monuments were closed to the public and dingy with accumulated dirt. A huge program of restoration and revitalization brought about a cultural renaissance, resulting also in the ebullient artistic and creative verve — especially in the field of music, but also in the performance and figurative arts — we can witness today.

Naples and the *presepio*

The dearest activity to Neapolitans is the making of manger scenes for Christmas. Far from being a Christmas-only preoccupation, Neapolitans have turned this into an art form — and the carving of figurines, as well as the preparation of details of the setting, is the permanent activity of a number of reputed artists. These figurines are collectors' items now. People save to buy them — the ones dressed in original 18th-century fabrics are quite expensive — and think about their displays for months. Unlike those crèches that are simply a little display of established characters, Neapolitan versions are alive with the passions and happenings of the historical and political present, and among the figures offered for sale, you will recognize such characters as Lady Diana and Madre Teresa di Calcutta, and even Gianni Versace! **Via San Gregorio Armeno**, in the *città antica*, is where most of the historic workshops are located; you will find not only characters, but also rocks, grottoes, miniature pumps to make "rivers," miniature street lamps, and so on. A vividly painted figure or figurine — some of them are life-size — can be a beautiful souvenir of Naples and Italy, but remember that these carvings don't come cheap: A shepherd dressed in 18th-century clothes will be priced in the hundreds of dollars. See "Shopping the Local Stores," later in this chapter, for more information.

and works by several other masters, such as Mantegna, Raphael, Titian, Caravaggio, and Botticelli. The nearby Borgia collection includes works by Mantegna and a number of Spanish artists. The **Neapolitan Gallery** on the third floor has more works by **Titian** (his *Annonciation*) and **Caravaggio** (his *Flagellation*), among others; the adjacent **D'Avalos** collection includes a celebrated 16th-century **tapestry series** depicting the Battle of Pavia. The contemporary gallery on the third and fourth floors holds works by Alberto Burri, Jannis Krounellis, Andy Warhol, and so on. We also recommend a visit to the second floor's **royal apartments,** which are full of priceless objects, tapestries, and porcelain, including a whole room — the *salottino di porcellana* — completely done in porcelain.

See map p. 386. Palazzo Capodimonte, Via Miano 1 and Via Capodimonte (park entrance). ☎ *081-7499111. Bus: 24 or R4 to Parco Capodimonte. Admission: 8€ ($10); 6.50€ ($7.80) after 2 p.m. Included on the artecard list. Audio guide: 4€ ($4.80). Open: Tues–Sun 8:30 a.m.–7:30 p.m. Ticket booth closes 1 hour earlier. Closed Jan 1 and Dec 25.*

Palazzo Reale
Piazza Plebiscito

The imposing neoclassical Royal Palace was designed by Domenico Fontana and built by the Bourbons in the 17th century; the eight statues on the facade depicting Neapolitan kings were added in the 19th century. The *palazzo* retains its glamour to this day, and was used as the venue for a G7 summit meeting in 1994. The **royal apartments** inside are quite splendid — richly appointed with marble floors, tapestries, frescoes, and baroque furniture — and the chapel holds the splendid **Presepio del Banco di Napoli** (manger scene), with characters carved by famous Neapolitan sculptors in the 18th century. The *palazzo's* most grandiose rooms house the **Vittorio Emanuele III Library,** accessible from a separate entrance on the ground floor. Originally established by Charles de Bourbon and later enlarged, it is the greatest in southern Italy, holding over 2 million volumes, stretching as far back as papyrus manuscripts from Herculaneum. Those are not on display, but you should definitely admire the gorgeous decorated public halls. To bring the place to life, we recommend taking the guided tour, also available in English.

See map p. 386. Piazza del Plebiscito 1. ☎ *081-5808111. Bus: R2 or R3 to Piazza Trieste e Trento. Admission: 4€ ($4.80), courtyard and gardens free. Included on the artecard list. Guided tour by reservation 3€ ($3.60). Open: Thurs–Tues 9:30 a.m.– 8 p.m. Ticket booth closes 1 hour earlier.*

Santa Chiara
Città Antica

Built at the beginning of the 14th century as the burial church for the Angevin dynasty, this majestic church is the heart of the large monastic complex of the Clares. The church was severely damaged by World War II bombing and an ensuing fire, and although much of the artwork that decorated the interior was lost, its architectural structure was restored to its original look. Among the several monuments inside, the **tomb of Roberto d'Angió** at the end of the nave — a beautiful example of Tuscan-style Renaissance sculpture — is the most magnificent. The **Choir of the Clares,** accessible from the sacristy, is where the nuns can sit protected from the public during mass; it was a splendid work of art decorated by Giotto — you can still admire some fragments and the gorgeous carved portal — but much was lost in the fire. Outside of the church to the back, you can visit the key attraction of the whole complex: the **Cloister of the Clares,** a uniquely beautiful cloister completely decorated with hand-painted majolica tiles. From the cloister, you can also access the **museum,** which holds artwork donated to the church as well as the archaeological excavations of ancient Roman thermal baths from the first century A.D.

See map p. 386. Via Santa Chiara 49. ☎ *081-5526280.* www.santachiara.info. *Metro: Dante; Bus: R1, R2, R3, or R4. Admission: Church free, cloister and museum 3€ ($3.60). Open: Church Thurs–Tues 9:30 a.m.–1 p.m. and 4–6 p.m., Sun 9 a.m.–1 p.m.; cloister and museum Mon–Sat 9:30 a.m.–1 p.m. and 2:30–5:30 p.m., Sun 9:30 a.m.–1 p.m.*

Sant'Anna dei Lombardi (Santa Maria di Monteoliveto)
Città Antica

Opening onto a charming *piazza* graced by the city's most beautiful **baroque fountain,** this 15th-century church was the favorite church of the Aragonese dynasty, which is why many of them are buried here. This is also why the artwork and architectural masterpieces here make this church a Renaissance gem. The elegant **Piccolomini Chapel** to the left houses the **tomb of Maria d'Aragona,** by Antonio Rossellino and

Benedetto da Maiano. The **Cappella Tolosa,** also to the left, decorated in the styles of Brunelleschi and della Robbia by Giuliano da Maiano, is a showcase of Neapolitan sculpture from the 15th and 16th centuries. The **Cappella Correale,** to the right, holds a beautiful *San Cristoforo* by Francesco Solimena over a superb marble altar by Benedetto da Maiano. In the sacristy are frescoes by Giorgio Vasari and helpers, as well as the spectacular wood inlay work by Giovanni da Verona (created 1506–10) depicting classical panoramas, musical instruments, and other scenes with thousands of tiny slivers of wood of various kinds and colors.

See map p. 386. Piazza Monteoliveto 44. ☎ *081-5513333. Metro: Dante; Bus: R1, R2, R3, or R4. Admission: Free. Open: Mon–Sat 9 a.m. to noon; Sat also 5:30–6:30 p.m.*

Finding more cool things to see and do

Naples has enough attractions to satisfy its visitors for weeks on end. Here are some more sights to explore:

✔ Built at the end of the 19th century (20 years after its larger Milanese counterpart), the **Galleria Umberto I** (Bus: R2 or R3 to Piazza Trieste e Trento) is a splendid example of the Liberty style (Italian Art Nouveau). Opening to the right of Via Toledo as you come from Piazza del Plebiscito, the glass-and-iron covered passage is an enormous airy space with a soaring glass ceiling, lined with graciously decorated buildings and elegant shops. Come to marvel at the architecture or to simply shop (see "Shopping the Local Stores," later in this chapter).

✔ Built by the Bourbons at the beginning of the 18th century, the **Teatro San Carlo** (Via San Carlo 93; ☎ 081-400300; Bus: R2 or R3 to Via San Carlo) is among Europe's most beautiful opera houses, a neoclassical jewel with an ornate gilded interior. It was also the first opera theater in the world and is said to have even better acoustics than Milan's famous La Scala. You can appreciate its architecture and decorations by taking the free guided tour (by reservation at ☎ 081-664545; www.itineranapoli.com), but of course you can also come for a performance to see the building in its full glory and hear for yourself (see "Living It Up After Dark," later in this chapter).

✔ The country house of the Duchess of Floridia, second wife of King Ferdinand II Bourbon, **Villa La Floridiana** (Via Domenico Cimarosa 77; ☎ 081-407881; Funivia to Vomero; Admission: 2.50€/$3; 10 percent discount with artecard; Open: Wed–Mon 8:30 a.m.–2 p.m.), is a very pleasant place indeed. The richly decorated halls house a **porcelain museum** that boasts the world's largest collection of Capodimonte porcelain, as well as other precious objects. The splendid park affords great views of the city and the bay.

✔ The dark and mysterious Prince Raimondo di Sangro of Sansevero, an alchemist from the 18th century, transformed his family chapel into an architectural marvel. The **Cappella di San Severo** (Via

Francesco De Sanctis 19; ☎ **081-5518470;** www.museosansevero. it; Metro: Dante; Admission: 6€/$7.20; 20 percent discount with artecard; Open: Mon–Sat 10 a.m.–6 p.m., Sun 10 a.m.–1 p.m.), in the *città antica,* contains some of the most strangely beautiful sculptures of the time, including the famous *Veiled Christ,* by the Neapolitan master Giuseppe Sanmartino. The crypt holds two mummified bodies — the work of the prince — showing their perfectly preserved circulatory systems.

✔ Less frequently visited than the Duomo, **San Domenico Maggiore** (Piazza San Domenico Maggiore, off Via Benedetto Croce; ☎ **081-449097;** Metro: Piazza Cavour; Admission: Free; Open: Daily 9 a.m. to noon and 5–7 p.m.) is still a splendid church. Built by the Angevins in the 13th century, its main facade is not on the *piazza* but inside a courtyard, according to their customs. The interior is graced by innumerable works of art, from the elegant Renaissance monumental tombs along the walls to the 14th-century frescoes and many paintings. From the transept, you can also visit the medieval church of **San Michele Arcangelo a Morfisa,** which was incorporated into the newer one. In the *piazza* is the **Guglia San Domenico,** one of the city's typical baroque stone spires — a pile of carved figures — erected at the end of the plague.

✔ In use between the second and ninth centuries, the **Catacombs of St. Gennaro** (Via Capodimonte 13, down a small alley running alongside the church Madre del Buon Consiglio; ☎ **081-7411071;** Bus: 24 or R4 to Via Capodimonte; Admission: 3€/$3.60) are particularly famous for the well-maintained frescoes decorating the large corridors and chapels. One of the most beautiful is the **Cripta dei Vescovi** on the upper level, decorated with fifth-century mosaics. Buried in these catacombs is San Gennaro, the patron saint of Naples — hence the name — whose remains were moved here in the fifth century. You can visit only by guided tour, Tuesday through Sunday at 9 a.m., 10 a.m., 11 a.m., and noon.

✔ The medieval church of **San Lorenzo Maggiore** (Piazza San Gaetano; ☎ **081-290580;** Metro: Cavour; Open: Mon–Sat 8 a.m. to noon and 5–7 p.m.) has important literary references, as it's where the poet Boccaccio (author of the *Decameron*) met his love, Fiammetta, back in 1334. The attached convent was also home to the great poet Francesco Petrarca (Petrarch) for a time. Originally built in the sixth century, the church enjoyed both a Renaissance and a baroque overhaul, which left untouched the beautiful 13th- and 14th-century frescoes, as well as the many carvings decorating the interior. From the cloister, you can access the very interesting archaeological excavations (www.sanlorenzomaggiorenapoli.it; Admission: 2€/$2.40; Open: Tues–Sun 9 a.m.–6 p.m.), descending to the Roman and Greek period: You'll see different layers, with the Greek merchant stalls at the bottom, then the ancient Roman market, a paleo-Christian basilica, and the medieval buildings.

✔ The neighborhood of **Mergellina** (Tram: 1; Bus: 140; Metro: Mergellina), to the west of Chiaia, lies along the waterfront, where you'll find the pleasure harbor and the hydrofoil terminal. Only a short distance from the city center, Neapolitans like to come here for dinner and ice cream by the sea, looking at the bay from under the shadow of the **Posillipo** towering promontory. If you want to do like the locals, try **Don Salvatore** (Via Mergellina 4/a; ☎ 081-681817; closed Wed in winter), a good *trattoria* housed in a former boat shed, or the more formal **Ciro a Mergellina** (Via Mergellina 18; ☎ 081-6 81780; closed Mon), which has better service as well as excellent pizza. At both places, you can enjoy nicely grilled fresh fish, accompanied by local vegetables, or else opt for the seafood pasta or *risotto*.

Seeing Naples by guided tour

The hop-on/hop-off buses operated by **City Sightseeing** (☎ 081-5517279; www.napoli.city-sightseeing.it) offer a great way to see the city as well as a good alternative to public transportation. Three one-hour itineraries start from Piazza Municipio/Parco Castello: **Line A** travels inland to Museo di Capodimonte (9:45 a.m.–6:45 p.m., every 45 minutes); **Line B** goes along the seaside to Posillipo (9:30 a.m.–7:30 p.m., every 45 minutes); and **Line C** heads to the Carthusian Monastery of San Martino on the Vomero (Sat–Sun and holidays 10 a.m.–7 p.m., every two hours). Check the schedule, as it changes often. You can get tickets on board for 16€ ($19) for adults and 8€ ($10) for children 5 to 15. Tickets are valid for both itineraries for 24 hours. You get a 10 percent discount if you have the **artecard** (see the beginning of the "Exploring Naples" section, earlier in this chapter).

At **Museo Aperto Napoli** (Via Pietro Colletta 85; ☎ 081-5636062; www.museoapertonapoli.com; Open: Daily 10 a.m.–6 p.m.), you can sign up for free self-guided walking tours (with a map and audio guide in six languages) of the *città antica*.

Suggested one-, two-, and three-day itineraries

Even for a short stay, consider purchasing the **artecard,** which gets you free and discounted admissions to attractions, unlimited public transportation, and a variety of other discounts (see the beginning of the "Exploring Naples" section, earlier in this chapter).

Naples in one day

It's impossible to see the best of Naples in one day, but you can hit some of the highlights; it only means that you'll have to return for more days next time! Begin in Piazza Municipio, taking in the **Castel Nuovo** — the huge fortress in the center of the square — and stopping just long enough to admire its magnificent portal. Head now for the **City Sightseeing** hop-on/hop-off bus to the side of the *piazza* and buy a ticket: Its three routes offer a great way to get an overview of the city and to move from attraction to attraction. Go directly up to the **Museo di Capodimonte,** where you've made advance reservations, and spend time exploring this splendid museum. After your visit, hop back on the bus and get off at **Porta Capuana** to have lunch at the **Pizzeria di Matteo.** After your taste of real Neapolitan pizza, take a stroll along Via dei Tribunali in the heart of the *città antica.* Stop at the **Caffetteria Pasticceria Gelateria G. Mazzaro** for a snack of Neapolitan coffee and pastries (see "Dining Out," earlier in this chapter) while you wait for the Duomo to open. After your visit to the **Duomo,** its **baptistery,** and its **Cappella di San Gennaro,** head for the **Museo Archeologico.** You can't skip this part — some of the ancient Roman artifacts here are the best in the world. Then climb back on your bus and, back in Piazza Municipio, switch to Line B for a sunset ride along the waterfront. Stop at **Castel dell'Ovo** on the way back and have dinner by the sea, taking in the romantic beauty of the bay. After your meal, stroll to **Piazza Plebiscito,** the most beautiful square in Naples, for your adieu to this magic city.

Naples in two days

Two days is a lot better than one — you'll be able to skip fewer attractions. Here's how we'd spend our time:

Day 1

Start off by following our "Naples in one day" itinerary, earlier in this chapter, up to and including the visit to the **Duomo,** but then dedicate more time to the old streets of the *città antica,* also visiting **Santa Chiara** and one or all of the minor churches — **Cappella San Severo, San Domenico Maggiore,** and **San Lorenzo Maggiore.** Get back on your bus at Piazza Bovio and finish the day as in the itinerary earlier in this chapter, with a scenic waterfront ride and dinner.

Day 2

Begin your day at **Santa Maria di Monteoliveto (Sant'Anna dei Lombardi),** maybe stopping for *caffè* and *sfogliatella* at the **Gran Caffè Gambrinus** on your way. Proceed then to the **Museo Archeologico,** where you'll spend the rest of your morning. Dedicate your afternoon to the **Riviera di Chiaia,** strolling the waterfront, and visiting the **Giardini Comunali.** End your stay in memorable fashion, with *aperitivo* at Piazza dei Martiri and dinner at **George's** in the Grand Hotel Parker's (see "Dining Out," earlier in this chapter).

Naples in three days

Follow our itinerary for "Naples in two days," earlier in this chapter. On your third day, devote your morning to a visit of **Castel Nuovo,** followed by a *funivia* ride up to the **Vomero** to see the splendid attractions up there. Visit **Villa La Floridiana** before having lunch at **Gorizia** (see "Dining Out," earlier in this chapter). Then proceed to the **Carthusian Monastery of San Martino;** you can then follow up with **Castel Sant'Elmo** to admire the sunset over the bay from its splendid vantage point, or descend to

Chiaia for some shopping. Alternatively, you can dedicate your whole day to one of the side trips we highlight in Chapter 19 — **Pompeii, Herculaneum,** or the **Campi Flegrei**— or catch a ferry to **Capri** (see Chapter 20).

Shopping the Local Stores

Though not as glitzy and ubiquitous as in Milan or Rome, shopping in Naples does offer some serious possibilities. You can find all the big and small names of Italian fashion here, as well as some local designers. Naples also excels in antiques, but you need to know what you're doing (the city is known for its experts in the tricky art of "antiquing," or making something new look old). Finally, Naples and the surrounding areas maintain a tradition of producing crafts — one specialty being **cameos** (delicately carved jewels using colored stone like agate or coral), the other being figurines for *presepi* **(manger scenes).** Both of these artistic traditions date back to the 18th century.

Best shopping areas

In the elegant area behind the **Chiaia** waterfront, you'll find all the big names of Italian fashion, such as Valentino, Versace, Ferragamo, and Prada, plus a lot of other nice boutiques. The best streets for such high-end shopping are **Via dei Mille, Piazza dei Martiri,** and **Via Calabritto.** Also in this area are many **antiques** dealers. **Via Domenico Morelli** is home of the city's most established dealers, specializing in 18th-century furniture and paintings. Another good area for shopping is **Via Toledo,** the animated street leading away from Piazza del Plebiscito.

What to look for and where to find it

Shops in Naples are generally open Monday through Saturday from 10:30 a.m. to 1 p.m. and from 4 or 4:30 to 7:30 or 8 p.m.

Accessories

Among the local designers, **Marinella** (Via Riviera di Chiaia 287; ☎ 081-7644214; Open: Mon–Sat 6:45 a.m.–8 p.m.) is the most famous. The specialty is cravats and ties, with a new collection offered almost every week.

Antiques

The **Fiera Antiquaria** (☎ 081-621951), in the Villa Comunale di Napoli on Viale Dohrn, is an important event held every third Saturday and Sunday of each month from 8 a.m. to 2 p.m. (except in Aug).

Two reputable antiques shops are **Regency House** (Via D. Morelli 36; ☎ 081-764-3640) and **Navarra** (Piazza dei Martiri; ☎ 081-764-3595). To get to these shops, take bus no. R3 to Riviera di Chiaia.

Cameos

In the **Galleria Umberto I,** off Via Toledo (see "Finding more cool things to see and do," earlier in this chapter), you can buy as well as see a demonstration of cameo and coral carving, at **Ascione 1855** (☎ 081-421111).

Chocolate

The most interesting shop in Naples is **Gay-Odin** (Via Toledo 214 and up the street at no. 427; ☎ 081-417843), a historic chocolate factory making delicious, 100-percent pure chocolate (what you usually get is 30-percent chocolate at best), and such daring concoctions as chocolate *con peperoncino* (with hot pepper): try it, it is great!

Presepi (Manger Figurines)

At **Gambardella Pastori** (Via San Gregorio Armeno 40; ☎ 081-5517107), you'll find a large array of manger figurines and accessories. Another good resource is **Giuseppe Ferrigno** (Via San Gregorio Armeno 8; ☎ 081-5523148). These are traditional workshops selling quality items, but nearby you'll also find cheaper plastic versions of the same thing.

Living It Up After Dark

Like other Italians, Neapolitans like to stroll in the evening, perhaps having an ice cream or sitting out on the terrace of a popular cafe. On the other hand, the lively local cultural life is also well worth sampling.

The performing arts

Seeing an opera at the **Teatro San Carlo** (Via San Carlo 98/f; ☎ 081-7972412 or 081-7972331; www.teatrosancarlo.it) is an unforgettable experience. This is a world-class venue (see "Finding more cool things to see and do," earlier in this chapter) that attracts the best international stars. The acoustics are excellent, and the program always includes some grandiose production. The season runs from December to June, with shows Tuesday through Sunday. Ticket prices range from 45€ to 110€ ($54–$132); you can get a 20 percent discount with the artecard.

Traditional Neapolitan songs are famous around the world — think *O Sole Mio* — and you can see some of the best performers at the **Trianon** (Piazza Vincenzo Calenda 9; ☎ 081-2258285). Tickets cost 5€ to 25€ ($6–$30), with 10 percent off if you have an artecard.

Live music

Naples has a tradition of music, and its pop scene is very lively with both new and more established local groups. The local sound is jazz mixed with traditional and ethnic influences. You can sample some of it at **Il Re Nudo** (Via Manzoni 126; ☎ 081-7146272) or **Vibes Cafe** (Via San Giovanni Maggiore Pignatelli 10; ☎ 081-5513984).

Clubs and discos

A real harbor town, Naples offers a lively nightlife scene with discos and clubs galore; they're mostly open Thursday through Saturday until 4 or 5 a.m. One of the most popular is **Chez Moi** (Via del Parco Margherita 13; ☎ 081-407526), a small, chic hangout in Chiaia. Nearby is **La Mela** (Via dei Mille; ☎ 081-4010270), where the best night is Thursday.

For a gay atmosphere, go to **Tongue** (Via Manzoni 202; ☎ 081-7690888), in the seaside suburb of Posillipo, where you'll find a mixed crowd with a large proportion of gays and lesbians. In the *città antica,* check out **Bar B** (Via Giovanni Manna, near the Duomo; ☎ 081-287681), which has an attached sauna.

Wine bars and cafes

Aperitivo and after-dinner pastries and ice cream are popular with locals; join them at the oldest cafe in Naples, the **Gran Caffè Gambrinus** (Via Chiaia 1; ☎ 081-417582; Bus: R2 or R3 to Piazza Trieste e Trento). The cafe has been beautifully restored to its full glory; the ornate gilded interior dates from the 1860s. If Gambrinus is too full, try the nearby **Caffè del Professore** (Piazza Trieste e Trento 46; ☎ 081-403041), less glitzy but also popular. Even more fashionable is **La Caffetteria** (Piazza dei Martiri; ☎ 081-7644243). Also trendy is the roof bar of the **Starhotel Terminus** (Piazza Garibaldi 91; ☎ 081-7793111).

If you feel like relaxing over a nice glass of *vino,* **Berevino** (Via Sebastiano 62; ☎ 081-290313) is an *enoteca* with lots of room and many wines to sample. With its beamed ceiling and warm interior, it will make you feel as if you've stepped into the countryside. Berevino also serves food and has a full bar.

Fast Facts: Naples

American Express

American Express business is handled by Every Tours (Piazza del Municipio 5; ☎ 081-5518564; Bus: R2 or R3 to Piazza del Municipio). It's open Monday through Friday from 9 a.m. to 1 p.m. and 3:30 to 7 p.m., Saturday from 9:30 a.m. to 1 p.m.

Area Code

The local area code is **081** (see "Telephone" in the "Fast Facts" section of Appendix A for more on calling to and from Italy).

ATMs

You'll find several banks with ATMs in the historic district, particularly along Via Toledo, Via Chiaia, and Corso Umberto I. You'll find a BNL (Banca Nazionale del Lavoro) linked to the PLUS network at Via Toledo 126 (☎ 081-799111), and another at Piazza dei Martiri 23.

Currency Exchange

There are three exchange offices at Piazza Garibaldi (Metro: Piazza Garibaldi) and four on Corso Umberto at nos. 44, 92, 212, and 292 (Bus: R2 to Corso Umberto). Thomas Cook is at Piazza del Municipio (Bus: R2 or R3 to Piazza del Municipio).

Doctors

Call the 24-hour Guardia Medica Specialistica at ☎ 081-431111, or contact any consulate to get a list of English-speaking doctors.

Embassies and Consulates

The U.S. Consulate is at Piazza della Repubblica (☎ 081-583-8111); the U.K. Consulate is at Via Francesco Crispi 122 (☎ 081-663-511). For other embassies and consulates, see Appendix A.

Emergencies

For an ambulance, call ☎ **118**, 081-7804296, or 081-5841481. For the fire department, call ☎ **115**. For first aid *(pronto soccorso)*, call ☎ **081-7520696**.

Hospitals

The Ospedale Fatebenefratelli is at Via Manzoni 220 (☎ 081-7697220).

Information

You'll find a small tourist info desk inside the Stazione Centrale train station (☎ 081-268799; Metro: Piazza Garibaldi), and larger ones at Via S. Carlo 9 (☎ 081-402394; www.inaples.it); and at Piazza del Gesù (☎ 081-5512701).

Internet Access

You'll find two Internet Point branches off Via Toledo, one at Vico Tre Re a Toledo 59/a (☎ 081-4976090) and another at Via Montecalvario 9.

Maps

All newsstands in the historic district carry maps (often the excellent but large *Pianta Generale* by N. Vincitorio); you can do well

with the wallet-sized *Mini-City,* sold at the bookshop of Palazzo Reale and other major museums.

Newspapers and Magazines

You can find foreign newspapers and magazines at the news kiosks, particularly the ones at the train station and near the U.S. Consulate. The best source for a calendar of events is the free monthly *QuiNapoli* (bilingual in English), distributed at the tourist info desks; you can also download it at www.inaples.it.

Pharmacies

The one in the Stazione Centrale train station (Piazza Garibaldi; ☎ 081-5548894; Metro: Piazza Garibaldi) is open most nights.

Police

Call ☎ **113**.

Post Office

The main post office *(ufficio postale)* is at Piazza Matteotti (☎ 081-5511456; Bus: R3 to Piazza Matteotti).

Restrooms

You'll find public restrooms inside museums and major attractions. Otherwise, your best bet is to go to a nice-looking cafe (you'll have to buy something, like a cup of coffee).

Safety

Pickpockets are common; keep an eye out on your belongings and your car. Occasional muggings occur on deserted and dark streets at night, but most criminal activity takes place in the poorer areas to the east and north of the historic district.

Smoking

In 2005, Italy passed a law outlawing smoking in most public places. Smoking is allowed only where there is a separate, ventilated area for nonsmokers. If you want to smoke at your table, call beforehand to make sure the restaurant or cafe you'll be visiting offers a smoking area.

Taxes

See Chapter 5 for information on IVA (Value Added Tax).

Taxi

You can walk to the taxi stands at the Duomo, Piazza Municipio, or Piazza Trieste e Trento, or call one of the five radio-taxi companies for pickup: ☎ 081-5707070, 081-5515151, 081-5564444, 081-5560202, or 081-5525252.

Transit Info

Contact Trenitalia (☎ 892021; www.trenitalia.it) for railroad information. Contact the Naples transportation authority (☎ 800-482644; www.ctpn.it) for information on local trains, buses, trams, the metro, and funiculars.

Weather Updates

Your best bet is the news on TV. (There's no phone number for weather forecasts in Italy, as there is in the U.S

Chapter 19

Going Beyond Naples: Three Day Trips

In This Chapter

▶ Checking out steam holes and ruins in the Campi Flegrei
▶ Seeing the eerie sights of Herculaneum
▶ Discovering the marvels of Pompeii

*R*ich in history and natural beauty, the region surrounding Naples is a favorite destination of antiquity lovers and seaside loungers in particular. While the famous sites of **Herculaneum** and **Pompeii** are today mainly interesting for their archaeological areas, the ancient Roman resort of **Baia** and busy **Pozzuoli,** in the volcanic natural park of the **Campi Flegrei,** have maintained their appeal and are still attracting visitors — not only for their Greek and ancient Roman ruins, but also for their splendid seaside scenery.

You can visit each destination as a day trip from Naples, but the area of the Campi Flegrei could also warrant a longer stay if you have the time.

Campi Flegrei

This volcanic area, lying to the west of Naples, was established as a protected natural park in 1993. Its attractions range from the archaeological sites of **Pozzuoli** to the dramatic ruins of **Cuma,** from the hot mud and steam holes in the volcano of the **Solfatara** to beautiful lakes and the underwater archaeological park of **Baia.**

Getting there

Pozzuoli, the area's main town, is about 18km (11 miles) from the center of Naples and is connected to the city by metro line no. 2; by the Cumana railroad — a frequent commuter line — from Piazza Montesanto in Chiaia (☎ 800-001616 in Italy); and by the scenic but slower bus no. 152, starting from Piazza Garibaldi in Naples and going through Santa Lucia and Chiaia. Allow about 15 to 20 minutes to get here by metro or rail, and an hour by bus. To reach the farthest attractions, your best bet is to take the

Archeobus (see later in this section). If you visit when the Archeobus isn't operating, you can take a taxi (same rates as in Naples; see Chapter 18) from the taxi stand at Piazza della Repubblica, in Pozzuoli (☎ 081-5265800), or the one at Piazzetta Centrale, in Bacoli (☎ 081-5235300) — or use the local **bus service** (☎ 800-001616 in Italy; www.sepsa.it) and the Cumana commuter train (see earlier in this paragraph) between Pozzuoli and Baia.

Taking a tour

The **Archeobus** (☎ 800-001616 in Italy; www.sepsa.it) is the park's official hop-on/hop-off bus tour. Tickets cost 8€ ($9.60) and are included with the artecard (see "Exploring Naples," in Chapter 18). The bus operates hourly, Friday through Sunday from 9 a.m. to 7 p.m., from Piazza della Repubblica in Pozzuoli (check again before your trip, as the schedule changes often). The whole loop takes 90 minutes, with 16 intermediary stops.

Seeing the sights

The whole area itself is the attraction, centered around a small bay with splendid views of the islands of Ischia and Procida. **Pozzuoli** is the main town and the park's entrance; it's a lively town on a picturesque bay, home to many locals who commute to Naples.

If you're planning to see several attractions in the Naples area, the best deal after the **artecard** (see "Exploring Naples," in Chapter 18) is the 5.50€ ($6.60) **combination ticket,** valid for two days and including the archaeological area and museum of Baia, the excavations of Cuma, Rione Terra, and the archaeological area in Pozzuoli.

Archaeological Area and Museum of Baia

Baia was a lively VIP resort in Roman times as well as an important town; its ruins are scattered over a large area adjacent to today's welcoming fishing town. The most interesting are the **Thermal Baths,** fabled in antiquity for their beauty and therapeutic properties. You can admire the pools and rooms, as well as the complicated hydraulic systems that worked underneath. From the baths, follow a footpath to the **Monumental Park,** the rest of the huge archaeological area — it covers over 14 hectares (35 acres) — which is still being excavated, exposing partially uncovered villas and imperial residences. The **museum,** housing the best findings from the archaeological area, is located in the **Aragonese Castle** on the promontory overlooking the town.

Thermal Baths: Via Sella di Baia 22. ☎ 081-8687592. Museum: Via Castello 39. ☎ 081-5233797. Admission: 4€ ($4.80); includes archaeological area of Pozzuoli and excavations of Cuma. Open: Tues–Sun Thermal baths 9 a.m. to 1 hour before sunset; museum 9 a.m.–8 p.m. Ticket booth closes 1 hour earlier. Closed Jan 1, May 1, and Dec 25.

Underwater Archaeological Park of Baia

Visiting the part of the ruins of Roman Baia that are submerged under the sea is a very evocative experience, whether you do it by glass-bottom boat or by scuba diving. The prices are the same, but the dive is unique and memorable; you'll need to be certified to do it (the dive is easy, as the ruins lie only a few feet underwater). The glass-bottom boat excursion is also very nice; departures are by the harbor.

Harbor of Baia. ☎ *081-5248169.* www.baiasommersa.it. *Admission: 35€ ($42), including boat and scuba equipment. Open: Mid-Mar to mid-Nov Tues–Sun 9:30 a.m.–1:30 p.m. and 3:30–7:30 p.m.*

Excavations of Cuma

Back when the ancient Greeks started taking over the Mediterranean, this is where they founded their first colony, in the eighth century B.C. The settlement rapidly evolved to become the most important city on this coast, and the little that remains today speaks of its past grandeur: its **acropolis** and part of the **fortified walls**, as well as a **necropolis**, an **amphitheater**, and a grandiose but mysterious tunnel excavated through the mountain. Known as **Sybilla's Cave**, it was for a long time believed to have been the cave where this priestess to Apollo officiated; in reality, it was probably a strategic construction. The view from the terraces is spectacular.

Via Monte di Cuma 3. ☎ *081-8543060. Admission: 4€ ($4.80); includes archaeological area of Pozzuoli and archaeological area and museum of Baia. Open: Daily 9 a.m. to 1 hour before sunset. Ticket booth closes 1 hour earlier. Closed Jan 1, May 1, and Dec 25.*

Archaeological Area of Pozzuoli

A Greek and then Roman town, Puteoli — as it was then called — surpassed Naples many times in size, commercial significance, and strategic importance, as you can see from its imposing ruins scattered throughout the modern town. The so-called **Temple of Serapis** by the harbor — actually the town's market and forum from the first century A.D. — is an elegant columned structure, once lined with shops and taverns with a temple in the middle; the whole thing was once submerged beneath sea level, but has now re-emerged due to the local phenomenon of bradisism (a slow movement of the earth's surface). The third largest after the Colosseum, the **Flavian Amphitheater** to the north of town is worth the detour; the walls and the vaulted ceilings under the arena are still preserved here, unlike the Colosseum's, where they have collapsed. The arena hosts special musical performances during the **Flavian Nights Festival** (☎ 081-7611221 for a schedule of events.)

Temple of Serapis: Via Roma 10. Amphitheater: Via Terracciano 75. ☎ *081-5266007. Admission: 4€ ($4.80); includes excavations of Cuma and archaeological area and museum of Baia. Open: Daily 9 a.m. to 1 hour before sunset. Closed Jan 1, May 1, and Dec 25.*

Rione Terra

The most suggestive ruin in Pozzuoli, this is the excavation of what was once the town's acropolis, which later sunk to below sea level. You can walk the streets underground and see the shops and taverns that lined them; you'll need to sign up for your visit in advance. We also recommend taking the 3.50€ ($4.20) guided tour.

Largo Sedile di Porta. ☎ *848-800288 or 06-39967050 for reservations. Admission 3€ ($3.60), plus 2€ ($2.40) reservations fee, children under 6 free. Open: Sat–Sun 9 a.m.–7 p.m.*

Solfatara

A 20-minute walk uphill, or a five-minute taxi ride from Pozzuoli, this is actually the large crater of a flattish volcano which was used as a spa back in the 19th century. You can see a series of impressive phenomena, from hissing steam holes to bubbling mud, not to mention the pervasive sulfurous smell. Quite hellish, but not to be missed!

Via Solfatara 161. ☎ *081-5262341.* www.solfatara.it. *Admission 5.50€ ($6.60); children under 4 free; 20 percent discount with artecard. Open: Daily 8:30 a.m.–7 p.m.*

Dining locally

Il Brontolone
$ Pozzuoli NEAPOLITAN

This restaurant features a good choice of local dishes, well prepared and moderately priced. We loved the simply prepared, very fresh, and very tasty seafood: The various catches of the day are displayed on ice, so you can choose your fish and how you'd like it prepared (baked with potatoes, grilled, or *all'acquapazza* — in a light herbed broth). The buffet of *antipasto* and side dishes is superb — you could create a whole meal from the tasty vegetables and seafood salads alone.

Via Campana 121. ☎ *081-5266510. Reservations recommended on weekends. Secondi: 6€–12€ ($7.20–$14). AE, DC, MC, V. Open: Tues–Sun noon to 3 p.m. and 7–11 p.m.*

Il Tucano
$ Baia NEAPOLITAN/PIZZA

Il Tucano is an excellent spot, right on the harbor, to have a quick bite. The very good pizza here is served "by the foot" — actually by the centimeter — so all you have to do is show how big a piece you want (you can use your hands). The restaurant also has a regular menu that lists several local specialties and pasta dishes.

Via Molo di Baia. ☎ *081-8545046. Reservations not necessary. Secondi: 8€–16€ ($9.60–$19). MC, V. Open: Tues–Sun noon to midnight.*

Vecchio Ulivo
$$ **Pozzuoli** NEAPOLITAN/SEAFOOD

Head here for a romantic dinner at moderate prices. Located in the town of Pozzuoli, this restaurant serves traditional food prepared with the freshest ingredients. If they're on the menu, we recommend the fish lasagna as well as the simple but delicious spaghetti with *cozze* (mussels).

Via Cupa della Fescina 35. ☎ *081-5241180. Reservations recommended. Secondi: 11€–14€ ($13–$17). AE, DC, MC, V. Open: Mon–Sat 7:30–11 p.m.*

Spending the night

Hotels in town tend to be very simple. This one is the best in the area:

Cala Moresca
$ **Bacoli**

A pleasant seaside resort with a picturesque location, this hotel is a short distance from Baia within a large park. The spacious guest rooms are luminous, each with a private balcony and functional modern furnishings. Bathrooms are good-sized and very well kept. Small children will enjoy the playground, while older ones and adults can hike or play tennis and squash. You can swim either in the pool or from the hotel's rocky beach.

Via Faro 44. ☎ *081-5235595. Fax: 081-5235557.* www.calamoresca.it. *Rates: 135€ ($162) double. Rates include buffet breakfast. AE, DC, MC, V. Free parking. Closed Dec 24–26.*

Herculaneum

Few archaeological sites are as moving as this town buried beneath volcanic mud after Mount Vesuvius erupted in A.D. 79. The mud preserved the houses to a remarkable extent, and the town has yielded great numbers of artifacts and sculptures, some of which are on display in the Archaeological Museum of Naples (see Chapter 18).

Getting there

From Naples, take either line of the **Circumvesuviana Train** (Corso Garibaldi; ☎ **800-053939;** www.vesuviana.it; Metro: Garibaldi) to the **Ercolano Scavi** stop; outside the station, you'll find a shuttle bus to the site. The 20-minute ride costs 1.70€ ($2); trains leave every half-hour.

Taking a tour

The agency **Every Tours** (Piazza del Municipio 5; ☎ **081-551-8564;** Metro: Garibaldi) — which serves as the American Express office in Naples — organizes day excursions to Herculaneum. Unless you are keen on bus tours, we much prefer getting to the archaeological area by ourselves and booking one of the official guided tours (see later in this section).

Seeing the sights

Unless you're visiting in the dead of winter, remember to bring a hat, plenty of sunscreen, and water. There are no trees among the ruins, and it can get really hot here. Remember to wear comfortable shoes as well.

If you have time to visit both Herculaneum and Pompeii, you can get a **combination ticket** for 18€ ($22); it is valid for three days and gives you access to three other archaeological sites in the Vesuvian area — Oplonti, Stabia, and Boscoreale. This is a good alternative to the 25€ ($30) **"3 days all sites" artcard** (see "Exploring Naples," in Chapter 18), which grants free admission to two attractions and a 50 percent discount on all others from an extensive list (including Pompeii, Herculaneum, and Paestum).

Archaeological Area

Smaller than Pompeii — about a third the size, according to experts — this was the glitzier seaside resort for VIPs during Roman times. It's been estimated that at the time of the eruption, Herculaneum was a town of about 5,000. Because it was covered in hard volcanic mud — and the new town was built over it — only a small part has been excavated, but what has been unearthed is highly interesting: rich and elaborate buildings, along with woodwork that's only partially burned. Among the most interesting public sites are the elegantly decorated **thermal baths** and the **Palestra,** a sports arena where games were staged to satisfy the spectacle-hungry denizens. The **Collegio degli Augustali,** lavishly adorned with marble floors and frescoes, had a custodian: He was found sleeping in his bed, which you can still see in his small room. The best example of private architecture is the **House of the Stags,** named for the sculpture found inside; it was an elegant town house overlooking the sea, built around atriums and terraces, and decorated extravagantly. The **House of the Latticework** was at the other end of the scale: It was where poor workers had their rooms, in a forerunner of project housing. The **House of the Mosaic of Neptune,** in contrast, belonged to a merchant — and you can see his shop lined with cabinets and merchandise still on his counter. *Tip:* We strongly recommend signing up for an official guided tour at the

Pack a picnic

There's little to eat at the excavation sites, so it's a good idea to pack a picnic lunch to bring along (don't forget plenty of water during the summer). If you want to eat in a restaurant, you'll have to head for the modern town of Ercolano, which is relatively poor, though it does have a few snack bars near the center.

Herculaneum

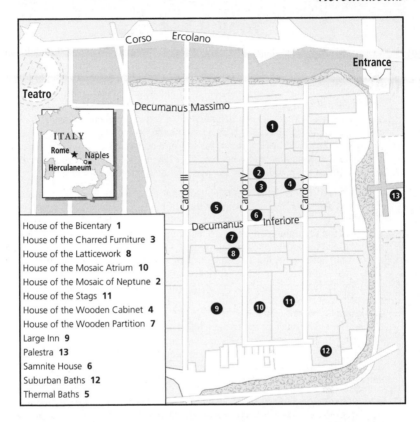

Corso Ercolano

Entrance

Teatro

Decumanus Massimo

ITALY

Rome ★ Naples
Herculaneum

Cardo III

Cardo IV

Cardo V

① ② ③ ④ ⑬

⑤ ⑥

Decumanus Inferiore

⑦

⑧

⑨ ⑩ ⑪

⑫

House of the Bicentary **1**
House of the Charred Furniture **3**
House of the Latticework **8**
House of the Mosaic Atrium **10**
House of the Mosaic of Neptune **2**
House of the Stags **11**
House of the Wooden Cabinet **4**
House of the Wooden Partition **7**
Large Inn **9**
Palestra **13**
Samnite House **6**
Suburban Baths **12**
Thermal Baths **5**

entrance (in high season, make reservations ahead): A number of the houses on the site have been gated to protect the very interesting remains within, and if you're on your own, you'll have to squint between the iron bars for a peek.

See map above. Corso Resina. ☎ *081-8575347 (reservations daily 10 a.m.–1:30 p.m.).* www.pompeiisites.org. *Admission: 10€ ($12). Included on the artecard list (see Chapter 18). Open: Daily Nov–Mar 8:30 a.m.–5 p.m.; daily Apr–Oct 8:30 a.m.–7:30 p.m. Last entrance 90 minutes earlier.*

Villa dei Papiri

Opened to the public in March 2004, this grandiose villa must have belonged to a wealthy, literate art lover: A library of thousands of papyrus rolls were found inside (giving the villa its current name), along with a large collection of sculptures. Extending for over 250m (820 ft.) along the coast, this villa was built around A.D. 60; you can visit both the lower and upper

Mount Vesuvius

Loved and feared by Neapolitans, **Mount Vesuvius (Vesuvio)** is the dormant volcano that dominates Naples and its bay to the southeast. Mount Vesuvius is the only continental volcano still active in Europe, and it is now a national park. Of the two major kinds of volcanoes — some slowly ooze magma, like the ones on Hawaii; others build and build up pressure inside and then blow their tops — Vesuvius is a topblower. Although Vesuvius has belched only a few puffs of smoke since the last real eruption in 1944, no one really knows whether the volcano is losing its punch or just biding its time. It had been dormant for centuries when it exploded in the great eruption of A.D. 79., which buried Pompeii and Herculaneum. It got everybody on their toes when it puffed again in 1999, just in case anyone thought it was extinct.

Luckily, one of the best (and the first) observatories for the study of volcanology is right here on the mountain, taking its pulse daily. From Naples, take the **Circumvesuviana Train** (Corso Garibaldi; ☎ 800-053939; www.vesuviana.it; Metro: Garibaldi) and get off at the **Ercolano** stop, about 15 minutes away. From there, an electric minibus will take you to the entrance of the park at 1,017m (3,106 ft.) altitude. The trip costs about 1.50€ ($1.80). Rising 1,281m (3,944 ft.), the slopes of Vesuvius are green with vineyards — producing the famous local wine, the amber-colored Lacrimae Christi — and they become more rugged only as you approach the top. At the entrance of the park (Admission: 4.50€/$5.40; Open: Daily 9 a.m.–sunset; last entrance one hour earlier), there is a **visitor center** (☎ 081-7775720) where you can sign up for a guided tour of the crater (3€/$3.60), as well as a historic *osteria* that was recently restored and is now open for business. A small shop sells local products, including wine. Nearby, at 608m (1,994 ft.), you can visit the **Vesuvian Observatory,** the top-notch center that has observed the volcano's activity day by day since around 1850. Attached to the observatory are the geological museum and a rich scientific library.

After entering the park, you'll follow a dirt trail to the crater. Closer to the top, the dirt trail becomes lava, which looks like typical black-and-purple rough pieces of stone. The trail circles the crater, but you'll need a guide to descend into it and look at the smoldering lava. From the top on a good day, you can enjoy a fantastic view of the Bay of Naples. The manageable uphill hike — up 264m (838 ft.) in altitude — takes about an hour; allow twice as much time if you choose to descend into the crater. You can also join an organized tour from Naples: **Every Tours** (Piazza del Municipio 5; ☎ 081-5518564) offers classic bus excursions, while **La Porta del Vesuvio** (☎ 081-274200; www.laportadelvesuvio.it; for reservations, call from 9 a.m.–1:30 p.m.) organizes scenic night tours of the crater as well as a nature trail hike (Sun at 11 a.m.).

floors, all decorated with rich mosaics and frescoes. Entrance is by guided tour only, and requires advance reservation. The visit takes about an hour.

A short distance west of the archaeological area. ☎ *081-7390963.* www.arethusa.net. *Admission: 2€ ($2.40). Open: By guided tour only Sat–Sun 9 a.m. to noon.*

Pompeii

Buried beneath volcanic ash and pumice stone in the A.D. 79 eruption of Mount Vesuvius, the ruins of Pompeii have been easier to excavate than those in Herculaneum (see earlier in the chapter), allowing archaeologists to bring nearly the whole town back to light. The huge site — four times larger than Herculaneum — is impressive indeed. The burning ashes suffocated people without burning them, transforming Pompeiians taking flight into human statues that are preserved now in the museum — an eerie and moving sight.

Getting there

From Naples, take the **Sorrento** line of the **Circumvesuviana Train** (Corso Garibaldi; ☎ **800-053939;** www.vesuviana.it; Metro: Garibaldi) to the **Pompei Scavi** stop (the Pompei stop on the other line is the modern town, which you don't want); the station is near the entrance to the archaeological area. The 45-minute ride costs 2.20€ ($2.60); trains leave every half-hour.

Taking a tour

If you prefer a classic bus tour, both **Every Tours** (Piazza del Municipio 5; ☎ **081-5518564;** Metro: Garibaldi) — the American Express branch in Naples — and **NapoliVision** (☎ **081-5595130;** www.napolivision.it) organize day trips to Pompeii.

We prefer booking one of the several guided tours offered by **Arethusa** (☎ **081-8616405;** www.arethusa.net) — the official tour provider of the archaeological area. Given the sheer size of the excavations, the tours are organized by theme, some of them seasonal: public life, private homes, merchants, grape harvest (we especially like this one, since you get to see — and sample — the wine production using 2,000-year-old techniques).

Seeing the sights

Even more so than for Herculaneum, you'll need water, comfortable shoes, and a hat and sunscreen (in good weather) to visit this large site in comfort.

If you're planning to visit more than one archaeological site in the area, you should take advantage of one of the available deals.

Certain attractions within the archaeological area — for instance, the Suburban Baths and the House of the Gilded Cupids (see later in this section) — require advance reservations. These reservations are free of charge, but need to be made at least 24 hours in advance by calling ☎ **081-8575347** daily between 10 a.m. and 1:30 p.m., or by going online to www.pompeiisites.org. If you're planning to sign up for both free tours recommended below, keep in mind that you'll need about 30 minutes to get from one to the other.

Archaeological Area

Pompeii was an important commercial town as well as a residential resort, and its urban fabric was a mix of elegant villas, shops, and more modest housing. The town was buried under volcanic ash and pumice stone that then solidified, which allowed the residents who had escaped to come back and salvage some of their treasures. Of course, this same situation also made it easier for the treasure hunters of later centuries to loot the place. In spite of all the scavengers, the city was very well preserved, and the archaeological excavations have uncovered much about the life of that time period. The excavated archaeological area is huge — about 44 hectares (109 acres) — representing about two-thirds of the original town; at the time of the eruption, Pompeii had about 35,000 inhabitants.

Organized around three points — the **Forum;** the **theater district** by the **triangular forum;** and the games and sports area with the **Palestra** and the **Amphitheater** — this large town followed the classic Roman grid of almost perpendicular streets, both residential and commercial, lined with taverns and shops.

Nearest to the entrance is the **Forum** — covering 5,388 sq. m (58,000 sq. ft.) — surrounded by three important buildings: the **Basilica** (the meeting hall, the city's largest single structure), the **Macellum** (covered goods market), and the **Temple of Jupiter.** Interestingly, the Forum was severely damaged in an earthquake 16 years before the eruption of Vesuvius, and you can see how parts of it had not yet been repaired when the final destruction came.

Farther along is the **theater district,** with the beautiful **Teatro Grande** — a structure that could hold 5,000 — and the smaller **Odeion,** for only about 1,000. Nearby are the **Stabian Baths,** the finest thermal baths to have survived from antiquity. Still in good condition, they are richly decorated with marble, frescoes, and mosaics.

At the other end of town are the **Amphitheater** — from 80 B.C., making it the oldest in the world — and the magnificent **Palestra,** the sports compound, with exercise areas and a swimming pool that must have been wonderful (it was huge and surrounded by plane trees — you can see the casts of the stumps).

Among the private homes, the most elegant is the **House of the Vettii,** belonging to two rich merchants, where you can admire a frescoed dining room in the shade that has become famous as Pompeiian red. The largest is the **House of the Faun,** named for the bronze statue of a dancing faun that was found there; the house takes up a city block and has four dining rooms and two spacious inner gardens.

Some buildings within the archaeological area can be visited only with advance reservations through www.arethusa.net. These include the beautifully decorated **House of the Gilded Cupids,** named after the delicate cupids painted on gilded glass in one of the bedrooms (20-minute visits scheduled daily 9 a.m.–6 p.m.), and the **Suburban Baths,** a set of private

Pompeii

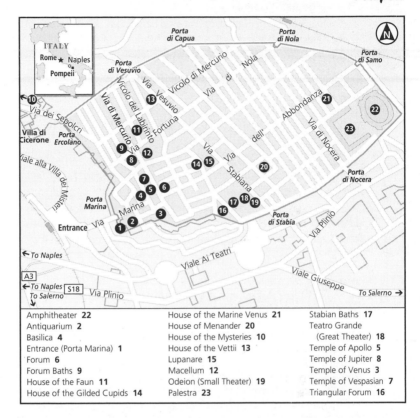

Amphitheater **22**	House of the Marine Venus **21**	Stabian Baths **17**
Antiquarium **2**	House of Menander **20**	Teatro Grande
Basilica **4**	House of the Mysteries **10**	(Great Theater) **18**
Entrance (Porta Marina) **1**	House of the Vettii **13**	Temple of Apollo **5**
Forum **6**	Lupanare **15**	Temple of Jupiter **8**
Forum Baths **9**	Macellum **12**	Temple of Venus **3**
House of the Faun **11**	Odeion (Small Theater) **19**	Temple of Vespasian **7**
House of the Gilded Cupids **14**	Palestra **23**	Triangular Forum **16**

thermal baths attached to a sumptuous villa, which opened to the public in 2002 (30-minute visits scheduled daily 10 a.m.–1:30 p.m.). These baths reveal the pleasure-oriented mind of the local population: Set in a splendid, panoramic spot by the western town wall overlooking the sea, they were used by men and women together, and the various halls and spaces were decorated with frescoes and mosaics.

About half a mile down Via dei Sepolcri, out of Porta Ercolano to the north-west of Pompeii's archaeological area, you can visit the **Villa dei Misteri (House of the Mysteries).** This was an elegant suburban villa once over-looking the sea (it has since receded). The most famous of its decorations are those of a medium-sized room with frescoes of ritual scenes related to the cult of Bacchus (Dionysus) — a cult inherited from the Greeks, along with its mysterious practices. The villa's architecture, with its dramatic terrace, is worth the detour.

Allow about four hours if you want to get a glimpse of everything. We strongly recommend taking an official guided tour (see earlier in this section); you can sign up at the ticket booth when you arrive, but we suggest making reservations ahead of time, especially if you're going to be here on a weekend in high season.

See map p. 421. Porta Marina, off Via Villa dei Misteri. ☎ *081-8575347 (reservations daily 10 a.m.–1:30 p.m.).* www.pompeiisites.org. *Admission: 10€ ($12). Included on the artecard list (see Chapter 18). Open: Daily Nov–Mar 8:30 a.m.–5 p.m.; daily Apr–Oct 8:30 a.m.–7:30 p.m. Last entrance 90 minutes earlier.*

Virtual Pompei

This is not an archaeological ruin, but rather a computerized way of reliving what Pompeii must have looked like in antiquity; the show is quite impressive and well done.

Via Plinio 105, in the modern town. ☎*/fax: 081-8610500.* www.virtualpompei.it. *Admission: 6€ ($7.20); 10 percent discount with artecard (see Chapter 18). Open: Daily 11:30 a.m.–5 p.m.*

Dining locally

The lively modern town offers many options, including bars, snack bars, and grocery shops; below are some of the most interesting restaurants.

Il Principe
$$ NEAPOLITAN/ANCIENT ROMAN

This is your chance to try — and hopefully enjoy — some ancient Roman concoctions. Take a seat in the Pompeian dining rooms or outdoors if it's pleasant, and taste both modern favorites — we recommend the spaghetti with mussels and the *fritto misto* (deep-fried calamari and shrimp) — as well as the sweet and spicy recipes from 2,000 years ago: The *lagane al garum* (fresh eggless pasta with anchovy sauce) was surprisingly tasty.

Piazza Bartolo Longo, in the center of modern Pompei. ☎ *081-8505566. Reservations recommended on weekends. Secondi: 13€–18€ ($16–$22). AE, DC, MC, V. Open: Tues–Sun 12:30–3 p.m.; Tues–Sat 8–11 p.m.*

Lucullus
$$ NEAPOLITAN

Only the décor is reminiscent of Roman times — you'll dine among statues and palm trees — while the menu is solid, traditional Neapolitan food, very well prepared. We enjoyed the buffet of *antipasti*, with a large choice of vegetable and seafood dishes. If you're tired of seafood, the well-rounded menu also includes several other choices; we recommend the grilled meats and the fettuccine with mushrooms.

Via Plinio 129, in modern Pompei. ☎ *081-8613055. Reservations recommended on weekends. Secondi: 7€–15€ ($8.40–$18). AE, DC, MC, V. Open: Wed–Mon noon to 3 p.m. and 7–11 p.m.*

Chapter 20

Sorrento, Capri, and the Amalfi Coast

In This Chapter

▶ Relaxing in picturesque Sorrento
▶ Taking in the sights in lovely Capri
▶ Living the good life on the Amalfi Coast

*E*nclosing the famous bay of Naples to the south, the Sorrento peninsula has been a place of pleasure since antiquity. Giving its name to the peninsula, the town of **Sorrento** is said to be the most picturesque on this coast. Only a short ferry ride away, the famed island of **Capri** (pronounced *Cap*-ry), favored by VIPs, makes a perfect getaway. Occupying the whole southern edge of the peninsula and opening onto the splendid bay of **Salerno** is the **Amalfi Coast,** a stretch of shore famous for its natural beauty, as well as for its picturesque towns of **Amalfi, Ravello,** and **Positano.**

If you have the time, the best way to enjoy each of these destinations is to spend the night, but you can also see the highlights as a day trip from Naples. Sorrento makes a good base for your explorations, or you can choose to move southward along the coast as we do in this chapter.

Sorrento

The favored destination of writers and artists — following in the footsteps of such illustrious predecessors as Emperor Augustus and Tiberius — Sorrento has not had its charm dulled by the crowds of visitors that populate its cobbled streets at the height of summer. You can enjoy a taste of it all in three to four hours.

Getting there

Sorrento is the last stop on the **Circumvesuviana Train** (Corso Garibaldi; ☎ 800-053939; www.vesuviana.it; Metro: Garibaldi) from Naples; the 50-minute ride costs about 3€ ($3.60). Trains depart every half-hour.

You can also get here by one of the frequent ferries from Naples and Capri, run by **Linee Marittime Partenopee** (☎ 081-55513236), **NLG** (☎ 081-5527209), and **Linee Lauro** (☎ 081-55522838). All are reputablez companies; you just need to choose the one leaving at a time that's convenient for you. Ferries arrive at the Marina Piccola by the waterside. You can then take the frequent shuttle bus for the steep climb to Piazza Tasso, in the heart of town.

If you're coming from the Capodichino airport in Naples, you can take one of the seven daily buses operated by **Curreri Viaggi** (☎ 081-8015420); the trip takes about an hour and costs 6€ ($7.20).

You'll find the local **tourist office** on Via Luigi de Maio, off Piazza Tasso (☎ 081-8074033; www.sorrentotourism.com).

Spending the night

Sorrento offers many hotel options, with the most expensive ones lining the waterfront. Here is our selection of the best in each price range.

Grand Hotel Excelsior Vittoria
$$ **Piazza Tasso**

Right in the heart of town is the grandest of all the elegant hotels in Sorrento — actually, one of the best in the world. Run by the same family who welcomed Lord Byron and Wagner through these same doors, it has shown it knows how to keep up with modern international standards. From the public spaces, furnished with the original 19th-century furniture, to the beautiful terraces, everything whispers taste, luxury, and relaxation. Guest rooms, which are palatial in size and décor, continue that theme. Guests can swim from the private pier off Marina Piccola, which is connected to the hotel by elevator, or in the pool in the private park.

Piazza Tasso 34. ☎ *081-8071044. Fax: 081-8771206.* www.exvitt.it. *Free parking. Rack rates: 315€–380€ ($378–$456) double. Rates include buffet breakfast. AE, DC, MC, V.*

Hotel Regina
$ **Marina Grande**

This simple hotel surrounded by a garden has a good location near the harbor, a short uphill walk from the heart of town. The affordable guest rooms are furnished with the basic comforts; all have balconies opening onto the garden or the sea. Note that all prices include a half-board plan, thus dinner is always included in your room rate, whether you choose to have it or not.

Via Marina Grande 10. ☎ *081-8782722. Fax: 081-8782721. Parking: 12€ ($14) in nearby garage. Rack rates: 95€–150€ ($114–$180) double. Rates include breakfast and dinner. AE, DC, MC, V. Closed Nov 15–Mar 31 and mid-Nov to Dec 24.*

Majestic Palace
$$ Sant'Agnello

Located on the shore, a 20-minute walk from the heart of Sorrento — technically in the adjacent small town of Sant'Agnello — this elegant hotel offers superior accommodations at moderate prices. The nicely furnished public spaces — a series of comfortable living rooms with a piano bar at night — and the outdoor pool nicely complement the large guest rooms, which have tiled floors and private balconies opening onto scenic views.

Via M Crawford 40. ☎ *081-8072050. Fax: 081-8772506.* www.majesticpalace.it. *Free parking. Rack rates: 148€–188€ ($178–$226) double. Rates include buffet breakfast. AE, DC, MC, V. Closed Jan 6–Mar 31 and mid-Nov to Dec 24.*

Dining locally

Sorrento is the place for romantic dinners. Although you may think that it's all in the atmosphere, the town also has a strong culinary tradition.

Canonico
$$ CREATIVE SORRENTINE

Located on Sorrento's main square, this is still a good spot for well-prepared traditional cuisine at reasonable prices. Try the *gnocchi alla sorrentina* (potato dumplings with tomato sauce and *bufala* mozzarella), a local specialty. The menu also offers a selection of seafood and meat dishes.

Piazza Tasso 5. ☎ *081-8783277. Reservations recommended. Secondi: 10€–21€ ($12–$25). AE, DC, MC, V. Open: Tues–Sun noon to 3 p.m. and 7:30–11 p.m.*

Caruso
$ SORRENTINE

This beacon of Sorrentine cuisine — a charming restaurant whose founder loved the famous Neapolitan tenor Caruso as much as he loved Sorrento — is where you'll find the best rendition of the local favorites. We loved the seafood lasagna and the ravioli with eggplant sauce, as well as the perfectly grilled fish of the day. The orange and walnut cake is heavenly.

Via Sant'Antonino 12. ☎ *081-8073156.* www.ristorantemuseocaruso.com. *Reservations recommended. Secondi: 16€–32€ ($19–$38). AE, DC, MC, V. Open: Daily 12:30–3:30 p.m. and 7:30–11:30 p.m.*

Il Buco
$ CREATIVE SORRENTINE

This is a real gourmet hide-out, where locals and visitors come to partake of the daily offerings from the imaginative chef. Housed in the atmospheric cellars of a convent, it also has a small outdoor terrace. The menu includes simple dishes with elaborate flavor combinations, such as the splendid seafood ravioli with sweet peppers. You can also choose one of the two

The best gelato on the coast

Gelato is our guilty pleasure, and we are hard to please — but we'd be perfectly happy to return again and again to **Davide II Gelataio** (Via Padre Reginaldo Giuliani 41; ☎ 081-8781337), which produces such enticing flavors as *delizia al limone* (lemon delight) — oh so delicious indeed — and *cioccolato ai canditi* (dark chocolate and candied orange peel). You'll have a hard time choosing: Davide makes some 60 different flavors.

tasting menus, one centered on meat for 48€ ($58) and the other on seafood for 55€ ($66).

Rampa Marina Piccola 5. ☎ *081-8782354. Reservations recommended. Secondi: 18€–25€ ($22–$30). AE, DC, MC, V. Open: Daily noon to 3:30 p.m. and 7:30–11:30 p.m. Closed Jan.*

Exploring Sorrento

At **Nautica Sic Sic** (Marina Piccola; ☎ 081-8072283; closed Nov–Apr) and at **Tony's Beach** (Marina Grande; ☎ 081-8785606), you can rent a boat with a driver to poke around the coast and discover the small secluded beaches. Figure on spending 20€ ($24) for about an hour.

The top attractions

Although little remains from medieval Sorrento, as it was destroyed in the 16th century, the old part of town is very picturesque. Narrow cobbled streets and pretty flower-ringed squares are set behind a dramatic cliff, overlooking the two harbors of Marina Grande and Marina Piccola.

Duomo

This is Sorrento's cathedral, dedicated to San Filippo and San Giacomo. Behind the simple Romanesque facade, flanked by a bell tower and decorated with four antique columns and a majolica clock, you'll find an elegant interior, adorned with original bas reliefs from the 14th and 15th centuries. The bishop's chair on display is an example of splendid wood intarsia work — a typical local craft (see later in this section).

Corso Italia 1. ☎ *081-8782248. Admission: free. Open: Daily 8 a.m. to noon and 4–8 p.m.*

Museo Correale

This interesting museum was the home of a local aristocratic family who donated it to the town, along with their collection of art. Besides the beauty of the villa itself, overlooking the sea, you'll find all the original furnishings as well as a collection that includes a few Flemish masters and a number of precious objects and valuable porcelains.

Via Correale, off Piazza Tasso. ☎ *081-8781846.* www.museocorreale.com. *Admission: 8€ ($10). Open: Wed–Mon 9 a.m.–2 p.m.*

San Francesco

This average 18th-century church hides a treasure inside: its splendid 14th-century cloister, done in the typical local mix of styles that merges Eastern influence with Western. On selected nights, the cloister becomes the beautiful setting for classical music concerts (see "Living it up after dark," later in this section).

Piazza Francesco Saverio Gargiulo. Admission: free. Open: Daily 8 a.m.–1 p.m. and 2–7 p.m.

More cool things to see and do

✔ If you like marquetry furniture, you'll be delighted by the display of the **Bottega della Tarsia Lignea Museum** (Via San Nicola 28; ☎ 081-8771942; Admission: 8€/$10; Open: Mon–Sat 10 a.m.–1 p.m.), housed in the 18th-century Palazzo Pomaranci Santomaso. You can admire the frescoes that decorate the ceilings as well as a collection of some of the best examples of this local traditional craft spanning the 19th century.

✔ **Swimming** is definitely one of the best things to do here, but don't expect soft sandy beaches: The rugged coast that makes this area so beautiful, and the sea so attractive, yields only a few tiny stretches of sand — like the one at **Marina Grande** — and some rocky beaches. Hotels have gotten around this dilemma by rigging **piers** that extend into the sea and are equipped with beach chairs and umbrellas. If you don't mind a pleasant hike, you can also head to **Punta del Capo,** with the best beach in town — and a few Roman ruins to top it all off. Take Via del Capo heading west out of town; the trail starts at Piazza Capo di Sorrento. Even easier: Hire a boat to take you there, and you can admire the coast along the way.

✔ Provided you can convince yourself to abandon your lounge chair, **hiking** is a major possibility here, with trails crisscrossing the promontory behind town. They're well marked, but local book-stores and newsstands also carry an excellent map.

Living it up after dark

In high season, Sorrento has a lively cultural life that's mostly centered on music, with concerts — mostly classical music but not exclusively — scheduled at major hotels and churches around town. At the tourist office (Via Luigi de Maio 35; ☎ 081-8074033; www.sorrentoturismo.com; Open: Mon–Sat 9 a.m.–6 p.m., plus July–Aug Sun 9 a.m.–12:30 p.m.), you can pick up the free magazine *Sorrentum,* the best source for infor-mation on all events.

How a myth begins

Established by the Etruscans and taken over by the Greeks, beautiful Sorrento was a thriving town. Such was the beauty of this peninsula — and so treacherous its seas — that it was believed to be the headquarters of the sirens, the half-woman/half-animal creatures who used their enchanted songs to lure mariners onto the rocks and to their destruction. Taken over by the Romans, Sorrento had already become an elegant resort by the first century B.C. At the end of the Roman Empire, the Goths occupied the town, but it was reconquered by the Byzantines in A.D. 552 and remained part of their Duchy of Naples until the 11th century. Though it succeeded in becoming an independent city-state for a few decades, it fell again, first under the Normans in 1133, and then the Angevins. With the Saracens continuously menacing this stretch of coast, Sorrento lived through difficult years until it was basically razed to the ground by the Saracens in 1558. The Sorrentines didn't lose their spirit, however, and immediately began reconstruction work, surrounding the town with a new set of walls and a number of watchtowers. Since then, Sorrento has kept up its role as enchanted land, attracting travelers and not letting them go — or at least keeping their hearts.

Some of the most sought-after tickets are those for the classical concerts held in the **cloister of San Francesco** (see "The top attractions," earlier in this chapter) and in the baroque chapel inside the **Albergo Cocumella** (Via Cocumella 7; ☎ 081-8782933; www.cocumella.com), the luxury hotel in Sant'Agnello, to the east of town.

If you prefer local folk music, you should not miss the **Sorrento Musical,** a festival of Neapolitan songs held March through October at **Teatro Tasso** (Piazza Sant'Antonino; ☎ 081-8075525; www.teatrotasso.com; ticket prices around 26€/$31), or the simpler events at the bar **Circolodei Forestieri** (Via Luigi de Maio 35; ☎ 081-8773012; Open: Mar–Oct).

For more modern entertainment, head to Piazza Tasso for one of the two nightclubs, **Fauno** (☎ 081-8781021; www.faunonotte.it; cover 25€/$30) — with DJ music and shows of **Tarantella** (the traditional and colorful local dance) — or **Matilda** (☎ 081-8773236; cover 10€/$12), with DJ music and a somewhat younger clientele. Or hit the pubs: The most popular in town are **Chaplin's Video Pub** (Corso Italia 8; ☎ 081-8072551) and the **English Inn** (Corso Italia 55; ☎ 081-8074357), but we also like the **Merry Monk** (Via Capo 6; ☎ 081-8772409), a bit farther away.

Fast Facts: Sorrento

Area Code

The local area code is **081** (see "Telephone" in the "Fast Facts" section of

Appendix A for more on calling to and from Italy).

ATMs

You'll find several banks with ATMs in town; one is the Deutsche Bank on Piazza Angelina Lauro 22, which also offers currency exchange.

Emergencies

For an ambulance, call ☎ 118; for the fire department, call ☎ 115; for road assistance, call ☎ 116.

Hospitals

The hospital is on Corso Italia 1 (☎ 081-5331111).

Police

Call ☎ 113.

Post Office

You'll find the post office on Corso Italia 210 (☎ 081-8781495; open Mon–Fri 8 a.m.– 6 p.m., Sat 8 a.m.–12:30 p.m.)

Taxi

You can get a taxi at one of the two stands in town: one by the harbor (☎ 081-8783527) and another at Piazza Tasso (☎ 081-8782204).

Capri and the Blue Grotto

Emperor Tiberius retreated to the island of Capri to concentrate on his own decadent pleasures. Idyllic in the off season, and full of charm in any season, Capri is just a short ferry ride away from Naples, Sorrento, Positano, or Amalfi. This famous island has been a haunt for eccentric characters (such as movie stars hiding out, artists in exile, and the like) for decades. Whether you stay for a day or a year, remember to bring very little luggage or expect to hire a porter when you land: The island is quite steep and you may have to walk up many steps to get to your hotel.

Getting there

From **Naples,** you can catch one of the frequent ferries at Molo Beverello, in the Stazione Marittima: **Metrò del Mare** (☎ **199-446644;** www.metro delmare.com) makes only one daily run on line MM4 (a 50-minute trip) to Capri at 4:25 p.m., with return from Capri at 10:50 a.m., but the ticket costs just 4.50€ ($5.40) and includes ground transportation for 45 minutes before and 45 minutes after the ferry link. Or you can take one of the four daily run by **Caremar** (☎ 081-5513882; www.caremar.it) for 6€ ($7.20); the trip takes 90 minutes. If you prefer the faster *aliscafo* **(hydrofoil)** — a 35-minute trip — SNAV (☎ 081-7612348; www.snav.it) and **NLG** (☎ 081-5527209; www.navlib.it) make several runs a day; a few are from Molo Beverello, but most are from the hydrofoil terminal in Mergellina; tickets are 12€ ($14).

From **Sorrento,** you can choose between hydrofoil or regular ferry; they all leave from Marina Piccola. The companies are **Caremar** and **NLG,** as from Naples (see earlier in this chapter), as well as **Linee Lauro** (☎ 081-5522838; www.alilauro.it) and **Linee Marittime Partenopee** (☎ 081-55513236). Tickets are 13€ ($16) for the hydrofoil and 7€ ($8.40) for the regular ferry.

You can also get to Capri from the Amalfi Coast with **Alicost** (☎ 081-7611004; www.alilauro.it) or **NLG** (see earlier in this chapter), which offer several daily runs by hydrofoil or ferry from **Positano** (hydrofoil 13€/$16; regular ferry 9€/$11), **Amalfi** (hydrofoil 14€/$17; ferry 10€/$12), and off Molo Manfredi in **Salerno** (hydrofoil 15€/$18; ferry 11€/$13).

Ferries and hydrofoils arrive at **Marina Grande** in Capri. From the ferry terminal, you can take a taxi (see "Fast Facts: Capri," at the end of this section) or the picturesque *funicolare* (**funicular**) up the steep coast to the town of Capri. Regular **bus** service also links Marina Grande, Capri, Marina Piccola, Anacapri, Faro (Lighthouse), and Grotta Azzurra. A regular ticket costs 1.30€ ($1.60) for either the bus or the funicular; you can also get a 60-minute ticket for 2.10€ ($2.50), valid for one funicular run and unlimited bus runs during the time limit, or a day pass for 6.70€ ($8), valid for two funicular rides and unlimited bus service.

You'll find the local **tourist office** at Piazzetta I. Cerio 11 (☎ **081-8375308**; www.capritourism.com).

Spending the night

If you want to stay overnight, hotels in Anacapri are cheaper and quieter, as they're set among the vineyards of the hills. If you'd like to be in the heart of things, though, Capri offers much more in the way of nightlife and glitzier hotels. If you're traveling in the off season when most hotels are closed, or arriving without a reservation, contact the tourist office for assistance (Piazzetta I. Cerio 11; ☎ **081-8375308**; www.capritourism.com).

Capri Palace
$$$$ Anacapri

The best hotel in Capri dominates the island from its location in Anacapri. The views are spectacular, and you won't even miss the sea while you relax in the splendid private gardens with swimming pool. Guest rooms are large and furnished in high-comfort modern style. Those with sea views have private balconies. All have spacious marble bathrooms with all the comforts. The best units have canopied beds and vaulted ceilings. The hotel's restaurant **L'Olivo,** is the best on the island.

Via Capodimonte 2b. ☎ *081-9780111. Fax: 081-8373191.* www.capripalace.com. *Rack rates: 400€–810€ ($480–$972) double. Rates include buffet breakfast. Closed Nov–Feb, but open 10 days for new year.*

Hotel La Minerva
$$ Capri

This small hotel offers great value: It's quiet, well run, and only steps from the center of town. All of the pleasant guest rooms are spacious and furnished in Mediterranean style. Most have sea views; all have private terraces that are delightfully filled with flowers in high season.

Via Occhio Marino 8. ☎ *081-8377067. Fax: 081-8375221.* www.laminervacapri. com. *Rack rates: 150€–270€ ($180–$324) double. Rates include breakfast. AE, DC, MC, V. Closed Jan–Feb.*

Hotel Luna
$$$$ Capri

The upscale Hotel Luna offers beautiful vistas of the bay and the Faraglioni (Capri's famous cliffs) from its location atop a cliff. Most guest rooms have private terraces overlooking the cliffs or gardens, and all are quite luxurious.

Viale Matteotti 3. ☎ *081-8370433. Fax: 081-8377459.* www.lunahotel.com. *Rack rates: 250€–395€ ($300–$474) double. Rates include buffet breakfast. Closed end of Oct to Easter.*

Dining locally

Even if restaurant dining is not your thing, consider going to Capri's best restaurant — **L'Olivo** (in the Capri Palace, reviewed earlier in this chapter)— for a superb dinner. Another option is the romantic **La Colombaia**, in the **Grand Hotel Quisiana** (Via Camerelle 2; ☎ **081-8370788**), the priciest hotel in Capri.

Cantinella
$$$ Capri CAPRESE

If you don't get too distracted by the great view of the Faraglioni, you will be able to enjoy the very good cuisine of this restaurant. Among the local dishes, the *paccheri con frutti di mare e rucola* (pasta with seafood and arugula) was excellent, as were the other homemade pastas. The fish *secondi* change daily; meat and vegetarian dishes are available as well. We enjoyed the eggplant, zucchini, and cheese carpaccio. Leave room for the delicious homemade desserts.

Viale Matteotti 8. ☎ *081-8370616. Reservations recommended. Secondi: 23€–42€ ($28–$50). AE, DC, MC, V. Open: Wed–Mon 12:30–3 p.m. and 7:30 p.m.–12:30 a.m.*

CasaNova
$$ Capri NEAPOLITAN/CAPRESE

Tucked away on a small street a short distance from Capri's *piazzetta,* this is one of our favorite restaurants on the island. The food is always fresh and well prepared, from the splendid and rich antipasto buffet to the large choice of meat and seafood dishes. The red snapper *all'acquapazza* (in a light herbed broth) and the *totanetti affogati* (baby squid stewed in herbs and wine) were very good, and so was the veal Sorrento.

Via Le Botteghe 46. ☎ *081-8377642. Reservations required for dinner. Secondi: 11€–25€ ($13–$30). AE, DC, MC, V. Open: Daily noon to 3 p.m. and 7–11 p.m. Closed Dec to mid-Mar.*

Rondinella
$$ Anacapri   CAPRESE/PIZZA

This excellent restaurant, right in the center of tranquil Anacapri, serves some of the best food on the island; an added perk is the chance to dine outdoors in good weather. Do try the *ravioli alla caprese* (with mozzarella, basil, and tomatoes) — it's the best we've had — and enjoy the local and fragrant bread with the daily catch or one of the meat dishes. We also highly recommend the pizza and the desserts: The *torta caprese* (almond cake) is a local specialty.

Via G. Orlandi 245, Anacapri. ☎ *081-8371223. Reservations necessary for dinner. Secondi: 12€–16€ ($14–$19). AE, DC, MC, V. Open: Daily noon to 3 p.m. and 7–11 p.m. Closed 2 weeks in Feb.*

Exploring Capri

Boat tours of the island leave from Marina Grande (where the ferries and hydrofoils from Naples arrive). A complete tour of the island will cost you about 19€ ($23) per person with either **Gruppo Motoscafisti** (www.motoscafisticapri.com) or **Laser Capri** (www.lasercaprisrl.com). Both companies offer other excursions as well, such as a short trip to the **Faraglioni**, Capri's famous cliffs.

The top attractions

Anacapri

This is the smaller of the two towns on the island and the one that's higher up. The steep climb from Capri could technically be done on foot (see "More cool things to see and do," later in this section), but it's a lot easier by taxi or bus — a hair-raising ride along the cliff road. The natural beauty of the place can be best enjoyed from the terraces of **Villa San Michele** (Via San Michele; ☎ **081-8371401;** www.sanmichele.org; Admission: 5€/$6; Open: Mar–Apr and Oct daily 9:30 a.m.–4:30 p.m., May–Sept daily 9 a.m.–6 p.m., Nov–Dec daily 10:30 a.m.–3:30 p.m.), the splendid 19th-century villa of Swedish doctor Axel Munthe.

Capri

This is the most picturesque — and largest — town on the island, a hive of activity, glamorous hotels, cafes, and shops. The heart of it all is the famous *piazzetta* (Piazza Umberto I) and the little streets around it; another popular spot is the terraces of the public gardens — the **Giardini di Augusto** — which afford superb views.

Grotta Azzurra (Blue Grotto)

Kids will love visiting this underwater cave that can be reached only by small rowboat, though some adults may find it a bit less comfortable. This natural wonder conjures up visions of pirates and buried treasure; Capri's top attraction, it is unfortunately so overrun with tourists that it is difficult to truly enjoy. The most common way to visit is to board one of the large motorboats leaving from Marina Grande, and then be shuttled in a small rowboat that takes only a few people at a time down to the entrance of the grotto, and under the narrow passage — so narrow and low that if you're not limber or if you have claustrophobia, you won't like it: The slow sinking of the grotto over time has reduced the opening to slightly more than 1m (3 ft.) above sea level.

Once inside, though, you'll immediately understand what all the commotion is about, and you'll even forget about the outrageous money you've paid to see it. The grotto was known to the ancients — you'll see a little landing just inside the entrance that dates back to Roman times, but was later lost to the world until an artist stumbled upon it in 1826. Inside the cavern, light refraction (the sun's rays entering from an opening under the water) creates incredible colors and a magical atmosphere — stunning, indeed. Alas, chances are you won't be able to stay as long as you'd like, because at the height of tourist season no lingering is allowed. For all these reasons, we think that the grotto, like Capri in general, should be seen in the off season, if possible.

Another way to reach the grotto is by taking the bus to the stop by Anacapri, hence skipping the motorboat ride. From there, you can directly take the rowboat ride. We much prefer this option. Technically, you could also swim inside the grotto — a wonderful experience if you're a good swimmer — but definitely not to be attempted in high season and during the hours of operation of the large motorboats and the incessant boat traffic. Whatever your means of access, you will need to pay the admission. Note that rowboat operators welcome, and deserve, a tip: Their rates have been officially blocked from any increases for many years.

Near the northwestern tip of the island. Admission: Grotto only 4€ ($4.80); rowboat ride 4.50€ ($5.40); boat tour from Marina Grande (including rowboat ride inside the grotto and admission) 17€ ($20); land excursion from Anacapri (including rowboat ride inside the grotto and admission) 8.10€ ($9.70). Rowboat operators welcome tips. Open: Daily 9 a.m. to 1 hour before sunset.

Marina Piccola and the Faraglioni

A tiny and picturesque harbor on the south shore of the island, this is where you can admire the **Faraglioni,** the tall cliffs off the island's southeastern tip, Capri's famous landmark. The local beach offers perfect views, but you can also hire a boat to take you closer to this natural attraction.

Monte Solaro

This is the highest point on the island. From Anacapri, you can take the chairlift up to the top, or walk up the trail. The views from up here are absolutely breathtaking, especially on a clear day, when you can see Mount Vesuvius and the entire bay.

Chairlift at Via Caposcuro 10, Anacapri. ☎ 081-8371428. Tickets: 4€ ($4.80) one-way, 5.50€ ($6.60) for the 12-minute round-trip ride. Ride operates Mar–Oct 9:30 a.m.– sunset; Nov–Feb 10:30 a.m.–3 p.m.

Villa Jovis

During his self-imposed exile here, Emperor Tiberius built several villas on the island, where he could enjoy all sorts of illicit pleasures far away from the prying eyes of the Roman Senate. The Villa Jovis, the palace where Tiberius lived, extended over several levels for an estimated 5,850 sq. m (63,000 sq. ft. — just a modest summer home), but is now only a romantic ruin from which you get beautiful views.

Viale Amedeo Maiuri, at the eastern tip of the island. www.villajovis.it. *Admission: 2€ ($2.40). Open: Daily 9 a.m.–sunset; ticket booth closes 1 hour earlier.*

More cool things to see and do

✔ Capri boasts beautiful cliffs and views of the sea, the Bay of Naples, and Vesuvius, which can be best enjoyed by going on a **hike.** If you're moderately fit, the windy roads climbing up the promontory offer fantastic vistas. The best and most popular trail is the **Scala Fenicia,** originally the only road connecting Anacapri to Capri, which was built by Greek colonists almost 3,000 years ago. This path is so steep that it's actually a staircase (*scala* means "stairs") with over 500 steps. We recommend you descend the stairs from Anacapri rather than climbing up from Capri.

✔ If you like **swimming,** you won't be disappointed: The water is beautiful and marvelously refreshing under the hot sun. Because Capri is very rocky, however, its beaches are small, and the easy-to-reach ones are beautiful but often crowded, such as those of **Marina Piccola** (where you can rent umbrellas and beach chairs). The best approach is to avail yourself of one of the small boats that will take you to a difficult-to-reach beach for about 10€ ($12). The **Bagni di Tiberio** is a nice sandy beach on the north side of the island, near the ruins of an ancient villa. You can take a boat there from Marina Grande or walk on a rough trail (allow about half an hour). The beach is freely accessible and not too crowded.

Shopping for local treasures

We know of people who come to Capri to shop — and there are indeed some nice clothing, accessories, and jewelry shops carrying merchandise that you wouldn't find on the mainland. The perfume maker **Carthusia** has two locations, one in Capri (Via Camerelle 10; ☎ 081-8370358) and one in Anacapri (Via Capodimonte 26; ☎ 081-8373668); it has made unique perfumes with local herbs and flowers since 1948. Another good store is **Canfora** (Via Camerelle 3; ☎ 081-8370487), which carries handmade, high-quality, good-looking sandals. If you're looking for prestigious jewelry, you should not miss **La Perla Gioielli** (Piazza Umberto I 21; ☎ 081-8370641), selling wonderful creations since 1936. We have only two words for you: Happy hunting!

Capri

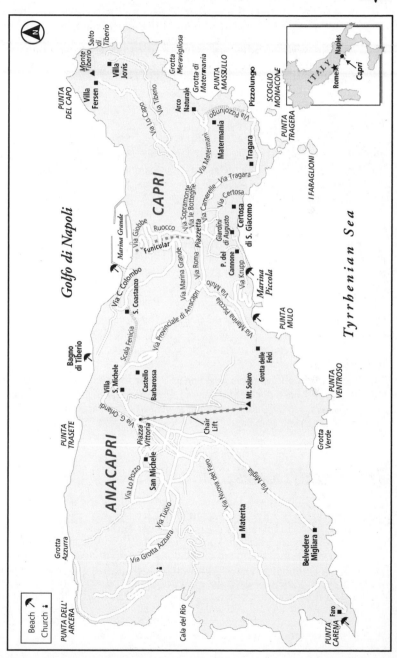

Living it up after dark

From May through September, Capri's nights come alive with visitors and locals who stroll in and out of the many cafes and clubs, taking advantage of the sweet air and joyful atmosphere. A popular nightclub is **Number Two** (Via Camerelle 1; ☎ **081-8377078**), good for dancing, but you'll see that any of the cafes and bars — including those of the major hotels — will do for a pleasant evening.

Fast Facts: Capri

Area Code

The local area code is **081** (see "Telephone" in the "Fast Facts" section of Appendix A for more on calling to and from Italy).

ATMs

You'll find a number of banks with ATMs on the island; the most central is the Banco di Roma, at Piazza Umberto I (☎ 081-8378743).

Emergencies

For an ambulance, call ☎ **118;** for the fire department, call ☎ **115.**

Hospitals

The hospital is at Via Provinciale Anacapri 5 (☎ 081-8381111). For a doctor after-hours and on holidays, call the Guardia Medica, at Via Maria delle Grazie 28 in Capri (☎ 081-8381239).

Internet Access

Capritech Internet Corner has two locations: in Capri at the Bar Gabbiano (Via Colombo 76; ☎ 081-8376531) and in Anacapri at the Bar Due Pini (Piazza Vittoria 3; ☎ 081-8371404).

Police

Call ☎ **113.**

Post Office

The main post office is at Via Roma 50 (☎ 081-9785233).

Taxi

You can call or walk to the taxi stands at Piazza Martiri dell'Ungheria (☎ 081-8370543) in Capri and Piazza Vittoria (☎ 081-8371175) in Anacapri.

The Amalfi Coast

The Amalfi Coast's terraced cliffs overlooking the sea are blanketed with lemon trees, olive groves, and vineyards interspersed with small villages and historic towns; its waters are clear and blue, lapping the small sand and rocky beaches, making it the perfect spot for an interesting and relaxing vacation. The queen of the coast is **Amalfi,** a small harbor town with a charming medieval center and mementos from its glorious past; followed by elegant **Ravello** — overlooking the sea from its own valley — and **Positano,** the most picturesque of all, with its small harbor opening between towering cliffs. Many other small villages would also be worthwhile if you had the time: You could stay here a week or spend only the day, depending on your interests and schedule.

The Amalfi Coast

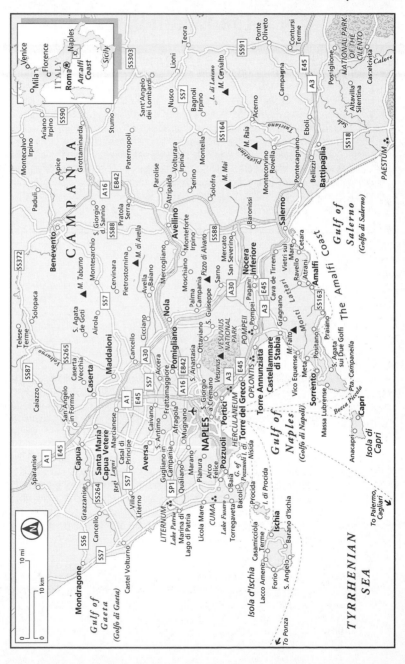

The Amalfi Drive

When this stretch of coast was discovered by tourists back in the 19th century — the famed road that winds along the cliffs (SS163) was built in 1840 — visitors were few and far between, and traveled slowly by horse-drawn carriages. When it became a fave destination for the jet set of the *Dolce Vita* and their artsy friends in the 1950s and early 1960s, tourists were rare, and the few lucky ones traveled in convertible cars with Sophia Loren by their side. If that's the image in your head when you picture yourself driving along the Amalfi Coast, well, think again: SS163 is still the same road (not any larger or more modern than back then) and the beauty of the place is still quite unspoiled, but the crazy traffic and noise on that narrow road are at times unbearable. You can still have your scenic drive, provided you're not the one driving, and you're doing it in the off season in the very early hours of the morning. Just hire a limousine service and have them take you; even better, skip the drive altogether and go for a hike instead.

Getting there

What makes this place beautiful is also what makes it difficult to get here: The road is narrow and winding, sometimes without a guard rail, and it's cut into the side of tall cliffs. Traffic and speeding locals (seemingly attached to your rear bumper) don't make it any easier. There are several ways to get to the Amalfi Coast, as we discuss later in this chapter — driving yourself is just not one of them.

By far the best way to visit the Amalfi Coast if you're coming for a day trip is hiring a car with a driver, which allows you to enjoy the scenic drive in complete comfort and at your own pace. **ANA Limousine Service** (Piazza Garibaldi 73; ☎ 081-282000) and **Italy Limousine** (☎ 081-8016184 or 335-6732245; www.italylimousine.it) in Naples, or **2golfi car service** (Via Deserto 30/e, Sant'Agata sui due Golfi; ☎ 339-8307748 or 338-5628649; www.duegolficarservice) near Sorrento, are all reliable companies that use new, air-conditioned cars and minivans, with trained English-speaking drivers who double as guides. Prices vary depending on your needs, the car you choose, and the number of people in your group, but the hourly rate is about 35€ ($42) for two people. You can arrange for pickup at your hotel, the Naples airport, the rail station, or Stazione Marittima.

Taking a ferry is the best way to get here if you have a little time on your hands. The newly created **Metrò del Mare** (☎ 199-446644; www.metro delmare.com) makes several daily runs to Amalfi and Positano (Apr–Sept only) from Molo Beverello in Naples; the trip to Positano takes 75 minutes on the express line (MM2) and about two hours on the local line (MM3); allow 25 extra minutes to Amalfi on either line. You can use the special ticket **Terra and Mare,** which includes ground transportation for 45 minutes before and 45 minutes after the ferry link for about 8.50€ ($10). The company **Alicost** (☎ **081-7611004**) offers year-round ferry service, as well as faster hydrofoil service during high season, to Positano and Amalfi from Sorrento and Capri. Rates vary depending on your destination and point of departure, but estimate about 14€ ($17) for the hydrofoil and 11€ ($13) on the regular ferry. Make reservations at least 24 hours in advance. **Cooperativa Sant'Andrea** (☎ **089-873190;** www. coopsantandrea.it) offers regular motorboat service from Sorrento and Salerno to Amalfi, Positano, and a number of points in between; tickets range from 5€ to 9€ ($6–$11), depending on the distance.

A cheaper way to get to this stretch of coast is by taking buses operated by **SITA** (☎ **081-5522176;** www.sita-on-line.it), which make daily runs from Naples, Sorrento, and Salerno to both Positano and Amalfi. Local lines to Ravello — and to a number of other villages and hamlets in the area — start from the SITA bus terminal at Piazza Flavio Gioia in Amalfi (☎ **089-871009**). The trip from Naples should cost about 4€ ($4.80) and take about two hours. The ride can be hair-raising at times — you'll be grateful that you're not driving the bus — but it's certainly panoramic.

Spending the night

The coast and its cliffs are dotted with places to stay, ranging from small hotels to beautiful resorts. Here are some of our favorites:

Casa Albertina
$$ Positano

The favorite hotel of Luigi Pirandello — the famous Sicilian writer and playwright — this small family-run house is a well-hidden gem in busy Positano. Each guest room is different from the others, simply furnished but with care and taste, and all have private balconies opening onto the sea. Bathrooms are not large, but do come with all the essentials. In high season, only a half-board plan is offered (all rates include dinner, whether you want it or not).

Via della Tavolozza 3. ☎ *089-875143. Fax: 089-811540.* www.casalbertina.it. *Parking: 22€ ($26) in a garage nearby. Rack rates: 230€–280€ ($276–$336) double. Rates include breakfast and dinner. AE, DC, MC, V.*

Hotel Lidomare
$ Amalfi

This moderately priced hotel near the beach is housed in a 13th-century building. The guest rooms are brightly decorated in typical Amalfitan style (tiles, strong colors, lots of sparkling white). Most rooms have air-conditioning, the bathrooms are small but very clean, and the staff is extremely friendly and welcoming to families with children.

Largo Duchi Piccolomini 9. ☎ *089-871332.* Fax: 089-871394. www.lidomare.it. Parking: 15€ ($18). Rack rates: 120€ ($144) double. Rates include breakfast. AE, MC, V.

Hotel Luna Convento
$$$$ Amalfi

With a splendid position on the promontory of Amalfi, overlooking the sea, this family-run hotel offers elegant and romantic accommodations. An ancient monastery founded by St. Francis in 1222, it was transformed into a hotel in 1822; you can still visit the original cloister and chapel, as well as the watchtower from 1564. The large and bright guest rooms are individually decorated, with whitewashed walls, fine fabrics, and vaguely Moorish-style furnishings. All rooms have views of the sea and large tiled bathrooms; some have private terraces. The hotel also has a large salt-water swimming pool, a solarium, and two excellent **restaurants,** one more upscale and the other less formal.

Via Pantaleone Comite 33. ☎ *089-871002.* Fax: 089-871333. www.lunahotel.it. Free parking. Rack rates: 240€ ($288) double. Rates include breakfast. AE, DC, MC, V.

Hotel San Pietro
$$$$ Positano

One of the best hotels in the world, this abode to the rich and famous is still family run with hard-to-find warmth and professional efficiency. The gorgeous public areas include terraces, a garden, a pool, and a private, elevator-accessible beach. You can relax in perfect style in the commodious guest rooms, bright with hand-painted tiles and cozy with antiques. The bathrooms are done in pink marble. The **restaurant** is one of the best in the region.

Via Laurito 2. ☎ *089-875455.* Fax: 089-811449. www.ilsanpietro.it. Free parking. Rack rates: 380€ ($456) double. Rates include buffet breakfast. AE, DC, MC, V. Closed Nov–Mar.

Palazzo Sasso
$$$$ Ravello

This is one of the oldest hotels in Ravello — it opened in 1880 — but it's been completely refurbished since closing down in the 1960s. Housed in an 11th-century *palazzo,* it is a haven of elegance and style, receiving its guest in rooms furnished with antiques and appointed with all the comforts, including spacious marble bathrooms. Some of the guest rooms have glorious views. The **restaurant** is one of the best in town.

Via San Giovanni del Toro 28. ☎ *089-818181.* Fax: 089-858900. www.palazzo sasso.com. Rack rates: 296€–590€ ($355–$708) double. Rates include buffet breakfast. AE, DC, MC, V. Free parking. Closed Nov to mid-Mar.

Villa Cimbrone
$$$ Ravello

Residence of the Vuillemier family, this villa welcomes a small number of guests in great luxury and privacy. Each room is unique and decorated with antiques; some of them have views over the park, while others have private terraces overlooking the sea. From Ravello, call the hotel; it will send a porter to carry your luggage to the hotel. The villa is an attraction in itself (see "The top attractions," later in this chapter), and its **restaurant** is both beautiful and excellent.

Via Santa Chiara 26. ☎ *089-857459. Fax: 089-857777.* www.villacimbrone.it. *Rack rates: 250€–450€ ($300–$540) double. Rates include breakfast. AE, DC, MC, V. Closed Dec–Mar.*

Dining locally
On the Amalfi Coast, the sea reigns, making this a paradise for seafood lovers. Besides the restaurants we describe later in this chapter, consider also those inside the best hotels reviewed earlier in this chapter, offering romantic locations and quality food.

Cumpà Cosimo
$$ Ravello   AMALFITAN

At this great family-run spot, you can order all the local home-style specialties, but at lower prices than in the more "resorty" restaurants. You will see locals with their families, especially at lunchtime on the weekend. The pasta is very good, as are the *secondi,* among which you'll find a worthwhile *zuppa di pesce* (fish stew) and a fine *fritto misto* (deep-fried mixed seafood). Half-portions and kid-friendly menu items will please the little ones.

Via Roma 44. ☎ *089-857156. Reservations recommended. Secondi: 11€–28€ ($13–$34). AE, DC, MC, V. Open: Tues–Sun 12:30–3 p.m. and 7:30–11 p.m.; Apr–Oct daily.*

Da Adolfo
$$ Positano   AMALFITAN/SEAFOOD

Located right on the beach of Laurito, a short boat ride from Marina Grande (the free shuttle boat, marked with a red fish, leaves every 30 minutes), this restaurant, which doubles as beach club, offers excellent food and a relaxed atmosphere. You can swim (a beach chair and umbrella rent for 7€/$8.40 per day) and delight in an array of seafood *antipasto* and seafood dishes. We recommend the delicious spaghetti with mussels as well as the *grigliata di pesce* (a choice of several kinds of grilled fish and seafood).

Spiaggetta di Laurito. ☎ *089-875022. Reservations recommended. Secondi: 12€–18€ ($14–$22 No credit cards accepted. Open: Daily noon to 3 p.m.; July–Aug also Sat 8 p.m. to midnight. Closed Oct–May.*

Da Gemma
$$$ Amalfi AMALFITAN

One of the most popular restaurants on this stretch of coast, Da Gemma has been serving repeat customers for over a century. It specializes in traditional dishes of the area: The *zuppa di pesce per due* (fish stew for two) is definitely a winner; the *fritto misto* is one of the lighter fried mixed seafoods we've tasted; and the *polipo* (tender octopus) is simply great. The homemade *crostata* (a thick bread topped with jam, a typical Italian home-style dessert), prepared with local citrus-fruit jam, also deserves a mention. Half-portions and child-friendly foods are available.

Via Fra Gerardo Sassi 9. ☎ *089-871345. Reservations required. Secondi: 16€–25€ ($19–$30). AE, DC, MC, V. Open: Thurs–Tues 12:30–2:45 p.m. and 7:45–10:30 p.m.; daily in summer. Closed mid-Jan to mid-Feb.*

Da Salvatore
$ Ravello AMALFITAN

This down-to-earth restaurant is a favorite hangout with locals as well as visitors. Everybody enjoys the traditional food prepared according to local family recipes, as well as the splendid setting with views from both the dining room and the garden terrace. We recommend the *gnoccoloni al pomodoro e basilico* (potato-based dumplings with fresh tomatoes and basil).

Via Boccaccio 2. ☎ *089-857227. Reservations recommended. Secondi: 12€–18€ ($14–$22 AE, V. Open: Tues–Sun noon to 3 p.m. and 7:30–11 p.m.; Apr–Oct daily.*

Donna Rosa
$$ Positano AMALFITAN

This pleasant restaurant on the outskirts of Positano serves traditional cuisine that's very carefully prepared. We recommend all the homemade pastas, served with local vegetables, and the daily catches — but you will not be limited to fish: Rather unusually for the region, the *secondi* include many very good meat choices such as *salsicce alla griglia* (grilled local sausages) and *agnello arrosto* (roasted lamb). You can dine on the terrace in nice weather.

Via Montepertuso 97. ☎ *089-811806. Reservations recommended. Secondi: 12€–21€ ($14–$25). AE, DC, MC, V. Open: Wed–Mon 12:30–2:30 p.m. and 7:30–10:30 p.m.; June, July, and Sept also closed Mon; Aug open daily. Closed 11 weeks Jan–Mar.*

La Caravella
$$$ Amalfi AMALFITAN/CREATIVE

If ever a restaurant deserved to be expensive, this is the one: The delicious concoctions are not only made from excellent ingredients, but also involve extremely complicated and time-consuming preparations. You will find such dishes as *panzerottini al nero di seppia ripieni di provola e scampi con salsa di calamaretti mignon ripieni di zucchine* (homemade squid-ink pasta filled with prawns and local cheese, with a sauce of zucchini-stuffed calamari) or *zuppetta di polpo con il pane fritto alle alghe* (octopus stew with homemade bread with seaweed).

Via Matteo Camera 12. ☎ *089-871029. Reservations required. Secondi: 20€–30€ ($24–$36). AE, DC, MC, V. Open: Wed–Mon noon to 2 p.m. and 7:30–10:30 p.m.; Aug daily. Closed 5 weeks in Nov–Dec.*

Exploring the Amalfi Coast

Beaches, seaside resorts, small farming villages up the cliffs, fishing villages by the sea — the Amalfi Coast is varied and beautiful. The attractions of the coast are mainly natural; people come to explore the spectacular cliffs, play in the sea, and eat delicious seafood.

The top attractions

Amalfi

The largest of the small towns on this stretch of coast, Amalfi is today a pleasant fishing harbor and resort. The medieval part of town — including the old harbor — is rich in monuments that are mementos of its past importance. The imposing **Duomo** (Piazza del Duomo; ☎ 089-871059; Free admission; Open: Daily Nov–Feb 10 a.m.–1 p.m. and 2:30–4:30 p.m.; Mar and Oct 9:30 a.m.–5 p.m.; Apr–June 9 a.m.–7 p.m.; July–Sept 9 a.m.–9 p.m.) — named in honor of Sant'Andrea — has a facade decorated with gold leaf and majolica and is flanked by a charming belltower finished in the 13th century. The portal is closed by a bronze door that is only slightly less famous that the one in the Duomo of Ravello (see later in this chapter), but still magnificent; the grandiose staircase leading to it was added

Amalfi's glory days

The first of Italy's maritime republics — the city-states that dominated the Mediterranean sea and its commerce starting in the tenth century — Amalfi once surpassed Pisa, Genoa, and Venice in both power and riches. Created in ancient Roman times, Amalfi declared its independence from the Byzantine empire in A.D. 839, as it had developed into an important commercial harbor thanks to its great strategic location. Its moment of glory came between the 10th and the 12th centuries, when it dominated the southern Mediterranean. When you walk the narrow streets of medieval Amalfi, imagine this as the cosmopolitan heart of the republic, where peoples from all over the known world intermingled and exchanged their goods. Amalfi's notables and VIPs mostly lived outside town, in the hills or nearby resorts; Ravello was the residence of some of the wealthiest merchant families of Amalfi. Even after the fall of the city-state by the hands of Pisa in 1135, it continued to be an important center for commerce with the East throughout the 13th century.

in the 18th century, when the Duomo was enlarged. To the left is the entrance of one of the most beautiful cloisters you'll ever see — the **Chiostro del Paradiso** (Admission: 3€/$3.60; Open: Daily June–Oct 9:30 a.m.–7 p.m.; Nov–May 9:30 a.m.–5 p.m.), which has a small collection of antiquities. It gives access to the **Chiesa del Crocifisso (Church of the Crucifix),** the original cathedral from the tenth century that was integrated into the Duomo. From the Church of the Crucifix, you can descend into the crypt containing the remains of St. Andrew. The apostle's face is missing: It was donated to the Cathedral of St. Andrew in Patras, Greece.

Off the main square, you can visit the ruins of the **medieval shipyard** (Via Matteo Camera, off Piazza Flavio Gioia; Free admission; Open: Easter–Sept 9 a.m.–8 p.m.), where the once-powerful city-state built its galleys. These were big ships moved by sails and oars — up to 120 for a 130-foot ship — used for both defense and commerce with the East through the Mediterranean. Near the end of Amalfi's period of glory in the 12th century, a series of violent sea storms (due to a seaquake) destroyed part of the shipyard, which was never rebuilt.

The republic was also famous for its **paper industry,** which produced a particularly kind of paper called *bambagina.* Paper from Amalfi was shipped all over Europe, and still is to this day: This art has been preserved in town, where descendants of the ancient master papermakers are still at work, producing paper of an almost forgotten quality. It's sold to the most exclusive paper shops in Europe and the U.S. The Vatican, for one, uses Amalfi paper for its official correspondence (see "The paper of Amalfi" sidebar, later in this chapter). We enjoyed visiting the workshop of **Antonio Cavaliere** (Via Fiume; ☎ 089-871954), whose trademark is paper with dried wildflowers caught between the fibers. His shop, open during regular business hours, is outfitted with the traditional equipment of the trade. The water for his craft still comes from the covered river that crosses town and was the key resource in the development of the paper industry in Amalfi.

You can actually follow that river inland and out of town toward the hills (start at Piazza del Duomo and head up Via Genova), where you can explore the **Valle dei Mulini (Valley of the Mills).** A pleasant and easy walk, the path stretches down the narrow valley of the river, along which the old paper mills are still visible. You can find out more about the industry at the very interesting **Museo della Carta (Museum of Paper),** Via delle Cartiere 23 (☎ 089-8304561; www.museodellacarta.it; Admission: 3.40€/$4.10; Open: winter Tues–Sun 9 a.m.–1 p.m., summer daily 10 a.m.–6 p.m.), filled with antique presses and yellowing manuscripts.

Besides paper, Amalfi is famous today for its **lemons.** Unique in size, sweetness, flavor, and color, the lemons of Amalfi are exported as rare gems to markets around Italy. If you come at harvest time, you can see lemons being processed all over town: turned into the famous *limoncello,* a sweet lemon liqueur, but also into delicious confections such as candied lemons, jams, and lemon ice cream.

 Limoncello has a very nice taste, but few people can drink it straight. If you buy a bottle, you will probably want to use it to flavor cakes, cookies, and other sweet preparations.

The paper of Amalfi

Called *bambagina*, Amalfi's paper is made from macerated cloth fibers, which are then filtered and pressed into large frames. Such an art was learned from the Arabs of the Middle East, with whom the Republic of Amalfi enjoyed flourishing commercial relationships. Researchers actually believe that the name *bambagina* is a distortion of the Arab town that perfected this paper-making technique, El Marubig. The paper industry developed in Amalfi in the 12th and 13th centuries, and continued its expansion through the Renaissance and into modern times. The first machines were introduced in the 18th century, and only the development of cheaper paper manufacturing from wood pulp, in the 19th and 20th centuries, drove the local industry nearly out of business. The higher quality of its product kept it alive, though, and Amalfi still produces and sells paper throughout the world, in spite of the harsh competition. What makes this paper so special is that its fibers are very soft, making it wonderful to handle and allowing special effects as in the work of Antonio Cavaliere (see earlier in this chapter), which would be impossible with the harsher and less flexible fibers making up other qualities of paper.

Positano

Positano is a seaside resort made exclusive by its topography. The westernmost of the three most famous towns on the Amalfi Coast, Positano is also the most dramatic. Built in the narrow gap between two mountains, the village slopes steeply to the Tyrrhenian Sea.

The village develops vertically and, as you'll soon discover, is impossibly steep. You may want to wear comfortable shoes without heels to climb the steep alleys and many ramps of steps.

Don't expect white Caribbean beaches here: The beach is gray and rather pebbly. The sea, however, is splendid. Just off the coast are the legendary Sirenuse Islands, Homer's siren islands in the *Odyssey,* which form the privately owned mini-archipelago of Li Galli (The Cocks).

This elegant resort village's small alleys are filled with boutiques, restaurants, and hotels. Aside from the picturesque alleys, the big attraction here — you'll notice it the moment you step into town — is the local style, known as **Positano Fashion.** Fabrics and particularly swimsuits — whether maillot, bikini, or thong — all have colorful and unique patterns. Because people here spend two-thirds of their time in swimsuits, this local industry has exploded. We know someone who buys her bikinis only in Positano, no matter how far she has to travel to get them!

Ravello

The only one of the major towns that's not on the coast, Ravello opens onto a splendid valley with intensive cultivation — vineyards and lemons and other fruit grow on its steep terraced flanks. The town has a feeling of subdued elegance, the evidence of its magnificent past — and its past and present exclusiveness. Celebrities and writers favor this town; the reigning celeb of the moment is Gore Vidal, who purchased a villa as a writing retreat.

Salerno

If you happen to be in the area, it would be a real shame to miss out on Salerno's little-visited and off-the-beaten-track attractions. From the splendid seafront promenade to the medieval city, graced by one of the most beautiful cathedrals in all southern Italy, Salerno does not disappoint. You can get here by train from Naples in 35 minutes (trains depart every 15 minutes from Stazione Centrale), or by ferry and hydrofoil from Sorrento, Capri, and the Amalfi Coast run by **Alicost** (☎ 089-234892) and **Travelmar** (☎ 089-2227979; from Amalfi, Positano, and Minori only). April through September, you can also get here from Naples via the **Metrò del Mare** (☎ 199-446644; www. metrodelmare.com), a two-hour ferry ride. You'll find one tourist office at Via Roma 258 (☎ 089-224744) and a smaller one inside the train station at Piazza Vittorio Veneto.

An Etruscan town founded in the sixth century B.C., Salerno grew in importance under the Romans to become one of the leading cultural centers in Italy. In medieval times and during the Renaissance, its medical school was the top research center in the whole Western world. It then lost its primacy, as Naples was made the capital of the Southern Kingdom and became progressively larger and more powerful, leaving Salerno to fall into quiet oblivion.

The second-most-important harbor in the region, after Naples, Salerno today is a modern town bustling with activity and a cultural life dominated by its important university. At its heart is the medieval town, centered around **Piazza Sedile del Campo** — the picturesque old market square — and the beautiful **Duomo** (Piazza Alfano I; ☎ 089-231387; Free admission; Open: Daily 10 a.m.–6 p.m.). This 11th-century cathedral is one of the most beautiful Romanesque churches in Italy, with delicate carvings decorating its halls and portals (the main one closes with a set of bronze doors from Constantinople). Inside, do not miss the monumental candle holder, mosaic, inlay, and carved masterpieces. Attached to the church is the **museum** (Via Monsignor Monterisi; ☎ 089-239126; Free admission; Open: Daily 9 a.m.–6 p.m.), well worth a visit to see the 12th-century *paliotto* (altar front) decorated with 54 carved panels. Four frames are missing; each is the coveted possession of a museum: Paris's Louvre, New York's Met, and the museums of Berlin and Budapest.

From Salerno, you can catch a regular bus (several companies leave from Piazza della Concordia, among them **SCAT**; ☎ 0974-838415) to nearby **Paestum.** You can also hire a car with driver — the best option if your time is limited — who will double as guide; one reliable company is **Leonardo D'Onofrio** (Via Cesare Pavese; also sign up for a guided tour). If you are at all interested in antiquity and don't have time to go to Sicily, Paestum is an all-important destination: Three magnificent temples, a few ruined abodes, and long sections of fortified walls are all that remain of this powerful Greek city, once dominating the whole of southern Italy. You can walk the walls — affording beautiful views of the sea — but the key attractions are the well-preserved temples, a striking and romantic sight, particularly at sunset, when the stone takes on a unique pink hue. Admission to the archaeological area (Via Magna Grecia; ☎ **0828-811023**; www.infopaestum.it; Open: Daily 9 a.m.–sunset) is 4€ ($4.80), plus 4€ ($4.80) for the museum (combination tickets 6.50€/$7.80), which is closed the first and third Monday of each month.

Another excursion is to the fantastic **Carthusian Monastery of Padula** (☎ **097-577484**; Open: Sun and holidays 8 a.m.–sunset, other days by appointment), a Renaissance and baroque masterpiece. This is rarely visited because of its remote location in the hills inland of Salerno, but it's worth your time. You can take a bus with **Curcio Viaggi** (☎ **089-254080**; www.curcioviaggi.it) from Piazza della Concordia in Salerno (and also from Firenze and Siena), or with **Autolinee SLA** (☎ **0973-21016**; www.slasrl.it) from the same *piazza* in Salerno or from Naples. The complex is huge, covering over 46,450 sq. m (500,000 sq. ft.), with gorgeous cloisters and elegant cells for the monks, the most beautiful of all being the apartments of the Prior, of course. It is worth visiting the **archaeological museum** (☎ **097-577745**; Admission: 3€/$3.60; Open: Daily Oct 1–Mar 31 9 a.m.–7 p.m.) to see the monastery's original library and reception halls, which house the exhibits.

You can stay in Salerno at the **Jolly Hotel delle Palme** (Lungomare Trieste 1; ☎ **089-225222**; www.jollyhotels.it) and dine very well at the elegant **Cenacolo** (Piazza Alfano I 4; ☎ **089-238818**; Open: Tues–Sun 12:30–3 p.m., Tues–Sat 7:30–11 p.m.), across from the Duomo, serving local cuisine with a creative twist. Or settle for simpler fare and excellent pizza at **Zi Renato** (Via Roma 170; ☎ **089-228018**; Open: Daily 12:30–3 p.m. and 7:30–10 p.m.). In Paestum, you can stay at **Mec Paestum** (Via Tiziano 23; ☎ **082-8722444**; www.mechotel.com).

The 11th-century **Duomo** (Piazza Vescovado; ☎ **089-858311**; Admission: Duomo free, Museum 2€/$2.40; Open: Daily winter 9 a.m.–1 p.m. and 4–7 p.m., summer 8:30 a.m.–1 p.m. and 3–8 p.m.) is a splendid Romanesque church, with a grandiose carved triple **portal** and an elegant bell tower from the 13th century. The **bronze door** closing the center arch of the portal was sculpted in 1179 by Barisano da Trani, and cast in Constantinople: It is one of Italy's most beautiful, rivaling the doors in Florence's Baptistery and Pisa's Duomo. Inside, to the left of the main altar, is the **Cappella di San Pantaleone,** the chapel of the patron saint of Ravello. It contains a relic of the saint (a cracked vessel with his blood, which miraculously fails to leak away when it liquefies once a year). The blood is a symbol of the saint's violent demise: He was beheaded in Nicomedia on July 27, 290. Ravello holds a festival on that day every year. The crypt houses a small museum, where the star of the show is the beautiful sculpture by the 13th-century artist Bartolomeo da Foggia, depicting the bust of Sichelgaita della Marra, a local noble woman.

To the right of the Duomo is the beautiful 13th-century **Villa Rufolo** (Piazza Vescovado; ☎ **089-857657**; Admission: 5€/$6; Open: Daily summer 9 a.m.–8 p.m., winter 9 a.m.–5 p.m.), with its splendid gardens that play host to part of the **Ravello Festival** (see later in this section). Although the renovations by its 19th-century Scottish owner somewhat altered the original beauty of the building, much of its architecture still deserves a visit, from the elegant entrance hall to the grand reception and main halls to the romantic loggias of the inner court. In the gardens, you can visit the **Terrazza Wagner,** where the German composer received his inspiration for the Klingsor Garden scene in his *Parsifal.* The views are truly splendid.

Going farther up from the center of town (a steep ten-minute walk), you can reach **Villa Cimbrone** (Via Santa Chiara 26; ☎ **089-858072;** Admission: 5€/$6; Open: Daily 9 a.m.–7 p.m., winter until sunset), the fruit of the extensive renovations of a 15th-century villa by an eccentric English lord, who bought it at the end of the 19th century. The views and the gardens are very beautiful — particularly the famous **Belvedere Cimbrone,** a terrace lined with statues and opening onto a breathtaking panorama stretching from Capri to Paestum, beyond Salerno. You can also visit part of the villa, which has been turned into a hotel and restaurant (see "Spending the night," earlier in this chapter). Ring the bell at the entrance, and a member of the staff will let you in and take you around.

More cool things to see and do

Many people drive the Amalfi Coast and stop at only one or two of the towns, usually Amalfi or Positano. But the smaller towns and destinations are worth exploring, too. Here are a few recommendations:

✔ About 5km (3.1 miles) west of Amalfi — on foot or by boat — is the **Grotta dello Smeraldo (Emerald Grotto),** an underwater grotto less famous than Capri's Blue Grotto, but to the eyes of some, even more beautiful. What's unique about this grotto is its ancient formation of stalactites and stalagmites, which have been partially invaded by seawater. As a result, some of the formations are submerged, creating fantastic effects of light and shade. The boat takes you inside and around this bizarre world. It's open daily from November through February from 9 a.m. to 4 p.m. and March through October from 9 a.m. to 7 p.m., weather permitting. The cave is accessible from the sea; regular launch service is available from **Molo Pennello** in Amalfi, from 9:30 a.m. to 4 p.m., for 10€ ($12) round-trip. Or from land, you can take the SITA bus (Amalfi–Positano line; get off at the km 26.4 milestone on SS163) and go down a steep staircase or take the elevator. Admission to the grotto is 5€ ($6) per person, which includes the elevator ride from the road down to sea level and the boat ride to and inside the cave.

✔ The Amalfi Coast is a seaside resort, so naturally you can enjoy its many small sandy beaches, sunbathe, and swim in the blue Mediterranean. The beach in Amalfi is nice but crowded; you'll do better in the small towns of **Maiori** and **Minori,** two villages nearby to the south and easily reached by SITA bus. In Positano, besides the large and crowded beach by Marina Grande in the center of town, you can access **Fornillo** to the west and three small beaches to the east, followed by the nice beach of **Laurito.**

✔ **Hiking** is the best way to enjoy this stretch of coast. One very pleasant trail takes you through ramps and alleys from the center of **Ravello** (by a small fountain at the left of Villa Rufolo) down to **Minori,** a village on the seashore; allow about half an hour for the descent and double that for the climb back (or take a bus back). Another easy trail is along the **Valle dei Mulini** in Amalfi, up to the so-called "ruined mill" about one hour uphill. You could then continue on the moderately difficult hike along the **Vallone delle Ferriere.** This valley, which has been declared a World Heritage Site by UNESCO, is a protected natural area where you can find some animal and vegetable species from the Quaternary and Tertiary period, before glaciation. The whole trail is 12km (7.4 miles) long. From Positano, you can take the famous **Via degli Incanti,** a trail that goes all the way to Amalfi — a distance of 25km (15.6 miles) — along the steep coast, or at least the section of it called **Sentiero degli Dei** (Trail of Gods), starting to the right of Chiesa Nuova in the north of town.

Living it up after dark

During the summer months, this whole stretch of coast comes alive with cultural events, mostly centered on music and the figurative arts. The music festivals, featuring everything from classical to jazz, animate the sweet summer nights. The most famous of all is the **Ravello Festival** (Via Roma 10–12; ☎ 089-858422 or 199-109910 for reservations; www. ravellofestival.com), attracting international artists and a crowd of connoisseurs. Held in Ravello from June to September, it offers a great number of concerts and performances by the big names — mostly, but not entirely, classical. Special series include the **Festival Wagneriano,** in Villa Rufolo, and the **Dawn Concerts,** held, well, at dawn (by 4 a.m.). The price of events ranges from free to about 130€ ($156), depending on the performance.

Concerts are scheduled in Amalfi as well; the most popular are those held in the **Chiostro del Paradiso,** in Amalfi's Cathedral, on Friday nights from July through September.

In Positano, **Summer Music** is a festival of chamber music that takes place from the end of August through September. For a schedule of events, contact the tourist office (☎ 089-875067; www.aziendaturismo positano.it).

Fast Facts: The Amalfi Coast

Area Code

The local area code is **089** (see "Telephone" in the "Fast Facts" section of Appendix A for more on calling to and from Italy).

ATMs

You'll find banks with ATMs along the main streets and in the main square of each of the major towns, including a Banco di

Napoli at Piazza dei Mulini in Positano (☎ 089-875797); a Monte dei Paschi di Siena at Piazza Duomo 6 in Ravello (☎ 089-857120); and a Deutsche Bank at Via delle Repubbliche Marinare 21 in Amalfi.

Emergencies

For an ambulance, call ☎ 118; for the fire department, call ☎ 115; for road assistance, call ☎ 116.

Hospitals

There are medical centers in Amalfi (Via Casamare; ☎ 089-871-449) and in Ravello (Guardia Medica Castiglione di Ravello; ☎ 089-877208).

Police

Call ☎ 113.

Post Office

Positano's *ufficio postale* is on Via Marconi (SS163) at Viale Pasitea (☎ 089-875863); Ravello's is at Piazza Vescovado; and Amalfi's is at Via delle Repubbliche Marinare (☎ 089-872996).

Part VII
Sicily

"I appreciate that our room looks out onto several Baroque fountains, but I had to get up 6 times last night to go to the bathroom."

In this part . . .

"You cannot understand Italy without seeing Sicily. Sicily is where you can find the key to everything." These words, which Goethe wrote in 1787, still hold true today. Visiting Sicily is a unique experience: It's a more intense version of Italy, where things from the past are preserved with a magic vitality and hit you with strength and clarity. It is also a splendid Mediterranean island where you can abandon yourself to the task of enjoying life, the food and wine, and the sea and sun.

In Chapter 21, we tell you everything you need to know about Palermo, Sicily's capital and southern Italy's largest art center. In Chapter 22, we present the other top destinations in Sicily: beautiful Taormina; sleepy and mysterious Syracuse; Agrigento, with its breathtaking Valley of the Temples; as well as a few side trips — Segesta, Selinunte, Piazza Armerina, and Catania — all rich in art and attractions.

Chapter 21

Palermo

In This Chapter

▶ Finding your way to and around Palermo
▶ Getting the best deals on lodging — and the best meals
▶ Enjoying the sights and activities

· ·

Sicily is a big chunk of Italy, both geographically and culturally. Palermo — the island's capital and a busy modern port — has been the political center of "new" Sicily since about 1060 onward. A unique melting pot of cultures — from Arab to Norman to Spanish — it is a city rich in stunning works of art and local character. Behind a decaying but elegant facade, you'll find some of the region's — and the country's — finest art, particularly in the splendid churches, but also in the good museums. Similarly, behind their more formal manners and customs, you'll get to know the Sicilians as a warm and welcoming people, ready to help you enjoy your visit.

You can see Palermo's highlights in one day, but we recommend you dedicate at least two days to this splendid city. Palermo is also a good starting point for exploring the rest of Sicily, especially if your time is limited and you want to take advantage of the numerous day excursions that are offered from here (see "Seeing Palermo by guided tour," later in this chapter).

Getting There

Sicily is well connected with the rest of Italy, as well as with major destinations in Europe and in the Mediterranean. The major ports of entry to the island are Palermo, described in this chapter, and Catania (see Chapter 22), each with an important harbor, airport, and, of course, train and bus stations.

By ferry

Of the many ways to get here, our favorite is the overnight ferry: Not only do you get to enjoy some fabulous views, but you can also comfortably sleep in your cabin and have more time for sightseeing the next day. Several ferry companies serve Sicily: **SNAV** (Via Giordano Bruno 84; ☎ 081-4285555 in Naples, 0766-366366 in Civitavecchia; www.snav.it) runs ferries daily from Naples and every other day from Civitavecchia (the harbor about one hour north of Rome and easily connected to the capital by very frequent train and bus service, as well as car service). **Tirrenia** (☎ 892123 in Italy, or 081-0171998 from abroad; www.tirrenia.it) operates daily overnight service from Naples. **Grimaldi Ferries** (☎ 081-496444; www.grimaldi‑ferries.com) offers weekly service between Salerno (on the Amalfi Coast) and Palermo. Rates vary depending on the season, the seats or cabin chosen, and whether you're bringing a car; they range from around 60€ to 150€ ($72–$180) per person. It takes about 11 hours to travel from Naples or Salerno to Palermo, and 13 hours from Civitavecchia.

By air

Flying is less romantic than taking the ferry, but it's a lot faster. Daily flights connect Palermo to all other destinations in Italy and most major destinations in Europe (from the U.S., you'll need a connecting flight). **Alitalia** (☎ 06-2222, or 800-223-5730 in the U.S.; www.alitalia.it or www.alitaliausa.com) has several flights a day from Italian cities to Sicily. **Meridiana** (☎ 892928 in Italy, or 0789-52682 from abroad; www.meridiana.it) may offer better deals from some Italian destinations.

All flights arrive at Palermo's airport, **Falcone Borsellino** (☎ 800-541880 or 091-7020111; www.gesap.it) — locally called **Punta Raisi** — located 31km (19 miles) west of Palermo. In the arrivals concourse, you'll find a bank with ATM, a currency-exchange office, and a tourist information desk; public transportation is just outside the terminal.

The airport is a 25-minute **taxi** ride to the center of town; expect to pay about 40€ ($48). The airport is also connected to the city by rail: **Trains** run every hour (every half-hour at peak times) and cost 4.50€ ($5.40). You can also take the **bus,** run by **Prestia & Comande** (☎ 091-586351), to Palermo's rail station; it departs every 30 minutes and makes five stops in town, including the modern harbor and the Teatro Politeama. It takes about half an hour and costs 5€ ($6).

By train

Sicily is served by train (☎ 892021; www.trenitalia.it) from all major destinations: Cars are put on a train ferry at Messina and then continue on to Palermo. The trips are long, but sleeping cars can be quite comfortable if you book a single, double, or triple cabin; regular *cuccetta* (sleeping berths) in a six-seat compartment are more cramped. The ride from Rome to Palermo takes 11 or 12 hours and costs about 90€ ($108). Trains arrive at Palermo's **Stazione Centrale,** at Piazza Giulio Cesare (☎ 091-6165914), on the southeastern edge of the historic district.

Sicily

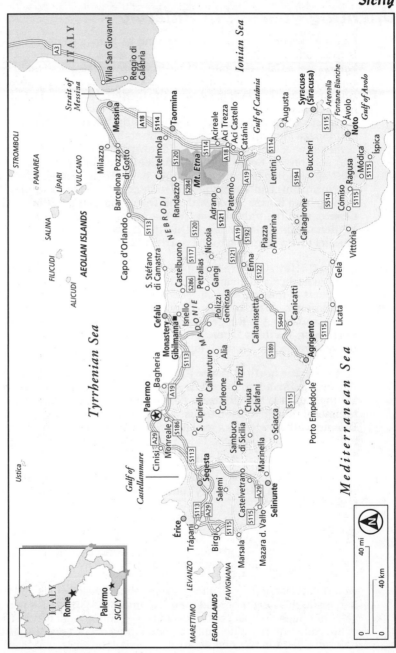

Orienting Yourself in Palermo

Palermo is a port city, organized around its busy waterfront: To the west is the modern harbor, with piers for large ships; to the east is the old harbor — La Cala — a rounded basin where sailing and fishing boats bob sleepily in the sun. **Via Francesco Crispi** is the major thoroughfare running along the waterfront from the modern harbor to La Cala. The historic district centers around and inland of the old harbor. To the east is **La Kalsa,** the ancient Arab quarters, with **Piazza Marina** by the harbor and **Piazza Magione** at its heart; to the south and west are the four *mandamenti* (neighborhoods) of the old town. This is neatly divided into four sections by **Corso Vittorio Emanuele** (running northeast to southwest and leading from the old harbor to the royal residence of Palazzo dei Normanni) and **Via Maqueda** (running northwest to southeast and leading from **Piazza Verdi,** with the Teatro Massimo, to **Piazza Giulio Cesare,** with the train station and bus terminal), intersecting at **Piazza Vigliena,** appropriately called **Quattro Canti** (Four Corners) by locals. Parallel to Via Maqueda to the north is **Via Roma.**

During the 19th century, the city expanded to the west, developing the modern harbor and, inland, a residential and commercial neighborhood. The heart of this more modern section of the historic district is **Piazza Castelnuovo,** with the Teatro Politeama, crossed by the continuation of Via Maqueda — **Via Ruggero VII** — and its further continuation to the northwest, **Via della Libertà,** the elegant avenue leading to the gardens of Villa Trabia and Giardino Inglese.

Farther to the north is **Monte Pellegrino,** a steep mountain overlooking the sea; up the hill to the south is **Monreale,** a separate town overlooking the city (it is to Palermo as Fiesole is to Florence). The great attraction here, enough in itself to justify your whole trip to Sicily, is the **Duomo,** with its cloister (see later in this chapter).

Introducing the neighborhoods

All of the neighborhoods below are safe. For tips on safety, see "Getting Around Palermo," and "Safety" under "Fast Facts: Palermo," both later in this chapter.

La Kalsa

The most famous — and once the most notorious — neighborhood in Palermo, this residential area of picturesque narrow streets stretches southeast of the old harbor. There was a time when visitors and locals wouldn't come here at all if they valued their lives: Crooks and thugs had made this neighborhood their headquarters. Today, it's perfectly safe (although do observe typical big-city caution) and is now the focus of an exuberant nightlife, cultural, and dining scene (see "Exploring Palermo," later in this chapter).

Palermo

ACCOMMODATIONS ■
Excelsior Palace **23**
Grande Albergo Sole **22**
Grand Hotel et des Palmes **10**
Grand Hotel Villa Igiea **1**
Hotel Gallery House **9**
Joli Hotel **8**
Massimo Plaza **13**
Principe di Villafranca **5**

DINING ◆
091 **32**
Antica Focacceria San Francesco **29**
Capricci di Sicilia **6**
Casa del Brodo **27**
Il Ristorantino **3**
La Cambusa **30**
Osteria dei Vespri **28**

ATTRACTIONS ●
Catacombe dei Cappuccini **18**
Cattedrale and Museo Diocesano **17**
Chiesa del Gesù (Casa Professa) **24**
Chiesa della Martorana **25**
Fontana Pretoria **26**
Galleria Regionale Siciliana (Palazzo Abatellis) **31**
La Cuba **19**
La Zisa **11**
Monte Pellegrino **2**
Museo Archeologico Regionale Salinas **14**
Oratorio del Rosario di San Domenico **16**
Oratorio di Santa Cita **15**
Palazzo dei Normanni and Cappella Palatina **20**
San Giovanni degli Eremiti **21**
Teatro Massimo **12**
Teatro Politeama **7**
Villa Malfitano **4**

Piazza Castelnuovo

Less picturesque than the old town, but much more elegant, this neighborhood was first developed in the late 19th century. This is the modern heart of Palermo, its streets lined with boutiques, restaurants, theaters, and, of course, hotels. The **Teatro Politeama,** where opera and ballet are staged (see "Living It Up After Dark," later in this chapter), is the rendezvous point for locals of every age, who meet here in noisy and colorful groups before heading for their evening destination, whether a restaurant or a simple stroll. One favorite stroll is along beautiful **Via Libertà,** which is lined with Liberty (Italian Art Nouveau) palaces.

Piazza Verdi

Dominated by the beautiful **Teatro Massimo,** where opera and concerts are presented, this neighborhood sits at the hinge of the old town of the Quattro Canti (see later) and the 19th-century district of Piazza Castelnuovo (see earlier). It shares some of the characteristics of each, preserving a historical feeling yet more stately and well maintained than the oldest neighborhoods in town. Centrally located, it is within walking distance of many attractions and is not far from the modern harbor, with its numerous hotels and restaurants.

Quattro Canti

The heart of the oldest part of town along with La Kalsa (see earlier), this is where you'll find most of the attractions in the historic district, including some of Palermo's most important monuments, such as **La Martorana, Palazzo dei Normanni,** and the **Cattedrale.** This area is home to many hotels and restaurants, an active nightlife scene, and lively shopping — including the famous **Vucciria open-air market.**

Finding information after you arrive

The main tourist office is at **Piazza Castelnuovo** 34, across from the Teatro Politeama (☎ **091-6058351;** www.palermotourism.com; Open: Mon–Fri 8:30 a.m.–2 p.m. and 3–6 p.m.); it maintains two tourist info points, one at the **airport** (☎ **091-591698;** Open: Mon–Fri 8 a.m. to midnight, Sat–Sun 8 a.m.–8 p.m.), and one at the **train station** on Piazza Giulio Cesare (☎ **091-6165914;** Open: Mon–Fri 8:30 a.m.–2 p.m. and 3–6 p.m.).

Getting Around Palermo

Modern Palermo sprawls between the mountains and the sea, but the historic district and its sights are fairly concentrated, making it easy to visit.

 Despite the police's best efforts, purse-snatchers (often operating from motor scooters) and pickpockets are a common reality. Backpacks are especially susceptible, as their bottoms can be easily sliced without your noticing it. Observe common big-city caution and, at night, avoid deserted, run-down streets, as muggings are not unheard of.

On foot

Palermo is an interesting city to discover on foot; the city layout is simple, making it easy to find your way. Among the hidden surprises of the back streets in the historic district are forlorn blocks with partially destroyed buildings — some by World War II bombings, others by earthquakes — that are still unrepaired. We have walked down some of these streets (by day) to look at the shuttered villas of the Sicilian aristocracy and never had any problem, but everyone has their own comfort level. If you don't feel comfortable, turn around and take a different street.

The free map from the tourist office is perfectly adequate for most visitors; if you want more detail, you can pick up a map with *stradario* (street directory) at most news kiosks.

By bus

Palermo's **bus system** (☎ 848-800817; www.amat.pa.it) is functional and well run. Regular bus tickets cost 1€ ($1.20) and are valid for two hours; you can save a little if you want to invest in a carnet of 20 individual tickets, selling for 19€ ($23); you can also get a **giornaliero** (day pass) for 3.50€ ($4.20). Tickets are sold at tobacconist stores and news kiosks around town; you can get a free bus map at the information office at Via Giusti 7 (Open: Mon–Wed 8 a.m.–1 p.m. and 3–5:30 p.m.; Thurs–Fri 8 a.m.–1 p.m.).

The three **electric minibus** lines (red, yellow, and green) are convenient for visiting all the important attractions in Palermo; they loop through the historic district Monday through Saturday from 7:45 a.m. to 7:30 p.m. and Sunday and holidays from 7:45 a.m. to 1:30 p.m. Use them as you would a hop-on/hop-off tour bus; the ticket costs 3€ ($3.60) and is valid for one day on all lines.

By taxi

Taxis are an excellent way to get around Palermo; you'll find taxi stands at all the major squares — Piazza Indipendenza, Piazza Verdi, Piazza Castelnuovo — as well as at the modern harbor and the train station. You can also be picked up anywhere by calling a radio taxi (☎ 091-225455 or 091-513311). The meter starts at 3.50€ ($4.20) and goes up 0.65€ (78¢) for every additional kilometer (⅗ mile); you'll also pay a 1.50€ ($1.80) night or holiday surcharge and, for radio-taxi calls, the meter reading from where your taxi came from to pick you up. However, expect to pay a few euro more than what the meter shows: Because official rates haven't been adjusted since 1995 (it's true, we checked), taxi drivers award themselves an inflation increase over what the meter reads.

It's a lot easier — and will avoid friction on both sides — if you ask the driver to estimate the charge for your destination upfront, rather than being surprised by an extravagant amount upon arrival. Ask the concierge at your hotel for the likely charge for your destination and, if need be, negotiate with the driver. If it doesn't sound reasonable, take another cab.

Staying in Style

Hotels in Palermo are mixed, ranging from old-fashioned accommodations that are remnants of a previous era (beware of those) to modern, up-to-international-standards hotels. Rates tend to be considerably lower than in other major Italian destinations such as Venice, Rome, and Florence, so you can stay in superior hotels without paying through the nose.

If you arrive without a reservation, check with the tourist office for assistance — it maintains information desks at the airport and the train station (see "Information" under "Fast Facts: Palermo," later in this chapter).

The top hotels

Baglio Conca d'Oro
$$$ Monreale

We're not great fans of staying out of the historic district when that's what you've come to see, but we have to make an exception for this wonderful place. Housed in a historic *baglio* (paper mill) on the slopes of the hill of Monreale, south of Palermo, it is located 10km (6 miles) away from the city center and only 3km (2 miles) from Monreale. Perfectly restored, the villa welcomes its guests in elegant public spaces done with frescoed ceilings and wooden beams; guest rooms are splendid, with a good mix of modern comforts and countryside elegance. The hotel's restaurant, **Absidi,** is quite good and open to the public. *Note:* If you're driving instead of taking a cab, be forewarned that the hotel is off the main road and not easy to find after dusk.

Via Aquino 19, Borgo Molara. ☎ *091-6406286. Fax:091-6408742.* www.baglioconca doro.com. *Free parking. Rack rates: 164€ ($199) double. Rates include buffet breakfast. AE, DC, MC, V.*

Grand Hotel et des Palmes
$$ Teatro Massimo

Once a private home, the Grand Hotel opened in 1874 and immediately became the place to stay in Palermo: Wagner finished writing his *Parsifal* here. The classically inspired lobby has marble floors, Greek columns, chandeliers, marble staircases, and original Art Nouveau furnishings. Guest rooms are spacious and grand, but not all of them have been updated, and some are rather staid. The excellent buffet breakfast is served in the Hall of Mirrors (Sala degli Specchi) — a superb hall used also for private receptions — and the hotel's restaurant, La Palmetta, serves lunch and dinner fare.

See map p. 457. Via Roma 398, 4 blocks northeast of the Teatro Politeama. ☎ *800-179217 or 091-6028111. Fax: 091-331545.* www.grandhoteletdespalmes.com. *Bus: Red line. Parking: $14€ ($15). Rack rates: 191€–232€ ($229–$278) double. Rates include buffet breakfast. AE, DC, MC, V.*

Grand Hotel Villa Igiea
$$$ Monte Pellegrino

The best hotel in Palermo is not only a hotel, but also a historic site: A former private villa on the outskirts of town, Villa Igiea is a masterpiece of the Sicilian Liberty (Italian Art Nouveau) style, completely designed — right down to the furnishings — by Sicilian architect Ernesto Basile. The hotel is surrounded by splendid terraced gardens overlooking the bay. It features two restaurants with a panoramic terrace, a piano bar, and a salt-water pool. The spacious guest rooms are as glamorous as the public areas, with elegant furnishings and fine fabrics; some offer glorious views and private terraces. Be aware that some of the cheaper rooms may not have been renovated and could be a bit worn, with aging bathrooms.

See map p. 457. Salita Belmonte 43. ☎ *091-6312111. Fax: 091-547654. Bus: 139 or 731. Free parking. Rack rates: 277€–385€ ($332–$462) double. Rates include buffet breakfast. AE, DC, MC, V.*

Joli Hotel
$ Piazza Castelnuovo

This modest hotel, on a quiet and stately square just north of the modern harbor, offers functional, comfortable accommodations within walking distance of all major attractions. Completely renovated in 2003, its guest rooms are done in simple modern style with compact (but not cramped) bathrooms and private terraces; some have views of Monte Pellegrino, the mountain overlooking Palermo. Although the hotel is small, it offers a pleasant lounge for guests.

See map p. 457. Via Michele Amari 11, 2 blocks southeast of the Teatro Politeama. ☎ */fax: 091-6111765.* www.hoteljoli.com. *Bus: Red line. Free parking. Rack rates: 88€–98€ ($106–$118) double. Rates include breakfast. AE, DC, MC, V.*

Massimo Plaza
$$ Teatro Massimo

Recently restored, this elegant hotel is one of the best in town, offering beautiful accommodations and an excellent location just across from the Teatro Massimo. The large guest rooms are outfitted with tasteful modern furniture, pastel walls, and wooden floors. Bathrooms are good-sized and have all the comforts. The kindness of the staff is a pleasant plus.

See map p. 457. Via Maqueda 437. ☎ *091-325657. Fax: 091-325711.* www.massimo plazahotel.com. *Bus: Red line. Rack rates: 200€ ($240). AE, DC, MC, V.*

Principe di Villafranca
$$$ Piazza Castelnuovo

This family-run boutique hotel offers palatial accommodations close to the heart of Palermo. Built in 1998, it has no historical claims, but it's decorated in style and comfort, creating a most welcoming and elegant atmosphere. Turkish carpets, wooden floors, fine upholstery, and some antique furnishings fill the hotel, which even has a fitness club. Guest rooms are large and stylish, with contemporary furnishings, Internet access, and good-sized marble or tiled bathrooms. The **Firriato** restaurant is excellent and a reputed gourmet destination (closed Sun).

See map p. 457. Via G. Turrisi Colonna 4. ☎ *091-6118523. Fax: 091-588-705.* www.principedivillafranca.it. *Bus: Red line. Rack rates: 239€ ($287). AE, DC, MC, V.*

Runner-up accommodations

Excelsior Palace

$$$ Piazza Verdi Striving to be one of the best hotels in Palermo, this historic choice — open since 1891 — was overhauled in 2005. Public spaces are grand; guest rooms are spacious and elegantly appointed, with a pleasant mix of modern furniture, good reproductions, and a few antiques. *See map p. 457. Corso Vittorio Emanuele 327.* ☎ *091-7909. Fax: 091-342139.* www.excelsiorpalermo.it.

Grande Albergo Sole

$$ Centro Storico Located near the Duomo and the Palazzo Reale, this is considered one of the best hotels in Palermo. It features an indoor garden and a terrace with a panoramic view. Guest rooms are even more welcoming since they underwent complete restorations in 2005. *See map p. 457. Corso Vittorio Emanuele 291.* ☎ *091-6041111. Fax: 091-6110182.* www.ghshotels.it.

Hotel Gallery House

$$ Piazza Castelnuovo Catering to savvy business travelers, this small hotel offers excellent value. Centrally located, yet on a quiet street, it provides welcoming service and accommodations. The good-sized guest rooms are appointed with quality furniture and an attention to modern comforts. You'll find Wi-Fi connections in every room. *See map p. 457. Via Mariano Stabile 136.* ☎ *091-6124758. Fax: 091-6124779.* www.hotelgalleryhouse.com.

Dining Out

Even within Italy, where every town seems to lay claim to a unique cuisine, Sicily is exceptional: The Sicilians perfected multiculturalism centuries ago, so here you can find pasta and meats seasoned with pistachio nuts, almonds, North African spices, and, because Sicily is an island, many culinary treasures from the sea (see Chapter 2 for details).

Two dining areas well worth checking out are **Piazza Marina,** behind the recreational harbor of La Cala, and the area around the **Teatro Politeama,** on Piazza Castelnuovo, where locals go for more traditional and elegant dining. In addition, some of the hotels reviewed earlier have excellent restaurants that are popular with locals.

091
$$$ La Kalsa   CREATIVE SICILIAN

This is our favorite gourmet restaurant in Palermo — your taste buds will be tickled by a cuisine that integrates traditional flavors with some of the best ingredients from elsewhere on the Italian peninsula. The colorful modern décor is welcoming, and we love the terrace in good weather. Your menu may include such dishes as swordfish and smoked-tuna pâté served with confit of fresh figs, or perhaps zucchini-stuffed lamb with garlic and fresh mint. The desserts are excellent, and if you like wine, you'll find a well-rounded list with some unusual bottles.

See map p. 457. Piazza Magione 10. ☎ 091-6177807. Reservations required. Bus: Yellow line. Secondi: 15€–22€ ($18–$26). AE, MC, V. Open: Mon–Sat 12:30–3 p.m. and 7:30–11 p.m. Closed Feb.

Antica Focacceria San Francesco
$ La Kalsa   SNACKS

More of a snack place than a restaurant, this eatery is a Palermo institution for those in the know. Here you'll find some delicious and difficult-to-find staples of Sicilian traditional fast food, served since 1834. The best is *panelle* (chickpea fritters), *arancini* (deep-fried stuffed rice balls), and the more recent addition of *focaccia farcita* (stuffed pizza). If you're daring, try the house specialty, deep-fried spleen sandwich, served with or without cheese (we prefer without, but also decided we could live very well without the whole thing altogether).

See map p. 457. Via A. Paternostro 58. ☎ 091-320624. Reservations not accepted. Bus: Yellow line. Sandwiches 3€–6€ ($3.60–$7.20). MC, V. Open: Daily 10 a.m. to midnight.

Capricci di Sicilia
$$ Piazza Castelnuovo   SICILIAN

Located in the more elegant part of the town center, Capricci di Sicilia is an excellent restaurant offering typical Sicilian recipes in a pleasant setting. Try the delicious *bucatini alle sarde e finocchietto selvatico* (pasta with sardines and wild fennel), *maccheroni alla Norma* (with eggplant), *involtini di pesce spada* (rolled and stuffed swordfish), and *trionfo di pesce azzurro* (several kinds of bluefish — grilled, sautéed, roasted, or poached). Finish your meal with *cassata* (sweet creamy cheese and candied fruit) — they make an awesome one here.

See map p. 457. Via Istituto Pignatelli 6, off Piazza Sturzo to the northwest of the Teatro Politeama. ☎ 091-327777. Reservations recommended. Bus: Red line. Secondi: 9–15€ ($11–$18). AE, DC, MC, V. Open: Tues–Sun 12:30–3 p.m. and 8–11 p.m. Closed lunch in Aug.

Casa del Brodo
$ Quattro Canti   SICILIAN

This *trattoria,* opened in 1890, claims to be the oldest in Palermo. Indeed, the dining room is very atmospheric, but the old-fashioned ambience isn't a bit ruined by the new air-conditioning. We love coming here for the buffet of *antipasti,* always including a large variety of traditional fish and vegetable specialties, as well as for the traditional *primi* — our faves are *pasta alla Norma* (with eggplant) and *pasta con le sarde* (with sardines) — and the well-prepared grilled fish. It gets very crowded at lunch, so come early.

See map p. 457. Corso Vittorio Emanuele 175, near the Vucciria market. ☎ *091-321655. Reservations recommended on weekends. Bus: Green, red, or yellow line. Secondi: 6.50€–15€ ($7.80–$18). DC, MC, V. Open: Oct–May Wed–Mon 12:30–3 p.m. and 7:30–11 p.m.; June–Sept closed Sun.*

Il Ristorantino
$$ Via della Liberta   SEAFOOD/SICILIAN

In the residential area a short distance north of the center, this is an excellent place to sample Sicily's seafood bounty. It hews more closely to tradition than the other restaurants reviewed in this section, but the seasonal menu includes some successful innovative touches. We loved the squid-ink pasta with seafood ragout, the mackerel with caper sauce, and the *polpettine di pesce azzurro al finocchio selvatico* (wild-fennel fish cakes). Desserts are also very good.

See map p. 457. Piazzale Alcide De Gasperi 19, off Via della Croce Rossa (continuation of Via della Liberta to the north). ☎ *091-512861. Reservations recommended. Bus: 101 or 106. Secondi: 14€–20€ ($17–$24). AE, DC, MC, V. Open: Tues–Sun 12:30–3 p.m. and 7:30–11 p.m.*

La Cambusa
$ La Kalsa   SICILIAN

We like to come here for typical home-style Sicilian fare — and we're not the only ones. La Cambusa is very popular with the people of La Cala (the marina across the street) and other Palermitans, so come early — Sicilians don't eat until 9 or even 9:30 p.m. in summer — or be prepared to wait. Try the superb *pasta con le sarde* (pasta with sardines, fennel, and tomato sauce) or the *pasta alla carrettiera* (the Sicilian version of pesto, with capers, almonds, and tomato), one of our all-time favorites. The grilled fish is always tasty.

See map p. 457. Piazza Marina 16. ☎ *091-584574. Reservations recommended on weekends. Bus: Red line. Secondi: 8€–14€ ($9.60–$17). MC, V. Open: Tues–Sun 12:30–3 p.m. and 7:30–11 p.m.*

Osteria dei Vespri
$$ La Kalsa   CREATIVE SICILIAN

Not everything in Palermo is traditional; this small *osteria* framed by the splendid Palazzo Ganci (made famous by the ball scenes of Visconti's

The Mafia

The region's reputation as headquarters of the Mafia and its bloody vendettas scared people away from Sicily, particularly in the 1970s and 1980s, when the internal fights between the new generation — mostly drug traffickers and thugs — and the old generation — the "men of honor," as they liked to call themselves — allowed the police to butt in and bring to justice many criminals. The magistrates stood up to the challenge, some at the cost of their lives (Giovanni Falcone and Paolo Borsellino were slaughtered in 1992), and started a crackdown that cleared much ground and lifted the heavy veil that had weighed upon the island for so long. Most of this is now history — you can even visit the **Mafia Museum** in Corleone (Palazzo Provenzano, Via Orfanatrofio 7; ☎ 091-8464907) — but as with all recent history, it has left scars that are slow to heal. The changes are tangible and far-reaching: The trials spawned a Sicilian renaissance that has brought about restoration and reopening of monuments that had been closed for decades, and, even more important, a jolt of cultural and economic energy that has given new life to the island.

movie *Il Gattopardo*) specializes in innovative cuisine, for which chef and proprietor Alberto Rizzo has become renowned. Try the soup made with local mushrooms, or perhaps the mushroom, potato, and thyme ravioli over cheese fondue with truffles and fresh parsley. The pork filet mignon in hazelnut crust is also worthwhile. In a land known for idiosyncrasy, Rizzo earns that reputation. The 45€ ($54) tasting menu is a great deal.

See map p. 457. Piazza Croce dei Vespri 6. ☎ *091-6171631.* www.osteriadei vespri.it. *Reservations required. Bus: Red line. Secondi: 9€–16€ ($11–$19). AE, DC, MC, V. Open: Mon–Sat 12:30–2:30 p.m. and 7:30–10:30 p.m. Closed 2 weeks in Aug.*

Exploring Palermo

If you're planning to visit several attractions in town, one good deal is the **combination ticket** to La Zisa, San Giovanni degli Eremiti, and the cloister of the Duomo of Monreale. It's valid for two days and sold at any of the participating attractions for 12€ ($14).

Discovering the top attractions

Just wandering around the historic district is fascinating — note the various styles and cultural overlays that bear witness to Palermo's variegated history. The old town, centered around **Piazza Vigliena,** is a sight unto itself; the small square is appropriately called *Teatro del Sole* (Theater of the Sun) because you can see the sun from sunrise to sunset, and it is very picturesque . . . but you should not miss the nearby **Piazza Bellini** — one of the most attractive squares in town — nor **Fontana Pretoria** on Piazza Pretoria, at the intersection of Via Vittorio Emanuele and Via Maqueda. Created for a Florentine villa, this magnificent 16th-century fountain was sold to the Palermo Senate when the villa's owner died. The nudes created a big scandal at the time, and for a while it was called the "Fountain of Shame."

Cattedrale and Museo Diocesano

Palermo's cathedral was built in 1185 atop a mosque that was itself built atop a Byzantine church. In this architectural sandwich, some material was reused; for example, in the portico is a column (first on the left) with an engraved inscription from the Koran, an unusual feature for a Catholic church. The church went through many renovations, but the Romanesque exterior is still original; this creates quite a shock when you go in and find yourself deep into baroque. Many masterpieces are hidden inside: Look for the bas-reliefs by Vincenzo and Fazio Gagini on the altar, and for the **Madonna with Child** by Francesco Laurana in the seventh chapel of the left nave (Laurana's famous sculpture of Eleanora d'Aragona is in the Galleria Regionale Siciliana — see later in this chapter). The **apses** are the only section of the interior that are still original from the 12th century.

From a door to the right of Santa Rosalia chapel inside the cathedral, or from the garden outside, you can access the **crypt** and the **treasury**; the latter contains a variety of precious objects, including chalices, vestments, and other utensils of the Catholic rite, as well as the **crown** of Constance of Aragon, the wife of Frederick II. The cathedral also houses the **tombs** of Sicily's kings and emperors, including those of Holy Roman Emperor Frederick II and Roger II.

Recently open to the public, the **Museo Diocesano** is housed in the beautiful archbishop's palace attached to the cathedral to the left (entrance on Via Matteo Bonello). It holds a great collection of religious art from the 12th to the 19th centuries.

See map p. 457. Piazza della Cattedrale, on Via Vittorio Emanuele. ☎ *091-3343736. www.cattedrale.palermo.it. Bus: Green line. Admission: Cathedral free; Crypt, treasury, and Museum 4.50€ ($5.40); Crypt and treasury only, 2.50€ ($3). Open: Cathedral, treasury, and crypt Mon–Sat 9:30 a.m.–1:30 p.m. and 2:30–5:30 p.m.; Cathedral also Sun and holidays 7:30 a.m.–1:30 p.m. and 4–7 p.m., but closed to visitors during mass; Museum Sun–Fri 9:30 a.m.–1:30 p.m., Sat 10 a.m.–6 p.m.*

Chiesa del Gesù

Most commonly called the **Casa Professa,** after the library attached to the church, this was the first church in Sicily founded by the Jesuits. Its interior is rich in **stucco work** by several members of the Serpotta family (famous Palermitan sculptors who operated between the 17th and the 18th centuries). We love the beautiful **marble inlays,** in a large range of colors, that decorate the altar and walls. The original Renaissance church, in the form of a Latin cross (a nave and two short aisles), was much changed in the following century by the Jesuit Natale Masuccio, who made it into one of the most ostentatious churches of the Sicilian baroque. The lavish decorations have been preserved despite the damage caused by a 1943 bombing, which partially destroyed the church.

See map p. 457. Piazza Casa Professa, off Via Ponticello from Via Maqueda. ☎ *091-6076223. Bus: Red line. Admission: Free. Open: Daily 7 a.m. to noon and 5–6:30 p.m.; no visits during mass. Open mornings only in Aug.*

Chiesa della Martorana

Built in 1143 by Giorgio di Antiochia, admiral to Ruggero II, this church was transformed during later centuries, but its stunning **Byzantine mosaics** were luckily preserved, magnificently depicting religious scenes from the life of Mary. The mosaic on the balustrade contains an interesting detail: It shows Roger II getting his crown directly from Christ and not from the pope — a direct political statement against the church in Rome. The name *Martorana* comes from the nearby convent, founded by the Martorana family. Tradition says that the nuns there invented the little marzipan fruits that today are a typical — and delicious — souvenir from Sicily. They still sell the original creations: bunches of grapes made of almond paste, each grape delicately painted with sugar, the stems made of candied orange peel covered in dark chocolate — a bit expensive, yes, but a treat fit for a king.

See map p. 457. Piazza Bellini 3, off Via Maqueda, near the Quattro Canti. ☎ *091-6161692. Bus: Red line. Admission: Free. Open: Mon–Sat 8 a.m.–1 p.m. and 3:30–5:30 p.m.; Sun and holidays 8:30 a.m.–1 p.m.*

Duomo di Monreale

Overlooking Palermo about 10km (6 miles) away, Monreale dominates the city from its beautiful hill. The great attraction here, enough in itself to justify your whole trip to Sicily, is the **Duomo,** with its **cloister.** This 12th-century Romanesque church is one of the most breathtaking in existence. It may not be exceptional for its Norman exterior — the Duomo in Palermo is more interesting — but the interior is extraordinary. The church is decorated with 6,000 sq. m (55,000 sq. ft.) of fabulous Byzantine **mosaics** depicting scenes from the Old and New Testaments; only in Constantinople — in the Hagia Sofia — did the Byzantines create a more extensive series of mosaics. The **floors** are also magnificent, made up of remarkable marble mosaics, and the **bronze doors** by Bonanno Pisano (designer of Pisa's famous tower) are masterpieces. You can also visit the treasury, with its collection of precious religious objects, and the terraces, from which you can enjoy pretty views over the attached cloister and the town.

Annexed to the church is the **cloister** from 1180, one of the most beautiful in Italy. A unique work of art, its 228 double columns are decorated with individual details, some with mosaic inlay and each with a different pattern; the carved stone capitals are amazingly intricate renderings of scenes such as battles, the punishment of the damned, and stories of obscure meaning with fanciful and incredibly detailed carvings. Allow about thirty minutes for the bus ride from Palermo and about an hour and a half for your visit.

Piazza del Duomo in Monreale. ☎ *091-6404413. Bus: 389 from Piazza Indipendenza, off the Palazzo dei Normanni in Palermo, to Piazza del Duomo, running every 20 minutes. Admission: Duomo free; treasury 2€ ($2.40); terraces 1.50€ ($1.80); cloister 6€ ($7.20). Open: Duomo daily summer 8 a.m.–6 p.m., winter 8 a.m.–12:30 p.m. and 3:30–6 p.m.; treasury and terraces daily 8 a.m.–12:30 p.m. and 3:30–6 p.m.; cloister Oct–Apr Mon–Sat 9 a.m. to noon and 3:30–5:30 p.m., Sun and holidays 9 a.m.–12:30 p.m., May–Sept daily 9 a.m.–7 p.m. Last entrance 30 minutes earlier.*

Galleria Regionale Siciliana

Housed in the 15th-century Palazzo Abatellis — in elegant late Catalan-Gothic style — this is the principal museum of Sicilian art from the 13th to the 18th centuries. Among the many treasures inside, the 15th-century **Triumph of Death** is a powerful and intriguing fresco that came from the hall of the 1330 Palazzo Sclafani in town: A skeleton on horseback fires arrows at pleasure seekers, rich prelates, and other sinners as the poor and ill look on (the two artists who did the fresco painted themselves in this group). The faces are incredibly expressive; Picasso could have done the horse's head. One of the words that comes to mind when seeing this work is "modern." It's unfortunate that its creator's identity is not known. Our favorite painting is Antonello da Messina's **Madonna Annunziata,** looking out from under a blue mantle, which displays the painter's uncanny ability to portray more than one emotion at the same time.

A bit of history

Although today Palermo may seem off the beaten track in terms of tourism, its treasures attest that it was once the center of an empire: Holy Roman emperor Frederick II (1194–1250) was born in Italy, and he made Palermo his capital. It eventually became one of the most renowned and magnificent courts in the Western world. Before that, Palermo had been an important Phoenician, Greek, Roman, and Byzantine harbor, but it was only with the Arabs, in the ninth century, that it gained importance in the Mediterranean. The new rulers made Palermo into Sicily's capital, gracing the flourishing commercial and cultural center with beautiful palaces and innumerable mosques (over 300, it is said). Little remains of that period: The Normans erased most traces of the Arab presence when they took over the city in 1072, transforming most of the palaces and churches with their own architectural style. Sicily was taken over by Spain in the 15th century and was reunited with Italy by the Bourbons in the 18th century.

Palermo suffered severe damage by earthquakes in the early 20th century and was bombarded in World War II; much of it seems to have never recovered. However, Palermo's intertwined traditions have left behind a city like no other in the world, where "multiculturalism" has flourished since the early Middle Ages.

Francesco Laurana's splendid marble **bust of Eleonora d'Aragona** is one of the most famous works in Sicily.

See map p. 457. Via Alloro, across the garden near Piazza Marina and off Via Quattro Aprile. ☎ *091-6230011.* www.regione.sicilia.it/beniculturali/ dirbenicult/PALAZZOABATELLIS. *Bus: Red line. Admission: 6€ ($7.20). Open: Daily 9 a.m.–1 p.m.; Tues–Fri also 2:30–7 p.m. Ticket booth closes 30 minutes earlier.*

La Kalsa

This is one of Palermo's oldest neighborhoods, created by the Arabs as their emir's walled citadel when they took over the island and the town in A.D. 831. Left undisturbed — and decaying — the neighborhood had become one of the most dangerous areas in Palermo until the late 1980s, when a successful plan of renovation and revitalization transformed it into a lively cultural destination, attracting intellectuals and artists as well as regular people who come for the many events, restaurants, and nightlife. Although some of the area still needs refurbishing, it is extremely interesting to explore.

La Kalsa developed around **Piazza Magione,** southeast of **Piazza Marina** and Palermo's old harbor, **La Cala.** The grandiose battle scene between Garibaldi and the Bourbons in the famous Visconti movie *Il Gattopardo (The Leopard)* was filmed on Piazza Magione. Piazza Marina is one of La Kalsa's main features, with its beautiful garden enclosed by elegant Liberty-style iron railings and graced by an impressive giant ficus. **Via Alloro** was the citadel's main street, as you can see from the once-elegant palaces lining it. Unfortunately, much of the Arabs' fine work was destroyed when the Spanish viceroys took over, adding their own architectural interpretations, and many of the later *palazzi* were damaged or destroyed by earthquakes and World War II, and are now mostly semi-abandoned. For an idea of what they looked like in their former splendor, visit **Palazzo Mirto** (Via Merlo 2; ☎ 091-6164751; Admission: 3€/$3.60; Open: Mon–Sat 9 a.m.–7 p.m., Sun and holidays 9 a.m.–1:30 p.m.), which was donated to the city with all its furnishings intact by the aristocratic family who occupied it for centuries.

Among the neighborhood's churches, visit **Santa Teresa** (Piazza Kalsa; ☎ 091-6171658; Open: Fri–Wed 7–11 a.m. and daily 4:30–6 p.m.), a good example of the irrepressible Sicilian baroque, lavishly decorated inside with stucco work by the famous Serpotta Sicilian sculptors; and the 13th-century **San Francesco d'Assisi** (Piazza San Francesco, off Via Merlo; ☎ 091-582370; open occasionally), with a superb 14th-century portal and handsome carvings inside its magnificent chapel Mastrantonio.

Unless you're a die-hard urbanite, check out La Kalsa during the daytime. Its dark alleys and decaying buildings can be intimidating at night.

Bordered by Via Maqueda, Corso Vittorio Emanuele, Via Lincoln, and the sea. Bus: Red and yellow lines.

Museo Archeologico Regionale Salinas

Built on the site of a monastery, this museum occupies several buildings and contains what is probably the most impressive archaeological collection in the country. Walking through its rooms is a good introduction to Sicily's ancient history, from pre-historic findings to Roman times. On the ground floor, you'll see the major art finds from Greek and Roman sites on the island, particularly from Tindari, Solunto, and Selinunte. One of the most famous pieces is the **head of Medusa.** The basement houses a reconstruction of **clay decorations** of a Greek temple, while in the Sala Marconi you'll find a partial reconstruction of the **cornice moldings** with lion heads from the Temple of Victory in Himera. The museum also holds beautiful **Roman bronze statues** — note in particular the bronze statue of a ram — and a fair amount of **Etruscan pottery** and other objects. Also remarkable are the **Phoenician works** dating from the fifth century B.C., including sarcophagi depicting human images.

See map p. 457. Piazza P. Olivella 24, between Via Roma and Via Maqueda. Bus: Red line. ☎ *091-6116805. Admission: 6€ ($7.20). Open: Daily 8:30 a.m.–1:45 p.m.; Tues–Fri also 2:30–6:30 p.m.*

Palazzo dei Normanni and Cappella Palatina

Built over an ancient Roman palace — itself probably built over a Carthaginian building — this *palazzo* embodies the island's culture of continuity in change. The imposing building was the castle and royal residence of the various powers that reigned over Palermo, from the Arab emir to the current Regional Assembly of Sicily. In the 12th century, the Normans remodeled the palace, which had been the residence of the Arab emir. It had four towers, of which only one remains today, the **Torre Pisana.** It was remodeled again in the 16th century as the residence of the Spanish viceroy. The royal apartments are open to the public, but because of the parliamentary meetings, access is restricted (see details later). On the third floor is the **Sala di Ruggero,** originally the bedroom of Ruggero II (1095–1154), with mosaics representing hunting scenes and striking animals and plant forms. On the second floor is the famous **Cappella Palatina (Palatine Chapel),** with its impressive decorations. The chapel, started by Ruggero II in 1132, took over ten years to complete and is a harmony of masterwork from different cultures — Arab artisans made the inlaid wooden ceilings (a type of work known as *muqarnas*), Sicilians did the stonecutting, and the mosaics are Byzantine. The walls and dome are completely covered with rich mosaics representing scenes from the Old Testament (the nave), Christ's life (the southern transept), and the lives of Peter and Paul (the aisles). Note the **candlestick** by the entrance — it's intricately carved from a single piece of stone and stands over 3.9m (13 ft.) tall.

See map p. 457. Piazza Indipendenza, off Corso Calatafimi, through the Porta Nuova. ☎ *091-7051111.* www.ars.sicilia.it. *Bus: Green line. Admission: Cappella 4€ ($4.80); Cappella and Palazzo 6€ ($7.20). Open: Palazzo Mon, Tues, and Sat 8:30 a.m. to noon and 2–5 p.m.; Sun and holidays 8:30 a.m.–2:30 p.m. Last entrance 30 minutes* *earlier. Cappella Palatina Mon–Sat 9 a.m. to noon and 2–5 p.m.; Sun 8:30–2 p.m. Last entrance 30 minutes earlier.*

Teatro Massimo

Begun in 1875 but not completed until 1897, this building cost a fortune and was Italy's largest and most splendid theater at a time when Palermo didn't even have a good hospital. The theater is a masterpiece of Liberty style (Italian Art Nouveau) and was designed by Gian Battista and Ernesto Basile, the famous Sicilian father-and-son Art Nouveau stylists. The stage and backstage measure 1,280 sq. m (12,000 sq. ft.), the second largest in Europe after the Opéra Garnier in Paris. Its greatest marvel is a **painted ceiling** with 11 panels that open like flower petals to let heat escape from the interior during intermissions. Since the building's conception, the only change that's been made is a new wood floor for better acoustics. The building was used not only as a theater, but also as a meeting place, and these rooms were the site of important business and political meetings. The most famous is the **Sala Pompeiana,** at the level of the second loggia, where the men would meet; it's designed so that the sound of voices would keep bouncing from wall to wall and not escape the room and disturb the performance. After being closed for 23 years of restoration work, the theater reopened in 1997.

See map p. 457. Piazza Verdi, west on Via Maqueda. ☎ *800-655858. Bus: Red line. Admission: 5€ ($6). Open: Tues–Sun 10 a.m.–3:30 p.m.*

Villa Malfitano

This great Liberty-style villa lies within one of the city's most spectacular gardens. It was built in 1886 by Joseph Whitaker, who arranged to have trees shipped from all over the world and planted around his villa. High society in Palermo flocked here for lavish parties — royalty came from as far away as Great Britain. The villa is still stocked with beautiful antiques

Santa Rosalia

If you happen to be in Palermo between July 11 and July 15, you'll be surprised by the enthusiastic celebrations of Palermo's patron saint, Santa Rosalia. The festivities commemorate the anniversary of the discovery of the saint's remains. Niece of Norman King Guglielmo II, Rosalia abandoned the palace (Palazzo dei Normanni, described earlier in this chapter) for a cave on Monte Pellegrino to live a life of prayer. Many centuries after her death, during the terrible plague epidemic of 1624, her bones were found and brought down the mountain. As the procession bringing her remains traversed the city, the epidemic miraculously stopped (a good reason to keep celebrating her!). During the festival, a religious procession — with a huge, beautifully decorated triumphal carriage carrying an orchestra — winds through the town. There's also a spectacular candlelit procession up Monte Pellegrino to Santa Rosalia's cave. The end of the festival is marked by great fireworks.

and furnishings of various styles and periods. The most beautiful of the rooms, the **Sala d`Estata (Summer Room),** is decorated with *trompe l'oeil* frescoes on the walls and ceiling.

See map p. 457. Via Dante 167. ☎ 091-6816133. Bus: 106 from Piazza Sturzo. Admission: 3€ ($3.60). Open: Mon–Sat 9 a.m.–1 p.m.

Finding more cool things to see and do

The major sites of Palermo are stunning, but there's still much more to see and do. Here are a few recommendations:

✔ The city has three much-visited traditional **food markets** (Open: Mon–Sat 6 a.m.–4 p.m.), where fruits, vegetables, meat, and fish provide an explosion of colors and flavors. **La Vucciria,** whose name comes from the French word *boucherie* ("meat store"), is in La Kalsa and runs along Via Argenteria to Piazza Garraffello. **Ballarò** is our favorite and Palermo's oldest, running from Piazza Casa Professa to Corso Tukory toward Porta Sant'Agata; it's connected to the market of Casa Professa, which sells shoes and secondhand clothing. Smaller **Il Capo** covers Via Carini and Via Beati Paoli, crossing Via Sant'Agostino and Via Cappuccinelle. All are best visited in the morning. Beware of potential purse-snatchers and pickpockets riding *motorini.*

✔ We fell in love with the work of Giacomo Serpotta, the Sicilian sculptor who excelled in the use of marble and polychrome, but became famous for his stucco work — his *putti* (cherubs) in particular. His masterpiece is the **Oratorio del Rosario di San Domenico** (Via dei Bambinai 2, off Via Roma; ☎ 091-6090308; www.campodivolo.it), which he lavishly decorated between 1714 and 1717 (inside you'll also find Anthony Van Dyck's *Madonna of the Rosary,* commissioned during the artist's stay in Palermo in 1624). Between 1687 and 1718, the Sicilian sculptor decorated the nearby **Oratorio di Santa Cita** (Via Valverde 3, off Via Squarcialupo, between Via Cavour and Via Roma, on the left of the church), creating a whole world of stucco figures and reliefs. Admission is 2.50€ ($3) for each; both are open Monday through Saturday from 9 a.m. to 1 p.m.

✔ One of the most famous sights of Palermo is **San Giovanni degli Eremiti** (Via dei Benedettini 3; ☎ 091-6515019; Admission: 6€/$7.20; Open: Mon–Sat 9 a.m.–7 p.m., Sun and holidays 9 a.m–1:30 p.m.). Although it is a Christian church, it was built at the height of the Arab-Norman style, and thus it was given five round red domes. The church is a ruin and the inside is open to the elements; once you've seen it from the outside, you have experienced most of its charm, although its 13th-century cloister is also quite nice.

✔ One of the few examples of Arab architecture left in town, **La Zisa** (Piazza Guglielmo il Buono; ☎ 091-6520269; Admission: 3€/$3.60; Open: Mon–Sat 9 a.m.–7 p.m., Sun and holidays 9 a.m.–1:30 p.m.) dates from 1165. Known for its elegant columns and mosaics, the palace was surrounded by a park with an artificial lake in which the building was reflected (a few hundred years before the Taj Mahal), small rivers, and ponds for fish. The origin of the name is uncertain — it may have belonged to an Arab noblewoman, Azisa, or may have been built for King Guglielmo I (William) using Arab techniques and hence named Al-Aziz, "The Magnificent." The surrounding garden has disappeared, but the building has been restored and houses a museum of **Islamic art,** including a rich collection of the characteristic carved wooden screens known as *musciarabia.*

✔ **La Cuba** (Corso Calatafimi 100, inside the Caserma Tukory; ☎ 091-590-299; Admission: 2€/$2.40; Open: Mon–Sat 9 a.m.–7 p.m., Sun 9 a.m.–1 p.m.), a dome surrounded by gardens, is another striking example of Arab and early Norman architecture. It was built by Guglielmo II in 1180 in the Park of Genoardo; its beauty was so famous that Boccaccio used it in the *Decameron.* The building is only one floor, organized around a central space with a star-shaped fountain. Today, only the external walls and giant arches remain.

✔ If you're into catacombs and you aren't squeamish, you will enjoy the **Catacombe dei Cappuccini** (Via Cappuccini 1; ☎ 091-212117; Admission: 1.50€/$1.80; Open: Mon–Sat 9 a.m. to noon and 3–5 p.m.), which were used as a burial spot until 1920. For some reason, these catacombs miraculously preserved the dead — or at least some of them — and they still contain 8,000 mummified bodies of aristocratic Sicilians and priests, still dressed in the costumes of their time. Needless to say, this is not a "kid-friendly" sight, unless you have teenagers.

✔ If you're visiting in high season, you may want to take a break from the art and hop onto bus no. 806 or 833 from Teatro Politeama to the **beach of Mondello** (a few miles west of town beyond Punta Raisi). A favorite with locals, it gets crowded at the height of summer (July and Aug) but is quite nice in the shoulder season (spring and fall), when the Mediterranean waters are mild enough for a swim.

Seeing Palermo by guided tour

The best bus tour in town is the **Giro Città** (☎ 091-6902690; www.amat. pa.it), a hop-on/hop-off loop starting from Teatro Politeama (Piazza Ruggero Settimo 9) daily at 9 a.m. Tickets cost 12€ ($14) per person (children under 12 ride free) and can be purchased directly on the bus. Another good option is **City Sightseeing** (☎ 091-589429; www.palermo. city-sightseeing.it), whose open double-decker buses depart on two loops every 30 minutes from Teatro Politeama; tickets cost 20€ ($24) for adults, 10€ ($12) for youths 6 to 15 (children under 6 go free).

You can also arrange for your own personal tour of the city with a local guide by contacting **AGT** (www.palermoguide.it; no phone); it charges 70€ ($84) for a two-hour "mini-tour" of the historic center of Palermo for up to eight people, or 120€ ($144) for half a day.

Several companies organize guided tours to all the major attractions in Sicily, departing from Palermo on a daily basis. **CST** (Compagnia Siciliana Turismo; Via A. Amari 124; ☎ **091-7439654**; www.compagnia sicilianaturismo.it) is one of the best; it offers guided bus tours of the island that include the Valley of the Temples in Agrigento, Piazza Armerina, and Mount Etna. Excursions depart from both Palermo and Taormina; those from Palermo are priced from about 20€ ($24).

Suggested one-, two-, and three-day itineraries

Palermo deserves as much time as you can give it. Here are our suggestions on how to manage the time you have.

Palermo in one day

You'll have only time for a quick bite of Palermo's attractions, but the taste will stay with you forever. After a nice breakfast of ice cream and brioche — a Sicilian tradition, delicious with coffee on the side — head for the **Cattedrale,** Palermo's Duomo. Keep up your strength, however, as you'll need to continue on to Palermo's most stunning attraction, the **Palazzo dei Normanni.** Visit the splendid royal apartments and the magnificent **Palatine Chapel** before lunch. Dedicate the afternoon to **Monreale** (a 30-minute bus ride from the Palazzo dei Normanni), visiting the superb **Duomo** and its **cloister,** one of the world's most beautiful. Return to Palermo for drinks and dinner: If you head for the waterfront in the neighborhood of **La Kalsa,** by the horseshoe-shaped old harbor, **La Cala,** you'll find some excellent restaurants, including the ones we recommend in **Piazza Marina** (see "Dining Out," earlier in this chapter).

Palermo in two days

In two days, you can start to savor Palermo and the best it has to offer. On your first day, follow our "Palermo in one day" itinerary, earlier. On your second day, start the morning with a visit to one of the historic open-air markets — **Il Capo, Ballarò,** or **La Vucciria** (see "Finding more cool things to see and do," earlier in this chapter) — and then proceed to the **Galleria Regionale Siciliana.** Afterward, admire the stuccowork of Serpotta at the **Casa Professa,** and then get a glimpse of the marvelous **Oratorio di Santa Cita.** Spend the afternoon exploring Palermo's more ancient past at the **Museo Archeologico Regionale.** Finish your day by taking in a performance at the **Teatro Massimo,** or cap off your evening with some other form of entertainment (see "Living It Up After Dark," later).

Palermo in three days

Follow the suggested itinerary for "Palermo in two days," earlier. On your third day, begin by exploring the beautiful rooms of the **Villa Malfitana** before proceeding on in the same direction toward **La Zisa.** After lunch, take in some more architectural marvels, or perhaps have a little adventure: Visit the **Grand Hotel Villa Igea** and head for the beach.

Living It Up After Dark

Nightlife in Palermo is like everything else on the island: intense and somewhat more deeply Italian than elsewhere in the country. Leisurely strolls take up a large share of locals' evenings, and — as Sicilians have a sweet tooth — you'll often find them chatting over a pastry or an ice cream as well. Try **Antico Caffè Spinnato** (Via Principe di Belmonte 115; ☎ 091-583231; Open: Daily 7 a.m.–1 a.m.) for luscious desserts and a historic décor — it's one of the oldest cafes in Palermo — or go for drinks, pastries, and splendid ice cream at **Caffè Mazzara** (Via Generale Vincenzo Magliocco; ☎ 091-321443; Open: Daily 7:30 a.m.–11 p.m.), only about a century old.

For more serious entertainment, head to **Teatro Politeama Garibaldi** (Piazza Ruggero Settimo; ☎ 091-6053315), which stages opera and ballet; tickets are reasonably priced at about 20€ to 40€ ($24–$48). The splendid **Teatro Massimo** (Piazza Verdi; ☎ 800-655858; www.teatromassimo.it) also hosts concerts and opera performances. The season runs from October through June.

We love the traditional **Teatro dei Pupi,** a typically Sicilian puppet theater. The *pupi* — dressed in armor and bright-colored fabrics — tell tales of Orlando and the Paladins of France and stage fights against the Saracens, in which the audience actively participates. This traditional art is slowly disappearing, and out of the ten companies that were present in Palermo a couple of decades ago, only a few still perform today. The best is the **Teatro Arte Cuticchio — Opera dei Pupi e Laboratorio** (Via Bara all'Olivella 95; ☎ 091-323400; www.figlidartecuticchio. com), performing November through June. Tickets cost 6€ ($7.20) for adults and 3€ ($3.60) for children; the theater also contains a museum with a collection of *pupi,* machines, and special effects.

You'll find more modern-minded crowds at **I Candelai** (Via Candelai 65; ☎ 091-327151; www.candelai.it), a club for the young and energetic that stages live concerts and DJ dancing — often the latest rock — and a variety of other events. Quieter and also popular is the well-established **Kandinsky** (Discesa Tonnara 4; ☎ 091-6376511). If your thing is jazz, don't miss **Lo Spasimo-Blue Brass** (Via Spasimo, off Piazza Magione; ☎ 091-6161486; www.thebrassgroup.it), the temple of jazz in town, housed in the beautiful setting of the ex-church Santa Maria dello Spasimo.

One of the best pubs, **Villa Niscemi** (Piazza Niscemi 55; ☎ 091-6880820), has music of various kinds, including, literally, pickup groups (instruments provided), and stays open into the wee hours. **Pub 88** (Via Candelai 88; ☎ 091-611-9967), just down the road from I Candelai, is a quieter place to have a drink and relax. At **Agricantus** (Via XX Settembre 82; ☎ 091-487117), you may find jazz playing in the background or a group performing a skit.

One of the few gay spots in town, **Exit** (Piazza San Francesco di Paola 40; ☎ **0348-781498**), is also the best one. It has a great disco-cum-pub-cum-cabaret.

Fast Facts: Palermo

Area Code

The local area code is **091** (see "Telephone" in the "Fast Facts" section of Appendix A for more on calling to and from Italy).

ATMs

Banks with ATMs abound in town; centrally located ones are Monte dei Paschi di Siena, at Piazza Castelnuovo 48 (☎ 091-581228), and Banca di Roma, at Via Mariano Stabile 245 (☎ 091-7436911).

Doctors

You can call the emergency doctor for tourists (Guardia Medica Turistica) at ☎ 091-532798.

Embassies and Consulates

The U.S. Consulate is at Via Vaccarini 1 (☎ 091-305857). The U.K. Consulate is at Via Cavour 117 (☎ 091-326412).

Emergencies

For an ambulance, call ☎ **118**. For the Red Cross ambulance, call ☎ **091-306-644**. For first aid *(pronto soccorso),* call ☎ **091-6661111**. For the fire department, call ☎ **115**.

Hospitals

The Ospedale Civico is at Via Carmelo Lazzaro (☎ 091-6062207).

Information

You'll find a tourist info desk at the airport (☎ 091-591698; Open: Mon–Fri 8 a.m. to midnight, Sat–Sun 8 a.m. to 8 p.m.). There are also two info desks in town: one at the

train station on Piazza Giulio Cesare (☎ 091-6165914), and one at Piazza Castelnuovo 34, across from the Teatro Politeama (☎ 091-583847; www.palermotourism.com); both are open Monday through Friday from 8:30 a.m. to 2 p.m. and 3 to 7 p.m.

Internet Access

Aboriginal Internet Café (Via Spinuzza 51; ☎ 091-6622229; www.aboriginalcafe.com) is centrally located, only a couple of blocks from the Teatro Massimo (it's also a center for extreme-sports enthusiasts and a bar, if that interests you). Two local bars, I Candelai and Villa Niscemi (see "Living It Up After Dark," earlier in this chapter), also offer Internet access.

Pharmacies

Several pharmacies are open after-hours; among the most central are the ones at Stazione Centrale train station (Via Roma 1; ☎ 091-6162117) and at Via Mariano Stabile 177, off Teatro Massimo (☎ 091-334482).

Police

Call ☎ **113**.

Restrooms

Museums have public toilets. The best bet for a restroom is to go to a nice-looking cafe (though you'll have to buy something, like a cup of coffee).

Safety

Palermo's historic districts are safe except for the pickpockets and purse-snatchers on *motorini.* They concentrate in tourist areas, on public transportation, and at crowded open-air markets, such as the Il Capo and the Vucciria; muggings are rare but could occur in the most deserted streets at night.

Smoking

In 2005, Italy passed a law outlawing smoking in most public places. Smoking is allowed only where there is a separate, ventilated area for nonsmokers. If you want to smoke at your table, call beforehand to make sure the restaurant or cafe you'll be visiting offers a smoking area.

Taxes

See Chapter 5 for information on IVA (Value Added Tax).

Taxi

Walk to one of the taxi stands in town — Piazza Indipendenza, Piazza Verdi, Piazza Castelnuovo, the modern harbor, or the railroad station — or call a radio-taxi company (☎ 091-225455 or 091-513311) for pickup.

Transit info

Contact Palermo's transportation authority, AMAT (☎ 091-6902690; www.amat.pa.it), for city bus and subway info; call AST (☎ 800-234163 in Italy, or 091-6882906) for out-of-town bus connections.

Weather Updates

Your best bet is the news on TV. (There's no phone number for weather forecasts in Italy, as there is in the U.S.)

Chapter 22

Taormina, Syracuse, and Agrigento

In This Chapter

▶ Touring Taormina

▶ Viewing the past and present in Syracuse

▶ Visiting the Valley of the Temples in Agrigento

S icily is a splendid island rich with many wonderful destinations. **Taormina** — a city that flourished during the Roman period and again from the 19th century on — stands out for its fabulous position between the sea and Etna, the snow-capped volcano, and for its **Greco-Roman Theater** — one of the greatest of antiquity. Rivaling Athens for importance during antiquity, **Syracuse** knew a second period of glory during the 17th and 18th centuries, which left their marks in the **archaeological area** and the baroque architectural jewel of **Ortigia.** Dominating the southern shore, **Agrigento** was another important Greek city, one of the most beautiful of the ancient world, graced by one of the most imposing complexes of temples, which has partly survived to this day.

If you have the time, you could spend a night in each of these destinations; otherwise, either Taormina and Palermo (see Chapter 21) makes an excellent base for visiting the rest of the island.

Taormina

On Sicily's eastern shore, south of Messina, Taormina was built on a breathtakingly beautiful site, overlooking the sea with nearby volcano Mount Etna smoldering in the background. A small town of about 10,000 residents, Taormina receives some 900,000 visitors per year — that's about 2,500 visitors a day — counting only those who stay overnight; many others just pass through for the day. You may find it odd that this was a haunt of Greta Garbo, who "wanted to be alone," but crowded as it may be, Taormina's unique charm remains untouched, especially in the off season.

Taormina

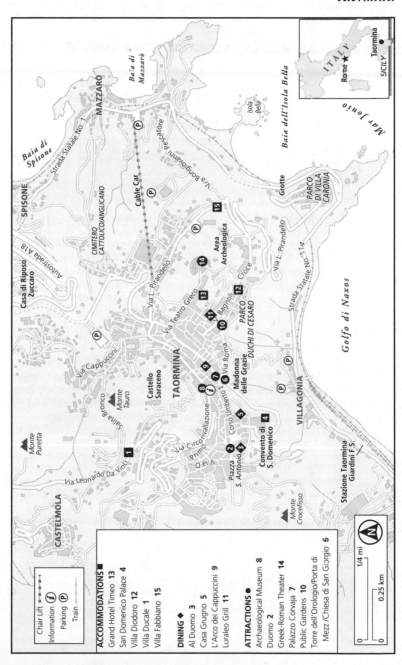

Chair Lift ┿┿┿┿┿
Information (i)
Parking (P)
Train ┼─┼─┼

ACCOMMODATIONS ■
Grand Hotel Timeo **13**
San Domenico Palace **4**
Villa Diodoro **12**
Villa Ducale **1**
Villa Fabbiano **15**

DINING ◆
Al Duomo **3**
Casa Grugno **5**
L'Arco dei Cappuccini **9**
Luraleo Grill **11**

ATTRACTIONS ●
Archaeological Museum **8**
Duomo **2**
Greek-Roman Theater **14**
Palazzo Corvaja **7**
Public Gardens **10**
Torre dell'Orologio/Porta di
Mezz /Chiesa di San Giorgio **6**

0 ┤ 1/4 mi
0 ┤ 0.25 km

Taormina makes an excellent base for visiting the rest of the region; many travel agencies based here offer guided tours to other destinations in Sicily (see "Exploring Taormina," later in this section).

Getting there

Taormina is 50km (30 miles) north of Catania (see later in this chapter) and 250km (150 miles) east of Palermo (see Chapter 21). **Catania,** a major harbor town on Sicily's eastern shore, is the most logical point of arrival, as it's linked to the mainland and other destinations in Europe and the Mediterranean by air and water.

Flights from most major destinations in Italy and Europe arrive at Catania's **Aeroporto Fontanarossa** (☎ **800-605656** in Italy; www. aeroporto.catania.it), only 4km (2½ miles) south of Catania town. Efficient and compact, the airport is well organized with a bank with ATM, a currency-exchange booth, and a tourist information desk in the arrivals concourse. Public transportation is right outside: You'll find the electric shuttle **Alibus** (☎ **800-018696**), which runs to the center of Catania every 20 minutes from 5 a.m. to midnight, and the bus operated by **Etna Trasporti** (☎ **095-532716**; www.etnatrasporti.it), which serves Taormina, a 75-minute ride away.

By ferry, **TTT Lines** (☎ **800-915365** in Italy, or 081 5752192; www.ttt lines.com) offers daily overnight service from Molo Angioino in Naples to Catania's harbor for 50€ to 150€ ($60–$180) per person. You can then take the easy 50-minute train ride from Catania rail station to Taormina.

Taormina is well linked by **train** service with the rest of Sicily and Italy (☎ **892021**; www.trenitalia.it). The **train station** (Via Nazionale; ☎ **0942-51026** or 0942-51511) is located a little down the hill, below Taormina's center, in Villagonia. From the station, you can take a **taxi** (☎ **0942-51150** or 0942-23800) or the electric shuttle.

If you're getting here by **car,** Taormina lies off the *autostrada* A18 from Catania to Messina. From Palermo, you'll have to take A19 to Catania, where you'll pick up A18. Taormina's center is pedestrian-only, so you'll have to leave your car at the entrance of town. The best place to park your car is just after the highway exit for Taormina, at **Parcheggio Lumbi** (☎ **0942-23605**), at the base of the hill; the cost is about 8€ ($9.60) for half a day and 13€ ($16) for 24 hours. A shuttle bus runs from the parking lot to town every few minutes. If you're spending the night, ask if your hotel has parking.

Spending the night

Taormina is a prime tourist destination in Italy, and the hotel standards are high here: You'll find accommodations for every budget and taste. The two luxury resorts in town — **Grand Hotel Timeo** (Via del Teatro Greco 59, by the Greek theater; ☎ **0942-23801**; www.framon-hotels. com; Rack rates: 490€/$588 double) and **San Domenico Palace** (Piazza

San Domenico 5, south of the Duomo; ☎ 0942-613111; www.san domenico.thi.it; Rack rates: 450€/$540 double) — the first and second hotels, respectively, to open in town back in the 19th century — are beautiful and will make for the perfect vacation, but you can also do very well in the more moderately priced accommodations.

Villa Diodoro
$$$ Centro

This elegant hotel is set in an attractive villa near the center of town, surrounded by its own garden. Guest rooms are spacious and tastefully decorated with fine fabrics and period furniture, including wrought-iron beds and Oriental carpets. Most of the rooms feature private terraces and gorgeous ocean views. Amenities include a swimming pool, a solarium, a bar, and a restaurant; in high season, a shuttle bus gets you to the Lido Caparena beach nearby.

See map p. 479. Via Bagnoli Croci 75. ☎ *0942-23312. Fax: 0942-23391.* www.gais hotels.com. *Free parking. Rack rates: 248€–314€ ($298–$377) double. Rates include breakfast. AE, DC, MC, V.*

Villa Ducale
$$$ Centro

Housed in a beautifully restored villa from the early 1900s, this small hotel offers splendid accommodations. From its unique position on the cliff, a ten-minute uphill walk from the center of town, it affords quiet and unique views. Guest rooms are full of charm, each with its own veranda opening onto a sea view. They're individually decorated in Sicilian style — terracotta floors, wrought-iron beds, whitewashed or pastel walls — with compact but pleasant tiled bathrooms. In high season, a shuttle bus takes guests to the beach.

See map p. 479. Via Leonardo da Vinci 60. ☎ *0942-28153. Fax: 0942-28710.* www. hotelvilladucale.it. *Parking: 10€ ($12). Rack rates: 250€ ($300) double. Rates include buffet breakfast. AE, MC, V.*

Villa Fabbiano
$$$ Centro

Set in a former private villa built to resemble a castle, this family-run hotel offers welcoming accommodations, friendly staff, and a quiet and romantic location. Guest rooms are spacious and bright, individually decorated with comfortable quality furnishings. The good-sized tiled bathrooms have all the comforts. The hotel's roof garden and the outdoor swimming pool, along with the large suites with private terraces, are a real plus for families with children. There's also an excellent **restaurant** here.

See map p. 479. Via Pirandello 81. ☎ *0942-626058. Fax: 0942-23732.* www.villa fabbiano.com. *Rack rates: 280€ ($336) double; suites 350€–420€ ($420–$504). Rates include buffet breakfast. MC, V. Closed Nov–Mar.*

Dining locally

You will find plenty of restaurants in this lively resort, catering to a variety of tastes; they are particularly easy to spot during the warm season, when tables overflow on small outdoor terraces and sidewalks. Many hotels also have excellent restaurants open to the public, such as the superb **Bougainvillées** inside the San Domenico Palace (see "Spending the Night," earlier in this chapter), serving regional specialties on its terrace with a breathtaking view of Mount Etna.

Al Duomo
$$ Centro   SICILIAN

Opening onto Piazza Duomo, this restaurant offers fine local cuisine that you can enjoy on the terrace with a view or inside the very pleasantly appointed dining room — or you can reserve a romantic table for two on the private balcony in summer. Excellent choices include the *tonno sott'olio fatto in casa* (home-preserved tuna in olive oil), *zuppa di ceci* (chickpea soup), *pasta ca' nocca* (pasta with anchovies, fried bread crumbs, and wild fennel), *braciole di pesce spada alla messinese* (swordfish steaks, Messina style), and *agnello "ngrassatu"* (roasted lamb chops). There is also a good selection of vegetarian dishes and great traditional desserts such as *cassata* (a ricotta, almond paste, and candied-fruit preparation) and *cannoli di ricotta*.

See map p. 479. Vico Ebrei 11, off Piazza Duomo. ☎ *0942-625656. Reservations recommended. Secondi: 12€–16€ ($14–$19). AE, DC, MC, V. Open: Tues–Sun noon to 3 p.m. and 7–11 p.m. Closed 4 weeks in Jan/Feb and 10 days in Dec.*

Casa Grugno
$$ Centro   CREATIVE SICILIAN

The best restaurant in Taormina, Casa Grugno offers delicious concoctions of high-quality ingredients. The menu changes often, but we strongly recommend the Marsala-flavored seafood bisque; the fusilli with lemon, fresh anchovies, capers, bread crumbs, and parsley; the house-smoked fish with a mango, citron, and ginger relish; and the jumbo shrimp over crispy pasta with citrus sauce.

See map p. 479. Via Santa Maria dei Greci. ☎ *0942-21208.* www.casagrugno.it. *Reservations recommended. Secondi: 16€–25€ ($19–$30). AE, DC, MC, V. Open: Mon–Sat 7 p.m. to midnight. Closed Nov–Feb.*

L'Arco dei Cappuccini
$ Centro   SICILIAN/SEAFOOD

In a perfect location just off the main street in the center of town, this restaurant offers a menu that changes daily according to the market offerings. There could be *gamberi marinati* (marinated shrimp), *fettuccine fresche con i crostacei appena pescati* (fresh homemade pasta with shellfish,

---

A contended place

In the fifth century B.C. Greek colonists founded Naxos (today the seaside resort of Giardini Naxos), on the shore below Mount Taurus — the mountain giving its name to Taormina — but the town was completely destroyed by the ruler of competing city-state Syracuse, Dionysius I. In 358 B.C., Andromachus decided to rebuild over the dramatic cliff overlooking the sea, and thus founded Taormina at its present location. The residents had thought it prudent to move to the top of the cliffs, but that didn't save them from further invasions. They certainly had a keen eye for the most picturesque location, though, and had become able politicians: The Greek city-state backed the Romans in the Punic Wars, who in return protected them from Syracuse. This resulted in a glorious period that stretched from the third century B.C. to the end of the Roman Empire; during this time, Taormina thrived and received the coveted status of Roman colony under Augustus. After the empire ended, the city of Taormina lost its protection: It was twice laid waste by the Arabs, until Roger II took over the city in 1078 for the Normans. After the Middle Ages, Taormina slowly sank into obscurity for several hundred years. It remained a forgotten medieval village until the end of the 18th century, when European artists, such as the German writer Goethe, began to celebrate it as the "ideal vista." Taormina's unique panorama, with the sea on one side and snow-capped Etna on the other, started attracting visitors from all over the world. Taormina became the place to be, appealing to the wealthy and glamorous until this day.

---

just harvested), *campanelle con pesce e zucchine* (pasta with fish and zucchini), or *pesce del giorno gratinato* (daily catch au gratin).

See map p. 479. Via Dietro Cappuccini 1. ☎ *0942-24893. Reservations recommended. Secondi: 8€–14€ ($9.60–$17). AE, DC, MC, V. Open: Thurs–Tues 12:30–2:30 p.m. and 7:30–10:30 p.m. Closed 1 week in Nov/Dec and 4 weeks in Jan/Feb.*

Luraleo Grill
$$ Centro   SICILIAN

The "grill" added to this establishment's name hasn't spoiled the romantic atmosphere of this pleasant restaurant with a nice terrace, nor substantially changed the menu, which continues to include a variety of Sicilian specialties. We're fond of the perfectly grilled fish — the reason behind that name change — and of the more adventurous dishes, such as the excellent risotto with salmon and pistachios.

See map p. 479. Via Bagnoli Croce 27. ☎ *0942-24279. Reservations recommended. Secondi: 11€–20€ ($13–$24). DC, MC, V. Open: Winter Thurs–Tues 12:15–3 p.m. and 7:15–11 p.m; summer daily.*

Exploring Taormina

Sais Tours (☎ 091-6265457; www.saistours.com) organizes guided tours and excursions to the nearby attractions of Mount Etna and Gole dell'Alcantara (see "More cool things to see and do," later in this section), as well as to the top attractions on rest of the island, including Palermo (see Chapter 21), Syracuse, Agrigento, and Piazza Armerina (see later in this chapter). **SAT Sicilian Airbus Travel** (Corso Umberto 73; ☎ 0942-24653; www.sat-group.it) offers a similar array of tours, including a nice bus-and-jeep sunset tour of Mount Etna, which we particularly recommend. **CST** (Corso Umberto 101; ☎ 0942-626088; www.compagnia sicilianaturismo.it) organizes guided tours to all major sights in Sicily, departing from both Taormina and Catania. Expect to pay between 35€ and 60€ ($42–$72) per person for a half- or full-day tour.

The top attractions

The medieval center of town is best enjoyed early in the morning or in the off season, when its streets are less crowded and noisy with happy visitors. If you feel overwhelmed by the hordes, just step into the side streets, lined with many magnificent villas owned by famous residents past and present.

Archaeological Museum

Opened in 2002, this museum is housed in the elegant **Palazzo della Badia Vecchia** — a beautiful example of Sicilian Gothic — and holds an important collection of artifacts from 19th-century excavations in Taormina and the nearby areas. Among its best pieces is the statue of a priestess to the cult of Isis from the second century A.D., found in the excavations of the church of San Pancrazio, where there was a Hellenistic temple.

See map p. 479. Via Circonvallazione 30. ☎ 0942-620112. Admission: 2.50€ ($3). Open: Daily 9 a.m.–1 p.m. and 4–8 p.m.

Corso Umberto 1

Taormina's central street stretches between **Porta Catania** and **Porta Messina;** these were the town's gates in Greek and Roman times. In medieval times, the town shrunk so much that they built another gate — the **Torre dell'Orologio (Clock Tower),** also appropriately called Porta di Mezzo (Middle Gate) — and abandoned Porta Messina. During the Renaissance, the town began expanding again, but it reoccupied the whole hourglass-shaped area of the Greek city only in modern times. The clock tower of the middle gate was rebuilt and attached to the **Chiesa di San Giorgio** in the 17th century, in a baroque remake.

Along Corso Umberto I are some of Taormina's most interesting monuments, such as the **Palazzo dei Duchi di Santo Stefano,** the best preserved of the town's Norman buildings, and the **Chiesa di Sant'Agostino,** a 16th-century church opening onto a nice square, **Largo IX Aprile,** above the sea (the church is closed to worship and used as the town library). Opening onto Piazza Santa Caterina is **Palazzo Corvaja,** one of the most interesting in town. Built between the 12th and 15th centuries around a preexisting Arab cubic tower — probably part of a fortress — in several additions, it has a crenellated structure and beautiful entrance staircase from the 12th century, plus a 15th-century wing (to the right) where the Sicilian Parliament met. Today, it houses the **Ethno-Anthropological**

Museum (☎ 0942-610274; Admission: 2.50€/$3; Open: Tues–Sun 9 a.m.–1 p.m. and 4–8 p.m.) and the **tourist office** (see "Information" under "Fast Facts: Taormina," later in this chapter).

Duomo

Built in the 12th century according to a Latin cross plan and dedicated to St. Nicola, this church was later remodeled — the central portal dates to 1633, while the lateral portals date to the 15th and 16th centuries, respectively. Inside, the nave is defined by gracious monolithic pink-marble columns topped by capitals decorated with a fish-scale pattern, recalling Sicily's maritime tradition. In front of the Duomo is the beautiful baroque **Fontana Monumentale,** built in 1635 with two-legged female centaurs.

See map p. 479. Piazza del Duomo, just off Corso Umberto. ☎ 0942-23123. Admission: Free. Open: Daily for mass, usually early morning and early evening.

Greek-Roman Theater

Seating a capacity of 5,000 people, this theater carved out of rock is second in Sicily only to Syracuse's (see later in this chapter) in both size and importance. It's the best preserved of all Greek and Roman theaters in Italy. Unusual for a Greek theater, the backdrop scene was a fixed structure: It represented a two-story house, part of which is still visible. Following the destiny of so many buildings of antiquity, part of the theater's materials were taken to construct other buildings, in this case by the Arabs and Normans, leaving modern-day visitors to imagine what it once looked like. During its glory days, the walls of the theater (only a portion in the back remains) were covered with marble and decorated with frescoes. Although the theater was Greek in origin, the Romans modified it for gladiator battles. A tunnel connected the cellar of the Roman arena with the outside; the orchestra of the theater was enlarged and closed off by a high podium in order to protect spectators. Today, the theater is famous for the performances held during the **Taormina Arte** (Via Pirandello 31; ☎ 0942-21142; Fax: 0942-23348), a summertime festival of cinema, theater, music, ballet, and video started in 1983.

See map p. 479. Via del Teatro Greco. ☎ 0942-23220. Admission: 4.50€ ($5.40). Open: Daily Apr–Sept 9 a.m.–7 p.m.; Oct–Mar 9 a.m.–4 p.m.

Public Gardens

These gardens were built by Miss Florence Trevelyan, who arrived in 1882, fell in love with the town, and bought a piece of land sloping toward the sea. She worked at transforming the land, training and employing local workers as gardeners. Within the gardens, she designed and built the **Victorian Follies** — bizarre toy houses built with red bricks and light-colored stone containing inlaid archaeological materials. Taorminians were fond of her, and when she died in 1902, they showered flowers upon her funeral procession. Her will forbade her heirs from ever building on or industrially cultivating the land.

See map p. 479. Via Bagnoli Croce, just below Corso Umberto. Admission: Free. Open: Daily sunrise–sunset.

Piazza Armerina and its glorious Roman villa

Inland from Taormina and Catania, and east of Palermo, lies a unique archaeological finding: **Villa del Casale** (☎ 0935-680036; www.piazza-armerina.it). This well-preserved ancient Roman rural villa — it was once a wealthy hunting lodge — hides a treasure trove of mosaics. The roofs and walls have collapsed, but since this villa was abandoned before the Middle Ages, it has come to us basically unchanged since Roman times. Its splendid mosaic floors are untouched, making for a unique experience. The visit takes about one hour and you can easily get here by organized tour from either Taormina or Palermo. If you're driving, take A19, exit at ENNA, and follow signs for PIAZZA ARMERINA; the archaeological area is just south of town near the ramps to the highway. Admission is 4€ ($4.80); hours are daily from 8 a.m. to sunset.

More cool things to see and do

✔ By the sea below Taormina lies the small seaside resort of **Mazzarò,** with its beautiful beaches and seafood restaurants. This is what most visitors to Taormina come for: to enjoy the beautiful sea. To the right of Mazzarò, at the center of a picturesque bay, is the **Isola Bella,** a protected nature refuge with its marine grottoes: Some people swim to it from the beach, but it's also great fun to hire a boat from Mazzarò and circle around the point to the bay. The best way to get down to the beach is via the *funivia* (cable car; ☎ 0942-23605) from Via Pirandello, in the center of Taormina. It runs every 15 minutes all day long (until 3 a.m. in summer); tickets are 3€ ($3.60) round-trip and 1.80€ ($2.15) one-way.

✔ We love taking a day trip to the great volcano **Etna,** which dominates the area around Taormina. Europe's biggest and most active volcano (the last eruptions were in 2001 and 2003), it is 3,300m (10,824 ft.) tall and still growing. Famous for its mega-eruptions — which ceased centuries ago — Etna's littlest grumbles and oozings can still wipe out vast areas and human settlements. The 1669 eruption not only took out chunks of the not-so-close-by town of Catania (amazingly, the deposits by the side of the highway south of town look as if they were made yesterday), but also extended the coastline about a kilometer (more than half a mile) into the sea. Etna isn't all lava and debris; parts of its north slopes are covered with a soaring conifer forest that took root in the rich soil. The easiest way to visit is via organized tour from Taormina (see earlier in this section); if you have a car, follow the signs for Linguaglossa and then Zafferana, where you take the small winding road to the **Rifugio Sapienza.** The cable car to the summit starts from Rifugio. If you want to see the craters up close and personal, you'll need an authorized guide: Book one at **Guide Alpine Etna Sud** (☎ 095-7914755), which will take you close enough to see the craters from a safe distance.

▶ If you're into the outdoors, you'll love the **Gole dell'Alcantara** (☎ **0942-989911;** www.parcoalcantara.it; Admission: 2.50€/$3; Open: Daily 9 a.m.–5 p.m.), a series of picturesque gorges, rapids, and falls created by a fast torrent, formally protected as a natural park since 2001. Its waters are incredibly cold — a unique phenomenon — and you'll need appropriate clothing (in summer, at least a bathing suit, towel, and aqua shoes). You can get here by guided tour (see earlier in this section), by car (off SS185, about 18km/11 miles from Taormina), or by bus from Taormina — **Interbus** (☎ **0942-625301**) leaves at 9:30 a.m., returns at 2:30 p.m., and charges 5€ ($6) round-trip. From the parking lot, an elevator takes you part of the way, and from May through September, you can climb the rest of the way (partly walking in the frigid waters).

Fast Facts: Taormina

Area Code

The local area code is **0942** (see "Telephone" in the "Fast Facts" section of Appendix A for more on calling to and from Italy).

ATMs

There are banks with ATMs on Corso Umberto, just before the Porta Messina to the north. You can also find banks in Giardini Naxos, the town next to Taormina.

Emergencies

For an ambulance, call ☎ **118;** for the fire department, call ☎ **115;** for first aid *(pronto soccorso),* call ☎ **0942-625-419;** for road assistance, call ☎ **116.**

Hospitals

The Ospedale Sirina is on Piazza San Francesco di Paola (☎ 0942-53-745).

Information

The tourist office (Azienda Autonoma di Soggiorno e Turismo) is inside the beautiful Palazzo Corvaja on Piazza Santa Caterina, off Corso Umberto to the west (☎ 0942-23243; www.comune.taormina.it). Hours are Monday through Saturday from 8 a.m. to 2 p.m. and 4 to 7 p.m.

Internet Access

You'll find an Internet cafe at Corso Umberto 214.

Pharmacies

A good central location is Dr. Verso, at Piazza IX Aprile 1 (☎ 0942-625866).

Police

There are two police forces in Italy; call either one. For the Polizia, call ☎ **113;** for the Carabinieri, call ☎ **112.**

Post Office

The *ufficio postale* is on Piazza Medaglie d'Oro (☎ 0942-23-010).

Catania

Almost unknown to foreign visitors, Catania is the second-largest town in Sicily after Palermo. Centered around an important harbor, it hides a baroque heart that rewards those who brave its belt of industrial — and quite ugly — developments.

The historic district is an apotheosis of baroque buildings, as the town was completely rebuilt after the earthquake of 1693. The most famous attraction in town is the **Duomo** (Piazza Duomo; ☎ 095-320044; Admission: Free; Open: Daily 7 a.m. to noon and 4:30– 7 p.m.), Catania's cathedral. Named for St. Agata, it is richly decorated with paintings and carvings. From Piazza Duomo and crossing the heart of the historic district, **Via Etnea** is lined with ornate buildings; follow it down to the **Giardini Bellini** (Piazza Roma), the beautiful public gardens named after the local opera composer Vincenzo Bellini (composer of *Norma*, among others) — a destination favored by locals, and one of the nicest gardens in Europe. Also worth a visit are the Greek theater and the Roman ruins, including the thermal baths and the forum.

You can eat very well at **Ambasciata del Mare** (Piazza Duomo 6; ☎ 095-341003; www.ambasciatadelmare.com; Open: Tues–Sun 12:30–3 p.m. and 7:30–11 p.m.), and even better at the **Osteria I tre Bicchieri** (Via San Giuseppe al Duomo 31; ☎ 095-7153540; www.osteriaitrebicchieri.it; Open: Mon–Sat 7:30–11 p.m.), both conveniently located near the beautiful Duomo. If you're planning to stay overnight, the **Excelsior Grand Hotel** (Piazza Giovanni Verga; ☎ 095-7476111; www.thi.it) is the best in town, followed by the **Katane Palace** (Via Camillo Finocchiaro Aprile 110; ☎ 095-7470702; www.katanepalace.it) with its excellent restaurant **Il Cuciniere**, one of the best on the island.

You'll find tourist information offices at the train station, the airport, and Via Etnea 63, in the center of town (☎ 095-7306233; www.apt.catania.it).

Syracuse

Close to Sicily's southeastern tip, Syracuse is a beautiful stone city shimmering somewhat sleepily by the sea. Its attractions range from an impressive Greek theater to the island of Ortigia, the town's baroque historic district. Staying overnight will allow you to see most of the local attractions, including a short visit to nearby Noto.

Getting there

Syracuse is easily reached from Catania, only 63km (39 miles) to the north (see the "Getting there" section in "Taormina," earlier in this chapter). From Catania's airport and town, **Interbus** (☎ 0935-565111; www.interbus.it) offers regular bus service to Syracuse (a 70-minute ride); it also has frequent bus service from Palermo (a three-and-a-half-hour ride). You can also take the **train** (☎ 892021; www.trenitalia.it) to Syracuse's **train station** (☎ 0931-69722), on the west side of town, about a 20-minute walk from either Ortigia or the Archaeological Zone; you'll find local buses and taxis outside. For radio-taxi pickup, call ☎ 0931-69722.

 If you're coming by **car,** beware of the dangerous 21km (13-mile) stretch on **SS114** (also labeled **E14** on European maps) between Catania and Syracuse, where the road reduces to two lanes. Much too narrow for the amount of traffic on it, locals speeding and passing each other turn it into a hair-raising, and potentially deadly, experience. State road **SS115** from Agrigento is picturesque, but a long haul.

Spending the night

Gran Bretagna
$ Ortigia

This small hotel in the heart of Ortigia was recently upgraded and restored, returning the public spaces and accommodations to their original splendor. Guest rooms are comfortable, some very large, and a few rooms still have the original ceiling frescoes from the 19th century. Bathrooms are modern and well kept.

Via Savoia 21. ☎ 0931-68765. www.hotelgranbretagna.it. *Rack rates: 106€ ($127) double. Rates include breakfast. AE, MC, V.*

 ### Grand Hotel
$$ Ortigia

This beautiful Liberty (Italian Art Nouveau) hotel offers pleasant and welcoming public areas and professional service. Guest rooms are large and bright, decorated with pastel colors and elegant furnishings. All have floors in beautiful checkered tiles or wood intarsia (inlay), and most rooms afford gorgeous views of the harbor and the sea. The spacious bathrooms are state-of-the-art.

Viale Mazzini 12. ☎ 0931-464600. Fax: 0931-464611. www.grandhotelsr.it. *Free parking. Rack rates: 225€ ($270) double. Rates include breakfast. AE, DC, MC, V.*

 ### Gutkowski Hotel
$ Ortigia

This hotel offers excellent accommodations and service at moderate prices. Guest rooms vary in size, but all are bright, outfitted with comfortable beds, and decorated in pastel colors in a modern yet welcoming style. Only five rooms have a sea view, so reserve in advance if you want to grab one of those — but be aware that they tend to be smaller.

Lungomare Vittorini 26. ☎ 0931-465861. Fax: 0931-480505. www.guthotel.it. *Free parking. Rack rates: 90€ ($108) double. Rates include breakfast. AE, DC, MC, V.*

Dining locally

You will find many small restaurants tucked away in the historic streets of Ortigia, but don't expect a lively scene as in Taormina; Syracuse has yet to become a crowded tourist destination.

Don Camillo
$ Ortigia SICILIAN/SEAFOOD

This welcoming restaurant is one of the few moderately priced gourmet destinations in Italy. We love the relaxing atmosphere and the kind service, both at the wine bar up front and in the more formal dining room in the back. The cuisine is simply excellent, heavily influenced by traditional recipes. Smoked local tuna and swordfish make a wonderful appetizer; we recommend the unique spaghetti with shrimp and sea urchins and the delicious *crespelle mediterranee* (crepes layered with eggplant, tomato, basil, and hot pepper) as a *primo,* followed by the daily catch. The wine list is extensive, with a number of superb choices.

Via Maestranza 96. ☎ *0931-67133. Reservations recommended. Secondi: 10€–15€ ($12–$18). AE, DC, MC, V. Open: Mon–Sat 12:30–2:30 p.m. and 7:30–10:30 p.m. Closed 2 weeks in Feb, 2 weeks in July, and 3 days at Christmas.*

Gambero Rosso
$$ Centro SICILIAN

This restaurant, in an old tavern near the harbor, is known for its seafood. It also has a terrace overlooking the port, adding to its popularity with local families on weekends. You'll find that children are welcome and half-portions are available here. Try the *cannelloni* (tubes of pasta filled with fish or meat) or one of the fish soups.

Via Eritrea 2, off to the right of Corso Umberto, just inland of the bridge leaving Ortigia. ☎ *0931-68546. Reservations recommended. Secondi: 14€–18€ ($17–$22). AE, DC, MC, V. Open: Fri–Wed 12:30–3 p.m. and 7:30–11 p.m.*

Ristorante Rossini
$$ Ortigia SICILIAN

This intimate restaurant, run by a renowned chef, offers a menu based mainly on seafood prepared in both traditional and imaginative ways. One specialty is *pesce alla stimpirata,* which creatively combines mint, garlic, and olive oil with fish. More familiar Sicilian-style preparations include roasted swordfish. The buffet *antipasto* is excellent.

Via Savoia 6. ☎ *0931-24317. Reservations recommended. Secondi: 14€–22€ ($17–$26). AE, DC, MC, V. Open: Wed–Mon noon to 2:30 p.m. and 7:30–11 p.m.*

Exploring Syracuse

The main attractions of Syracuse lie at some distance from one another: At one end of town is the archaeological area with the Greek and Roman

Siracusa

When the Corinthians founded Syracuse in the eighth century B.C., they established their first settlement by the island of Ortigia, home to the mythical nymph Calypso, who kept Odysseus captive for seven years. The city-state flourished around its beautiful harbor, perfectly positioned for trade. It rapidly gained increasing control over the eastern and western Mediterranean, to the point of rivaling the great cities of the mother country, and particularly Athens. Syracuse rose to become the Mediterranean's greatest power under its forceful tyrants (particularly Dionysius I). However, during the Punic Wars, Syracuse was caught between a rock and a hard place — the Romans and the Carthaginians. The Roman siege lasted two years, and in 215 B.C. they finally overwhelmed Syracuse, despite the clever devices that Archimedes, the city's most famous son, constructed to thwart them and their siege engines. Archimedes died in the Roman siege, and Syracuse wound up on the losing side. It lost all its importance at that point and never recovered.

ruins, while by the sea is the island of Ortigia. It's about a 40-minute walk between each attraction; you'll want to take the bus or, even easier, call a taxi (see "Fast Facts: Syracuse," later in this chapter).

For the best guided tours, contact **Siracusa Tours** (Viale Armando Diaz 12; ☎ 0931-65881; www.siracusatour.it).

The top attractions

Museo Archeologico Regionale Paolo Orsi

This is the best archaeological museum in Sicily. Every time period is represented in the large, well-organized collection, from prehistoric objects to an extensive Hellenistic collection from Syracuse's heyday. The single most famous piece is the second-century-B.C. *Venus Anadyomene,* which — though headless — powerfully evokes the birth of the goddess from the sea. The pre-Greek vases are lovely, too.

In the gardens of the Villa Landolina, Viale Teocrito 66, near the Zona Archeologica. ☎ *0931-464022. Bus: 4, 5, 12, or 15 to Viale Teocrito. Admission: 6€ ($7.20). Open: Tues–Sat 9 a.m.–6 p.m.; Sun 9 a.m.–1 p.m.*

Ortigia

Today connected to the mainland by a bridge — Ponte Nuovo — this island in the heart of Syracuse's harbor is where the city began back in the eighth century B.C. With its Greek ruins and baroque *palazzi*, it is the heart of the historic district. Actually, one could say that it *is* the historic district, since, until the end of the 19th century, Ortigia was still all there was of Syracuse; the mainland area contained only the rail station and the Greek ruins.

As you cross the Ponte Nuovo, you will first see the remains of the **Temple of Apollo,** built in the sixth century B.C., reduced now to just a few columns. Walk up Via Savoia to **Porta Marina** (Seaside Gate) and enter the old town. If you proceed along the stone border of the harbor, you'll find the romantic **Fonte Aretusa:** This — according to the myth — is the very spring into which the nymph Arethusa was turned in order to escape the fiery advances of Alfeo, the marine god who was trying to seduce her. He then turned into a river so their waters could mingle together. Famous since antiquity for its almost magical qualities, this spring — separated from the sea only by a stone wall — is rich in freshwater fish.

Head back to the center of Ortigia to admire the seventh-century **Duomo** (Piazza del Duomo; ☎ 0931-65328; Admission: Free; Open: Daily 8 a.m. to noon and 4–7 p.m.), built on the remains of the Greek temple to Athena (Minerva to the Romans). You can still see 12 of the temple's columns incorporated into the church structure. Farther to the southeast, you'll find beautiful **Piazza Archimede,** the heart of Ortigia, graced by a stately baroque fountain. Nearby is the splendid **Palazzo Bellomo,** which houses the **Galleria Regionale** (Via Capodieci 16; ☎ 0931-69511; Admission: 3€/$3.60; Open: Mon–Sat 9 a.m.–1:30 p.m., Sun 9 a.m.–12:30 p.m.). Built in the 13th century and remodeled in the 15th, this elegant *palazzo* holds a large collection of Sicilian figurative art stretching from the Byzantine period to the 18th century. The most important piece is Antonello da Messina's famous *Annunciation.* (Note that the *palazzo* was still closed for restoration at press time, but is scheduled to reopen imminently.) At the tip of the island is the **Castello Maniace** (☎ 0931-464420; Admission: 2€/$2.40; Open: Mon–Sat 8:30 a.m.–1 p.m.), an imposing defensive structure dating back to the 12th century.

In the harbor, off Largo XXV Luglio and Ponte Nuovo.

Parco Archeologico della Neopolis (Archaeological Area)

On the western edge of modern Syracuse lies the **Neopolis** ("new town" in Greek, as opposed to the old settlement of Ortigia). Created at the height of Syracuse's glory, it was practically abandoned during the town's decline in Roman times; thus its ruins are well preserved. The archaeological area is large, encompassing two theaters and the quarries from which stone was excavated to build all the monuments in the old town.

Beware of the sun in the hot months — walking around the ruins at high noon can quickly exhaust and dehydrate you. Bring water, wear a hat, and put on your most comfortable shoes.

The star of the park is the **Greek Theater,** dating back to the fifth century B.C. Carved out of the hillside, it is very well preserved and a magical place to attend a show. Indeed, thanks to the **Italian Institute of Ancient Drama** (INDA, Corso G. Matteotti 29; ☎ 800-907080 in Italy, or 0931-67415; www.indafondazione.org), this theater comes to life again in even-numbered years, when classical plays by Aeschylus, Euripides, and other Greek playwrights are staged as they were 2,500 years ago. The season usually runs from May to June, and tickets cost about 30€ ($36). In odd-numbered years, plays are presented at the theater of Segesta (see "Segesta and

Segesta and Selinunte

Sicily is the land of Greek temples — if you're into ancient ruins, you'll be delighted by the gorgeous sites of Segesta and Selinunte. **Selinunte** lies 122km (76 miles) southwest of Palermo and 113km (70 miles) west of Agrigento. Once a prosperous Greek colony established by Syracusans, it was destroyed by Hannibal in 409 B.C. The archaeological area (Admission: 4.50€/$5.40; Open: Daily 9 a.m.–sunset) feels like a dinosaur cemetery, with the huge stone structures of the once splendid acropolis lying on the ground, scattered here and there. Part of temple C was re-erected in 1925. The easiest way to visit is by guided tour from Palermo (see Chapter 21) or by car, but you can also get here by public transportation: Take a train (☎ 892021; www.trenitalia.it) from Palermo to Castelvetrano, and then switch to a bus operated by **Autoservizi Salemi** (☎ 0923-981120) to get to Selinunte.

The temple — yes, there's only one — in **Segesta** is still standing, and it's a unique sight indeed. All alone in a field on a hill, it's one of the best preserved Greek temples in the world. The archaeological site (Admission: 4€/$4.80; Open: Daily 9 a.m.–7 p.m.; last entrance one hour earlier) lies only 74km (46 miles) southwest of Palermo and is easily reached by train (☎ 892021; www.trenitalia.it) — the train station is 1km (⅔ mile) away — or by guided tour from Palermo (see Chapter 21). Up nearby Mount Barbaro lies the ancient Greek theater, which comes alive in summer with modern and classic plays. Bus service from Palermo is organized for these shows; check with the tourist office for a schedule of events.

Selinunte" sidebar, later in this chapter). The tunnels you see in the stage area aren't original; they were dug later by the Romans so they could use the theater for their blood sports.

On the other side of the hill, you can visit the **Latomia del Paradiso,** one of the stone quarries that served the city. Once a huge grotto, its roof collapsed in the 1693 earthquake, leaving a hole covering many acres and a few stone pillars sticking up here and there. Some of the grottoes still exist, including the **Grotta dei Cordari,** used in later centuries for ropemaking, and the **Orecchio di Dionisio (Dionysius's Ear),** a deep, very tall, pitch-black cave with unique acoustics (try tearing up a piece of paper). The story that the tyrant Dionysius used the cave to eavesdrop on conversations is a myth; the painter Caravaggio was said to have given the cave its name (perhaps he made up the story, too).

Nearby is the **Roman Amphitheater,** built during the reign of Augustus and partially carved from the rock. Like other Roman theaters, it was used for life-and-death battles between humans and animals, and was sometimes flooded and filled with crocodiles and other friendly creatures for water fights. What you see today is only the bottom story — try to imagine how it looked when the top of the theater reached the present height of the surrounding trees. Holy Roman Emperor Charles V is the bad guy of many stories about Italy, and Syracuse is no exception. He did more damage than the earthquake and is responsible for turning this theater into a quarry. During his North African campaigns, he destroyed many of the Roman ruins for material to build fortifications.

Via Augusto, off the intersection of Corso Gelone and Viale Teocrito. ☎ **0931-65068.** *Bus: 4, 5, or 6 to Parco Archeologico. Admission: 6€ ($7.20). Open: Mon–Sat 9 a.m.–sunset (last entrance 2 hours before sunset); Sun and holidays 9 a.m.–1 p.m.*

More cool things to see and do

✔ In summer, Syracuse is boiling hot. Head for the beach, like the locals do. **Arenella** is the closest (only about 8km/5 miles south of the historic district), but **Fontane Bianche** (19km/12 miles away in the same direction) is the best. You can easily get there by public transportation (bus no. 23 from Riva della Posta). If you're driving, take SS115 and follow the signs.

✔ The famous town of **Noto,** which is easy to reach via guided tour or by bus — service is offered by **Interbus** (☎ **0935-565111** or 0931-66710; www.interbus.it) — lies only 32km (20 miles) southwest of Syracuse off *autostrada* A18, a 50-minute ride from the historic district of Syracuse. A wonderful example of Sicilian baroque, the town was reduced to rubble by the 1693 earthquake — the same one that destroyed the whole southeast of Sicily — and the town's notables decided to rebuild a completely new town 16km (10 miles) south of its original location. The reconstruction happened very rapidly — in about 45 years — and the result was a town remarkably uniform in style, a real rarity in Italy where you can usually see the layers of history. Faithful to pure baroque standards, Noto was built on a regular street grid; many important Sicilian artists contributed to the reconstruction, and the whole town is considered a work of art. Carvings of grotesque animals and figures support the balconies, and all the buildings were constructed of a golden-yellow stone. Noto underwent a restoration that started in 1997, leaving it more beautiful than ever. The **tourist office,** where you can also get a map of the town, is in the center at Piazza XIV Maggio (☎ **0931-573779;** Open: Summer daily 9 a.m.–1 p.m. and 3:30–6:30 p.m., winter Mon–Sat 8 a.m.–2 p.m. and 3:30–6:30 p.m.).

Fast Facts: Syracuse

Area Code

The local area code is **0931** (see "Telephone" in the "Fast Facts" section of Appendix A for more on calling to and from Italy).

Emergencies

For an ambulance, call ☎ **118;** for the fire department, call ☎ **115;** for road assistance, call ☎ **116.**

Information

You'll find a tourist info office at Via San Sebastiano 45 (☎ 0931-481200; www.apt-siracusa.it). There are additional locations at Via Maestranza 33 (☎ 0931-464255) and at the Archaeological Area on Piazzale Paradiso (☎ 0931-60510).

Police

Call ☎ 113.

Post Office

The main *ufficio postale* is at Piazza Riva della Posta 15, to the left of the main bridge in Ortigia (☎ 0931-68973). It's open Monday

through Friday from 8:10 a.m. to 6:30 p.m., Saturday from 8:10 a.m. to 1 p.m.

Taxis

You can call or walk to one of the taxi stands: at the train station (☎ 0931-69722) or at Piazza Pancali, by the bridge to Ortigia (☎ 0931-60980).

Agrigento and the Valley of the Temples

Dominating the southern shore, Agrigento was another important Greek city-state, and one of the most beautiful of the ancient world. Founded in 581 B.C., it was deeply admired by the Greek poet Pindar. Agrigento reached great heights in art and culture in the third century B.C., but saw its fortunes wax and wane with those of the Roman Empire. Its Valley of the Temples is one of the most dramatic classical sites in the Mediterranean: A high plateau overlooking the sea holds the most impressive Greek ruins in existence outside Greece, and is reason enough to come to Sicily. Farther up the hill from the ruins stands modern Agrigento, a small town that most visitors bypass.

Getting there

Several companies in both Taormina and Palermo offer tours (see Chapter 21 and earlier in this chapter), but you can easily get to Agrigento on your own. **Trains** (☎ 892021; www.trenitalia.it) arrive at Agrigento rail station, on Piazza Guglielmo Marconi (☎ 0922-725669); the trip from Palermo takes one and a half hours and costs about 7€ ($8.40). You can also take a **bus: AST** (☎ 800-234163 in Italy, or 091-6882906) and **Omnia** (☎ 0922-596490) serve Agrigento from Palermo town, whereas **Licata** (☎ 0922-401360) connects Agrigento with Palermo's airport, Falcone Borsellino/Punta Raisi. If you're coming by **car,** Agrigento lies 126km (79 miles) south of Palermo. You can take the shorter but narrower SS121/189 connecting Palermo to Agrigento, or the A19 *autostrada* connecting Palermo to Caltanissetta (and then follow the directions to Agrigento and take SS640 for the remaining 60km/37 miles).

The Valley of the Temples is 3km (2 miles) south of Agrigento; a shuttle-bus service connects the archaeological area with the train station in Agrigento, or you can take a taxi (see "Fast Facts: Agrigento," later in this chapter).

Spending the night

Dioscuri Bay Palace
$$ **San Leone**

If you're going to spend the night in Agrigento, why not stay near the beach and swim in the beautiful waters? Only 2.5km (1½ miles) from the Valley of the Temples, this modern hotel is on a delightful small bay, with a view of the temples. The spacious guest rooms are furnished in modern Mediterranean style, with bright whitewashed walls and tiled floors.

Lungomare Falcone e Borsellino 1, San Leone (off SS115, toward the sea from the Valle dei Templi). ☎ *0922-406111. Fax: 0922-411297.* www.framon-hotels.com. *Rack rates: 170€–200€ ($204–$240) double. Rates include breakfast. AE, DC, MC, V.*

Foresteria Baglio della Luna
$$$ Valle dei Templi

Near the Valley of the Temples, this hotel is located in a perfectly restored manor house built around a medieval watchtower. It offers stylish accommodations with individually decorated guest rooms opening onto either the cobblestone courtyard or the valley of the temples. The restaurant, Dehor, is excellent (see "Dining locally," later in this section).

Valle dei Templi, Contrada Maddalusa on SS640 at km 4,150. ☎ *0922-511061. Fax: 0922-598802.* www.bagliodellaluna.com. *Rack rates: 300€ ($360) double. Rates include breakfast. AE, DC, MC, V.*

Dining locally

As in the rest of Sicily, the cuisine of Agrigento relies heavily on seafood. In addition, Agrigento is at the center of the almond-growing industry, so almonds are used in a variety of preparations.

Dehor
$$ Valle dei Templi   CREATIVE SICILIAN

One of the best restaurants in Sicily, Dehor offers creative concoctions and an elegant setting. The seasonal menu may include such delicacies as grilled tuna with herbed couscous, bell-pepper fondue, and mint/cherry-tomato purée, or perhaps *crema ghiacciata di mandorle e fichi secchi e miele al profumo di vecchio Marsala Florio* (iced almond cream with figs, honey, and aged Marsala wine sauce).

In the Foresteria Baglio della Luna hotel, Valle dei Templi, Contrada Maddalusa on SS640 at km 4,150. ☎ *0922-511061. Reservations recommended. Secondi: 15€–22€ ($18–$26). AE, DC, MC, V. Open: Daily 12:30–2:30 p.m. and 7:30–10:30 p.m.*

Trattoria dei Templi
$$$ Valle dei Templi   SICILIAN

This is an old-fashioned restaurant, down to the absence of a full written menu — your waiter will tell you the delicious daily specials — and up to the professional and kind service. We love the appetizer buffet, overflowing with fish and vegetables dishes based on local traditions (it's also a big hit with children, who get to see and choose what they want), but we never miss the excellent spaghetti with clams or the tasty seafood ravioli. Half-portions are available for children. The kitchen and staff will strive to meet all your special needs.

The Greek temple

The Greek temple was conceived as the habitation of a god and always opened to the east because the god's statue had to face the rising sun (symbol of the beginning of light and life) and never the sunset (symbol of the night and death). Over a high rectangular platform with steps, the classic temple has a perimeter of columns and an inside wall enclosing three rooms: the *pronaos* (entrance), the *naos* (the cell with the statue of the god), and the *opistodomos* (where the treasure, the votive gifts, and the archives of the temple were kept). In fact, temples were so sacred that citizens used to leave their valuables there, thus using them as safes.

Strada Panoramica dei Templi 15. ☎ *0922-403110. Reservations recommended. Secondi: 15€–20€ ($18–$24). AE, DC, MC, V. Open: Sat–Thurs 12:30–3 p.m. and 7:30–11 p.m. Closed Sun July–Aug; closed 2 weeks in July.*

Exploring Agrigento

The best time of year to explore Agrigento is in February, during the **Festival of the Almond Flower,** held between the first and second Sundays in the month, and celebrating the early coming of spring. The whole valley is graced by the almond trees in blossom. Folklore groups from around the whole island, as well as from other places in Italy and Europe, meet in town for a rich series of shows and concerts. Check with the local tourist office (☎ **0922-20454**) for a calendar of events.

You can get a **combination ticket** for the archaeological area and the museum for 10€ ($12)

The top attractions

 ### Valley of the Temples

The archaeological area is vast and has very few trees. Bring comfortable shoes and, if you're visiting in high season, a hat, sunscreen, and at least a quart of water per person. Packing a picnic lunch to enjoy by the ruins is also a good idea if your time is limited. The valley is at its most dramatic at sunrise or sunset (when the temperature is also cooler). You will need two to three hours for your visit.

Entering the archaeological area from the **Porta Aurea** (a gate in the Greek walls), you'll find the three best-preserved temples — Hercules, Concord, and Juno — to your right, while the Temple of Jupiter and the Temple of Castor and Pollux are by the river on your left.

You'll have to use your imagination to fully appreciate the massive **Temple of Jupiter,** built to celebrate the gratitude of the people of Agrigento for their 480-to-479 B.C. victory over the Carthaginians at Himera. One of the largest temples of antiquity, it covered approximately 6,317 sq. m

Agrigento and the Valley of the Temples

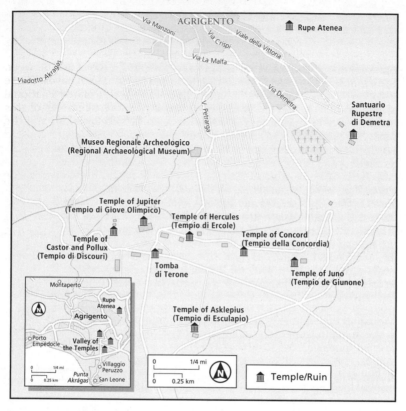

(68,000 sq. ft.) and was 32m (108 ft.) tall. Each of the columns rose 26m (55 ft.) and measured 4.1m (14 ft.) at the base; probably alternated with the columns were the Telamons (or Atlases, human figures supporting a structure). Each of these giants measured 7.5m (25 ft.) high, as you can see from the whole one lying flat on the ground; a better preserved one is in the Regional Museum (see later in this section). Little remains also of the **Temple of Castor and Pollux,** built between 480 and 460 B.C. to honor the twin sons of Jupiter and Leda (queen of Sparta), protectors of athletes, hospitality, and sailors in difficulty. Of the 34 columns, only 4 remain standing (at the corner of the temple); these were restored in the 19th century. Nearby are the few remains of the **Tempio di Vulcano.**

The temples on the other side of the entrance are much better preserved and remain an impressive sight. The **Temple of Hercules** is one of the most beautiful and the largest of the temples on this side: It occupied an area of about 2,043 sq. m (22,000 sq. ft.). Hercules was highly revered in Sicily and particularly in Agrigento; the god of strength, he was thought to free people from nightmares and unwanted erotic stimuli. Nine columns are still standing, thanks to the generosity of the English Captain Hardcastle, who paid for their restoration in the 1920s. The temple was richly decorated with reliefs and sculptures; the columns were painted white to simulate marble, whereas the cornice was decorated in red, blue, and turquoise. The **Temple of Concord,** built around 430 B.C., is remarkably well preserved. Transformed into a church as far back as A.D. 597, 12 arches were opened in the walls of the temple, while the space between the columns was walled in to make it into a church with three naves. These alterations were reversed in 1743, when the temple was declared a national monument and restored. It's one of the best-preserved temples of this period, along with the one of Hera in Paestum (see Chapter 20) and the Theseion in Athens. The **Temple of Juno** is also well preserved. Built in 450 to 440 B.C. in honor of Juno (Hera) — the mother goddess and protectress of marriage and fertility — it has 34 columns and a maximum height of 15m (50 ft.). It rises on a pretty hill, near one of the few trees on this side of the archaeological area.

See map p. 498. Piazzale dei Templi/Posto di Ristoro, off SS115 connecting Siracusa to Trapani. ☎ *0922-497226. Bus: 8, 9, 10, or 11. Admission: 6€ ($7.20). Open: Hill of the temples (Juno, Concord, and Hercules) Mon–Fri 8:30 a.m.–10 p.m., Sat–Sun and holidays 8:30 a.m. to midnight; Temples of Jupiter and Castor and Pollux daily 9 a.m.– 7 p.m. Ticket booth closes 30 minutes earlier.*

Regional Archaeological Museum

Located in Contrada San Nicola, near the archaeological area, this museum contains a large collection of Greek artifacts, many of which were found during the excavations in the Valley of the Temples. Besides the ample number of Greek vases, an interesting piece is one of the Telamons (human figures supporting a structure) from the Temple of Jupiter (see earlier in this section), which is in much better shape than the one on the ground at the temple.

Via dei Templi, Zona Archeologica. ☎ *0922-401565. Admission: 6€ ($7.20). Open: Mon–Fri 9 a.m.–7 p.m.; Sun–Mon 9 a.m.–1 p.m.*

More cool things to see and do

✔ In Contrada Caos, a village to the southeast of Agrigento, you can visit the **Casa Natale di Pirandello** (☎ **0922-511102;** Admission: 2.60€/$3.10; Open: Daily 8 a.m.–8 p.m.; last entrance for the promenade to the pine one hour before sunset), the house where the famous Italian writer Luigi Pirandello was born in 1867. Pirandello received the Nobel prize for literature in 1934; in his best-known novel — *Six Characters in Search of an Author* — Pirandello explored the theme of the mask that everyone must wear to have a role in society. The grounds are beautiful; for a great view, take the walk to the site's famous pine tree growing alone on a beautiful spot — it's where the author's ashes are buried.

✔ In Contrada San Nicola, between modern Agrigento and the Valley of the Temples, lies the **church of San Nicola** (Via dei Templi;

Admission: Free; Open: Daily 8 a.m.–1 p.m.). Built in the 12th century, this church offers a perfect view of the temples. Inside, at the center of the second chapel, is the famous third-century *Sarcofago di Fedra,* one of the most gracious examples of Greek sculpture in existence. It evokes the myth of Phaedra and Ippolyte — a sad story of unrequited love in which the rejected Phaedra is delirious while Ippolyte goes hunting; he is then killed in an accident.

Fast Facts: Agrigento

Area Code

The local area code is **0922** (see "Telephone" in the "Fast Facts" section of Appendix A for more on calling to and from Italy).

Emergencies

For an ambulance, call ☎ **118;** for the fire department, call ☎ **115;** for road assistance, call ☎ **116.**

Hospitals

You'll find the hospital San Giovanni di Dio in Contrada Consolita (☎ 0922-492111).

Information

You'll find tourist info desks at Via Cesare Battisti 15 (☎ 0922-20454;

www.agrigento-sicilia.it) and Via Empedocle 73 (☎ 0922-20391).

Police

Call ☎ **113.**

Post Office

The main post office is at Piazza Vittorio Emanuele (☎ 0922-595150). It's open Monday through Friday from 8:10 a.m. to 6:30 p.m., Saturday from 8:10 a.m. to 1 p.m.

Taxis

You can call for pickup or walk to the taxi stand at the rail station (☎ 0922-26670) or at Piazzale Aldo Moro (☎ 0922-21899).

Part VIII
The Part of Tens

The 5th Wave   By Rich Tennant

"So far you've called a rickshaw, a unicyclist and a Zamboni. I really wish you'd learn the Italian word for taxicab."

In this part . . .

In this part, we've included a few other things that will be useful to you and help you have the splendid vacation you deserve.

Think you can't possibly make do in Italy knowing only ten Italian words? Believe it or not, you can — and in Chapter 23, we give you ten key words to help you converse with the natives. In Chapter 24, we tell you about ten Italian artists, perhaps the greatest ones of all, and certainly some whose work you will encounter over and over during your visit.

Chapter 23

Non Capisco: The Top Ten Expressions You Need to Know

● ●

In This Chapter

▶ Using salutations
▶ Asking questions
▶ Knowing lifesavers

● ●

*T*raveling in a country where you don't know the language can be intimidating, but trying to speak the language can be amusing, at the very least. Local people often appreciate it if you at least make the effort. And you'll find that Italian is a fun language to try to speak. If you're ready for more, check out Appendix B for a glossary of architectural and menu terms.

Per Favore

Meaning "please," *per favore* (*pehr* fah-*voh*-reh) is the most important expression you can know. With it, you can make useful phrases such as *"Un caffè, per favore"* ("A coffee, please") and *"Il conto, per favore"* ("The bill, please"). There's no need for verbs, and it's perfectly polite!

Grazie

Grazie (*grah*-tsee-eh) means "thank you"; if you want to go all out, use *grazie mille* (*mee*-leh), meaning "a thousand thanks." Say it clearly and loudly enough to be heard. Saying *grazie* is always right and puts people in a good mood. *Grazie* has other uses as well: Italians often use it as a way to say goodbye or mark the end of an interaction. It's particularly useful when you don't want to buy something from an insistent street vendor: Say *"Grazie,"* and walk away.

Permesso

Meaning "excuse me" (to request passage or admittance), *permesso* (pehr-*mehs*-soh) is of fundamental importance on public transportation. When you're in a crowded bus and need to get off, say loudly and clearly, *"Permesso!"* and people will clear from your path (or feel less irritated as you squeeze your way through). The same thing applies in supermarkets, trains, museums, and so on. Of course, you may be surrounded by non-Italians, so the effect may be a little lost on them.

Scusi

Scusi (*scoo*-zee) means "excuse me" (to say you're sorry after bumping into someone) and is more exactly *mi scusi,* but the shortened form is the one most people use. Again, it's a most useful word in any crowded situation. You'll note that Italians push their way through a narrow passage with a long chain of *"Scusi, permesso, mi scusi, grazie, permesso . . ."* It's very funny to hear. *Scusi* has another important use: It's the proper way to attract somebody's attention before asking a question. Say *"Scusi?"* and the person will turn toward you in benevolent expectation. Then it's up to you.

Buon Giorno and Buona Sera

Buon giorno (bwon *djor*-no), meaning "good day," and its sibling *buona sera* (*bwon*-a *sey*-rah), meaning "good evening," are of the utmost importance in Italian interactions. Italians always salute one another when entering or leaving a public place. Do the same, saying it clearly when entering a store or restaurant. Occasionally, these words can also be used as forms of goodbye.

Arrivederci

Arrivederci (ah-ree-vey-*der*-chee) is the appropriate way to say goodbye in a formal occasion — in a shop, at a bar or restaurant, or to friends. If you can say it properly, people will like it very much: Italians are aware of the difficulties their language poses for foreigners.

You'll hear the word *ciao* (chow), the familiar word for goodbye, used among friends (usually of the same age). Note that using the word *ciao* with someone you don't know is considered quite impolite!

Dov'è

Meaning "where is," *dov'è* (doe-*vay*) is useful for asking for directions. Because the verb is included, you just need to add the thing you're looking for: *"Dov'è il Colosseo?"* ("Where is the Colosseum?") or *"Dov'è la stazione?"* ("Where is the train station?").

Quanto Costa?

Meaning "How much does it cost?", *Quanto costa?* (*quahn*-to *koss*-tah) is of obvious use all around Italy, for buying anything from a train ticket to a Murano glass chandelier.

Che Cos'è?

Meaning "What is it?", *Che cos'è?* (kay *koss*-ay) will help you buy things, particularly food, and know what you're buying. But it could also be useful in museums and other circumstances. But then the tricky part begins: understanding the answer. If you don't understand the answer, you can get the person to repeat it by saying the next phrase on our list:

Non Capisco

Non capisco (nohn kah-*pees*-koh) means "I don't understand." There's no need to explain this one: Keep repeating it and Italians will try more and more imaginative ways to explain things to you.

Chapter 24

Ten Great Italian Artists

In This Chapter
▶ Knowing who's who
▶ Charting the careers of the masters
▶ Getting background on what you'll be seeing

Admittedly, hundreds of books have been written about the great figures of Italian art, so any choice of ten figures is apt to be personal. However, some artists would be on everybody's list: Leonardo, Michelangelo, Raffaelo . . . This chapter is intended to give you some background to attach to the names that you will encounter again and again during your travels in Italy.

Giotto

Immortalized by Dante in the *Divine Comedy,* Giotto di Bondone (1266 or 1276–1337) was born in a village not far from Florence, and went on to become an apprentice of the great painter Cimabue. He was famous in his own time and in later centuries came to be known as the father of modern painting. A practitioner of the Gothic style, he departed from the serene but flat and static mode of Byzantine painting and the somber, otherworldly beauty of medieval art. In works such as his masterpiece, the **Scrovegni Chapel** in Padua (see Chapter 17), he depicted human beings with a passion and emotion not seen since classical times, and paved the way for the Renaissance in the following century.

Donatello

In a sense, Donatello (1386–1466) did for sculpture what Giotto did for painting: pulled it out of the Middle Ages and gave it a new realism and psychological accuracy. He developed a new technique, *schiacciato,* which used flattened, shallow carving to make relief sculpture more pictorial and more like painting. Donatello executed works in marble, bronze, and wood, and many of these pieces survive in his native Florence, where he spent most of his long life. His crowning achievement is probably the carvings for the sacristy in the **Basilica di San Lorenzo;** the **Bargello** museum has two of his statues of *David,* one in bronze and the other in marble (see Chapter 13).

Giovanni Bellini

Born to an artistic family (his father and brother were painters, and his sister married Andrea Mantegna), Giovanni Bellini (1430–1516) began as a painter of austere religious pictures in the late Gothic tradition. He later developed one of the most recognizable styles and had a lasting effect on Venetian painting. His masterpiece is reputed to have been the large historical paintings he did for the hall of the Maggior Consiglio in Venice, but these were destroyed by fire in 1577. However, his luminosity and exquisite colors are fully on display in religious artworks (such as his famous Madonnas) and other pieces preserved in the museums and churches of **Venice** (see Chapter 16).

Leonardo da Vinci

Leonardo (1452–1519) grew up on his father's estate in Vinci, a Tuscan town under the rule of Florence. He was apprentice to the Florentine painter Andrea del Verrocchio. Leonardo later left Florence for Milan, where he spent 17 years. His genius for observation manifested itself in portrayals of the human figure, such as the *Mona Lisa,* that were psychologically real to the point of being uncanny, while also showing a revolutionary sense of physicality, based on a profound grasp of anatomy. His use of *chiaroscuro* (contrast between light and dark) influenced later painters. Leonardo's attention to nature led him to become a scientist, engineer, and inventor as well. Leonardo's life and work are perhaps the most perfect expression of the spirit of the Renaissance. His *Last Supper* in **Milan** (see Chapter 17), though much damaged, is a pilgrimage site for art lovers.

Michelangelo

Michelangelo Buonarotti (1475–1564), like Leonardo, was a great painter but many other things as well, including an architect; **St. Peter's** in Rome (see Chapter 12) received its final form and its dome from him. This architectural masterpiece also contains his painterly masterpiece, the frescoes of the **Cappella Sistina (Sistine Chapel),** and his sculptural masterpiece, the **Pictà.** A tempestuous genius, Michelangelo was often embroiled in conflict. His patrons included Lorenzo de' Medici and Pope Julius II. Julius's successor, Leo X, was actually a son of Lorenzo and longtime friend of Michelangelo, and he employed the artist in the **Medici Chapels** in Florence (see Chapter 13). His use of color and monumental modeling of the human form pointed ahead to the style known as Mannerism.

Raphael

In a short lifetime, Raffaelo Sanzio (1483–1520) left a profound mark on European painting. He had already shown great talent as a draftsman before he was out of his teens. After studying painting with Perugino and other artists, he moved to Florence and fell under the spell of Leonardo da Vinci. But Raffaelo's figures have a radiant, peaceful composure that is all his own; his images have often been described as "sublime." Some of his finest work is in the rooms he frescoed at the **Vatican** for Pope Julius II (see Chapter 12). It is less well known that Raffaelo was very interested in archaeology and was appointed commissioner of antiquities for the city of Rome. He died on his birthday at the age of 37; his tomb is in the Pantheon.

Titian

Tiziano Vecellio (circa 1488–1576) moved to Venice with his brother at the age of nine and was apprenticed to a mosaicist. He found his true calling, however, when he began to study under the greatest Venetian painter of the time, Giovanni Bellini. Titian became famous for his depictions of mythological and idyllic scenes, powerful and revealing portraits (like the one of Pope Paul III and family in the Capodimonte museum in **Naples** — see Chapter 18), and stunning religious works such as the revolutionary *Assumption* in the Frari church in **Venice** (see Chapter 16), a truly glorious painting.

Tintoretto

Jacopo Robusti (1518–94) was nicknamed *"tintoretto"* ("little dyer") because his father was a silk dyer. His unmistakable mature style involved dynamic, loose brushwork and a palette that could almost be described as moody. He was a colossal talent, the leading Mannerist painter of the time, and his presence is felt everywhere in **Venice,** particularly in **Scuola Grande di San Rocco,** which he literally filled with large canvasses (see Chapter 16). Inspired by Michelangelo and Titian, Tintoretto was nonetheless a unique and startlingly original painter, whose work is above all passionate.

Gian Lorenzo Bernini

If anyone personifies the baroque period, it is Bernini (1598–1680). Although born in Naples, he did his major work in Rome, where one can hardly turn around without stumbling on one of his masterworks. He developed a style that combined the psychological realism of earlier Renaissance sculptors with heightened decoration. His **baldaquin** inside **St. Peter's** in Vatican City (see Chapter 12), a giant gilt-and-bronze canopy over four stories tall, has been called the first baroque monument. His fountain in the **Piazza Navona** is one of the most beautiful in Rome, while the **Galleria Borghese** contains several sculptures of incredible mastery in which he made marble behave like flesh. Bernini was so famous that when he visited the court of French king Louis XIV in 1665, crowds lined the streets to see him.

Caravaggio

One of the most beloved of Italian artists, Michelangelo Merisi da Caravaggio (1572–1610) appeals to the modern imagination for his romantic, tragic life as well as for his intense and unique art. He was considered a wild spirit by his contemporaries, and he befriended both prostitutes (some of whom were his models) and criminals. However, he was also protected and encouraged by cardinal Francesco del Monte. His religious paintings were often rejected for their emotional intensity and overpowering sensual impact (many can be found in the churches of **Rome** and in the **Galleria Borghese** — see Chapter 12). He fled Rome after a killing, or duel, which remains shadowy; he died soon thereafter. The lurid details of his life, however, are less important than his extraordinary use of light and shade, brilliant depiction of bodies in motion, and tremendous fusion of naturalistic art and spiritual faith.

Quick Concierge

Fast Facts

American Express

The Rome office is at Piazza di Spagna 38 (☎ 06-67641; Metro: Line A to Spagna); the Florence office is at Via Dante Alighieri 22R (☎ 055-50981); the Venice office is at Salizzada San Moisè, 1471 San Marco (☎ 041-5200844); the Milan office is at Via Brera 3 (☎ 02-876674); the Naples office is at Piazza Municipio 5 (☎ 081-5512007); and the Palermo office is at Via E. Amari 40 (☎ 091-587144).

ATMs

ATMs are available everywhere in the centers of towns. Most banks are linked to the Cirrus network. If you require the Plus network, your best bet is the BNL (Banca Nazionale del Lavoro; www.bnl.it), but ask your bank for a list of locations before leaving on your trip.

Automobile Club

Contact the Automobile Club d'Italia (ACI) at ☎ 06-4477 for 24-hour information and assistance. For **road emergencies** and assistance in Italy, dial ☎ **116**.

Baby Sitters

Hotels in Italy rarely offer structured activities for children, but do use professional agencies to provide their guests baby-sitting services on request. See individual chapters for local agencies where applicable.

Business Hours

Shops are usually open Monday through Saturday from 9 a.m. to 1 p.m. and 4 to 7:30 p.m.; grocery and other food stores are also closed on Wednesday or Thursday afternoon, while apparel and other shops are closed on Monday mornings. Offices are usually open Monday through Friday from 8:30 a.m. to 1 p.m. and 2:30 to 5:30 p.m.; banks close about an hour earlier, and some are open Saturday mornings as well.

Credit Cards

Contact the following offices if your card is lost or stolen: American Express (☎ 06-7220348, 06-72282, or 06-72-461; www.americanexpress.it); Diners Club (☎ 800-864064866 in Italy; www.dinersclub.com); MasterCard (☎ 800-870866 in Italy; www.mastercard.com); or Visa (☎ 800-819014 in Italy; www.visaeu.com)

Currency Exchange

You can find exchange bureaus (marked CAMBIO/CHANGE/WECHSEL) at airports and major train stations.

Customs

U.S. citizens can bring back $800 worth of merchandise duty-free. You can mail yourself $200 worth of merchandise per day and $100 worth of gifts to others — alcohol and tobacco excluded. You can bring on the plane 1 liter of alcohol and 200 ciga-rettes or 100 cigars. The $800 ceiling doesn't apply to artwork or antiques (antiques must be 100 years old or more). You're charged a flat rate of 10 percent duty on the next $1,000 worth of purchases — for special items, the duty is higher. Make sure that you have your receipts handy. Agricultural restrictions are severely enforced: no fresh products, no meat prod-ucts, no dried flowers; other foodstuffs are allowed only if they're canned or in airtight sealed packages. For more information, contact the U.S. Customs Service, 1301 Pennsylvania Ave. NW, Washington, DC 20229 (☎ 877-287-8867) and request the free pamphlet *Know Before You Go,* which is also available on the Web at www. customs.gov.

Canadian citizens are allowed a Can$750 exemption and can bring back, duty-free, 200 cigarettes, 2.2 pounds of tobacco, 40 imperial ounces of liquor, and 50 cigars. In addition, you're allowed to mail gifts to Canada from abroad at the rate of Can$60 a day, provided they're unsolicited and don't contain alcohol or tobacco (write on the package "Unsolicited Gift, Under $60 Value"). Declare all valuables on the Y-38 form before your departure from Canada, including serial numbers of valuables that you already own, such as expensive for-eign cameras. You can use the $750 exemption only once a year and only after an absence of seven days. For more infor-mation, contact the Canada Border Services Agency (☎ 800-461-9999 in Canada, or 204-983-3500 or 506-636-5064; www.cbsa-asfc.gc.ca).

There's no limit on what U.K. citizens can bring back from an EU country, as long as the items are for personal use (this includes gifts), and the necessary duty and tax have already been paid. However, Customs law sets out guidance levels. If you bring in more than these levels, you may be asked to prove that the goods are for your own use. Guidance levels on goods bought in the EU for your own use are: 800 cigarettes, 200 cigars, 1 kilogram smoking tobacco, 10 liters of spirits, 90 liters of wine (of this not more than 60 liters can be sparkling wine), and 110 liters of beer. For more information, contact HM Customs and Excise, Passenger Enquiry Point, 2nd Floor Wayfarer House, Great South West Road, Feltham, Middlesex, TW14 8NP (☎ 0845-010-9000 in the U.K., or 44-208-929-0152 from outside the U.K.; www.hmce.gov.uk).

Australian citizens are allowed an exemp-tion of A$400 or, for those under 18, A$200. Personal property mailed back home should be marked "Australian Goods Returned" to avoid payment of duty. Upon return to Australia, you can bring in 250 cigarettes or 250 grams of loose tobacco, plus 1.125 liters of alcohol. If you're return-ing with valuable goods you already own, such as foreign-made cameras, you should file form B263. A helpful brochure, avail-able from Australian consulates or Customs offices, is *Know Before You Go.* For more information, contact Australian Customs Services, GPO Box 8, Sydney NSW 2001 (☎ 02-9213-2000 or 1300-363-263 in Australia, 612-6275-6666 from out-side Australia; www.customs.gov.au).

New Zealand citizens have a duty-free allowance of NZ$700. If you're over 17, you can bring in 200 cigarettes, 50 cigars, or 250 grams of tobacco (or a mix of all three if their combined weight doesn't exceed 250 grams), plus 4.5 liters of wine and beer, or 1.125 liters of liquor. New Zealand cur-rency doesn't carry import or export restrictions. Fill out a certificate of export, listing the valuables you're taking out of the country (that way, you can bring them back without paying duty). You can find the answers to most of your questions in a free pamphlet available at New Zealand consulates and Customs offices: *New Zealand Customs Guide for Travellers, Notice no. 4.* For more information, contact New Zealand Customs, The Custom House, 17–21 Whitmore St. Box 2218, Wellington (☎ 04-473-6099; www.customs.govt.nz).

Driving

If you have a breakdown or any other **road emergencies,** call ☎ **116** (road emergencies and first aid of the Italian Automobile Club), or call the **police** emergency number (☎ **113** or **112**).

Electricity

Electricity in Italy is 220 volts. To use your appliances, you need a transformer. Remember that plugs are different, too: The prongs are round, so you also need an adapter. You can buy an adapter kit at an electronics store before you leave.

Embassies and Consulates

Rome is the capital of Italy and, therefore, the seat of all the embassies and consulates, which maintain a 24-hour referral service for emergencies: United States (☎ 06-46741), Canada (☎ 06-445981), Australia (☎ 06-852721), New Zealand (☎ 06-4402928), United Kingdom (☎ 06-7482441), Ireland (☎ 06-6979121).

Emergencies

For an ambulance or first aid, call ☎ **118**; for the fire department, call ☎ **115**.

Information

See "Where to Get More Information," later in this appendix, and in individual destination chapters throughout this book.

Internet Access

Refer to the "Fast Facts" section in individual destination chapters.

Language

Italians speak Italian, and although many know a bit of English, it is not widely understood. Luckily, you can survive with very little knowledge of the Italian language (see Chapter 23 for a few choice terms), especially because Italians are very friendly and ready to help foreigners in difficulty. However, you'll greatly enhance your experience if you master more than a dozen basic expressions. A good place to start your studies is *Italian For Dummies* (Wiley).

Liquor Laws

There are no liquor laws in Italy. That is, anybody is free to drink, but drinking and driving is forbidden, as is displaying drunken behavior. The law against disturbing the *quiete pubblica* (public quiet) is strict, and getting drunk and loud in bars, streets, and even private homes is not tolerated. You can buy alcohol in all supermarkets and grocery stores, open usually from 9 a.m. to 1 p.m. and 4 to 7 p.m.

Maps

The free maps distributed at tourist information desks are usually adequate. If you want something more detailed, you can buy maps at local newsstands, kiosks, and tobacconists — they all carry a good selection.

Police

Call ☎ **113** from anywhere in Italy.

Post Office

Each town has at least one post office, usually in the center. Mail in Italy used to be notoriously unreliable, and many visitors still prefer to use the Vatican post office while they're visiting St. Peter's in Rome (it's the same price as Italian post offices, but faster). But Italian mail has gotten a lot better with the introduction of

Posta Prioritaria (express/priority). A letter to the U.S. costs 0.80€ (96¢) and can take as little as four to five days to get there. Beware, though, that postcards are always sent via the equivalent of U.S. third-class mail and will take a long time to arrive; if you want your postcard to arrive more quickly, slip it into an envelope and send it letter rate. Also, make sure you put your mail in the right mailbox: The ones for international mail are blue, whereas the red ones are for national mail. The new priority mail also applies to packages; however, it is expensive and you may be better off using a private carrier like UPS or DHL, which will guarantee your delivery, especially for valuables.

Safety

Italy is very safe, but petty theft is common. Pickpockets abound in tourist areas, on public transportation, and in crowded open-air markets. Purse-snatchers on motor scooters are less common than they used to be — Palermo is the only city where they're still prevalent. Avoid carrying your bag on the street side of the sidewalk, lest a thief zip by on a scooter. Instead, keep your bag on the non-street side, or between you and your companion. Observe common big-city caution: Keep your valuables in your hotel's safe, don't be distracted, watch your belongings, don't count your money in public, and avoid displaying valuable jewelry and electronic equipment. There are areas of poverty where a wealthy-looking tourist with an expensive camera may be mugged after dark, but those are usually on the outskirts of cities. (We indicate seedy areas, when applicable, in individual destination chapters.)

If you're a woman traveling alone in Italy — especially if you're young and fair-haired — you will attract attention from young (and sometimes not-so-young) Italian men.

They'll give obvious and often vocal indication of their admiration; in fact, they may approach you and try to charm you. However, it's unlikely that someone will touch you, let alone harm you. Still, it's a good idea to ignore and not make eye contact with anyone who approaches you, lest you be thought promiscuous. The way you dress will also have an effect: Italians have a stricter dress code than Americans do, and the farther south you go, the more traditional the society is. You'll see a lot of female skin displayed, but only when women are accompanied by a man. If you're alone, you may want to cover up a bit.

Smoking

In 2005, Italy passed a law outlawing smoking in most public places. Smoking is allowed only where there is a separate, ventilated area for nonsmokers. If you want to smoke at your table, call beforehand to make sure the restaurant or cafe you'll be visiting offers a smoking area.

Taxes

See Chapter 5 for information on IVA (Value Added Tax).

Telephone

To call Italy from the U.S., dial the international access code, **011**; then Italy's country code, **39**; and then the **area code** followed by the local telephone number. Area codes for land lines in Italy can have different numbers of digits — 06 for Rome, 055 for Florence, 0583 for Lucca, and so on — but always begin with 0; cellular lines instead always have three-digit area codes beginning with 3 (340, 338, and so on depending on the company network). Toll-free numbers have an **800** or **888** area code (you'll be tempted to add a 1, but it doesn't work). Some paying services use three-digit codes beginning with 9. Also, some companies have their own special numbers that don't conform to any of the preceding standards and that are local calls from anywhere in Italy, such as the railroad info line of Trenitalia (☎ 892021).

To make a call within Italy, always use the area code — including 0 if any — for both local and long distance. Public pay phones in Italy take a *carta telefonica* (telephone card), which you can buy at a *tabacchi* (tobacconist, marked by a sign with a white *T* on a black background), bar, or newsstand. The cards can be purchased in different denominations, from 2€ to 7.50€ ($2.40–$9). Tear off the perforated corner, stick the card in the phone, and you're good to go. A local call in Italy costs 0.10€ (12¢).

To call abroad from Italy, dial the international access code, **00**; then the country code of the country that you're calling (1 for the United States and Canada, 44 for the United Kingdom, 353 for Ireland, 61 for Australia, 64 for New Zealand); and then the local area code and phone number. Make sure you have a high-value *carta telefonica* before you start; your 5€ won't last long if you call San Diego at noon. Lower rates apply after 11 p.m. and before 8 a.m. and on Sundays. The best option for calling home, though, is using your own calling card linked to your home phone. Some calling cards offer a toll-free access number in Italy; for those that don't, you must put in a *carta telefonica* to dial the access number (you're usually charged only for a local call or not at all). Check with your calling-card provider before leaving on your trip. You can also make collect calls: For AT&T, dial ☎ 800-1724444 and then your U.S. phone number, area code first; for MCI, dial ☎ 800-905825; and for Sprint, dial ☎ 800-172405 or 800-172406. To make a collect call to a country

other than the United States, dial ☎ 170. Directory assistance for calls within Italy is free: Dial ☎ 12. International directory assistance is a toll call: Dial ☎ 176. Remember that calling from a hotel is convenient but usually expensive, as various surcharges apply.

Time Zone

In terms of standard time zones, Italy is six hours ahead of eastern standard time in the United States: When it is 6 a.m. in New York, it is noon in Italy. Daylight saving time goes into effect in Italy each year from the end of March to the end of September.

Tipping

Tipping is customary as a token of appreciation as well as a polite gesture on most occasions. A 10 to 15 percent service charge is usually included in your restaurant bill (check the menu when you order — if the service is included, it will be marked at the beginning or at the end as *servizio incluso*), but it is customary to leave an additional 5 to 10 percent if you appreciated the meal. If the service is not included, leave 15 to 25 percent. In bars, leave a 5 percent tip at the counter and a 10 to 15 percent tip if you sit at a table. Bellhops who carry your bags will expect about 1€ ($1.20) per bag, and you may want to leave a small tip for housekeeping in your hotel; cabdrivers will expect 10 to 15 percent of the fare.

Weather Updates

Before you go, you can check a Web site such as www.cnn.com or www.weather.com. Once in Italy, your best bet is to watch the news on TV (there's no number for weather forecasts, as there is in the U.S.).

Toll-Free Numbers and Web Sites

Airlines that fly to and around Italy

Air France
☎ 800-237-2747
www.airfrance.com

Air New Zealand
☎ 800-737-000
www.airnewzealand.com

Air One
☎ 199-207080 in Italy, or ☎ 06-488800 from abroad
www.flyairone.it

Air Sicilia
☎ 06-650171046

Alitalia
☎ 1478-65643 in Italy, or 06-65643
☎ 800-223-5730 in the U.S.
☎ 800-361-8336 in Canada
☎ 0990-448-259 in the U.K.
☎ 020-7602-7111 in London
☎ 1300-653-747 or 1300-653-757 in Australia
www.alitalia.it or www.alitaliausa.com in the U.S.

American Airlines
☎ 800-433-7300
www.aa.com

British Airways
☎ 800-247-9297 in the U.S.
☎ 0345-222-111 or 0845-77-333-77 in the U.K.
www.british-airways.com

Cathay Pacific
☎ 131-747 in Australia
☎ 0508-800454 in New Zealand
www.cathaypacific.com

Continental Airlines
☎ 800-525-0280
www.continental.com

Delta Air Lines
☎ 800-221-1212
www.delta.com

Lufthansa
☎ 800-645-3880 in the U.S.
www.lufthansa-usa.com

Meridiana
☎ 892928 in Italy
☎ 0789-52682 from abroad
www.meridiana.it

Northwest Airlines
☎ 800-225-2525
www.nwa.com

Qantas
☎ 800-227-4500 in the U.S.
☎ 612-9691-3636 in Australia
www.qantas.com

United Airlines
☎ 800-241-6522
www.united.com

US Airways
☎ 800-428-4322
www.usairways.com

Car-rental agencies

Auto Europe
☎ 800-223-5555 in the U.S.
☎ 800-334440 in Italy
www.autoeurope.com

Avis
☎ 800-331-1212 in the U.S.
☎ 06-41999 in Italy
www.avis.com

Europe by Car
☎ 800-223-1516 in the U.S.
www.europebycar.com

Europcar
☎ 800-014410 or 06-65010879 in Italy
www.europcar.it

Hertz
☎ 800-654-3001 in the U.S.
☎ 199-112211 in Italy
www.hertz.com

Kemwel
☎ 800-678-0678 in the U.S.
www.kemwel.com

National/Maggiore
☎ 800-227-7368 in the U.S.
☎ 1478-67067 in Italy
www.maggiore.it

Sixt
☎ 888-749-8227 in the U.S.
☎ 199-100666 in Italy
www.e-sixt.it or
www.sixtusa.com in the U.S.

Hotel chains in Italy

Best Western
☎ 800-780-7234 in the U.S. and
Canada
☎ 0800-39-31-30 in the U.K.
☎ 131-779 in Australia
☎ 0800-237-893 in New Zealand
www.bestwestern.com or
www.bestwestern.it

Hilton Hotels
☎ 800-HILTONS
www.hilton.com

Holiday Inn
☎ 800-HOLIDAY
www.holiday-inn.com

ITT Sheraton
☎ 800-325-3535
www.sheraton.com

Jolly Hotels
☎ 800-017-703 in Italy
☎ 800-221-2626 in the U.S.
☎ 800-247-1277 in New York
☎ 800-237-0319 in Canada
☎ 0800-731-0470 in the U.K.
www.jollyhotels.it

Sofitel
☎ 02-2951-2280 in Italy
☎ 800-SOFITEL in the U.S. and
Canada
☎ 020-8283-4570 in the U.K.
☎ 800-642-244 in Australia
☎ 0800-44-44-22 in New Zealand
www.sofitel.com or www.
accor-hotels.it

(Sofitel is part of the giant Accor group, representing 3,400 hotels in several chains. You can connect to all of them through ☎ 800-221-4542 in the U.S. and Canada, or ☎ 0208-283-4500 in the U.K.; www.accor.com.)

Where to Get More Information

For more information on Italy, you can visit the tourist offices and Web sites listed in this section.

Visitor information

The Italian Government Tourist Board, ENIT (www.enit.it), maintains a Web site where you can find all kinds of cultural and practical information — including hotel listings, addresses, and Web sites of local tourist offices. It also maintains liaison offices abroad where you can get brochures and other information (all offices are open Mon–Fri 9 a.m.–5 p.m. local time):

✔ **New York** (630 Fifth Ave., Suite 1565, New York, NY 10111; ☎ 212-245-5618 or 212-245-4822; Fax: 212-586-9249; enitny@italian tourism.com)

✔ **Chicago** (500 N. Michigan Ave., Suite 2240, Chicago, IL 60611; ☎ 312-644-0996 or 312-644-0990; Fax: 312-644-3019; enitch@ italiantourism.com)

✔ **Los Angeles** (12400 Wilshire Blvd., Suite 550, Los Angeles, CA 90025; ☎ 310-820-9807 or 310-820-1898; Fax: 310-820-6357; enitla@ earthlink.net)

✔ **Toronto** (175 Bloor St., Suite 907, South Tower, Toronto M4W3R8 Ontario; ☎ 416-925-4822; Fax: 416-925-4799; enit.canada@on. aibn.com)

✔ **London** (1 Princes St., London, WIB 2AY; ☎ 0207-399-3562; Fax: 0207-493-6695; italy@italiantouristboard.co.uk)

✔ **Sydney** (Level 26, 44 Market St. NSW 2000 Sydney; ☎ 02-9262-1666; Fax: 02-9262-1677; enitour@ihug.com.au)

You can also contact the following local tourist boards:

✔ **Agrigento** (AAPIT, Viale della Vittoria 255, 92100 Agrigento; ☎ 0922-401352; Fax: 0922-25185)

✔ **Amalfi** (AACST, Corso Roma 19, 84011 Amalfi; ☎ 0898-71107; Fax: 0898-72619)

✔ **Assisi** (APT, Piazza del Comune 27, 06081 Assisi; ☎ 075-812450; Fax: 075-813727; www.umbria2000.it)

✔ **Capri** (AACST, Piazzetta Italo Cerio 11, 80073 Capri; ☎ 081-8370424; Fax: 081-8370918; www.capritourism.com)

✔ **Cinque Terre** (APT, Viale Mazzini 47, 19100 La Spezia; ☎ 0187-770900; www.aptcinqueterre.sp.it)

✔ **Firenze (Florence)** (APT, Via A. Manzoni 16, 50121 Firenze; ☎ 055-23320; Fax: 055-2346286; www.firenzeturismo.it)

✔ **Gaiole in Chianti** (Via Ricasoli 50, 53013 Gaiole in Chianti; ☎ 0577-749-605; www.siena.turismo.toscana.it)

✔ **Greve in Chianti** (Pro Loco, Via Luca Cino 1, 50022 Greve in Chianti; ☎ 055-854-6287)

✔ **Lucca** (APT, Piazza Guidiccioni 2, 55100 Lucca; ☎ 0583-91991; Fax: 0583-490766; www.luccaturismo.it)

✔ **Milano (Milan)** (APT, Via Marconi 1, 20123 Milano; ☎ 02-725241; Fax: 02-72524250; www.milanoinfotourist.com)

✔ **Napoli (Naples)** (AACST, Palazzo Reale, 80132 Napoli; ☎ 081-2525711; Fax: 081-418619; www.inaples.it)

✔ **Padova (Padua)** (APT, Riviera Dei Mugnai 8, 35137 Padova; ☎ 049-8767911; Fax: 049-650794; www.turismopadova.it)

✔ **Palermo** (AAPIT, Piazza Castelnuovo 34, 90141 Palermo; ☎ 091-586122; Fax: 091-582788; www.palermotourism.com)

✔ **Perugia** (APT, Via Mazzini 6, 06121 Perugia; ☎ 075-5728937; Fax: 075-5739386; www.perugia.umbria2000.it)

✔ **Pisa** (APT, Via Pietro Nenni 24, 56124 Pisa; ☎ 050-929777; Fax: 050-929764; www.pisa.turismo.toscana.it or www.comune.pisa.it/turismo)

✔ **Positano** (AACST, Via del Saracino 4, 84017 Positano; ☎ 089-875067; Fax: 089-875760)

✔ **Ravello** (AACST, Piazza Duomo 10, 84101 Ravello; ☎ 089-857096; Fax: 089-857977; www.ravellotime.it)

✔ **Roma (Rome)** (APT, Via Parigi 11, 00185 Roma; ☎ 06-488991; Fax: 06-4819316; www.romaturismo.it)

✔ **San Gimignano** (Pro Loco, Piazza Duomo 1, 53037 San Gimignano; ☎ 0577-940008; Fax: 0577-940903; www.sangimignano.com)

✔ **Siena** (APT, Piazza del Campo 56; ☎ 0577-280-551; Fax: 0577-281041; www.terresiena.it)

✔ **Siracusa (Syracuse)** (APT, Via San Sebastiano 43, 96100 Siracusa; ☎ 0931-481200; Fax: 0931-67803; www.apt-siracusa.it)

✔ **Spoleto** (IAT, Piazza della Libertà 7, 06049 Spoleto; ☎ 0743-49890; Fax: 0743-46241; www.umbria2000.it)

✔ **Taormina** (AACST, Piazza Santa Caterina, 98039 Taormina; ☎ 0942-23243; Fax: 0942-24941; www.gate2taormina.com)

✔ **Venezia (Venice)** (APT, Castello 4421, 30122 Venezia; ☎ 041-5298711; Fax: 041-5230399; www.turismovenezia.it)

✔ **Verona** (APT, Via delle Franceschine 10, 37122 Verona; ☎ 045-8068680; Fax: 045-8003638; www.tourism.verona.it)

✔ **Vatican/Holy See** (Ufficio Informazioni Turistiche, Piazza San Pietro, 00163 Roma; ☎ 06-69884466)

Newspapers and magazines about Italy

If you love Italy and would like a taste of the rest of the country besides its capital, you can browse one of the following magazines. These are the best Italian magazines about Italy in English; you can get them at Amazon.com, by subscription, or from some bookstores in the U.S.

✔ **The American** (www.theamericanmag.com), published in Italy for expatriates, is a 48-page monthly covering all of Italy. It has interesting articles and extensive event listings.

✔ **Bell'Italia** (www.bellitalia.it) is a monthly magazine with gorgeous print quality. It's dedicated to discovering the most beautiful natural, cultural, and artistic destinations in Italy.

✔ **Events in Italy** (Lungarno Corsini 6, 50123 Firenze; www.events-italy.it) is a beautiful bimonthly magazine that focuses on cultural and social events in Italy.

✔ **ItalyItaly Magazine** (Piazza Principe di Piemonte 9, Magliano Romano (RM), 00060; www.italyitalymagazine.com) is an elegant travel and lifestyle magazine about Italy, available by subscription (contact the magazine directly, or in the U.S.: American Multimedia Corporation; P.O. Box 1255, New York, NY 10116; ☎ 800-984-8259).

Online resources

You can also get excellent information at the following Web sites:

✔ **Ciao Italy** (www.ciao-italy.com) provides links to a variety of Web sites, from museums to local news.

✔ **Dolce Vita** (www.dolcevita.com) is all about style — as it pertains to fashion, cuisine, design, and travel. Dolce Vita is a good place to stay up-to-date on trends in modern Italian culture.

✔ **In Italy Online** (www.initaly.com) provides information on all sorts of accommodations in Italy (country villas, historic residences, convents, and farmhouses) and includes tips on shopping, dining, driving, and viewing art.

✔ **Italian Tourist Web Guide** (www.itwg.com) lists new itineraries each month for art lovers, nature buffs, wine enthusiasts, and other Italophiles. It features a searchable directory of accommodations, transportation tips, and city-specific lists of restaurants and attractions.

✔ **Welcome to Italy** (www.wel.it) is a good source for all kinds of visitor information about Italy, from the cultural (monuments and history) to the practical (hotels and restaurants), with some curiosities thrown into the mix.

Glossary of Architectural and Menu Terms

● ●

Knowing Your Nave from Your Ambone

Ambone: A pulpit, either serpentine or simple in form, erected in an Italian church.

Apse (*abside* in Italian): The half-rounded extension behind the main altar of a church; Christian tradition dictates that it be placed at the eastern end of an Italian church, the side closest to Jerusalem.

Atrium (*atrio* in Italian): A courtyard, open to the sky, in an ancient Roman house; the term also applies to the courtyard nearest the entrance of an early Christian church.

Baldachin, baldaquin, or ciborium (*baldacchino* in Italian): Columned stone canopy, usually placed above the altar of a church.

Baptistery (*battistero* in Italian): A separate building or a separate area in a church where the rite of baptism is held.

Basilica: Any rectangular public building, usually divided into three aisles by rows of columns. In ancient Rome, this architectural form was frequently used for places of public assembly and law courts; later, Roman Christians adapted the form for many of their early churches.

Calidarium: The steam room of a Roman bath.

Campanile: A bell tower, often detached, of a church.

Capital (*capitello* in Italian): The four-sided stone at the top of a column, often decoratively carved. The classical Greek architectural styles included three orders: Doric, Ionic, and Corinthian.

Caryatid (*cariatide* in Italian): Column carved into a standing female figure.

Cathedral (*cattedrale* in Italian): The church where a bishop has his seat.

Cavea: The curved row of seats in a classical theater; the most prevalent shape is that of a semicircle.

Cella: The sanctuary, or most sacred interior section, of a Roman pagan temple.

Chancel: The section of a church containing the altar.

Cherub or cupid (*amorino* in Italian): Personification of the mythological god of love as a chubby and winged naked child armed with bow and arrows.

Cloister (*chiostro* in Italian): A courtyard ringed with a gallery of arches or lintels set atop columns.

Cornice: The horizontal flange defining the uppermost part of a building, especially in classical or neoclassical facades.

Cortile: Courtyard or backyard.

Crypt (*cripta* in Italian): A church's underground chapel, mostly used as a burial place, usually below the choir.

Cupola: A dome.

Duomo: A town's most important church, usually also a cathedral.

Forum (*foro* in Italian): The main square and principal gathering place of any Roman town, usually surrounded by the city's most important temples and civic buildings.

Hypogeum (*ipogeo* in Italian): Subterranean structure. The adjective is *hypogee,* describing any subterranean structure, a temple, a chamber, a chapel; often used as a tomb.

Loggia: Roofed balcony or gallery.

Narthex: The anteroom, or enclosed porch, of a Christian church.

Nave (*navata* in Italian): Each of the longitudinal sections of a church or basilica, divided by walls, pillars, or columns.

Palazzo: A palace or other important building.

Pergamo: Pulpit.

Piano nobile: The floor of a *palazzo* designated for the owner's use (usually the second floor), as opposed to the floors used by the house staff and for other services.

Pietra dura: Semiprecious stone, such as amethyst and lapis lazuli.

Pieve: A parish church.

Portico: A porch with columns on at least one side, usually for decorative purposes.

Presbytery (*presbiterio* in Italian): Area around the main altar of a church, elevated and separated by columns or, in the oldest churches, by a screen (transenna), which was traditionally reserved for the bishop and the officiating clergy.

Pulvin (*pulvino* in Italian): A typical structure of Byzantine architecture consisting of a four-sided stone, often in the shape of a truncated pyramid and often decorated with carvings of plants and animals, which connected the capital to the above structure.

Putto: Artistic representation of a naked small child or cherub, especially common in the Renaissance.

Stucco: A building compound composed of sand, powdered marble, lime, and water, applied to a surface to make it smooth, or used to create a decorative relief.

Telamone: Structural column carved into a standing male form; female versions are called caryatids.

Terme: Thermal baths or spa, such as the ancient Roman ones.

Timpano: Tympanum: the triangular wall — sometimes decorated with reliefs — between the cornice and the roof.

Transenna: Screen (usually in carved marble) separating the presbytery from the rest of an early Christian church.

Travertine (*travertino* in Italian): Type of porous limestone that is white, pale yellow, or pale reddish in color, commonly found in central Italy.

Dining in Italy, from Acqua Pazza to Zuppa Inglese

Acqua pazza: Light herbed broth used to poach fish.

Agnello: Lamb, usually grilled or baked; in Rome it is also called *abbacchio*.

Agnolotti: Crescent-shaped filled pasta similar to ravioli.

Al cartoccio: A cooking method by which fish, seafood, or vegetables are baked in a parchment envelope with herbs.

Anguilla: Eel.

Antipasto: Succulent tidbits served at the beginning of a meal (before the pasta); it may include sliced cured meats, seafood (especially shellfish), and cooked and seasoned vegetables.

Aragosta: Mediterranean type of lobster.

Arancini: Deep-fried balls of seasoned rice filled with cheese or meat, a typical Sicilian snack.

Arrosto: Roasted meat.

Babà: A spongy cake, similar to brioche, that is soaked in rum and served with pastry cream.

Baccalà: Dried and salted codfish, usually prepared as a stew.

Bagna cauda: Spicy, well-seasoned sauce, heavily flavored with anchovies, used as a dip for raw vegetables; literally translated as "hot bath."

Bistecca alla fiorentina: Delicious thick T-bone steak from the Chianina cow, a unique and protected species of cow, traditionally raised in southern Tuscany; served grilled with a seasoning of olive oil and herbs.

Bollito misto: Assorted boiled meats served on a single platter.

Braciola: In the rest of Italy, this means chop, usually lamb or pork; in Naples, it refers to an *involtino* filled with raisins and pine nuts and cooked with the *ragù*.

Brasato: Beef braised in white wine with vegetables.

Bresaola: Air-cured spiced beef.

Bruschetta: Toasted peasant-style bread, seasoned with olive oil and garlic and often topped with tomatoes.

Bucatini: Thick, hollow spaghetti.

Cacciucco ali livornese: Seafood stew.

Calzone: Filled pocket of pizza dough, usually stuffed with ham and cheese, and sometimes other ingredients. It can be baked or fried.

Cannelloni: Tubes of fresh pasta dough stuffed with meat, fish, or vegetables and then baked with cheese, tomato sauce, and sometimes béchamel (creamy white sauce).

Cappelletti: Small ravioli ("little hats") stuffed with meat or cheese.

Caprese: Sliced fresh tomatoes and mozzarella cheese, seasoned with fresh basil, pepper, and olive oil.

Carciofi: Artichokes.

Carpaccio: Thin slices of raw beef, seasoned with olive oil, lemon, pepper, and slivers of Parmesan. Sometimes raw fish is served in the same style, but without the cheese.

Cassata alla siciliana: Rich, sweet, and creamy dessert that combines layers of sponge cake, sweetened ricotta cheese, and candied fruit, bound together with chocolate coating and almond paste.

Cervello al burro nero: Brains in black-butter sauce.

Cima alla genovese: Baked filet of veal rolled into a tube-shaped package containing eggs, mushrooms, and sausage.

Cinghiale: Wild boar.

Coniglio alla cacciatora: Rabbit cooked in wine with olives and herbs.

Coppa: A kind of cured meat sausage.

Cotoletta alla milanese: Deep-fried breaded veal cutlet.

Cozze: Mussels.

Crostini: Toasted bread with savory toppings.

Fagioli: White beans.

Fave: Fava beans, usually eaten fresh.

Fegato alla veneziana: Venetian version of sautéed liver and onions.

Fiordilatte: A type of mozzarella cheese made with cow's milk.

Focaccia: Thick pizza dough baked with salt, olive oil, and rosemary.

Fontina: Rich cow's-milk cheese.

Fresella: Dry, rustic whole-wheat bread seasoned with fresh tomatoes, fresh basil, salt, and olive oil. The special bread is sold in the shape of large, flat doughnut-shaped rounds.

Frittata: Italian omelet.

Fritto misto: A deep-fried medley of small fish and seafood, most commonly squid and shrimp.

Frutti di mare: Translated "fruits of the sea," it refers to all shellfish.

Fusilli: Spiral-shaped pasta; the traditional version is fresh and homemade.

Gelato (produzione propria): Ice cream (homemade).

Gnocchi: Dumplings usually made from potatoes *(gnocchi alla patate)* or from semolina *(gnocchi alla romana),* often stuffed with combinations of cheese, spinach, vegetables, or whatever combinations strike the chef's fancy. Traditionally served with a tomato sauce.

Gorgonzola: One of the most famous blue-veined cheeses of Europe — strong, creamy, and aromatic.

Granita: Flavored ice, usually with lemon, coffee, or almond.

Insalata di mare: Seafood salad (usually including octopus or squid) seasoned with olive oil, lemon or vinegar, and fresh herbs and spices.

Involtini: Thinly sliced beef, veal, pork, eggplant, or zucchini that is rolled, stuffed, and sautéed, often served in a tomato sauce.

Lepre: Hare.

Melanzane: Eggplant.

Minestrone: Thick vegetable-and-bean soup served with bread or pasta and Parmesan cheese.

Mortadella: A kind of cured meat sausage, fashioned into huge cylinders and seasoned with black peppercorns and pistachio nuts, from which the American lunch meat bologna was derived.

Mozzarella di bufala: Typically from Campania, this is a non-fermented fresh cheese, exclusively made from fresh buffalo milk. It is boiled and then kneaded into a round ball. What is called *mozzarella* in the rest of Italy and abroad is mere *fiordilatte,* a similar kind of cheese made with cow's milk.

Osso buco: Sliced beef or veal shank slowly braised in a wine sauce.

Pancetta: Italian bacon.

Panelle: Chickpea fritters, a typical Sicilian street snack.

Panettone: Rich, sweet, yellow-colored bread studded with raisins and candied fruit and served traditionally for Christmas.

Panna: Heavy cream, used as an ingredient in sauces, or served whipped for dessert with *gelato* or fruit.

Pansotti: Similar to ravioli, stuffed with greens, herbs, and cheeses, traditionally served with a walnut sauce.

Panzerotti: Large, half-moon-shaped ravioli with a savory or a sweet filling, in which case they are deep-fried.

Pappardelle: Wide strips of fresh pasta.

Parmigiano: Parmesan, a hard and salty yellow cheese usually grated over pastas and soups but also eaten alone; the best is *Parmigiano Reggiano,* while *Grana Padano* is a paler imitation.

Pastiera: Traditional Neapolitan thick pie filled with a creamy mixture of wheat grains, ricotta, and candied orange peels.

Peperoni: Green, yellow, or red sweet peppers (not to be confused with the American pepperoni).

Pesce spada: Swordfish.

Pesto: Seasoning made of finely chopped fresh basil, garlic, Parmesan cheese, and olive oil; sometimes with pine nuts and potatoes.

Piccata al Marsala: Thin escalope of veal sautéed with Marsala sauce.

Piselli al prosciutto: Peas with strips of ham.

Pizza: Served as individual rounds or by weight from large square pans; the most common varieties include *margherita* (tomato sauce, mozzarella cheese, fresh basil); *marinara* (tomato sauce and oregano); *napoletana* — note that in Naples this is called *romana* (tomato sauce, mozzarella cheese, anchovies); *capricciosa* (tomato sauce, mozzarella cheese, mushrooms, ham, black olives, egg, and artichoke); and *quattro stagioni* (same ingredients as above, but neatly arranged into four slices).

Pizzaiola: Sliced beef or filet of fish cooked with tomatoes, garlic, and oregano.

Polenta: Italian-style grits made from cornmeal flour and water.

Polipetti: Squid.

Polla alla cacciatora: Chicken stewed with wine and herbs, and often tomatoes and olives as well.

Pollo all diavola: Highly spiced grilled chicken.

Polpo or polipo: Octopus.

Ragù: Meat-based tomato sauce.

Ravioli: Squares of fresh pasta dough filled with ricotta cheese, herbs, and greens, or with seafood, meats, or vegetables.

Ricotta: A fresh soft cheese made from sheep's milk; lesser quality is made with cow's milk.

Risotto: Italian Arborio rice cooked with wine, fresh herbs, and other ingredients to a creamy consistency.

Risotto alla milanese: Risotto seasoned with saffron and beef marrow.

Risotto alla pescatora: Risotto seasoned with seafood and sometimes a little tomato sauce.

Salsa verde: A sauce made of chopped parsley, lemon juice and/or vinegar, garlic, and sometimes capers and anchovies, usually served with cold meats.

Saltimbocca: Sliced veal layered with prosciutto and sage and sautéed in oil; it is so tasty that its Italian name literally translates as "jump in your mouth."

Salvia: Sage.

Scaloppina alla Valdostana: Escalope of veal stuffed with cheese and ham.

Scaloppine: Thin slices of veal coated in flour and sautéed in butter and oil.

Semifreddo: A frozen dessert made of ice cream with sponge cake.

Seppia: Cuttlefish (a kind of squid); its black ink is used for flavoring pasta dough, pasta sauces, and risotto.

Sfogliatella: A flaky pastry filled with a sweet ricotta mixture.

Soffritto: In Naples, a traditional tomato sauce made with pork tidbits cooked at length with olive oil and red pepper; in the rest of Italy, a sauté of thinly sliced onions and herbs.

Sogliola: Sole.

Spaghetti: A long, round, thin pasta, variously served — *al ragù* (meat sauce), *al soffritto* (see earlier), *al pomodoro* (with fresh tomatoes), *ai frutti di mare* (with a medley of sautéed seafood), and *alle vongole* (with clam sauce) are some of the most common.

Spiedini: Skewers of fish or meat cooked over an open flame.

Strangolapreti: Thick, elongated bits of fresh pasta dough, usually served with sauce; the name is literally translated as "priest-choker."

Stufato: Braised meat — usually beef — in white wine with vegetables.

Tagliatelle: Flat egg noodles.

Tonno: Tuna.

Torta Caprese: A rich chocolate and almond cake.

Tortelli: Pasta dumplings stuffed with ricotta and spinach or other greens.

Tortellini: Rounds of fresh pasta dough stuffed with minced and seasoned meat, served in soups or with sauce.

Trenette: Thin noodles, often served with pesto sauce.

Trippa alla Fiorentina: Beef tripe (stomach).

Vermicelli: Thin spaghetti.

Vitello tonnato: Sliced roasted veal smothered in tuna sauce, served cold.

Zabaglione or zabaione: Whipped egg yolks with sugar and Marsala, served as a warm custard or ice cream.

Zampone: Pig's shank and foot skin stuffed with seasoned pork meat, served boiled and sliced, traditionally with lentils.

Zuccotto: A liqueur-soaked sponge cake, molded into a dome and layered with chocolate, nuts, and whipped cream.

Zuppa inglese: Sponge cake soaked in custard.

Index

• A •

A la Vecia Cavana, 318
AAA, 74
AARP, 87
Accademia, 176
accommodations. *See also* Florence
   accommodations; Rome
   accommodations
  Agrigento, 495–496
  Amalfi Coast, 439–441
  apartment rentals, 84
  Assisi, 285–286
  budget planning, 52–54
  Campi Flegrei, 415
  Capri, 430–431
  Catania, 488
  Chianti region, 264
  Cinque Terre, 247–248
  cost-cutting tips, 57
  discounts, 81–83
  Internet access, 95
  Lucca, 226–228
  major chains, 516
  Milan, 367–370
  Naples, 54, 389–392
  options, 78–80
  overview, 78
  Padua, 348–352
  Palermo, 460–462
  Perugia, 277–278
  Pisa, 235–237
  pricing guide, 2–3, 80–81
  rating system, 80
  reservations, 83–84
  Salerno, 447
  San Gimignano, 256–258
  Siena, 265–268
  Sorrento, 424–425
  Spoleto, 293–294
  Syracuse, 489
  Taormina, 480–481
  top picks, 12
  Venice, 12, 58, 310–317
  Verona, 358–360
acqua pazza, 522

Ae Oche, 318
agnello, 522
agnolotti, 522
Agricantus, 475
Agrigento, 21, 495–500
agriturismo, 80
Agriturismo.it, 84
Air Canada, 65
Air France, 66
Air Sicilia, 73
air travel
  budget planning, 52, 53
  cost-cutting tips, 56, 57
  deep vein thrombosis, 94
  to Florence, 175–176
  in Italy, 72–73
  to Italy, 64–67
  itinerary challenges, 35
  to Lucca, 226
  major carriers, 515
  to Milan, 366
  to Naples, 381–382
  package tours, 70–71
  to Palermo, 454
  to Pisa, 234
  to Rome, 101–103
  security, 97–98, 102
  to Taormina, 480
  travel times between cities, 73
  to Venice, 302
  to Verona, 358
al cartoccio, 522
Al Covo, 319
Al Duomo, 482
Al Marsili, 268
Al Ristoro dei Vecchi Macelli, 237
Albergo Cesàri Hotel, 114
Albergo del Senato, 114
Albergo Ristorante Adriano, 161
Albergo Santa Chiara, 115
Alberto Ciarla, 125
alcohol, 25, 58, 512. *See also specific
  types*
Alexanderplatz, 169
Alitalia, 64–65, 72

Amalfi Coast
  accommodations, 439–441
  archaeological sites, 11
  attractions, 443–449
  map, 437
  nightlife, 449
  overview, 34, 436
  restaurants, 441–443
  tourist information, 449–450
  travel to, 438–439
Amalfi (town), 443–444
ambone, 500
ambulance, 93
American Airlines, 65, 71
American Express, 61, 62
Anacapri, 432
Anatomy Theater, 356
Ancient Roman Emperor Hadrian's
  Villa, 160
Angelino ai Fori, 125
Angelo Rasi, 352
anguilla, 523
Antica Besseta, 319
Antica Focacceria San Francesco, 463
Antica Locanda Leonardo, 377
Antica Locanda Sturion, 310
Antica Trattoria Da Bruno, 237
Antica Trattoria Papei, 269
Antiche Dimore, 275
Antico Caffè della Pace, 170
Antico Caffè delle Mura, 228
Antico Caffè Spinnato, 475
Antico Martini, 320
antipasti, 23, 24, 523
antique shopping, 165, 375, 406
Antonio e Antonio, 392
apartment, 84
Apollinare, 294
Appian Line, 161
apse, 520
aqueduct, 297
Ar Montarozzo, 126–127
Arab cuisine, 131
aragosta, 523
arancini, 28, 463, 523
Arcangelo, 125
Arch of Septimius Severus, 151
Arch of Titus, 151
Archaeological Museum
  Agrigento, 499
  Florence, 213
  Naples, 396
  Palermo, 470

Spoleto, 297
Syracuse, 491
Taormina, 484
top picks, 10
Archaeological Park of the Appian
  Way, 158
archaeological site, 11, 13, 47–48, 55.
  See also specific sites
Arche Scaligere, 362
architecture, 20–22, 79. *See also
  specific buildings*
Arena (Roman Amphitheater), 11, 362,
  493–494
Arethusa, 419
Armando al Pantheon, 126
arrosto, 523
Arsenale, 337
art
  churches, 55
  exhibitions, 40
  festival, 485
  Florence attractions, 175, 200–210
  Florence shopping, 218
  galleries, 159, 165–166, 342
  Renaissance movement, 19
art museum. *See also* museum
  Lucca, 230
  Milan, 372–374
  Naples, 398–399, 402–403
  Padua, 354
  Palermo, 468–469
  Perugia, 282
  Pisa, 241–243
  Rome, 145–148
  San Gimignano, 261
  Siena, 271–274
  top picks, 9–10
  Venice, 328–331
  Verona, 363
artist, famous, 506–509
Ascione, 407
Assisi, 284–292
astronomy, 242
ATM, 59–61, 105
atrium, 520
attractions. *See also* Florence
  attractions; Rome attractions;
  specific attractions
  Amalfi Coast, 443–449
  Assisi, 288–291
  budget planning, 52, 55
  Campi Flegrei, 412–414
  Capri, 432–434

Cinque Terre, 249, 250–253
Herculaneum, 416–418
Lucca, 229–233
Naples, 395–404
Padua, 353–357
Palermo, 465–473
Perugia, 280–283
Pisa, 238–244
Pompeii, 419–422
San Gimignano, 260–261
senior discounts, 87
Siena, 269–275
Sorrento, 426–428
Spoleto, 296–298
Syracuse, 490–494
Taormina, 483–487
top picks, 9–11
Verona, 361–365
Aventino, 106
Avogaria, 320

• B •

babà, 523
babysitting, 86, 510
baccalà, 318, 523
Baffetto, 127
Baglio Conca d'Oro, 460
bagna cauda, 523
Baia, 413
Baires, 131
bakery, 24
baldacchino, 151, 520
baldaquin, 520
ballet, 169, 475
bank, 60, 61
baptistery
  definition, 520
  Padua, 354
  Pisa, 239
  Rome, 151
  San Giovanni, 270
  St. John, 197, 200
bar
  Florence, 219
  Milan, 376
  overview, 24
  Rome, 170–172
  Siena, 275
  Sorrento, 428
  Venice, 344
Bargello Museum, 201

basilica, 10, 520
Basilica della Porziuncola, 291
Basilica di S. Maria Assunta, 260–261
Basilica di San Francesco, 289–290
Basilica di San Marco, 10, 335–336
Basilica di San Zeno Maggiore, 363
Basilica di Santa Chiara, 290
Basilica di Santa Maria del Fiore,
  201–202
Basilica di sant'Ambrogio, 374
Basilica di Sant'Anastasia, 365
Basilica di Sant'Antonio, 353–354
Basilica of Constantine and
  Maxentius, 151
beach
  Amalfi Coast, 448
  Capri, 434
  Cinque Terre, 252
  Palermo, 473
  Sorrento, 427
  Syracuse, 494
  Taormina, 486
  Venice, 338
bed-and-breakfast, 80, 83
Bel Soggiorno, 257–258
Belcore, 190–191
Bellini, Giovanni (artist), 507
Bernini Bristol, 115
Bernini, Gian Lorenzo (artist), 508–509
Biglietto Cumulativo, 270
Biglietto Fiesole Musei, 213
biking, 70, 253
Birreria Viennese, 131
biscotti, 26
bistecca alla fiorentina, 523
Bistrot d'Hubert, 131
Blue Grotto (Grotta Azzurra), 432–433
boat race, 38
boat tour
  Capri, 432, 433
  Cinque Terre, 250
  Padua, 353
  Pisa, 244
  Rome, 159, 162
  Sorrento, 426
boat travel, 246, 302
bollito misto, 127, 523
Bolognese, 127
books, 29–30, 86, 166
Botanical Garden, 357
Bottega dei Ragazzi, 212
Bottega della Tarsia Lignea
  Museum, 427

Boutique del Gelato, 322
braciola, 523
Brandi, 392–393
brasato, 523
bread, 24, 58
breakfast, 57, 80
Brera district (Milan), 375, 376
Brera Picture Gallery, 10, 372
bresaola, 523
bridge
  Florence, 210
  Spoleto, 297
  Venice, 329–330, 332
  Verona, 363
Bridge of Sighs, 329–330
British Airways, 65, 66
bruschetta, 24, 523
Buca di San Francesco, 286, 288
Buca di Sant'Antonio, 228–229
Buca Mario dal 1886, 191
bucatini, 126, 523
bucket shop, 66
budget, 51–58, 319
Buonarotti, Michelangelo (artist), 507
Burano, 338, 341
bus tour
  Blue Grotto, 433
  Florence, 214
  Rome, 161
  San Gimignano, 260
  Siena, 269
  Verona, 361
bus travel
  Agrigento, 495
  Amalfi Coast, 439
  Assisi, 285
  budget planning, 52
  Campi Flegrei, 411–412
  Capri, 430
  disabled travelers, 87
  Florence, 176, 182–183, 222
  general information, 68, 74
  Lucca, 226
  Milan, 367
  Naples, 382, 389
  Palermo, 454, 459
  Perugia, 276
  Rome, 104, 112–113
  San Gimignano, 256
  Siena, 262
  Sorrento, 424
  Spoleto, 293

Syracuse, 488
Taormina, 480
ticket purchase, 112
Venice, 302

• C •

Ca' d'Andrean, 247
Ca' d'Oro, 325, 328
Ca' Rezzonico, 328
cab. *See* taxi
cabaret, 170
cable car, 389
cacciucco ali livornese, 523
cafeteria, 24
Caffè del Professore, 408
Caffè della Signoria, 294
Caffè dell'Ussero, 244
Caffè Florian, 344
Caffè Greco, 170
Caffè Mazzara, 475
Caffè Pedrocchi, 356–357
Caffè Quadri, 344
Caffè Rosati, 170
Caffetteria Pasticceria Gelateria G.
  Mazzaro, 394
Cala Moresca, 415
calendar of events, 38–42
Calendimaggio, 39
calidarium, 142, 520
Calmiere, 360
calzone, 523
cameo, 14, 406, 407
campanile, 520
Campi Flegrei, 412–415
Campo de' Fiori, 106
Campo dei Miracoli, 239
Camposanto Monumentale, 239–240
Canadian passport, 91
canal, Padua, 356
canal, Venice
  neighborhood orientation, 303–304
  tourist information, 336–337
  travel by, 307
Cannaregio, 304
cannelloni, 490, 523
Canonico, 425
Cantina Tirolese, 131
Cantinella, 431
Cantinetta Antinori Tornabuoni, 191
Cantinetta del Verrazzano, 193
capital, 520

Capitoline Museums, 139
capitone, 352
Capodimonte, 385
Cappella del Sacro Chiodo, 274
Cappella di San Severo, 402–403, 403
Cappella Palatina, 22, 470
Cappella Pazzi, 211
cappelletti, 523
Cappun Magru in Casa di Marin, 248
caprese, 27, 524
Capri, 12, 89, 431–436
Capri Palace, 12, 430
Capricci di Sicilia, 463
Capuchin convent, 251
car rental, 75–77, 103, 515–516
car travel
  Amalfi Coast, 438
  Assisi, 285
  budget planning, 53
  Cinque Terre, 246
  driving emergencies, 512
  Florence, 177
  general information, 74–77
  Lucca, 226
  Milan, 377
  Naples, 382
  Padua, 348
  Perugia, 277
  Pisa, 234
  Rome, 102–104
  safety, 76, 77
  San Gimignano, 256
  Siena, 265
  Spoleto, 293
  Syracuse, 489
  Taormina, 480
  travel times between cities, 73
  Venice, 303
  Verona, 358
Caracalla Baths, 142–143
carciofi, 129, 524
Caribbean cuisine, 131
Carnevale, 39, 339
carpaccio, 524
carriage ride, 253
Carta Agile, 182–183
Carta Rail Plus, 73
Carthusian Monastery of Padula, 447
Carthusian Monastery of San Martino
  and Museum, 396–397
Cartiera Latina, 158
Caruso, 425

caryatid, 520
Casa Albertina, 439
Casa del Brodo, 464
Casa di Giulietta (Juliet's House), 364
Casa di Romeo (House of Romeo), 364
Casa Grugno, 482
Casa Natale di Giacomo Puccini, 233
Casa Natale di Pirandello, 499
Casa Valdese, 115
CasaNova, 431
cash, 60
casino, 339, 344
cassata alla siciliana, 28, 463, 524
cast iron, 342
Castel dell'Ovo, 397
Castel Nuovo, 397–398
Castel Sant'Angelo, 143
Castel Sant'Elmo, 397
Castello di Brolio, 264
Castello di Spaltenna, 264
Castello di Uzzano, 264
Castello Sforzesco, 373
Castello (Venice), 304
Castelvecchio, 363
castle. See specific castles
Catacombe dei Cappuccini, 473
Catacombs of San Callisto, 143
Catacombs of St. Gennaro, 403
Catania, 64–67, 488
cathedral. See church
Cathedral of San Lorenzo, 281
Cattedrale di San Martino, 230
Cattedrale di Santa Maria Assunta, 240
cavea, 521
Cavolo Nero, 192
CDW (Collision Damage Waiver), 76
cella, 521
cellphone, 94–95
cemetery, 239–240
cena, 23
Centrale RistoTheatre, 170
Centro Guide Turistiche Milano, 372
Centro Guide-Associazione Guide
  Turistiche, 269
cervello al burro nero, 524
Cesarina, 127
chancel, 521
Charly's Saucière, 131
Checco er Carettiere, 128
cherub, 521
Chiaia, 385
chianti, 27

Chianti region, 263–264. *See also*
    specific locations
Chiesa del Gesù, 466–467
Chiesa del Redentore, 339
Chiesa della Martorana, 467
Chiesa di San Pietro, 298
children. *See* family travel
chocolate, 283, 376, 407
church. *See also* duomo; *specific
    churches*
  Agrigento, 499–500
  Amalfi Coast, 444
  architectural styles, 21, 22
  Assisi, 289–290, 291
  Cinque Terre, 250, 251, 252–253
  dress code, 22, 139
  interior art, 55
  Lucca, 230–232
  Milan, 373–374
  Naples, 398–399, 402–403
  Padua, 353–354, 356
  Palermo, 466–468, 469, 472
  Perugia, 283
  Pisa, 243
  San Gimignano, 260–261
  Siena, 270–271
  Sorrento, 427
  Spoleto, 296–297, 298
  top attractions, 10–11
  Venice, 334–336, 338, 339
  Verona, 362, 363, 365
ciborium, 520
Cibreo, 13, 192
cima alla genovese, 524
Cinque Terre, 33, 245–254
Cipriani and Palazzi, 12, 311
Ciro a Mergellina, 404
Ciro a Santa Brigida, 393
Città antica, 385
Civic Museum, 261, 397–398
cloister, 444, 521
clothing
  Amalfi shopping, 445
  Capri shopping, 434
  dress code, 22
  Florence shopping, 216, 217
  Herculaneum tour, 419
  hiking precautions, 492
  Milan shopping, 375
  Naples shopping, 406
  Rome shopping, 164, 166, 167
  shopping budget, 55
  top souvenirs, 14

club
  budget planning, 56
  Capri, 436
  Florence, 219
  Milan, 376
  Naples, 408
  Palermo, 475
  Rome, 170, 171
  Sorrento, 428
  Venice, 344
Collegio del Cambio, 280–281
Collegio della Mercanzia, 281
Collision Damage Waiver (CDW), 76
Colosseo, 106
Colosseum, 11, 144
commuter train, 103–104
Compagnia dei Vinattieri, 269
Compagnia di Navigazione Ponte San
    Angelo, 159, 162
Compagnia Siciliana Turismo, 69
COMPARK, 303
concert. *See also* music festival
  Amalfi Coast, 449
  budget planning, 56
  Florence, 218
  Lucca, 232
  Milan, 376
  Naples, 407–408
  Palermo, 475
  Rome, 169
  Sorrento, 428
  spring celebrations, 39
Concorso Ippico Internazionale, 40
coniglio alla cacciatora, 524
consolidator, 66
Consorzio Agrario Pane and Co., 193
Consorzio Battellieri di Padova e
    Riviera del Brenta, 356
Continental airlines, 65, 71
contorno, 23
convent, 251
Coop supermarket, 319
Cooperativa il Navicello, 244
Cooperativa San Marco/Alilaguna, 302
coppa, 524
cornice, 521
Corniglia, 250–251
Coronas Café, 195
Corso Umberto I, 484–485
Corte Sconta, 320–321
cortile, 521
costume shop, 339, 343

cotoletta alla Milanese, 27, 524
Council Travel, 89
cozze, 524
CraccoPeck, 13, 370
crafts. *See specific crafts*
crèche (presepi), 41, 400, 407
credit card, 2, 60–61, 510
credit-reporting agency, 62
crêpes, 191
Crisco, 220
Croce di Malta, 186
crostini, 26, 524
crowds, 301, 336
crypt, 521
cultural museum, 150
Cuma excavations, 413
Cumpà Cosimo, 441
cupid, 521
cupola, 521
currency, 3, 58–59, 102
customs
    Florence, 176
    Naples, 382
    overview, 510–511
    Rome, 102
    Venice, 302

• *D* •

Da Adolfo, 441
Da Benito e Gilberto, 128
da Caravaggio, Michelangelo Merisi
    (artist), 509
Da Gemma, 442
Da Giggetto, 128–129
Da Raffaele, 321
Da Salvatore, 442
da Vinci, Leonardo (artist), 407
Daiwing 5 Terre Immersioni, 253
dance
    clubs, 171, 219, 376
    festivals, 39, 40, 297
    performances, 218
Dante Taberna de' Gracchi, 129
David (Michelangelo), 203
Davide Il Gelataio, 426
day trip
    Campi Flegrei, 412–415
    Etna, 486
    Herculaneum, 415–418
    overview, 411
    Pompeii, 419–422

Dehor, 496
Delta Vacations, 71
Desirée, 186
dessert, 23, 25
di Bondone, Giotto (artist), 506
Diners Club, 62
Dioscuri Bay Palace, 495–496
disability, traveler with, 87–88, 308
disco, 219, 376, 408
Discoteca Flamingo, 220
discount
    accommodations, 81–83
    air travel to Italy, 65–66
    cost-cutting tips, 56–58
    Milan shopping, 375
    Padua attractions, 353
    Rome attractions, 139
    senior travelers, 87
    student travelers, 89
    Venice attractions, 324–325
    Verona attractions, 361, 362
Discover Card (credit card), 2
Ditirambo, 129
diving, 253, 413
doctor, 93
Dolce & Gabbana, 375
Domus Aurea, 144
Don Camillo, 490
Don Chisciotte, 192
Don Salvatore, 404
Donatello (artist), 506–507
Donna Rosa, 442
Dorandò, 258–259
Dorsoduro, 304, 306
dress code, 22, 139, 153
driver's license, 74, 92
driving rules, 75–76
driving tour, 177
duomo. *See also* church
    Assisi, 290
    Catania, 488
    definition, 521
    Florence, 180, 201–202
    Milan, 10, 373
    Naples, 11, 398–399
    Padua, 354
    Palermo, 467–468
    Perugia, 281
    Pisa, 240
    Ravello, 447
    Salerno, 446
    San Gimignano, 260–261

duomo *(continued)*
  Siena, 271
  Sorrento, 426
  Spoleto, 296–297
  Syracuse, 492
  Taormina, 485
Duomo di Monreale, 11, 467–468
Duomo di San Rufino, 290

• E •

Eau Vive, 131
e-mail, 96
embassy
  Florence, 220
  Naples, 409
  overview, 512
  Palermo, 476
  Venice, 345
embroidery, 217, 275
Emerald Grotto (Grotta dello
    Smeraldo), 448
emergency situation, 93, 512
emperor, 18–19
Emperor Constantine, 18
Epifania holiday, 38
Er Faciolaro, 129
Eremo delle Carceri, 291
escorted tour. *See also specific types*
  Campi Flegrei, 412
  disabled travelers, 88
  family travel, 86
  Florence, 213–214
  Herculaneum, 415–416, 418
  Naples, 404
  overview, 68–70
  Padua, 353, 356
  Palermo, 473–474
  Pisa, 239, 244
  Pompeii, 419
  Rome, 161–162
  San Gimignano, 260
  Taormina, 483–484, 486
  Venice, 330, 339–340
Estate Romana Festival, 168
ethnic cuisine, 26–28, 70
Ethnological Missionary Museum, 156
Etna volcano, 486
Eurailpass, 68
euro, 51, 56, 58–59, 60
Eurochocolate, 283

Eurolines, 68
Europa Hotels, 83
European Central Bank, 60
Europeo di Mattozzi, 393
event calendar, 38–42
Excelsior Palace, 462
Exhibition of Azaleas, 39
Expedia, 67, 83

• F •

fagioli, 26, 524
Falcone Borsellino, 454
fall, 37–38
family travel
  babysitting, 86, 510
  cost-cutting tips, 57
  escorted tour, 86
  itinerary, 45–47
  resources, 86
  tips for success, 85–86
Faraglioni, 433
farm, 84
Fattoria la Parrina, 126
fave, 524
fegato alla veneziana, 27, 524
Ferragosto holiday, 41
Ferrara, 130
ferry service
  Amalfi Coast, 438–439
  Capri, 429, 430
  general information, 74
  to Italy, 68
  Naples, 382
  Palermo, 453–454
  Sorrento, 424
  Taormina, 480
  Venice, 308–309
Festa del Redentore, 41
Festa di San Ranieri, 243
festival. *See also* music festival
  dance, 39, 40
  film, 41
  Florence, 212–213
  flower, 497
  opera, 41
  seasonal, 40, 168
Fiaschetteria Toscana, 321
Fiera Antiquaria, 406
Fiesole, 180, 213
figurine, 14, 400, 407

film, 30–31, 41
finocchietto, 28, 523
fiordilatte, 524
fireworks, 39, 41, 42
Florence
  art treasures, 175
  event calendar, 39, 40
  guided tours, 213–214
  historical events, 19, 200
  itineraries, 214–215
  neighborhoods, 177–181
  nightlife, 218–220
  overview, 33, 175
  street numbering, 183
  tourist information, 181–182, 220–222
  travel in, 182–183
  travel to, 64–67, 175–177
Florence accommodations. See also
  accommodations
  Croce di Malta, 186
  Desirée, 186
  Grand Hotel Cavour, 186
  Grand Hotel Villa Medici, 186–187
  Hermitage Hotel, 190
  Hotel Bellettini, 187
  Hotel De La Pace, 187
  Hotel Mario's, 190
  Hotel Savoy, 187
  Il Guelfo Bianco, 188
  J. K. Place, 188
  Loggiato dei Serviti, 188
  Machiavelli Palace, 188–189
  map, 184–185
  Monna Lisa, 189
  overview, 183
  Palazzo Benci, 189
  Relais Santa Croce, 189
  top picks, 12
  Torre Guelfa, 190
  Westin Excelsior, 190
Florence attractions. See also
  attractions; specific attractions
  art displays, 200–210
  bridge, 210
  churches, 10
  festivals, 212–213
  gardens, 208
  map, 198–199
  monastery, 210–211
  overview, 197
  reservations, 197

shopping, 14, 215–218
soccer events, 213
Florence Baths, 220
Florence restaurants. See also
  restaurants
  Belcore, 190–191
  Buca Mario dal 1886, 191
  Cantinetta Antinori Tornabuoni, 191
  Cantinetta del Verrazzano, 193
  Cavolo Nero, 192
  Cibreo, 192
  Coronas Café, 195
  Don Chisciotte, 192
  Gelateria Carabè, 195
  Gelateria Vivoli, 195
  Giannino in San Lorenzo, 193
  Il Cantastorie, 193–194
  Il Cantinone, 194
  La Carabaccia, 194
  map, 184–185
  Narbone, 193
  Oliviero, 194
  Osteria del Caffè Italiano, 195
  Osteria Ganino, 195–196
  overview, 190
  Pane e Vino, 196
  Perchè No, 195
  Ristorante Ricchi, 196
  top picks, 13
  Trattoria Boboli, 196
  Trattoria Garga, 196–197
  Trattoria Le Mossacce, 197
Florentine Chamber Orchestra, 218
focaccia, 28, 524
Fontana Maggiore, 282
Fontebella Hotel, 285–286
fontina, 524
Foresteria Baglio della Luna, 496
Forno Food e Cafè, 126
Fortezza da Basso, 180
forum, 521
fountain, 153, 159, 261, 401–402
Four Seasons hotel, 12, 367, 370
French cuisine, 131, 191
Fresco Museum, 365
fresella, 524
frittata, 191, 524
fritto misto, 422, 524
frutti di mare, 524
funicular, 389, 430
fusilli, 525

• *G* •

Galileo (astronomer), 242
Galleria Borghese, 9, 145
Galleria degli Uffizi, 10, 202–203
Galleria dell'Accademia
    (Michelangelo's *David*), 203
Galleria Doria Pamphili, 159
Galleria Nazionale d'Arte Antica in
    Palazzo Barberini, 145–146
Galleria Nazionale d'Arte Moderna, 146
Galleria Regionale Siciliana, 468–469
Galleria Umberto I, 402, 407
Gallerie dell'Accademia, 10, 328–329
Gambardella Pastori, 407
Gambero Rosso, 248–249, 490
Garage San Marco, 303
Garden Hotel, 265
gardens. *See specific gardens*
Gattopardo Relais, 123
gay and lesbian travelers
    festivals, 168
    Florence bars, 219–220
    Milan bars, 376
    Naples bars, 408
    overview, 88–89
    Palermo bars, 476
    Rome bars, 171–172
    Rome shopping, 166
    Venice bars, 344
Gay Village, 168
Gay-Odin, 407
Gelateria alla Scala, 128
Gelateria Carabè, 195
Gelateria Cecere, 128
Gelateria dei Gracchi, 128
Gelateria Vivoli, 195
gelato
    definition, 525
    Florence, 195
    Rome, 25, 128
    Sorrento, 426
    Venice, 322
George's, 393–394
ghetto, 110, 337
Giannino in San Lorenzo, 193
Giardino Giusti, 365
Gioco del Ponte, 243
Gioco di Calcio Storico Fiorentino,
    40, 213
Giolitti, 128
Giotto's Bell Tower, 203, 206

Giovanni da Verrazzano, 264
Giroscopio.com, 82
Giuseppe Ferrigno, 407
glass artwork, 14, 338, 341
Glass Museum, 338
gloves, 217
gnocci, 425, 525
gold jewelry, 217
Gole dell'Alcantara, 487
gondola ride, 13, 336–337
Good Friday holiday, 39
gorgonzola, 525
Gorizia, 394
GoToMyPC, 96
Gran Bretagna, 489
Grand Hotel, 489
Grand Hotel Cavour, 186
Grand Hotel de la Minerve, 118
Grand Hotel et des Palmes, 460
Grand Hotel Excelsior Vittoria, 424
Grand Hotel Parker's, 12, 390
Grand Hotel Timeo, 12, 480
Grand Hotel Vesuvio, 12, 390
Grand Hotel Villa Igiea, 461
Grand Hotel Villa Medici, 186–187
Grande Albergo Sole, 462
granita, 28, 525
Grappolo d'Oro—Zampanò, 130
Greek cuisine, 131
Greek temple, 11, 493, 497–499
Greek-Roman Theater, 485
Gregorian Egyptian Museum, 156
Gregorian Etruscan Museum, 156
Greve in Chianti, 264
Gritti Palace, 317
Grotta Azzurra (Blue Grotto), 432–433
Grotta dello Smeraldo (Emerald
    Grotto), 448
grotto. *See specific grottoes*
Guglia San Domenico, 403
guided tour. *See* escorted tour
Gulf of Naples, 13–14
Gustavo, 258
Gusto, 130
Gutkowski Hotel, 489

• *H* •

Hamasei, 131
Hasekura, 131
Herculaneum, 11, 415–418
Hermitage Hotel, 190

hiking
  Amalfi Coast, 449
  Assisi, 291
  Capri, 433, 434
  Cinque Terre, 252
  clothing, 492
  Sorrento, 427
  Taormina, 487
  tours, 70
history
  Amalfi, 443
  Florence, 200
  Italian tourism, 1
  itinerary, 47–48
  main events, 15–20
  Naples, 399
  opera, 208
  Palermo, 468
  Perugia, 281
  Pisa, 240
  Rome cafes, 170
  San Gimignano, 259
  Sorrento, 428
  Syracuse, 491
  Taormina, 483
  Venice, 334
Holy See, 111
Home-Sanctuary of Saint Caterina, 275
horse racing, 13, 40, 273
horseback riding, 253
hospital
  Agrigento, 500
  Amalfi Coast, 450
  Assisi, 292
  Capri, 436
  Cinque Terre, 253
  disabled travelers, 88
  Florence, 220
  Lucca, 233
  Milan, 377
  Naples, 409
  Padua, 357
  Palermo, 476
  Perugia, 284
  Pisa, 244
  Rome, 135
  San Gimignano, 262
  Siena, 276
  Sorrento, 429
  Spoleto, 298
  Taormina, 487
  Venice, 345
  Verona, 366

Hostaria Da Nerone, 131
Hotel Aleph, 123
Hotel Antica Torre, 268
Hotel Arenula, 118
Hotel Art, 118
Hotel Aurora, 358, 360
Hotel Bellettini, 187
Hotel Campiello, 311
Hotel Capo d'Africa, 119
Hotel Celio, 119
Hotel Colomba d'Oro, 360
Hotel Colombina, 311
Hotel Columbia, 124
Hotel De La Pace, 187
Hotel de Russie, 12, 120
Hotel Dei Mellini, 119
Hotel des Bains, 338
Hotel Do Pozzi, 317
Hotel Falier, 317
Hotel Farnese, 120
Hotel Fiori, 120
Hotel Forte, 121
Hotel Gabbia D'Oro, 360
Hotel Gallery House, 462
Hotel Gattapone, 293
Hotel Grand'Italia, 348
Hotel Hassler, 124
Hotel Ilaria, 226–227
Hotel La Minerva, 430–431
Hotel Leonardo, 235
Hotel Lidomare, 439–440
Hotel Lilium, 121
Hotel Luna, 431
Hotel Luna Convento, 440
Hotel Manzoni, 370
Hotel Marina Piccola, 247
Hotel Mario's, 190
Hotel Metropole, 314
Hotel Miramare, 390
Hotel Nardizzi, 124
Hotel Olimpia, 317
Hotel Parlamento, 121
Hotel Plaza, 348, 352
Hotel Porto Roca, 247–248
Hotel Regina, 370, 424
Hotel Relais dell'Orologio, 235
Hotel Rex, 391
Hotel San Cassiano Ca' Favretto, 314
Hotel San Luca, 293–294
Hotel San Pietro, 12, 440
Hotel Santa Maria, 121–122
Hotel Sant'Anna, 124
Hotel Santo Stefano, 314

Hotel Savoy, 12, 187
Hotel Subasio, 286
Hotel Teatropace 33, 122
Hotel Umbra, 286
Hotel Violino d'Oro, 315
House of Romeo (Casa di Romeo), 364
housewares, 217
hydrofoil, 429, 430, 439
hypogeum, 521

• I •

I Candelai, 475
I Monaci, 288
I Re di Napoli, 394
identity theft, 62
Il Brontolone, 414
Il Buco, 425–426
Il Cantastorie, 193–194
Il Cantinone, 194
Il Convento, 391
Il Convivio Troiani, 131–132
Il Desco, 13, 361
Il Drappo, 132
Il Falchetto, 278
Il Giglio, 229
Il Guelfo Bianco, 188
Il Guru, 131
Il Luogo di Aimo e Nadia, 371
Il Principe, 422
Il Ristorantino, 464
Il Tartufo, 296
Il Tucano, 414
Il Vigneto, 248
Indian cuisine, 131
InfoHub Specialty Travel Guide, 70
insalata di mare, 525
insurance. *See specific type*
Internet
  access, 95–97, 512
  resources, 519
  specials, 56
involtini, 525
Irish pub, 171, 219, 428
Isola Bella, 486
itinerary
  accommodation prices, 53
  ancient history focus, 47–48
  challenges, 35–36
  escorted tour, 69

family travel, 45–47
Florence, 214–215
Naples, 404–406
one-week options, 43–44
Palermo, 474
Rome, 162–164
two-week options, 44–45
Venice, 340–341

• J •

Japanese cuisine, 131
jazz
  festival, 40, 168
  Florence, 219
  Palermo, 475
  Rome, 170
  Venice, 344
jewelry, 167, 217, 406, 434
Jewish neighborhood, 110, 337
Joia, 371
Joli Hotel, 461
Jolly Hotel delle Palme, 447
Juliet's House (Casa di Giulietta), 364
Juliet's Tomb, 365

• K •

Kandinsky, 475
Keats–Shelley Memorial House, 149

• L •

La Calcina, 315
La Cambusa, 464
La Cantinella, 395
La Cantinetta, 264
La Carabaccia, 194
La Caravella, 442–443
La Casina Valadier, 132
La Cuba, 473
La Fortezza, 288
La Kalsa, 456, 469
La Mangiatoia, 259
La Pergola, 12
La Pergola of the Rome Cavalieri
  Hilton, 133
La Porta del Vesuvio, 418
La Taverna, 278–279

La Zisa, 472–473
Labor Day holiday, 39
lace, 338, 343
language, 28, 503–505, 512
L'Antico Forno di Piazza Trevi, 126
L'Antico Pozzo, 258
L'Arco dei Cappuccini, 482–483
Lazzi, 226
Le Cafe, 344
Le Logge, 269
Le Terrazze, 259–260
Leaning Tower of Pisa, 33, 241
leather goods, 167, 217
lemon harvest, 444
lepre, 525
liability insurance, 76–77
library, 401
Lido, 338
linen, 217, 275
lire, 51
Lo Spasimo-Blue Brass, 475
Locanda ai Santi Apostoli, 315
Locanda Cairoli, 122
Locanda L'Elisa, 226
Locanda Novecento, 316
loggia, 521
Loggia del Consiglio, 364
Loggiato dei Serviti, 188
L'Opera, 280
Lucca, 223–233
Lucca in Musica festival, 232
Lucullus, 422
Lufthansa, 66
luggage, 57, 92–93, 97
lunch, 22–23, 57
Lungolanotte, 371
Luraleo Grill, 483

• **M** •

Maccheroni, 133
Machiavelli Palace, 188–189
Macondo, 131
Mafia organization, 20, 465
magazine, travel, 87, 88, 518–519
Maggio Musicale Fiorentino, 39,
    212–213, 218
Majestic Hotel Toscanelli, 352
Majestic Palace, 425
Manarola, 251
manger scene, 400, 407

map
  Agrigento, 498
  Amalfi Coast, 437
  Assisi, 287
  Capri, 435
  car travel in Italy, 76
  Chianti region, 263
  Herculaneum, 417
  Lucca, 227
  Milan, 368–369
  Naples, 383, 386–387
  Padua, 350–351
  Palermo, 457
  Perugia, 279
  Pisa, 236
  Pompeii, 421
  Salerno, 383
  San Gimignano, 257
  Sicily, 455
  Siena, 266–267
  Spoleto, 295
  Taormina, 479
  Tuscany overview, 224–225
  Umbria overview, 224–225
  Valley of the Temples, 498
  Vatican museums, 156–158
  Verona, 359
maps, Florence
  accommodations, 184–185
  attractions, 198–199
  neighborhoods, 178–179
  purchase locations, 182, 221
  restaurants, 184–185
  Uffizi Gallery, 204–205
maps, Rome
  accommodations, 116–117
  attractions, 140–141
  neighborhoods, 108–109
  purchase locations, 113
maps, Venice
  accommodations, 312–313
  attractions, 326–327, 333
  disabled travelers, 308
  neighborhoods, 305
  purchase locations, 345
Marina Piccola, 433
marine park, 253
Marinella, 406
market, 126, 193, 216, 238, 472
mask, 343
Massimo Plaza, 461

MasterCard, 61, 62
Mausoleum of Cecilia Metella, 158
Mazzarò, 486
Mec Paestum, 447
medical insurance, 92
Medici Chapels, 206
melanzane, 525
Mercato Centrale, 193
Mercure Angioino, 391
Mergellina, 404
Meridiana, 72
Met de l'Hotel Metropole, 321–322
Michelangelo (artist), 203, 507
Michelangelo's dome, 155
midday meal, 22, 57
Milan
  accommodations, 367–370
  churches, 10
  ethnic cuisine, 27
  historical events, 19
  location, 349
  map, 368–369
  museums, 10
  nightlife, 376
  overview, 34, 347, 365
  restaurants, 13, 370–372
  shopping, 375
  top accommodations, 12
  tourist information, 377
  travel in, 367
  travel to, 64–67, 366–367
minestrone, 525
Mirabelle de l'Hotel Splendide
  Royal, 133
monastery, 396–397, 447
Monna Lisa, 189
Monte Solaro, 433
Monterosso al Mare, 251
mortadella, 525
mosaic art, 218
Moss Rehab Hospital, 88
Mount Subasio, 291
Mount Vesuvius, 415–418
ovies, 30–31
zzarella di bufala, 27, 525
icipal Casino, 344
no glass, 14, 338, 341
Civici Eremitani, 355–356
Aperto Napoli, 404
Archeologico Regionale Paolo
rsi, 491

Museo Archeologico Regionale
  Salinas 470
Museo Bandini, 213
Museo Capitolare, 281
Museo Civico, 271
Museo Civico d'Arte, 363
Museo Correale, 426–427
Museo degli Innocenti, 212
Museo del Duomo, 373
Museo del Risorgimento, 357
Museo della Casa Buonarroti, 212
Museo delle Sinopie, 241–242
Museo dell'Opera del Duomo, 206–207,
  242, 272
Museo dell'Opera di Santa Croce, 211
Museo di Capodimonte, 10, 399–400
Museo di Roma, 150
Museo Diocesano di Arte Sacra, 274
Museo Diocesano (Palermo), 466
Museo Ebraico, 337
Museo Marciano, 335
Museo Teatrale della Scala, 375
museum. *See also* art museum
  budget planning, 55
  Campi Flegrei, 412
  Florence, 201, 206–207, 210–213
  free admission event, 40
  Lucca, 230–233
  Milan, 10, 375
  Naples, 10, 396–400
  Padua, 357
  Palermo, 465
  Perugia, 280–281, 283
  reservations, 98
  Rome, 9, 139, 142, 159
  Salerno, 446, 447
  San Gimignano, 261
  Sorrento, 426, 427
  Spoleto, 297, 298
  Taormina, 484–485
  top picks, 9–10
  Vatican, 9, 156–158
  Vatican options, 156–158
  Venice, 10, 325, 337, 338
  Verona, 365
Museum of Baia, 412
Museum of Ethno-History, 397
Museum of the Basilica, 374
music festival. *See also* concert;
  festival
  events calendar, 39, 40
  Florence, 218

Lucca, 232
Perugia, 283
Ravello, 449
Rome, 168
Sorrento, 428
Spoleto, 40, 292, 297
music museum, 159

• N •

Naples
accommodations, 54, 389–392
attractions, 395–404
churches, 11
escorted tour, 404
ethnic cuisine, 27–28
history, 399
map, 383, 386–387
museums, 10
neighborhoods, 384–388
nightlife, 407–408
overview, 34, 381
restaurants, 54, 392–395, 404
shopping, 406–407
top attractions, 10, 11, 13–14
tourist information, 408–410
travel in, 388–389
travel to, 64–67, 382–384
Napoleonic era, 20
Narbone, 193
narthex, 521
National Archaeological Museum of
Umbria, 283
National Etruscan Museum of Villa
Giulia, 146
National Gallery of Umbria, 282
National Museum of Musical
Instruments, 159
National Museum of San Matteo,
242–243
National Museum of Spoleto, 298
National Roman Museum, 9, 139,
147–148
nature refuge, 486
Navarra, 406
nave, 521
Navona, 106–107
Negroni drink, 219
newspaper, 518–519
nightlife. *See* bar; club; *specific types of
performing arts*

Northwest/KLM Airlines, 65
Nostra Signora della Salute, 253
Nostra Signora di Montenero, 253
Nostra Signora di Soviore, 252
Noto, 494
Nuova Idea International, 376

• O •

Oliviero, 194
110 Open, 161
opera
budget planning, 56
event calendar, 40
festival, 41
history, 208
Lucca, 232, 233
Milan, 374–375
Naples, 402, 407
Palermo, 471, 475
Rome, 169
Oratorio del Rosario di San
Domenico, 472
Oratorio di San Bernardino, 274, 282
Oratorio di Santa Cita, 472
Orbitz, 67
Oriental Express, 131
Orsanmichele, 207
Ortigia, 491–492
osso buco, 525
Osteria ai 4 Feri, 322
Ostaria ai Vetrai, 338
Osteria alle Testiere, 322
Osteria da Fiore, 13, 323
Osteria dei Cavalieri, 238
Osteria dei Vespri, 464–465
Osteria del Caffè Italiano, 195
Osteria del Gambero, 280
Osteria di Santa Marina, 323
Osteria Ganino, 195–196
Osteria Speroni, 352
Ostia Antica, 160, 162
Ouzerie, 131

• P •

package tour, 57, 70–71
Padua, 34, 348–357
Paestum, 11, 446–447
Pagliaccio, 133–134

Palatine Hill, 147
Palatine Museum, 147
Palatino train, 68
palazzo, 78, 81, 84, 521
Palazzo Alabardieri, 391
Palazzo Alexander, 227–228
Palazzo Altemps, 147–148
Palazzo Benci, 189
Palazzo Braschi, 150
Palazzo dei Normanni, 470
Palazzo dei Priori, 282
Palazzo del Bo, 356
Palazzo del Giglio, 316
Palazzo del Governo, 363
Palazzo del Popolo, 261
Palazzo della Ragione, 354–355,
    363–364
Palazzo Dragoni, 294
Palazzo Ducale, 329–330
Palazzo Mansi and Pinacoteca
    Nazionale, 230–231
Palazzo Massimo alle Terme, 148
Palazzo Medici Riccardi, 212
Palazzo Nuovo, 142
Palazzo Pitti and Giardino di Boboli,
    207–208
Palazzo Ravizza, 268
Palazzo Reale, 400–401
Palazzo Sant'Angelo, 316
Palazzo Sasso, 12, 440
Palazzo Senatorio, 142
Palazzo Vecchio, 208–209
Palazzo Vendramin-Calergi, 344
Palermo
    accommodations, 460–462
    attractions, 465–473
    churches, 11
    escorted tour, 473–474
    event calendar, 40
    history, 468
    map, 457
    neighborhoods, 456–458
    nightlife, 475–476
    overview, 35, 453
    restaurants, 462–465
    safety, 458, 476–477
    tourist information, 458, 476–477
    travel in, 458–459
    travel to, 64–67, 453–454
Palio delle Contrade, 13, 40, 41,
    272–273

Palio di San Rufino, 41
pancetta, 525
panelle, 28, 463, 525
panettone, 525
panna, 525
pansotti, 525
Pantheon, 13, 106–107, 148–149
panzerotti, 526
paper goods
    Amalfi Coast, 444, 445
    Florence shopping, 218
    Rome, 167–168
    top picks, 14
    Venice shopping, 343
pappardelle, 526
Parco Archeologico della Neopolis, 492
Parco della Musica, 169
parmigiano, 526
Passeggiata delle Mura, 232
passport, 86, 90–92, 97
Pasticceria Marchini, 322
Pasticceria Scaturchio, 394
Pasticceria Tonolo, 322
pastiera, 526
pastry, 322, 394
Peggy Guggenheim Collection, 330–331
pensione, 80
Pensione Accademia Villa
    Maravegie, 317
Pentagramma, 296
peperoni, 526
Per Bacco, 353
Perchè No, 195
performing arts. *See specific types*
perfume, 434
pergamo, 521
personal accident insurance, 76–77
Perugia, 276–284
Perugina Factory Museum, 283
pesce spada, 526
pesto, 526
piano nobile, 521
Pianura Padana, 34
Piazza Castelnuovo, 458
Piazza dei Signori, 363–364
Piazza del Carmine, 180
Piazza del Comune, 290–291
Piazza del Plebiscito, 385
Piazza del Popolo, 107
Piazza della Cisterna, 260
Piazza della Repubblica, 107

Piazza della Signoria, 180–181, 209
Piazza delle Erbe, 364
Piazza delle Vettovaglie, 238
Piazza di Siena, 159
Piazza di Spagna, 107
Piazza di Spagna and the Spanish
  Steps, 149
Piazza Garibaldi, 385
Piazza Navona, 149–150
Piazza San Marco, 331, 333
Piazza San Pietro, 154
Piazza Santo Spirito, 181
Piazza Verdi, 458
Pica, 128
piccata al Marsala, 526
Piccolo Hotel Puccini, 228
Piccolomini Library, 271
pickpocket, 62, 63, 388, 409
picnic lunch, 126, 193, 238, 416
Pierreci, 138
pietra dura, 521
pieve, 264, 522
Pinacoteca, 10, 156
Pinacoteca Ambrosiana, 374
Pinacoteca Nazionale, 273
Pincio Gardens, 159
Pisa
  accommodations, 235–237
  attractions, 238–244
  escorted tour, 239
  history, 240
  map, 236
  overview, 223, 234
  restaurants, 237–238
  top picks, 33
  tourist information, 244–245
  travel to, 226, 234
Pisa Centrale, 234
piselli al prosciutto, 526
pizza, 24, 27, 126, 526
Pizza a Taglio, 126
Pizza Al Taglio, 126
Pizza Forum, 126
Pizza (restaurant), 126
Pizza Rustica, 126
PizzaBuona, 126
pizzaiola, 526
Pizzeria Di Matteo, 394
Pizzeria Ivo, 134
PlanetAudio guide, 339–340
poetry, 247

Poggibonsi, 256
polenta, 27, 526
polipetti, 526
polla alla cacciatora, 526
pollo all diavola, 526
polpi al coccio, 27
polpo, 526
Pompeii, 11, 14, 419–422
Ponte delle Torri, 297
Ponte di Rialto, 332
Ponte Scaligero, 363
Ponte Vecchio, 210, 217
porcelain, 14, 402
portico, 522
Porziuncola, 291
Positano, 445
post office, 512–513
Pozzuoli archaeological site, 413
pranzo, 22
Prati, 107
Prefecture of the Papal Household, 154
presbytery, 522
Presentation of Mary in the Temple, 41
presepi (crèche), 41, 400, 407
Priceline, 67, 83
Principe di Villafranca, 461–462
prison, 330
promenade, 232
Puccini, 229
pulvin, 522
puppet theater, 475
putto, 522

• *Q* •

Qantas, 65
Quartieri Spagnoli, 388
Quattro Canti, 458

• *R* •

rack rate, 54, 82–83
ragù, 526
Rail Europe, 68, 73
rainfall, 36
Raphael (artist), 508
Ravello, 449, 445–446
ravioli, 353, 526
Regata Storica, 41
Regata sull'Arno, 38

Regatta of the Great Maritime
   Republics, 39
Regency House, 406
Regina Viarum, 158
Regional Archaeological Museum, 499
Relais Santa Chiara, 258
Relais Santa Croce, 189
Renaissance era, 19, 21, 243
Repubblica, 107
reservation
   accommodations, 83–84
   cost-cutting tips, 57
   discount air travel, 65–66
   ferry service, 74
   Florence attractions, 197
   Herculaneum, 419–420
   museums, 98
   Rome attractions, 138
   Vatican attractions, 138
restaurants. *See also* Florence
   restaurants; Rome restaurants
   Agrigento, 496–497
   Amalfi Coast, 441–443
   Assisi, 286–288
   budget planning, 54
   Campi Flegrei, 414–415
   Capri, 431–432
   Catania, 488
   Chianti region, 264
   Cinque Terre, 248–250
   cost-cutting tips, 57, 58
   dining hours, 24
   ethnic cuisines, 25–29
   etiquette, 25
   Lucca, 228–229
   meal overview, 22–24
   Milan, 13, 370–372
   Naples, 54, 392–395, 404
   Padua, 352–353
   Palermo, 462–465
   Perugia, 278–280
   Pisa, 237–238
   Pompeii, 422
   pricing guide, 2–3
   Salerno, 447
   San Gimignano, 258–260
   Siena, 268–269
   smoking policies, 26
   Sorrento, 425–426
   Spoleto, 294–296
   Syracuse, 490

Taormina, 482–483
tipping, 25
top picks, 12–13
types, 23–24
Venice, 54, 317–324, 338, 344
Verona, 360–361
restroom, 79
ricotta, 527
Riomaggiore, 251
Rione Terra, 414
Ripa del Sole, 249
risotto, 27, 527
risotto alla milanese, 527
risotto alla pescatora, 527
Ristorante Ricchi, 196
Ristorante Rossini, 490
Riviera del Brenta, 356
RoadPost, 95
Robusti, Jacopo (artist), 508
Rocca Albornoziana, 297–298
Rocca Maggiore, 291
Rocca Paolina, 283
Roma Cristiana, 161
Roman Amphitheater (Arena), 11, 362,
   493–494
Roman Arena, 355
Roman Forum, 150–151
Roman Summer Festival, 40
Roman Theater and Archaeological
   Museum, 297
Rome. *See also* Vatican
   archaeological sites, 11
   dress code, 139
   Easter holiday, 39
   ethnic cuisine, 25–26, 131
   event calendar, 39, 40, 42
   historical events, 15–20
   neighborhoods, 105–110
   nightlife, 168–172
   overview, 32–33, 101
   safety, 136
   tourist information, 110–111, 135–137
   travel in, 111–113
   travel to, 64–67, 101–105
   vacation itineraries, 162–164
Rome accommodations. *See also*
   accommodations
   Albergo Cesàri Hotel, 114
   Albergo del Senato, 114
   Albergo Santa Chiara, 115
   Bernini Bristol, 115

budget planning, 53
Casa Valdese, 115
Gattopardo Relais, 123
Grand Hotel de la Minerve, 118
Hotel Aleph, 123
Hotel Arenula, 118
Hotel Art, 118
Hotel Capo d'Africa, 119
Hotel Celio, 119
Hotel Columbia, 124
Hotel de Russie, 120
Hotel Dei Mellini, 119
Hotel Farnese, 120
Hotel Fiori, 120
Hotel Forte, 121
Hotel Hassler, 124
Hotel Lilium, 121
Hotel Nardizzi, 124
Hotel Parlamento, 121
Hotel Santa Maria, 121–122
Hotel Sant'Anna, 124
Hotel Teatropace 33, 122
Locanda Cairoli, 122
map, 116–117
overview, 113–114
Rose Garden Palace, 122–123
top hotels, 12
travel to, 103–105
Villa San Pio, 123
Rome attractions. *See also* attractions;
   specific attractions
baths, 142–143
castles, 143
catacombs, 143
discounts, 139
fountains, 153, 159
gardens, 159
map, 140–141
reservations, 138
shopping, 162–168
Vatican options, 153–158
Rome restaurants. *See also* restaurants
Albergo Ristorante Adriano, 161
Alberto Ciarla, 125
Angelino ai Fori, 125
Ar Montarozzo, 126–127
Arcangelo, 125
Armando al Pantheon, 126
Baffetto, 127
Baires, 131
Birreria Viennese, 131

Bistrot d'Hubert, 131
Bolognese, 127
budget planning, 54
Cantina Tirolese, 131
Cesarina, 127
Charly's Saucière, 131
Checco er Carettiere, 128
Da Benito e Gilberto, 128
Da Giggetto, 128–129
Dante Taberna de' Gracchi, 129
Ditirambo, 129
Eau Vive, 131
Er Faciolaro, 129
Fattoria la Parrina, 126
Ferrara, 130
Gelateria alla Scala, 128
Gelateria Cecere, 128
Gelateria dei Gracchi, 128
Giolitti, 128
Grappolo d'Oro — Zampanò, 130
Gusto, 130
Hamasei, 131
Hasekura, 131
Hostaria Da Nerone, 131
Il Convivio Troiani, 131–132
Il Drappo, 132
Il Guru, 131
La Casina Valadier, 132
La Pergola of the Rome Cavalieri
   Hilton, 133
Maccheroni, 133
Macondo, 131
Mirabelle de l'Hotel Splendide
   Royal, 133
Naturist Club CMI, 131
Oriental Express, 131
Ouzerie, 131
overview, 124
Pagliaccio, 133–134
Pica, 128
Pizza, 126
Pizza a Taglio, 126
Pizza Al Taglio, 126
Pizza Forum, 126
Pizza Rustica, 126
PizzaBuona, 126
Pizzeria Ivo, 134
Sant'Andrea, 134
Sora Lella, 134
Surya Mahal, 131
top picks, 12

Rondinella, 432
Rose Garden Palace, 122–123
rowing competition, 39, 41
Royal Victoria, 235

• *S* •

Sagra Musicale Lucchese, 232
Salerno, 383, 446–447
salsa verde, 527
saltimbocca, 52, 527
salvia, 527
San Domenico church, 283
San Domenico Palace, 12, 480–481
San Francesco al Corso, 365
San Francesco at Cinque Terre, 251
San Francesco at Sorrento, 427
San Frediano, 231
San Gimignano, 256–262
San Giorgio Maggiore, 339
San Giovanni Battista, 251
San Giovanni church, 231
San Giovanni degli Eremiti, 472
San Giovanni in Laterano and Cloister, 151–152
San Lorenzo, 210
San Lorenzo church, 251
San Lorenzo Maggiore, 403
San Marco monastery, 210–211
San Marco (Venice), 306
San Michele Arcangelo a Morfisa, 403
San Michele in Foro, 231
San Pietro, 13, 107, 250
San Polo, 306
Santa Chiara, 401
Santa Croce, 181, 211, 306
Santa Fina Chapel, 260–261
Santa Lucia, 388
Santa Margherita di Antiochia, 251
Santa Maria Assunta, 296–297
Santa Maria della Salute, 333
Santa Maria della Scala, 274
Santa Maria della Spina, 243
Santa Maria delle Grazie, 374
Santa Maria di Monteoliveto, 401–402
Santa Maria e Donato, 338
Santa Maria Gloriosa dei Frari, 334–335
Santa Maria in Trastevere, 159
Santa Maria Maggiore, 160
Santa Maria Novella, 181, 211
Santa Maria Sopra Minerva, 21

Santa Rosalia procession, 40, 471
Sant'Agostino, 261
Sant'Andrea, 134
Sant'Anna dei Lombardi, 401–402
Santo Spirito, 212
Sanzio, Raffaelo (artist), 508
Savonarola, Girolamo (reformer), 209
scaloppina alla Valdostana, 527
scaloppine, 527
Schiaffini, 104
Scoppio del Carro, 39
Scrovegni Chapel, 355–356
seafood, 26–28, 317–318
seasons, 36–42, 53, 57
Segesta, 21, 493
Selinunte, 493
semifreddo, 527
Senatorial Palace, 142
senior traveler, 86–87
seppia, 527
Settembre Lucchese, 41, 232
Settimana della Cultura, 40
sfogliatella, 27, 527
Shaw Guides, 70
ship travel, 303, 382
shipyard, 337, 444
shoes, 167
shopping
    budget planning, 55
    Capri, 434
    Florence, 14, 215–218
    Milan, 375
    Naples, 406–407
    Rome, 162–168
    Siena, 275
    tax, 62
    top souvenirs, 14
    Venice, 341–343
shuttle bus, 103, 104, 302, 366, 382
Sicilian Barocco style, 22
Sicily. *See also specific locations*
    escorted tour selection, 69
    ethnic cuisine, 28–29
    map, 455
    overview, 34–35, 453
    top attractions, 11, 14
Siena, 265–275
Silver Stud, 220
Sistine Chapel, 156
SitaSightseeing, 239
smoking, 26, 79, 513

soccer, 40, 213
soffritto, 527
sogliola, 527
Solfatara, 414
Sora Lella, 134
Sorrento, 423–429
Sorrento Musical, 428
South American cuisine, 131
southern Tuscany. *See* Tuscany
souvenir, 14, 58
spaghetti, 527
spiedini, 527
Spoleto, 40, 293–298
Spoleto Festival, 40, 292, 297
spring, 37
St. Clare, 289, 290
St. Francis of Assisi, 41, 288–289
St. Mark's Basilica, 10, 22, 335–336
St. Mark's Bell Tower, 331–332
St. Peter's Basilica, 10, 154–155
Stanze di Raffaello, 156
Starhotel Terminus, 392
Stazione Marittima, 303
strangolapreti, 527
street numbering, 183, 309
stucco, 522
student travelers, 89, 325
stufato, 527
subway, 111–112, 367, 389
Sulga, 285
Surya Mahal, 131
swimming, 427, 434
Swiss cuisine, 131
Syracuse, 488–495

• T •

Tabularium, 142
tagliatelle, 528
Talmone, 283
Taormina, 478–487
tax, 62
taxi
  Agrigento, 500
  Assisi, 292
  Capri, 436
  Cinque Terre, 246
  Florence, 221
  Lucca, 233
  Milan, 367, 376
  Naples, 382, 384, 389, 410

Padua, 357
Palermo, 454, 459, 477
Perugia, 284
Pisa, 245
Rome, 102–103, 113, 137
  scams, 103, 384
Siena, 265, 276
Sorrento, 429
Syracuse, 495
Venice, 302, 346
Verona, 366
Teatro Arte Cuticchio, 475
Teatro Comunale, 181, 218
Teatro dei Pupi, 475
Teatro del Giglio, 232
Teatro del Sale, 219
Teatro della Scala, 374–375, 376
Teatro dell'Opera, 169
Teatro Greco-Romano (Greco-Roman
  Theater), 14
Teatro Marcello, 110
Teatro Massimo, 471, 475
Teatro Olimpico, 169
Teatro Politeama Garibaldi, 475
Teatro Romano and Museo Civico, 213
Teatro San Carlo, 402, 407
Teatro Tasso, 428
Teatro Verdi, 218
telamone, 522
telephone, 3, 94–95, 513–514
temperature, 36–38
temple, 11, 21. *See also specific temples*
Temple of Jupiter, 11
terme, 522
theft protection insurance, 77
thermal baths, 412, 416, 420–421
Ticinese/Navigli district (Milan), 376
Ticketeria, 138
time zone, 514
timpano, 522
Tin Box Club, 220
Tintoretto (artist), 508
tipping, 25, 54, 169, 514
tiramisù, 25
Titian (artist), 508
Tivoli, 160
tomato sauce, 25
tomb, 155, 362, 365
Tombolini, 164
tonno, 482, 528
Torre dei Lamberti, 364

Torre del Mangia, 271
Torre delle Ore, 233
Torre dell'Orologio, 331
Torre di Santa Maria, 244
Torre Grossa, 261
Torre Guelfa, 190
Torre Guelfa della Cittadella
    Vecchia, 244
Torre Guinigi, 232–233
torta Caprese, 528
tortelli, 361, 528
tortellini, 528
Torture Instruments Museum, 261
Toti Globe Theatre in Villa
    Borghese, 168
tourist information
  Agrigento, 500
  Amalfi Coast, 449–450
  Assisi, 292
  Capri, 436
  Catania, 488
  Cinque Terre, 253–254
  Florence, 181–182
  Lucca, 233
  Milan, 377
  Naples, 408–410
  overview, 516–518
  Padua, 357
  Palermo, 458, 476–477
  Perugia, 284
  Pisa, 244–245
  Rome, 110–111, 135–137
  San Gimignano, 262
  Siena, 275–276
  Sorrento, 428–429
  Spoleto, 298
  Syracuse, 494–495
  Taormina, 487
  Venice, 306–307, 345–346
  Verona, 365–366
traghetto, 309
Tragicomica di Gualtiero dell'Osto, 339
train travel
  Agrigento, 495
  Assisi, 285
  budget planning, 53
  Campi Flegrei, 411–412
  Cinque Terre, 245
  Florence, 176–177
  Herculaneum, 415–418
  to and in Italy, 68, 73
  itinerary challenges, 36
  Lucca, 226
  Milan, 366
  Naples, 382
  Padua, 348
  Palermo, 454
  Perugia, 276
  Pisa, 234
  Pompeii, 419
  Rome, 103–105
  San Gimignano, 256
  Siena, 262, 264, 274
  Sorrento, 423–424
  Spoleto, 293
  Syracuse, 488
  Taormina, 480
  ticket purchase, 112
  travel times between cities, 73
  Venice, 302
  Verona, 358
Trajan's Market, 152
tram
  Milan, 367, 372
  Naples, 389
  Rome, 112–113
transenna, 522
Trattoria alla Madonna, 323
Trattoria Boboli, 196
Trattoria dei Templi, 496–497
Trattoria di Giovanni Rana —
    Tre Corone, 361
Trattoria Garga, 196–197
Trattoria Gianni Franzi, 249–250
Trattoria Le Mossacce, 197
Trattoria Milanese, 372
Trattoria San Omobono, 238
Trattoria Tre Spiedi, 324
travel agency, 67, 69
travel insurance, 69, 92–93
traveler's checks, 61, 102
Travelocity, 67, 83
travertine, 522
trenette, 528
Trenitalia train service, 68, 73, 245
Treno Natura, 274
Trevi, 110
Trevi Fountain, 153
Trianon, 407
trip-cancellation insurance, 92

trippa alla Fiorentina, 528
truffle, 26
Tuscany. *See also specific Tuscan locations*
    architecture, 21
    driving tour, 177
    ethnic cuisine, 26–27, 191
    overview, 33, 223, 255–256

• U •

Ufficio Guide Turistiche, 213
Uffizi Gallery, 202–203, 204–205
Umbria. *See also specific locations*
    architecture, 21
    ethnic cuisine, 26
    event calendar, 40
    overview, 33, 255–256
Umbria Jazz Festival, 40, 283
underwater archaeological park, 413
United Vacations, 71
US Airways, 65, 71

• V •

Valley of the Temples, 11, 495–500
vaporetto, 308–309
Vatican. *See also* Rome
    attractions, 153–158
    dress code, 22, 153
    location, 107
    museums, 9, 156–158
    reservations, 138
    tourist information, 111
Vatican Information Office, 153
Vecchio Ulivo, 415
Vecellio, Tiziano (artist), 508
vegetarian cuisine, 131
Venere Net, 82
Venetian Ghetto, 337
Venetian Gothic style, 22
Venice
    accommodations, 12, 53, 310–317
    architectural style, 22
    churches, 10
    escorted tour, 330
    ethnic cuisine, 27
    event calendar, 39, 41
    historical events, 19
    history, 334

itinerary, 340–341
    museums, 10
    neighborhoods, 303–306
    nightlife, 343–344
    overview, 33–34, 301
    restaurants, 54, 317–324, 338, 344
    safety, 346
    shopping, 341–343
    top attractions, 10, 13
    topography, 329
    tourist information, 306–307, 345–346
    travel in, 307–310
    travel to, 64–67, 301–303
Venice Biennial, 40
Venice International Film Festival, 41
vermicelli, 528
Vernazza, 251
Verona
    accommodations, 358–360
    archaeological sites, 11
    attractions, 361–365
    bus tour, 361
    location, 349
    overview, 34, 347, 358
    restaurants, 360–361
    top restaurants, 13
    tourist information, 365–366
    travel to, 358
Vesuvian Observatory, 418
Villa Borghese, 159
Villa Capodimonte, 392
Villa Cimbrone, 441
Villa dei Papiri, 417–418
Villa dei Quintili, 158
Villa del Casale, 486
Villa d'Este, 160
Villa Diodoro, 481
Villa Ducale, 481
Villa Fabbiano, 481
Villa Farnesina, 160
Villa Guinigi, 232
Villa Jovis, 434
Villa Kinzica, 235, 237
Villa La Floridiana, 402
Villa La Principessa, 226
Villa Malfitano, 471–472
Villa Niscemi, 475
Villa Rosa di Boscorotondo, 264
Villa San Pio, 123
vineyard, 250, 264, 445
Vini da Gigio, 324

Visa, 61, 62
vitello tonnato, 528
Vittorio Emanuele III Library, 401
volcano. *See specific sites*
Vomero, 388

• *W* •

walking
  in Florence, 182
  in Naples, 388–389
  in Palermo, 459
  in Rome, 113
  in Venice, 307–308
walking tour, 162, 213, 404, 444
wallet, 61, 62–63
water bus, 308–309
water taxi, 302, 309–310
weather, 36–38, 514
Westin Excelsior, 190
wheelchair, 87–88, 308

wine
  cost-cutting tips, 58
  etiquette, 25
  Milan bars, 376
  Naples, 28, 408
  Rome, 26, 170–171
  Sicily, 29
  Siena, 275
  tours, 70
  Tuscany, 27
  Venetian, 27
  Venice, 344

• *Z* •

zabaglione, 25, 528
zampone, 528
Zi Renato, 447
Zibaldone, 283
zuccotto, 528
zuppa inglese, 528

USINESS, CAREERS & PERSONAL FINANCE

Grant Writing

Home Buying

0-7645-5307-0   0-7645-5331-3 *†

Also available:
- Accounting For Dummies †
  0-7645-5314-3
- Business Plans Kit For Dummies †
  0-7645-5365-8
- Cover Letters For Dummies
  0-7645-5224-4
- Frugal Living For Dummies
  0-7645-5403-4
- Leadership For Dummies
  0-7645-5176-0
- Managing For Dummies
  0-7645-1771-6

- Marketing For Dummies
  0-7645-5600-2
- Personal Finance For Dummies *
  0-7645-2590-5
- Project Management
  For Dummies
  0-7645-5283-X
- Resumes For Dummies †
  0-7645-5471-9
- Selling For Dummies
  0-7645-5363-1
- Small Business Kit For Dummies *†
  0-7645-5093-4

OME & BUSINESS COMPUTER BASICS

Windows XP

Excel 2003

0-7645-4074-2   0-7645-3758-X

Also available:
- ACT! 6 For Dummies
  0-7645-2645-6
- iLife '04 All-in-One Desk Reference
  For Dummies
  0-7645-7347-0
- iPAQ For Dummies
  0-7645-6769-1
- Mac OS X Panther Timesaving
  Techniques For Dummies
  0-7645-5812-9
- Macs For Dummies
  0-7645-5656-8
- Microsoft Money 2004 For Dummies
  0-7645-4195-1

- Office 2003 All-in-One Desk
  Reference For Dummies
  0-7645-3883-7
- Outlook 2003 For Dummies
  0-7645-3759-8
- PCs For Dummies
  0-7645-4074-2
- TiVo For Dummies
  0-7645-6923-6
- Upgrading and Fixing PCs
  For Dummies
  0-7645-1665-5
- Windows XP Timesaving
  Techniques For Dummies
  0-7645-3748-2

OOD, HOME, GARDEN, HOBBIES, MUSIC & PETS

Feng Shui

Poker

0-7645-5295-3   0-7645-5232-5

Also available:
- Bass Guitar For Dummies
  0-7645-2487-9
- Diabetes Cookbook For Dummies
  0-7645-5230-9
- Gardening For Dummies *
  0-7645-5130-2
- Guitar For Dummies
  0-7645-5106-X
- Holiday Decorating For Dummies
  0-7645-2570-0
- Home Improvement All-in-One
  For Dummies
  0-7645-5680-0

- Knitting For Dummies
  0-7645-5395-X
- Piano For Dummies
  0-7645-5105-1
- Puppies For Dummies
  0-7645-5255-4
- Scrapbooking For Dummies
  0-7645-7208-3
- Senior Dogs For Dummies
  0-7645-5818-8
- Singing For Dummies
  0-7645-2475-5
- 30-Minute Meals For Dummies
  0-7645-2589-1

NTERNET & DIGITAL MEDIA

Digital Photography

Starting an eBay Business

0-7645-1664-7   0-7645-6924-4

Also available:
- 2005 Online Shopping Directory
  For Dummies
  0-7645-7495-7
- CD & DVD Recording For Dummies
  0-7645-5956-7
- eBay For Dummies
  0-7645-5654-1
- Fighting Spam For Dummies
  0-7645-5965-6
- Genealogy Online For Dummies
  0-7645-5964-8
- Google For Dummies
  0-7645-4420-9

- Home Recording For Musicians
  For Dummies
  0-7645-1634-5
- The Internet For Dummies
  0-7645-4173-0
- iPod & iTunes For Dummies
  0-7645-7772-7
- Preventing Identity Theft
  For Dummies
  0-7645-7336-5
- Pro Tools All-in-One Desk
  Reference For Dummies
  0-7645-5714-9
- Roxio Easy Media Creator
  For Dummies
  0-7645-7131-1

* Separate Canadian edition also available
† Separate U.K. edition also available
Available wherever books are sold. For more information or to order direct: U.S. customers
visit www.dummies.com or call 1-877-762-2974.
U.K. customers visit www.wileyeurope.com or call 0800 243407. Canadian customers visit
www.wiley.ca or call 1-800-567-4797.

SPORTS, FITNESS, PARENTING, RELIGION & SPIRITUALITY

0-7645-5146-9   0-7645-5418-2

Also available:
- Adoption For Dummies
  0-7645-5488-3
- Basketball For Dummies
  0-7645-5248-1
- The Bible For Dummies
  0-7645-5296-1
- Buddhism For Dummies
  0-7645-5359-3
- Catholicism For Dummies
  0-7645-5391-7
- Hockey For Dummies
  0-7645-5228-7

- Judaism For Dummies
  0-7645-5299-6
- Martial Arts For Dummies
  0-7645-5358-5
- Pilates For Dummies
  0-7645-5397-6
- Religion For Dummies
  0-7645-5264-3
- Teaching Kids to Read
  For Dummies
  0-7645-4043-2
- Weight Training For Dummies
  0-7645-5168-X
- Yoga For Dummies
  0-7645-5117-5

TRAVEL

0-7645-5438-7   0-7645-5453-0

Also available:
- Alaska For Dummies
  0-7645-1761-9
- Arizona For Dummies
  0-7645-6938-4
- Cancún and the Yucatán
  For Dummies
  0-7645-2437-2
- Cruise Vacations For Dummies
  0-7645-6941-4
- Europe For Dummies
  0-7645-5456-5
- Ireland For Dummies
  0-7645-5455-7

- Las Vegas For Dummies
  0-7645-5448-4
- London For Dummies
  0-7645-4277-X
- New York City For Dummies
  0-7645-6945-7
- Paris For Dummies
  0-7645-5494-8
- RV Vacations For Dummies
  0-7645-5443-3
- Walt Disney World & Orlando
  For Dummies
  0-7645-6943-0

GRAPHICS, DESIGN & WEB DEVELOPMENT

0-7645-4345-8   0-7645-5589-8

Also available:
- Adobe Acrobat 6 PDF
  For Dummies
  0-7645-3760-1
- Building a Web Site For Dummies
  0-7645-7144-3
- Dreamweaver MX 2004
  For Dummies
  0-7645-4342-3
- FrontPage 2003 For Dummies
  0-7645-3882-9
- HTML 4 For Dummies
  0-7645-1995-6
- Illustrator CS For Dummies
  0-7645-4084-X

- Macromedia Flash MX 2004
  For Dummies
  0-7645-4358-X
- Photoshop 7 All-in-One Desk
  Reference For Dummies
  0-7645-1667-1
- Photoshop CS Timesaving
  Techniques For Dummies
  0-7645-6782-9
- PHP 5 For Dummies
  0-7645-4166-8
- PowerPoint 2003 For Dummies
  0-7645-3908-6
- QuarkXPress 6 For Dummies
  0-7645-2593-X

NETWORKING, SECURITY, PROGRAMMING & DATABASES

0-7645-6852-3   0-7645-5784-X

Also available:
- A+ Certification For Dummies
  0-7645-4187-0
- Access 2003 All-in-One Desk
  Reference For Dummies
  0-7645-3988-4
- Beginning Programming
  For Dummies
  0-7645-4997-9
- C For Dummies
  0-7645-7068-4
- Firewalls For Dummies
  0-7645-4048-3
- Home Networking For Dummies
  0-7645-42796

- Network Security For Dummies
  0-7645-1679-5
- Networking For Dummies
  0-7645-1677-9
- TCP/IP For Dummies
  0-7645-1760-0
- VBA For Dummies
  0-7645-3989-2
- Wireless All In-One Desk Reference
  For Dummies
  0-7645-7496-5
- Wireless Home Networking
  For Dummies
  0-7645-3910-8